Programming Concepts and Methods

IFIP – The International Federation for Information Processing

IFIP was founded in 1960 under the auspices of UNESCO, following the First World Computer Congress held in Paris the previous year. An umbrella organization for societies working in information processing, IFIP's aim is two-fold: to support information processing within its member countries and to encourage technology transfer to developing nations. As its mission statement clearly states,

> IFIP's mission is to be the leading, truly international, apolitical organization which encourages and assists in the development, exploitation and application of information technology for the benefit of all people.

IFIP is a non-profitmaking organization, run almost solely by 2500 volunteers. It operates through a number of technical committees, which organize events and publications. IFIP's events range from an international congress to local seminars, but the most important are:

- the IFIP World Computer Congress, held every second year;
- open conferences;
- working conferences.

The flagship event is the IFIP World Computer Congress, at which both invited and contributed papers are presented. Contributed papers are rigorously refereed and the rejection rate is high.

As with the Congress, participation in the open conferences is open to all and papers may be invited or submitted. Again, submitted papers are stringently refereed.

The working conferences are structured differently. They are usually run by a working group and attendance is small and by invitation only. Their purpose is to create an atmosphere conducive to innovation and development. Refereeing is less rigorous and papers are subjected to extensive group discussion.

Publications arising from IFIP events vary. The papers presented at the IFIP World Computer Congress and at open conferences are published as conference proceedings, while the results of the working conferences are often published as collections of selected and edited papers.

Any national society whose primary activity is in information may apply to become a full member of IFIP, although full membership is restricted to one society per country. Full members are entitled to vote at the annual General Assembly, National societies preferring a less committed involvement may apply for associate or corresponding membership. Associate members enjoy the same benefits as full members, but without voting rights. Corresponding members are not represented in IFIP bodies. Affiliated membership is open to non-national societies, and individual and honorary membership schemes are also offered.

Programming Concepts and Methods PROCOMET '98

IFIP TC2 / WG2.2, 2.3 International Conference on Programming Concepts and Methods (PROCOMET '98) 8–12 June 1998, Shelter Island, New York, USA

Edited by

David Gries

Dept of Computer Science
Cornell University, Ithaca
USA

and

Willem-Paul de Roever

Institute of Computer Science & Applied Mathematics
Christian-Albrechts-University of Kiel
Germany

SPRINGER-SCIENCE+BUSINESS MEDIA, B.V.

First edition 1998

Originally published by Chapman & Hall in 1998

Thomson Science is a division of International Thomson Publishing I(T)P®

ISBN 978-1-4757-6299-0 ISBN 978-0-387-35358-6 (eBook)
DOI 10.1007/978-0-387-35358-6

A catalogue record for this book is available from the British Library

∞ Printed on permanent acid-free text paper, manufactured in accordance with ANSI/NISO Z39.48-1992 (Permanence of Paper).

CONTENTS

Preface

This book constitutes the Proceedings of the IFIP Working Conference PROCOMET'98, held 8–12 June 1998 at Shelter Island, N.Y. The conference is organized by the two IFIP TC 2 Working Groups 2.2 *Formal Description of Programming Concepts* and 2.3 *Programming Methodology.* WG2.2 and WG2.3 have been organizing these conferences every four years for over twenty years.

The aim of such Working Conferences organized by IFIP Working Groups is to bring together leading scientists in a given area of computer science. Participation is by invitation only. As a result, these conferences distinguish themselves from other meetings by extensive and competent technical discussions.

PROCOMET stands for *Programming Concepts and Methods*, indicating that the area of discussion for the conference is the formal description of programming concepts and methods, their tool support, and their applications. At PROCOMET working conferences, papers are presented from this whole area, reflecting the interest of the individuals in WG2.2 and WG2.3.

In response to the call for papers, 58 submissions were received. Each submission was carefully refereed by at least three people. The total number of referees was 110. The selection of papers from these submissions was carried out by the Program Committee, consisting of

Eike Best, Manfred Broy, Ernie Cohen, Philippe Darondeau, Rocco De Nicola, Willem-Paul de Roever (co-chair), David Gries (co-chair), Furio Honsell, Jim Horning, Ian Hayes, Jay Misra, Carroll Morgan, Ernst-Rüdiger Olderog, Benjamin Pierce, Amir Pnueli, Anders Ravn, Fred Schneider, Michel Sintzoff, Bernhard Steffen, Andrzej Tarlecki, Frits Vaandrager, and Pamela Zave,

by means of exchange of e-mails, resulting in 24 accepted papers (some of which were selected partly because of the heated discussions they generated during four weeks of Byzantine Agreement).

These Proceedings contain revised versions of the selected papers. They represent the most recent developments in a wide spectrum of research topics centering around programming:

- Compositional approaches to specification and verification,
- Specification, verification, and development of concurrent systems, in particular of reactive, real-time, and hybrid systems,
- Abstraction and refinement methods in specification and verification,
- Semantics of specification and programming concepts,

Programming Concepts and Methods D. Gries, & W-P. de Roever (Eds.)

- Logical and algebraic foundations of specification and verification,
- Design of verification support tools, and
- Practical software-engineering issues in using programming concepts and methods.

IFIP's Technical Committee 2 has requested that its working groups open themselves up more to applications of the theories that they help to develop. This has led, amongst other things, to having invited speakers who emphasize this shift of direction within their work.

The process of selecting papers and editing this volume would have been impossible were it not for the around-the-clock and through-the-weekend support of Martin Steffen of the University of Kiel. We are extremely grateful for his work. We also thank Kathy Germana of Stony Brook for her assistance in organizing the conference.

The referees —including those who preferred to remain anonymous, the members of the Program Committee, and the additional referees mentioned below— are to be commended for their timely and careful reviews of the submissions.

Finally, we gratefully acknowledge support for this workshop from the United States National Science Foundation.

Willem-Paul de Roever, Kiel, Germany, Program Committee Co-chair
David Gries, Ithaca, N.Y., USA, Program Committee Co-chair
Scott Smolka, Stony Brook, N.Y., USA, Organizer
Rance Cleaveland, North Carolina, USA, Co-organizer

REFEREES

The following referees (together with some who preferred to remain anonymous) helped the Program Committee in evaluating the submitted papers:

Martín Abadi
Fabio Alessi
Rajeev Alur
Eric Badouel
Christel Baier
Johan van Benthem
Albert Benveniste
Gérard Berry
Frank de Boer
Jürgen Bohn
Mario Bravetti
Max Breitling
Ed Brinksma
Olaf Burkart
Bettina Buth
Michael Butler
Luca Cardelli
Edmund M. Clarke
Corky Cartwright
Rowan Davies
Mariangiola Dezani-Ciancaglini
Peter van Emde Boas
E. Allen Emerson
Kai Engelhardt
Colin Fidge
Clemens Fischer
Paul Gardiner
Jaco Geldenhuys
Pietro Di Gianantonio
Rob van Glabbeek
Patrice Godefroid
Ursula Goltz
Mohamed G. Gouda
Burkhard Graves
Jan Friso Groote
Orna Grumberg
Hans Hansson
Wim H. Hesselink
Martin Hofmann
Thomas Jensen
Bengt Jonsson
Joost-Pieter Katoen
S. Kleuker
Ron Koymans
Sandeep Kulkarni
Yassine Lakhnech
K. Rustan M. Leino
Andrew Martin
Merro Massimo
Erich Mikk
Ugo Montanari
Olaf Müller
Kedar Namjoshi
Rob Nederpelt
Ray Nickson
Catuscia Palamidessi
Larry C. Paulson
Doron A. Peled
Jan Peleska
Carsta Petersohn
Frank Pfenning
Andrew M. Pitts
Patrice Quinton
S. Ramesh
Christian Retoré
J.J.M.M. Rutten
Davide Sangiorgi
Bernhard Schätz
Michael Schenke
Emil Sekerinski
Natarajan Shankar
Michael Siegel
Morten H. Sørensen
Martin Steffen
Wolfgang Thomas
R.J. Trefler
Antti Valmari
Moshe Y. Vardi
Dennis Volpano
Martin Wirsing
Pierre Wolper
Joakim von Wright
Job Zwiers

1
Extended static checking (Invited Lecture)

K.R.M. Leino
Digital Systems Research Center
130 Lytton Avenue
Palo Alto, CA 94301, USA
rustan@pa.dec.com

Abstract
Extended static checking (ESC) is a static program analysis technique that attempts to find common programming errors like null-dereferences, array index bounds errors, type cast errors, deadlocks, and race conditions. An ESC tool is powered by program verification technology, yet it feels to the programmer like a type checker because of the limited ambition of finding only certain kinds of errors. This talk reports on some of the research results of and the current state of the Extended Static Checking project at DEC SRC.

BIOGRAPHY

Dr. K. Rustan M. Leino is a computer science researcher at DEC SRC, where his research has centered around programming tools, languages, semantics, and specifications, with focus on modular, object-oriented software. He is currently the project leader for ESC/Java, a programming tool that uses program semantics to find common errors in programs. He holds a BA in Computer Science from The University of Texas at Austin and an MS and PhD in Computer Science from Caltech. Before graduate school, he worked as a technical lead in Windows/NT at Microsoft.

Programming Concepts and Methods D. Gries, & W-P. de Roever (Eds.)

2

From Lattices to Practical Formal Hardware Verification

(Invited Lecture)

C. Seger
Strategic CAD Labs, Intel Corporation
5200 N.E. Elam Young Pkwy.
Hillsboro, OR 97124-6497 USA
cseger@ichips.intel.com

Abstract

Symbolic Trajectory Evaluation (STE) is a model checking algorithm that mixes the use of lattice structures with binary decision diagrams. In addition to this algorithmic decision procedure for the logic, there is also a sound and complete set of inference rules for the logic. Together, these make STE an attractive candidate for a verification system. In this talk we will briefly introduce the underlying theory of STE. We will then discuss the challenges we faced in making STE the basic model checker in the Voss hardware verification system and how the inference rules were used to extend the capabilities of the system. The emphasis of the talk will be on the process of taking a nice theory and making it practically useful.

BIOGRAPHY

Dr. Carl Seger received his M.A.Sc. in Engineering Physics from Chalmer's University of Technology, Sweden, in 1985 and his M.Math and Ph.D. degrees in Computer Science from the University of Waterloo, Canada, in 1986 and 1988 respectively. After two years as Research Associate at Carnegie Mellon University he became an Assistant Professor in the Department of Computer Science at the University of British Columbia, Canada, and in 1995 he became Associate Professor. He was a visiting professor at Intel in the summer of 1995 and joined Intel full time in December 1995. Dr. Seger's main research interests are formal hardware verification and asynchronous circuits. He is the author of the Voss hardware verification system and is co-author of *Asynchronous Circuits* (Springer Verlag, 1995).

Programming Concepts and Methods D. Gries, & W-P. de Roever (Eds.)

3

Programming with Tabling in XSB

(Invited Lecture)

D.S. Warren
Computer Science
State University of NY at Stony Brook
Stony Brook, NY 11794-4400 USA
warren@CS.SunySB.edu

Abstract

I describe how XSB, a tabling Prolog system, can be used effectively to program useful tasks in a variety of domains. The presentation is through the use of examples, with examples being taken from some of the following areas: traditional dynamic programming problems, finite state automata theory, context-free language recognition, parsing and analysis, recursive aggregation, meta-interpreters, program analysis and abstract interpretation, model checking, and abduction.

Program analysis and model checking will be emphasized.

BIOGRAPHY

David Scott Warren received his PhD in Computer Science from the University of Michigan in 1979. He then joined the faculty at the University at Stony Brook where he is currently Professor of Computer Science and chair of the Computer Science Department. For the past fifteen years his research has centered around a variety of topics in the area of logic programming. He has more than 60 publications, is co-author of a major book in the area, and has advised 16 students who have completed their PhD degrees. He has been a leading Principal Investigator of three major multi-million dollar institutional infrastructure grants from NSF and numerous smaller grants. Professor Warren has been active in the logic programming community, serving on many conference program committees. He is the Past President of the Association for Logic Programming, an international professional organization of approximately 1000 members.

Programming Concepts and Methods D. Gries, & W-P. de Roever (Eds.)

4

Verifying Electronic Control Units — today and tomorrow

(Invited Lecture)

W. Damm
OFFIS, Embedded Systems Division, Germany
werner@egk.informatik.uni-oldenburg.de

Abstract

Electronic Control Units (ECUs) are in almost every non-trivial physical system you use today —automotive, telecommunication, avionics, you name it. Software design for ECUs that gives life to such systems is growing exponentially, with ECU development costs even dominating development costs for the total system in some domains. For example, today's cars contain 60–100 ECUs, whose development costs are 12–35% of the total cost.

ECU designs constitute an excellent challenge for formal methods. They often realize safety critical functions, need to deliver their response under hard real-time constraints, are most often hybrid in nature, and are increasingly realized in a distributed fashion.

This talk reports on results on verifying industrial ECU designs both in avionics and automotive and discusses challenges in extending the power of the currently available verification technology.

BIOGRAPHY

Dr. Werner Damm received his Ph.D. in computer science at the RWTH Aachen, Germany, in 1981. He has been a professor in the Computer Science Department, the University of Oldenburg, since 1987 and holds the Chair for Computer Architecture. He is member of the Board of Directors of the OFFIS research institute, which is dedicated to technology transfer, in particular in the domain of embedded systems. He has been leading several industrial projects within OFFIS on hardware verification and verification of safety critical embedded systems. His research interests include multiprocessor systems, semiformal specification methods, synthesis, and verification. He has been serving on program committees of the CAV, CHARME, CHDL, PARLE and EURO-VHDL conferences, is an associate editor of the *Journal on Formal Methods in System Design*, and is a member of IFIP WG10.5.

Programming Concepts and Methods D. Gries, & W-P. de Roever (Eds.)

5

Teaching Calculational Logic (Education Session)

D. Gries
Computer Science, Upson Hall
Cornell University
Ithaca, NY 14853, USA
gries@cs.cornell.edu

Abstract

For the past four years, we have been teaching logic and discrete math at the freshman-sophomore college level using an approach that regards logic as a basic tool —instead of as just another academic subject. We strive to give students a skill in using the propositional and predicate calculi and then to exercise that skill thoroughly in teaching other topics of discrete math. Almost all proofs are done formally, using a calculational logic in which substitution of equals for equals is the main inference rule.

In this talk, we present the calculational logic and discuss our experiences with the approach. Our main message is that this approach can do far better than the conventional one in dispelling students' fears of math and in turning students on to logic.

BIOGRAPHY

David Gries received a BS from Queens College, NY, in 1960, an MS from Illinois in 1962, and a *Dr. rer. nat.* from MIT (Munich Institute of Technology, now the Munich Technical University), Germany, in 1966, all in mathematics. He was an assistant professor of computer science at Stanford 1966–1969 and has been at Cornell since 1969. His research has been in compilers, programming methodology, programming languages, and logic. He is known for his texts in compiler writing (1971), introductory programming (1973), formal development of programming (1981), and logic and discrete math (1993). He holds the major education awards from ACM, ACM SIGCSE, IEEE, and IFIP and is a Cornell Weiss Presidential Fellow.

Programming Concepts and Methods D. Gries, & W-P. de Roever (Eds.)

6

Types for Trees

F. Barbanera, M. Dezani-Ciancaglini
Università degli studi di Torino
Dipartimento di Informatica, C.so Svizzera 185, 10149 Torino, Italia
Email: barba, dezani@di.unito.it

F.J. de Vries
Computer Science Division, ETL
1-1-4 Umezono, Tsukuba, Ibaraki 305 Japan, E-mail: ferjan@etl.go.jp

Abstract

We introduce a type assignment system which is parametric with respect to five families of trees obtained by evaluating λ-terms (Böhm trees, Lévy-Longo trees, ...). Then we prove, in an (almost) uniform way, that each type assignment system fully describes the observational equivalences induced by the corresponding tree representation of terms. More precisely, for each family of trees two terms have the same tree if and only if they get assigned the same types in the corresponding type assignment system.

Keywords

Böhm trees, approximants, intersection types.

1 INTRODUCTION

A theory of functions like the λ-calculus, which provides a foundation for the functional programming paradigm in computer science, can be seen essentially as a theory of "programs". This point of view leads naturally to the intuitive idea that the meaning of a λ-term (program) is represented by the amount of "meaningful information" we can extract from the term by "running it". The formalization of "the information" obtained from a term requires first the definition of what is, in a λ-term, a "stable relevant minimal information" directly observable in the term. This is the token of information which cannot be altered by further reductions but can only be added upon. (As an example the reader may think of the calculation of the $\sqrt{2}$. The calculation process merely adds decimals to the already calculated decimal expansion).

All stable relevant minimal information produced during a computation can quite naturally be represented as a tree. This tree then embodies the total information hidden in the original term. There are many such a tree representation in literature, depending on the possible notions of stable relevant minimal information; the

Programming Concepts and Methods D. Gries, & W-P. de Roever (Eds.)

most commonly used being *top* trees (or Berarducci trees (Berarducci 1996)), *weak* trees (or Lévy-Longo trees (Sangiorgi 1994)), *head* trees (or Böhm trees (Barendregt 1984)), *eta* trees and *infinite eta* trees (infinite eta trees are in one-one correspondence with Nakajima trees (Nakajima 1975)). Hence the various notions of tree represent different notions of *meaning* of a term (in particular they also specify different notions of *undefined* value).

This apparently vague intuition is substantiated by results starting with (Wadsworth 1976), which show that there exist precise correspondences between the tree representations of terms and the local structures (or equivalently the λ-theories) of certain λ-models ((Barendregt 1984), Chapter 19). In particular, such correspondences amount to the fact that two λ-terms have the same tree representation iff they are equal in the λ-model. For example,

- the infinite eta trees represent the local structure of Scott's D_∞ model as defined in (Scott 1972) (this result is proved in (Wadsworth 1976));
- the eta trees represent the local structure of the inverse limit model defined in (Coppo et al. 1987);
- the head trees represent the local structure of Scott's P_ω model as defined in (Scott 1976) (a discussion on this topic can be found in (Barendregt 1984), Chapter 19);
- the weak trees were introduced by Longo in (Longo 1983) (following (Lévy 1976)), who proved that they represent the local structure of Engeler models as defined in (Engeler 1981).

Orthogonally, the results about observational equivalences confirm this operational intuition of *dynamically* evolving meanings of terms encorporated in the tree representations. For instance in (Wadsworth 1976) Wadsworth shows that two λ-terms M, N have the same infinite Böhm tree iff for all contexts $C[\,]$ the following holds:

$$C[M] \text{ has a head normal form } \Leftrightarrow C[N] \text{ has a head normal form.}$$

The same property holds even considering eta trees and normal forms (Hyland 1976). Weak trees correspond, instead, to the observational equivalence with respect to weak head normal forms in suitably enriched versions of the λ-calculus (Sangiorgi 1994, Boudol et al. 1996, Dezani et al. 1997).

λ-terms represent programs which themselves are *static* entities and as such can be "handled", in contrast to the more ineffable computations. It would be very useful if these dynamic aspects could be analysed with tools dealing with static entities like terms and types. Type assignment disciplines are typical static tools, much used in the programming practice to check decidable properties of programs.

There are several results showing how very powerful typing disciplines can be devised that, at the (of course expected) price of being undecidable, can be used to analyze the dynamic world. For instance the observational equivalences induced by a number of tree representations of terms.

- Each inverse limit λ-model is isomorphic to a filter model, i.e. to a model in which the meanings of terms are sets of derivable intersection types (Coppo et al. 1983).

- Two terms have the same Böhm tree iff they have the same set of types in the standard intersection type discipline (Barendregt et al. 1983), as proved in (Ronchi della Rocca 1982).
- Two terms have the same Lévy-Longo tree iff they have the same set of types in the type discipline with union and intersection of (Dezani et al. to appear), as proved in (Dezani et al. 1997).
- Two terms have the same Berarducci trees iff they have the same set of types in a type assignment system with applicative types (Berarducci et al. to appear).

In the present paper we design one type assignment system for each of the five families of trees mentioned above (more precisely, a type assignment system (almost) parametric with respect to these five families.) For each family of trees we show that two terms have the same tree if and only if they get assigned the same types in the corresponding type assignment system.
This is a new result for the eta trees and the infinite eta trees. Moreover, our proof method unifies the earlier proofs mentioned above, while making the following improvements:

- we simplify the types of (Ronchi della Rocca 1982) since we do not consider infinite type variables;
- we do not allow the union type constructor which is considered instead in (Dezani et al. 1997);
- the applicative types are build starting from just one constant instead of two (this last is the choice of (Berarducci et al. to appear)).

All the type systems we introduce (but that representing Beraducci trees) induce filter λ-models in the sense of (Barendregt et al. 1983). Clearly the theories of these filter models coincide with the equalities of the corresponding trees. So as byproduct we obtain alternative proofs of the characterizations of the theories of Scott's D_∞ model (Wadsworth 1976) and of the filter λ-model (Ronchi della Rocca 1982). Notice that these new proofs (unlike the original ones) are constructive, in the sense that, whenever two terms have different interpretations, we build a compact d such that d approximates only the interpretation of one of thc two terms. Really d is the principal filter induced by a type which can be deduced only for one of the two terms.

The long-term goal of this research is to find answers to the question "what can be added to the pure λ-calculus in order to internally discriminate terms having different trees?", which can be formulated for each family of trees.
An intersection type assignment system played a crucial role to show that observational equivalence in lazy concurrent λ-calculus is equivalent to Lévy-Longo tree equality (Dezani et al. 1997). We hope that similar results can be obtained for the other families of trees. This would justify the present choices. A very limited number of type constants and type constructors allows us to search for a proof along the following lines.
Suppose we were able to define for each type α a test term T_α such that $T_\alpha M$ converges iff M has type α. Then we would obtain an observational equivalence which coincides with the tree equality (see (Boudol 1994)).

The paper is organized as follows. In Section 2 we shall recall the various definitions of tree. Moreover, we shall introduce the notion of *approximant*. In Section 3 we shall describe the type assigment systems which will be used for our main result and we shall give a theorem of approximation stating that a term has a type iff there exists an approximant of the term which has the same type. Section 4, instead, contains our main result.
Syntax, basic notation on the λ-calculus and the usual conventions on variables to prevent explicit mentioning of α-conversion are as in (Barendregt 1984).

The proofs we omitted for reasons of space can be found in the full version of the paper which can be obtained from the URL:
ftp://lambda.di.unito.it/pub/dezani/tm.ps.gz.

2 TREES AND APPROXIMANTS

In this section we recall the various notions of trees which can be obtained by evaluating λ-terms. As briefly discussed in the introduction, in order to describe trees, it is natural to formalize first the intuitive possible notions of *stable relevant minimal information* coming out of a computation (naturally inducing different notions of *meaningless term* (Kennaway et al. 1996)).
If during a computation we get the following terms, their underlined parts will remain stable during the rest (if any) of the computation: $\underline{x}M_1 \ldots M_m$, $\underline{\lambda x.}M$, $P\underline{@}Q$ (where @ is the explicit representation of the operation of application and P is a term which will never reduce to an abstraction.) Having a *stable* part in a computation, however, does not necessarily mean that we consider it *relevant*. For instance, we could consider an abstraction $(\underline{\lambda x.}M)$ relevant only in case M is of the form $\lambda y_1 \ldots y_n.zN_1 \ldots N_m$ $(n, m \geq 0)$. This means that we can end up with different notions of what a *stable relevant minimal information* is.
In order to formalize such notions it is possible to define for each notion a reduction relation such that

(a) if a term can produce a stable relevant minimal information we can get it by means of the given reduction relation;

(b) the computation process represented by the reduction relation stops once a stable relevant minimal information is obtained.

In the following we give a number of such reduction relations for λ-terms present in the literature. All of them are proper restrictions of the usual β-reduction relation.

Definition 1 *Given the following axioms and rules:*

(β)	$(\lambda x.M)N \to M[N/x]$
(η)	$\lambda x.Mx \to M$ *if* $x \notin FV(M)$
(ν)	$M \to N \;\Rightarrow\; ML \to NL$
$(\nu)_t$	$M \to N \;\Rightarrow\; ML \to NL$ (*proviso M is not a* strong zero term*).

*That is, it cannot be reduced to a weak head normal form (as defined in Definition 2.2.) by means of the reduction relation induced by the (β) rule (Berarducci 1996). Such terms are called *unsolvables of order* 0 in (Longo 1983) and *strongly unsolvables* in (Abramsky et al. 1993).

$$(\xi) \qquad M \to N \ \Rightarrow\ \lambda x.M \to \lambda x.N$$

we can define the following reduction relations on λ-terms.

(top reduction) $\to_t$ *is the relation relation induced by* (β) *and* $(\nu)_t$
(weak head reduction) $\to_w$ *is the reduction relation induced by* (β) *and* (ν)
(head reduction) $\to_h$ *is the reduction relation induced by* (β), (ν) *and* (ξ)
(eta head reduction) $\to_e$ *is the reduction relation induced by* (β), (ν), (ξ) *and* (η).

The weak head reduction is better known as lazy reduction (Abramsky et al. 1993).

The sets of terms in normal form with respect to the above defined reduction relations can be described syntactically. Such description makes explicit the different intended notion of stable minimal relevant information.

Definition 2 *1. A* top normal form* *is a term of one of the following three kinds:*

(a) an application term of the form $xM_1 \dots M_m$ $(m \geq 0)$*;*
(b) an abstraction term $\lambda x.M$*;*
(c) an application term of the form MN*, where* M *is a strong zero term.*

2. *A* weak head normal form *is a term of one of the following two kinds:*

(a) an application term of the form $xM_1 \dots M_m$ $(m \geq 0)$*;*
(b) an abstraction term $\lambda x.M$.

3. *A* head normal form *is a term of the following kind:*

(a) $\lambda x_1 \dots x_n.yM_1 \dots M_m$ $(m, n \geq 0)$.

4. *An* eta head normal form *is a term of the following kind:*

(a) $\lambda x_1 \dots x_n.yM_1 \dots M_m$ $(m, n \geq 0)$,
where $x_n \not\equiv M_m$ *or* $x_n \in FV(yM_1 \dots M_{m-1})$.

Notice that the sets of normal forms in the above definition are presented in a proper inclusion order, i.e. the set of top normal forms includes that of weak normal forms, etc.

Example 3 *Let* $\mathbf{\Delta_n} \equiv \lambda x.\underbrace{x \dots x}_{n}$ *and* $\mathbf{\Omega_n} \equiv \underbrace{\mathbf{\Delta_n} \dots \mathbf{\Delta_n}}_{n}$*. Moreover, let* $Q \equiv \lambda x.f(xx)$, $R \equiv \lambda zxy.x(zzy)$ *and* $\mathbf{\Delta_2^\eta} \equiv \lambda xy.xxy$*. Then*

1. *For each* $n \geq 2$ *the term* $\mathbf{\Omega_n}$ *is an example of strong zero term.*
2. $\mathbf{\Omega_2}$ *is not a top normal form, while* $\mathbf{\Omega_n}$ *(for* $n \geq 3$*) are top normal forms that cannot reduce to weak head normal forms.*
3. $\lambda x.\mathbf{\Omega_2}$ *is a weak head normal form which cannot reduce to head normal form.*
4. $\mathbf{\Delta_2^\eta}$ *is a head normal form but it is not an eta head normal form.*
5. $\lambda f.f(QQ)$ *and* $\lambda xy.x(RRy)$ *are eta head normal forms.*

---

*called *root stable form* in (Kennaway et al. 1997).

Following (Berarducci 1996) we say that a term is *mute* iff it does not have a top normal form.
With this definition we can represent in tree notation all the various related kinds of information we can distract from a term. Given a term M for each of the four reduction relations we can try to reduce M to normal form. If it has no normal form then no information is obtainable out of M and its tree is $\bot$. Otherwise, put the information so obtained in a node and build the children of such a node by repeating this process on the various subterms of the normal form. In case of head normal forms this amounts to the usual construction of Böhm trees.

Definition 4 (i) *The* top tree $\mathcal{T}_t(M)$ *of a term* M *is defined by cases as follows:*

– *if* $M \twoheadrightarrow_t xN_1 \ldots N_m$ $(m \geq 0)$, *then:*

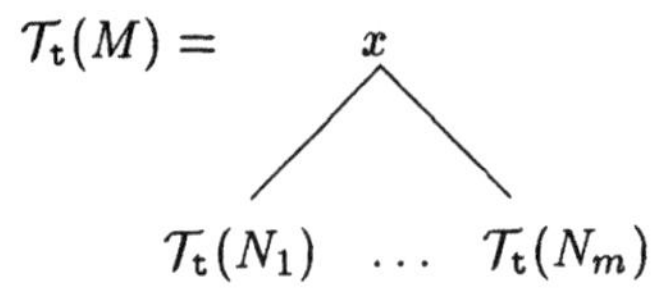

– *if* $M \twoheadrightarrow_t \lambda x.N$, *then:*

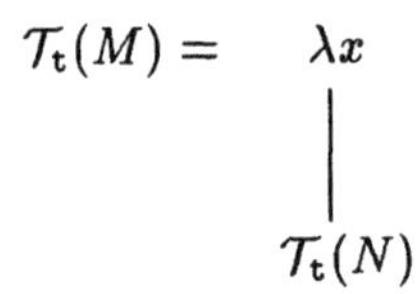

– *if* $M \twoheadrightarrow_t NP$, *where* N *is a strong zero term, then:*

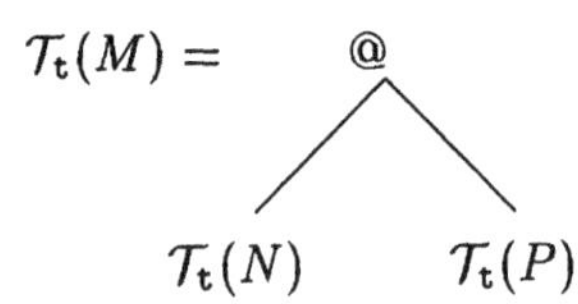

– *otherwise:* $\mathcal{T}_t(M) = \bot$

(ii) *The* weak tree $\mathcal{T}_w(M)$ *of a term* M *is defined by cases as follows:*

– *if* $M \twoheadrightarrow_w xN_1 \ldots N_m$ $(m \geq 0)$, *then:*

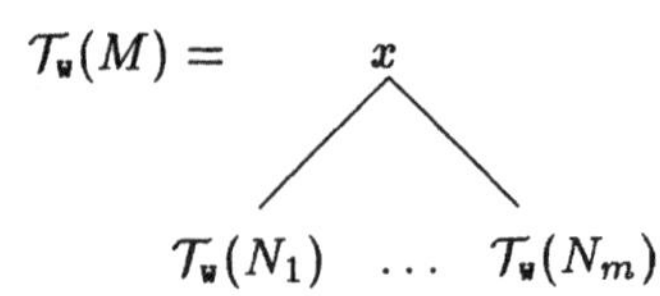

– *if* $M \twoheadrightarrow_w \lambda x.N$, *then:*

$$\mathcal{T}_{\mathtt{w}}(M) = \begin{array}{c}\lambda x\\ | \\ \mathcal{T}_{\mathtt{w}}(N)\end{array}$$

– *otherwise:* $\mathcal{T}_{\mathtt{w}}(M) = \bot$

(iii) *The* head tree $\mathcal{T}_{\mathtt{h}}(M)$ *of a term* M *is defined by cases as follows:*

– *if* $M \twoheadrightarrow_{\mathtt{h}} \lambda x_1 \ldots x_n.yN_1 \ldots N_m$ $(n, m \geq 0)$, *then:*

$$\mathcal{T}_{\mathtt{h}}(M) = \begin{array}{c}\lambda x_1 \ldots x_n.y\\ \diagup \quad \diagdown \\ \mathcal{T}_{\mathtt{h}}(N_1) \quad \ldots \quad \mathcal{T}_{\mathtt{h}}(N_m)\end{array}$$

– *otherwise:* $\mathcal{T}_{\mathtt{h}}(M) = \bot$

(iv) *The* eta tree $\mathcal{T}_{\mathtt{e}}(M)$ *of a term* M *is defined by cases as follows:*

– *if* $M \twoheadrightarrow_{\mathtt{e}} \lambda x_1 \ldots x_n.yN_1 \ldots N_m$ $(n, m \geq 0)$, *where* $x_n \not\equiv N_m$ *or* $x_n \in FV(yN_1 \ldots N_{m-1})$, *then:*

$$\mathcal{T}_{\mathtt{e}}(M) = \begin{array}{c}\lambda x_1 \ldots x_n.y\\ \diagup \quad \diagdown \\ \mathcal{T}_{\mathtt{e}}(N_1) \quad \ldots \quad \mathcal{T}_{\mathtt{e}}(N_m)\end{array}$$

– *otherwise:* $\mathcal{T}_{\mathtt{e}}(M) = \bot$

Finally the fifth family of trees we shall consider in this paper is the family of the *infinite η-normal forms* of head trees (and hence of eta trees as well), as defined in (Barendregt 1984). In order to give the definition of *infinite η-normal form*, we need first to recall briefly the definition of *infinite η-expansion* of a variable.

Given a variable x one can consider a (possibly) infinite tree resulting by the limit of a series of expansions like the following one:

$$x \;{}_{\eta}\!\leftarrow \mathcal{T}_{\mathtt{h}}(\lambda z_0.xz_0) \;{}_{\eta}\!\leftarrow \mathcal{T}_{\mathtt{h}}(\lambda z_0.x(\lambda z_1.z_0z_1)) \;{}_{\eta}\!\leftarrow \ldots$$

We denote by $T \geq_\eta x$ the fact that T is a (possibly) infinite η-expansion of x. We refer to (Barendregt 1984) (10.2.10) for a formal definition of $\geq_\eta$.

Definition 5 *Let T be a head tree, i.e. $T \equiv \mathcal{T}_{\mathtt{h}}(M)$ for some M. The* infinite η-normal form *of T, $\infty\eta(T)$, is defined as follows:*

$$\infty\eta(\bot) = \bot$$

$$\infty\eta\left(\begin{array}{c} \lambda x_1 \ldots x_n.y \\ /\backslash \\ T_1 \ldots T_m \end{array}\right) = \begin{cases} \infty\eta\left(\begin{array}{c} \lambda x_1 \ldots x_{n-1}.y \\ /\backslash \\ T_1 \ldots T_{m-1} \end{array}\right) & \begin{array}{l} \text{if } x_n \leq_\eta T_m \text{ and} \\ x_n \notin FV(T_i), \\ 1 \leq i \leq m-1 \end{array} \\ \begin{array}{c} \lambda x_1 \ldots x_n.y \\ /\backslash \\ \infty\eta(T_1) \ldots \infty\eta(T_m) \end{array} & \text{otherwise} \end{cases}$$

It is possible now to define *infinite eta trees.*

Definition 6 *The* infinite eta tree $\mathcal{T}_{\mathtt{i}}(M)$ *of a term M is defined as* $\infty\eta(\mathcal{T}_{\mathtt{e}}(M))$.

As recalled in the introduction, the interest of the above tree representations is that they represent the local structure (or, equivalently, the λ-theory) of different λ-models.
As usual when dealing with (possibly) infinite structures, one can consider finite approximations. In our case, we can get approximations by pruning our trees. We need to add a constant in our language ($\bot$) in order to represent the (possibly infinite) parts of the trees that have been pruned. An approximation of a tree then represents certain finite stable information that can be extracted from a term.
Given a notion of tree, approximations of a tree can be represented as terms in a slightly enriched λ-calculus.

Let $\Lambda_\bot$ be the set of terms obtained by adding the symbol $\bot$ to the syntax of the pure λ-calculus.
We extend the notion of $\rightarrow_\dagger$-reduction ($\dagger \in \{\mathtt{t}, \mathtt{w}, \mathtt{h}, \mathtt{e}\}$) to $\Lambda_\bot$ by adding the clauses

$$\bot M \rightarrow \bot \quad \text{for } \dagger \in \{\mathtt{w}, \mathtt{h}, \mathtt{e}\}, \quad \lambda x.\bot \rightarrow \bot \quad \text{for } \dagger \in \{\mathtt{h}, \mathtt{e}\}.$$

Definition 7 *For $\dagger \in \{\mathtt{t}, \mathtt{w}, \mathtt{h}, \mathtt{e}\}$, we define $\mathcal{A}_\dagger \subseteq \Lambda_\bot$ as the set of normal forms with respect to $\rightarrow_\dagger$. $\mathcal{A}_{\mathtt{i}}$ is defined to be equal to $\mathcal{A}_{\mathtt{e}}$.*

We denote by $\mathcal{A}_\dagger^{(n)}$ ($\dagger \in \{\mathtt{t}, \mathtt{w}, \mathtt{h}, \mathtt{e}, \mathtt{i}\}$) the set of approximate normal forms with at most n symbols.
$(M)_\dagger^{(h)}$ ($\dagger \in \{\mathtt{t}, \mathtt{w}, \mathtt{h}, \mathtt{e}, \mathtt{i}\}$) denotes the approximate normal form representing the tree obtained out of $\mathcal{T}_\dagger(M)$ by cutting it at height h and putting as leaves at the end of the cut edges the constant $\bot$.
It is trivial to verify that $(M)_\dagger^{(h)} \in \mathcal{A}_\dagger$ for all M. Since the tree representations easily extend to approximate normal forms, we define $(A)_\dagger^{(h)}$ similarly. For instance,

by looking at $\mathcal{T}_{\mathtt{t}}(\mathbf{\Delta_3\Delta_3})$, it is easy to verify that $(\mathbf{\Delta_3\Delta_3})_{\mathtt{t}}^{(h)}$ for $h = 0, 1, 2, 3$ are $\bot$, $\bot\bot$, $\bot\bot(\lambda x.\bot)$ and $\bot\bot(\lambda x.\bot)(\lambda x.x\bot\bot)$.

There is a natural partial order between approximants which can be easily formalized by induction.

Definition 8 *For* $\dagger \in \{\mathtt{t}, \mathtt{w}, \mathtt{h}, \mathtt{e}, \mathtt{i}\}$, *the relation* $\preceq_\dagger$ *is the least partial order on* $\mathcal{A}_\dagger$, *such that:*

(a) $\bot \preceq_\dagger A$;
(b) *if* $A \preceq_\dagger A'$, *then* $\lambda x.A \preceq_\dagger \lambda x.A'$;
(c) *if* $A_i \preceq_\dagger A'_i$ *for* $i = 1, \ldots, n$, *then* $A_1 \ldots A_n \preceq_\dagger A'_1 \ldots A'_n$.

It is trivial to verify that $(M)_\dagger^{(h)} \preceq_\dagger (M)_\dagger^{(h+1)}$ for all h.

It is possible to associate to a λ-term, for any possible notion of stable minimal relevant information, the sets of its approximants, that is the set of all the finite approximations of its corresponding tree.

Definition 9 *For* $\dagger \in \{\mathtt{t}, \mathtt{w}, \mathtt{h}, \mathtt{e}, \mathtt{i}\}$ *the* set $\mathcal{A}_\dagger(M)$ of approximants of M *is defined by:*

$$\mathcal{A}_\dagger(M) = \{A \in \mathcal{A}_\dagger \mid \exists h.\ A \preceq_\dagger (M)_\dagger^{(h)}\}.$$

For example $\mathcal{A}_{\mathtt{t}}(x(\mathbf{\Omega_3 I})(\mathbf{II}))$ contains $\bot \preceq_{\mathtt{t}} x\bot\bot \preceq_{\mathtt{t}} x(\bot\mathbf{I})\mathbf{I} \preceq_{\mathtt{t}} x(\bot\mathbf{\Delta_3 I})\mathbf{I} \preceq_{\mathtt{t}} x(\bot\mathbf{\Delta_3\Delta_3 I})\mathbf{I} \preceq_{\mathtt{t}} \ldots$.

It is natural to expect that our different notions of trees and approximants represent the very same concepts, that is that they formalize the same observational behaviours of λ-terms.

Theorem 10 *For* $\dagger \in \{\mathtt{t}, \mathtt{w}, \mathtt{h}, \mathtt{e}, \mathtt{i}\}$ *and for any* M, N:

$$\mathcal{T}_\dagger(M) = \mathcal{T}_\dagger(N) \ \textit{ iff } \ \mathcal{A}_\dagger(M) = \mathcal{A}_\dagger(N).$$

One can show also that $\mathcal{T}_\dagger(M)$ is the least upper-bound of $\mathcal{A}_\dagger(M)$ wrt $\preceq_\dagger$.

It is possible to extend each partial order $\preceq_\dagger$ to a partial order $\sqsubseteq_\dagger$ naturally inducing an equivalence relation on sets of approximants. Such equivalence can be proved to coincide with the identity relation on sets of approximants and hence (by Theorem 10) to coincide with the identity on trees.

Definition 11 *1. Let* $\sqsubseteq_{\mathtt{t}}$ *be the relation* $\preceq_{\mathtt{t}}$.

2. *For* $\dagger \in \{\mathtt{w}, \mathtt{h}\}$ *the relation* $\sqsubseteq_\dagger$ *is the least partial order on* $\mathcal{A}_\dagger$ *which satifies clauses (a),(b),(c) of* $\preceq_\dagger$ *and, moreover,*

   (d) $\lambda y.xA_1 \ldots A_n y \sqsubseteq_\dagger xA_1 \ldots A_n$ *for all variables* $y \notin FV(xA_1 \ldots A_n)$ $(1 \leq i \leq n)$.

3. *For* $\dagger \in \{\mathtt{e}, \mathtt{i}\}$ *the relation* $\sqsubseteq_\dagger$ *is the least partial order on* $\mathcal{A}_\dagger$ *which satifies clauses (a),(b),(c) of* $\preceq_\dagger$ *and, moreover,*

   (d) *if* $A \sqsubseteq_\dagger xA_1 \ldots A_n y$ *where* $y \notin FV(xA_1 \ldots A_n)$, *then* $\lambda y.A \sqsubseteq_\dagger xA_1 \ldots A_n$;

(e) $xA_1 \ldots A_n \sqsubseteq_\dagger \lambda z_1 \ldots z_m.xA_1 \ldots A_n B_1 \ldots B_m$, *where* $x \notin \{z_1, \ldots, z_m\}$ *and* $B_j \not\equiv \bot$ *for* $1 \leq j \leq m$.

Definition 12 *For* $\dagger \in \{\mathtt{t}, \mathtt{w}, \mathtt{h}, \mathtt{e}, \mathtt{i}\}$ *and any two terms* M *and* N *we define:*
$\mathcal{A}_\dagger(M) \simeq_\dagger \mathcal{A}_\dagger(N) \Leftrightarrow$ *for all* $A \in \mathcal{A}_\dagger(M)$ *there is* $B \in \mathcal{A}_\dagger(N)$ *such that* $A \sqsubseteq_\dagger B$, *and vice versa.*

Lemma 13 *For* $\dagger \in \{\mathtt{t}, \mathtt{w}, \mathtt{h}, \mathtt{e}, \mathtt{i}\}$,

$$\mathcal{A}_\dagger(M) \simeq_\dagger \mathcal{A}_\dagger(N) \;\; \textit{iff} \;\; \mathcal{A}_\dagger(M) = \mathcal{A}_\dagger(N) \;\; \textit{iff} \;\; \mathcal{T}_\dagger(M) = \mathcal{T}_\dagger(N).$$

The main motivation for the introduction of $\sqsubseteq_\dagger$ is that it can be proved to be compatible with the typings that we shall introduce in the next section.

3 TYPES AND TYPE ASSIGNMENT SYSTEMS

As stated in the introduction, our static tools to analyse trees (or, equivalently, their corresponding sets of approximants) will be type assignment systems, in particular type assignment systems using intersection-type-like disciplines.
In type assignment systems one derives statements of the form $M : \alpha$, where a term M gets assigned a type α and α represents a certain finite information about M.
Roughly speaking, a type will be used as a description of a particular notion of normal form. Hence, it is not possible to use a unique set of types to deal with all the trees defined in the previous section. We shall need, instead, three sets of types: $\mathbf{Types}_\mathtt{t}$ to characterize $\mathcal{T}_\mathtt{t}$, $\mathbf{Types}_\mathtt{wh}$ to characterize $\mathcal{T}_\mathtt{w}$ and $\mathcal{T}_\mathtt{h}$, and $\mathbf{Types}_\mathtt{ei}$ to characterize $\mathcal{T}_\mathtt{e}$ and $\mathcal{T}_\mathtt{i}$.
After defining these sets of types, in this section we shall define an order $\leq_\dagger$ parameterized by the notion of tree. Then—parametrized by this order— our type assignment systems will be defined (almost) uniformly for all notions of tree. All these type assignment systems will be able to detect that a term carries no information: $\mathcal{T}_\dagger(M) = \bot$ if and only if ω is the only type that the type system related to $\mathcal{T}_\dagger$ can assign to M.
In the following, we shall use the following notation: if $\dagger \in \{\mathtt{t}, \mathtt{w}, \mathtt{h}, \mathtt{e}, \mathtt{i}\}$, then

$$\ddagger = \begin{cases} \mathtt{t} & \text{if } \dagger = \mathtt{t} \\ \mathtt{wh} & \text{if } \dagger = \mathtt{w} \text{ or } \dagger = \mathtt{h} \\ \mathtt{ei} & \text{if } \dagger = \mathtt{e} \text{ or } \dagger = \mathtt{i}. \end{cases}$$

3.1 Types

Let us begin with $\mathbf{Types}_\mathtt{t}$. To describe a top normal form which is the application of two terms, following (Berarducci et al. to appear) we introduce a particular type constructor: the application $\alpha\beta$ between two types α and β. In the intended interpretation a term has type $\alpha\beta$ if its top normal form is the application of two terms, the

first one of type α and the second one of type β. We differ from (Berarducci et al. to appear) since we build types starting only from the unique constant ω, i.e. we don't introduce a new type constant to be interpreted as the set of all strong zero terms.
We have to prevent the presence of inconsistent types. For example, $\omega\omega$ says that a top normal form is the application of two terms, the first one being a strong zero term, whereas $\omega \to \omega$ says that a top normal form is an abstraction. So we need to prevent their intersection $\omega\omega \wedge (\omega \to \omega)$.
To describe $\mathbf{Types}_{\mathtt{t}}$ we can define first a set of "pretypes" and then restrict it.

In writing types we assume the following precedence between operators: application, intersection, arrow. Moreover, $\alpha \to \beta^n \to \gamma$ is short for $\alpha \to \underbrace{\beta \ldots \to \beta}_{n} \to \gamma$.

Definition 14 (Pretypes) *The set of pretypes* **PTypes** *is defined by the grammar:*

$$P ::= \omega \mid P \to P \mid PP \mid P \wedge P.$$

Definition 15 ($\mathbf{Types}_{\mathtt{t}}$) *Given $\alpha \in$ **PTypes**, we define two predicates $\alpha \in \mathbf{Types}_{\mathtt{t}}$ and $\alpha \notin \mathbf{Types}_{\mathtt{t}}$ by simultaneous induction on α by stipulating that $\alpha \in \mathbf{Types}_{\mathtt{t}}$ iff one of the following conditions holds (and $\alpha \notin \mathbf{Types}_{\mathtt{t}}$ iff all the conditions do not hold):*

(Universal kind) α is ω.
(Arrow kind) α is a finite intersection of the form $\bigwedge_{i\in I}(\alpha_i \to \beta_i)$ where $\alpha_i, \beta_i \in \mathbf{Types}_{\mathtt{t}}$ and for all $J \subseteq I$ either $\bigwedge_{j\in J}\beta_j \in \mathbf{Types}_{\mathtt{t}}$ or $\bigwedge_{j\in J}\alpha_j \notin \mathbf{Types}_{\mathtt{t}}$.
(Applicative kind) α is $\omega\beta$, or α is a finite intersection of the form $\bigwedge_{i\in I}\alpha_i\beta_i$ where $\bigwedge_{i\in I}\beta_i \in \mathbf{Types}_{\mathtt{t}}$, and $\bigwedge_{i\in I}\alpha_i \in \mathbf{Types}_{\mathtt{t}}$ is of applicative kind.
If $\alpha \in \mathbf{Types}_{\mathtt{t}}$, then $\omega \wedge \alpha \in \mathbf{Types}_{\mathtt{t}}$: the kind of $\omega \wedge \alpha$ is defined to be the kind of α.

In what follows we shall consider only types. α, β, γ will range over types of any kind, σ, τ, ρ will range over types of arrow kind (*arrow types*), π, μ, ν will range over types of applicative kind (*applicative types*).

To describe normal forms other than top normal forms, applicative types are not needed. Moreover, since all the intersections are meaningful, the definition of $\mathbf{Types}_{\mathtt{wh}}$ and $\mathbf{Types}_{\mathtt{ei}}$ can be given in a direct way.
However, for weak head normal forms and head normal forms, we need to have a new constant, ζ, representing λ-free terms *. Roughly speaking, ζ can be seen as the collapse of all the applicative types.

Definition 16 ($\mathbf{Types}_{\mathtt{wh}}$) *The set of types* $\mathbf{Types}_{\mathtt{wh}}$ *is defined by the grammar:*

$$T_{\mathtt{wh}} ::= \omega \mid \zeta \mid T_{\mathtt{wh}} \to T_{\mathtt{wh}} \mid T_{\mathtt{wh}} \wedge T_{\mathtt{wh}}.$$

* Sangiorgi in (Sangiorgi 1994) proves that $\lambda x.xx$ and $\lambda x.x(\lambda y.xy)$ have the same types when types are built starting from ω using arrow and intersection type constructors. Clearly these terms have different weak and head trees.

In order to define $\mathbf{Types}_{\mathtt{ei}}$, since terms are considered modulo η, we are forced to equate all atomic types to intersections of arrow types. This means that another type constant, ϑ, is needed.

Definition 17 ($\mathbf{Types}_{\mathtt{ei}}$) *The set of types $\mathbf{Types}_{\mathtt{ei}}$ is defined by the grammar:*

$$T_{\mathtt{ei}} ::= \omega \mid \zeta \mid \vartheta \mid T_{\mathtt{ei}} \to T_{\mathtt{ei}} \mid T_{\mathtt{ei}} \wedge T_{\mathtt{ei}}.$$

3.2 Type preorders

On the sets of types of the previous subsection we define five preorder relations which all take into account the meaning of ω as universal type, of $\to$ as function space constructor, and of $\wedge$ as intersection. These five preorders have also distinguished clauses which make them suitable to describe the different trees.

The preorder $\leq_{\mathtt{t}}$ defined on $\mathbf{Types}_{\mathtt{t}}$ reflects the interpretation of applicative types. The preorder $\leq_{\mathtt{h}}$ defined on $\mathbf{Types}_{\mathtt{wh}}$ equates ω to $\omega \to \omega$, since we want to take into account the reduction $\lambda x.\bot \to \bot$. The preorders $\leq_{\mathtt{e}}$ and $\leq_{\mathtt{i}}$ equate all atomic types to arrow types. They differ since in $\leq_{\mathtt{i}}$ the left argument of this arrow type is always ω, while this is not true for $\leq_{\mathtt{e}}$. This difference is essential to mimic either infinite or finite η-reductions, as we shall see later.

Definition 18 *1. Let $\leq_{\mathtt{t}}$ be the smallest binary relation over $\mathbf{Types}_{\mathtt{t}}$ such that:*

- *(a) it is a preorder in which $\wedge$ is the meet and ω is the top;*
- *the arrow satisfies:*

$$(b)\ \alpha \to \omega \leq \omega \to \omega; \quad (c)\ (\alpha \to \beta) \wedge (\alpha \to \gamma) \leq \alpha \to \beta \wedge \gamma;$$

$$(d)\ \alpha \geq \alpha' \text{ and } \beta \leq \beta' \text{ imply } \alpha \to \beta \leq \alpha' \to \beta'.$$

- *the applicative types satisfy:*

$$(e)\ \pi\alpha \wedge \pi'\alpha' \leq (\pi \wedge \pi')(\alpha \wedge \alpha'); \quad (f)\ \pi \leq \pi' \text{ and } \alpha \leq \alpha' \text{ imply } \pi\alpha \leq \pi'\alpha'.$$

2. *Let $\leq_{\mathtt{w}}$ be the smallest binary relation over $\mathbf{Types}_{\mathtt{wh}}$ which satisfies the clauses (a)-(d) above.*
3. *Let $\leq_{\mathtt{h}}$ be the smallest binary relation over $\mathbf{Types}_{\mathtt{wh}}$ which satisfies the clauses (a)-(d) above and moreover:*

$$(g)\ \omega \leq \omega \to \omega.$$

4. *Let $\leq_{\mathtt{e}}$ be the smallest binary relation over $\mathbf{Types}_{\mathtt{ei}}$ which satisfies the clauses (a)-(d), (g) above and moreover:*

$$(h)\ \zeta \leq \vartheta \to \zeta \leq \zeta; \quad (i)\ \vartheta \leq \zeta \to \vartheta \leq \vartheta.$$

5. *Let $\leq_{\mathtt{i}}$ be the smallest binary relation over $\mathbf{Types}_{\mathtt{ei}}$ which satisfies the clauses (a)-(d), (g) above and moreover:*

$$(l)\ \zeta \leq \omega \to \zeta \leq \zeta; \quad (m)\ \vartheta \leq \omega \to \vartheta \leq \vartheta.$$

$\alpha =_{\dagger} \beta$ is short for $\alpha \leq_{\dagger} \beta$ and $\beta \leq_{\dagger} \alpha$, where $\dagger \in \{\mathtt{t}, \mathtt{w}, \mathtt{h}, \mathtt{e}, \mathtt{i}\}$.

Notice that clause (b) is derivable from clause (g), so we can eliminate clause (b) from the definitions of $\leq_{\mathtt{h}}, \leq_{\mathtt{e}}, \leq_{\mathtt{i}}$.

For example we have $\omega \wedge \alpha =_{\dagger} \alpha$ for every type $\alpha \in \mathbf{Types}_{\ddagger}$ where $\dagger \in \{\mathtt{t}, \mathtt{w}, \mathtt{h}, \mathtt{e}, \mathtt{i}\}$, $(\omega \to \omega) \wedge \sigma =_{\mathtt{t}} \sigma$ for every arrow type $\sigma \in \mathbf{Types}_{\mathtt{t}}$, $(\omega \to \omega) \wedge \alpha =_{\dagger} \alpha$ for every type $\alpha \in \mathbf{Types}_{\ddagger}$ (proviso that $\alpha \neq_{\mathtt{w}} \omega$ when $\dagger = \mathtt{w}$) where $\dagger \in \{\mathtt{w}, \mathtt{h}, \mathtt{e}, \mathtt{i}\}$, and $\omega\omega \wedge \pi = \pi$ for every applicative type $\pi \in \mathbf{Types}_{\mathtt{t}}$.

3.3 Type assignment systems

For each preorder introduced in the previous subsection, we define a type assignment system associating λ-terms to the corresponding set of types. As said at the beginning of this section, these systems can be defined *almost* uniformly. In fact there are six rules which are common to all systems and which are standard in intersection type disciplines. The type assignment systems $\{\vdash_{\dagger}\}_{\dagger \in \{\mathtt{w},\mathtt{h},\mathtt{e},\mathtt{i}\}}$ are defined by such six rules, by instantiating rule $(\leq_{\dagger})$ with the corresponding preorder. However, to define $\vdash_{\mathtt{t}}$ we have to deal with applicative types, and hence we need two extra rules: (ωapp) and (app). Moreover, a rule (Eq_{β}) is needed as well, since applicative types are not invariant under β-expansion of subjects. For example, without (Eq_{β}) we have $\vdash \mathbf{\Omega}_2\mathbf{I}\!:\omega(\omega \to \omega)$, but $\not\vdash (\lambda xy.y\mathbf{\Delta}_2 x)\mathbf{I}\mathbf{\Delta}_2\!:\omega(\omega \to \omega)$.

A *basis* Γ is a (finite or infinite) set of statements of the shape $x : \alpha$, with distinct variables as subjects. In writing $\Gamma, x : \alpha$ we assume that x does not occur in Γ. We denote by $\mathcal{B}_{\mathtt{t}}, \mathcal{B}_{\mathtt{wh}}, \mathcal{B}_{\mathtt{ei}}$ the sets of bases whose predicates belong to $\mathbf{Types}_{\mathtt{t}}$, $\mathbf{Types}_{\mathtt{wh}}$, and $\mathbf{Types}_{\mathtt{ei}}$, respectively.

Definition 19 (Type assignment systems) *Let us consider the following axioms and rules (where M, N are terms or approximate normal forms)*

$$(\mathrm{Ax})\ \Gamma, x\!:\alpha \vdash x\!:\alpha \qquad\qquad (\omega)\ \Gamma \vdash M\!:\omega$$

$$(\to \mathrm{I})\ \frac{\Gamma, x\!:\alpha \vdash M\!:\beta}{\Gamma \vdash \lambda x.M\!:\alpha \to \beta} \qquad\qquad (\to \mathrm{E})\ \frac{\Gamma \vdash M\!:\alpha \to \beta \quad \Gamma \vdash N\!:\alpha}{\Gamma \vdash MN\!:\beta}$$

$$(\wedge \mathrm{I})\ \frac{\Gamma \vdash M\!:\alpha \quad \Gamma \vdash M\!:\beta}{\Gamma \vdash M\!:\alpha \wedge \beta} \qquad\qquad (\leq_{\dagger})\ \frac{\Gamma \vdash M\!:\alpha \quad \alpha \leq_{\dagger} \beta}{\Gamma \vdash M\!:\beta}$$

$$(\omega app)\ \frac{M \textit{ is a strong zero term} \quad \Gamma \vdash N\!:\alpha}{\Gamma \vdash MN\!:\omega\alpha} \qquad (app)\ \frac{\Gamma \vdash M\!:\pi \quad \Gamma \vdash N\!:\alpha}{\Gamma \vdash MN\!:\pi\alpha}$$

$$(Eq_{\beta})\ \frac{\Gamma \vdash N\!:\alpha \quad M =_{\beta} N}{\Gamma \vdash M\!:\alpha}.$$

1. The type assignment system $\vdash_{\mathtt{t}}$ is defined by the axioms and rules (Ax), (ω),

$(\rightarrow \mathrm{I})$, $(\rightarrow \mathrm{E})$, $(\wedge \mathrm{I})$, (ωapp), (app), (Eq_β), *and* $(\leq_{\mathtt{t}})$, *where* $\Gamma \in \mathcal{B}_{\mathtt{t}}$ *and* $\alpha, \beta \in$ $\mathbf{Types}_{\mathtt{t}}$.

2. *The type assignment system* $\vdash_\dagger$ *for* $\dagger \in \{\mathtt{w}, \mathtt{h}, \mathtt{e}, \mathtt{i}\}$ *is defined by the axioms and rules* (Ax), (ω), $(\rightarrow \mathrm{I})$, $(\rightarrow \mathrm{E})$, $(\wedge \mathrm{I})$, *and* $(\leq_\dagger)$, *where* $\Gamma \in \mathcal{B}_\ddagger$ *and* $\alpha, \beta \in$ $\mathbf{Types}_\ddagger$.

Since terms are considered modulo α-conversion, the weakening rule is admissible. Moreover we have $\Gamma_{|M} \vdash_\dagger M{:}\alpha$ whenever $\Gamma \vdash_\dagger M{:}\alpha$, where $\Gamma_{|M} = \{x{:}\beta \in \Gamma \mid x \in FV(M)\}$ for $\dagger \in \{\mathtt{t}, \mathtt{w}, \mathtt{h}, \mathtt{e}, \mathtt{i}\}$.

We want to consider unions of bases taking the intersections of the types with the same subjects. Since not all intersections of types in $\mathbf{Types}_{\mathtt{t}}$ are types, we need to allow in this case only unions of compatible bases, according to the following definition. For the other sets of types any two arbitrary bases are compatible.

Definition 20 *Let* $\ddagger \in \{\mathtt{t}, \mathtt{wh}, \mathtt{ei}\}$. *We say that two bases* $\Gamma, \Gamma' \in \mathcal{B}_\ddagger$ *are* compatible *if and only if* $x : \alpha \in \Gamma$ *and* $x : \beta \in \Gamma'$ *imply* $\alpha \wedge \beta \in \mathbf{Types}_\ddagger$. *If* Γ *and* Γ' *are compatible bases we define their union* $\uplus$ *as:*

$$\Gamma \uplus \Gamma' \quad = \quad \{x : \alpha \wedge \beta \mid x : \alpha \in \Gamma \text{ and } x : \beta \in \Gamma'\}.$$

Accordingly we define: $\Gamma \Subset \Gamma' \;\Leftrightarrow\; \exists \Gamma''.\, \Gamma \uplus \Gamma'' = \Gamma'$.

Notice that $x : \alpha \wedge \omega \in \Gamma \uplus \Gamma'$ whenever $x : \alpha \in \Gamma$ and $x \notin Dom(\Gamma')$, since by convention we get $x{:}\omega \in \Gamma'$. Similarly when $x : \beta \in \Gamma'$ and $x \notin Dom(\Gamma)$.

As expected, we have generation lemmas for all the given type assignment systems. Due to the presence of rule (Eq_β), in the generation lemma for $\vdash_{\mathtt{t}}$ we need to consider approximate normal forms instead of arbitrary terms.

Lemma 21 (Generation Lemma for $\vdash_{\mathtt{t}}$)

1. $\Gamma \vdash_{\mathtt{t}} \bot{:}\alpha$ *implies* $\alpha =_t \omega$;
2. *If* $\Gamma \vdash_{\mathtt{t}} A{:}\alpha$, $\alpha \neq_t \omega$, *and*
   (a) $A \equiv x$, *then* $x : \beta \in \Gamma$ *for some* $\beta \leq_{\mathtt{t}} \alpha$;
   (b) $A \equiv \lambda x.A'$, *then* $\alpha =_t \bigwedge_{i \in I}(\alpha_i \rightarrow \beta_i)$ *and* $\forall i \in I\; \Gamma, x : \alpha_i \vdash_{\mathtt{t}} A' : \beta_i$;
   (c) $A \equiv xA_1 \ldots A_n A'$, *then there is* β *such that* $\Gamma \vdash_{\mathtt{t}} A'{:}\beta$, *and either* $\Gamma \vdash_{\mathtt{t}} xA_1 \ldots A_n{:}\beta \rightarrow \alpha$, *or* $\alpha \geq_t \pi\beta$ *and* $\Gamma \vdash_{\mathtt{t}} xA_1 \ldots A_n{:}\pi$ *for some* π;
   (d) $A \equiv \bot A_1 \ldots A_n A'$, *then there is* β *such that* $\Gamma \vdash_{\mathtt{t}} A'{:}\beta$, $\alpha \geq_t \pi\beta$ *and* $\Gamma \vdash_{\mathtt{t}} \bot A_1 \ldots A_n{:}\pi$ *for some* π.
3. *If* $\Gamma \vdash_{\mathtt{t}} A{:}\alpha$ *and* $\Gamma \vdash_{\mathtt{t}} A{:}\beta$, *then* $\alpha \wedge \beta \in \mathbf{Types}_{\mathtt{t}}$.

Lemma 22 (Generation Lemma for $\vdash_\dagger$) *Let* $\dagger \in \{\mathtt{w}, \mathtt{h}, \mathtt{e}, \mathtt{i}\}$.

1. $\Gamma \vdash_\dagger \bot{:}\alpha$ *implies* $\alpha =_\dagger \omega$;
2. $\Gamma \vdash_\dagger x{:}\alpha$ *iff* $x : \beta \in \Gamma$ *for some* $\beta \leq_\dagger \alpha$;

3. $\Gamma \vdash_\dagger \lambda x.M:\alpha$ *(and* $\alpha \neq_{\mathtt{w}} \omega$ *when* $\dagger = \mathtt{w}$*) iff* $\alpha =_\dagger \bigwedge_{i\in I}(\alpha_i \to \beta_i)$ *and* $\forall i \in I$ $\Gamma, x : \alpha_i \vdash_\dagger M : \beta_i$*;*
4. $\Gamma \vdash_\dagger MN:\alpha$ *iff there is* β *such that* $\Gamma \vdash_\dagger M:\beta \to \alpha$*, and* $\Gamma \vdash_\dagger N:\beta$*.*

With a standard proof we can show that rule (Eq_β) is admissible in the systems $\vdash_\dagger$ for $\dagger \in \{\mathtt{w}, \mathtt{h}, \mathtt{e}, \mathtt{i}\}$.

Our type assignment systems enjoy the approximation theorem, i.e. we can deduce a type for a term M iff we can deduce this type for an approximant of M, w.r.t. the relative notion of approximant (Theorem 23). Such a theorem, having an interest also by itself, will be used in the next section to show that our type assignment systems are tools to analyse the observational behaviour represented by trees.

The Approximation Theorem can be proved by means of a variant of Tait's "computability" technique (Tait 1967) by defining sets of "approximable" and "computable" terms.

Theorem 23 (Approximation Theorem) *Let* $\dagger \in \{\mathtt{t}, \mathtt{w}, \mathtt{h}, \mathtt{e}, \mathtt{i}\}$*.*
$\Gamma \vdash_\dagger M : \alpha$ *iff there is* $A \in \mathcal{A}_\dagger(M)$ *such that* $\Gamma \vdash_\dagger A : \alpha$*.*

4 CORRESPONDENCE BETWEEN TREES AND TYPINGS

In this section we present the main result of the paper, namely that our type assignment systems can be used to analyse the observational behaviour represented by trees. As recalled in the introduction, similar results are present in the literature for particular notions of tree.

We shall provide an (almost) uniform proof for a theorem which considers other trees besides the ones of the results recalled above. More precisely, we shall prove that $\vdash_\dagger$ derives the same types for two terms M, N iff M, N have the same $\dagger$-trees, where $\dagger \in \{\mathtt{t}, \mathtt{w}, \mathtt{h}, \mathtt{e}, \mathtt{i}\}$.
In order to prove this property, we follow an approach similar to (Dezani et al. 1997) and to (Berarducci et al. to appear) in that we do not allow an infinite set of type variables. The expressive power needed for our purposes and that could be provided by an infinity of type variables can be obtained instead by defining, as we shall do, an infinite set of constant types. These constants will also allow to define the characteristic pairs $\langle basis; type\rangle$ for approximate normal forms.
The key idea is that characteristic pairs give us sufficient information to discriminate between approximate normal forms obtained by pruning (in a suitable way) different trees.

We introduce three different sets of type constants, one for each set of types $\mathbf{Types}_{\mathtt{t}}$,
$\mathbf{Types}_{\mathtt{wh}}$ and $\mathbf{Types}_{\mathtt{ei}}$. It is easy to verify that each one of these constants belong to the corresponding set of types.

Definition 24 *1. Let* $\theta = (\omega\omega \to \omega \to \omega) \wedge ((\omega \to \omega) \to \omega\omega)$. *We define* ϕ_0 *as the type* $\omega(\omega\omega \to \theta)$ *and inductively* $\phi_{i+1} \equiv \phi_i\theta$.

2. *Define* $\psi_i^{(n)} = (\zeta \to \omega^i \to \zeta \to \omega^{n-i} \to \zeta) \wedge \zeta$ *for all* $i \leq n$.
3. *Define* $\chi_i^{(n)} = \zeta \to \vartheta^i \to \zeta \to \vartheta^{n-i} \to \zeta \to \vartheta \wedge \zeta$ *for all* $i \leq n$.

We need to consider special kinds of bases which allow us to distinguish occurrences of different variables or even different occurrences of the same variable. More precisely in presence of applicative types it suffices to give different types to occurrences of different variables, but in all other cases we need to give also different types to different occurrences of the same variable.

Definition 25 *1. We define* $\Gamma_{\mathtt{t}} \in \mathcal{B}_{\mathtt{t}}$ *as the basis* $\{x_n : \phi_n \mid n \in \mathtt{N}\}$.

2. $\Gamma \in \mathcal{B}_{\mathtt{wh}}$ *is a* special basis *of degree* n *if each type declaration in* Γ *has the form* $x : \bigwedge_{i \in I}(\alpha_1^{(i)} \to \ldots \to \alpha_{n_i}^{(i)} \to \psi_i^{(n)})$ *where* $n_i \leq n$ *for all* $i \in I$ *and moreover each* $\psi_i^{(n)}$ *occurs only once as last type.*
3. $\Gamma \in \mathcal{B}_{\mathtt{ei}}$ *is a* generalized special basis *of degree* n *if each type declaration in* Γ *has the form* $x : \zeta$ *or* $x : \bigwedge_{i \in I}(\alpha_1^{(i)} \to \ldots \to \alpha_{n_i}^{(i)} \to \zeta^n \to \chi_i^{(n)})$ *where* $n_i \leq n$ *for all* $i \in I$ *and moreover each* $\chi_i^{(n)}$ *occurs only once as last type.*

Notice that $\Gamma_{\mathtt{t}}$ contains only applicative types, while special basis and generalized special basis contain only arrow types and atomic types.

We associate now to each approximate normal form $A \in \mathcal{A}_\dagger$ a basis $\Gamma \in \mathcal{B}_\ddagger$ and a type $\gamma \in$ **Types**$_\ddagger$ for $\dagger \in \{\mathtt{t}, \mathtt{w}, \mathtt{h}, \mathtt{e}, \mathtt{i}\}$. We call the pair $\langle \Gamma; \gamma \rangle$ the $\dagger$-characteristic pair of A.

Definition 26 *Let* $A \in \mathcal{A}_{\mathtt{t}}$.

1. *The* t-characteristic type $ct_{\mathtt{t}}(A)$ *of* A *is defined as follows.*
   (a) $ct_{\mathtt{t}}(\lambda x_i.A) = \phi_i \to ct_{\mathtt{t}}(A)$,
   (b) $ct_{\mathtt{t}}(\bot A_1 \ldots A_n) = \omega ct_{\mathtt{t}}(A_1) \ldots ct_{\mathtt{t}}(A_n)$,
   (c) $ct_{\mathtt{t}}(x_i A_1 \ldots A_n) = \phi_i ct_{\mathtt{t}}(A_1) \ldots ct_{\mathtt{t}}(A_n)$.
2. *The* t-characteristic pair $cp_{\mathtt{t}}(A)$ *of* A *is* $\langle \Gamma_{\mathtt{t}}; ct_{\mathtt{t}}(A) \rangle$.

Definition 27 *Let* $A \in \mathcal{A}_\dagger^{(n)}$ *for* $\dagger \in \{\mathtt{w}, \mathtt{h}, \mathtt{e}, \mathtt{i}\}$.
The $\dagger$-characteristic pair *of degree* n $pp_\dagger^{(n)}(A)$ *of* A *is defined as follows.*

1. *If* $pp_\dagger^{(n)}(A) = \langle \Gamma, x : \beta; \alpha \rangle$, *then* $pp_\dagger^{(n)}(\lambda x.A) = \langle \Gamma; \beta \to \alpha \rangle$.
2. *If* $pp_\dagger^{(n)}(A) = \langle \Gamma; \alpha \rangle$ *and* x *does not occur in* Γ, *then* $pp_\dagger^{(n)}(\lambda x.A) = \langle \Gamma; \omega \to \alpha \rangle$.
3. *If* $pp_\dagger^{(n)}(A) = \langle \Gamma_i; \alpha_i \rangle$ *where* $i \leq k$ *and* $\Gamma = \biguplus_{i=1}^k \Gamma_i$ *is a special basis of degree* n, *then* $pp_\dagger^{(n)}(\bot A_1 \ldots A_k) = \langle \Gamma; \omega\alpha_1 \ldots \alpha_k \rangle$.

4. *If* $\dagger \in \{\mathtt{w}, \mathtt{h}\}$, $pp_{\dagger}^{(n)}(A_i) = \langle \Gamma_i; \alpha_i \rangle$ *where* $i \le k$ *and* $\Gamma = \biguplus_{i=1}^{k} \Gamma_i \uplus \{x: \alpha_1 \to \ldots \to \alpha_k \to \psi_j^{(n)}\}$ *is a special basis of degree* n, *then* $pp_{\dagger}^{(n)}(xA_1 \ldots A_k) = \langle \Gamma; \psi_j^{(n)} \rangle$. *(In particular when* $k = 0$ *we obtain* $pp_{\dagger}^{(n)}(x) = \langle \{x: \psi_j^{(n)}\}; \psi_j^{(n)} \rangle$*).*
5. *If* $\dagger \in \{\mathtt{e}, \mathtt{i}\}$, $pp_{\dagger}^{(n)}(A_i) = \langle \Gamma_i; \alpha_i \rangle$ *where* $i \le k$ *and* $\Gamma = \biguplus_{i=1}^{k} \Gamma_i \uplus \{x: \alpha_1 \to \ldots \to \alpha_k \to \zeta^n \to \chi_j^{(n)}\}$ *is a generalized special basis of degree* n, *then* $pp_{\dagger}^{(n)}(xA_1 \ldots A_k) = \langle \Gamma; \zeta^n \to \chi_j^{(n)} \rangle$. *(In particular when* $k = 0$ *we obtain* $pp_{\dagger}^{(n)}(x) = \langle \{x: \zeta^n \to \chi_j^{(n)}\}; \zeta^n \to \chi_j^{(n)} \rangle$*).*

Notice that we can always choose the Γ_i in such a way the conditions of the previous definition are satisfied.

We can now prove that, in all cases, if the $\dagger$-characteristic pair of A is $\langle \Gamma; \gamma \rangle$, and if we deduce $\Gamma \vdash_{\dagger} B: \gamma$ (and some conditions on the number of symbols of B or of $(B)_{\dagger}^{(h)}$, where h is the height of the tree of A, hold), then $A \sqsubseteq_{\dagger} B$, where $\sqsubseteq_{\dagger}$ has been defined in Definition 11.

Lemma 28 *1. If* $\Gamma_{\mathtt{t}} \vdash_{\mathtt{t}} A: \phi_i$ *then* $A \equiv x_i$.
2. *If* $\Gamma_{\mathtt{t}} \vdash_{\mathtt{t}} A: \pi\alpha$ *and* $\pi\alpha \ne \phi_i$ *for all* i, *then* $A \equiv A_1 A_2$ *with* $\Gamma_{\mathtt{t}} \vdash_{\mathtt{t}} A_1: \pi$ *and* $\Gamma_{\mathtt{t}} \vdash_{\mathtt{t}} A_2: \alpha$.
3. *If* $\Gamma_{\mathtt{t}} \vdash_{\mathtt{t}} A: \phi_i \to \alpha$, *then* $A \equiv \lambda x_i.A'$ *and* $\Gamma_{\mathtt{t}} \vdash_{\mathtt{t}} A': \alpha$.
4. *If* $\Gamma_{\mathtt{t}} \vdash_{\mathtt{t}} B: ct_{\mathtt{t}}(A)$ *then* $A \sqsubseteq_{\mathtt{t}} B$.

Lemma 29 *Let* $\dagger \in \{\mathtt{w}, \mathtt{h}\}$, $A \in \mathcal{A}_{\dagger}^{(n)}$ *and* $pp_{\dagger}^{(n)}(A) = \langle \Gamma; \alpha \rangle$. *Then* $B \in \mathcal{A}_{\dagger}$ *and* $\Gamma \vdash_{\dagger} B: \alpha$ *imply* $A \sqsubseteq_{\dagger} B$.

Lemma 30 *Assume* $\dagger \in \{\mathtt{e}, \mathtt{i}\}$, $A, B \in \mathcal{A}_{\dagger}$. *Let* h *be the height of* $\mathcal{T}_{\dagger}(A)$, *and* n *be such that* $A, (B)_{\dagger}^{(h)} \in \mathcal{A}_{\dagger}^{(n)}$. *Then* $pp_{\dagger}^{(n)}(A) = \langle \Gamma; \alpha \rangle$ *and* $\Gamma \vdash_{\dagger} B: \alpha$ *imply* $A \sqsubseteq_{\dagger} B$.

Theorem 31 (Main Theorem) *For* $\dagger \in \{\mathtt{t}, \mathtt{w}, \mathtt{h}, \mathtt{e}, \mathtt{i}\}$ *the following conditions are equivalent:*

1. $\mathcal{T}_{\dagger}(M) = \mathcal{T}_{\dagger}(N)$;
2. $\Gamma \vdash_{\dagger} M: \alpha$ *iff* $\Gamma \vdash_{\dagger} N: \alpha$ *for all* Γ, α.

Proof. (1.)$\Rightarrow$(2.). If M and N have the same trees, then they have the same sets of approximate normal forms, and therefore the same types by the Approximation Theorem.

(2.)$\Rightarrow$(1.). If $\mathcal{T}_{\dagger}(M) \ne \mathcal{T}_{\dagger}(N)$, then by Lemma 13 we can find an approximate normal form A such that $A \in \mathcal{A}_{\dagger}(M)$ and there is no $B \in \mathcal{A}_{\dagger}(N)$ such that $A \sqsubseteq_{\dagger} B$ (or vice versa). If $\dagger = \mathtt{t}$ we have by the Approximation Theorem and Lemma 28(4.) that $\Gamma_{\mathtt{t}} \vdash_{\mathtt{t}} M: ct_{\mathtt{t}}(A)$ and $\Gamma_{\mathtt{t}} \nvdash_{\mathtt{t}} N: ct_{\mathtt{t}}(A)$. If $\dagger \in \{\mathtt{w}, \mathtt{h}\}$ let n be so big that $A \in \mathcal{A}_{\dagger}^{(n)}$ and $\langle \Gamma; \alpha \rangle = pp_{\dagger}^{(n)}(A)$. We have by the Approximation Theorem and Lemma 29 that $\Gamma \vdash_{\dagger} M: \alpha$ and $\Gamma \nvdash_{\dagger} N: \alpha$. If $\dagger \in \{\mathtt{e}, \mathtt{i}\}$, let h be the height of $\mathcal{T}_\dagger(A)$ and n be so big that $A, (N)^{(h)}_\dagger \in \mathcal{A}^{(n)}_\dagger$. This implies $(B)^{(h)}_\dagger \in \mathcal{A}^{(n)}_\dagger$ for all $B \in \mathcal{A}(N)$. Moreover let $\langle \Gamma; \alpha \rangle = pp^{(n)}_\dagger(A)$. We have by the Approximation Theorem and Lemma 30 that $\Gamma \vdash_\dagger M : \alpha$ and $\Gamma \not\vdash_\dagger N : \alpha$. $\square$

In all cases we get a discrimination algorithm, i.e. for two arbitrary terms M, N with different $\dagger$-trees, we can always find a basis Γ and a type α such that $\Gamma \vdash_\dagger M : \alpha$ and $\Gamma \not\vdash_\dagger N : \alpha$, or vice versa. The less easy case is that of $\dagger \in \{\mathtt{e}, \mathtt{i}\}$. In this case we take an approximate normal form A such that $A \in \mathcal{A}_\dagger(M)$ and there is no $B \in \mathcal{A}_\dagger(N)$ such that $A \sqsubseteq_\dagger B$ (or vice versa). Let h be the height of $\mathcal{T}_\dagger(A)$ and n be so big that $A, (N)^{(h)}_\dagger \in \mathcal{A}^{(n)}_\dagger$. This implies $(B)^{(h)}_\dagger \in \mathcal{A}^{(n)}_\dagger$ for all $B \in \mathcal{A}(N)$. Now we can choose $\langle \Gamma; \alpha \rangle = pp^{(n)}_\dagger(A)$.

Acknowledgements. This paper has strongly benefited from comments and remarks by the Anonymous Referees. Matteo Sereno has been of great help in solving some LaTeX compilation problems.
The first author expresses his gratitude to Roberto Nobilio and Valeria Bosso for interesting discussions. The second author thanks Masako Takahashi for hospitality and enlightening discussions. The third author, whose work has been supported by a COE grant of the Science and Technology Agency of Japan, thanks Yoshiki Kinoshita for introducing him to the ETL environment, and Vincent van Oostrom for fruitful discussions.

REFERENCES

Abramsky S.. Domain theory in logical form. *Ann. of Pure and Appl. Logics*, 51, 1991, 1-77.

Abramsky S., Ong C.-H.L.. Full abstraction in the lazy λ-calculus. *Info. and Comp.* 105, 1993, 159-267.

Alessi F. Type preorders. CAAP'94, *LNCS* 787, Springer-Verlag, Berlin, 1994, 37-51.

Barendregt H.. The Lambda Calculus Its Syntax and Semantics. Studies in Logic 103, North-Holland, Amsterdam, 1984.

Barendregt H., Coppo M., Dezani-Ciancaglini M.. A filter lambda model and the completeness of type assignment. *J. Symbolic Logic* 48, 1983, 931-940.

Berarducci A.. Infinite Lambda-calculus and Non-sensible Models. *Logic and Algebra*, Lecture Notes in Pure and Applied Mathematics 180, Marcel Dekker Inc., 1996, 339-378.

Berarducci A., Dezani-Ciancaglini M.. Infinite lambda-calculus and types. *Theor. Comp. Sci.*, to appear.

Boudol G.. A lambda calculus for (strict) parallel functions. *Info. and Comp.* 108, 1994, 51-127.

Boudol G., Laneve C.. The discriminating power of multiplicities in the λ-calculus. *Info. and Comp.* 126(1), 83–102, 1996.

Coppo M., Dezani-Ciancaglini M., Honsell F., Longo G.. Extended type structures and filter lambda models. *Logic Colloquium '82*, North-Holland, Amsterdam, 1983, 241-262.

Coppo M., Dezani-Ciancaglini M., Venneri B.. Principal type schemes and λ-calculus semantics. *To H.B.Curry, Essays on Combinatory Logic, Lambda Calculus and Formalism*, Academic Press, New York, 1980, 535-560.

Coppo M., Dezani-Ciancaglini M., Zacchi M.. Type theories, normal forms and $\mathcal{D}_\infty$ lambda models. *Info. and Control* 72(2), 1987, 85-116.

Dezani-Ciancaglini M., de'Liguoro U., Piperno A.. Filter models for conjunctive-disjunctive λ-calculus. *Theor. Comp. Sci.* 170(1-2), 1996, 83–128.

Dezani-Ciancaglini M., de'Liguoro U., Piperno A.. A filter model for concurrent λ-calculi. *SIAM J. of Comp.*, to appear.

Dezani-Ciancaglini M., Tiuryn J., Urzyczyn P.. Discrimination by parallel observers. *LICS '97*, IEEE Comp.Soc. Press, Los Alamitos, 1997, 396–407.

Engeler E.. Algebra and combinators. *Algebra Universalis* 13(3), 1981, 389-392.

Hyland M.. A syntactic characterization of the equality in some models of the λ-calculus. *J. London Math.Soc.* 12(2), 1976, 361-370.

Kennaway J. R., Klop J. W Sleep R., de Vries F.J.. Transfinite reductions in orthogonal term rewriting systems. *Info. and Comp.* 119(1), 1995, 18-38.

Kennaway R., Klop J. W., Sleep R., de Vries F.J.. Infinitary lambda calculus. *Theor. Comp. Sci.*, 175(1), 1997, 93-126.

Kennaway J.R., van Oostrom V., de Vries F.J.. Meaningless terms in rewriting. ALP'96, *LNCS* 1139, Springer-Verlag, Berlin, 1996, 254-268.

Lévy J.J.. An algebraic interpretation of the $\lambda - \beta - \mathbf{K}$-calculus and an application of the labelled λ-calculus. *Theor. Comput. Sci.* 2(1), 97–114, 1976.

Longo G.. Set theoretical models of lambda calculus: theory, expansions and isomorphisms. *Ann. of Pure and Appl. Logic* 24, 153-188, 1983.

Nakajima R.. Infinite normal forms for the λ-calculus. LCCST, LNCS 37, Springer-Verlag, Berlin, 1975, 62-82

Ronchi della Rocca S.. Characterization theorems for a filter lambda model. *Info. and Control* 54, 1982, 201-216.

Sangiorgi D.. "The lazy λ-calculus in a concurrency scenario. *Info. and Comp.* 111(1), 120-153, 1994.

Scott D.S.. Continuous lattices. TAGL, *LNM* 274, Springer-Verlag, Berlin, 1972, 97-136.

Scott D.S.. Data types as lattices. *Siam J. Comput.* 5, 1976, 522-587.

Scott D.S.. Domains for denotational semantics. ICALP'82, *LNCS* 140, Springer-Verlag, Berlin, 1982, 577-613.

Tait W.W.. Intensional interpretation of functionals of finite types I. *J. Symbolic Logic* 32, 1967, 198-212.

Wadsworth C.P.. The relation between computational and denotational properties for scott's D_∞ models of the λ-calculus. *Siam J. Comput.* 5, 1976, 488-521.

BIOGRAPHY

FRANCO BARBANERA was born in Latina (3 Nov. 1963). Ph.D. at the University of Torino. Assistant professor at the University of Torino since 1992.

MARIANGIOLA DEZANI-CIANCAGLINI was born in Torino (22 Dec. 1946). Ph.D. at the University of Nijmegen. Full professor at the University of Torino since 1981. Member of IFIP W.G.2.2 on "Formal Description of Programming Concepts", of the Editorial Board of "Information and Computation", of the "Academia Europaea" and of LICS Advisory Board.

FER-JAN DE VRIES received his Ph.D from the University of Utrecht in 1989. After a six year stay at CWI in Amsterdam he went to Japan as a visiting researcher at NTT and Hitachi. Currently he is projectleader of the Rewriting Group of the El.Lab. in Tsukuba, Japan.

7

Structures for lazy semantics

O. Bastonero, A. Pravato, S. Ronchi della Rocca
Università degli studi di Torino
Dipartimento di Informatica, C.so Svizzera 185, 10149 Torino, Italia
Email: bastone, pravato, ronchi@di.unito.it

Abstract

The paper explores different approaches for modeling the lazy λ-calculus, which is a paradigmatic language for studying the operational behaviour of programming languages, like Haskell, using a call-by-name and lazy evaluation mechanism. Two models for lazy λ-calculus in the coherence spaces setting are built. They give a new insight in the behaviour of the language since their local structures are different from the one of all existing models in the literature. In order to compare different models, a class of models for lazy λ-calculus is defined, namely, the lazy regular models class. All the models adequate for the lazy λ-calculus studied in the literature belong to this class.

Keywords

Lazy Lambda Calculus, Denotational Semantics, Coherent Spaces.

1 INTRODUCTION

Different structures have been explored for building models for the standard λ-calculus, like Scott domains, Engeler's algebras, DI-domains, filter models and coherence spaces. This richness has been very useful for grasping unexpected operational properties of λ-calculus. Indeed, it has been proved that there are λ-theories which can be modeled in Scott's domains but not in coherence spaces (Bastonero & Gouy to appear) and vice-versa (Bastonero 1996).

In this paper we are interested in studying structures for modeling the lazy λ-calculus. The lazy λ-calculus, formally introduced in Abramsky & Ong (1993), can be seen as a paradigm for programming languages, like Haskell (Hudak, Jones & Wadler 1992), using a call-by-name and a lazy evaluation mechanism. An evaluation mechanism is call-by-name when parameters are passed to a function before to be evaluated, moreover it is lazy when a procedure is evaluated only when its parameters are supplied. The syntax and the reduction rule of the lazy λ-calculus coincide with the syntax and reduction rule of the classical λ-calculus, but in this calculus a particular reduction strategy is introduced. This strategy leads to the concept of "value", namely a term on which the computation induced by the strategy stops. The set of values of the lazy λ-calculus contains all the abstraction terms, which formal-

Programming Concepts and Methods D. Gries, & W-P. de Roever (Eds.)

ize the notion of "procedure". Consequently, strictly speaking, all the models of the classical λ-calculus are models also for the lazy one, but we are interested in such models which are adequate with respect to the operational semantics modeling the call-by-name lazy evaluation mechanism. Models for lazy λ-calculus, adequate w.r.t. its operational semantics, have been studied in Longo (1983) and Abramsky & Ong (1993). The model of Longo ($\mathcal{M}_L$) is built in the Engeler's algebras setting, while the model of Abramsky and Ong ($\mathcal{M}_{AO}$) is built in the Scott's domains setting (they present it also as filter domain). These models have a very different local structure, namely, the theory of $\mathcal{M}_L$ is strictly included in the one of $\mathcal{M}_{AO}$, and neither the former nor the latter of the two models is fully abstract.

There is not, until now, a model for lazy λ-calculus built in the coherence spaces setting. Perhaps this depends on the fact that, since coherence spaces have been presented by Girard as a simplification of Scott domains, it would have been natural to mimic the Abramsky and Ong construction in the coherence spaces setting. But, this is not easy, since $\mathcal{M}_{AO}$ is based on the *lifting* constructor, which has not a natural corresponding construction in coherence spaces. And indeed, in order to mimic the lifting construction for modeling the lazy call-by-value evaluation in coherence spaces, Honsell and Lenisa defined a different notion of coherence space, the pointed coherence space (Honsell & Lenisa 1993).

Inside cartesian closed categories whose objects are cpo and morphisms are continuous functions, we define a class of models for lazy λ-calculus, the class of "lazy regular models", to which both the previous recalled models belong. All the models belonging to this class share important properties, like the approximation property. The definition of lazy regular models points out that a model for λ-calculus is adequate w.r.t. the lazy operational semantics if it is based on a domain $\mathcal{D}$ such that $(\mathcal{D} \Rightarrow \mathcal{D})$ is a retract of $\mathcal{D}$ (where $(\mathcal{D} \Rightarrow \mathcal{D})$ represents the function space from $\mathcal{D}$ to itself) and, if $\phi : \mathcal{D} \rightarrow (\mathcal{D} \Rightarrow \mathcal{D})$ and $\psi : (\mathcal{D} \Rightarrow \mathcal{D}) \rightarrow \mathcal{D}$ are the immersion, projection pair, $\psi(\bot_{(\mathcal{D}\Rightarrow\mathcal{D})}) \neq \bot_{\mathcal{D}}$. Let call *strict* a retraction of this kind. In fact the lifting construction is the easiest way of building a strict retraction in Scott domains. Consequently, in order to build a strict retraction in the coherence space setting, it is sufficient to have $\mathcal{D} \approx T(\mathcal{D} \Rightarrow \mathcal{D})$, where T is the interpretation of any additive or modal constructor. We exhibit two models of lazy λ-calculus, $\mathcal{M}_1$ and $\mathcal{M}_2$, built over the coherence space which is the minimal solution of the equation $\mathcal{D} \approx I\&(\mathcal{D} \Rightarrow_s \mathcal{D})$, where I is the coherence space with just one atom (interpreting the unity of the tensor product), $\&$ is the additive (cartesian) product, and $(\mathcal{D} \Rightarrow_s \mathcal{D})$ is the coherence space representing the stable functions from $\mathcal{D}$ to $\mathcal{D}$. In the paper we use a primitive constructor $(\cdot)_\emptyset$, isomorphic to $I\&\_$, that we call *pseudo-lifting*. Such a constructor can be viewed as a restricted power-domain construction.

It turns out that these two models give a new insight in the operational behaviour of the lazy λ-calculus. We prove that $\mathcal{M}_1$ has the same theory as $\mathcal{M}_L$, and we conjecture that $\mathcal{M}_2$ has the same theory as $\mathcal{M}_{AO}$. But the two new defined models have a local structure which is different from both the one of $\mathcal{M}_L$ and $\mathcal{M}_{AO}$. In particular, in all models all the unsolvable of infinite order are equated, but in $\mathcal{M}_L$ and $\mathcal{M}_{AO}$ such unsolvables are the greatest element, while in both $\mathcal{M}_1$ and $\mathcal{M}_2$ they are a maximal element, not comparable with any solvable term. An unsolvable of infinite order converges whatever sequence of arguments it is applied, while for a solvable term there is at least one sequence of arguments making it converging and at least one sequence making it diverging. Looking at the lazy λ-calculus as the tool for studying the "core" of lazy call-by-name real programming languages, an unsolvable of infinite order represents a program converging to an *undetermined* value, while a solvable term is such that it produces a particular, specified, value when applied to some sequence of arguments. Ong, in Ong (1992), interpreted the fact that the unsolvable of infinite order are the top in $\mathcal{M}_L$ and $\mathcal{M}_{AO}$, by the fact that they represent an *over-specified* value. This is reasonable, but the two models we exhibit show that it is possible to have a more refined interpretation, when undetermined and determined values are interpreted in not comparable points.

As far as the full-abstraction problem is concerned, no one of the two models is fully-abstract: indeed, to $\mathcal{M}_2$ the counter-example used in Theorem 8.1.1 of Abramsky & Ong (1993) can be applied, inducing that $\mathcal{M}_1$ too is not fully-abstract.

An example of model for lazy (but this time *call-by-value*) computation built using a modal construction in the category of coherence spaces and linear functions, can be found in Pravato, Ronchi della Rocca & Roversi (1995).

2 LAZY MODELS

In this section we will define the lazy λ-calculus and its models. Moreover, we will introduce a class of models, particularly suitable for our purposes.

Let Λ be the set of terms of the pure (i.e. without constants) λ-calculus built out from a denumerable set *Var* of variables. I.e., terms of Λ are generated by the following grammar: $M ::= x \mid MM \mid \lambda x.M$ where x ranges over *Var*. Let $\Lambda^o \subseteq \Lambda$ be the set of closed terms.

Let $\Rightarrow_\beta$ denote the contextual transitive and reflexive closure of the β-reduction rule $\rightarrow_\beta$ on terms, defined as: $(\lambda x.M)N \rightarrow_\beta M[N/x]$. Let denote with $=_\beta$ the symmetric contextual transitive and reflexive closure of $\rightarrow_\beta$.

Definition 1 *Let Val* $= \{\lambda x.M \mid M \in \Lambda\} \subseteq \Lambda$.
i) The notion of lazy convergence *for closed terms of the λ-calculus is defined through a logical system proving judgements of the shape:* $M \Downarrow_{lazy} P$ *where* $M \in \Lambda^o$ *and* $P \in$ *Val.*
The rules of the system hare the following:

$$\frac{}{\lambda x.M \Downarrow_{lazy} \lambda x.M}(abs) \qquad \frac{M \Downarrow_{lazy} \lambda x.P \qquad P[N/x] \Downarrow_{lazy} Q}{MN \Downarrow_{lazy} Q}(app)$$

Let $M \Downarrow_{lazy}$ *(read:* M *is* valuable *or* M converges*) be an abbreviation for* $\exists P.M \Downarrow_{lazy} P$*, and* $M \Uparrow_{lazy}$ *(*M diverges*) be an abbreviation for* $\nexists P.M \Downarrow_{lazy} P$*. Notice that this notion of convergence is a particular β-reduction strategy, namely if* $M \Downarrow_{lazy} P$*, then* $M \Rightarrow_\beta P$.

ii) The lazy operational preorder *on* Λ *is defined as follows: for all* $M, N \in \Lambda$
$M \sqsubseteq_{lazy} N \Leftrightarrow (\forall C[.] \,.\, C[M], C[N] \in \Lambda^o \,.\, C[M] \Downarrow_{lazy} \Rightarrow C[N] \Downarrow_{lazy})$
Let $\approx_{lazy}$ *be the equivalence induced by* $\sqsubseteq_{lazy}$.

In order to model the lazy convergence of the λ-calculus, a semantic account of the notion of valuable terms must be given. This can be done by enriching the well–known set–theoretical definition of λ-calculus model in Hindley-Longo style, see Hindley & Longo (1980), by explicitly introducing a subset V of the interpretation domain, where all valuable terms have to be interpreted.

Definition 2 *A* model for the lazy λ-calculus *is a 4-tuple* $\mathcal{M} = (D, \bullet, V, [\![\cdot]\!])$ *where: D together with* $\bullet$ *is an applicative structure, i.e., it is a set with at least two elements equipped with a binary operation* $\bullet : D^2 \to D$, $V \subseteq D$ *is the set of* semantic values, $[\![\cdot]\!] : \Lambda \to \mathbf{Env} \to D$ *is the* interpretation function, *where* **Env** *is the set of* environments, *(i.e. maps* $\rho : Var \to D$*), such that* $(D, [\![\cdot]\!])$ *is a model for the pure* λ*-calculus, and* $(M \in Val \Longrightarrow \forall \rho \in \mathbf{Env} \,.\, [\![M]\!]_\rho \in V)$.

The semantic equivalence of terms in $\mathcal{M}$ *is defined as usual: given* $M, N \in \Lambda$,
$\mathcal{M} \models M = N \iff (\forall \rho \in \mathbf{Env} \,.\, [\![M]\!]_\rho = [\![N]\!]_\rho)$.

Remember that a model $\mathcal{M}$ for a given λ-calculus is *adequate* w.r.t. a $\approx$ operational semantics if and only if $\mathcal{M} \models M = N$ implies $M \approx N$. The following proposition gives an equivalent notion of equivalence for lazy models, based on the notion of semantics values.

Proposition 3 *A model* $\mathcal{M} = (D, \bullet, V, [\![\cdot]\!])$ *for the lazy* λ*-calculus is adequate for the lazy operational equivalence* $\approx_{lazy}$ *if:* $\forall M \in \Lambda^o \,.\, ([\![M]\!] \in V \Longrightarrow M \Downarrow_{lazy})$.

Remark 4 In Abramsky & Ong (1993) we find a general definition of a model of the lazy λ-calculus in a different but equivalent style, starting from the basic notion of applicative structure equipped with a partial evaluation function. They require explicitly that a model for the lazy λ-calculus be adequate w.r.t. $\approx_{lazy}$. If Definition 2 was modified by adding the condition of Proposition 3, so requiring explicitly the adequacy, then the resulting definition would be equivalent to the one given in Abramsky & Ong (1993). We chosed to have adequacy as an additional condition for sake of uniformity with the standard λ-calculus treatment. And indeed, there is just one definition of what is a λ-calculus model, but a given model may be adequate or not w.r.t. a given operational semantics. For example, the standard D_∞ Scott's model is adequate w.r.t. the operational semantics induced by a call-by-name reduction machine (whose values are the head-normal-forms), but it is not adequate to the one induced by the normalizing machine (whose values are all the normal-forms). An example of a model adequate w.r.t. this last operational semantics is the model described in Coppo, Dezani-Ciancaglini & Zacchi (1987).

2.1 Lazy regular models

For our purposes, we need to consider only a particular class of models for the lazy λ-calculus, the $lazy\text{-}regular$-models, based on the notion of domains. All the models we are interested in belong to this class. We will prove that all lazy-regular models are adequate w.r.t. the given operational semantics. First of all, let recall the definition of $regular$ model for λ-calculus as given in Bastonero & Gouy (to appear).

Let **C** be a closed cartesian category (c.c.c.) with enough points. Let $\Rightarrow$: $\mathbf{C} \times \mathbf{C} \to \mathbf{C}$ be the bifunctor such that, for all objects A, B, the object $A \Rightarrow B$ internalizes the set $\mathbf{Hom_C}(A, B)$ of morphisms from the object A to the object B, through the operation $\Lambda_{A,B,C} : \mathbf{Hom_C}(A \times B, C) \to \mathbf{Hom_C}(A, (B \Rightarrow C))$ and the *evaluation morphism*: $ev_{B,C} : (B \Rightarrow C) \times B \to C$, for each C (see Asperti & Longo (1991) for details).

Definition 5 *A regular category* **C** *is a c.c.c. such that: every object* A *of* **C** *is a pointed complete partial order w.r.t. the order relation* $\leq_A$, *where* $\bot_A$ *denotes the minimum point; the morphisms of* **C** *are continuous functions.*

For each morphism f from an object A to an object B, $\Lambda(f)$ is a shortening for $\Lambda_{\mathbb{I},A,B}(f \circ \lambda_A)$ (where λ_A is the isomorphism between A and $\mathbb{I} \times A$, taking $\mathbb{I}$ as the unity of the cartesian product $\times$) which is the point in $A \Rightarrow B$ corresponding to f. Conversely, Λ^{-1} will be used as a shortening for $\Lambda^{-1}_{\mathbb{I},A,B}$.

Definition 6 *Let* $\mathcal{D}$ *be a reflexive object of a regular category, namely, an object such that* $\mathcal{D} \rhd (\mathcal{D} \Rightarrow \mathcal{D})$ *through the retraction pair* (ϕ, ψ). $\mathcal{D}$ *is an applicative structure once defined a binary operator* $\bullet$ *in the following way:*
$\forall d_1, d_2 \in \mathcal{D} \, . \, d_1 \bullet d_2 = (\Lambda^{-1}(\phi(d_1)))(d_2)$.
Then $\mathcal{M} = (D, \bullet, [\![\cdot]\!])$ *is a* regular model *of* λ*-calculus, where the interpretation function is defined as follows:*

- $[\![x]\!]_\rho = \rho(x)$;
- $[\![MN]\!]_\rho = (\Lambda^{-1}(\phi([\![M]\!]_\rho)))([\![N]\!]_\rho)$;
- $[\![\lambda x.M]\!]_\rho = \psi(\Lambda(d \in \mathcal{D} \mapsto [\![M]\!]_{\rho[d/x]}))$.

Definition 7 *Let* $\mathcal{M} = (D, \bullet, [\![\cdot]\!])$ *be a regular model.*

i) The set of projections *of* $\mathcal{M}$ *is the set of points* $p \in \mathcal{D}$ *such that:* $p \leq_{\mathcal{D}} \psi(\Lambda(d \in \mathcal{D} \mapsto d))$ *and* $p = \psi(\Lambda(d \in \mathcal{D} \mapsto p \bullet (p \bullet d)))$. *Let us notice that for every projection* p *we have:* $\forall d \in \mathcal{D} \, . \, p \bullet d = p \bullet (p \bullet d)$.

ii) $\mathcal{M}$ *is* stratified *if there exists an increasing sequence of projections* $p_0 \leq_{\mathcal{D}} p_1 \leq_{\mathcal{D}} p_2 \leq_{\mathcal{D}} \cdots$ *in* $\mathcal{D}$ *such that:*

- $\bigsqcup_n p_n = \psi(\Lambda(d \in \mathcal{D} \mapsto d))$,
- $p_{n+1} \bullet d_1 \bullet d_2 = p_n \bullet (d_1 \bullet (p_n \bullet d_2))$ *for all* $d_1, d_2 \in \mathcal{D}$,
- $p_0 \bullet d = \bot_{\mathcal{D}}$ *for all* $d \in \mathcal{D}$.

Definition 8 *A* lazy regular model $\mathcal{M} = (\mathcal{D}, \bullet, \mathcal{V}, [\![\cdot]\!])$ *is a model for the lazy λ-calculus (as in Definition 2) where:*

i) $(\mathcal{D}, \bullet, [\![\cdot]\!])$ *is a stratified regular model;*

ii) $\psi : (\mathcal{D} \Rightarrow \mathcal{D}) \to \mathcal{D}$ *is not strict, i.e.,* $\psi(\bot_{(\mathcal{D}\Rightarrow\mathcal{D})}) \neq \bot_{\mathcal{D}}$,

iii) $\bot_{\mathcal{D}} \notin \mathcal{V}$.

Since every regular model is built over a partial order, we can now extend the notion of adequacy. Namely a lazy regular model $\mathcal{M} = (\mathcal{D}, \bullet, \mathcal{V}, [\![\cdot]\!])$ is adequate for $\sqsubseteq_{lazy}$ if and only if $\mathcal{M} \models M \sqsubseteq N$ implies $M \sqsubseteq_{lazy} N$, where $\mathcal{M} \models M \sqsubseteq N$ means $\forall \rho. [\![M]\!]_\rho \leq_{\mathcal{D}} [\![N]\!]_\rho$.

Theorem 9 *Every lazy regular model is adequate for the lazy operational preorder* $\sqsubseteq_{lazy}$.

Proof. In the following section we will prove that every lazy regular model enjoys an approximation property w.r.t. a suitable notion of approximants. The adequacy is a direct consequence of this fact. □

3 APPROXIMATION IN LAZY REGULAR MODELS

In this section we establish that the notion of *Lévy–Longo preorder*, introduced in Longo (1983) by adapting an idea of Lévy (Lévy 1975), is a key one for speaking about the theories of lazy regular models. Namely, the Lévy–Longo preorder is included in the local theory of every lazy regular model. The proof of this last point is an immediate consequence of the fact that all the lazy regular models share an approximation property w.r.t. the same notion of approximant, which is an adaptation of the one introduced by Hyland (Hyland 1976) and Wadsworth (Wadsworth 1978) for analyzing Scott's D_∞ model. The approximation property says that the interpretation of a term is the supremum of the interpretations of a set of normal forms in an extended language (its *approximants*).

3.1 Approximation Theorem

Let the $\lambda(\Omega)$-calculus be the following extension of the pure λ-calculus obtained by adjoining to set of variable the constant Ω. The rewriting rules are the β-rule and also the Ω-rule defined by: (Ω) $\quad \Omega M \to_\Omega \Omega$.
Every lazy regular model $(\mathcal{D}, \bullet, \mathcal{V}, [\![\cdot]\!])$ can be extended to $\Lambda(\Omega)$ posing $[\![\Omega]\!]_\rho = \bot_{\mathcal{D}}$.

Definition 10 *Let* $M \in \Lambda$.

$A \in \Lambda(\Omega)$ *is an* approximation *of* M*, and we write* $A \, app \, M$*, if* A *is obtained from* M *by substituting* Ω *for some subterm of* M.

Let $\mathcal{N}_{\beta\Omega} \subseteq \Lambda(\Omega)$ *be the set of* βΩ*-normal forms. The set of* approximants *of* M *is the set* $\mathcal{A}(M) = \{A \in \mathcal{N}_{\beta\Omega} \mid \exists M'.(M \Rightarrow_\beta M') \wedge (A \, app \, M')\}$.

It is immediate to verify that the terms of $\mathcal{N}_{\beta\Omega}$ have either the shape $\lambda x_1 \ldots x_n.\Omega$ or $\lambda x_1 \ldots x_n.xA_1 \ldots A_p$, where $A_i \in \mathcal{N}_{\beta\Omega}$ (for $p \geq 0, n \geq 0$).

For lazy regular models an approximation theorem holds. It can be proved by adapting the proof given in Ong (1992) (theorem 4.8) for a class of models of lazy λ-calculus which is properly included in our class.

Theorem 11 (Approximation Theorem) *Let $\mathcal{M} = (\mathcal{D}, \bullet, \mathcal{V}, [\![\cdot]\!])$ be a lazy regular model. For all $\rho \in$ **Env** and $M \in \Lambda$, $[\![\mathcal{A}(M)]\!]_\rho$ is directed in $\mathcal{D}$ and $[\![M]\!]_\rho = \bigsqcup\{[\![A]\!]_\rho \mid A \in \mathcal{A}(M)\}$.*

3.2 Lazy preorders

In order to introduce some notions of Lazy preorders, we need to recall the notion of order of an unsolvable.

An unsolvable term M is of *order 0* if $\not\exists P.M =_\beta \lambda x.P$. An unsolvable term M is *of order n* ($n > 0$) if n is the maximum m such that $\exists P.M =_\beta \lambda x_1 \ldots x_m.P$. If such an n does not exist, then M is *unsolvable of infinite order*.

Let us recall the Lévy-Longo preorder ($\sqsubseteq_{LT}$) given in Longo (1983) and studied in Ong (1992), and the $\sqsubseteq_{PSE}$ preorder, defined in Ong (1992). Moreover we need to define a new preorder between terms, the stable lazy one, denoted by $\sqsubseteq_{LS}$, for studying the local structure of the models we will introduce later.

Definition 12 *$M \sqsubseteq_i N$ if and only if $\forall k \geq 0.M \sqsubseteq_i^k N$ where $i \in \{LT, LS, PSE\}$ and $M \sqsubseteq_i^k N$ is so defined:*

- *$M \sqsubseteq_i^0 N$ always holds;*
- *$M \sqsubseteq_{LT}^{k+1} N$ if and only if:*
  (i) M is unsolvable of order n and $\exists P \in \Lambda$ s.t. $N =_\beta \lambda x_1 \ldots x_n.P$, or
  (ii) M is unsolvable of infinite order and N is unsolvable of infinite order, or
  (iii) $M =_\beta \lambda x_1 \ldots x_n.yM_1 \ldots M_p$ and $N =_\beta \lambda x_1 \ldots x_n.yN_1 \ldots N_p$ and $\forall 1 \leq i \leq p.M_i \sqsubseteq_{LT}^k N_i$;
- *$M \sqsubseteq_{PSE}^{k+1} N$ if and only if:*
  (i) M is unsolvable of order n and $\exists P \in \Lambda$ s.t. $N =_\beta \lambda x_1 \ldots x_n.P$, or
  (ii) N is unsolvable of infinite order, or
  (iii) $M =_\beta \lambda x_1 \ldots x_n.yM_1 \ldots M_p$ and $N =_\beta \lambda x_1 \ldots x_{n+q}.yN_1 \ldots N_{p+q}$ and $\forall 1 \leq i \leq p.M_i \sqsubseteq_{PSE}^k N_i$ and $\forall 1 \leq j \leq q.x_{n+j} \sqsubseteq_{PSE}^k N_{p+j}$.
- *$M \sqsubseteq_{LS}^{k+1} N$ if and only if:*
  (i) M is unsolvable of order n and $\exists P \in \Lambda$ s.t. $N =_\beta \lambda x_1 \ldots x_n.P$, or
  (ii) M is unsolvable of infinite order and N is unsolvable of infinite order, or
  (iii) $M =_\beta \lambda x_1 \ldots x_n.yM_1 \ldots M_p$ and $N =_\beta \lambda x_1 \ldots x_{n+q}.yN_1 \ldots N_{p+q}$ and $\forall 1 \leq i \leq p.M_i \sqsubseteq_{LS}^k N_i$ and $\forall 1 \leq j \leq q.x_{n+j} \sqsubseteq_{LS}^k N_{p+j}$.

All the three preorders share the property that they equate all the unsolvables of infinite order. By the way, such unsolvables are the greatest element in $\sqsubseteq_{PSE}$, while in both $\sqsubseteq_{LT}$ and $\sqsubseteq_{LS}$ they are maximal elements, not the top. As far as solvable terms are concerned, $M \Rightarrow_\eta N$ implies $N \sqsubseteq_i M$ ($i \in \{LS, PSE\}$), while this implication does not hold for $\sqsubseteq_{LT}$.

Proposition 13 $\sqsubseteq_{LT} \subset \sqsubseteq_{LS} \subset \sqsubseteq_{PSE}$ *and they induce the same equivalence relation.*

Theorem 14 *Let $\mathcal{M}$ be a lazy regular model and let $M, N \in \Lambda$.*
$M \sqsubseteq_{LT} N \Longrightarrow (\mathcal{M} \models M \sqsubseteq N)$.

Proof. (Sketch) Using the characterisation of approximants, we show that if $M \sqsubseteq_{LT} N$ then $\mathcal{A}(M) \subseteq \mathcal{A}(N)$. Then the thesis follows from the approximation theorem. □

Let $\mathcal{M} = (\mathcal{D}, \bullet, \mathcal{V}, [\![\cdot]\!])$ be a lazy regular model. We denote with $\mathcal{M} \models \eta^-$ the fact that for all $d \in \mathcal{D}$, $\mathcal{M} \models d \sqsubseteq \lambda x.dx$.

Theorem 15 *Let $\mathcal{M}$ be a lazy regular model such that $\mathcal{M} \models \eta^-$. Let $M, N \in \Lambda$.*
$M \sqsubseteq_{LS} N \Longrightarrow (\mathcal{M} \models M \sqsubseteq N)$.

Proof. (Sketch) Let $M \sqsubseteq_{LS} N$, then $M \sqsubseteq_{LT} N'$ with $N \Rightarrow_\eta N'$. By theorem 14, $\mathcal{M} \models M \sqsubseteq N'$ and, by induction, using the fact that $\mathcal{M} \models \eta^-$ and the continuity, $\mathcal{M} \models M \sqsubseteq N$. □

4 LAZY REGULARITY IN COHERENCE SPACES

Let us consider the category **Stab**, whose objects are *coherence spaces* and whose morphisms are *stable functions*, which can be easily proved to be regular. For what concerns the notions relative to coherence spaces and stability, we refer the reader to Girard, Lafont & Taylor (1989).

4.1 The models $\mathcal{M}_1$ and $\mathcal{M}_2$

If D is a coherence space, let us denote with $|D|$ its set of atoms (ranged over by α, β, γ,...), and by $comp_D \subseteq |D| \times |D|$ the compatibility relation. Elements of D are subsets of compatible atoms, and will be denoted by $a, b, c, \ldots$. The bottom elements is the empty set ($\emptyset$). We also denote by $(D_1 \Rightarrow_s D_2)$ the coherence space whose elements are the traces of the stable functions from D_1 to D_2. Let us recall that the trace of a stable function f from D_1 to D_2 is the set $tr(f) \subseteq (D_1)_{\mathrm{fin}} \times |D_2|$ (where $(D_1)_{\mathrm{fin}}$ denotes the set of all the finite elements of D_1) defined as:
$tr(f) = \{(a_0, \beta) \mid \forall a.(\beta \in f(a) \Rightarrow a_0 \subseteq a)\}$
where, if $(a, \beta), (a', \beta') \in \mathcal{F}$ and $a \cup a' \in D_1$ then both $comp_{D_2}(\beta, \beta')$ and if

$\beta = \beta'$ then $a = a'$. A stable function f is completely determined by its trace $tr(f)$ in the following way: $f(a) = \{\beta \mid \exists a_0 \subseteq a.(a_0, \beta) \in tr(f)\}$.

Now, in order to define lazy regular models in **Stab** we introduce an endofunctor $(\cdot)_\emptyset$.

Definition 16 *Let us define the* pseudo-lifting *functor:* $(\cdot)_\emptyset$: **Stab** $\to$ **Stab** *as:*

- *if D is a coherence space, then $D_\emptyset$ is the coherence space whose set of atoms is: $|D_\emptyset| = \{a \mid a \subseteq \mathcal{P}_{fin}(|D|), \#a \leq 1\}$ and whose compatibility relation is defined by: $\forall a, b \in |D_\emptyset|.(a, b) \in comp_{D_\emptyset} \Leftrightarrow a \cup b \in D$ ($\#a$ denotes the cardinality of the set a),*
- *if f is a stable function from D_1 to D_2, then $f_\emptyset$ is the stable function from $(D_1)_\emptyset$ to $(D_2)_\emptyset$ whose trace is: $tr(f_\emptyset) = \{(\{\emptyset\}, \emptyset)\} \cup \{(\tilde{a}, \{\alpha\}) \mid (a, \alpha) \in tr(f)\}$ where, if $a = \{\alpha_1, \ldots, \alpha_n\}$ with $n > 0$, then $\tilde{a} = \{\{\alpha_1\}, \ldots, \{\alpha_n\}\}$, while $\tilde{\emptyset} = \{\emptyset\}$.*

Note that the atom $\emptyset$ is compatible with all other atoms of $D_\emptyset$, according to the definition above. Moreover, for every coherence space D, $D_\emptyset \rhd D$ through both the retraction pair (out^1_D, in_D) and (out^2_D, in_D), where:
- $in_D : D \to D_\emptyset$ is defined as: $in_D(a) = \{\{\alpha\} \mid \alpha \in a\} \cup \{\emptyset\}$, whose trace is: $tr(in_D) = \{(\{\alpha\}, \{\alpha\}) \mid \alpha \in |D|\} \cup \{(\emptyset, \emptyset)\}$.
- for $i \in \{1, 2\}$, $out^i_D : D_\emptyset \to D$, are defined as: $out^1_D(b) = \{\alpha \mid \{\alpha\} \in b\}$, whose trace is $tr(out^1_D) = \{(\{\{\alpha\}\}, \alpha) \mid \alpha \in |D|\}$, $out^2_D(b) = \{\alpha \mid \{\alpha\} \in b \text{ and } \emptyset \in b\}$, whose trace is $tr(out^2_D) = \{(\{\{\alpha\}, \emptyset\}, \alpha) \mid \alpha \in |D|\}$. Note that the behaviour of out^1_D and out^2_D is the same when they are applied to elements in the range of in_D.

Remark 17 It is routine to check that $D_\emptyset$ is isomorphic to $I \& D$, where I is the coherence space with just one atom.

We now define two lazy regular models. Both are based on the coherence space $\mathcal{D}$, minimum solution of the domain equation $D \approx (D \Rightarrow_s D)_\emptyset$. Such a solution $\mathcal{D}$ can be obtained by the inverse limit construction, namely, $\mathcal{D} \approx \lim_{\leftarrow} \langle D_n, j_n \rangle$, where $|D_0| = \emptyset$ and $D_{n+1} = (D_n \Rightarrow_s D_n)_\emptyset$, and the initial immersion-projection pair is (i_0, j_0), where $i_0 = x \in D_0 \mapsto \emptyset$, and $j_0 = x \in D_1 \mapsto \emptyset$. Let (F, G) be the resulting isomorphism pair. Using the fact that $(\mathcal{D} \Rightarrow_s \mathcal{D})_\emptyset \rhd (\mathcal{D} \Rightarrow_s \mathcal{D})$, through the retraction pairs $(out^1_{\mathcal{D}\Rightarrow_s\mathcal{D}}, in_{\mathcal{D}\Rightarrow_s\mathcal{D}})$ and $(out^2_{\mathcal{D}\Rightarrow_s\mathcal{D}}, in_{\mathcal{D}\Rightarrow_s\mathcal{D}})$, we define the retraction $D \rhd (D \Rightarrow_s D)$ through the retraction pairs (ϕ^i, ψ), for $i \in \{1, 2\}$, where $\phi^i = out^i_{\mathcal{D}\Rightarrow_s\mathcal{D}} \circ F$ and $\psi = G \circ in_{\mathcal{D}\Rightarrow_s\mathcal{D}}$. Hence, we obtain two different regular models. Based on these regular models are the lazy regular models $\mathcal{M}_1$ and $\mathcal{M}_2$ that we will define after the following remark:

Remark 18 Since the isomorphism pair (F, G) defined above, we can characterize the set of atoms $|\mathcal{D}|$ as it was the set of atoms $|(\mathcal{D} \Rightarrow_s \mathcal{D})_\emptyset|$. Furthermore, reasoning modulo isomorphism, if $\gamma \in |\mathcal{D}|$, then $\gamma = \emptyset$, or else $\gamma = \{(a, \alpha)\}$, where $a \in \mathcal{D}$, a finite and $\alpha \in |\mathcal{D}|$.

Let $\mathcal{M}_1 = (\mathcal{D}, \bullet_1, \mathcal{V}, [\![\cdot]\!]^1)$ and $\mathcal{M}_2 = (\mathcal{D}, \bullet_2, \mathcal{V}, [\![\cdot]\!]^2)$ be defined as follows:

a) $\mathcal{V} = \{a \in \mathcal{D} \mid \emptyset \in a\}$,
b) $d_1 \bullet_1 d_2 = \{\alpha \mid \exists a \subseteq d_2.\{(a, \alpha)\} \in d_1\}$,
c) $d_1 \bullet_2 d_2 = \{\alpha \mid \exists a \subseteq d_2.\{\emptyset, \{(a, \alpha)\}\} \subseteq d_1\}$,
d) the interpretation functions $[\![\cdot]\!]^1$ and $[\![\cdot]\!]^2$ are obtained by instantiating, in the definition given after Definition 6, ϕ by ϕ^1 and ϕ^2, and considering $\Lambda(d \in \mathcal{D} \mapsto [\![M]\!]^i_{\rho[d/x]})$ as a notation for the trace:
$\{(a, \alpha) \mid a \text{ is the minimal finite } a' \in \mathcal{D} \text{ s.t. } \alpha \in [\![M]\!]^i_{\rho[a'/x]}\}$.

Proposition 19 *$\mathcal{M}_1$ and $\mathcal{M}_2$ are lazy regular models.*

Proof. We must prove just that $\mathcal{M}_1$ and $\mathcal{M}_2$ satisfy Definition 8.

First of all, they must be models for the lazy λ-calculus. In order to prove this, only point 2 of Definition 2 needs a verification. This is immediate since if $M \in Val$ then, for each ρ, $[\![M]\!]^i_\rho = \psi(\Lambda(f))$, for a given $f : \mathcal{D} \to \mathcal{D}$. Since $\psi = G \circ in_{\mathcal{D} \Rightarrow_s \mathcal{D}}$ and $\emptyset \in in_{\mathcal{D} \Rightarrow_s \mathcal{D}}(d)$ for each $d \in (\mathcal{D} \Rightarrow_s \mathcal{D})$, speaking modulo the isomorphism G, $\emptyset \in [\![M]\!]^i_\rho$.

Secondly, we prove that they are stratified. We make the prove only for $\mathcal{M}_2$, since for $\mathcal{M}_1$ the proof is similar, but simpler.

First of all, let us define the rank of an atom in $|\mathcal{D}|$ as the following integer: $\text{rg}(\emptyset) = 0$, $\text{rg}(\{(a, \alpha)\}) = \max\{\max\{\text{rg}(\beta) \mid \beta \in a\}, \text{rg}(\alpha)\} + 1$.

If $a \in \mathcal{D}$ is finite, then $\text{rg}(a)$ denotes $\max\{\text{rg}(\beta) \mid \beta \in a\}$. We denote by $|\mathcal{D}|_n$ the set of atoms of $\mathcal{D}$ whose rank is smaller of equal to n.

The interpretation of the identity term $\lambda x.x$ is given by, (omitting G, up to the isomorphism), $\{\{(\{\alpha\}, \alpha)\} \mid \alpha \in |\mathcal{D}|\} \cup \{\emptyset\}$.

We take as p_n, for $n \geq 0$, the following points:
$p_n = \{\gamma \in [\![\lambda x.x]\!]_{\rho_0} \mid \gamma \in |\mathcal{D}|_n\} = \{\{(\{\alpha\}, \alpha)\} \mid \text{rg}(\alpha) < n\} \cup \{\emptyset\}$.

Let us notice that for all $n \in \mathbf{N}$ and $d \in \mathcal{D}$:
$p_{n+1} \bullet_2 d = \{\alpha \mid \alpha \in d, \text{rg}(\alpha) \leq n\} = d \cap |\mathcal{D}|_n$ and $p_0 = \{\emptyset\}$.

Thus $p_0 \bullet_2 d = \emptyset$ and $p_1 \bullet_2 d = \{\emptyset\}$ iff $\emptyset \in d$.

Now we can proof that, for all $n \in \mathbf{N}$, p_n is a projection. We must check the two points of Definition 7 *i)*. The first point is obvious, by the definition of p_n above. The second one is given by:

if $n > 0$:

$$\begin{aligned} p_n &= \{\{(a, \alpha)\} \mid \alpha \in a \cap |\mathcal{D}|_{n-1}, a \text{ is minimal}\} \cup \{\emptyset\} \\ &= \{\{(a, \alpha)\} \mid \alpha \in p_n \bullet_2 (p_n \bullet_2 a), a \text{ is minimal}\} \cup \{\emptyset\} \\ &= G(in_{\mathcal{D} \Rightarrow_s \mathcal{D}}(\Lambda(d \in \mathcal{D} \mapsto p_n \bullet_2 (p_n \bullet_2 d)))), \end{aligned}$$

and $p_0 = \{\emptyset\} = G(in_{\mathcal{D} \Rightarrow_s \mathcal{D}}(\Lambda(d \in \mathcal{D} \mapsto \emptyset))) = G(in_{\mathcal{D} \Rightarrow_s \mathcal{D}}(\Lambda(d \in \mathcal{D} \mapsto p_0 \bullet_2 (p_0 \bullet_2 d))))$.

By the definition of p_n above, the sequence $(p_n)_{n \geq 0}$ is increasing in $\mathcal{D}$ and $\bigsqcup_n p_n =$

$G(in_{\mathcal{D}\Rightarrow_s\mathcal{D}}(\Lambda(d \in \mathcal{D} \mapsto d)))$ and $p_0 \bullet_2 d = \emptyset$ for every $d \in \mathcal{D}$. Moreover, for all $n \in \mathbf{N}$ and $d_1, d_2 \in \mathcal{D}$:

i) by points 2 and 3 above $p_1 \bullet_2 d_1 \bullet_2 d_2 = \{\emptyset\} \bullet_2 d_2 = \emptyset = p_0 \bullet_2 (d_1 \bullet_2 (p_0 \bullet_2 d_2))$,

ii) if $n > 0$,

$$\begin{aligned} p_{n+1} \bullet_2 d_1 \bullet_2 d_2 &= \{\alpha \mid \exists a \subseteq d_2.\{\{(a,\alpha)\},\emptyset\} \subseteq d_1 \cap |\mathcal{D}|_n\} \\ &= \{\alpha \mid \exists a \subseteq d_2 \cap |\mathcal{D}|_{n-1}.\{\{(a,\alpha)\},\emptyset\} \subseteq d_1\} \cap |\mathcal{D}|_{n-1} \\ &= p_n \bullet_2 (d_1 \bullet_2 (p_n \bullet_2 d_2)). \end{aligned}$$

So $\mathcal{M}_2$ is stratified. (The proof for $\mathcal{M}_1$ differs just in the behaviour of $\bullet_1$.)

Now we must prove that $\mathcal{M}_1$ and $\mathcal{M}_2$ satisfy Definition 8 *ii)* and *iii)*. By definition of $\psi = G \circ in_{\mathcal{D}\Rightarrow_s\mathcal{D}}$, $\emptyset \in \psi(\Lambda(d \in \mathcal{D} \mapsto \emptyset))$. Moreover, by definition of $\mathcal{V}$, $\emptyset \notin \mathcal{V}$.
□

Proposition 20 $\mathcal{M}_1 \models \eta^-$ *while* $\mathcal{M}_2 \not\models \eta^-$.

4.2 Lazy stable type assignment systems

In this section we define, for each one of the previous defined models, a type system, for reasoning in a finitary way on the interpretation of terms. Namely types are names for points of the models, and a type can be assigned to a term if and only if the corresponding point is equal to (or less than) the interpretation of the term itself. As will be shown in the following, this finitary representation of the behaviour of the interpretation function, together with the approximation theorem, will be very useful for studying the local structure of the models.

Definition 21 *The set* $\mathcal{T}$ *of* types *is defined inductively starting from a type constant* ν*, in the following way:*

- $\nu \in \mathcal{T}$,
- $[\sigma_1, \ldots, \sigma_n] \to \sigma \in \mathcal{T}$ *if* $\sigma, \sigma_1, \ldots, \sigma_n \in \mathcal{T}$ *and* $(\mathtt{comp}(\sigma_i, \sigma_j))_{(1 \le i,j \le n)}$, *where* $n \geq 0$ *and* comp *is formalized as in Figure 1 (see Honsell & Ronchi della Rocca (1990)).*

Types are considered modulo the equivalence:
$[\sigma_1, \ldots, \sigma_n] \to \sigma \sim [\sigma_{s(1)}, \ldots, \sigma_{s(n)}] \to \sigma$, *for every permutation* s *of* $\{1, \ldots, n\}$.

Definition 22 *Let* $t : \mathcal{T}/\!\sim\, \to |\mathcal{D}|$ *be defined as:*

- $t(\nu) = \emptyset$ *and* $t([\sigma_1, \ldots, \sigma_n] \to \sigma) = \{(\{t(\sigma_1), \ldots, t(\sigma_n)\}, t(\sigma))\}$ $\quad (n \geq 0)$.

Property 23 *i) t is injective and surjective.*
ii) $\mathtt{comp}(\sigma, \sigma') \iff comp_{\mathcal{D}}(t(\sigma), t(\sigma'))$.

Definition 24 *i) Let a basis be a set of assumptions of the shape* $x : \sigma$, *where* $x \in Var$ *and* $\sigma \in \mathcal{T}$. *The* domain *of a basis* B *of the form* $\{x_1 : \sigma_1, \ldots, x_n : \sigma_n\}$

Judgements: $\texttt{comp}(\sigma, \sigma')$ $\quad\texttt{nonc}(\sigma, \sigma')$
where $\sigma, \sigma' \in \mathcal{T}$. The first judgement states the compatibility, while the second states the non compatibility.

Rules:

$$\frac{}{\texttt{comp}(\nu, \sigma)}(1) \qquad \frac{\sigma_1 \sim \sigma_2}{\texttt{comp}(\sigma_1, \sigma_2)}(2) \qquad \frac{\texttt{comp}(\sigma, \sigma')}{\texttt{comp}(\sigma', \sigma)}(3) \qquad \frac{\texttt{nonc}(\sigma, \sigma')}{\texttt{nonc}(\sigma', \sigma)}(4)$$

$$\frac{(\texttt{comp}(\sigma_i, \sigma'_j))_{\forall i,j \in \{1,\ldots,m\}} \quad \sigma \sim \sigma' \quad [\sigma_1 \ldots \sigma_n] \to \sigma \not\sim [\sigma'_1 \ldots \sigma'_m] \to \sigma'}{\texttt{nonc}([\sigma_1 \ldots \sigma_n] \to \sigma, [\sigma'_1 \ldots \sigma'_m] \to \sigma')}(5)$$

$$\frac{(\texttt{comp}(\sigma_i, \sigma'_j))_{\forall i \in \{1,\ldots,n\}, \forall j \in \{1,\ldots,m\}} \quad \texttt{nonc}(\sigma, \sigma')}{\texttt{nonc}([\sigma_1 \ldots \sigma_n] \to \sigma, [\sigma'_1 \ldots \sigma'_m] \to \sigma')}(6)$$

$$\frac{\exists i, j \in \{1, \ldots, \max\{n, m\}\} \,.\, \texttt{nonc}(\sigma_i, \sigma'_j)}{\texttt{comp}([\sigma_1 \ldots \sigma_n] \to \sigma, [\sigma'_1 \ldots \sigma'_m] \to \sigma')}(7)$$

$$\frac{(\texttt{comp}(\sigma_i, \sigma'_j))_{\forall i \in \{1,\ldots,n\}, \forall j \in \{1,\ldots,m\}} \quad \texttt{comp}(\sigma, \sigma') \quad \sigma \not\sim \sigma'}{\texttt{comp}([\sigma_1 \ldots \sigma_n] \to \sigma, [\sigma'_1 \ldots \sigma'_m] \to \sigma')}(8)$$

Figure 1 Formalizing the compatibility relation

is the set dom$(B) = \{x_1, \ldots, x_n\}$, *and for each* $x \in dom(B)$, $B(x)$ *is defined as* $\{\sigma \mid x : \sigma \in B\}$.

ii) A consistent basis *is a basis* B *such that for each* $\{x : \sigma, x : \sigma'\} \subseteq B$, $\texttt{comp}(\sigma, \sigma')$.

iii) The two type assignment systems prove judgements of the shapes:
$B \vdash_1 M : \sigma \qquad\qquad B \vdash_2 M : \sigma$
where B *is a consistent basis,* $M \in \Lambda$ *and* $\sigma \in \mathcal{T}$. *The rules are the following:* $(i \in \{1, 2\})$

$$\frac{}{\{x : \sigma\} \vdash_i x : \sigma}(ax) \qquad \frac{}{\vdash_i \lambda x.M : \nu}(lazy)$$

$$\frac{B \cup \{x : \sigma_1, \ldots, x : \sigma_n\} \vdash_i M : \tau \quad n \geq 0 \quad x \notin dom(B)}{B \vdash_i \lambda x.M : [\sigma_1, \ldots, \sigma_n] \to \tau}(\to I)$$

$$\frac{B \vdash_1 M : [\sigma_1, \ldots, \sigma_n] \to \tau \quad (B_i \vdash_1 N : \sigma_i)_{1 \leq i \leq n} \quad B \cup (\bigcup_{1 \leq i \leq n} B_i) \text{ is a consistent basis} \quad n \geq 0}{B \cup (\bigcup_{1 \leq i \leq n} B_i) \vdash_1 MN : \tau}(\to E_1)$$

$$\frac{\begin{array}{c} B' \vdash_2 M : \nu \\ B \vdash_2 M : [\sigma_1, \ldots, \sigma_n] \to \tau \quad (B_i \vdash_2 N : \sigma_i)_{1 \leq i \leq n} \\ B' \cup B \cup (\bigcup_{1 \leq i \leq n} B_i) \text{ is a consistent basis} \quad n \geq 0 \end{array}}{B' \cup B \cup (\bigcup_{1 \leq i \leq n} B_i) \vdash_2 MN : \tau} (\to E_2)$$

(note that the rules of the two systems coincide, but the rule $(\to E)$).

Let $\vdash_i M : \sigma$ be an abbreviation for $\emptyset \vdash_i M : \sigma$,

Definition 25 *Let us denote, for all environments ρ, ρ',*
$dom(\rho) = \{x \in Var \mid \rho(x) \neq \emptyset\}$ and $\rho \sqsubseteq \rho' \Leftrightarrow (\forall x \in Var. \rho(x) \subseteq \rho'(x))$
and $\rho \sqsubset \rho' \Leftrightarrow (\rho \sqsubseteq \rho'$ and $\rho \neq \rho')$.
We say that two environments ρ, ρ' are compatible *if $\forall x \in Var$, $\rho(x) \cup \rho'(x) \in \mathcal{D}$. Moreover, we define $\rho \sqcap \rho'$ as the environment such that for all $x \in Var$, $(\rho \sqcap \rho')(x) = \rho(x) \cap \rho'(x)$.*

Lemma 26 *Let γ be a type, M be a term and ρ, ρ' be two compatible environments. If $t(\gamma) \in [\![M]\!]_\rho$ and $t(\gamma) \in [\![M]\!]_{\rho'}$, then $t(\gamma) \in [\![M]\!]_{\rho \sqcap \rho'}$.*

Proof. By a straightforward induction on M using stability. □

The following theorem states the soundness and completeness of the above type assignment systems w.r.t. the two models $\mathcal{M}_1$ and $\mathcal{M}_2$.

Theorem 27 *i) (Soundness) Let B be a consistent basis, $M \in \Lambda$ and $\sigma \in \mathcal{T}$. If $B \vdash_i M : \sigma$, then $t(\sigma) \in [\![M]\!]^i_{\rho_B}$, where $\rho_B(x) = \{t(\sigma) \mid \sigma \in B(x)\}$. Moreover ρ_B is minimal among the environments $\rho \in Env$ such that $\sigma \in [\![M]\!]^i_{\rho}$, $(i \in \{1,2\})$.*
ii) (Completeness) Given $M \in \Lambda$ and an environment $\rho \in Env$, $t(\sigma) \in [\![M]\!]^i_\rho$ implies that there is a consistent basis B such that $B \vdash_i M : \sigma$ and $B \subseteq B_\rho$, where $B_\rho(x) = \{x : \sigma \mid t(\sigma) \in \rho(x)\}$, $(i \in \{1,2\})$.

Proof. (Soundness) By induction on the derivation of $B \vdash_i M : \sigma$. We will just give the proof for the system $\vdash_2$ in case the last applied rule is $(\to E)$. The other cases are simpler.

Let $M \equiv PQ$ for some P and Q and let the basis $B \equiv B' \cup B'' \cup \bigcup_{i \in I} B_i$ for some B', B'', B_i's where $I = \{1, \ldots, n\}$. Moreover, $B' \vdash P : \nu$, $B'' \vdash P : [\sigma_1, \ldots, \sigma_n] \to \sigma$ and $B_i \vdash Q : \sigma_i$ for all $i \in I$. By induction we have:
$\emptyset \in [\![P]\!]_{\rho_{B'}}$ and $\rho_{B'}$ minimal,
$\{(a, t(\sigma))\} \in [\![P]\!]_{\rho_{B''}}$ and $\rho_{B''}$ minimal, where $a = \{t(\sigma_i) \mid i \in I\}$,
and $t(\sigma_i) \in [\![Q]\!]_{\rho_{B_i}}$ and ρ_{B_i} minimal, for all $i \in I$.
By monotonicity $a \subseteq [\![Q]\!]_{\rho_B}$, $\{(a, t(\sigma))\} \in [\![P]\!]_{\rho_B}$ and $\emptyset \in [\![P]\!]_{\rho_B}$. So, $t(\sigma) \in [\![PQ]\!]_{\rho_B}$. Moreover, ρ_B is minimal, indeed if $t(\sigma) \in [\![PQ]\!]_{\rho'}$ with $\rho' \sqsubset \rho_B$, we have $b = \{t(\gamma_1), \ldots, t(\gamma_p)\}$ for some p, such that $\{(b, t(\sigma))\}, \emptyset \in [\![P]\!]_{\rho'}$ and $t(\gamma_i) \in [\![Q]\!]_{\rho'}$ $(1 \leq i \leq p)$. By monotonicity if $\{(b, t(\sigma))\} \in [\![P]\!]_{\rho'}$ then $\{(b, t(\sigma))\} \in$

$[\![P]\!]_{\rho_B}$, and hence, by stability, $a = b$. Since $\rho_{B'}, \rho_{B''}, \rho_{B_i}, \rho' \sqsubseteq \rho_B$ then all these environments are compatible each other. By Lemma 26, $\emptyset \in [\![P]\!]_{\rho_{B'} \cap \rho'}$, $\{(a, t(\sigma))\} \in [\![P]\!]_{\rho_{B''} \cap \rho'}$ and for all i, $t(\gamma_i) \in [\![Q]\!]_{\rho_{B_i} \cap \rho'}$. Since $\rho' \sqsubset \rho_B$ we have: (i) $\rho_{B'} \cap \rho' \sqsubset \rho_{B'}$ or (ii) $\rho_{B''} \cap \rho' \sqsubset \rho_{B''}$ or (iii) $\rho_{B_i} \cap \rho' \sqsubset \rho_{B_i}$. By minimality of $\rho_{B'}$, $\rho_{B''}$ and ρ_{B_i} we have a contradiction.

(Completeness)

By induction on M. We will make the proof only for the model $\mathcal{M}_2$ because for the other model the proof is similar, but simpler.

$M \equiv x$. $t(\sigma) \in [\![x]\!]_\rho$ means $t(\sigma) \in \rho(x)$. Taking $B = \{x : \sigma\}$ we have $B \subseteq B_\rho$ and $B \vdash x : \sigma$.

$M \equiv PQ$. Since $[\![PQ]\!]_\rho = out^2_{\mathcal{D}_{\Rightarrow_s}\mathcal{D}}(F([\![P]\!]_\rho))([\![Q]\!]_\rho)$, $t(\sigma) \in [\![PQ]\!]_\rho$ implies (by definition of $out^2_{\mathcal{D}_{\Rightarrow_s}\mathcal{D}}$) $\emptyset \in [\![P]\!]_\rho$, $\{(a, t(\sigma))\} \in [\![P]\!]_\rho$ and $a \subseteq [\![Q]\!]_\rho$ for some a. Take $a = \{t(\sigma_1), \ldots, t(\sigma_n)\}$. By induction, $B' \vdash P : \nu$, $B'' \vdash P : [\sigma_1, \ldots, \sigma_n] \rightarrow \sigma$, $B_i \vdash Q : \sigma_i$ for all $i \in \{1, \ldots, n\}$, with $B', B'', B_i \subseteq B_\rho$. Using Rule *($\rightarrow$ E)* we have $B' \cup B'' \cup \bigcup_i B_i \vdash M : \sigma$ and $B' \cup B'' \cup \bigcup_i B_i \subseteq B_\rho$.

$M \equiv \lambda x.Q$ $t(\sigma) \in [\![\lambda x.Q]\!]_\rho$ implies two cases:

1. $\sigma \sim \nu$. Then $\vdash M : \nu$, by Rule *(lazy)*.
2. $\sigma \sim [\sigma_1, \ldots, \sigma_n] \rightarrow \tau$ with $n \geq 0$.
   Since $[\![\lambda x.Q]\!]_\rho = \{\{(b, \alpha)\} \mid b \text{ minimal s.t. } \alpha \in [\![Q]\!]_{\rho[b/x]}\} \cup \{\emptyset\}$, $t(\sigma) \in [\![\lambda x.Q]\!]_\rho$ implies $t(\tau) \in [\![Q]\!]_{\rho[a/x]}$ with $a = \{t(\sigma_1), \ldots, t(\sigma_n)\}$ ($a = \emptyset$ if $n = 0$). By induction, $B \vdash Q : \tau$ with $B \subseteq B_{\rho[a/x]}$. Since $B = B_1 \cup \{x : \sigma_1, \ldots, x : \sigma_n\}$ with $x \notin dom(B_1)$, for some B_1, using Rule *($\rightarrow$ I)*, $B_1 \vdash M : [\sigma_1, \ldots, \sigma_n] \rightarrow \tau$ and $B_1 \subseteq B_\rho$.

□

In the types setting the set of semantics values $\mathcal{V}$ is the set of all closed terms having a type ν. In fact it is easy to verify that $M \in \Lambda^o$ and $M \Downarrow_{lazy}$ implies $\vdash_i M : \nu$ ($i \in \{1, 2\}$).

The Approximation Theorem can be rewritten in the types setting in the following way:

Let $M \in \Lambda$, B be a consistent basis and σ be a type.

$B \vdash_i M : \sigma \iff \exists A \in \mathcal{A}(M).B \vdash_i A : \sigma$. ($i \in \{1, 2\}$).

4.3 Local structure of $\mathcal{M}_1$ and $\mathcal{M}_2$

In this subsection we give a complete characterization of the local structure of the model $\mathcal{M}_1$. Moreover we will give some properties of the local structure of $\mathcal{M}_2$. Both the approximation theorem and the type system describing the interpretation of terms are useful tools for proving these properties.

First, by Proposition 20 and Theorem 15, we know that:

Fact 28 *For each* $M, N \in \Lambda$, $M \sqsubseteq_{LS} N \Longrightarrow \mathcal{M}_1 \models M \sqsubseteq N$.

The order relation $\sqsubseteq_{LS}$ can be easily extended to approximants just posing $\Omega \sqsubseteq_{LS} A$, for every A.

Remark 29 For each $A, A' \in \mathcal{N}_{\beta\Omega}$, if $A \sqsubseteq_{LS} A'$ and $A' \sqsubseteq_{LS} A$, then $A \equiv A'$.

Lemma 30 *Let* $M, N \in \Lambda$.
$(\forall A \in \mathcal{A}(M)\,.\,\exists A' \in \mathcal{A}(M)\,.\,A \sqsubseteq_{LS} A') \Longrightarrow M \sqsubseteq_{LS} M'$.

Proof. If N or M is unsolvable then the result follows immediately.

Otherwise, $M =_\beta \lambda x_1 \ldots x_m.yM_1 \ldots M_q$ and $N =_\beta \lambda x_1 \ldots x_n.zN_1 \ldots N_p$, then it is easy to check that, for a given l, $n = m + l$, $p = q + l$, $y \equiv z$, $\forall i \leq q.\forall A \in \mathcal{A}(M_i).\exists A' \in \mathcal{A}(N_i).A \sqsubseteq_{LS} A'$ and $\forall j \leq l.\forall A \in \mathcal{A}(x_{m+j}).\exists A' \in \mathcal{A}(N_{q+j}).A \sqsubseteq_{LS} A'$. Then the result follows by induction. □

Main Lemma 31 *Let* $A, A' \in \mathcal{N}_{\beta\Omega}$.
i) $\mathcal{M}_1 \models A \sqsubseteq A' \quad \Longleftrightarrow \quad A \sqsubseteq_{LS} A'$.
ii) $\mathcal{M}_1 \models A = A' \quad \Longrightarrow \quad A \equiv A'$.

Proof. i) The proof uses a "semantic separability" property on approximants and it is given in the appendix.

ii) Immediate from i) using Remark 29. □

We can now characterize the local structure of $\mathcal{M}_1$.

Theorem 32 *Let* $M, N \in \Lambda$.
i) $\mathcal{M}_1 \models M = N \Longleftrightarrow M \approx_{LT} N$.
ii) $\mathcal{M}_1 \models M \sqsubseteq N \Longleftrightarrow M \sqsubseteq_{LS} N$.

Proof. ii) ($\Leftarrow$) By Fact 28.
($\Rightarrow$) $\mathcal{M}_1 \models M \sqsubseteq N$
$\Rightarrow \forall B, \sigma.(B \vdash_1 M : \sigma \Rightarrow B \vdash_1 N : \sigma)$ by Theorem 27
$\Rightarrow \forall B, \sigma.((\exists A \in \mathcal{A}(M).B \vdash_1 A : \sigma) \Rightarrow (\exists A' \in \mathcal{A}(N).B \vdash_1 A' : \sigma))$ by Approximation Theorem
$\Rightarrow \forall A \in \mathcal{A}(M).\exists A' \in \mathcal{A}(N).A \sqsubseteq_{LS} A'$ by the Main Lemma
$\Rightarrow M \sqsubseteq_{LS} N$ by Lemma 30
i) By *ii)* using the fact that $\approx_{LS} = \approx_{LT}$ (Proposition 13). □

As far as the model $\mathcal{M}_2$ is concerned, we can state the following properties:

Theorem 33 *i)* $M \sqsubseteq_{LT} N \Rightarrow (\not\Leftarrow) \mathcal{M}_2 \models M \sqsubseteq N$;
ii) $M \approx_{LT} N \Rightarrow (\not\Leftarrow) \mathcal{M}_2 \models M = N$;

iii) $M \sqsubseteq_{LS} N \not\Rightarrow \mathcal{M}_2 \models M \sqsubseteq N$;
iv) $M \sqsubseteq_{PSE} N \not\Rightarrow \mathcal{M}_2 \models M \sqsubseteq N$.

Proof. i) ($\Rightarrow$) follows from Theorem 14.
A counterexample for ($\Leftarrow$) is $\mathcal{M}_2 \models \lambda x.xx = \lambda x.x(\lambda y.xy)$ (it can be easily checked using the $\vdash_2$ type system).
ii) ($\Rightarrow$) follows from i). A counterexample for ($\Leftarrow$) is the same as in the preceding point.
iii) follows from the fact that $\mathcal{M}_2 \not\models \eta^-$. For example $x \sqsubseteq_{LS} \lambda y.xy$ while, if we consider any environment ρ such that $\emptyset \notin \rho(x)$, $\rho(x) \not\subseteq \lambda y.\rho(x)y = \{\emptyset\}$ in $\mathcal{M}_2$.
iv) Let O_∞ be any unsolvable of infinite order. Then $\mathcal{M}_2 \not\models \lambda x.x \sqsubseteq O_\infty$, while, for all term M, $M \sqsubseteq_{PSE} O_\infty$. □

5 COMPARISON WITH RELATED WORK

In this section we will recall the models of the lazy λ-calculus studied in the literature and we will compare their local structures with the models $\mathcal{M}_1$ and $\mathcal{M}_2$ defined in the present paper.

Longo model The Longo's model $\mathcal{M}_L$ defined in Longo (1983) is based on the *free PSE-algebra* (see Engeler (1981)) built over a given set A, namely the pair $D_A = (\mathcal{P}(B), \bullet)$ where $B = \bigcup_n B_n$ with $B_0 = A$ and $B_{n+1} = B_n \cup \{(b, \beta) \mid b \in \mathcal{P}_{fin}(B_n), \beta \in B_n\}$ and $d_1 \bullet d_2 = \{\alpha \mid \exists a \in \mathcal{P}_{fin}(d_2).(a, \alpha) \in d_1\}$. Defining the set V as $\mathcal{P}(B) \setminus \emptyset$, it is easy to show that $\mathcal{M}_L = (\mathcal{P}(B), \bullet, V, [\![\cdot]\!]^A)$ is a lazy regular model where ψ and ϕ are defined as: $\psi(f) = \{(a, \alpha) \mid \alpha \in f(a)\} \cup A$ and $\phi(a) = \{(b, \beta) \mid (b, \beta) \in a\}$, for each continuous function f from $\mathcal{P}(B)$ to itself and $a \in \mathcal{P}(B)$. As an immediate consequence of Theorem 32 we have that the theory of $\mathcal{M}_1$ *is* the theory of $\mathcal{M}_L$. Moreover, the local structure of $\mathcal{M}_1$ *is strictly included* in the one of $\mathcal{M}_L$, whose local structure is proved in Ong (1992) to be characterized by $\sqsubseteq_{PSE}$.

Abramsky-Ong model The Abramsky–Ong model, defined in Abramsky & Ong (1993), has been built starting from a regular model in the category **CPO**, whose objects are Scott's domains and whose morphisms are continuous functions, exploiting the canonical solution $\mathcal{D}_{AO}$ of the domain equation $D \approx (D \Rightarrow D)_\perp$, where $(\cdot)_\perp$ is the usual *lifting* functor on **CPO**. Letting *in* and *out* as the constructor and destructor of lifting and (F, G) be the resulting isomorphism pair of the above equation, it is easy to check that $\mathcal{M}_{AO} = (\mathcal{D}_{AO}, \bullet, \mathcal{V}, [\![\cdot]\!]^{AO})$ is a lazy regular model where $\mathcal{V} = \mathcal{D}_{AO} \setminus \{\perp_{\mathcal{D}_{AO}}\}$ and $\phi = out_{(\mathcal{D}_{AO} \Rightarrow_c \mathcal{D}_{AO})} \circ F$ and $\psi = G \circ in_{(\mathcal{D}_{AO} \Rightarrow_c \mathcal{D}_{AO})}$. It has been showed in Abramsky & Ong (1993) that the theory of $\mathcal{M}_{AO}$ strictly includes the theory of the Longo's $\mathcal{M}_L$ and so also the one of $\mathcal{M}_1$. We conjecture both that the theory of $\mathcal{M}_{AO}$ strictly includes the one of $\mathcal{M}_2$ and the local structure of $\mathcal{M}_{AO}$ (containing the $\sqsubseteq_{PSE}$ preorder) is different from the one of $\mathcal{M}_2$ (see Theorem 33).

APPENDIX: PROOF OF THE MAIN LEMMA

For shortening, we use small letter, like a, instead of writing $[\sigma_1,\ldots,\sigma_n]$ for given types $\sigma_1,\ldots,\sigma_n \in \mathcal{T}$. For $a \equiv [\sigma_1,\ldots,\sigma_n]$, $a \rightarrow \sigma$ denotes the type $[\sigma_1,\ldots,\sigma_n] \rightarrow \sigma$. Using this notation we can say that every type is of the shape $a_1 \rightarrow \cdots \rightarrow a_n \rightarrow \nu$ with $n \geq 0$ and for all $i \in \{1,\ldots,n\}$, $a_i \equiv [\sigma^i_1,\ldots,\sigma^i_{n_i}]$ with $n_i \geq 0$ and $\sigma^i_j \in \mathcal{T}$ for $j < n_i$, and we write $\vec{[]}^p \rightarrow \sigma$, for $p \geq 0$ and type σ, for denoting the type:

$\vec{[]}^0 \rightarrow \sigma = \sigma$ if $p = 0$ and $\underbrace{[] \rightarrow \cdots \rightarrow []}_{p>0} \rightarrow \sigma$ if $p \geq 1$.

Moreover, let us write $\alpha \epsilon a$ for $\alpha = \sigma_i$ for some $i \in \{1,\ldots,n\}$,

Definition 34 *Given a type $\sigma \in \mathcal{T}$, we define $l(\sigma) \in \mathbf{N}$ as: $l(\sigma) = 0$ if $\sigma \sim \nu$ and $1 + l(\tau)$ if $\sigma \sim [\sigma_1,\ldots,\sigma_n] \rightarrow \tau$, for $n \geq 0$.*

The following fact will be used in the proof:

- let M be a term. If $\sigma \sim a_1 \rightarrow \cdots \rightarrow a_n \rightarrow \nu$ and $\tau \sim b_1 \rightarrow \cdots \rightarrow b_p \rightarrow \nu$ then ($n = 0$ or $p = 0$ or $p \neq n$) $\Rightarrow$ $\mathtt{comp}(\sigma, \tau)$.

Now we are ready to sketch the proof of the main lemma:
Firstly we claim that $\vdash_1$ (denoted by $\vdash$ in this section) satifies the subformula property for approximants' derivations. Let A an approximant and let d be a proof of $B \vdash A : \sigma$. Then for every subderivation d' of d, if d' proves $B' \vdash A' : \sigma'$ then both σ' and every type in B' are subformula of either σ or a type in B. This property is easily proved by induction on derivation for approximants.

Proof. (*Part* $\Longrightarrow$) It can be proved that $A \not\sqsubseteq_{LS} A'$ implies that there is at least one typing for A which is not a typing for A'. Then, the thesis follows from the completeness of the type assignment system for $\mathcal{M}_1$. The proof is a boring, but straightforward, induction on the definition of $A \not\sqsubseteq_{LS} A'$. It is not difficult to distinguish, by the type assignment system, two terms whose shapes are $A \equiv \lambda x_1 \ldots x_n.yA_1 \ldots A_p$ and $A' \equiv \lambda x_1 \ldots x_m.zA'_1 \ldots A'_q$ with either $y \not\equiv z$ or $n > m$ or $n - p \neq m - q$. So we just deal with the most difficult case which is the following:

- $A \equiv \lambda x_1 \ldots x_n.zA_1 \ldots A_p$ and $A' \equiv \lambda x_1 \ldots x_n.zA'_1 \ldots A'_p$ and $\exists i \leq n.A_i \not\sqsubseteq_{LS} A'_i$.

By induction $\exists B, \sigma$ such that $B \vdash A_i : \sigma$ and $B \not\vdash A'_i : \sigma$. Let $\mu = \vec{[]}^{i-1} \rightarrow [\sigma] \rightarrow \vec{[]}^{p-i} \rightarrow \tau$ where $\tau \in \mathcal{T}$ such that $l(\tau) > m + s + r$ where $m = \max\{l(\eta);$ where η is any subtype of either σ or a type in B $\}$, $s = \max\{q;$ q arity of an occurence of z in A'_i $\}$ and $r = max\{k;$ k number of abstractions in a subterm of $A'_i\}$. Let us consider $B_1 = \{z : \mu\}$. Then (see the fact given just before this proof), $\mathtt{comp}(\mu, \alpha)$ for all $z : \alpha \in B$, hence $B \cup B_1$ is a consistent basis and $B \cup B_1 \vdash zA_1 \ldots A_p : \tau$. By n applications of Rule ($\rightarrow I$), we have $B' \vdash A : a_1 \rightarrow \cdots \rightarrow a_n \rightarrow \tau$, where, for all $i \leq n$, $a_i \equiv [\alpha^i_1,\ldots,\alpha^i_{n_i}]$ with $n_i \geq 0$, $\forall j \leq n_i.x_i : \alpha^i_j \in B \cup B_1$. (Let notice that B' can be empty.) We want to show that this typing is not possible for A'. If, by absurd, $B' \vdash A' : a_1 \rightarrow \cdots \rightarrow a_n \rightarrow \tau$, then $B \cup B_1 \vdash zA'_1 \ldots A'_p : \tau$. Then, by Rule $(\to E)$, there are B'_p and B''_p such that: $B'_p \vdash zA'_1 \ldots A'_{p-1} : a_p \to \tau$ and $B''_p \vdash A'_p : \alpha$ for all $\alpha \epsilon a_p$.

Similarly, for all $i < p$, there are B'_i and B''_i such that: $B'_i \cup B''_i = B'_{i+1}$ and $B'_1 \vdash z : a_1 \to \cdots \to a_p \to \tau$ and $B''_i \vdash A'_i : \alpha$ for all $\alpha \epsilon a_i$.

Hence, $B'_1 \cup \bigcup_{1 \leq i \leq p} B''_i = B \cup B_1$. So $B'_1 = \{z : a_1 \to \cdots \to a_p \to \tau\}$. Let us show that $B'_1 \not\subseteq B$. Indeed, $l(\tau) > \max_{z:\alpha \in B}\{l(\alpha)\}$ and $l(a_1 \to \cdots \to a_p \to \tau) \geq l(\tau)$. Thus, $B'_1 = B_1$ and $a_1 \to \cdots \to a_p \to \tau = \mu$, which implies $B''_i \vdash A'_i : \sigma$, and since for all $j \leq p$ $(j \neq i).a_j \equiv []$, we have $B''_j = \emptyset$ and $B \vdash A'_i : \sigma$ or $B \cup \{z : \mu\} \vdash A'_i : \sigma$. By induction the first case is not possible. Let us suppose that the second case is true. Then there exists $zP_1 \ldots P_s$ subterm of A'_i, a base $B' \subseteq B$, a subtype ρ of μ such that $B' \cup \{z : \mu\} \vdash zP_1 \ldots P_s : \rho$ is proved by a subderivation of $B \cup \{z : \mu\} \vdash A'_i : \sigma$ and $B' \not\vdash zP_1 \ldots P_s : \rho$ (the premise on z used for typing $zP_1 \ldots P_s$ is μ). Three cases are possible: $A'_i \equiv \lambda z_1 \ldots z_r.zP_1 \ldots P_s$ or there is $y'Q_1 \ldots Q_l$ subterm of A'_i and, for some q $(1 \leq q \leq l)$, $Q_q \equiv \lambda z_1 \ldots z_r.zP_1 \ldots P_s$ with the variable y' either free or bound in A'_i. We consider only the last case with y' bound. The other case is similar but easier. Then $y'Q_1 \ldots Q_l$ is a subterm of $\lambda y'.Q$, which is a subterm of A'_i, and there is a subderivation of the derivation proving $B \cup \{z : \mu\} \vdash A'_i : \sigma$, whose conclusion is $B'' \vdash \lambda y'.Q : b \to \eta$ for some b and η. So there is a type $b_1 \to \cdots \to b_l \to \eta'$ belonging to b and a type $c_1 \to \cdots \to c_r \to \rho$ belonging to b_p. By the subformula property for approximants $b \to \eta$ is a subtype either of σ or of a premise in $B \cup \{z : \mu\}$. We deduce that $l(b \to \eta) \geq l(\mu) - s + r$ which is against the hypothesis on the length of μ.

(*Part* $\Longleftarrow$) By induction following the definition of $\sqsubseteq_{LS}$ and using the Theorem 27, □

REFERENCES

Abramsky, S. & Ong, C.-H. L. (1993), 'Full abstraction in the lazy lambda calculus.' *Information and Computation* **105**(2), 159–267.

Asperti, A. & Longo, G. (1991), *Categories, Types and Structures.* Foundations of Computing, The MIT Press.

Bastonero, O. (1996), *Modèle fortement stables du lambda-calcul et résultats d'incomplétude.* PhD thesis, Université Paris VII.

Bastonero, O. & Gouy., X. (To Appear), 'Strong stability and the incompleteness of the class of stable models', *Annals of Pure and Applied Logic* .

Coppo, M., Dezani-Ciancaglini, M. & Zacchi, M. (1987), 'Type theories, normal forms and D_∞ lambda models.' *Information and Control* **72**(2), 85 – 116.

Engeler, E. (1981), 'Algebras and combinators.' *Algebra Universalis* **13**, 389 – 392.

Girard, J.Y., Lafont, Y. & Taylor, P. (1989), *Proofs and Types.* Cambridge University Press.

Hindley, J. R. & Longo, G. (1980), 'Lambda-calculus models and extensionality.' *Z. Math. Logik Grundlag. Math.* **26**, 289 – 310.

Honsell, F. & Lenisa, M. (1993), Some results on the full-abstraction problem for restricted λ-calculi, *in* Proceedings of 18th. Symposium on MFCS'93, 'LNCS 711', Poland, Springer-Verlag, pp. 84 – 104.

Honsell, F. & Ronchi della Rocca, S. (1990), Reasoning about interpretations in qualitative lambda models, *in* M. Broy & C. Jones, eds, 'IFIP Working Group 2.2/2.3 Working Conference on Programming Concepts and Methods', Sea of Galilee, Israel, North-Holland, pp. 505–521.

Hudak, P., Jones, S. P. & Wadler, P. (1992), 'Report on the programming language haskell.' *SIGPLAN Notices* **27**(5).

Hyland, Y. (1976), 'A syntactic characterization of the equality in some models of the lambda calculus.' *Journal of London Mathematical Society* **12**(2), 83 – 95.

Lévy, J.-J. (1975), An algebraic interpretation of the $\lambda\beta$K-calculus and a labelled λ-calculus, *in* G. Goos & J. Hartmanis, eds, 'λ-Calculus and Computer Science Theory, Lecture Notes in Computer Science 37', Springer-Verlag, Berlin, DE, pp. 147–165.

Longo, G. (1983), 'Set-theoretical models of lambda calculus: Theories, expansions and isomophisms.' *Annals of Pure and Applied Logic* **24**, 153–188.

Ong, C.-H. L. (1992), Lazy lambda calculus: Theories, models and local structure characterization, *in* W. Kuich, ed., 'Automata, Languages and Programming, LNCS 623', Springer Verlag.

Pravato, A., Ronchi della Rocca, S. & Roversi, L. (1995), Categorical semantics of the call-by-value lambda-calculus, *in* 'Proceeding of the Second International Conference of Typed Lambda Calculi and Application, TLCA'95, LNCS 902', Edinburgh, U.K., Springer-Verlag, pp. 302 –318.

Wadsworth, C. P. (1978), 'Approximate reductions and λ-calculus models.' *SIAM Journal of Computing* **7**(3), 337 – 356.

BIOGRAPHY

Olivier Bastonero was born in Paris (France) in 1966. Master in mathematics at the University Paris VII in 1990. Ph.D in Mathematics at the University of Paris VII in December 1996.

Alberto Pravato was Born in Venizia (Italia) in 1967. Master in Computer Science at the University of Udine (Italia) in the 1991. Ph.D in Computer Science at the University of Turin (Italia) in 1997.

Simona Ronchi della Rocca was born in Bra (Italia) in 1946. Master in Physics at the University of Torino in 1969. Full Professor of "Foundation of Computer Science" at the University of Torino since 1987.

8

A proof theory of asynchronously communicating sequential processes

F. S. de Boer[1], *N. Francez*[2], *M. van Hulst*[3], *F. A. Stomp*[4]
[1] *Utrecht University*, [2] *The Technion*, [3] *Intel Corporation*, [4] *University of California*
[1] *Department of Computer Science, P.O. Box 80089, 3508 TB Utrecht, The Netherlands. frankb@cs.ruu.nl.*
[2] *Department of Computer Science, Haifa 32000, Israel. francez@cs.technion.ac.il.*
[3] *Santa Clara, CA 95052-8119, USA. mvanhuls@mipos2.intel.com.*
[4] *Department of Computer Science, Davis, CA 95616, USA. stomp@cs.ucdavis.edu.*

Abstract

We present a compositional Hoare logic for distributed systems in which communication is asynchronous via unbounded FIFO channels. Our main result is that the noncompositional proof method for (synchronous) CSP of Apt, Francez, and de Roever applied to asynchronous communication allows a simple compositional formulation in which the so-called cooperation test can be fully incorporated in the local verification of the (sequential) components of the system. Thus, the resulting method enables (verified) local specifications of the components, which may be augmented with auxiliary variables, to be combined into a global specification without any test involving the way those local specifications have been derived.

The applicability of our approach is demonstrated by a correctness proof of a distributed program for leader election.

Keywords

Asynchronous communication, compositional reasoning, distributed computing

1 INTRODUCTION

Hoare logics have been developed for and applied successfully to a variety of sequential programming constructs (see for an overview [1]). For the parallel programming language CSP a Hoare logic is presented in [3]. The proof

Programming Concepts and Methods D. Gries, & W-P. de Roever (Eds.)

method in [3] is based on the proof-theoretical ideas first introduced in [18] for a parallel programming language based on communication via shared variables. Characteristic of this method is its two-leveled structure: In the first level the (sequential) components of a system are verified using *assumptions* about the communication statements; these assumptions in general involve *auxiliary variables.* The second level consists of checking whether the assumptions introduced in the first level for the various components are mutually consistent with respect to a *global invariant.* This test is called the *cooperation test.* Since this test involves information of the internal structure of the local proofs of the correctness of the sequential components, this proof method is not compositional.

The results

In this paper we develop a *compositional* Hoare logic for distributed systems composed of processes which communicate asynchronously via unbounded FIFO (First In First Out) channels.

Our main result is that the noncompositional proof method of [3] applied to ACSP (Asynchronously Communicating Sequential Processes) allows a formulation in which the cooperation test can be fully incorporated in the verification of the (sequential) components of a system. More specifically, compositionality is obtained by the introduction of a generalization of the usual Hoare logic for sequential programs. This generalization consists of the addition of a global invariant to local specifications. Such generalized Hoare triples involve a rely/guarantee style of reasoning ([13]) and as such are to be distinguished from the specification formalism of I-logic ([20]). The verified local specifications then can be logically combined into a global specification, without any additional test involving the way these local specifications are derived (as usually codified in proof outlines). As such the resulting proof method is compositional (assuming the following definition: A proof system is called compositional if the specification of a compound programming construct can be derived from specifications of its constituent parts without any further information about the structure of these parts). The applicability of the proof method is demonstrated by proving correctness of a distributed leader election algorithm.

We prove in the full paper that the method is sound and (relative) complete. To obtain a (relative) complete proof method for ACSP *auxiliary variables* are needed to describe and reason about dynamic control properties.

Comparison with related work

The first proof method for ACSP was proposed in [22] and [23]. That method extends the system presented in [17] for synchronous CSP. These systems are not compositional because of the tests for *satisfaction* and *interference-freedom*. A proof method in the same spirit has been proposed by Camp, Kearns, and Ahuja [9] to reason about communication through *flush-channels*, which generalize conventional asynchronous channels.

Compositional Hoare logics for CSP have been developed in [24] and [26]. The Hoare logic of [26] has been applied to ACSP in [20]. Other similar compositional proof systems for reasoning about asynchronous communication have been presented in [6, 14, 25, 21]. Francez [10] gives on overview of many existing proof methods for sequential and parallel/distributed programs. Compositionality in the above-mentioned systems is achieved by the incorporation of certain logical variables which range over *histories*, i.e. sequences of communication events. Characteristic of our method on the other hand is that it allows compositional reasoning based on *arbitrary* auxiliary variables. In other words, it does not force the user (of the method) to use only one particular kind of auxiliary variables like history variables. Instead, our method allows to verify a concurrent system in terms of auxiliary variables which are appropriate for the specification of the particular correctness problem considered. Since in general histories complicate the reasoning process while in many real-life examples simple boolean 'flags' as auxiliary variables already suffice, compositional proof methods, which allow auxiliary variables of any kind, like the one presented in this paper, are clearly more flexible and thus more useful in practice.

The generalization of Hoare logic introduced in this paper is based on the specification of the *reactive behaviour* of a component of a concurrent system in terms of a *global invariant*. In [15] and [16] a generalization of Hoare logic has been developed which is also based on the use of invariants in the specification and verification of concurrent systems. The logic of [15] however involves the use of built-in *location* variables and consequently it does not provide for a more flexible use of arbitrary auxiliary variables. Moreover, in this paper we present a formal semantic justification of generalized Hoare logic in terms of *reactive sequences*. Such sequences have been introduced in [4] as a general compositional model for concurrent systems based on asynchronous communication. The formal semantic justification of our generalization of Hoare logic allows for simple proofs of soundness and completeness, which are given in the full paper. Basically these proofs generalize in a straightforward manner the corresponding proofs of soundness and completeness (see [1]) of the standard Hoare logic of sequential programs.

The plan of the paper

In the next section we introduce our programming language of asynchronously communicating sequential processes. We present our proof system for reasoning about partial correctness properties of programs in Section 3. In Section 4, we prove correctness of a distributed leader election program. Finally, Section 5 draws some conclusions.

2 PROGRAMMING LANGUAGE

In this section we define the syntax and the semantics of the programming language. The semantics describes the behaviour of asynchronously communicating processes. Processes interact only via directed communication channels which are implemented by unbounded FIFO-buffers. A process can send a value along a channel or it can receive a value along a channel. The value sent along a channel is appended to the buffer which implements that channel, whereas receiving a value along a channel consists of retrieving the first element from its corresponding buffer. Thus values are received along a channel in the same order as they have been sent along that channel. A process is suspended when it tries to receive a value along an empty channel. Since buffers are assumed to be unbounded sending values can always take place.

2.1 Syntax

We assume given a set *Pvar* of (program) variables, and a set C of channel names with typical element $c, \ldots$. The sets *Pvar* and C are assumed to be disjoint.

The syntax of a statement, which can be executed by a (sequential) process, is defined by the following grammar:

$$S \ ::= \ x := e \mid c!!e \mid c??x \mid S_1; S_2 \mid [\!]_i[g_i \rightarrow S_i] \mid \star [\!]_i[g_i \rightarrow S_i]$$

In the above, e denotes an expression, and A denotes some fixed and finite set (of indices.) (The syntactic structures of expressions and of indices are left unspecified.)

The assignment statement $x := e$ has its usual meaning (e.g. we assume that the execution of an assignment terminates properly). Sending the value of expression e along channel c is described by the *send-statement* $c!!e$, whereas receiving a value along channel c and recording that value in variable x is described by the *receive-statement* $c??x$. We sometimes refer to a receive- or a send-statement as an IO statement. Sequential composition is denoted by ';'. The statement $[\!]_i[g_i \rightarrow S_i]$ is called a *guarded conditional.* It consists of a (finite number of) guarded statements $g_i \rightarrow S_i$. Every *guard* is either a boolean expression b or a sequential composition $b; c??x$, for some boolean condition b and some receive-statement $c??x$. (The syntactic structure of boolean expressions is left unspecified.) Guard b is enabled in some state, if it evaluates to true in that state. If enabled, execution of such a guard is equivalent to the execution of a skip-statement. Guard $b; c??x$ is enabled in some state, if in that state b evaluates to true and channel c is not empty. If enabled, execution of such a guard is equivalent to the execution of $c??x$. The execution of a guarded conditional $[]_i[g_i \rightarrow S_i]$ consists of the execution of some enabled guard g_i and the execution of S_i thereafter. If there exists no enabled guard, then the execution of the guarded conditional suspends. The *guarded iteration* $\star[]_i[g_i \rightarrow S_i]$ consists of repeatedly executing the guarded selection $[]_i[g_i \rightarrow S_i]$ until all the boolean parts of the guards are false (and the iteration terminates). Note that we do not have send-statements in guards. However this does not reduce the expressive power as in CSP ([8]) because the execution of a send-statement does not depend on the environment.

In order to reason about programs, we may possibly have to expand them by (assignments to) *auxiliary* variables. These variables are not allowed to affect the flow of control of the original program. They are used only to reason about dynamic control properties. Related with the notion of auxiliary variables is that of a *bracketed section*. Bracketed sections are used to render the sequential composition of an IO-statement and an assignment to an auxiliary variable *atomic*, so that it is irrelevant whether an *invariant* holds in between. The formal definition of this notion can be found in the full paper and is similar to the corresponding notion as defined in [3].

Definition 1 A parallel program is of the form $[S_1 \parallel \ldots \parallel S_n]$ with the following restrictions: The statements S_i do not share program variables, channels are unidirectional and connect exactly one sender and one receiver. Formally we assume a partitioning of the set $Pvar$ of program variables into sets $Pvar_i$ (here i ranges over the natural numbers.) Also, we assume a partitioning of the set $IOvar = \{c??, c!! \mid c \in C\}$ of *input/output* variables into sets $IOvar_i$. Let $Pvar(S)$ be the set of program variables of S and let $IOvar(S)$ be the set of those input/output variables for which there occurs a corresponding input/output statement in S, e.g. $IOvar(c??x) = \{c??\}$. We then impose on any program $P = [S_1 \parallel \ldots \parallel S_n]$ the syntactic restriction that $Pvar(S_i) \subseteq PVar_i$ and $IOvar(S_i) \subseteq IOvar_i$.

2.2 Semantics

We define the semantics of the programming language in terms of a structured operational semantics. We first define the notion of a state.

Definition 2 A state assigns values to all program variables and all input/output variables. Define $\Sigma = (Pvar \cup IOvar) \rightarrow (Val \cup Val^*)$, where Val denotes some domain of values and Val^* denotes the set of all finite sequences over Val. We impose the restriction that program variables are mapped to values; and that input/output variables are mapped to sequences of values. Elements of Σ are called states and denoted by $\sigma, \ldots$.

The idea is that $\sigma(c??)$ denotes the sequence of values received along channel c, whereas $\sigma(c!!)$ denotes the sequence of values sent along channel c.

Definition 3 The transition relation $S \stackrel{\langle\sigma,\sigma'\rangle}{\Longrightarrow} S'$ is defined in terms of the stucture of S. It describes an execution step of S in state σ which results in σ'. The statement S' denotes the remaining statement to be executed. We present the following two cases (the symbol E below denotes termination, the append operation is denoted by '$\cdot$', and the operation f applied to a sequence gives its first element):

Output statements are described by a transition

$$c!!e \stackrel{\langle\sigma,\sigma'\rangle}{\Longrightarrow} E$$

where $\sigma' = \sigma\{\sigma(c!!)\cdot\sigma(e)/c!!\}$, i.e. the state which results from σ by assigning to the output variable $c!!$ the sequence obtained by appending the value of e (in σ) to $\sigma(c!!)$.

Let $\sigma(c)$ denote the suffix of $\sigma(c!!)$ corresponding to its prefix as given by $\sigma(c??)$ (so $\sigma(c)$ presents the contents of the buffer).

Input statements then are described by a transition

$$c??x \stackrel{\langle\sigma,\sigma'\rangle}{\Longrightarrow} E$$

provided $\sigma(c)$ is nonempty. Here $\sigma' = \sigma\{\sigma(c??)\cdot v/c??, v/x\}$, where $v = f(\sigma(c))$. So σ' results from assigning the first element to be read, i.e. $f(\sigma(c))$, to x and updating the input variable $c??$ by appending this element to the sequence of values read sofar.

We define the semantics of a statement S as the set of (finite) sequences, so-called *reactive* sequences, of elements of $\Sigma \times \Sigma$ generated by the above transition relation (such sequences are introduced in [4] as a general model for asynchronous communication).

Definition 4 For $w = \langle\sigma_1,\sigma_1'\rangle\cdots\langle\sigma_n,\sigma_n'\rangle \in (\Sigma\times\Sigma)^*$, $S \stackrel{w}{\Longrightarrow} E$ holds if there exist statements $S_1,\ldots,S_n$ such that $S_1 = S$, $S_n = E$ and, for $1 \le i < n$, $S_i \stackrel{\langle\sigma_i,\sigma_i'\rangle}{\Longrightarrow} S_{i+1}$. For any statement S with $Pvar(S) \subseteq Pvar_m$ and $IOvar(S) \subseteq IOvar_m$, the semantics $\mathcal{M}(S) \subseteq (\Sigma\times\Sigma)^*$ is defined by

$$\mathcal{M}(S) = \{w \mid S \stackrel{w}{\Longrightarrow} E \text{ and } w \text{ is } m\text{-connected}\}$$

where sequence $\langle\sigma_1,\sigma_1'\rangle\cdots\langle\sigma_n,\sigma_n'\rangle$ is m-connected if for all $1 \le i < n$, σ_{i+1} and σ_i' agree on all the variables in $Pvar_m$ and $IOvar_m$. By $\mathcal{M}(S)(\sigma)$ we denote the set of sequences $\langle\sigma_1,\sigma_1'\rangle\cdots\langle\sigma_n,\sigma_n'\rangle$ with $\sigma = \sigma_1$.

A sequence in set $\mathcal{M}(S)$ represents a computation of S in some environment. The environmental steps in a sequence $\langle\sigma_1,\sigma_1'\rangle\cdots\langle\sigma_n,\sigma_n'\rangle$ are represented by the 'gaps' $\langle \sigma_i', \sigma_{i+1} \rangle$. The requirement of m-connectedness guarantees that the environment does not affect the (program and input/output) variables controlled by S.

Definition 5 For any program $P = [S_1 \parallel \dots \parallel S_n]$, the semantics $\mathcal{M}(P) \subseteq \Sigma \times \Sigma$ of P is defined by

$$\mathcal{M}(P) = \alpha(\mathcal{M}(S_1) \parallel \dots \parallel \mathcal{M}(S_n)),$$

where the abstraction operator α returns the set of pairs $\langle \sigma, \sigma' \rangle$ of initial and final states of all *connected* sequences, such that for all channels c in the program $\sigma(c??) \leq \sigma(c!!)$ holds. An element $\langle \sigma_1, \sigma_1' \rangle \cdots \langle \sigma_n, \sigma_n' \rangle$ of $(\Sigma \times \Sigma)^*$ is called connected if $\sigma_i' = \sigma_{i+1}$, for $1 \leq i < n$. The semantic operator $\parallel$ denotes the usual operation of interleaving. By $\mathcal{M}(P)(\sigma)$ we denote the set of states σ' such that $\langle \sigma, \sigma' \rangle \in \mathcal{M}(P)$. (Thus, if $\sigma(c??)$ is not a prefix of $\sigma(c!!)$ for some channel c in program P, then $M(P)(\sigma) = \emptyset$ holds.)

3 PROOF SYSTEM

In this section we present axioms and proof rules for formally reasoning about programs.

3.1 Correctness formulas

We assume given some logic to reason about properties of states. The vocabulary of the logic includes the set of program variables and input/output variables, and function/predicate symbols describing operations/relations on the domain *Val* of values and the domain *Val** of sequences (of values). Assertions of the underlying logic are denoted by $p, q, \ldots$. By $\sigma \models p$ we denote that assertion p holds in σ. Validity of an assertion p is denoted by $\models p$.

Local correctness formulas are of the form $I : \{p\}S\{q\}$, for assertions p, q, I and statement S. Here, I is an assertion which describes certain invariant properties of computations of S starting in a state satisfying p. W.r.t. a local correctness formula $I : \{p\}S\{q\}$, it is implicitly assumed that $PVar(S, p, q) \subseteq Pvar_n$ and $IOvar(S, p, q) \subseteq IOvar_n$, for some n. Invariant I may refer to arbitrary input/output variables, but is allowed to refer only to those program variables of S which occur as auxiliary variables. Informally, $I : \{p\}S\{q\}$ is valid iff

> every terminating computation of S in a parallel environment, which guarantees I at each interleaving point, preserves I and results in a state satisfying postcondition q, if initially p holds.

Global correctness formulas are of the form $\{p\}P\{q\}$, for assertions p, q and program P. The correctness formula $\{p\}P\{q\}$ holds if every terminating computation of P in a state satisfying precondition p results in a state satisfying postcondition q.

We now turn to the formal semantics of correctness formulas:

Definition 6 Let $\mathcal{M}_{\leq}(S)$ denote the prefix closure of $\mathcal{M}(S)$, i.e. it consists of $\mathcal{M}(S)$ plus all the prefixes of sequences of $\mathcal{M}(S)$. We define $\models I : \{p\}S\{q\}$ iff for every sequence $w = \langle\sigma_1, \sigma_1'\rangle \cdots \langle\sigma_n, \sigma_n'\rangle \in \mathcal{M}_{\leq}(S)$, such that $\sigma_1 \models p$ and $\sigma_i \models I$, for $1 \leq i \leq n$, we have that $\sigma_i' \models I$, for $1 \leq i \leq n$; and if $w \in M(S)$ then $\sigma_n' \models q$.

Invariant I in local correctness formula $I : \{p\}S\{q\}$ thus provides for a kind of *rely/guarantee* style specification: If the states produced by the environment, i.e. the states σ_i, $i = 1, \ldots, n$, in the definition above, all satisfy the invariant I then the process guarentees that I is preserved by its local state-changes, i.e. I holds in σ_i', $i = 1, \ldots, n$. Note that although local correctness formulas have the same format as formulas in I-logic [20], their interpretations are different (in I-logic the invariant is used actually only for describing nonterminating behaviours, whereas in our logic the invariant is essential for compositionality).

Definition 7 For global correctness formula $\{p\}P\{q\}$, $\models \{p\}P\{q\}$ holds iff for all $\langle\sigma, \sigma'\rangle \in \mathcal{M}(P)$ with $\sigma \models p$ we have that $\sigma' \models q$ is satisfied.

This is the standard partial correctness interpretation of correctness formulas in Hoare logics.

3.2 Axioms and rules

Next we discuss the axioms and rules of the proof system. We have the following axiom for assignments:

Axiom 1 *(assignment)* $\quad I : \{p[e/x]\}x := e\{q\}$

Here $p[e/x]$ denotes the result of substituting all free occurrences of x in p by e. Since the invariant I does not refer to program variables (except for the auxiliary variables, but these occur only in bracketed sections for which we have different rules), I is on purely syntactic grounds preserved by the assignments.

The following axiomatization of input/output statements closely mirrors their semantics.

Rule 1 *(output)*

$$\frac{(I \wedge p) \rightarrow (I \wedge q)[c!! \cdot e/c!!]}{I : \{p\}c!!e\{q\}}$$

The output rule thus states that the local specification $I : \{p\}c!!e\{q\}$ can be derived if the assertion $I \wedge p$ implies the assertion obtained from $I \wedge q$ by replacing every occurrence of the output variable $c!!$ by the sequence term $c!! \cdot e$. The term $c!! \cdot e$ records the fact that the value of e has been sent.

In order to axiomatize input statements we assume in the logic a binary sequence operator '$-$' such that $s - s'$ denotes the suffix of s as determined by s' (in case s' is a prefix of s, otherwise the result is undefined) and an unary sequence operator f which yields the first element of a sequence. In the rule below the term c stands for $c!! - c??$, i.e. it represents the contents of the buffer, the values sent but not yet read.

Rule 2 *(input)*

$$\frac{(I \wedge p \wedge c \neq \epsilon) \rightarrow (I \wedge q)[f(c)/x, c?? \cdot f(c)/c??]}{I : \{p\}c??x\{q\}}$$

The input rule thus states that the local specification $I : \{p\}c??e\{q\}$ can be derived if the assertion $I \wedge p$ together with the assumption that the buffer c is nonempty (formally described by $c \neq \epsilon$) implies the assertion obtained from $I \wedge q$ by replacing every occurrence of the variable x by the term $f(c)$, which denotes by definition the first element to be read, and by replacing every occurrence of the input variable $c??$ by the sequence term $c?? \cdot f(c)$, which records that the first element of the buffer c has been read.

The straightforward generalization of the above rules to bracketed sections are ommitted but can be found in the full paper.

The following rules for sequential composition, the guarded statement and the guarded iteration are the usual ones, except for the addition of invariant I.

Rule 3 *(sequential composition)*

$$\frac{I : \{p\}S_1\{r\},\ I : \{r\}S_2\{q\}}{I : \{p\}S_1; S_2\{q\}}$$

For notational convenience we treat the case of the conditional with only guards of the form $b; c??x$.

Rule 4 *(guarded conditional)*

$$\frac{I : \{p \wedge b_i\}c_i??x_i; S_i\{q\}}{I : \{p\}[\!]_i[b_i; c_i??x_i \rightarrow S_i]\{q\}}$$

Rule 5 *(guarded iteration)*

$$\frac{I : \{p\}[\!]_i[g_i \rightarrow S_i]\{p\}}{I : \{p\} \star [\!]_i[g_i \rightarrow S_i]\{p \wedge \bigwedge_i \neg b_i\}}$$

Moreover we have the following consequence rule.

Rule 6 *(Local consequence rule)* $$\frac{(I \wedge p) \rightarrow p',\ I : \{p'\}S\{q'\},\ (I \wedge q') \rightarrow q}{I : \{p\}S\{q\}}$$

It is important to note that the rely/guarantee style of specification inherent in the interpretation of the invariant does *not* allow a weakening of the invariant in the above consequence rule.

We have the following simple rule for parallel composition:

Rule 7 *(parallel composition)* $$\frac{I : \{p_i\}S_i\{q_i\}\ i = 1, ..., n}{\{I \wedge \bigwedge_{i=1}^{n} p_i\}[S_1 \parallel ... \parallel S_n]\{I \wedge \bigwedge_{i=1}^{n} q_i\}}$$

Note that the rule does not involve any additional test on the way the local specifications of the components have been derived.

We conclude the exposition of the proof system with the global consequence rule, the auxiliary variables rule, the FIFO rule and the elimination rule.

Rule 8 *(global consequence rule)* $$\frac{p \rightarrow p',\ \{p'\}P\{q'\},\ q' \rightarrow q}{\{p\}P\{q\}}$$

Rule 9 *(auxiliary variables rule)* $$\frac{\{p\}P'\{q\}}{\{p\}P\{q\}}$$

where P is obtained from P' by deleting all assignments to the auxiliary variables. It is assumed that the postcondition q does not refer to the auxiliary variables of P'.

Rule 10 *(FIFO rule)* $$\frac{\{p \wedge c?? \leq c!!\}P\{q\}}{\{p\}P\{q\}}$$

where channel c occurs in program P, and '$\leq$' denotes the prefix relation on sequences.

Rule 11 *(elimination rule)* $$\frac{\{p\}P\{q\}}{\{\exists x.p\}P\{q\}}$$

provided x is a variable not occurring in P or q.

The following small (toy) examples of correctness proofs illustrate some characteristic reasoning patterns of asynchronous communication. First we consider the case of a simple communication:

$$\{c?? = \epsilon \wedge c!! = \epsilon\}c!!e \parallel c??x\{x = e\}$$

This correctness formula states that after the execution of $c!!e \parallel c??x$ in a state which satisfies $c?? = \epsilon \wedge c!! = \epsilon$, that is, no values have been sent nor read yet, the value of x equals that of e. We take as global invariant the assertion $c?? \leq c!!$. Now, since

$$(c?? \leq c!! \wedge c?? = \epsilon \wedge c \neq \epsilon) \rightarrow (c?? \cdot f(c) \leq c!! \wedge (c?? \cdot f(c))[1] = f(c))$$

(given a term t which denotes a sequence of values, $t[n]$, with n an arithmetic expression, denotes the nth element of t), we have by the input rule

$$c?? \leq c!! : \{c?? = \epsilon\}c??x\{c??[1] = x\}$$

Similarly we derive by the output rule that

$$c?? \leq c!! : \{c!! = \epsilon\}c!!e\{c!![1] = e\}$$

An application of the rule for parallel composition and the global consequence rule (observe the use of the global invariant $c?? \leq c!!$ in the application of the consequence rule) then finishes the proof.

Next we consider the case of a computation which deadlocks:

$$\{c = \epsilon \wedge d = \epsilon\}c??x; d!!e \parallel d??y; c!!e'\{\mathit{false}\}$$

We take as global invariant I the precondition $c = \epsilon \wedge d = \epsilon$: Since $(I \wedge c \neq \epsilon) \rightarrow \mathit{false}$ (and similarly $(I \wedge d \neq \epsilon) \rightarrow \mathit{false}$) we derive by the input rule

$$I : \{\mathit{true}\}c??x\{\mathit{false}\}$$

(and a similar correctness formula for $d??y$). An application of the rule for sequential composition and the rule for parallel composition then finishes the proof.

The following example illustrates the use of auxiliary variables:

$$\begin{gathered}(\mathit{true} \rightarrow c??x; d!!0 \,\square\, \mathit{true} \rightarrow d!!1; c??x)\\ \parallel \\ (\mathit{true} \rightarrow d??y; c!!0 \,\square\, \mathit{true} \rightarrow c!!1; d??y)\end{gathered}$$

Assuming that all the input/output variables $(c??, c!!, d??, d!!)$ are initialized to the empty sequence, we have upon termination the following possible combinations of values of x and y:

$$(x = 1 \wedge y = 0) \vee (x = 1 \wedge y = 1) \vee (x = 0 \wedge y = 1) \tag{1}$$

That is, the combination $(x = 0 \wedge y = 0)$ is excluded because the two first branches of the parallel components cannot be activated during one computation. In order to prove this we need the introduction of auxiliary variables. A possible way to do so is described below:

$$\begin{gathered}\mathit{true} \rightarrow \langle c??x; h_1 := 0\rangle; d!!0 \,\square\, \mathit{true} \rightarrow \langle d!!1; h_1 := 1\rangle; c??x\\ \parallel \\ \mathit{true} \rightarrow \langle d??y; h_2 := 0\rangle; c!!0 \,\square\, \mathit{true} \rightarrow \langle c!!1; h_2 := 1\rangle; d??y\end{gathered}$$

Thus the auxiliary variables h_1 and h_2 simply indicate which branches have been selected. Assuming that all the input/output variables $(c??, c!!, d??, d!!)$ are initialized to the empty sequence and that h_1 and h_2 are initialized to, say -1, we can derive the postcondition (1), using the global invariant I

$$\neg(h_1 = 0 \wedge h_2 = 0) \wedge (d!! = \epsilon \rightarrow h_2 \neq 0) \wedge (c!! = \epsilon \rightarrow h_1 \neq 0)$$

First observe that I holds initially, since $h_1 = h_2 = -1$ holds initially by assumption. Let us now highlight the main points in the proof of the invariance of I over the branch

$$true \rightarrow \langle c??x; h_1 := 0\rangle; d!!0$$

First we have to show that I holds after $\langle c??x; h_1 := 0\rangle$. Since h_1 becomes 0 we thus have to show that h_2 is different from 0. But locally we know that $d!! = \epsilon$, this then together with I gives us that indeed $h_2 \neq 0$. Next we have to argue that I holds after $d!!0$: Just observe that $d!! \neq \epsilon$ holds after its execution. The proof of the invariance of I over the other branches is similar. The information that h_1 and h_2 cannot be 0 at the same time now can be used to eliminate the combination $x = 0 \wedge y = 0$ upon termination. The involves basically the same reasoning pattern as in the above example $c!!e \parallel c??x$, and is therefore omitted.

It can be shown that the last example cannot be proved correct with input/output variables only. This demonstrates that auxiliary variables (apart from the built-in input/output variables) are needed in general to reason about nondeterministic programs. In [7] however it is shown that when programs are restricted to deterministic control structures, input/output variables suffice.

4 EXAMPLE

We now demonstrate the applicability of our proof system by proving correct a *distributed program for leader election.*

Consider program P=$[S_1 \parallel \ldots \parallel S_n]$ with

$$
\begin{array}{l}
S_i = z_i := 0;\ y_i := 0;\ c_i!!(x_i, 0);\\
\quad *[y_i \neq \infty; c_{i-1}??(y_i, hop_i);\ [x_i = y_i \rightarrow z_i := 1; y_i := \infty;\ c_i!!(\infty, hop_i + 1)\\
\qquad\qquad\qquad\qquad\qquad\qquad \Box\\
\qquad\qquad\qquad\qquad\qquad\qquad x_i > y_i \rightarrow skip\\
\qquad\qquad\qquad\qquad\qquad\qquad \Box\\
\qquad\qquad\qquad\qquad\qquad\qquad x_i < y_i \rightarrow c_i!!(y_i, hop_i + 1)\\
\qquad\qquad\qquad\qquad\qquad\qquad]\\
\quad]
\end{array}
$$

Figure 1 Distributed Leader Election.

In this program, there are n+1 processes, $n > 1$ arranged in a ring, with channel c_i connecting S_i to S_{i+1}. Addition and subtraction involving such indices i is done modulo $n+1$. Each process S_i has a local variable x_i (all indices are explicit, for readability). Distinct variables x_i and x_j represent distinct integer values. Here '∞' denotes a value larger than all integers. In addition, each process has a local variable z_i whose initial value is irrelevant. Upon termination, it is required that there exists *exactly one* index i_0, such that $z_{i_0} = 1$, and $z_j = 0$, for all $j \neq i_0$. The idea is to choose as the 'leader' S_{i_0} such that $x_{i_0}=max\{x_k \mid 1 \leq k \leq n\}$, i.e., the index of the process with the largest value of x_i.

Each process sends its value x_i to the right, and propagates to the right any received value x larger than its own x_i. The maximal value x_{i_0} is the only one to traverse the whole ring. When it arrives back to its origin, a '∞' message is sent around the ring to terminate all other processes. The second component *hop* in message (x, hop) records the number of hops, i.e., the distance that x has traversed in the ring. (This component as well as the variables hop_i, $i = 1, \ldots, n$, have been added only to simplify the correctness proof. Strictly speaking, they are not needed.) It is assumed that for i=0, $\cdots$, n, $x_i < \infty$ holds, and that ∞ and pairs such as (x, hop) can be encoded as natural numbers to conform to the syntax of programs.

The correctness assertion we want to establish is:

$$\begin{array}{ll} & \{\bigwedge_{i=0}^{n}(c_i = \epsilon \wedge x_i = X_i \neq \infty \wedge \bigwedge_{j=0}^{n}(j \neq i \Rightarrow X_j \neq X_i))\} \\ (*) \vdash & P \\ & \{\bigvee_{i=1}^{n}(z_i = 1 \wedge \bigwedge_{j=0}^{n}(j \neq i \Rightarrow (z_j = 0 \wedge X_i > X_j)))\}. \end{array}$$

For this example, there is no need to introduce bracketed sections.

Let p_i=$c_{i-1}??$=$c_i!!$=ϵ $\wedge$ x_i=$X_i$$\neq$$\infty$ $\wedge$ $\bigwedge_{j=0}^{n}(j \neq i \Rightarrow X_j \neq X_i)$, for $i = 1, \ldots, n$; and let I=$\bigwedge_{i=1}^{n} c_i?? \leq c_i!!$ We construct local correctness assertions for each S_i. We have:

(1) $\{c_{i-1}?? = c_i!! = \epsilon \wedge x_i = X_i \neq \infty \wedge \bigwedge_{j=0}^{n}(j \neq i \Rightarrow X_j \neq X_i)\}$
$\vdash I$: $z_i := 0$
$\{z_i = 0 \wedge c_{i-1}?? = c_i!! = \epsilon \wedge x_i = X_i \neq \infty \wedge \bigwedge_{j=0}^{n}(j \neq i \Rightarrow X_j \neq X_i)\}$

as a consequence of (*assignment*), and

(2) $\{z_i = 0 \wedge c_{i-1}?? = c_i!! = \epsilon \wedge x_i = X_i \neq \infty \wedge \bigwedge_{j=0}^{n}(j \neq i \Rightarrow X_j \neq X_i)\}$
$\vdash I$: $y_i := 0$
$\{y_i = 0 \wedge z_i = 0 \wedge c_{i-1}?? = c_i!! = \epsilon \wedge x_i = X_i \neq \infty$
$\wedge \bigwedge_{j=0}^{n}(j \neq i \Rightarrow X_j \neq X_i)\}$

as a consequence of (*assignment*), and

(3) $\{y_i = 0 \wedge z_i = 0 \wedge c_{i-1}?? = c_i!! = \epsilon \wedge x_i = X_i \neq \infty$
$\wedge \bigwedge_{j=0}^{n}(j \neq i \Rightarrow X_j \neq X_i)\}$
$c_i!!(x_i, 0)$
$\{y_i = 0 \wedge z_i = 0 \wedge c_{i-1}?? = \epsilon \wedge c_i!! =< (x_i, 0) > \wedge x_i = X_i \neq \infty$
$\wedge \bigwedge_{j=0}^{n}(j \neq i \Rightarrow X_j \neq X_i)\}$

as a consequence of (*output*).

To proceed we, obviously, need a loop invariant L_i. It comprises a number of conjuncts formulated below. (We have named these conjuncts for convenience.) For a sequence h and value x, $x \in h$ denotes that x occurs in h; $h[i]$ denotes the ith element of h, provided that $1 \leq i \leq | h |$ holds; and $last(h)$ denotes $h[| h |]$.

Define L_i by the conjunction of

$$
\begin{array}{ll}
\text{(A)} & x_i{=}X_i{\neq}\infty \wedge (z_i{=}0 \vee z_i{=}1) \wedge \bigwedge_{j=0}^{n}(j \neq i \Rightarrow X_j \neq X_i). \\
\text{(B)} & z_i{=}1 \Rightarrow y_i{=}\infty. \\
\text{(C)} & (\exists hop.\ (x_i,\ hop){\in}\ c_{i-1}??) \Leftrightarrow z_i{=}1. \\
\text{(D)} & \forall x, hop.\ ((x,\ hop){\in}\ c_i!! \Rightarrow x{\geq}x_i). \\
\text{(E)} & \forall hop.((\infty, hop) \in c_i!! \Rightarrow \quad (hop \neq 0 \\
 & \qquad \wedge (\quad (\infty, hop-1) \in c_{i-1}?? \\
 & \qquad\quad \vee (x_i, hop-1) \in c_{i-1}??))). \\
\text{(F)} & \forall x, hop.\ ((x,\ hop){\in}\ c_i!! \Rightarrow \quad (x{=}x_i \wedge hop{=}0) \\
 & \qquad \vee (x{=}\infty \wedge hop{>}0) \\
 & \qquad \vee ((x,\ hop-1) \in c_{i-1}?? \wedge hop{>}0)). \\
\text{(G)} & y_i = \infty \Rightarrow \exists hop \geq 0.\ ((x_i, hop) \in c_{i-1}?? \vee (\infty, hop) \in c_{i-1}??).
\end{array}
$$

The loop invariant is established indeed:

$$
\begin{array}{ll}
\text{(4)} & (\quad y_i{=}0 \wedge z_i{=}0 \wedge c_{i-1}?? = \epsilon \wedge c_i!! = <(x_i, 0)> \\
 & \quad \wedge\ x_i{=}X_i{\neq}\infty \wedge \bigwedge_{j=0}^{n}(j \neq i \Rightarrow X_i{\neq}X_j)) \\
 & \Rightarrow L_i.
\end{array}
$$

We show in some detail that L_i serves as an invariant for the loop in S_i. First, we introduce assertion ALT_i, holding prior to the branching points in S_i. It also comprises several numbered conjuncts. ALT_i is the conjunction of (A), (D), and

$$
\begin{array}{ll}
\text{(B}'\text{)} & z_i{=}0, \\
\text{(C}'\text{)} & \forall hop, k.\ (1{\leq}\ k <| c_{i-1}?? | \Rightarrow (x_i,\ hop) \neq c_{i-1}??[k]), \\
\text{(E}'\text{)} & \forall hop. \quad ((\infty,\ hop){\in}\ c_i!! \\
 & \quad \Rightarrow (\quad hop{\neq}0 \\
 & \qquad \wedge\ \exists k.(1{\leq}k{<}|c_{i-1}??| \wedge (\quad (\infty, hop{-}1){=}c_{i-1}??[k] \\
 & \qquad\qquad \vee (x_i,\ hop{-}1){=}c_{i-1}??[k]))), \\
\text{(F}'\text{)} & \forall x, hop.\ (x,\ hop){\in}\ c_i!! \Rightarrow \quad (x{=}x_i \wedge hop{=}0) \\
 & \qquad \vee (x{=}\infty \wedge hop{>}0) \\
 & \qquad \vee\ \exists k.\ (1{\leq}k{<}|c_{i-1}??| \wedge (x, hop{-}1){=}c_{i-1}??[k] \\
 & \qquad\qquad \wedge\ hop{>}0), \\
\text{(G}'\text{)} & y_i = \infty \Rightarrow \exists hop \geq 0.\exists k.(\quad 1 \leq k <| c_{i-1}?? | \\
 & \qquad \wedge ((x_i, hop){=}c_{i-1}??[k] \vee (\infty, hop){=}c_{i-1}??[k])), \\
\text{(H}'\text{)} & c_{i-1}?? \neq \epsilon \wedge last(c_{i-1}??){=}(y_i,\ hop_i) \wedge hop_i{\geq}0.
\end{array}
$$

We note that

(5) $\vdash \{L_i \wedge y_i \neq \infty\}\ c_{i-1}??(y_i, hop_i)\ \{ALT_i\}$

is obtained via (*input*). We next consider the separate directions.
For the first direction we reason as follows:

$$
\begin{array}{ll}
(6) & \{ALT_i \wedge x_i = y_i\} \\
& \vdash z_i{:=}1 \\
& \{(\text{A}) \wedge z_i = 1 \wedge (C') \wedge (D) \wedge (E') \wedge (F') \wedge (G') \wedge (H') \wedge x_i = y_i\}. \\
(7) & \{(A) \wedge z_i = 1 \wedge (C') \wedge (D) \wedge (E') \wedge (F') \wedge (G') \wedge (H') \wedge x_i = y_i\} \\
& \vdash y_i := \infty \\
& \{(A) \wedge z_i = 1 \wedge y_i = \infty \wedge (C') \wedge (D) \wedge (E') \wedge (F') \wedge\ c_{i-1}?? \neq \epsilon \\
& \qquad \wedge\ last(c_{i-1}??) = (x_i, hop_i) \\
& \qquad \wedge\ hop_i \geq 0\}. \\
(8) & \{(A) \wedge z_i = 1 \wedge y_i = \infty \wedge (C') \wedge (D) \wedge (E') \wedge (F') \wedge\ c_{i-1}?? \neq \epsilon \\
& \qquad \wedge\ last(c_{i-1}??) = (x_i, hop_i) \\
& \qquad \wedge\ hop_i \geq 0\} \\
& c_i!!(\infty, hop_i + 1) \\
& \{L_i\}.
\end{array}
$$

Thus, the first direction re-establishes L_i.
The second direction also re-establishes L_i, since we have

(9) $\vdash \{ALT_i\ \wedge\ x_i{>}y_i\}\ skip\ \{L_i\}$.

Finally, we have

(10) $\{ALT_i\ \wedge\ x_i{<}y_i\}\ c_i!!(y_i,\ hop_i{+}1)\ \{L_i\}$.

Therefore, the third direction re-establishes L_i, too.

By combining the above local correctness assertions, we obtain that $\vdash I : \{p_i\}S_i\{q_i\}$ holds for $q_i = (L_i \wedge y_i = \infty)$, $i = 1, \ldots, n$.

Application of the parallel composition rule then yields $\vdash \{I \wedge \bigwedge_{i=1}^{n} p_i\}\ P\ \{I \wedge \bigwedge_{i=1}^{n} q_i\}$. By repeatedly applying the *FIFO* rule, we obtain that $\vdash \{\bigwedge_{i=1}^{n} p_i\}\ P\ \{I \wedge \bigwedge_{i=1}^{n} q_i\}$ holds.

We now derive correctness formula (*) to be established for the leader election program by application of the global consequence rule. It suffices to prove that $I \wedge \bigwedge_{i=1}^{n} q_i$ implies $\{\bigvee_{i=1}^{n}(z_i = 1 \wedge \bigwedge_{j=1}^{n}(j \neq i \Rightarrow (z_j = 0 \wedge X_i > X_j)))\}$.

To do so, assume $I \wedge \bigwedge_{i=1}^{n} q_i$ holds. Since q_i has been defined as $L_i \wedge y_i = \infty$ and L_i has been defined as the conjunction of (A), $\cdots$, (G), for all i=1, $\cdots$, n, we get from clause (G) that

(i) for all $i = 1, \cdots, n$, there exists some $hop \geq 0$ with $(x_i, hop) \in c_{i-1}?? \vee (\infty, hop) \in c_{i-1}??$.

From this we derive by *reductio ad absurdum* that

(ii) for some $j = 1, \cdots, n$, and for some $hop \geq 0$, $(x_j, hop) \in c_{j-1}??$ holds.

Suppose that (ii) is not the case. Then, for all $j = 1, \cdots, n$, and for all $hop \geq 0$, $(x_j, hop) \notin c_{j-1}??$ holds. Consider an arbitrary $k \in \{1, \cdots, n\}$. From (i) we obtain that there exists some $hop_0 \geq 0$, such that $(\infty, hop_0) \in c_{k-1}??$. From I, $(\infty, hop_0) \in c_{k-1}!!$ is obtained. Then (E) implies that for some hop_1 with $hop_0 > hop_1 \geq 0$, $(x_{k-1}, hop_1) \in c_{k-2}?? \vee (\infty, hop_1) \in c_{k-2}??$ is true. Because (ii) is assumed to be false, $(\infty, hop_1) \in c_{k-2}??$ follows. By repeating this process ad infinitum we find an infinite decreasing sequence $hop_0 > hop_1 > \cdots$ of natural numbers, which is impossible. We conclude that (ii) is satisfied.

Now, consider an arbitrary $i_0 \in \{1, \cdots, n\}$ such that for some $hop \geq 0$, $(x_{i_0}, hop) \in c_{i_0-1}??$ holds. From (C) we obtain that $z_{i_0}=1$ is true; I implies that for some $hop \geq 0$, $(x_{i_0}, hop) \in c_{i_0-1}!!$ holds. Then, $x_{i_0} \geq x_{i_0-1}$ follows from (D). From (A) and (F) we obtain that for some $hop \geq 0$, $(x_{i_0}, hop) \in c_{i_0-2}??$. Continuing this way, we get $(x_{i_0}, hop) \in c_{i_0-1}?? \Rightarrow \bigwedge_{1 \leq j \leq n} x_{i_0} \geq x_j$. Together with (A) this proves uniqueness of i_0; and hence the righthandside of the implication we wished to prove.

Consequently, correctness of the distributed leader election program follows from rule (*Consequence*). This concludes our proof, and hence this section.

5 CONCLUSION

We have presented a compositional Hoare logic for distributed systems in which processes conmmunicate asynchronously via (unbounded) FIFO buffers. We have applied the proof system to a distributed leader election program, in order to demonstrate the applicability of our method. It has been argued that our method is preferable over other methods presented in the literature for reasoning about asynchronously communicating systems because it allows the use of *arbitrary* auxiliary vriables. In the full paper the proof system is shown to be sound and (relative) complete.

We remark here that the proof system can be easily extended to reasoning about nonterminating computations by introducing global correctness formulas of the form $I : \{p\}P\{q\}$ and interpreting the invariant with respect to all the (finite prefixes of) computations including the infinite ones. Due to lack of space we refer to the full paper for the details.

In [5] it is shown that auxiliary variables are no longer needed if one restricts to parallel systems of *deterministic* sequential processes. Moreover, in

[7] it shown that restricting to local nondeterminism allows for a further *decomposition* of the global invariant.

In the future we intend to apply our method to larger programs, using interactive proof checkers like PVS [19].

ACKNOWLEDGEMENT

We are grateful to Hagit Attiya for her help in the example proof.

REFERENCES

[1] Apt, K. R. (1981) Ten years of Hoare's logic: A survey-part I. ACM Transactions of Programming Languages and Systems, Vol. 3, No. 4., pp. 431–483.

[2] Apt, K. R. (1983) Formal justification of a proof system for communicating sequential processes. Journal of the ACM, Vol. 30, pp. 197–216.

[3] Apt, K. R., Francez, N., and de Roever, W.-P. (1980), A proof system for communicating sequential processes. ACM Transactions of Programming Languages and Systems, Vol. 2, No. 3, pp. 359–385.

[4] de Boer, F. S., Kok, J. N., Palamidessi, C., and Rutten, J. J. M. M. (1991) The failure of failures: Towards a paradigm for asynchronous communication. Proceedings of the Second International Conference on Concurrency Theory, Lecture Notes in Computer Science 527, pp. 111–126, Amsterdam, The Netherlands.

[5] de Boer, F. S. and van Hulst, M. (1994) Partial correctness of asynchronously communicating processes. Proceedings of Mathematical Foundations of Computer Science 1994.

[6] de Boer, F. S. and van Hulst, M. (1995) A compositional proof system for asynchronously communicating processes. Proceedings of Mathematics of Program Construction.

[7] de Boer, F. S. and van Hulst, M. (1996) Local nondeterminism in asynchronously communicating processes. Proceedings of Formal Methods Europe 1996.

[8] Bougé, L. (1988) On the existence of symmetric algorithms to find leaders in networks of communicating sequential processes. Acta Informatica, Vol. 25, pp. 179–201.

[9] Camp, T., Kearns, P., and Ahuja, M. (1993) Proof rules for flush channels. IEEE Transactions on Software Engineering, Vol. 19, No. 4, pp. 366–378.

[10] Francez, N. (1992) Program verification. Addison Wesley.

[11] Francez, N. and Stomp, F. A. (1993) A proof system for asynchronously communicating processes. Technical Report 722, The Technion, Department of Computer Science.

[12] Francez, N. and Stomp, F. A. (1994) A proof system for asynchronously communicating processes. Technical Memorandum, AT&T Bell Laboratories, December 1994.

[13] Jones, C. B. (1981) Development methods for computer programs including a notion of interference. PhD thesis, Oxford University Computing Laboratory.

[14] Jonsson, B. (1985) A model and proof system for asynchronous networks. Proceedings of the 4th ACM Annual Symposium on Principles of Distributed Computing, pp. 49–58.

[15] Lamport, L. (1980) The 'Hoare logic' of concurrent programs. Acta Informatica 14 (1980), pp. 21-37.

[16] Lamport, L. and Schneider, F. B. (1984) The "Hoare logic" of CSP, and all that. ACM Transactions on Programming Languages and Systems, Vol. 6, No. 2, April 1984, pp. 281–296.

[17] Levin, G. M. and Gries, D. (1981) Proof techniques for communicating sequential processes. Acta Informatica 15, pp. 281–302.

[18] Owicki, S. and Gries, D. (1976) An axiomatic proof technique for parallel programs. Acta Informatica 6, pp. 319–340.

[19] Owre, S, Rushby, J., and Shankar, N. (1992) PVS: A prototype verification system. Proceedings of the 1th Conference on Automated Deduction, Lecture Notes in Artificial Intelligence, Vol. 607, Springer-Verlag, pp. 748–752.

[20] Pandya, P. K. (1988) Compositional verification of distributed Programs. PhD thesis, Tata Institute of Fundamental Research, Homi Bhabha Road, Bombay 400 005, INDIA.

[21] Pandya, P. K. and Joseph, M. (1991) P-A logic – a compositional proof system for distributed programs. Distributed Computing 5, pp. 37–54.

[22] Schneider, F. B. (1982) Proof rules for message passing, logics and models of concurrent systems. NATO ASI Series, Vol. F 13, Springer-Verlag, 1985. Lecture Notes in Computer Science 190, pp. 234–254.

[23] Schlichting, R. D. and Schneider, F. B. (1984) Using message passing for distributed programming, proof rules and disciplines. ACM Transactions of Programming Languages and Systems, Vol. 6, No. 3, pp. 402–431.

[24] Soundararajan, N. (1983) Correctness proofs for CSP programs. Theoretical Computer Science, Vol. 24.

[25] Zhou, P. and Hooman, J. (1992) A proof theory for asynchronously communicating real-time systems. Proceedings of the 13th Real-Time Systems Symposium.

[26] Zwiers, J. (1989) Compositionality, concurrency and partial correctness. Lecture Notes in Computer Science 321.

6 BIOGRAPHIES

Frank de Boer: His main current research interests concern semantics and logics of parallel programming languages, real-time extensions of concurrent constraint programming, and multi-agent systems.
Nissim Frances: His research interests include formal semantics of natural language, computational linguistics, semantics of programming languages, program verification, concurrent and distributed programming, and logic programming.
Marten van Hulst: He received his PhD in 1995 at the University of Utrecht. In his thesis *compositional verification of parallel programs* Marten applied epistemic logic to the verification of CSP-like languages.
Frank Stomp: His research interests are in the areas of program verification, with an emphasis on distributed computation. He has also done work on software development.

9

Bisimulations in the Join-Calculus

M. Boreale
Dipartimento di Scienze dell'Informazione, Università "La Sapienza," Via Salaria 113, 00198 Roma, Italy. michele@dsi.uniroma1.it

*C. Fournet**
INRIA Rocquencourt, BP 105, 78153 Le Chesnay Cedex, France. Cedric.Fournet@inria.fr

*C. Laneve**
Dipartimento di Scienze dell'Informazione, Università di Bologna, Mura Anteo Zamboni 7, 40127 Bologna, Italy. laneve@cs.unibo.it

Abstract

We develop a theory of bisimulation in the join-calculus. We introduce a refined operational model that makes interactions with the environment explicit, and we discuss the impact of the lexical discipline of the join-calculus on its extensional semantics. We propose several formulations of bisimulation and we establish that all formulations yield the same equivalence. We prove that this equivalence is finer than barbed congruence, but that both relations coincide in the presence of name-testing.

Keywords

Asynchronous processes, barbed congruence, bisimulation, chemical abstract machine, join-calculus, pi-calculus

1 INTRODUCTION

The join-calculus is a recent formalism for modeling mobile systems [7, 6]. Its main motivation is to relate two crucial issues in concurrency: distributed implementation and formal semantics. To this end, the join-calculus enforces a strict lexical discipline over the channel names that appear in processes: names can be sent and received, but their communication capabilities cannot be affected by the receivers. This is the *locality property.*

Locality yields a simpler distributed model, because the communication primitives of the calculus can be directly implemented via standard primitives of asynchronous systems [6, 9]. It also plays a prominent role in the design of implicit type systems for the join-calculus, because all contravariant occurrences of names are static [8]. In this paper, we show that locality strongly affects the treatment of bisimulation, and provides a semantics simpler than other proposals in the literature.

---

*This work is partly supported by the ESPRIT CONFER-2 WG-21836

Programming Concepts and Methods D. Gries, & W-P. de Roever (Eds.)

In order to reason about distributed processes, we must equip the join-calculus with semantics that have both a sensible discriminating power and some convenient proof techniques. The usual approach in concurrency is to focus on elementary forms of interaction between the process and its environment. Formally, this is achieved through the definition of two notions that are common to most process calculi: a *reduction relation* $\rightarrow$ that represents internal evolution and an *observation predicate* $\Downarrow_a$ that detects the ability of interacting at a given channel. Based on these two notions, numerous observational semantics can be defined. As regards discriminating power, it would be adequate to test the observation predicate under all possible contexts; indeed, the resulting *trace-based semantics* are relevant to many practical issues in distributed programming, especially when one is not interested in the branching structure of processes. In order to establish trace-based equivalences, however, one must cope with quantification over both contexts and traces, which makes the proofs particularly difficult [12].

To tackle these problems, it is convenient to consider behavioral equivalences that are finer and easier to check, possibly using them as indirect proof techniques for coarser semantics. Among these, bisimulation-based semantics are especially convenient, because co-inductive proofs need only to consider single reduction steps instead of traces [15]. *Barbed bisimilarity* has been proposed in [14] as a uniform basis to define sensible behavioral equivalences on different process calculi. This is the approach chosen for the join calculus in [7, 6], where *barbed congruence* is defined as the coarsest congruence that is a barbed bisimulation. Yet, checking that two processes are barbed congruent still requires explicit quantification over all contexts. Indeed, most proofs of [7] have to analyze in details how contexts and processes get intertwined, and to partition their reductions accordingly. This makes routine or automated checking of these properties problematic.

In this paper, we introduce a labeled operational model for the join calculus, and we equip it with the standard *weak bisimulation* [15], which enjoys the usual, purely co-inductive proof technique on labeled transitions. Then, we use weak bisimulation to establish several sensible equalities between join-calculus processes. We also consider alternate definitions of this equivalence and relate weak bisimulation to barbed congruence, showing that the difference between the two semantics is precisely due to the absence of a name-matching operator. A more precise account of our work follows.

The original semantics of the join-calculus is based on the *reflexive chemical abstract machine* (RCHAM) [7], which only accounts for the internal evolution of processes. In order to shape labeled bisimulation upon join-calculus, we first propose the *open* RCHAM, a refined operational semantics that explicitly models interaction with the environment. Via these interactions, the environment can get acquainted with local names of the process that are emitted at free names—the *extrusions*—and can later emit on these names—the *intrusions* ("intrusion" has another technical meaning in [13]). Due to the principle of locality, intrusions and extrusions occur on disjoint sets of names. To keep track of the environment's acquaintance with local names, definitions—the technical device for defining the computational steps of RCHAM's—are marked with extruded names as soon as these extrusions happen. In turn, intrusions are allowed on these extruded names. The resulting open syntax for the join-calculus has processes of the form $\mathsf{def}_S\ D \ \mathsf{in}\ P$, where S is a set of names defined by D and extruded to the environment. This also induces a refined chemical machine, called the open RCHAM.

Let us illustrate what locality means in our setting. The process $\mathsf{def}_{\{x\}}\ x\langle u\rangle \triangleright P \ \mathsf{in}\ x\langle v\rangle$ defines a name x such that, whenever a message $x\langle u\rangle$ is received, a fresh copy of process P is started. The name x is marked as extruded; the environment can therefore send messages on x to trigger copies of the process P. However, the environment cannot interfere with the definition of x; in particular, the message $x\langle v\rangle$ cannot be consumed by the environment, and as a consequence any sensible equivalence $\approx$ would identify the two processes below:

$$\mathsf{def}_{\{x\}}\ x\langle u\rangle \triangleright P \ \mathsf{in}\ x\langle v\rangle \quad \approx \quad \mathsf{def}_{\{x\}}\ x\langle u\rangle \triangleright P \ \mathsf{in}\ P\{^v/_u\}$$

Weak bisimulation is obtained by applying the standard definition to the open RCHAM. Weak bisimilarity is stable under renaming, is a congruence over contexts of the open calculus, and it suitably abstracts from the actual structure of the join-patterns. For instance, it is insensitive to buffering, as it is expected for an asynchronous semantics.

The open RCHAM allows intrusion of messages on every name that has been extruded; this clause embeds asynchrony in the operational semantics, but it also generates extraneous transitions in case these messages are not used by the process. That is, our model hides the actual receiving capabilities of the process, although this information is available from the syntax of the process. Unfortunately, weak bisimulation cannot benefit from this information, and needs to consider numerous useless intrusions.

To reduce the size of our model, we modify the open RCHAM and equip it with an alternative equivalence called *asynchronous bisimulation.* The new chemical machine restricts intrusions to sets of messages that immediately trigger a reaction rule; this technical device significantly augments the blocking capability of processes. Asynchronous bisimulation allows the intrusion of several messages at the same time, instead of single ones. We prove that weak bisimulation and asynchronous bisimulation coincide, which validates the use of asynchronous bisimulation in proofs.

The last characterization of bisimulation is given in terms of barbed congruence. The barbed congruence of [7] is strictly coarser than weak bisimulation, because contexts of barbed congruence have no internal name-testing capability, while labels of weak bisimulation separates distinct names that exhibit the same behavior. This is actually the only difference between the two equivalences. To establish this, we augment the join-calculus with a name-matching operator and we show that (a variant of) barbed congruence coincides with weak bisimulation.

Beside its use as a proof technique, our semantics yields a better understanding of the join-calculus, and provides a basis for comparing it with other calculi, which are usually equipped with weak bisimulations, and especially with the asynchronous π-calculus [5]. In these calculi, asynchrony means that message outputs have no continuation, and thus that there is no direct way to detect that a message has been received. Noticeably, the usual weak bisimulation of the π-calculus has too much discriminating power, and separates processes with the same behavior (e.g., $0 \not\approx x(u).\overline{x}\langle u\rangle$); several remedies are considered in [11, 1]. Our bisimulations for the join-calculus make use of similar accommodations, but they yield simpler semantics, mostly because locality constrains interaction with the environment. This prunes the number of transitions to consider, and rules out processes such as $z(x).x(u).\overline{x}\langle u\rangle$ where x is used by the environment both for input and output.

The rest of the paper is organized as follows. In Section 2 we introduce our language and its model. In Section 3 we define weak bisimulation in this setting, we give examples, and we study its basic properties. In Section 4 we introduce asynchronous bisimulation, and we prove that it coincides with weak bisimulation. In Section 5 we relate our bisimulations to barbed congruence, and study the impact of name-testing. In Section 6 we discuss related work for the asynchronous π-calculus. We conclude in Section 7. Due to space limitations, the proofs are omitted; they can be found in the full paper [2].

2 THE OPEN JOIN-CALCULUS

In this section, we define the open join-calculus and its operational semantics as extensions of the join-calculus and the RCHAM of [7].

Syntax and Scopes. Let $\mathcal{N}$ be a countable set of *names* ranged over by $x, y, u, v, \ldots$; tuples of names are noted $u_i{}^{i \in 1..p}$ or simply $\widetilde{u}$. Names can carry fixed-length messages, and we assume a recursive sorting discipline on names that avoids arity mismatch, in the style of [16]. We consider only well-sorted terms, and we assume an infinite number of names of each sort. We omit the sorting discipline, as it is not important to understand the contents of the paper.

The open join-calculus processes A and the join-calculus processes P, the definitions D, and the *join-patterns* J are the terms defined as follows:

$$
\begin{array}{lcl@{\qquad\qquad}lcl}
A & \stackrel{\text{def}}{=} & 0 & P & \stackrel{\text{def}}{=} & 0 \\
 & & x\langle u_i{}^{i\in 1..p}\rangle & & & x\langle u_i{}^{i\in 1..p}\rangle \\
 & & A \mid A & & & P \mid P \\
 & & \mathsf{def}_S\ D \ \mathsf{in}\ A & & & \mathsf{def}\ D\ \mathsf{in}\ P \\
D & \stackrel{\text{def}}{=} & J \triangleright P & J & \stackrel{\text{def}}{=} & x\langle u_i{}^{i\in 1..p}\rangle \\
 & & D \wedge D & & & J \mid J
\end{array}
$$

A process P can be the inert process 0, a message sent on a name x that carries a tuple of names $\widetilde{u}$, a parallel composition of processes, or the definition of local names and the process within their scope; a definition D is a conjunction of reaction rules $J \triangleright P$ that associate join-patterns J to guarded processes P; the intended meaning is that, whenever messages match the pattern J, the guarded process P can be triggered. An open process A is like a process, except that it has open definitions at top-level instead of local ones. The open definition $\mathsf{def}_S\ D \mathsf{\ in\ } \ldots$ exhibits a subset S of names defined by D that are visible from the environment: the *extruded names.* When omitted, the index set S is empty (no extruded names so far). We identify such open definitions $\mathsf{def}_\emptyset\ D \mathsf{\ in\ } P$ with local definitions $\mathsf{def}\ D \mathsf{\ in\ } P$.

Definition 1 *We partition names in terms as follows:* visible names *are either* free names $\mathsf{fv}[D]$, $\mathsf{fv}[A]$ *or* extruded names $\mathsf{xv}[A]$*;* local names *are either* received names $\mathsf{rv}[J]$ *or* defined names $\mathsf{dv}[J], \mathsf{dv}[D]$.

$$
\begin{array}{llll}
J: & \mathsf{rv}[x\langle\widetilde{v}\rangle] \stackrel{def}{=} \{u \in \widetilde{v}\} & & \mathsf{rv}[J \mid J'] \stackrel{def}{=} \mathsf{rv}[J] \uplus \mathsf{rv}[J'] \\
 & \mathsf{dv}[x\langle\widetilde{v}\rangle] \stackrel{def}{=} \{x\} & & \mathsf{dv}[J \mid J'] \stackrel{def}{=} \mathsf{dv}[J] \uplus \mathsf{dv}[J'] \\
D: & \mathsf{dv}[J \triangleright P] \stackrel{def}{=} \mathsf{dv}[J] & & \mathsf{dv}[D \wedge D'] \stackrel{def}{=} \mathsf{dv}[D] \cup \mathsf{dv}[D'] \\
 & \mathsf{fv}[J \triangleright P] \stackrel{def}{=} \mathsf{dv}[J] \cup (\mathsf{fv}[P] \setminus \mathsf{rv}[J]) & & \mathsf{fv}[D \wedge D'] \stackrel{def}{=} \mathsf{fv}[D] \cup \mathsf{fv}[D'] \\
A: & \mathsf{fv}[A \mid A'] \stackrel{def}{=} (\mathsf{fv}[A] \setminus \mathsf{xv}[A']) \cup (\mathsf{fv}[A'] \setminus \mathsf{xv}[A]) & & \mathsf{fv}[0] \stackrel{def}{=} \emptyset \\
 & \mathsf{xv}[A \mid A'] \stackrel{def}{=} \mathsf{xv}[A] \uplus \mathsf{xv}[A'] & & \mathsf{xv}[0] \stackrel{def}{=} \emptyset \\
 & \mathsf{fv}[\mathsf{def}_S\, D \mathsf{\ in\ } A] \stackrel{def}{=} (\mathsf{fv}[A] \cup (\mathsf{fv}[D] \setminus \mathsf{xv}[A])) \setminus \mathsf{dv}[D] & & \mathsf{fv}[x\langle\widetilde{v}\rangle] \stackrel{def}{=} \{x, \widetilde{v}\} \\
 & \mathsf{xv}[\mathsf{def}_S\, D \mathsf{\ in\ } A] \stackrel{def}{=} S \uplus \mathsf{xv}[A] & & \mathsf{xv}[x\langle\widetilde{v}\rangle] \stackrel{def}{=} \emptyset
\end{array}
$$

The above definition induces well-formed conditions on terms, which are made more explicit below. As usual, the operator $\uplus$ means disjoint union. In the whole paper, we consider processes modulo α-conversion on *bound names*, namely received names and defined non-extruded names, and we always assume that:

1. join-patterns are linear: as in the join-calculus of [7], both defined variables and received variables appear at most once in every join pattern. The restriction on received variables rules out name-matching. The restriction on defined variables does not affect expressiveness (cf. [7, 10]) but significantly simplifies our definitions;
2. sets of names extruded by different open sub-processes are disjoint—these names are defined in different definition;
3. open definitions $\mathsf{def}_S\ D \mathsf{\ in\ } P$ define all their extruded names ($S \subseteq \mathsf{dv}[D]$).

The *interface* of an open process A consists of two disjoint sets of names: free names $\mathsf{fv}[A]$ used in A to send messages out, and extruded names $\mathsf{xv}[A]$ used by the environment to send message in.

A *global renaming* σ is a substitution on the interface of open processes that is injective on the image of extruded names (for all names $x \in \mathsf{xv}[A]$, $y \in \mathsf{xv}[A] \cup \mathsf{fv}[A]$, if $x\sigma = y\sigma$ then $x = y$).

Open chemistry. Let us introduce the operational semantics of the open join-calculus through an example. It will also explain the dynamic role played by the index S in a definition. Consider the process $\mathsf{def}_\emptyset\ x\langle\rangle \triangleright y\langle\rangle \ \mathsf{in}\ z\langle x\rangle$. The interface contains no extruded name and two free names y, z. The message $z\langle x\rangle$ can be consumed by the environment, thus exporting x.

$$\mathsf{def}_\emptyset\ x\langle\rangle \triangleright y\langle\rangle \ \mathsf{in}\ z\langle x\rangle \quad \xrightarrow{\{x\}\overline{z}\langle x\rangle} \quad \mathsf{def}_{\{x\}}\ x\langle\rangle \triangleright y\langle\rangle \ \mathsf{in}\ 0\ .$$

Once x is known from the environment, it cannot be considered local anymore—the environment can emit on x—, but is not free either—the environment cannot modify or extend its definition. A new transition is enabled:

$$\mathsf{def}_{\{x\}}\ x\langle\rangle \triangleright y\langle\rangle \ \mathsf{in}\ 0 \quad \xrightarrow{x\langle\rangle} \quad \mathsf{def}_{\{x\}}\ x\langle\rangle \triangleright y\langle\rangle \ \mathsf{in}\ x\langle\rangle$$

Now the process can input some more messages on x, and also perform the two transitions below to emit on y:

$$\begin{array}{lcl} \mathsf{def}_{\{x\}}\ x\langle\rangle \triangleright y\langle\rangle \ \mathsf{in}\ x\langle\rangle & \longrightarrow & \mathsf{def}_{\{x\}}\ x\langle\rangle \triangleright y\langle\rangle \ \mathsf{in}\ y\langle\rangle \\ & \xrightarrow{\{\}\overline{y}\langle\rangle} & \mathsf{def}_{\{x\}}\ x\langle\rangle \triangleright y\langle\rangle \ \mathsf{in}\ 0 \end{array}$$

In order to model the interactions with the environment, we extend the RCHAM model defined in [7]. This is accomplished by means of two dual operations: *extrusion* of defined names on free names, and *intrusion* of messages sent on previously extruded names. The explicit bookkeeping of extruded names is performed by suitably augmenting the chemical solutions.

Formally, let the functions $\mathsf{dv}[\cdot], \mathsf{fv}[\cdot], \mathsf{xv}[\cdot]$ be extended to multisets of terms in the expected way. *Open chemical solutions*, ranged over by $\mathcal{S}, \mathcal{T}, \ldots$, are triples $(\mathcal{R}, S, \mathcal{A})$, written $\mathcal{R} \vdash_S \mathcal{A}$, where

- $\mathcal{A}$ is a multiset of open processes with disjoint sets of extruded names;
- $\mathcal{R}$ is a multiset of definitions such that $\mathsf{dv}[\mathcal{R}] \cap \mathsf{xv}[\mathcal{A}] = \emptyset$;
- $S \subseteq \mathsf{dv}[\mathcal{R}]$ is a set of extruded names.

The definitions of free and extruded names are lifted to solutions in this way: $\mathsf{fv}[\mathcal{R} \vdash_S \mathcal{A}] \stackrel{\mathrm{def}}{=} (\mathsf{fv}[\mathcal{R}] \cup \mathsf{fv}[\mathcal{A}]) \setminus \mathsf{dv}[\mathcal{R}]$ and $\mathsf{xv}[\mathcal{R} \vdash_S \mathcal{A}] \stackrel{\mathrm{def}}{=} S \uplus \mathsf{xv}[\mathcal{A}]$.

The chemical rules for the open RCHAM are given in Table 1; they define families of transitions $\rightharpoonup$, $\leftharpoondown$, $\rightarrow$, $\xrightarrow{\alpha}$, $\alpha \in \{S\overline{x}\langle\widetilde{v}\rangle, x\langle\widetilde{v}\rangle\}$ between open solutions. As usual, each chemical rule mentions only the processes and the definitions it involves, and the transition applies to every chemical solution $\mathcal{S}$ whose multisets contain these processes and definitions.

Let us comment on the rules. The first five rules are those of the RCHAM. The structural rules that define the inverse transitions $\rightharpoonup$ and $\leftharpoondown$ are unchanged, except for Rule S-DEF that performs some extra bookkeeping on extruded

S-NIL	$\Vdash 0$	$\rightleftharpoons$	$\Vdash$	
S-PAR	$\Vdash A \mid A'$	$\rightleftharpoons$	$\Vdash A,\ A'$	
S-AND	$D \wedge D \Vdash$	$\rightleftharpoons$	$D,\ D' \Vdash$	
S-DEF	$\Vdash_S \mathsf{def}_{S'}\ D \ \mathsf{in}\ A$	$\rightleftharpoons$	$D\sigma \Vdash_{S \uplus S'} A\sigma$	
RED	$J \triangleright P \Vdash J\rho$	$\longrightarrow$	$J \triangleright P \Vdash P\rho$	
EXT	$\Vdash_S x\langle v_i{}^{i \in 1..p}\rangle$	$\xrightarrow{S'\overline{x}\langle v_i{}^{i\in 1..p}\rangle}$	$\Vdash_{S \cup S'}$	
INT	$\Vdash_{\{x\} \cup S}$	$\xrightarrow{x\langle v_i{}^{i\in 1..p}\rangle}$	$\Vdash_{\{x\} \cup S} x\langle v_i{}^{i \in 1..p}\rangle$	

Side conditions on the reacting solution $\mathcal{S} = (\mathcal{R} \Vdash_S \mathcal{A})$:

S-DEF	σ replaces $\mathsf{dv}[D] \setminus S'$ with distinct fresh names.
RED	ρ substitutes names for $\mathsf{rv}(J)$;
EXT	x is free, and $S' = \{v_i \mid i \in 1..p\} \cap (\mathsf{dv}[\mathcal{R}] \setminus S)$;
INT	$v_i^{i\in 1..p}$ are either free, or fresh, or extruded.

Table 1 The open RCHAM of the open-join-calculus

names. The reduction rule RED says when a message can trigger a process in a definition. In the sequel, $\rightleftharpoons$ is the symmetric relation $\rightharpoonup \cup \leftharpoondown$ that contains all structural moves, its transitive closure $\rightleftharpoons^*$ is called structural equivalence; $\Rrightarrow$ is the relation $\rightleftharpoons \cup \rightarrow$ that gathers all silent moves.

The two last rules model interaction with the context. According to rule EXT, messages can be emitted at free names; messages can export defined names that were not previously known to the environment, thus causing the scope of their definitions to be opened. This is made explicit through the label S' that appears on the transition. Our rule resembles the Open rule for restriction in the π-calculus [13], with an important restriction due to locality: messages are either emitted on free names, to be consumed by EXT, or on names defined in the open solution, to be consumed by RED.

The intrusion rule INT can be viewed as a disciplined version of one of the Input rule for the asynchronous π-calculus proposed by Honda and Tokoro [11]: the latter allows intrusion of arbitrary messages at any stage, whereas our rule allows intrusion of messages only on defined-extruded names.

Notation Let $\mathcal{S}$ be the open solution $\mathcal{R} \vdash_S \mathcal{A}$ and $M = \prod x\langle\widetilde{v}\rangle$ be a parallel composition of messages that can be intruded using Rule INT. Then $\mathcal{S} \mid M$ is the open solution $\mathcal{R} \vdash_S \mathcal{A},\ M$. The *restriction* on extruded names is partially defined as

$$(\mathcal{R} \vdash_{S \uplus S'} \mathcal{A}) \setminus S' \quad \stackrel{\text{def}}{=} \quad \mathcal{R} \vdash_S \mathcal{A}\,.$$

Formally, the original RCHAM of [7] is the restriction of our open RCHAM that operates on chemical solutions with no extruded variables, and that uses every chemical rule except EXT and INT.

When applied to open solutions, the structural rules capture the intended meaning of extruded names: messages sent on extruded names can be moved inside or outside of their defining process. Assuming x has been extruded ($x \in S \cup S' \cup \mathsf{xv}[A]$), and modulo α-conversion to avoid clashes with the arguments ($\{\widetilde{v}\} \cap \mathsf{dv}[D] \subseteq S'$), we have

$$\vdash_S \; x\langle\widetilde{v}\rangle \,|\mathsf{def}_{S'}\; D \;\mathsf{in}\; A \quad \rightleftharpoons^* \quad \vdash_S \; \mathsf{def}_{S'}\; D \;\mathsf{in}\; (x\langle\widetilde{v}\rangle \,|\, A)$$

Remark 2 *In its original presentation [7], the join-calculus is equipped with an auxiliary labeled transition system. Its intent, however, is quite different from ours. It is used to give an alternative, syntactic description of chemical reduction steps; transitions are labeled by whole reaction rules; these large labels are discarded when the transition applies within a definition that contains the reaction rule. In contrast, our open* RCHAM *provides an extensional semantics of the calculus; labels are much simpler than definitions, and we do not define silent steps as matching labeled transitions plus hiding.*

3 WEAK BISIMULATION

The join-calculus has been "opened" to support the standard notion of bisimulation for process calculi [15]. In this section, we define this equivalence for open solutions and we investigate its properties.

Definition 3 *A symmetric relation $\mathcal{R}$ over open solutions is a* weak bisimulation *if, whenever $\mathcal{S} \;\mathcal{R}\; \mathcal{T}$, then*

- *if $\mathcal{S} \rightleftharpoons^* \rightarrow \rightleftharpoons^* \mathcal{S}'$ then $\mathcal{T} \Rrightarrow^* \mathcal{T}'$ and $\mathcal{S}' \;\mathcal{R}\; \mathcal{T}'$;*
- *if $\mathcal{S} \rightleftharpoons^* \xrightarrow{\alpha} \rightleftharpoons^* \mathcal{S}'$ then $\mathcal{T} \Rrightarrow^* \xrightarrow{\alpha} \Rrightarrow^* \mathcal{T}'$ and $\mathcal{S}' \;\mathcal{R}\; \mathcal{T}'$,*
  for all labels α of shape $x\langle\widetilde{v}\rangle$ or $S\overline{x}\langle\widetilde{v}\rangle$ where names in S are fresh in $\mathcal{T}$.

Let $\approx$ be the largest weak bisimulation. We shall write $A \approx B$ for $(\emptyset \Vdash A) \approx (\emptyset \Vdash B)$.

As an immediate consequence of its definition, weak bisimulation is an equivalence relation, and we can tell whether two processes are bisimilar by reasoning on their synchronization tree, without the need to exhibit discriminating contexts. For example, $x\langle u\rangle \not\approx x\langle v\rangle$ because they perform emissions with different labels. Likewise, $x\langle y\rangle \not\approx \mathsf{def}\; z\langle u\rangle \triangleright y\langle u\rangle \;\mathsf{in}\; x\langle z\rangle$ because the first process emits a free name (label $\overline{x}\langle y\rangle$) while the latter emits a local name that gets extruded (label $\{z\}\overline{x}\langle z\rangle$). The following properties should convince the reader that $\approx$ is a reasonable semantics for the join-calculus.

Bisimilarity and chemical interface. The set of extruded names $\mathsf{xv}[\mathcal{S}]$ is the input interface of the solution $\mathcal{S}$, and rule INT makes weak bisimulation sensitive to it: $\mathcal{S} \approx \mathcal{T}$ implies $\mathsf{xv}[\mathcal{S}] = \mathsf{xv}[\mathcal{T}]$.

To check this property, let us consider the partition of open RCHAMs induced by $\mathsf{xv}[\cdot]$. The resulting classes are stable for all chemical rules except EXT, and in particular, any solution is structurally equivalent to a "fully-heated" (containing only simple reaction rules and messages) solution with the same extruded variables; by definition of INT, a fully-heated solution can perform a transition with label $x\langle\widetilde{v}\rangle$ if and only if $x \in \mathsf{xv}[\mathcal{S}]$.

Conversely, rule EXT defines the only transitions that can separate solutions with the same extruded names. Obviously, open solutions whose derivatives never perform EXT are bisimilar if and only if they have the same extruded names to begin with, and this provides some "garbage-collection" properties such as $\mathsf{fv}[P] = \emptyset$ implies $P \approx 0$.

Equivalent definitions. The following examples show that weak bisimulation is largely insensitive to the shape of join-patterns.

Weak bisimulation is insensitive to buffering, as one expects from an asynchronous semantics. For instance we have:

$$\mathsf{def}_S\ D \ \mathsf{in}\ A \quad \approx \quad \mathsf{def}_S\ x\langle\widetilde{u}\rangle \triangleright x'\langle\widetilde{u}\rangle \wedge D' \ \mathsf{in}\ A$$

where $x \in \mathsf{dv}[D]$, x' is a fresh name, and D' is obtained from D by substituting $x'\langle\widetilde{v}\rangle$ for $x\langle\widetilde{v}\rangle$ in every join-pattern. We also have:

$$\mathsf{def}_S\ J \triangleright P \wedge D \ \mathsf{in}\ A \quad \approx \quad \mathsf{def}_S\ J \triangleright x\langle\widetilde{\mathsf{rv}[J]}\rangle \wedge x\langle\widetilde{\mathsf{rv}[J]}\rangle \triangleright P \wedge D \ \mathsf{in}\ A$$

where x is a fresh name and $\widetilde{\mathsf{rv}[J]}$ is a tuple that conveys the names in $\mathsf{rv}[J]$.

These properties of asynchrony are easy to prove (it suffices to consider the relation that contains processes that differ only because of a buffering reduction, which is included in a bisimulation, or equivalently, to use the bisimulation up-to expansion proof technique of [19]). Notice, however, that buffering of partial join-patterns would not usually preserve bisimulation, because it affects the branching structure of processes.

It is well-known that weak bisimulation is insensitive to divergence; for instance $0 \approx \mathsf{def}\ x\langle\rangle \triangleright x\langle\rangle \ \mathsf{in}\ x\langle\rangle$. Likewise, any reversible synchronization is invisible; for instance, we can temporarily grab arbitrary messages J within a definition D

$$\mathsf{def}_S\ D \ \mathsf{in}\ A \quad \approx \quad \mathsf{def}_S\ J \triangleright J' \wedge J' \triangleright J \wedge D \ \mathsf{in}\ A$$

where $\mathsf{dv}[J] \subseteq \mathsf{dv}[D]$, $\mathsf{dv}[J']$ fresh, and $\mathsf{rv}[J'] = \mathsf{rv}[J]$.

Another standard property of bisimulation is that it is not possible to observe the internal state of processes. As mentioned in [7] for the weaker barbed congruence, we have

$$\mathsf{def}_S\ J \triangleright P \ \mathsf{in}\ A \quad \approx \quad \mathsf{def}_S\ J|s\langle\widetilde{v}\rangle \triangleright P|s\langle\widetilde{v}\rangle \ \mathsf{in}\ A|s\langle\widetilde{v}\rangle$$

where s is a fresh name and $\{\widetilde{v}\} \cap \mathsf{rv}[J] = \emptyset$. Indeed, there is always one available message $s\langle\widetilde{v}\rangle$ that conveys the same names, that were initially bound in a process *within the same scope.* This equality suffices to prove interesting properties with regards to our scoping rules: if we take $\{\widetilde{v}\} = \mathsf{dv}[J] \cup \{s\}$, then all occurrences of names of $\mathsf{dv}[J]$ that appeared in P—we call them recursive occurrences—are now bound as received variables. Up-to bisimulation, we can therefore eliminate recursion from every definition. If we take $\{\widetilde{v}\} = (\mathsf{fv}[P] \cup \{s\}) \setminus \mathsf{rv}[J]$, then all names in P are now bound as received variables, which is reminiscent of lambda-lifting in the λ-calculus. In combination with the forthcoming congruence properties, this validates a compilation scheme for the join-calculus that would replace every process by an equivalent process with simpler binders (either receptions or immediate definitions).

3.1 Renaming and Congruence properties

The rest of the section is devoted to proving that weak bisimulation is indeed a congruence. This is not very surprising since our calculus has no operator for external choice. Nevertheless the proof is not completely standard and some interesting properties are required. In order to establish that weak bisimulation is persistent under global renaming, we first study the correspondence between transitions in a chemical solution $\mathcal{S}$ and transitions in $\mathcal{S}\sigma$, where σ is a global renaming.

Lemma 1 *Let $\mathcal{S}$ be an open solution and σ be a global renaming for $\mathcal{S}$.*

1. *$\mathcal{S} \rightleftharpoons^* \rightarrow \rightleftharpoons^* \mathcal{T}$ implies $\mathcal{S}\sigma \rightleftharpoons^* \rightarrow \rightleftharpoons^* \mathcal{T}\sigma$; conversely, $\mathcal{S}\sigma \rightleftharpoons^* \rightarrow \rightleftharpoons^* \mathcal{T}$ implies $\mathcal{S} \rightleftharpoons^* \xrightarrow{S_1 \overline{x_1}\langle\widetilde{v}_1\rangle} \xrightarrow{y_1\langle\widetilde{v}_1\rangle} \cdots \xrightarrow{S_n \overline{x_n}\langle\widetilde{v}_n\rangle} \xrightarrow{y_n\langle\widetilde{v}_n\rangle} \rightleftharpoons^* \rightarrow \rightleftharpoons^* \mathcal{S}'$, where $n \geq 0$ and, for all $i \leq n$, $\sigma(x_i) = \sigma(y_i)$ and $\mathcal{T} = (\mathcal{S}' \setminus (\bigcup_{i=1 \ldots n} S_i))\sigma$;*
2. *$\mathcal{S} \rightleftharpoons^* \xrightarrow{x\langle\widetilde{v}\rangle} \rightleftharpoons^* \mathcal{T}$ if and only if $\mathcal{S}\sigma \rightleftharpoons^* \xrightarrow{(x\langle\widetilde{v}\rangle)\sigma} \rightleftharpoons^* \mathcal{T}\sigma$;*
3. *if $\sigma(x)$ is free for $\mathcal{S}\sigma$, $\mathcal{S} \rightleftharpoons^* \xrightarrow{S\overline{x}\langle\widetilde{v}\rangle} \rightleftharpoons^* \mathcal{T}$ implies $\mathcal{S}\sigma \rightleftharpoons^* \xrightarrow{(S\overline{x}\langle\widetilde{v}\rangle)\sigma} \rightleftharpoons^* \mathcal{T}\sigma$; conversely, $\mathcal{S}\sigma \rightleftharpoons^* \xrightarrow{S\overline{x}\langle\widetilde{v}\rangle} \rightleftharpoons^* \mathcal{T}$ implies $\mathcal{S} \rightleftharpoons^* \xrightarrow{S'\overline{x'}\langle\widetilde{v}'\rangle} \rightleftharpoons^* \mathcal{S}'$, where $\mathcal{S}'\sigma \rightleftharpoons^* \mathcal{T}$ and $(S'\overline{x'}\langle\widetilde{v}'\rangle)\sigma = S\overline{x}\langle\widetilde{v}\rangle$.*

The statements in the above lemma are natural, except perhaps for the last part of Case 1. This case occurs when an internal step consumes messages on extruded names $\sigma(x_i)$ where x_i are free names in the initial solution $\mathcal{S}$. For every such message that is consumed in the internal step, this is mimicked as an extrusion on x_i followed by an intrusion on y_i.

Corollary 2 *$\mathcal{S} \approx \mathcal{T}$ implies $\mathcal{S}\sigma \approx \mathcal{T}\sigma$ for every global renaming σ.*

The congruence property essentially relies on this proposition; its proof is standard.

Rules S-JOIN, S-AND, S-DEF, EXT are as in Table 1;		
INT-J	$J \triangleright P \Vdash_S M \xrightarrow{M'} J \triangleright P \Vdash_S P\rho$	
Side condition:	$J\rho \rightleftharpoons^* M \mid M', \quad Dom(\rho) = \mathsf{rv}[J],$	
	$\mathsf{dv}[M'] \subseteq S, \quad \mathsf{rv}[M']$ free, fresh or extruded.	

Table 2 The J-open RCHAM of the open join calculus

Theorem 1 *Weak bisimulation is a congruence.*

4 ASYNCHRONOUS BISIMULATION

In order to prove that two chemical solutions are bisimilar, the large number of multiset configurations to consider is a nuisance; for example, a process with an extruded name already has an infinite set of configurations, even if no "real" computation is ever performed. Indeed, for checking the obvious equivalence

$$\mathsf{def}\ x\langle u\rangle|y\langle v\rangle \triangleright P\ \mathsf{in}\ z\langle x\rangle \ \approx\ \mathsf{def}\ x\langle u\rangle \mid y\langle v\rangle \triangleright Q\ \mathsf{in}\ z\langle x\rangle$$

one is confronted to infinite models on both sides, with a distinct chemical solution for every multiset of messages that have been intruded on x so far. This flaw in our definition of bisimulation motivates the following alternative formulation.

We refine the open RCHAM by allowing inputs only when they trigger some guarded process. Thus, we augment the blocking ability of inputs. For example, the two processes above become inert, and trivially bisimilar.

If we apply this refinement keeping the previous labels for input, however, we obtain a dubious result. The solution $x\langle\rangle|y\langle\rangle|z\langle\rangle \triangleright P \Vdash_{\{x,y\}} z\langle\rangle$ can transit inasmuch as it first inputs the two messages $x\langle\rangle$ and $y\langle\rangle$, then performs a silent step that consumes them together with the local message $z\langle\rangle$ already in the solution. Yet, neither $x\langle\rangle$ nor $y\langle\rangle$ alone can trigger the process P, and therefore this solution would becomes inert too. This suggests the use of *join*-inputs on x and y in new reduction steps such that

$$x\langle\rangle \mid y\langle\rangle \mid z\langle\rangle \triangleright P \Vdash_{\{x,y\}} z\langle\rangle \xrightarrow{x\langle\rangle \mid y\langle\rangle} x\langle\rangle \mid y\langle\rangle \mid z\langle\rangle \triangleright P \Vdash_{\{x,y\}} P\ .$$

On the other hand, the solution $x\langle\rangle|y\langle\rangle|z\langle\rangle \triangleright P \Vdash_{\{x\}} z\langle\rangle$ is truly inert, since P can never be triggered. Here join-inputs have a greater blocking ability than atomic inputs, and our refinement suppresses all input transitions.

4.1 The J-open RCHAM

The J-open RCHAM is defined in Table 2, by replacing the intrusion rule. Unlike the previous rule INT, the new rule INT-J permits intrusion of messages only if they are immediately used to trigger a process in a definition. This is formalized by allowing labels M' that are multisets of messages, and by handling them as partial join-patterns: if the solution can supply a complementary join-pattern M such that the combination $M \mid M'$ matches the join-pattern in a reaction rule, then the transition occurs and triggers this reaction rule. As for INT, we restrict intrusions in M' to messages on extruded names. Note that rule RED is now subsumed by rule INT-J where $M' = 0$, although we keep the distinction between internal moves and proper input moves in the following discussion.

The same chemical solution now has two different models: for instance, $x\langle\rangle|y\langle\rangle \triangleright P \vdash_{\{x\}}$ has no transition in the J-open RCHAM, while it has infinitely many $\xrightarrow{x\langle\rangle}$ transitions in the open RCHAM In the sequel, we shall keep the symbol $\xrightarrow{\alpha}$ for the open RCHAM and use $\xrightarrow{\alpha}_J$ for the J-open RCHAM; the subscript J is dropped whenever no ambiguity can arise.

As a direct consequence of the definitions of the J-open semantics, we have the following relation between our two models:

Proposition 3 *The intrusions of the J-open RCHAM and those of the open RCHAM are related as follows:*

1. $\mathcal{S} \xrightarrow{x_1\langle\widetilde{v}_1\rangle \mid \cdots \mid x_n\langle\widetilde{v}_n\rangle}_J \mathcal{S}'$ *implies* $\mathcal{S} \xrightarrow{x_i\langle\widetilde{v}_1\rangle} \cdots \xrightarrow{x_n\langle\widetilde{v}_n\rangle} \rightleftharpoons^* \rightarrow \mathcal{S}'$.
2. *For any A, if* $A \mid x\langle\widetilde{u}\rangle \rightleftharpoons^* \xrightarrow{M}_J \rightleftharpoons^* B$, *then either* $A \rightleftharpoons^* \xrightarrow{M}_J \rightleftharpoons^* A'$ *with* $A' \mid x\langle\widetilde{u}\rangle \rightleftharpoons^* B$, *or* $A \rightleftharpoons^* \xrightarrow{M'}_J \rightleftharpoons^* B$ *with* $M' \rightleftharpoons^* M \mid x\langle\widetilde{u}\rangle$.

All other transitions are common to both chemical machines.

Asynchronous bisimulation

We now try to shape the definition of weak bisimulation (Definition 3) to the new J-open RCHAM. Consider for instance the two processes:

$$P = \mathsf{def}\ x\langle\rangle \triangleright a\langle\rangle \wedge a\langle\rangle|y\langle\rangle \triangleright R\ \mathsf{in}\ z\langle x,y\rangle \qquad Q = \mathsf{def}\ x\langle\rangle|y\langle\rangle \triangleright R\ \mathsf{in}\ z\langle x,y\rangle$$

With the previous underlying model (open RCHAM), P and Q are weakly bisimilar, but with the new one (J-open RCHAM) this is not true anymore, because, after emitting on z, P can input on $x\langle\rangle$ while Q cannot. If we equip the J-open RCHAM with the weak bisimulation of Section 3, Q becomes inert after the extrusion on z because join inputs are not considered. But if we consider the weak bisimulation that uses join-input labels instead of single ones, Q can input on $x\langle\rangle|y\langle\rangle$ while P cannot, and P and Q are still separated. It turns out that weak bisimulation discriminates too much in the J-open RCHAM.

In order to avoid detection of the structure of join patterns, weak bisimulation must be weakened further on. At least, we must consider that a process simulate another one even if it does not immediately consume a join-input.

Definition 4 *A symmetric relation $\mathcal{R}$ over* J-*open* RCHAM*s is an* asynchronous bisimulation *if, whenever $\mathcal{S}\ \mathcal{R}\ \mathcal{T}$, then*

- $\mathsf{xv}[\mathcal{S}] = \mathsf{xv}[\mathcal{T}]$
- *if $\mathcal{S} \rightleftharpoons^* \xrightarrow{S\bar{x}\langle\tilde{v}\rangle} \rightleftharpoons^* \mathcal{S}'$ and names in S are fresh in $\mathcal{T}$, then $\mathcal{T} \Rrightarrow^* \xrightarrow{S\bar{x}\langle\tilde{v}\rangle} \Rrightarrow^* \mathcal{T}'$ and $\mathcal{S}'\ \mathcal{R}\ \mathcal{T}'$;*
- *if $\mathcal{S} \rightleftharpoons^* \xrightarrow{M} \rightleftharpoons^* \mathcal{S}'$, then $\mathcal{T} \mid M \Rrightarrow^* \mathcal{T}'$ and $\mathcal{S}'\ \mathcal{R}\ \mathcal{T}'$.*

Let $\approx_a$ be the largest asynchronous bisimulation. We write $A \approx_a B$ for $(\emptyset \Vdash \{A\}) \approx_a (\emptyset \Vdash \{B\})$.

Let us show the equality $P \approx_a Q$, where P and Q are the processes at the beginning of this section. Both P and Q perform the same emission, therefore it suffices to prove

$$A = \mathsf{def}_{\{x,y\}}\ x\langle\rangle \triangleright a\langle\rangle \ \wedge\ a\langle\rangle|y\langle\rangle \triangleright R \ \mathsf{in}\ 0 \quad \approx_a \quad B = \mathsf{def}_{\{x,y\}}\ x\langle\rangle|y\langle\rangle \triangleright R \ \mathsf{in}\ 0$$

Observe that $A \xrightarrow{x\langle\rangle} A'$, while $B \not\xrightarrow{x\langle\rangle}$. Nevertheless, it is possible to prove that $A' \approx_a \mathsf{def}_{\{x,y\}}\ x\langle\rangle \mid y\langle\rangle \triangleright R\ \mathsf{in}\ x\langle\rangle$. Hence, bisimilarity can be still achieved, by delaying the actual use of a message. Conversely, there is B' such that $B \xrightarrow{x\langle\rangle \mid y\langle\rangle} B'$, while this move cannot be mimicked by A. Again, one can prove that B' is asynchronous bisimilar to $\mathsf{def}_{\{x,y\}}\ x\langle\rangle \triangleright a\langle\rangle \ \wedge\ a\langle\rangle \mid y\langle\rangle \triangleright R\ \mathsf{in}\ R$, which is a derivative of $A \mid x\langle\rangle \mid y\langle\rangle$. All other transitions are the same, and we can conclude that $P \approx_a Q$.

Remark 5 *In the definition of asynchronous bisimulation, it is necessary to require that related solutions have the same extruded names. Otherwise, Definition 3 would not carry over asynchronous bisimulation, as for instance the open deadlocked solution $x\langle\rangle|y\langle\rangle \triangleright P \Vdash_{\{y\}}$ would be equivalent to the empty solution $\Vdash_\emptyset$.*

The relations $\approx$ (over open RCHAMs) and $\approx_a$ (over J-open RCHAMs) do match; this is a direct consequence of Proposition 3.

Theorem 2 $\approx_a = \approx$.

5 THE DISCRIMINATING POWER OF MATCHING

The semantics of the join-calculus in [7] is *barbed congruence*. We recall the definition, and refer to [7] for discussion.

Definition 6 *The* output barb $\Downarrow_x$ *is a predicate over open* RCHAMs *that tests for the potential emission on the free name x:*

$$\mathcal{S} \Downarrow_x \quad \stackrel{def}{=} \quad \exists S, \widetilde{v} \text{ such that } \mathcal{S} \mathrel{\overset{\rightharpoonup}{\underset{\leftharpoondown}{\Rightarrow}}}^* \xrightarrow{S\overline{x}\langle\widetilde{v}\rangle}$$

A symmetric relation $\mathcal{R}$ over open RCHAMs *is a* barbed bisimulation *if whenever $\mathcal{S}\ \mathcal{R}\ \mathcal{T}$ the following holds:*

- *If $\mathcal{S} \Downarrow_x$ then $\mathcal{T} \Downarrow_x$;*
- *If $\mathcal{S} \rightleftharpoons^* \rightarrow \rightleftharpoons^* \mathcal{S}'$ then $\mathcal{T} \mathrel{\overset{\rightharpoonup}{\underset{\leftharpoondown}{\Rightarrow}}}^* \mathcal{T}'$ and $\mathcal{S}'\ \mathcal{R}\ \mathcal{T}'$.*

Let $\dot{\approx}_b$ be the largest barbed bisimulation. As usual, this induces an equivalence on open terms, also noted $\dot{\approx}_b$: $A \dot{\approx}_b A' \stackrel{def}{=} \emptyset \vdash_\emptyset \{A\} \dot{\approx}_b \emptyset \vdash_\emptyset \{A'\}$.

A barbed congruence *is a barbed bisimulation that is also a congruence for open join-calculus contexts. Let $\approx_b$ be the largest barbed congruence.*

Weak bisimulation is a congruence and a barbed bisimulation, and thus a barbed congruence ($\approx \subset \approx_b$). This containment is strict, as can be seen from the paradigmatic example of barbed congruence:

$$x\langle z\rangle \quad \approx_b \quad \mathsf{def}\ u\langle v\rangle \triangleright z\langle v\rangle\ \mathsf{in}\ x\langle u\rangle$$

That is, emitting a free name z is the same as emitting a bound name u that forwards all the messages it receives to z, and the two processes are indistinguishable, up-to an extra internal move for every use of z. These two processes are distinguished by weak bisimulation, however, because their respective extrusion labels reveal that z is free and u is extruded.

Nevertheless, barbed congruence can easily be equipped with such a discriminating power, provided it can use richer contexts. To this end, we extend the syntax of the join-calculus with the standard name-matching prefix of [13].

$$A \stackrel{\text{def}}{=} \cdots \mid [x=y]\, A \qquad\qquad P \stackrel{\text{def}}{=} \cdots \mid [x=y]\, P$$

Accordingly, we extend our chemical machines with a new reduction rule.

$$\text{MATCH} \qquad\qquad \vdash [x=x]\, A \rightarrow \vdash A$$

Observe that barbed congruence can now separate $x\langle z\rangle$ from $\mathsf{def}\ u\langle v\rangle \triangleright z\langle v\rangle$ in $x\langle u\rangle$ by using the context $C[\,] = \mathsf{def}\ x\langle y\rangle \triangleright [y=z]\, a\langle\rangle\ \mathsf{in}\ [\,]$.

The usual drawback of name matching is that global renamings do not preserve weak bisimulation anymore: Corollary 2 is false in the extended calculus, and for instance $0 \approx [x=y]\, x\langle\rangle$, while after applying the renaming $\{^x/_y\}$, $0 \not\approx [x=x]\, x\langle\rangle$. Accordingly, bisimulation is not a congruence anymore; it is easy to check that the context $C[\,] \stackrel{\text{def}}{=} \mathsf{def}\ z\langle x,y\rangle \triangleright [\,]\ \mathsf{in}\ z\langle u,u\rangle$ separates the two processes above.

In order to retain the full congruence property, we may consider the coarsest equivalence contained into $\approx$ and closed under renaming. It is possible to prove, in the same style of Theorem 1, that this equivalence is indeed a congruence; however this equivalence is not a bisimulation.

Alternatively, we consider equivalences that are not full congruences. To this aim, we define the set of *evaluation contexts* $C[\,] \stackrel{\text{def}}{=} [\,] \mid C[\,]|P \mid \mathsf{def}\ D\ \mathsf{in}\ C[\,]$ up to structural congruence.

Lemma 4 *$\approx$ is a congruence with respect to evaluation contexts.*

We define *barbed equivalence* $\dot{\approx}_{be}$ over open join-calculus processes with matching as the largest barbed bisimulation that is a congruence for all evaluation contexts. We have

Theorem 3 $\dot{\approx}_{be} = \approx$.

6 A COMPARISON WITH THE π-CALCULUS

The join-calculus can be considered as a disciplined version of the asynchronous π-calculus, where the syntax enforces locality in the usage of names. Still, both calculi have a lot in common, and our semantics largely draw upon the bisimulations developed for the π-calculus [13, 14, 19, 11, 1]. In this section, we relate our definitions to previous proposals in the literature, and we compare the equivalences obtained by applying similar definitions to both the join-calculus and the π-calculus.

In the sequel, we use the following grammar for asynchronous π-calculus processes.

$$P \ ::= \ 0 \ \mid \ \overline{x}\langle v\rangle \ \mid \ x(y).P \ \mid \ \nu x.P \ \mid \ !P \ \mid \ P|P$$

We refer to [5] for the definition of its semantics. We recall the basic reduction step, which matches complementary pairs of emission and reception, and substitutes actual names for the variables in the receiving process:

$$\overline{x}\langle v\rangle \mid x(y).Q \longrightarrow Q\{^{y}/_{v}\}$$

Other transitions render intrusion or extrusion of messages, and their labels carry the same information than those we use in the open RCHAM. In particular output labels explicitly mention names that are being extruded.

The join-calculus and the asynchronous π-calculus have the same expressive power, at least up-to barbed congruence [7]. Their treatment of names, however, are quite different. In the open join-calculus, we partition the visible names of a process into names for extrusions (*free names*), which do not have a local definition, and names for intrusions and internal reduction (*extruded names*), which do have a local definition. As a result, interaction with the environment has more structure, and this significantly prunes the number of transitions that are enabled, even before introducing join-message labels.

In the π-calculus, on the contrary, a free name can always be used for intrusion, extrusion and internal reduction. Furthermore, a received name can be re-defined, as in $x(y).y(z).P$. In this respect, the barbed equivalence of Section 5 is illuminating. Consider the rough π-calculus encodings of the processes mentioned in its example, namely $\overline{x}\langle z\rangle$ and $\nu u.(!u(v).\overline{z}\langle v\rangle \mid \overline{x}\langle u\rangle)$. These two processes are not barbed congruent, and this can be established using a context that invalidates our locality property. For example, if we choose the context

$$C[\cdot] \stackrel{\text{def}}{=} \nu x, z.(x(a).a(u).\overline{u}\langle\rangle \mid \overline{z}\langle b\rangle \mid [\cdot])$$

we obtain that $C[\overline{x}\langle z\rangle] \Downarrow_b$ and $C[\nu u.(!u(v).\overline{z}\langle v\rangle \mid \overline{x}\langle u\rangle)] \not\Downarrow_b$. As could be expected, locality restricts the discriminating power of observers.

We now compare the observational semantics for the open join calculus with previous proposals for the asynchronous π-calculus, notably [11] and [1]. In these works, a major issue is to accommodate the semantics inherited from the standard π-calculus [13] to asynchrony. As message-output is not a prefix anymore, emitters in contexts cannot detect whether a message is actually read. Technically, this leads to a special treatment of input actions, either in the definition of transitions or in the definition of bisimulation.

In [11], Honda and Tokoro take as observational semantics the standard notion of weak bisimulation. As a consequence, they are forced to change the intensional semantics. Let us discuss this issue with a paradigmatic example. Take for instance the π-calculus processes 0 and $x(u).\overline{x}\langle u\rangle$. In order to progress, the process $x(u).\overline{x}\langle u\rangle$ has to consume an emission $\overline{x}\langle v\rangle$, thus exhibiting a new emission $\overline{x}\langle v\rangle$. The same happens for the process 0 that "takes" $\overline{x}\langle v\rangle$ and "gives" the same $\overline{x}\langle v\rangle$ (just nothing is consumed or produced). Therefore 0 and $x(u).\overline{x}\langle u\rangle$ should be reasonably equated in an asynchronous regime: indeed, they are barbed congruent. However, standard bisimulation obviously discriminates between 0 and $x(u).\overline{x}\langle u\rangle$. To cope with this problem, Honda and Tokoro adopt an operational model where asynchrony of communication with the environment is rendered as the total receptiveness of the process. In other words, any message can be intruded from the environment at any moment, using extended structural equivalence in combination with the rule:

$$\text{INPUT} \qquad\qquad 0 \xrightarrow{x\langle v\rangle} \overline{x}\langle v\rangle \ .$$

The intrusion rule of the open-RCHAM is reminiscent of this kind of operational semantics, with two important differences: (i) Our rule INT can be used only with names that have previously been extruded, and there are finitely many of them; conversely, their input rule immediately yields an infinite transition system; and (ii) extraneous inputs in the join calculus are not observable: if they are not used by the process, they can safely be garbage-collected, as we are not faced with the problem of contexts that attempt to read back their emissions.

In [1], Amadio *et al.* take the opposite approach. They keep the standard synchronous semantics, and they modify the notion of bisimulation. For two processes to be bisimilar, they do not require that every input on one side be necessarily simulated by an input of the other side. Rather, they introduce a *delay* clause in bisimulation, by which an input can be simulated by adding a new message in parallel on the other side. This is crucial, for example, for proving that 0 is bisimilar to $x(u).\,\overline{x}\langle u\rangle$. Their resulting asynchronous bisimulation offers three advantages: it eliminates the need for total receptiveness, it is consistent with external sum, and it relies on a widely-used semantics.

Our asynchronous bisimulation presented in Section 4 relies on similar motivations—handling asynchrony in the definition of bisimulation with a relaxed clause for intrusions—, but the clause we use is different from theirs: we deal with multiple intrusions, and we allow the simulating process to perform arbitrary internal moves after parallel composition with the intruded messages; in their terminology, this would place our equivalence between 1-bisimulation and asynchronous bisimulation. Notice, also, that the J-open RCHAM equipped with asynchronous bisimulation is not meant to be a standard semantics, but rather a technical device to reduce the branching of the underlying transition system. Arguably, the open RCHAM gives a more intuitive meaning to extruded names.

From a technical point of view, we often discuss the same, standard properties (stability through renaming, congruence, relation with barbed bisimulation); as we compare our work to the formal treatment of bisimulation in the π-calculus, we observe that locality makes most proofs simpler: it forbids the detection of messages carried on defined names, and reduces the number of cases to consider in the interaction between transitions and global renamings.

Weak bisimulation and asynchronous bisimulation coincide in the open join-calculus, for simple reasons. In contrast, the correspondence between the bisimulations of [11] and those of [1], discussed in details in the latter, is a delicate issue; it is unclear, for instance, whether both approaches yield the same relation in the weak case.

Independently, several notions of locality somehow related to the join-calculus have also been considered in a pure π-calculus setting. In [4], a fragment of the π-calculus is considered where received names cannot be used for input (i.e., cannot be redefined) and it is proven that this language can be compositionally compiled into a very simple, substitution-free calculus. The condition of transmitting only names with output capabilities is further strengthened into *uniform receptiveness* in [20] by also demanding that names are available in input-replicated form as soon as created. Uniform receptiveness is actually the locality property, which is formulated by syntactic means in join-calculus and by means of a typing system in [20] for the π-calculus.

7 CONCLUSIONS

In this paper we have developed the theory of bisimulation for the join-calculus. We started from the initial definitions of [7], which are purely based on internal reductions and observational equivalence; we provided extensions of the RCHAM that encompass intrusions and extrusions, in two different styles, and we studied for each style a relevant definition of bisimulation.

Asynchronous bisimulation, and more specifically its ground variant, is best suited for proofs, as it relies on smaller synchronization trees. In contrast with barbed congruence, bisimulation is therefore "easy" to check, and should be amenable to automated verification by means of the existing algorithms (see, for instance, [21] and [17]).

As regards the comparison between the π-calculus and the join-calculus, there are fully abstract encodings up to barbed congruence [7], but it would be interesting to know what is the status between the open join-calculus equipped with weak bisimulation and the asynchronous π-calculus.

The precise role of name-testing deserve further investigation. The coincidence of weak bisimilarity and barbed equivalence only holds in the presence of matching, which invalidates useful process equalities. Thus, numerous useful properties of the join-calculus as a programming language are not directly captured by weak bisimulation. Instead, they may be proved by using first an encoding of name-testing, then weak bisimulation techniques. Of course, it would be interesting to find direct, purely co-inductive characterization of barbed equivalence in the absence of matching. This issue is addressed in [3] in a π-calculus setting. Finally, one may wonder whether our approach carries over the full distributed join-calculus of [6].

Acknowledgments We thank Jean-Jacques Lévy, Uwe Nestmann, and especially Georges Gonthier for their fruitful comments.

REFERENCES

[1] R. M. Amadio, I. Castellani, and D. Sangiorgi. On bisimulations for the asynchronous π-calculus. RR 2913, INRIA, June 1996. A shorter version appeared in [18].

[2] M. Boreale, C. Fournet, and C. Laneve. Bisimulations in the join-calculus. Available electronically (`ftp://ftp.cs.unibo.it/pub/laneve/equiv.ps.gz`), Oct. 1997.

[3] M. Boreale and D. Sangiorgi. Bisimulation in name-passing calculi without matching. Submitted for publication, Dec. 1997.

[4] M. Boreale. On the expressiveness of internal mobility in name-passing calculi. In Montanari and Sassone [18].

[5] G. Boudol. Asynchrony and the π-calculus (note). Rapport de Recherche 1702, INRIA Sophia-Antipolis, May 1992.

[6] C. Fournet, G. Gonthier, J.-J. Lévy, L. Maranget, and D. Rémy. A calculus of mobile agents. In Montanari and Sassone [18].

[7] C. Fournet and G. Gonthier. The reflexive chemical abstract machine and the join-calculus. In *Proceedings of POPL '96*, pages 372–385. ACM, Jan. 1996.

[8] C. Fournet, C. Laneve, L. Maranget, and D. Rémy. Implicit typing à la ML for the join-calculus. In A. Mazurkiewicz and J. Winkowski, editors, *Proceedings of the 8th International Conference on Concurrency Theory*, volume 1243 of *LNCS*, Warsaw, Poland, 1–4 July 1997.

[9] C. Fournet and L. Maranget. The join-calculus language. Available electronically (`http://pauillac.inria.fr/join`), June 1997.

[10] C. Fournet. *A calculus for distributed programming.* PhD thesis, Ecole Polytechnique, Palaiseau, 1998. Forthcoming.

[11] K. Honda and M. Tokoro. On asynchronous communication semantics. In P. Wegner, M. Tokoro, and O. Nierstrasz, editors, *Proceedings of the ECOOP '91 Workshop on Object-Based Concurrent Computing*, volume 612 of *LNCS*, pages 21–51, 1992.

[12] C. Laneve. May and must testing in the join-calculus. Technical Report UBLCS 96-04, University of Bologna, March 1996. Revised: May 1996.

[13] R. Milner, J. Parrow, and D. Walker. A calculus of mobile processes, parts I and II. *Information and Computation*, 100:1–40 and 41–77, Sept. 1992.

[14] R. Milner and D. Sangiorgi. Barbed bisimulation. In W. Kuich, editor, *Proceedings of ICALP '92*, volume 623 of *LNCS*, pages 685–695, Vienna, 1992.

[15] R. Milner. *Communication and Concurrency.* Prentice Hall, New York, 1989.

[16] R. Milner. The polyadic π-calculus: a tutorial. In F. L. Bauer, W. Brauer, and H. Schwichtenberg, editors, *Logic and Algebra of Specification.* Springer-Verlag, 1993.

[17] U. Montanari and M. Pistore. Checking bisimilarity for finitary π-calculus. In I. Lee and S. A. Smolka, editors, *Proceedings of the 6th International Conference on Concurrency Theory*, volume 962 of *LNCS*, 1995.

[18] U. Montanari and V. Sassone, editors. *Proceedings of the 7th International Conference on Concurrency Theory*, volume 1119 of *LNCS*, Pisa, Italy, 26–29 Aug. 1996.

[19] D. Sangiorgi and R. Milner. The problem of "weak bisimulation up to". In W. R. Cleaveland, editor, *Proceedings of CONCUR'92*, volume 630 of *LNCS*, pages 32–46, 1992.

[20] D. Sangiorgi. The name discipline of uniform receptiveness. In P. Degano, R. Gorrieri, and A. Marchetti-Spaccamela, editors, *Proceedings of ICALP '97*, volume 1256 of *LNCS*, pages 303–313, 1997. Also Technical Report, INRIA Sophia-Antipolis, December 1996.

[21] B. Victor and F. Moller. The mobility workbench – a tool for the π-calculus. In *CAV'94*, volume 818 of *LNCS*, pages 428–440, 1994.

Michele Boreale is a researcher at Università "La Sapienza", Rome, where he got the PhD in 1995. His research interests concern formal methods for the specification and the verification of concurrent systems.
Cédric Fournet is completing his PhD at INRIA Rocquencourt. His research interests are distributed programming, mobile agents, and process calculi.
Cosimo Laneve is a researcher at University of Bologna. He got the PhD in 1993 at the University of Pisa. His research interests include semantics and implementation of functional and concurrent languages, types.

10

Using State Space Exploration and a Natural Deduction Style Message Derivation Engine to Verify Security Protocols

E. M. Clarke, S. Jha, and W. Marrero
Carnegie Mellon University
{emc, sjha, marrero}@cs.cmu.edu

Abstract

As more resources are added to computer networks, and as more vendors look to the World Wide Web as a viable marketplace, the importance of being able to restrict access and to insure some kind of acceptable behavior even in the presence of malicious adversaries becomes paramount. Many researchers have proposed the use of security protocols to provide these security guarantees. In this paper, we develop a method of verifying these protocols using a special purpose *model checker* which executes an exhaustive state space search of a protocol model. Our tool also includes a natural deduction style derivation engine which models the capabilities of the adversary trying to attack the protocol. Because our models are necessarily abstractions, we cannot *prove* a protocol correct. However, our tool is extremely useful as a debugger. We have used our tool to analyze 14 different authentication protocols, and have found the previously reported attacks for them.

Keywords

Model checking, security protocols, authentication, natural deduction

1 INTRODUCTION

The growth of such entities as the Internet and the World Wide Web have demonstrated the large demand for electronic access to information and for electronic transactions. However, both service providers and consumers need to have some guarantees about reasonable behavior, such as preventing unauthorized access and guaranteeing confidentiality, in the presence of malicious adversaries. Numerous protocols that take advantage of cryptography have been proposed that claim to solve many of the security issues.

Typically, these protocols can be thought of as a set of principals which send messages to each other. The hope is that by requiring agents to produce

Programming Concepts and Methods D. Gries, & W-P. de Roever (Eds.)

a sequence of messages, the security goals of the protocol can be achieved. For example, if a principal A receives a message encrypted with a key known only by principals A and B, then principal A should be able to conclude that the message originated from principal B or from itself. However, it would be incorrect to conclude that principal A is talking to principal B. An adversary could be replaying a message overheard during a previous conversation between A and B. So, depending on the security goal of this simple example protocol, the protocol may or may not be secure.

Because the reasoning behind the correctness of these protocols can be subtle, a number of researchers have turned to formal methods to prove protocols correct. One approach has been the use of belief logics to express and deduce security properties [4, 10]. Recently, some researchers have tried to automate the deduction process using theorem provers [5, 11]. Others have provided a rigorous mathematical proof for the correctness of a protocol [2, 26]. Many have tried using formal models to analyze security protocols. Some have developed deductive systems or proof methodologies for their models [1, 3, 6, 7, 9, 20, 25, 27] while others have tried automated search techniques to try to find an error in a model of the protocol [12, 14, 15, 17, 18, 19].

Our approach is also based on model checking and automated search. In this paper we describe a special purpose model checker with two orthogonal components. The first is a *state exploration component*. Each honest agent is described by the sequence of actions that it takes during a run of the protocol, and can be viewed as a finite-state machine. A trace of the actions performed by the asynchronous composition of these state machines corresponds to a possible execution of the protocol by the agents. By performing an exhaustive search of the state space of the composition, we can determine if various security properties are violated.

The second component is the message *derivation engine* which is used to model what the adversary is allowed to do. The derivation engine can be viewed as a simple natural deduction theorem prover for constructing valid messages. We describe the operations that can be performed on messages with a set of inference rules. Because these operations are invertible, each has both an introduction rule and an elimination rule. As in the case of other natural deduction systems, this property guarantees the existence of normalized derivations. For this inference system, the existence of normalized derivations allows for an efficient algorithm for determining whether a message is valid or not.

The standard adversary capabilities found in the literature, which evolved from the Dolev and Yao model [6], fit easily into this framework. The adversary can intercept messages, misdirect messages, and generate new messages using encryption, decryption, concatenation (pairing), and projection. Anytime a message is sent, the adversary intercepts the message and adds it to the set of assumptions it can use to derive new messages. Whenever an honest agent receives a message, the message must have been generated by the derivation engine.

This separation of functionality results in a very intuitive model of computation. In particular, having a black box derivation engine to model the adversary makes the model checker both easier to use and easier to describe and reason about. Unlike term rewriting systems, we do not need to construct a set of rewrite rules to model how an adversary can manipulate participants to generate new messages. In contrast to methods based solely on state space exploration, we need not encode the capabilities of the adversary as a state machine. While a new compiler now provides this feature for the FDR model checker [14], in our system, the capabilities of the adversary are incorporated directly into the model checker itself.

The inclusion of a message derivation engine also means that we do not need to specify ahead of time which messages or which types of messages the model will consider. In theory, the adversary is free to generate any message in an attempt to deceive an honest agent. Moreover, the use of a natural deduction engine allows us to introduce inference rules for new operations, such as XOR and hash functions, easily. Because the derivation engine is an orthogonal component, a new one could be substituted without changing how we model protocols. Finally, we believe this natural deduction framework sheds light on the reasons for the perfect encryption and atomic key assumptions which are frequently made when formal methods are used in this area.

2 INTUITION

In order to concentrate on the security of the protocol itself as opposed to the security of the cryptosystem used, the vast majority of research in this area has made the following "perfect encryption" assumptions.

- The decryption key must be known in order to extract the plain-text from the cipher-text.
- There is enough redundancy in the cryptosystem that a cipher-text can only be generated using encryption with the appropriate key. This also implies that there are no encryption collisions. If two cipher-texts are equal, they must have been generated from the same plain-text using the same key.

While the assumptions are obviously not true, they are, in practice, reasonable. They are important because they allow us to abstract away the cryptosystem and analyze the protocol itself. The drawback is that an attack that takes advantage of a particular property of a specific cryptosystem cannot be found.

We have developed a model checking scheme for the verification of security protocols, and we make use of the same "perfect encryption" assumptions.

We have a very intuitive model which captures the basic idea of message generation and communication. Each role in the protocol, whether the initiator, responder, or server, is described using a sequence of simple commands, such as SEND, RECEIVE, and NEWSECRET, which describe how it interacts with the network during a protocol run.

Once we have a sequence of actions for each of the participants we take their asynchronous composition to get the full model of the protocol. There is also an unspecified participant which we call the adversary. The adversary models an untrusted communication medium as well as any malicious agents. When messages are sent, they are always intercepted by the adversary, who can then forward them (possibly to someone other than the intended participant). The adversary is also allowed to send messages while impersonating a trusted principal. The adversary may even be selected as a participant in a protocol run.

A *run* of the protocol will then consist of some interleaving of actions from a set of participants (a single session for each role) and from the adversary. A *trace* is the interleaving of one or more runs. We can analyze a trace to determine if the security of the protocol was compromised. In particular we can check if the adversary ever learns a secret or if some principal A believes it has completed a run with principal B, while principal B has not participated in the run. In general, a set of security requirements can be specified in some kind of logic and then the trace can be checked to see if any of these requirements are violated.

To verify that a protocol is correct, all the possible traces must be checked. We can think of a trace as an alternating sequence of global states and actions. The global state will consist of the local state of each participant together with the state of the adversary. Because the length of each run is finite, and we only consider a small number of runs, each trace must necessarily be finite as well. If we can also insure that the number of different traces is finite, then the entire search space will be finite, and we can do an exhaustive search to insure that no reachable state violates the security specification. We will discuss this in more detail in section 5.

3 THE SPECIFICATION

There are two kinds of properties that we currently are interested in. The first is a kind of secrecy property. We provide the model checker with a set of terms which the adversary is not allowed to obtain. During the verification, we simply check that the adversary does not have possession of any of the terms in this set. The second property is a temporal property which occurs quite frequently in the literature and which Woo and Lam call *correspondence* [27]. The correspondence relation $X \hookrightarrow Y$ is satisfied if every X event is preceded by a Y event, and there is a one-to-one mapping from X events to Y events.

Many security properties can be expressed as a correspondence relation, and the vast majority of the properties verified in the literature (typically authentication properties) can be expressed as correspondence properties as well. For example, Woo and Lam express authentication by the property that if principal A has finished a protocol run with B, then principal B has at least started a protocol run with A. (Principal B has indeed participated in the protocol) [27]. Mitchell and others check for this property by insuring that if principal A has entered its final state then principal B is no longer in its initial state [19]. Lowe checks that the action $R\_running.A.B$ (meaning that B is running a protocol in response to A) occurs before the action $I\_commit.A.B$ (meaning that A has successfully completed a protocol run with B) [13]. Others have checked a weaker property in which the mapping between events need not be one-to-one [12, 24], although these methodologies could check the stronger property as well. There has also been work done on *intensional* specifications which insure that a protocol behaves "as intended," and so necessarily depend on the protocol [23]. It is also easy to see how certain properties of electronic commerce protocols could be expressed this way. For instance, one may want to check that a merchant provides a service only after a client has paid for it and that a client's account is debited only after the merchant has provided the service. Indeed, Leduc and others have verified a kind of electronic commerce protocol by checking for six safety properties which are all expressed as correspondence relations [12].

In order to check for this kind of property, we will augment the global state with counters. For each correspondence property $X \hookrightarrow Y$ we will maintain a separate counter which will keep track of the difference between the number of Y events and X events. If this counter ever turns negative (i.e. there are more X events than Y events) then the correspondence property will be violated at that point (there will be no one-to-one mapping from X events to Y events). Conversely, as long as the counter never goes negative there is always a one-to-one mapping from X events to Y events.

4 MESSAGES

Typically, the messages exchanged during the run of a protocol are constructed from smaller sub-messages using pairing and encryption. The smallest such sub-messages (i.e. they contain no sub-messages themselves) are called *atomic messages*. There are four kinds of *atomic messages*.

- *Keys* are used to encrypt messages. Keys have the property that every key k has an inverse k^{-1} such that for all messages m, $\{\{m\}_k\}_{k^{-1}} = m$. (Note that for symmetric cryptography the decryption key is the same as the encryption key, so $k = k^{-1}$.)
- *Principal names* are used to refer to the participants in a protocol.
- *Nonces* are randomly generated numbers. The intuition is that since they are randomly generated, any message containing a nonce can be assumed

to have been generated after the nonce was generated. (It is not an "old" message.)
- *Data* which plays no role in how the protocol works but which is intended to be communicated between principals.

Let $\mathcal{A}$ denote the space of *atomic messages*. The set of all messages $\mathcal{M}$ over some set of atomic messages $\mathcal{A}$ is defined inductively as follows:

- If $a \in \mathcal{A}$ then $a \in \mathcal{M}$. (Any *atomic message* is a message.)
- If $m_1 \in \mathcal{M}$ and $m_2 \in \mathcal{M}$ then $m_1 \cdot m_2 \in \mathcal{M}$. (Two messages can be paired together to form a new message.)
- If $m \in \mathcal{M}$ and key $k \in \mathcal{A}$ then $\{m\}_k \in \mathcal{M}$. (A message M can be encrypted with key k to form a new message.)

Because keys have inverses, we take this space modulo the equivalence $\{\{m\}_k\}_{k^{-1}} = m$. It is also important to note that we make the following perfect encryption assumption. The only way to generate $\{m\}_k$ is from m and k. In other words, for all messages m, m_1, and m_2 and keys k, $\{m\}_k \neq m_1 \cdot m_2$, and $\{m\}_k = \{m'\}_{k'} \Rightarrow m = m' \wedge k = k'$.

We also need to consider how new messages can be created from already known messages by encryption, decryption, pairing (concatenation), and projection. The following rules capture this relationship by defining how a message can be derived from some initial set of information I.

1. If $m \in I$ then $I \vdash m$.
2. If $I \vdash m_1$ and $I \vdash m_2$ then $I \vdash m_1 \cdot m_2$. (pairing)
3. If $I \vdash m_1 \cdot m_2$ then $I \vdash m_1$ and $I \vdash m_2$. (projection)
4. If $I \vdash m$ and $I \vdash k$ for key k, then $I \vdash \{m\}_k$. (encryption)
5. If $I \vdash \{m\}_k$ and $I \vdash k^{-1}$ then $I \vdash m$. (decryption)

While this defines the derivability relation $\vdash$, it is not clear if checking $I \vdash m$ is decidable. We will return to this question in section 7.

5 THE MODEL

We now define the model formally by describing how the overall global state and the individual principal local states are defined, as well as by describing how actions update the state. The model consists of the asynchronous composition of a set of named, communicating processes which model the honest agents and the adversary. The state of an honest principal is determined by the bindings for its local variables, and by its "program counter." Each run of an honest principal involved in the protocol is modelled as one of these processes and is described by a sequence of actions it is to perform. The initial state of the bindings is assumed to be empty.

The adversary is modelled differently. First, it is not bound to follow any protocol, so it doesn't make sense to describe it as a sequence of actions. At any point in time it is allowed to perform any "realistic" action, which includes intercepting all messages and sending any messages it can generate. The state of the adversary process is completely determined by the set of messages it "knows" and so we model the adversary by keeping track of acquired messages and by using a derivation engine that describes how it can create new messages.

More formally, each honest principal is modelled as a triple $\langle N, p, B\rangle$, where:

- $N \in$ *names* is the name of the principal.
- p is a process (similar in style to CSP) given as a sequence of actions to be performed.
- B: $vars(N) \rightarrow \mathcal{M}$ is a set of bindings for $vars(N)$, the set of variables appearing in principal N,

We model the adversary as the pair $\langle Z, I\rangle$, where:

- $Z \in$ *names* is the name of the adversary.
- $I \subseteq \mathcal{M}$ is a set of all messages known by the adversary either as initial information or by eavesdropping. Recall that $\mathcal{M}$ is the set of all possible messages.

The global state is then maintained as the composition of the participating principals, along with the adversary process, a list of secrets, and a set of counters, one for each correspondence relation we are checking. More formally, the global state is a triple $\langle \Pi, C, S\rangle$, where:

- Π is the product of the individual principals and the adversary process. This product is asynchronous, yielding an interleaving semantics, with the restriction that processes synchronize with the adversary on messages.
- C is a set of counters one for each correspondence relation. For each relation $X_i \hookrightarrow Y_i$, there is a counter $C_i \in \mathbb{N}$ whose value is equal to the difference between the number of Y_i events and X_i events that have occurred along the trace so far.
- $S \subseteq \mathcal{M}$ is a set of messages that are are considered secrets. These are the set of words that the adversary is not allowed to know. This set usually includes things like the private keys that principals use to communicate with a server.

The specific actions that a principal may perform can be divided into internal actions and communication actions. The internal actions are performed asynchronously. Any principal is allowed to perform an internal action and interleaving is used to model all possible behaviors when multiple principals can make a transition. We define a transition relation $\rightarrow$ between principals such that $\mathbf{A} \rightarrow \mathbf{B}$ if and only if principal $\mathbf{A}$ can take an action and become a principal that behaves like $\mathbf{B}$.

Communication actions consist of send and receive actions. Communication actions always involve the adversary who controls the network. The action can be thought of as a synchronous transition involving the adversary and the honest principal performing the action. Each receive action corresponds to a message being sent from the adversary to an honest principal and can augment the honest principal's bindings. Each send action corresponds to a message being sent by an honest principal and being received or intercepted by the adversary, thus possibly increasing the set of messages "known" by the adversary. These communication actions are also interleaved with the possible actions of other processes.

The adversary is always willing to receive any messages from any principal, and so send actions are always enabled. When a principal performs a send action, the adversary adds the new message to its local store and the principal takes the following transition:

$$\langle A,\ \textsc{send}(s\text{-}msg).q', B_A\rangle \quad \rightarrow \quad \langle A, q', B_A\rangle$$

In order for a receive action to take place, the message from the adversary must match the message being received. A message *s-msg* $\in I$ from the adversary matches a message template *r-msg* from principal $\mathbf{B} = \langle B, q, B_B\rangle$, if there exists a substitution σ_B: *vars*$(B) \rightarrow \mathcal{M}$ extending B_B ($B_B \subseteq \sigma_B$), such that *s-msg* $= \sigma_B($*r-msg*$)$. If the messages match, then the following transition can be taken:

$$\langle B,\ \textsc{receive}(r\text{-}msg).q', B_B\rangle \quad \rightarrow \quad \langle B, q', \sigma'_B\rangle$$

where σ'_B is the smallest substitution satisfying the conditions above. Because we require that *s-msg* match *r-msg*, if there is already a pair (*var*, *val*) in B for some *var* appearing in *r-msg*, then the corresponding value in *s-msg* must be *val*. In other words, messages received by honest agents must be consistent with their view of the protocol. Thus the updates to B only add new bindings and never change previous bindings.

For the most part internal actions are used to create new information. For example, NEWSECRET is used to create a nonce or session key, and bind it to a variable. Secrets are globally distinct, and each NEWSECRET action creates a secret that has not appeared up to that point in the protocol. The new binding is added to the principal's set of bindings.

$$\langle A, \textsc{newsecret}(var).p', B\rangle \quad \rightarrow \quad \langle A, p', B'\rangle$$

where $B' = B[var \leftarrow val]$ when *val* is the new value generated by the action.

Finally, we have four special actions BEGINIT, ENDINIT, BEGRESPOND, and ENDRESPOND. These are used to mark the beginning and the end of a principal's participation in a protocol. They have no effect on the state of the principal taking the action. However, the purpose of these actions is to check the correspondence relations, such as $A.\text{ENDINIT}(B) \hookrightarrow B.\text{BEGRESPOND}(A)$ which will maintain a counter in the global state. If this relation is satisfied, then we know that if the principal named A finishes the protocol with B then the principal named B has participated in the protocol with A. We also check that if B finishes, A has participated.

The actions a particular honest principal may make are restricted to the sequence of actions *p* that represent its role in the protocol. The adversary has no such restriction and is allowed to make any action at any time, provided that it can only send a message *s-msg* to an honest principal if it can derive it ($I \vdash s\text{-}msg$). We also place a bound on the number of NEWSECRET actions the adversary can perform, because otherwise the state space would become infinite. In all the protocols we have analyzed, no principal ever checks to see if a key or nonce is new, and so the adversary for these examples never has to take any NEWSECRET actions.

6 SEARCH ALGORITHM

Recall that a trace is an alternating sequence of global states and actions, and that we are interested in checking all possible traces. Clearly, everything in the model is finite except for the set of messages that the adversary can generate. If we can show that the adversary never generates an infinite set of messages, then the entire model is finite and we can perform a depth-first search to check all possible traces of the model, and check that none violate the security properties.

The only times we consider the set of messages the intruder can generate are when we check if it contains a secret, and when we check if the adversary can generate a message that an honest principal is waiting to receive. In the first case, we have a finite set of messages to check, and we prove in section 7 that this is decidable. The later case involves matching against a pattern and in the majority of cases the pattern is restrictive enough to limit the derivation to a finite number of matches (because there are a finite number of atomic messages). In general, however, this need not be the case. In particular, just by using multiple encryption, the set of messages the adversary can generate is infinite. Researchers have used different methods to restrict the model to a finite state space. Lowe restricts the set of messages that the intruder can learn to the set of all atoms along with the set of all encrypted components appearing in protocol messages [14]. Others place type restrictions on variables appearing in messages [8, 12, 19]. Still others solve rewrite equations that can be used to prove that entire families of messages cannot be generated [16,

$$\frac{m_1 \qquad m_2}{m_1 \cdot m_2} \cdot\mathcal{I} \qquad\qquad \frac{m_1 \cdot m_2}{m_1} \cdot\mathcal{E}_l \qquad \frac{m_1 \cdot m_2}{m_2} \cdot\mathcal{E}_r$$

$$\frac{m \qquad k}{\{m\}_k} \{\}_k\mathcal{I} \qquad\qquad \frac{\{m\}_k \qquad k^{-1}}{m} \{\}_k\mathcal{E}$$

Figure 1 Derivation rules for messages

18]. We plan to augment our matching algorithm to allow for message types; however, we currently limit the state space by placing a bound on the length of the derivations that can be used to find messages that match a variable during the matching process. In this way, we can find "type errors", where, for example, an attack might occur because an honest agent expects to receive a key and accepts a nonce instead. In practice we have been able to get away with a derivation length of 1. Hence, we only generate finite sets of messages, thus the entire state space is finite, and we can use depth first-search to perform an exhaustive search.

7 NORMALIZED DERIVATIONS

In section 4 we discussed how new messages can be generated from known messages using a set of derivation rules. This standard set of adversary capabilities which have evolved from the Dolev and Yao model [6], and which are used by a number of model checkers, fit quite naturally into our framework. In section 5 we discuss when it is necessary to check if the intruder can derive a message. In this section we prove the decidability of this problem by exploiting its similarity to natural deduction and using the idea of normalized derivations. A good discussion of natural deduction and the idea of normalized derivations can be found in [22].

We will assume that the reader is familiar with derivation trees and so we will not formalize them here. We will say that a particular message m is derivable from a set of information I, if there exists a valid derivation tree using the inference rules in Figure 1, such that m appears at the bottom of the tree and all messages appearing at the top of the tree are contained in I. An example of such a tree can be found in Figure 2.

Note that in general there is more than one derivation tree for some message m. While all derivations trees are finite, their sizes are unbounded. In order to prove the decidability of checking $I \vdash m$ we would like to show that there is

$$\dfrac{\dfrac{\dfrac{\{a\}_k \cdot b}{\{a\}_k}\cdot\mathcal{E}_l \qquad k^{-1}}{a}\{\}_k\mathcal{E} \qquad \dfrac{\{a\}_k \cdot b}{b}\cdot\mathcal{E}_r}{a \cdot b}\cdot\mathcal{I}$$

Figure 2 A derivation tree for $\{\{a\}_k \cdot b, k^{-1}\} \vdash a \cdot b$

always a *normalized derivation* of bounded size for which we can search. Unlike normalized derivations in natural deduction, this normalized derivation will have the additional property that all elimination rules ($\cdot\mathcal{E}_l$, $\cdot\mathcal{E}_r$, $\{\}_k\mathcal{E}$) appear above all introduction rules ($\cdot\mathcal{I}$, $\{\}_k\mathcal{I}$). A similar idea for placing bounds on the lengths of derivations can be found in [3, 11, 15, 20]. However, this framework allows for an straightforward translation into a proof search algorithm and explains the reasons behind certain assumptions made about the message space, in particular, the perfect encryption assumption and the atomic key assumption.

Each message construction operation (pairing and encryption) is characterized by a pair of inference rules. One is an introduction rule that creates a new message whose principal connective is that operation. For example the $\{\}_k\mathcal{I}$ rule creates a new encrypted message $\{m\}_k$ from the message m and the key k. The second is an elimination rule that removes that particular operation from the compound message. For example the $\cdot\mathcal{E}_l$ rule takes a message $m_1 \cdot m_2$ and returns its left component m_1. The intuition behind normalized derivations is that an instance of an elimination rule appearing immediately below an instance of the corresponding introduction rule gains no new information. So we transform such a derivation into a smaller derivation in which we eliminate this redundant step.

Using terminology similar to that found in [22], we will call the key k in an instance of the inference rule $\{\}_k\mathcal{E}$ a *minor premise.* Any other premise is a *major premise.* A message that appears in a derivation tree T as the conclusion of an introduction rule and as a major premise of an elimination rule is a *maximum message.* A derivation tree is a *normalized derivation* if it contains no maximum message. We now show that we can transform any derivation tree T into a normalized derivation tree T' by eliminating maximum messages one at a time.

Let T be a derivation tree that is not atomic, and let M be a maximum message in T. Then T', a reduction of T at M is constructed from T using one of the rules below, depending on the form of M. In the diagrams, Π is what would remain of T after removing M and everything above it, while Σ_1, Σ_2, and Σ_3 represent sequences of derivation trees.

·-reduction $(i = 1, 2)$

$$\begin{array}{c} \dfrac{\dfrac{\dfrac{\Sigma_1}{m_1} \qquad \dfrac{\Sigma_2}{m_2}}{m_1 \cdot m_2}}{m_i} \\ \Pi \end{array} \qquad \Rightarrow \qquad \begin{array}{c} \dfrac{\Sigma_i}{m_i} \\ \Pi \end{array}$$

$\{\}_k$-reduction

$$\begin{array}{c} \dfrac{\dfrac{\dfrac{\Sigma_1}{m} \qquad \dfrac{\Sigma_2}{k}}{\{m\}_k} \qquad \dfrac{\Sigma_3}{k^{-1}}}{m} \\ \Pi \end{array} \qquad \Rightarrow \qquad \begin{array}{c} \dfrac{\Sigma_1}{m} \\ \Pi \end{array}$$

Theorem 1 *Any derivation tree T for m depending on assumptions A can be transformed into a normalized derivation tree T' for m depending on the same assumptions A.*

Proof: We proceed by induction on the number of maximum messages. If T has no maximum messages then it is already normalized and we are done. Otherwise, take any maximum message M. Because of the perfect encryption assumption, M cannot be the conclusion of an introduction rule for one operator and a major premise in the elimination rule for the other operator. Therefore, one of the reduction rules applies to M. After applying the appropriate reduction rule, we have removed one maximum message and we have not introduced any new ones. The result is a derivation tree for m that depends on the same assumptions and which has one less maximum message. By the induction hypothesis this new derivation tree can be properly transformed.

In fact, the structure of these derivations trees is even more restricted.

Theorem 2 *No introduction rule appears above an elimination rule in a normalized derivation tree.*

Proof: By the definition of normalized, no message appears as the conclusion of an introduction rule and a major premise of an elimination rule. Therefore, we only need consider minor premises. The only minor premises are keys. Recall that we restricted keys to be atomic; therefore, no key can appear as the conclusion of an introduction rule. Hence no message can appear as the conclusion of an introduction rule and a premise of an elimination rule. It follows that no introduction rule appears above an elimination rule.

This theorem provides a simple explanation for the atomic key restriction. As we shall see, this theorem also leads to an efficient algorithm for deciding $I \vdash m$.

8 INFORMATION ALGORITHMS

Theorem 2 suggests an efficient algorithm for determining if $I \vdash m$. Since all elimination rules appear above all introduction rules in a normalized derivation, we can first construct I^*, the closure of the initial set of assumptions I under all elimination rules. We then do a backwards search for a derivation of m from I^* using only introduction rules. (We will use $I^* \vdash_{\mathcal{I}} m$ to denote that such a derivation tree exists.) We will now prove termination and correctness of this algorithm.

Theorem 3 *$I \vdash m$ iff $I^* \vdash_{\mathcal{I}} m$ (Correctness)*

Proof: ($\Rightarrow$) Consider the case when $I \vdash m$. Let T be a normalized derivation tree for m from I. By removing all elimination rules, we get a new tree T' for m from $I \cup \Delta$, where Δ is the set of all the messages appearing at the top of T' that are not in I. So T' is a derivation tree for $I \cup \Delta \vdash_{\mathcal{I}} m$. By construction, each $\delta_i \in \Delta$ can be derived from I using only elimination rules so $I \cup \Delta \subseteq I^*$. Therefore T' is also a derivation tree for $I^* \vdash_{\mathcal{I}} m$.

($\Leftarrow$) Consider the case when $I^* \vdash_{\mathcal{I}} m$. By definition, $I \vdash i$ for each $i \in I^*$. Therefore, we can transform the tree T' for $I^* \vdash_{\mathcal{I}} m$ into a tree T for $I \vdash m$ by placing a derivation tree T_i for $I \vdash i$ above each message $i \notin I$ at the top of T'.

Theorem 3 proves the correctness of our algorithm. To prove termination, consider all the messages that are generated during the derivation. The elimination rules start from the assumptions and generate only sub-messages. Since the original messages are finite length, and since there are only a finite number of them, the process of closing under elimination rules terminates. Now consider the backwards search using introduction rules. Since these rules are applied backwards, the new major premise messages we search for must be sub-messages, and so that part of the search terminates when we reach a message in I^* or we reach an atomic message that is not in I^*. The minor premises we search for are all atomic keys, and so clearly, that involves a simple scan of I^* as well. Therefore, the entire algorithm terminates.

The implementation of this algorithm is given in the following two figures. In Figure 3 we consider how to update the adversary's set of information when

```
funct add(I, m)
  foreach i ∈ I do
    if i = {x}_y ∧ m = y^-1
      then I := add(I, x)
           if y ∈ I then I := I − i fi
    fi
  od
  if m ∈ A
    then return I ∪ {m}
  elsif m = x · y
      then return add(add(I, x), y)
  elsif m = {x}_y ∧ y^-1 ∈ I
      then if y ∈ I
             then return add(I, x)
             else return add(I ∪ {m}, x)
           fi
  else
      return I ∪ {m}
  fi
```

Figure 3 Augmenting the adversary's knowledge

it learns a new message. Anytime the adversary gains a new message, we add it to the set of messages it currently has and we close this set under elimination rules while also removing "redundant" messages. Figure 4, describes how to search for a derivation of m from I^* using only introduction rules. This search involves first checking if $m \in I^*$. If this fails, then we recursively search for the components of m.

```
funct in(I, m)
  if m ∈ I
    then return true
  elsif m = x · y
      then return in(I, x) ∧ in(I, y)
  elsif m = {x}_y
      then return in(I, x) ∧ in(I, y)
  else
      return false
  fi
```

Figure 4 Searching the adversary's knowledge

9 WOO AND LAM EXAMPLE

We now analyze a protocol published by Woo and Lam in [28]. The protocol is given below:

1. $A \rightarrow B : A$
2. $B \rightarrow A : N_b$
3. $A \rightarrow B : \{N_b\}_{K_{as}}$
4. $B \rightarrow S : \{A \cdot \{N_b\}_{K_{as}}\}_{K_{bs}}$
5. $S \rightarrow B : \{A \cdot N_b\}_{K_{bs}}$

Here A is the initiator, B is the responder, and S is a server. In message one, A initiates the protocol by sending B its name. B replies in message two with a nonce. In message three, A encrypts the nonce with the secret key it shares with the server and sends it back to B. B then concatenates this with A's name, encrypts the whole thing with its private key with the server and sends it to the server in message four. In the last message, the server can decrypt using both keys to recover the original nonce and return it to B along with A's name and encrypted with B's key.

In order to use our model checker, we first isolate which actions are performed by A, which actions are performed by B, and which are performed by S. We then write a short sequence of actions which make up each participant's role in the protocol. The process description for principal B can be found in Figure 5. The descriptions for the other honest agents are similar. All that remains is to specify the initial state of the adversary's local store. Initially, the adversary knows the names of all agents and its own secret key with the server.

In just a few seconds, our model checker finds the following attack:

1. $I(A) \rightarrow B : A$
2. $B \rightarrow I(A) : N_b$
3. $I(A) \rightarrow B : N_b$
4. $B \rightarrow I(S) : \{A \cdot N_b\}_{K_{bs}}$
5. $I(S) \rightarrow B : \{A \cdot N_b\}_{K_{bs}}$

In this case B is the only honest agent participating in the protocol. The adversary pretends to be both the server S and the other honest agent A. In the end, B believes that A has participated in a run of the protocol, while A has not participated at all. The error occurs in step 3 of the protocol. B is waiting for a message that is encrypted with a key it does not possess; therefore, B has no idea what the message should look like. The adversary can replay the message B sent in step 2 and B will accept it as coming from A in step 3. B then generates message 4 by concatenating this message with A's name and encrypting with the secret key it shares with the server. The problem now is that this message just sent by B in step 4, is the exact message B is expecting from the server in step 5. So again, the adversary just replays this message to B in order to complete the attack.

This example demonstrates a type of attack that depends on the fact that an agent cannot differentiate between one kind of message and another. In this example, the responder does not possess the key K_{as} and so cannot tell in step 3 whether the message it receives is encrypted or not. Actually, the situation is worse, since we assume that B knows nothing about the message it receives and could actually accept *any* message at this point. However, not all messages generate an attack. By accepting its own nonce in step 3, B generates and sends in step 4 the exact message it is expecting in step 5. It is this interplay that allows the attack.

This kind of attack illustrates one of the trade-offs involved when trying to make the message space finite. When we look at the model of the responder in this protocol in Figure 5, we notice that the second receive performed by the responder consists of a single message variable. This is because, as discussed above, from the responder's point of view, this message could be anything. If we place a type restriction on this variable, so that it can only unify against an encrypted nonce, the attack discussed here would not be found. However, this variable matches an infinite number of messages derivable by the adversary and so we must somehow limit the set of messages we consider. In this case, the attack is found even if we limit the size of the derivations that the adversary is allowed to perform when generating messages to a single step (i.e. to messages directly contained in I^*).

```
((begrespond (*var* a))
 (receive (*var* a)
          (*var* a))
 (newsecret (*var* nb))
 (send (*var* a)
       (*var* nb))
 (receive (*var* a)
  (*var* tos))
 (send s
       (encrypt (*secret* b)
       (concat (*var* a) (*var* tos))))
 (receive s
  (encrypt (*secret* b)
   (concat (*var* a) (*var* nb))))
 (endrespond (*var* a)))))
```

Figure 5 Process description for the responder

10 CONCLUSION

The prototype model checker described here has successfully discovered previously published errors in protocols. When run on correct protocols, the model checker takes a bit longer because it ends up exploring the entire reachable state space, but for the examples investigated so far, with a single session for each role, the system still terminates in about a minute. We are confident that this kind of exhaustive simulation is a feasible and useful technique for verifying security protocols. However, there are still many extensions that can be investigated and implemented as well as additional experiments to be carried out.

Despite the fact that there is a simple and straightforward translation from protocol descriptions in the literature into our modelling language, this process is tedious and prone to error. We are currently developing a better interface that would allow protocols to be specified exactly the same way they are specified in the literature. We are also working on defining a logic in which to specify the properties we are interested in checking. We are investigating how to add other message operations such as XOR and encryption with non-atomic keys. While these extensions should be possible, it is not clear how these additions will affect the efficiency of the decision procedure for message derivations.

Efficiency is also an important concern. Currently, the model checker runs in an acceptable amount of time. As we begin to increase the number of concurrent protocol runs, and as we increase the complexity of the model checker itself, we can expect the execution time to increase dramatically. Techniques that increase the efficiency of the model checker are necessary to combat this increase in complexity. In particular, it has become clear that a number of operations can be thought of as independent of each other, in the sense that they can be swapped in the execution trace without affecting the rest of the trace. This leads us to believe that partial order techniques [21] can be applied. The increase in efficiency, ease of use, and expressibility will prove useful in analyzing more complex protocols, including electronic commerce protocols.

Finally, there is the problem of how many runs to check. Because the size of the model grows exponentially with the number of runs, it would be ideal to be able to limit the search to only one or two runs. Inspired by the kind of analysis done by Lowe [13], we are investigating a framework in which one can analyze and prove bounds on the number of runs that need to be checked. We use a kind of dependence graph on the messages that the adversary needs to generate. For some simple protocols, we have been able to argue that if there is a flaw in a protocol, then that flaw will be discovered by a model checker on a model with only one run. We plan to continue investigating this methodology with the hope of being able to automate it as well.

ACKNOWLEDGEMENTS

The authors would like to thank Natarajan Shankar and Carsten Schürmann for helpful discussions regarding normalized derivations and for feedback on an earlier version of this paper.

REFERENCES

[1] M. Abadi and A. Gordon. A calculus for cryptographic protocols the spi calculus. In *Proceedings of the Fourth ACM Conference on Computer and Communications Security*, April 1997. To appear.

[2] M. Bellare and P. Rogaway. Provably secure session key distribution–the three party case. In *Proceedings of the 27th Annual ACM Symposium on Theory of Computing*, pages 57–66, 1995.

[3] D. Bolignano. An approach to the formal verification of cryptographic protocols. In *Proceedings of the 3rd ACM Conference on Computer and Communication Security*, 1996.

[4] M. Burrows, M. Abadi, and R. Needham. A logic of authentication. Technical Report 39, DEC Systems Research Center, February 1989.

[5] D. Craigen and M. Saaltink. Using EVES to analyze authentication protocols. Technical Report TR-96-5508-05, ORA Canada, 1996.

[6] D. Dolev and A. Yao. On the security of public key protocols. *IEEE Transactions on Information Theory*, 29(2):198–208, March 1989.

[7] J. W. Gray and J. McLean. Using temporal logic to specify and verify cryptographic protocols (progress report). In *Proceedings of the 8th IEEE Computer Security Workshop*, 1995.

[8] N. Heintze, D. Tygar, J. Wing, and H. Wong. Model checking electronic commerce protocols. In *Proceedings of the USENIX 1996 Workshop on Electronic Commerce*, pages 146–164, 1996.

[9] N. Heintze and J. Tygar. A model for secure protocols and their compositions. *IEEE Transactions on Software Engineering*, 22(1):16–30, January 1996.

[10] R. Kailar. Accountability in electronic commerce protocols. *IEEE Transactions on Software Engineering*, 22(5), May 1996.

[11] D. Kindred and J. M. Wing. Fast, automatic checking of security protocols. In *USENIX 2nd Workshop on Electronic Commerce*, 1996.

[12] G. Leduc, O. Bonaventure, E. Koerner, L. Léonard, C. Pecheur, and D. Zanetti. Specification and verification of a TTP protocol for the conditional access to services. In *Proceedings of the 12th J. Cartier Workshop on Formal Methods and their Applications: Telecommunications, VLSI and Real-Time Computerized Control System*, October 1996.

[13] G. Lowe. Breaking and fixing the Needham-Schroeder public-key protocol using FDR. In *Tools and Algorithms for the Construction and*

Analysis of Systems, volume 1055 of *Lecture Notes in Computer Science*, pages 147–166. Springer-Verlag, 1996.

[14] G. Lowe. Casper: A compiler for the analysis of security protocols. In *Proceedings of the 1997 IEEE Computer Society Symposium on Research in Security and Privacy*, pages 18–30, 1997.

[15] W. Marrero, E. Clarke, and S. Jha. Model checking for security protocols. Technical Report CMU-CS-97-139, Carnegie Mellon University, 1997.

[16] C. Meadows. A model of computation for the NRL protocol analyzer. In *Proceedings of the 1994 Computer Security Foundations Workshop*. IEEE Computer Society Press, June 1994.

[17] C. Meadows. The NRL protocol analyzer: An overview. In *Proceedings of the Second International Conference on the Practical Applications of Prolog*, 1994.

[18] J. Millen. The Interrogator model. In *Proceedings of the 1995 IEEE Symposium on Security and Privacy*, pages 251–260. IEEE Computer Society Press, 1995.

[19] J. C. Mitchell, M. Mitchell, and U. Stern. Automated analysis of cryptographic protocols using murϕ. In *Proceedings of the 1997 IEEE Symposium on Security and Privacy*. IEEE Computer Society Press, 1997.

[20] L. Paulson. Proving properties of security protocols by induction. In *Proceedings of the 1997 IEEE Computer Society Symposium on Research in Security and Privacy*, pages 70–83, 1997.

[21] D. Peled. All from one, one for all, on model-checking using representatives. In *Proceedings of the Fifth International Conference on Computer Aided Verification*, Lecture Notes in Computer Science, pages 409–423. Springer-Verlag, 1993.

[22] D. Prawitz. *Natural Deduction: A Proof-Theoretical Study*. Almqvist & Wiksell, 1965.

[23] A. W. Roscoe. Intensional specifications of security protocols. In *9th Computer Security Foundations Workshop*, 1996.

[24] S. Schneider. Security properties and CSP. In *Proceedings of the 1996 IEEE Computer Society Symposium on Research in Security and Privacy*, 1996.

[25] S. Schneider. Verifying authentication protocols with CSP. In *Proceedings of the 1997 IEEE Computer Society Symposium on Research in Security and Privacy*, 1997.

[26] V. Shoup and A. Rubin. Session key distribution using smart cards. In *Proceedings of Eurocrypt*, 1996.

[27] T. Y. C. Woo and S. S. Lam. A semantic model for authentication protocols. In *Proceedings of the IEEE Symposium on Research in Security and Privacy*, 1993.

[28] T. Y. C. Woo and S. S. Lam. A lesson on authentication protocol design. In *Operating Systems Review*, pages 24–37, 1994.

Edmund M. Clarke received a B.A. degree in mathematics from the University of Virginia in 1967, an M.A. degree in mathematics from Duke University in 1968, and a Ph.D. degree in Computer Science from Cornell University in 1976. After receiving his Ph.D., he taught in the Department of Computer Science, Duke University, for two years. In 1978 he moved to Harvard University where he was an Assistant Professor of Computer Science in the Division of Applied Sciences. He left Harvard in 1982 to join the faculty in the Computer Science Department at Carnegie Mellon University. He was appointed Full Professor in 1989. In 1995 he became the first recipient of the FORE Systems Professorship, an endowed chair in the School of Computer Science.

Dr. Clarke's interests include software and hardware verification and automatic theorem proving. In his Ph.D. thesis he proved that certain programming language control structures did not have good Hoare style proof systems. In 1981 he and his Ph.D. student Allen Emerson first proposed the use of *Model Checking* as a verification technique for finite state concurrent systems. His research group pioneered the use of Model Checking for hardware verification. Symbolic Model Checking using BDDs was also developed by his group. This important technique was the subject of Kenneth McMillan's Ph.D. thesis, which received an ACM Doctoral Dissertation Award. In addition, his resarch group developed the first parallel resolution theorem prover (Parthenon) and the first theorem prover to be based on a symbolic computation system (Analytica).

Dr. Clarke has served on the editorial boards of Distributed Computing and Logic and Computation and is currently an editor-in-chief of Formal Methods in Systems Design. He is on the steering committees of two international conferences, Logic in Computer Science and Computer-Aided Verification. He is a Fellow of the Association for Computing Machinery, a member of the IEEE Computer Society, Sigma Xi, and Phi Beta Kappa.

Somesh Jha is a post-doctoral fellow in the Robotics Institute at Carnegie Mellon University. Somesh Jha received his B. Tech in Electrical Engineering from IIT Delhi, India, Masters in Computer Science from Penn State, and Ph.D. in Computer Science from Carnegie Mellon University. Somesh has also worked as a computer consultant for four years. He has worked as a consultant for IBM, AT&T, and UPS. His main areas of interests are in formal methods with applications to communication protocols, software engineering, and multi-agent systems. He is also interested in computational finance and application of economics to software engineering decision making.

Will Marrero is a graduate student in the School of Computer Science at Carnegie Mellon University. Will Marrero received his B.A. in mathematics and computer science from Columbia University in 1992. He has worked as a summer intern doing formal verification at Intel and at Cadence. His main areas of interest are formal methods as applied to security protocols, communication protocols, and hardware design.

11

Programming Language Semantics in Foundational Type Theory

K. Crary
Cornell University
Ithaca, New York 14853
crary@cs.cornell.edu

Abstract

There are compelling benefits to using foundational type theory as a framework for programming language semantics. I give a semantics of an expressive programming calculus in the foundational type theory of Nuprl. Previous type-theoretic semantics have used less expressive type theories, or have sacrificed important programming constructs such as recursion and modules. The primary mechanisms of this semantics are ***partial types,*** for typing recursion, ***set types,*** for encoding power and singleton kinds, which are used for subtyping and module programming, and ***very dependent function types,*** for encoding signatures.

Keywords

Semantics, program verification, type theory, functional programming

1 INTRODUCTION

Type theory has become a popular framework for formal reasoning in computer science and has formed the basis for a number of automated deduction systems, including Automath, Nuprl, HOL and Coq, among others. In addition to formalizing mathematics, these systems are widely used for the analysis and verification of computer programs. To do this, one must draw a connection between the programming language used and the language of type theory; however, these connections have typically been informal translations, diminishing the significance of the formal verification results.

Formal connections have been drawn in the work of Reynolds (1981) and Harper and Mitchell (1993), each of whom sought to use type-theoretic analy-

Programming Concepts and Methods D. Gries, & W-P. de Roever (Eds.)

sis to explain an entire programming language. Reynolds gave a type-theoretic interpretation of Idealized Algol, and Harper and Mitchell did the same for a simplified fragment of Standard ML. Recently, Harper and Stone (1998) have given such an interpretation of full Standard ML (Revised) (Milner *et al.*, 1997). However, in each of these cases, the type theories used were not sufficiently rich to form a foundation for mathematical reasoning; for example, they were unable to express equality or induction principles. On the other hand, Kreitz (1997) gave an embedding of a fragment of Objective CAML into the foundational type theory of Nuprl. However, this fragment omitted some important constructs, such as recursion and modules.

The difficulty has been that the same features of foundational type theories that make them so expressive also restrict the constructs that may be introduced into them. For example, as I will discuss below, the existence of induction principles precludes the typing of *fix* that is typical in programming languages. In this paper I show how to give a semantics to practical programming languages in foundational type theory. In particular, I give an embedding of a small but expressive programming language into a Martin-Löf-style type theory. This embedding is simple and syntax-directed, which has been vital for its use in practical reasoning.

The applications of type-theoretic semantics are not limited to formal reasoning about programs. Using such a semantics it can be considerably easier to prove desirable properties about a programming language, such as type preservation, than with other means. We will see two such examples in Section 4.4. The usefulness of such semantics is also not limited to one particular programming language at a time. If two languages are given type-theoretic semantics, then one may use type theory to show relationships between the two, and when the semantics are simple, those relationships need be no more complicated than the inherent differences between the two. This is particularly useful in the area of type-directed compilation. The process of type-directed compilation consists (in part) of translations between various typed intermediate languages. Embedding each into a common foundational type theory provides an ideal framework for showing the invariance of program meaning throughout the compilation process.

This semantics is also useful even if one ultimately desires a semantics in some framework other than type theory. Martin-Löf type theory is closely tied to a structured operational semantics and has denotational models in many frameworks including partial equivalence relations (Allen, 1987; Harper, 1992), set theory (Howe, 1996) and domain theory (Rezus, 1985; Palmgren and Stoltenberg-Hansen, 1989). Thus, foundational type theory may be used as a "semantic intermediate language."

The paper is organized as follows: Section 2 presents the paper's object language, λ^K. This object language is a small programming calculus, not a practical programming language, so a formal elaborator must be invoked to relate these results to a full programming language. I do not present such an

kinds	κ	$::=$	$\mathit{Type}_i \mid \Pi\alpha{:}\kappa_1.\kappa_2 \mid \mathcal{P}_i(c) \mid \mathcal{S}_i(c) \mid$ $\{\ell_1 \triangleright \alpha_1 : \kappa_1, \ldots, \ell_n \triangleright \alpha_n : \kappa_n\}$
constructors	c	$::=$	$\alpha \mid \lambda\alpha{:}\kappa.c \mid c_1[c_2] \mid \{\ell_1 = c_1, \ldots, \ell_n = c_n\} \mid$ $\pi_\ell(c) \mid c_1 \rightarrow c_2 \mid c_1 \Rightarrow c_2 \mid$ $\forall\alpha{:}\kappa.c \mid \{\ell_1 : c_1, \ldots, \ell_n : c_n\}$
terms	e	$::=$	$x \mid \lambda x{:}c.e \mid e_1 e_2 \mid \Lambda\alpha{:}\kappa.e \mid e[c] \mid$ $\{\ell_1 = e_1, \ldots, \ell_n = e_n\} \mid \pi_\ell(e) \mid \mathit{fix}_c(e)$
kind contexts	Δ	$::=$	$\bullet \mid \Delta[\alpha : \kappa]$
type contexts	Γ	$::=$	$\bullet \mid \Gamma[x : c]$

Figure 1 λ^K Syntax

elaborator in this paper, but see Harper and Stone (1998) for a presentation of such an elaborator. Section 3 contains an overview of Nuprl, the foundational type theory I use in this paper. Section 4 contains the embedding that is the central technical contribution of the paper. Section 5 discusses promising directions for future work. Finally, Section 6 contains brief concluding remarks. Due to space limitations, many technical details have been omitted; these may be found in the companion technical report (Crary, 1998b).

2 THE λ^K PROGRAMMING CALCULUS

As a case study to illustrate my technique, I use a predicative variant of λ^K, the high-level typed intermediate language in the KML compiler (Crary, 1998c). In this section we discuss λ^K. In the interest of brevity, the discussion assumes knowledge of several well-known programming constructs.

The syntax rules of λ^K appear in Figure 1. The overall structure of the calculus is similar to the higher-order polymorphic lambda calculus (Girard, 1972) augmented with records at the term and type constructor level (and their corresponding types and kinds), and a fixpoint operator at the term level. In addition to the kind *Type*, the kind level also includes, for any type τ, the power kind $\mathcal{P}(\tau)$, which includes all subtypes of τ, and the singleton kind $\mathcal{S}(\tau)$, which includes only τ. The kind level also contains the dependent function kind $\Pi\alpha{:}\kappa_1.\kappa_2$ and the dependent record kind $\{\ell_1 \triangleright \alpha_1 : \kappa_1, \ldots, \ell_n \triangleright \alpha_n : \kappa_n\}$ where each ℓ_i is an external name (or label) and each α_i is an internal name (or binding occurrence; see Harper and Lillibridge (1994) for discussion of internal and external names). Evaluation is intended to be call-by-value. The type level includes a type constructor $\Rightarrow$ for total functions and polymorphic functions are also required to be total.

To make this calculus predicative, the type-oriented kinds have level annotations i (i.e., Type_i, $\mathcal{P}_i(\tau)$ and $\mathcal{S}_i(\tau)$), which are integers ≥ 1. Each kind contains only types whose levels are strictly less than the given annotation, where the level of a type is the highest level annotation used within it. For $\mathcal{P}_i(\tau)$ or $\mathcal{S}_i(\tau)$ to be well-formed, the level of τ must be less than i. This mechanism is somewhat awkward, and is used to allow the calculus to be embedded in a predicative type theory. Section 5 contains some discussion of alternatives.

The static semantics of λ^K is given by four judgements (details appear in the companion technical report). The subkinding judgement $\Delta \vdash_K \kappa_1 \sqsubseteq \kappa_2$ indicates that (in kind context Δ) every type constructor in κ_1 is in κ_2. The constructor equality judgement $\Delta \vdash_K c_1 = c_2 : \kappa$ indicates that c_1 and c_2 are equal as members of kind κ. The typing judgement $\Delta; \Gamma \vdash_K e : c$ indicates that (in kind context Δ and type context Γ) the term e has type c. Finally, the valuability judgement (Harper and Stone, 1998) $\Delta; \Gamma \vdash_K e \downarrow c$ indicates that the term e has type c and evaluates without computational effects (in this setting this means just that it terminates).

The λ^K calculus used in the KML compiler also includes operators for constructing higher-order modules similar to those of Harper and Lillibridge (1994). Space limitations prevent a discussion of those features here. However, much of the functionality of the module system is derived from the kind structure described above. Modules are discussed in detail in the companion technical report.

3 THE LANGUAGE OF TYPE THEORY

The type theory I use in this paper is the Martin-Löf-style type theory of Nuprl. A thorough discussion of Nuprl is beyond the scope of this paper, so the intent of this section is to give an overview of the programming features of type theory. It is primarily those programming features that I will use in the embedding. The logic of types is obtained through the propositions-as-types isomorphism (Howard, 1980), but this will not be critical to our purposes. Detailed discussions of type theory, including the logic of types, appear in Martin-Löf (1982) and Constable (1991), and Nuprl specifically is discussed in Constable *et al.* (1986). As in the previous section, the discussion here assumes knowledge of several well-known programming constructs.

As base types, the theory contains integers (denoted by $\mathbb{Z}$), booleans (denoted by $\mathbb{B}$), strings (denoted by *Atom*), and the trivial type *Top* (which contains every well-formed term, and in which all well-formed terms are equal). Complex types are built from the base types using various type constructors such as disjoint unions (denoted by $T_1 + T_2$), dependent products (denoted by $\Sigma x{:}T_1.T_2$) and dependent function spaces (denoted by $\Pi x{:}T_1.T_2$). When x does not appear free in T_2, we write $T_1 \times T_2$ for $\Sigma x{:}T_1.T_2$ and $T_1 \to T_2$ for $\Pi x{:}T_1.T_2$.

This gives an account of most of the familiar programming constructs other

	Type Formation	Introduction	Elimination
universe i	$\mathbb{U}_i$ (for $i \geq 1$)	type formation operators	
disjoint union	$T_1 + T_2$	$inj_1(e)$ $inj_2(e)$	$case(e, x_1.e_1, x_2.e_2)$
function space	$\Pi x{:}T_1.T_2$	$\lambda x.e$	$e_1 e_2$
product space	$\Sigma x{:}T_1.T_2$	$\langle e_1, e_2 \rangle$	$\pi_1(e)$ $\pi_2(e)$
integers	$\mathbb{Z}$	$\ldots, -1, 0, 1, 2, \ldots$	assorted operations
booleans	$\mathbb{B}$	*true*, *false*	if-then-else
atoms	*Atom*	string literals	equality test ($=_A$)
top	*Top*		

Figure 2 Type Theory Syntax

than polymorphism. To handle polymorphism we want to have functions that can take types as arguments. These can be typed with the dependent types discussed above if one adds a type of all types. Unfortunately, a single type of all types is known to make the theory inconsistent (Girard, 1972), so instead the type theory includes a predicative hierarchy of universes, $\mathbb{U}_1, \mathbb{U}_2, \mathbb{U}_3$, etc. The universe $\mathbb{U}_1$ contains all types built up from the base types only, and the universe $\mathbb{U}_{i+1}$ contains all types built up from the base types and the universes $\mathbb{U}_1, \ldots, \mathbb{U}_i$. In particular, no universe is a member of itself.

Unlike λ^K, which has distinct syntactic classes for kinds, type constructors and terms, Nuprl has only one syntactic class for all expressions. As a result, types are first class citizens and may be computed just as any other term. For example, the expression *if* b *then* $\mathbb{Z}$ *else Top* (where b is a boolean expression) is a valid type. Evaluation is call-by-name, but the constructions in this paper may also be used in a call-by-value type theory with little modification.

To state the soundness of the embedding, we will require two assertions from the logic of types. These are equality, denoted by $t_1 = t_2$ *in* T, which states that the terms t_1 and t_2 are equal as members of type T, and subtyping, denoted by $T_1 \sqsubseteq T_2$, which states that every member of type T_1 is in type T_2 (and that terms equal in T_1 are equal in T_2). A membership assertion, denoted by $t \in T$, is defined as $t = t$ *in* T. The basic judgement in Nuprl is $H \vdash_\nu P$, which states that in context H (which contains hypotheses and declarations of variables) the proposition P is true. Often the proposition P will be an assertion of equality or membership in a type.

The basic operators discussed above are summarized in Figure 2. The reader is referred to Crary (1998c) for their dynamic semantics and the inference rules for the $\vdash_\nu$ judgement. Note that the lambda abstractions of Nuprl are untyped, unlike those of λ^K. In addition to the operators discussed here, the type theory contains some other less familiar type constructors: the partial type, set type and very dependent function type. In order to better motivate these type constructors, we defer discussion of them until their point of relevance.

4 A TYPE-THEORETIC SEMANTICS

I present the embedding of λ^K into type theory in three parts. In the first part I begin by giving embeddings for most of the basic type and term operators. These embeddings are uniformly straightforward. Second, I examine what happens when the embedding is expanded to include *fix*. There we will find it necessary to modify some of the original embeddings of the basic operators. In the third part I complete the semantics by giving embeddings for the kind-level constructs of λ^K. The complete embedding is summarized in Figures 4, 5 and 6.

The embedding itself could be formulated in type theory, leaving to metatheory only the trivial task of encoding the abstract syntax of the programming language. Were this done, the theorems of Section 4.4 could be proven within the framework of type theory. For simplicity, however, I will state the embedding and theorems in metatheory.

4.1 Core Embedding

he embedding is defined as a syntax-directed mapping (denoted by $[\![\cdot]\!]$) of ^{K} expressions to terms of type theory. Recall that in Nuprl all expressions e terms; in particular, types are terms and may be computed just as any her term. Many λ^K expressions are translated directly into type theory:

$$\begin{aligned} [\![x]\!] &\stackrel{\text{def}}{=} x \\ [\![\alpha]\!] &\stackrel{\text{def}}{=} \alpha \\ c.e]\!] &\stackrel{\text{def}}{=} \lambda x.[\![e]\!] \\ e_2]\!] &\stackrel{\text{def}}{=} [\![e_1]\!][\![e_2]\!] \\ c_2]\!] &\stackrel{\text{def}}{=} [\![c_1]\!] \rightarrow [\![c_2]\!] \end{aligned} \qquad (1)$$

happens here except that the types are stripped out of lambda ab- is to match the syntax of Nuprl. Functions at the type constructor level are equally easy to embed, but I defer discussion of them until Section 4.3.

Since the type theory does not distinguish between functions taking term arguments and functions taking type arguments, polymorphic functions may be embedded just as easily, although a dependent type is required to express the dependency of c on α in the polymorphic type $\forall\alpha{:}\kappa.c$:

$$\begin{aligned}
[\![\Lambda\alpha{:}\kappa.e]\!] &\stackrel{\text{def}}{=} \lambda\alpha.[\![e]\!] \\
[\![e[c]]\!] &\stackrel{\text{def}}{=} [\![e]\!][\![c]\!] \\
[\![\forall\alpha{:}\kappa.c]\!] &\stackrel{\text{def}}{=} \Pi\alpha{:}[\![\kappa]\!].[\![c]\!]
\end{aligned} \tag{2}$$

Just as the type was stripped out of the lambda abstraction above, the kind is stripped out of the polymorphic abstraction. The translation of the polymorphic function type above makes use of the embedding of kinds, but except for the elementary kind *Type* I defer discussion of the embedding of kinds until Section 4.3. The kind Type_i, which contains level-i types, is embedded as the universe containing level-i types:

$$[\![\mathit{Type}_i]\!] \stackrel{\text{def}}{=} \mathbb{U}_i \tag{3}$$

Records A bit more delicate than the above, but still fairly simple, is the embedding of records. Field labels are taken to be members of type *Atom*, and then records are viewed as functions that map field labels to the contents of the corresponding fields. For example, the record $\{\mathtt{x} = 1, \mathtt{f} = \lambda x{:}\mathit{int}.x\}$, which has type $\{\mathtt{x} : \mathit{int}, \mathtt{f} : \mathit{int} \to \mathit{int}\}$, is embedded as

$$\lambda a.\, \mathit{if}\ a =_A \mathtt{x}\ \mathit{then}\ 1\ \mathit{else}\ \mathit{if}\ a =_A \mathtt{f}\ \mathit{then}\ \lambda x.x\ \mathit{else}\ \mathit{junk} \tag{4}$$

where $a =_A a'$ is the equality test on atoms, which returns a boolean when a and a' are atoms, and *junk* is an arbitrary member of *Top*.

Since the type of this function's result depends upon its argument, this function must be typed using a dependent type:

$$\Pi a{:}\mathit{Atom}.\, \mathit{if}\ a =_A \mathtt{x}\ \mathit{then}\ \mathbb{Z}\ \mathit{else}\ \mathit{if}\ a =_A \mathtt{f}\ \mathit{then}\ \mathbb{Z} \to \mathbb{Z}\ \mathit{else}\ \mathit{Top} \tag{5}$$

In general, records and record types are embedded as follows:

$$
\begin{array}{rcl}
[\![\{\ell_1 = e_1, \ldots, \ell_n = e_n\}]\!] & \stackrel{\text{def}}{=} & \lambda a.\ \textit{if } a =_A \ell_1 \textit{ then } [\![e_1]\!] \\
& & \quad \vdots \\
& & \quad \textit{else if } a =_A \ell_n \textit{ then } [\![e_n]\!] \\
& & \quad \textit{else junk} \\
[\![\pi_\ell(e)]\!] & \stackrel{\text{def}}{=} & [\![e]\!]\,\ell \\
[\![\{\ell_1 : c_1, \ldots, \ell_n : c_n\}]\!] & \stackrel{\text{def}}{=} & \Pi a{:}Atom.\ \textit{if } a =_A \ell_1 \textit{ then } [\![c_1]\!] \\
& & \qquad \vdots \\
& & \qquad \textit{else if } a =_A \ell_n \textit{ then } [\![c_n]\!] \\
& & \qquad \textit{else Top}
\end{array} \tag{6}
$$

Note that this embedding validates the desired subtyping relationship on records. Since $\{\mathtt{x} : \mathit{int}, \mathtt{f} : \mathit{int} \to \mathit{int}\} \sqsubseteq \{\mathtt{x} : \mathit{int}\}$, we would like the embedding to respect the subtyping relationship: $[\![\{\mathtt{x} : \mathit{int}, \mathtt{f} : \mathit{int} \to \mathit{int}\}]\!] \sqsubseteq [\![\{\mathtt{x} : \mathit{int}\}]\!]$. Fortunately this is the case, since every type is a subtype of *Top*, and in particular the part of the type relating to the omitted field, *if* $a = \mathtt{f}$ *then* $\mathbb{Z} \to \mathbb{Z}$ *else* Top, is a subtype of Top.

4.2 Embedding Recursion

The usual approach to typing recursion, and the one used in λ^K, is to add a *fix* construct with the typing rule:

$$
\frac{H \vdash_\nu e \in T \to T}{H \vdash_\nu \mathit{fix}(e) \in T} \tag{wrong}
$$

In effect, this adds recursively defined (and possibly divergent) terms to existing types. Unfortunately, such a broad fixpoint rule makes Martin-Löf type theories inconsistent because of the presence of induction principles. An induction principle on a type specifies the membership of that type; for example, the standard induction principle on the natural numbers specifies that every natural number is either zero or some finite iteration of successor on zero. The ability to add divergent elements to a type would violate the specification implied by that type's induction rule.

One simple way to derive an inconsistency from the above typing rule uses the simplest induction principle, induction on the empty type *Void*. The induction principle for *Void* indirectly specifies that it has no members:

$$
\frac{H \vdash_\nu e \in \mathit{Void}}{H \vdash_\nu e \in T} \tag{7}
$$

However, it would be easy, using *fix*, to derive a member of *Void*: the identity function can be given type *Void* $\rightarrow$ *Void*, so $\mathit{fix}(\lambda x.x)$ would have type *Void*. Invoking the induction principle, $\mathit{fix}(\lambda x.x)$ would be a member of every type and, by the propositions-as-types isomorphism, would be a proof of every proposition. It is also worth noting that this inconsistency does not stem from the fact that *Void* is an empty type; similar inconsistencies may be derived (with a bit more work) for almost every type.

It is clear, then, that *fix* cannot be used to define new members of the basic types. How then can recursive functions be typed? The solution is to add a new type constructor for ***partial types*** (Constable and Smith, 1987; Smith, 1989; Crary, 1998c). For any type T, the partial type $\overline{T}$ is a supertype of T that contains all the elements of T and also all divergent terms. (A *total* type is one that contains only convergent terms.) The induction principles on $\overline{T}$ (Smith, 1989; Constable and Crary, 1997) are different than those on T, so we can safely type *fix* with the rule:*

$$\frac{H \vdash_{\nu} e \in \overline{T} \rightarrow \overline{T} \quad H \vdash_{\nu} T \ \mathit{admissible}}{H \vdash_{\nu} \mathit{fix}(e) \in \overline{T}} \tag{8}$$

We use partial types to interpret the possibly non-terminating computations of λ^K. When (in λ^K) a term e has type τ, the embedded term $[\![e]\!]$ will have type $\overline{[\![\tau]\!]}$. Moreover, if e is valuable, then $[\![e]\!]$ can still be given the stronger type $[\![\tau]\!]$. Before we can embed *fix* we must re-examine the embedding of function types. In Nuprl, partial functions are viewed as functions with partial result types:†

$$\begin{aligned} [\![c_1 \rightarrow c_2]\!] &\stackrel{\text{def}}{=} [\![c_1]\!] \rightarrow \overline{[\![c_2]\!]} \\ [\![c_1 \Rightarrow c_2]\!] &\stackrel{\text{def}}{=} [\![c_1]\!] \rightarrow [\![c_2]\!] \\ [\![\forall \alpha{:}\kappa.c]\!] &\stackrel{\text{def}}{=} (\alpha{:}[\![\kappa]\!]) \rightarrow [\![c]\!] \end{aligned} \tag{9}$$

Note that, as desired, $[\![\tau_1 \Rightarrow \tau_2]\!] \sqsubseteq [\![\tau_1 \rightarrow \tau_2]\!]$, since $[\![\tau_2]\!] \sqsubseteq \overline{[\![\tau_2]\!]}$. If partial polymorphic functions were included in λ^K, they would be embedded as $\Pi\alpha{:}[\![\kappa]\!].\overline{[\![c]\!]}$.

Now suppose we wish to *fix* the function f which (in λ^K) has type $(\tau_1 \rightarrow \tau_2) \rightarrow (\tau_1 \rightarrow \tau_2)$, and suppose, for simplicity only, that f is valuable. Then $[\![f]\!]$

*The second subgoal, that the type T be ***admissible,*** is a technical condition related to the notion of admissibility in LCF. This condition is required because fixpoint induction can be derived from the recursive typing rule (Smith, 1989). However, all the types used in the embedding in this paper are admissible, so I ignore the admissibility condition in this paper. Additional details appear in Crary (1998a).

†This terminology can be somewhat confusing. A total type is one that contains only convergent expressions. The partial *function* type $T_1 \rightarrow \overline{T}_2$ contains functions that *return* possibly divergent elements, but those functions themselves converge, so a partial function type is a total type.

has type $(\llbracket\tau_1\rrbracket \to \overline{\llbracket\tau_2\rrbracket}) \to \overline{\llbracket\tau_1\rrbracket \to \overline{\llbracket\tau_2\rrbracket}}$. This type does not quite fit the *fix* typing rule, which requires the domain type to be partial, so we must coerce $\llbracket f\rrbracket$ to a fixable type. We do this by eta-expanding $\llbracket f\rrbracket$ to gain access to its argument and then eta-expanding that argument:

$$\lambda g.\llbracket f\rrbracket(\lambda x.g\,x) \in \overline{\llbracket\tau_1\rrbracket \to \overline{\llbracket\tau_2\rrbracket}} \to \overline{\llbracket\tau_1\rrbracket \to \overline{\llbracket\tau_2\rrbracket}} \tag{10}$$

Eta-expanding g ensures that it terminates, changing its type from $\overline{\llbracket\tau_1\rrbracket \to \overline{\llbracket\tau_2\rrbracket}}$ to $\llbracket\tau_1\rrbracket \to \overline{\llbracket\tau_2\rrbracket}$. The former type is required by the *fix* rule, but the latter type is expected by $\llbracket f\rrbracket$. Since the coerced $\llbracket f\rrbracket$ fits the *fix* typing rule, we get that $\mathit{fix}(\lambda g.\llbracket f\rrbracket(\lambda x.g\,x))$ has type $\overline{\llbracket\tau_1\rrbracket \to \overline{\llbracket\tau_2\rrbracket}}$, as desired. Thus we may embed the *fix* construct as:

$$\llbracket \mathit{fix}_c(e)\rrbracket \stackrel{\text{def}}{=} \mathit{fix}(\lambda g.\llbracket e\rrbracket(\lambda x.g\,x)) \tag{11}$$

Strictness In λ^K, a function may be applied to a possibly divergent argument, but in my semantics functions expect their arguments to be convergent. Therefore we must change the embedding of application to compute function arguments to canonical form before applying the function. (Polymorphic functions are unaffected because all type expressions converge (Corollary 4).) This is done using the sequencing construct $\mathit{let}\ x = e_1\ \mathit{in}\ e_2$ which evaluates e_1 to canonical form e_1' and then reduces to $e_2[e_1'/x]$. The sequence term diverges if e_1 or e_2 does and allows x be given a total type:

$$\frac{H \vdash_\nu e_1 \in \overline{T_2} \quad H[x : T_2] \vdash_\nu e_2 \in \overline{T_1}}{H \vdash_\nu \mathit{let}\ x = e_1\ \mathit{in}\ e_2 \in \overline{T_1}} \tag{12}$$

Application is then embedded in the expected way:

$$\llbracket e_1 e_2\rrbracket \stackrel{\text{def}}{=} \mathit{let}\ x = \llbracket e_2\rrbracket\ \mathit{in}\ \llbracket e_1\rrbracket\, x \tag{13}$$

A final issue arises in regard to records. In the embedding of Section 4.1, the record $\{\ell = e\}$ would terminate even if e diverges. This would be unusual in a call-by-value programming language, so we need to ensure that each member of a record is evaluated:

$$\begin{array}{lcl} \llbracket\{\ell_1 = e_1, \ldots, \ell_n = e_n\}\rrbracket & \stackrel{\text{def}}{=} & \mathit{let}\ x_1 = \llbracket e_1\rrbracket\ \mathit{in} \cdots \\ & & \mathit{let}\ x_n = \llbracket e_n\rrbracket\ \mathit{in} \\ & & \lambda a.\ \mathit{if}\ a =_A \ell_1\ \mathit{then}\ x_1 \\ & & \quad\vdots \\ & & \quad \mathit{else\ if}\ a =_A \ell_n\ \mathit{then}\ x_n \\ & & \quad \mathit{else\ junk} \end{array} \tag{14}$$

4.3 Embedding Kinds

The kind structure of λ^K contains three first-order kind constructors. We have already seen the embedding of the kind *Type*; remaining are the power and singleton kinds. Each of these kinds represents a collection of types, so each will be embedded as something similar to a universe, but unlike the kind Type_i, which includes all types of the indicated level, the power and singleton kinds wish to exclude certain undesirable types. The power kind $\mathcal{P}_i(\tau)$ contains only subtypes of τ and the singleton kind $\mathcal{S}_i(\tau)$ contains only types that are equal to τ; other types must be left out.

The mechanism for achieving this exclusion is the *set type* (Constable, 1985). If S is a type and $P[\cdot]$ is a predicate over S, then the set type $\{z : S \mid P[z]\}$ contains all elements z of S such that $P[z]$ is true. With this type, we can embed the power and singleton kinds as:*

$$\begin{aligned} [\![\mathcal{P}_i(c)]\!] &\stackrel{\text{def}}{=} \{T : \mathbb{U}_i \mid T \sqsubseteq [\![c]\!] \wedge [\![c]\!] \mathrel{\mathit{in}} \mathbb{U}_i\} \\ [\![\mathcal{S}_i(c)]\!] &\stackrel{\text{def}}{=} \{T : \mathbb{U}_i \mid T = [\![c]\!] \mathrel{\mathit{in}} \mathbb{U}_i\} \end{aligned} \tag{15}$$

Among the higher-order type constructors, functions at the type constructor level and their kinds are handled just as at the term level, except that function kinds are permitted to have dependencies but need not deal with partiality or strictness:

$$\begin{aligned} [\![\lambda\alpha{:}\kappa.c]\!] &\stackrel{\text{def}}{=} \lambda\alpha.[\![c]\!] \\ [\![c_1[c_2]]\!] &\stackrel{\text{def}}{=} [\![c_1]\!][\![c_2]\!] \\ [\![\Pi\alpha{:}\kappa_1.\kappa_2]\!] &\stackrel{\text{def}}{=} \Pi\alpha{:}[\![\kappa_1]\!].[\![\kappa_2]\!] \end{aligned} \tag{16}$$

Dependent Record Kinds For records at the type constructor level, the embedding of the records themselves is analogous to those at the term level (except that there is no issue of strictness):

$$\begin{aligned} [\![\{\ell_1 = c_1, \ldots, \ell_n = c_n\}]\!] &\stackrel{\text{def}}{=} \lambda a.\ \mathit{if}\ a =_A \ell_1\ \mathit{then}\ [\![c_1]\!] \\ &\qquad\ \vdots \\ &\qquad \mathit{else\ if}\ a =_A \ell_n\ \mathit{then}\ [\![c_n]\!] \\ &\qquad \mathit{else\ junk} \\ [\![\pi_\ell(c)]\!] &\stackrel{\text{def}}{=} [\![c]\!]\,\ell \end{aligned} \tag{17}$$

However, the embedding of this expression's kind is more complicated. This is because of the need to express dependencies among the fields of the de-

*The second clause in the embedding of the power kind ($[\![c]\!]$ *in* $\mathbb{U}_i$) is used for technical reasons that require that well-formedness of $\mathcal{P}_i(\tau)$ imply that $\tau : \mathit{Type}_i$.

pendent record kind. Recall that the embedding of a non-dependent record type already required a dependent type; to embed a dependent record type will require expressing even more dependency. Consider the dependent record kind $\{\ell \triangleright \alpha : \mathit{Type}_1, \ell' \triangleright \alpha' : \mathcal{P}_1(\alpha)\}$. We might naively attempt to encode this like the non-dependent record type as

$$\begin{aligned} &\Pi a{:}Atom.\ \mathit{if}\ a =_A \ell\ \mathit{then}\ \mathbb{U}_1\ \mathit{else} \\ &\qquad \mathit{if}\ a =_A \ell'\ \mathit{then}\ \{T : \mathbb{U}_1 \mid T \sqsubseteq \alpha \wedge \alpha\ \mathit{in}\ \mathbb{U}_1\}\ \mathit{else}\ \mathit{Top} \end{aligned} \qquad \text{(wrong)}$$

but this encoding is not correct; the variable α is now unbound. We want α to refer to the contents of field ℓ. In the encoding, this means we want α to refer to the value returned by the function when applied to label ℓ. So we want a type of functions whose return type can depend not only upon their arguments but upon their own return values!

The type I will use for this embedding is a *very dependent function type* (Hickey, 1996). This type is a generalization of the dependent function type (itself a generalization of the ordinary function type) and like it, the very dependent function type's members are just lambda abstractions. The difference is in the specification of a function's return type. The type is denoted by $\{f \mid x{:}T_1 \rightarrow T_2\}$ where f and x are binding occurrences that may appear free in T_2 (but not in T_1).

As with the dependent function type, x stands for the function's argument, but the additional variable f refers to the function itself. A function g belongs to the type $\{f \mid x{:}T_1 \rightarrow T_2\}$ if g takes an argument from T_1 (call it t) and returns a member of $T_2[t, g/x, f]$.*

For example, the kind $\{\ell \triangleright \alpha : \mathit{Type}_1, \ell' \triangleright \alpha' : \mathcal{P}_1(\alpha)\}$ discussed above is encoded as a very dependent function type as:

$$\begin{aligned} &\{f \mid a{:}Atom \rightarrow \mathit{if}\ a =_A \ell\ \mathit{then}\ \mathbb{U}_1\ \mathit{else} \\ &\qquad \mathit{if}\ a =_A \ell'\ \mathit{then}\ \{T : \mathbb{U}_1 \mid T \sqsubseteq f\,\ell \wedge f\,\ell\ \mathit{in}\ \mathbb{U}_1\}\ \mathit{else}\ \mathit{Top}\} \end{aligned} \qquad (18)$$

To understand where this type constructor fits in with the more familiar type constructors, consider the "type triangle" shown in Figure 3. On the right are the non-dependent type constructors and in the middle are the dependent type constructors. Arrows are drawn from type constructors to weaker ones that may be implemented with them. Horizontal arrows indicate when a weaker constructor may be obtained by dropping a possible dependency from a stronger one; for example, the function type $T_1 \rightarrow T_2$ is a degenerate form of the dependent function type $\Pi x{:}T_1.T_2$ where the dependent variable

*To avoid the apparent circularity, in order for $\{f \mid x{:}T_1 \rightarrow T_2\}$ to be well-formed we require that T_2 may only use the result of f when applied to elements of T_1 that are less than x with regard to some well-founded order. This restriction will not be a problem for this embedding because the order in which field labels appear in a dependent record kind is a perfectly good well-founded order.

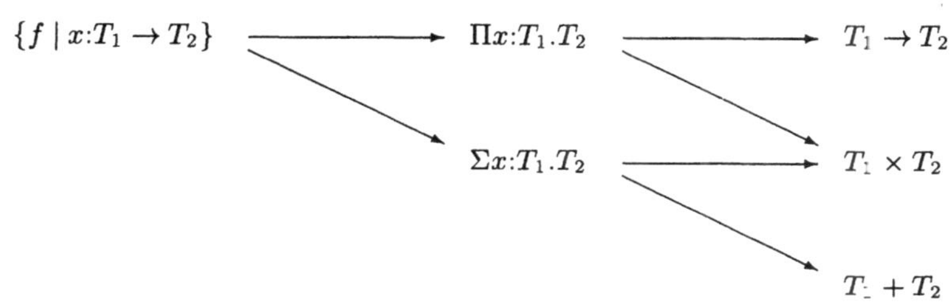

Figure 3 The Type Triangle

x is not used in T_2. Diagonal arrows indicate when a weaker constructor may be implemented with a stronger one by performing case analysis on a boolean; for example, the disjoint union type $T_1 + T_2$ is equivalent to the type $\Sigma b{:}\mathbb{B}.\ \mathit{if}\ b\ \mathit{then}\ T_1\ \mathit{else}\ T_2$.

If we ignore the very dependent function type, the type triangle illustrates how the basic type constructors may be implemented by the dependent function and dependent product types. The very dependent function type completes this picture: the dependent function is a degenerate form where the f dependency is not used, and the dependent product may be implemented by switching on a boolean. Thus, the very dependent function type is a single unified type constructor from which all the basic type constructors may be constructed.

In general, dependent record kinds are encoded using a very dependent function type as follows:

$$\begin{aligned}
&[\![\{\ell_1 \rhd \alpha_1 : \kappa_1, \ldots, \ell_n \rhd \alpha_n : \kappa_n\}]\!] \\
&\quad\stackrel{\text{def}}{=}\quad \{f \mid a{:}\mathit{Atom} \to \mathit{if}\ a =_A \ell_1\ \mathit{then}\ [\![\kappa_1]\!] \\
&\qquad\qquad\qquad\qquad\quad \mathit{else\ if}\ a =_A \ell_2\ \mathit{then}\ [\![\kappa_2]\!][f\,\ell_1/\alpha_1] \\
&\qquad\qquad\qquad\qquad\quad \vdots \\
&\qquad\qquad\qquad\qquad\quad \mathit{else\ if}\ a =_A \ell_n\ \mathit{then} \\
&\qquad\qquad\qquad\qquad\qquad [\![\kappa_n]\!][f\,\ell_1 \cdots f\,\ell_{n-1}/\alpha_1 \cdots \alpha_{n-1}] \\
&\qquad\qquad\qquad\qquad\quad \mathit{else}\ \mathit{Top}\}
\end{aligned} \tag{19}$$

4.4 Properties of the Embedding

I conclude my presentation of the type-theoretic semantics of λ^K by examining some of the important properties of the semantics. We want the embedding to validate the intuitive meaning of the judgements of λ^K's static semantics. If κ_1 is a subkind of κ_2 then we want the embedded kind $[\![\kappa_1]\!]$ to be a subtype

$$
\begin{array}{rcl}
[\![\alpha]\!] & \stackrel{\text{def}}{=} & \alpha \\
[\![\lambda\alpha{:}\kappa.c]\!] & \stackrel{\text{def}}{=} & \lambda\alpha.[\![c]\!] \\
[\![c_1[c_2]]\!] & \stackrel{\text{def}}{=} & [\![c_1]\!][\![c_2]\!] \\
[\![\{\ell_1 = c_1, \ldots, \ell_n = c_n\}]\!] & \stackrel{\text{def}}{=} & \lambda a.\ \mathit{if}\ a =_A \ell_1\ \mathit{then}\ [\![c_1]\!] \\
& & \quad \vdots \\
& & \quad \mathit{else\ if}\ a =_A \ell_n\ \mathit{then}\ [\![c_n]\!] \\
& & \quad \mathit{else\ junk} \\
& & \text{(where } a \text{ does not appear free in } c_i\text{)} \\
[\![\pi_\ell(c)]\!] & \stackrel{\text{def}}{=} & [\![c]\!]\,\ell \\
[\![c_1 \to c_2]\!] & \stackrel{\text{def}}{=} & [\![c_1]\!] \to \overline{[\![c_2]\!]} \\
[\![c_1 \Rightarrow c_2]\!] & \stackrel{\text{def}}{=} & [\![c_1]\!] \to [\![c_2]\!] \\
[\![\forall\alpha{:}\kappa.c]\!] & \stackrel{\text{def}}{=} & \Pi\alpha{:}[\![\kappa]\!].[\![c]\!] \\
[\![\{\ell_1 : c_1, \ldots, \ell_n : c_n\}]\!] & \stackrel{\text{def}}{=} & \Pi a{:}\mathit{Atom}.\ \mathit{if}\ a =_A \ell_1\ \mathit{then}\ [\![c_1]\!] \\
& & \qquad \vdots \\
& & \qquad \mathit{else\ if}\ a =_A \ell_n\ \mathit{then}\ [\![c_n]\!] \\
& & \qquad \mathit{else\ Top} \\
& & \text{(where } a \text{ does not appear free in } c_i\text{)}
\end{array}
$$

Figure 4 Embedding Types

of $[\![\kappa_2]\!]$; if c_1 and c_2 are equal in kind κ, we want the embedded constructors $[\![c_1]\!]$ and $[\![c_2]\!]$ to be equal (in $[\![\kappa]\!]$); and if e has type τ we want $[\![e]\!]$ to have type $\overline{[\![\tau]\!]}$ (and $[\![\tau]\!]$ if e is valuable). This is stated in Theorem 1:

Theorem 1 (Semantic Soundness) *Suppose* $\Delta = [\alpha_1 : \kappa_1] \cdots [\alpha_n : \kappa_n]$ *and* $\Gamma = [x_1 : c_1] \cdots [x_m : c_m]$, *then the following implications hold:*

1. *If* $\Delta \vdash_K \kappa \sqsubseteq \kappa'$ *then* $\alpha_1{:}[\![\kappa_1]\!], \ldots, \alpha_n{:}[\![\kappa_n]\!] \vdash_\nu ([\![\kappa]\!] \sqsubseteq [\![\kappa']\!] \wedge [\![\kappa]\!] \in \mathbb{U}_{level(\kappa)+1} \wedge [\![\kappa']\!] \in \mathbb{U}_{level(\kappa')+1})$.
2. *If* $\Delta \vdash_K c = c' : \kappa$ *then* $\alpha_1{:}[\![\kappa_1]\!], \ldots, \alpha_n{:}[\![\kappa_n]\!] \vdash_\nu [\![c]\!] = [\![c']\!]$ *in* $[\![\kappa]\!]$.
3. *If* $\Delta; \Gamma \vdash_K e : c$ *then* $\alpha_1{:}[\![\kappa_1]\!], \ldots, \alpha_n{:}[\![\kappa_n]\!], x_1{:}[\![c_1]\!], \ldots, x_m{:}[\![c_m]\!] \vdash_\nu [\![e]\!] \in \overline{[\![c]\!]}$.
4. *If* $\Delta; \Gamma \vdash_K e \downarrow c$ *then* $\alpha_1{:}[\![\kappa_1]\!], \ldots, \alpha_n{:}[\![\kappa_n]\!], x_1{:}[\![c_1]\!], \ldots, x_m{:}[\![c_m]\!] \vdash_\nu [\![e]\!] \in [\![c]\!]$.

Proof. By induction on the derivations of the λ^K judgements.

We may observe two immediate consequences of the soundness theorem. One is the desirable property of type preservation: evaluation does not change

$$
\begin{aligned}
[\![x]\!] &\stackrel{\text{def}}{=} x \\
[\![\lambda x{:}c.e]\!] &\stackrel{\text{def}}{=} \lambda x.[\![e]\!] \\
[\![e_1 e_2]\!] &\stackrel{\text{def}}{=} \mathit{let}\ x = [\![e_2]\!]\ \mathit{in}\ [\![e_1]\!]\, x \\
&\qquad \text{(where } x \text{ does not appear free in } e_1\text{)} \\
[\![\Lambda\alpha{:}\kappa.e]\!] &\stackrel{\text{def}}{=} \lambda\alpha.[\![e]\!] \\
[\![e[c]]\!] &\stackrel{\text{def}}{=} [\![e]\!][\![c]\!] \\
[\![\{\ell_1 = e_1, \ldots, \ell_n = e_n\}]\!] &\stackrel{\text{def}}{=} \mathit{let}\ x_1 = [\![e_1]\!]\ \mathit{in} \\
&\qquad \vdots \\
&\qquad \mathit{let}\ x_n = [\![e_n]\!]\ \mathit{in} \\
&\qquad \lambda a.\ \mathit{if}\ a =_A \ell_1\ \mathit{then}\ x_1 \\
&\qquad\qquad \vdots \\
&\qquad\qquad \mathit{else\ if}\ a =_A \ell_n\ \mathit{then}\ x_n \\
&\qquad\qquad \mathit{else\ junk} \\
&\qquad \text{(where } x_i \text{ does not appear free in } e_j\text{)} \\
[\![\pi_\ell(e)]\!] &\stackrel{\text{def}}{=} [\![e]\!]\,\ell \\
[\![\mathit{fix}_c(e)]\!] &\stackrel{\text{def}}{=} \mathit{fix}(\lambda g.[\![e]\!](\lambda x.g\, x)) \\
&\qquad \text{(where } g \text{ does not appear free in } e\text{)}
\end{aligned}
$$

Figure 5 Embedding Terms

the type of a program. The evaluation of t in one step to t' is denoted by $t \mapsto t'$. Type preservation of λ^K (Corollary 3) follows directly from soundness and type preservation of Nuprl (Proposition 2).

Proposition 2 *If* $\vdash_\nu t \in T$ *and* $t \mapsto^* t'$ *then* $t' \in T$.

Proof. Not difficult, but outside the scope of this paper (see Crary (1998c)).

Corollary 3 (Type Preservation) *If* $\vdash_K e : \tau$ *and* $[\![e]\!] \mapsto^* t$ *then* $t \in [\![\tau]\!]$.

Another consequence of the soundness theorem is that the phase distinction (Harper *et al.*, 1990) is respected in λ^K: all type expressions converge and therefore types may be computed in a compile-time phase. This is expressed by Corollary 4:

Corollary 4 (Phase Distinction) *If* $\vdash_K c : \kappa$ *then there exists canonical* t *such that* $[\![c]\!] \mapsto^* t$.

Proof. For any well-formed λ^K kind κ, the embedded kind $[\![\kappa]\!]$ can easily be

$$
\begin{aligned}
[\![\mathit{Type}_i]\!] &\stackrel{\text{def}}{=} \{T : \mathbb{U}_i \mid T \ \mathit{admissible}\} \\
[\![\mathcal{P}_i(c)]\!] &\stackrel{\text{def}}{=} \{T : \mathbb{U}_i \mid T \sqsubseteq [\![c]\!] \wedge [\![c]\!] \ \mathit{in} \ \mathbb{U}_i \wedge T \ \mathit{admissible}\} \\
&\qquad \text{(where } T \text{ does not appear free in } c\text{)} \\
[\![\mathcal{S}_i(c)]\!] &\stackrel{\text{def}}{=} \{T : \mathbb{U}_i \mid T = [\![c]\!] \ \mathit{in} \ \mathbb{U}_i \wedge T \ \mathit{admissible}\} \\
&\qquad \text{(where } T \text{ does not appear free in } c\text{)} \\
[\![\Pi\alpha{:}\kappa_1.\kappa_2]\!] &\stackrel{\text{def}}{=} \Pi\alpha{:}[\![\kappa_1]\!].[\![\kappa_2]\!]
\end{aligned}
$$

$$
\begin{aligned}
&[\![\{\ell_1 \triangleright \alpha_1 : \kappa_1, \ldots, \ell_n \triangleright \alpha_n : \kappa_n\}]\!] \\
&\stackrel{\text{def}}{=} \quad \{f \mid a{:}\mathit{Atom} \to \mathit{if}\ a =_A \ell_1 \ \mathit{then}\ [\![\kappa_1]\!] \\
&\qquad\qquad \mathit{else\ if}\ a =_A \ell_2 \ \mathit{then}\ [\![\kappa_2]\!][f\,\ell_1/\alpha_1] \\
&\qquad\qquad \vdots \\
&\qquad\qquad \mathit{else\ if}\ a =_A \ell_n \ \mathit{then} \\
&\qquad\qquad\quad [\![\kappa_n]\!][f\,\ell_1 \cdots f\,\ell_{n-1}/\alpha_1 \cdots \alpha_{n-1}] \\
&\qquad\qquad \mathit{else}\ \mathit{Top}\} \\
&\text{(where } f, a \text{ do not appear free in } \kappa_i\text{)}
\end{aligned}
$$

Figure 6 Embedding Kinds

shown to be a total type. (Intuitively, every type is total unless it is constructed using the partial type constructor, which is not used in the embedding of kinds.) The conclusion follows directly.

5 DIRECTIONS FOR FUTURE INVESTIGATION

One important avenue for future work is to extend the semantics in this paper to explain stateful computation. One promising device for doing this is to encode stateful computations as monads (Peyton Jones and Wadler, 1993), but this raises two difficulties. In order to encode references in monads, all expressions that may side-effect the store must take the store as an argument. The problem is how to assign a type to the store. Since side-effecting functions may be in the store themselves, the store must be typed using a recursive type, and since side-effecting expressions take the store as an argument, that recursive type will include *negative* occurrences of the variable of recursion. Type theory may express recursive types with only positive occurrences, but to allow negative occurrences is an open problem.*

The other main problem arising with a monadic interpretation of state has

*See Birkedal and Harper (1997) for a promising approach that may lead to a solution of this problem.

to do with predicativity. If polymorphic functions may be placed into the store, every function type, when monadized to take the store as an argument, will have a level as high as the highest level appearing in the store. Consequently, those monadized function types will not be valid arguments to some type abstractions when they should be. The obvious solution to this problem is to restrict references to be built with level-1 (non-polymorphic) types only. A more general solution would be to use a type theory with impredicative features. In addition to solving this problem, this would also eliminate the need for level annotations in the source calculus. The type theory of Mendler (1987) provides such impredicative features and is quite similar to Nuprl; I have not used that framework in this paper out of desire to use a simpler and more standard theory. The Calculus of Constructions (Coquand and Huet, 1988) also supplies impredicative features and could likely also support the semantics in this paper.

6 CONCLUSION

Aside from its advantages for formal program reasoning, embedding programming languages into type theory allows a researcher to bring the full power of type theory to bear on a programming problem. For example, Crary (1997) used a type-theoretic interpretation to expose the relation of power kinds to a nonconstructive set type. Adjusting this interpretation to make the power kind constructive resulted in a proof-passing technique used to implement higher-order coercive subtyping in KML.

Furthermore, the simplicity of the semantics makes it attractive to use as a mathematical model similar in spirit, if not in detail, to the Scott-Strachey program (Scott and Stratchey, 1971). This semantics works out so neatly because type theory provides built-in structure well-suited for analysis of programming. Most importantly, type theory provides structured data and an intrinsic notion of computation. Non-type-theoretic models of type theory can expose the "scaffolding" when one desires the details of how that structure may be implemented.

As a theory of structured data and computation, type theory is itself a very expressive programming language. Practical programming languages are less expressive, but offer properties that foundational type theory does not, such as decidable type checking. I suggest that it is profitable to take type theory as a foundation for programming, and to view practical programming languages as *tractable approximations* of type theory. This paper illustrates how to formalize these approximations. This view not only helps to *explain* programming languages and their features, as I have done in this paper, but also provides a greater insight into how we can bring more of the expressiveness of type theory into programming languages.

REFERENCES

Allen, S. (1987) A non-type-theoretic definition of Martin-Löf's types. In *Second IEEE Symposium on Logic in Computer Science*, pages 215–221, Ithaca, New York.

Birkedal, L. and Harper, R. (1997) Relational interpretations of recursive types in an operational setting. In *Theoretical Aspects of Computer Software.*

Constable, R., Allen, S., Bromley, H., Cleaveland, W., Cremer, J., Harper, R., Howe, D., Knoblock, T., Mendler, N., Panangaden, P., Sasaki, J., and Smith, S. (1986) *Implementing Mathematics with the Nuprl Proof Development System.* Prentice-Hall.

Constable, R. L. (1985) Constructive mathematics as a programming logic I: Some principles of theory. In *Topics in the Theory of Computation*, volume 24 of *Annals of Discrete Mathematics*, pages 21–37. Elsevier. Selected papers of the International Conference on Foundations of Computation Theory 1983.

Constable, R. L. (1991) Type theory as a foundation for computer science. In *Theoretical Aspects of Computer Software 1991*, volume 526 of *Lecture Notes in Computer Science*, pages 226–243, Sendai, Japan. Springer-Verlag.

Constable, R. L. and Crary, K. (1997) Computational complexity and induction for partial computable functions in type theory. Technical report, Department of Computer Science, Cornell University.

Constable, R. L. and Smith, S. F. (1987) Partial objects in constructive type theory. In *Second IEEE Symposium on Logic in Computer Science*, pages 183–193, Ithaca, New York.

Coquand, T. and Huet, G. (1988) The calculus of constructions. *Information and Computation*, **76**:95–120.

Crary, K. (1997) Foundations for the implementation of higher-order subtyping. In *1997 ACM SIGPLAN International Conference on Functional Programming*, pages 125–135, Amsterdam.

Crary, K. (1998a) Admissibility of fixpoint induction over partial types. Technical report, Department of Computer Science, Cornell University.

Crary, K. (1998b) Programming language semantics in foundational type theory. Technical Report TR98-1666, Department of Computer Science, Cornell University.

Crary, K. (1998c) *Type-Theoretic Methodology for Practical Programming Languages.* PhD thesis, Department of Computer Science, Cornell University, Ithaca, New York. Forthcoming.

Girard, J.-Y. (1972) *Interprétation fonctionelle et élimination des coupures de l'arithmétique d'ordre supérieur.* PhD thesis, Université Paris VII.

Harper, R. (1992) Constructing type systems over an operational semantics. *Journal of Symbolic Computation*, **14**:71–84.

Harper, R. and Lillibridge, M. (1994) A type-theoretic approach to higher-order modules with sharing. In *Twenty-First ACM SIGACT-SIGPLAN Symposium on Principles of Programming Languages*, pages 123–137, Portland, Oregon.

Harper, R. and Mitchell, J. C. (1993) On the type structure of Standard ML. *ACM Transactions on Programming Languages and Systems*, **15**(2):211–252.

Harper, R., Mitchell, J. C., and Moggi, E. (1990) Higher-order modules and the phase distinction. In *Seventeenth ACM SIGACT-SIGPLAN Symposium on Principles of Programming Languages*, pages 341–354, San Francisco.

Harper, R. and Stone, C. (1998) A type-theoretic interpretation of Standard ML. In *Proof, Language and Interaction: Essays in Honour of Robin Milner*. The MIT Press. To appear.

Hickey, J. J. (1996) Formal objects in type theory using very dependent types. In *Foundations of Object Oriented Languages 3*.

Howard, W. (1980) The formulas-as-types notion of construction. In Seldin, J. P. and Hindley, J. R., editors, *To H.B. Curry: Essays on Combinatory Logic, Lambda-Calculus and Formalism*, pages 479–490. Academic Press.

Howe, D. J. (1996) Semantic foundations for embedding HOL in Nuprl. Technical report, Bell Labs.

Kreitz, C. (1997) Formal reasoning about communications systems I. Technical report, Department of Computer Science, Cornell University.

Martin-Löf, P. (1982) Constructive mathematics and computer programming. In *Sixth International Congress of Logic, Methodology and Philosophy of Science*, volume 104 of *Studies in Logic and the Foundations of Mathematics*, pages 153–175. North-Holland.

Mendler, P. F. (1987) *Inductive Definition in Type Theory*. PhD thesis, Department of Computer Science, Cornell University, Ithaca, New York.

Milner, R., Tofte, M., Harper, R., and MacQueen, D. (1997) *The Definition of Standard ML (Revised)*. The MIT Press, Cambridge, Massachusetts.

Palmgren, E. and Stoltenberg-Hansen, V. (1989) Domain interpretations of intuitionistic type theory. U.U.D.M. Report 1989:1, Uppsala University, Department of Mathematics.

Peyton Jones, S. L. and Wadler, P. (1993) Imperative functional programming. In *Twentieth ACM SIGACT-SIGPLAN Symposium on Principles of Programming Languages*, Charleston, South Carolina.

Reynolds, J. C. (1981) The essence of Algol. In de Bakker, J. W. and van Vliet, J. C., editors, *Proceedings of the International Symposium on Algorithmic Languages*, pages 345–372, Amsterdam. North-Holland.

Rezus, A. (1985) Semantics of constructive type theory. Technical Report 70, Informatics Department, Faculty of Science, Nijmegen, University, The Netherlands.

Scott, D. and Strachey, C. (1971) Toward a mathematical semantics for computer languages. In *Proceedings of the Symposium on Computers and Automata*, volume 21 of *Microwave Research Institute Symposia Series*. Polytechnic Institute of Brooklyn.

Smith, S. F. (1989) *Partial Objects in Type Theory*. PhD thesis, Department of Computer Science, Cornell University, Ithaca, New York.

BIOGRAPHY

Karl Crary earned his B.S. in Computer Science from Carnegie Mellon University in 1993 and is now a Ph.D. candidate at Cornell University. His main interests include programming language design and semantics, type theory, and typed compilation.

12
An Algebraic Approach to the Specification of Stochastic Systems (Extended Abstract)

P. R. D'Argenio[1,*], *J.-P. Katoen*[2], *and E. Brinksma*[1]

[1]*Dept. of Computer Science. University of Twente.*
P.O.Box 217. 7500 AE Enschede. The Netherlands.
`{dargenio,brinksma}@cs.utwente.nl`

[2]*Lehrstuhl für Informatik VII. University of Erlangen-Nürnberg.*
Martensstrasse 3. D-91058 Erlangen. Germany.
`katoen@informatik.uni-erlangen.de`

Abstract

We introduce a framework to study stochastic systems, i.e. systems in which the time of occurrence of activities is a general random variable. We introduce and discuss in depth a stochastic process algebra (named ♤) adequate to specify and analyse those systems. In order to give semantics to ♤, we also introduce a model that is an extension of traditional automata with clocks which are basically random variables: the stochastic automata model. We show that this model and ♤ are equally expressive. Although stochastic automata are adequate to analyse systems since they are finite objects, they are still too coarse to serve as concrete semantic objects. Therefore, we introduce a type of probabilistic transition system that can deal with arbitrary probability spaces. In addition, we give a finite axiomatisation for ♤ that is sound for the several semantic notions we deal with, and complete for the finest of them. Moreover, an expansion law is straightforwardly derived.

Keywords

Stochastic process algebras, stochastic automata, probabilistic transition systems, probabilistic bisimulations, real-time systems.

1 INTRODUCTION

In the world of performance modelling, many models have been defined to analyse and simulate systems such as queuing networks, stochastic Petri-nets, or generalised semi-Markov processes. It has been argued many times that,

---

*Supported by the NWO/SION project 612-33-006.

Programming Concepts and Methods D. Gries, & W-P. de Roever (Eds.)

with these models, the difficulty of the design and analysis of a system grows rapidly with the size and complexity of the system itself.

In the last few years, this phenomenon has drawn the attention of many researchers into extending process algebras with stochastic and real-time features [16, 11, 13, 4, 6, 5, ...]. The so called *stochastic process algebras* considerably simplify the tractability of complex systems because, in this framework, systems do not need to be modelled as a whole, but as a composition of small subsystems. Another advantage is that stochastic process algebras not only allow to study the performance of a system, but also its functionality.

In this article, we have a three-folded purpose: we discuss a probabilistic transition system model based on general distributions, we introduce a stochastic automata model which borrows ideas from both timed automata [2, 14] and generalised semi-Markov processes (GSMP, for short) [26, 10], and finally we introduce and discuss in depth a stochastic process algebra.

Probabilistic transition systems (PTS, for short) have been widely studied in the context of discrete probabilities [25, 17, 12, 19, 23, 9, ...]. However, the case with general distributions has received scant attention [13, 22]. In the first part of our paper we define probabilistic transition systems that deal with any kind of probabilistic spaces, including thus discrete, continuous, and singular. This generality allows the specification of real–time systems in which time constraints are not necessarily deterministic but dependent on random variables. Our definition is basically a generalisation and formalisation of [13].

Although PTSs are an adequate framework for the understanding of processes with stochastic behaviour, they are highly infinite which makes them too difficult to deal with. Therefore, we also introduce the so-called *stochastic automata*. A stochastic automaton is an automaton extended with clocks. Clocks are variables which take some random value which is set according to a given probability distribution. Once set, clocks count down, and when they reach value zero, they may enable certain transitions in the automaton. We define the semantics of stochastic automata in terms of PTSs. In fact, we define two different kinds of semantics: one when the stochastic automaton is regarded as a *closed* system, i.e., when the system is complete by itself and no external interaction is required, and the other when it is regarded as an *open* system, that is, a system that cooperates with the environment or is intended to be part of a larger system. Interpretation of stochastic automata as closed systems is adequate for the final analysis of the system, e.g. to study the performance or to verify the whole system. Instead, the interpretation as open systems is appropriate to study compositionality and to analyse how systems behave in contexts.

Compositionality is a major drawback in many existing models for performance analysis such as queuing networks, stochastic Petri nets, or GSMPs, specially, in non-Markovian models. On the contrary, stochastic automata offer an appropriate framework to straightforwardly compose systems. In fact, because of its simplicity, we use stochastic automata as the underlying semantics of a stochastic process algebra that allows to express general distributions. Actually, the stochastic automata model and the process algebra turn out to be equally expressive. In this way, the process algebra can be regarded as a language to describe stochastic automata. This result closely follows the methodology of [7] where a process calculus for timed automata was introduced. Since a stochastic automaton can be executed using discrete event simulation techniques, the process algebra is called SPADES standing for *stochastic process algebra for discrete event simulation*, but we just write ♤.

Usually, the semantics of stochastic process algebras such as TIPP [11, 15], PEPA [16], and EMPA [4], is defined in terms of extended transition systems, which basically associate a distribution function to each transition. However, the inherent interleaving characteristic of transition systems demands a careful treatment of the definition of parallel composition. In traditional interleaving process algebras like CCS [18] the expansion law plays an important role: it says how parallel composition can be decomposed in terms of more primitive operations, namely, prefixing and non-deterministic choice. Stochastic process algebras extend prefixing into $a_F; P$ where F is a distribution function which determines the probability of the random delay after which the action a can happen. In this setting, the expansion law does no longer hold in general. To face this problem, the community has come up with different solutions.

A first proposal, and the most widely accepted, has been to restrict the attention to exponential distributions. Their memoryless property restores the expansion law [16, 15, 4]. Others have faced the general case [11, 13, 20] but the underlying semantic object usually becomes cumbersome and infinite, which makes it intractable. An alternative solution is to drop the expansion law by moving to true concurrency models [6], but for simple recursive processes, their semantic representations are infinite.

We propose a more elegant solution for ♤. We separate the stochastic information from the action name. (We remark that a similar approach has been used in [13].) Instead of writing $a_F; P$, we write $\{\!|x_F|\!\}(\{x_F\}\mapsto a; P)$. The operator $\{\!|x_F|\!\}\ldots$ sets the clock x_F according to the distribution function F, and the operation $\{x_F\}\mapsto\ldots$ prevents the prefixing $a; P$ to happen until clock x_F has expired (i.e., reached value 0). This separation of concerns gives as a result a straightforward expansion law, and moreover, it introduces more expressive power. We observe that in principle *any* kind of (continuous, discrete, ...) distribution function is allowed in this model, while we maintain a finite semantic object in a reasonable way (comparable to regular processes in CCS).

The paper is organised as follows. Section 2 discusses probabilistic transition systems and probabilistic bisimilarity for general probability spaces. In Section 3, we define the stochastic automata model and study its semantics. In Section 4, we discuss ♤ in depth including its semantics and axiomatisation. We discuss related work and further research in Section 5.

The complete report of this article, including proofs, rigorous definitions, and detailed technicalities, is given in [8].

2 PROBABILISTIC TRANSITION SYSTEMS

In this section, we introduce the notion of probabilistic transition systems and probabilistic bisimulation.

Preliminaries. Let $\mathbb{N}$ be the set of non-negative integers. Let $\mathbb{R}$ be the set of real numbers and $\mathbb{R}_{\geq 0}$ the set of non-negative reals. For $n \in \mathbb{N}$, let $\mathbb{R}^n$ denote the nth Cartesian product of $\mathbb{R}$. In particular, $\mathbb{R}^0 \stackrel{\text{def}}{=} \{\emptyset\}$.

A *probability space* is a structure $(\Omega, \mathcal{F}, P)$ where Ω is a *sample space*, $\mathcal{F}$ is a σ*-algebra* on Ω, and P is a *probability measure* on $\mathcal{F}$. In this work, we consider only probability spaces isomorphic to some Borel space defined in a real hyper-space, whose coordinates come from independent random variables. We denote by $\mathcal{R}(F_1, \ldots, F_n)$ the probability space $(\mathbb{R}^n, \mathcal{B}(\mathbb{R}^n), P_n)$ where $\mathcal{B}(\mathbb{R}^n)$ is the Borel algebra on $\mathbb{R}^n$ and P_n is the unique probability measure obtained from $F_1, \ldots, F_n$, a given family of distribution functions. In particular, if $n = 0$, $\mathcal{R}()$ is the trivial probability space $(\{\emptyset\}, \{\emptyset, \{\emptyset\}\}, P_0)$ with P_0 in the obvious way. We refer to [24] for further reading.

Let $\mathcal{P} = (\Omega, \mathcal{F}, P)$ be a probability space. Let $\mathcal{D} : \Omega \to \Omega'$ be an injective function. We lift $\mathcal{D}$ to subsets of Ω as usual: $\mathcal{D}(A) \stackrel{\text{def}}{=} \{\mathcal{D}(a) \mid a \in A\}$ and define $\mathcal{F}' \stackrel{\text{def}}{=} \{\mathcal{D}(A) \mid A \in \mathcal{F}\}$. Now, it is clear that, $\mathcal{D}(\mathcal{P}) \stackrel{\text{def}}{=} (\mathcal{D}(\Omega), \mathcal{F}', P \circ \mathcal{D}^{-1})$ is also a probability space. Since $\mathcal{D}(\mathcal{P})$ is basically the same probability space as $\mathcal{P}$, we say that $\mathcal{D}$ is a *decoration* and we refer to $\mathcal{D}(\mathcal{P})$ as the *decoration of* $\mathcal{P}$ *according to* $\mathcal{D}$. Decoration functions are a key concept in the probabilistic part of the stochastic automata semantics.

Probabilistic transition systems. We introduce a transition system with probabilistic information. We allow any kind of probability spaces, including continuous distributions. The definition of our model is inspired by [12] and [13], although we do not consider explicit timed transitions.

Definition 1 Let *Prob*(H) denote the set of probability spaces $(\Omega, \mathcal{F}, P)$ such that $\Omega \subseteq H$. A *probabilistic transition system* (PTS for short) is a structure $\mathcal{T} = (\Sigma, \Sigma', \sigma_0, \mathcal{L}, T, \longrightarrow)$ where

1. Σ and Σ' are two disjoint sets of *states*, with the *initial state* $\sigma_0 \in \Sigma$. States in Σ are called *probabilistic* and states in Σ' are *non-deterministic*.
2. $\mathcal{L}$ is a set of *labels*.
3. $T : \Sigma \to \mathit{Prob}(\Sigma')$ is the *probabilistic transition relation*.
4. $\longrightarrow \subseteq \Sigma' \times \mathcal{L} \times \Sigma$ is the *labelled (or non-deterministic) transition relation*. We denote $\sigma' \xrightarrow{\ell} \sigma$ for $\langle \sigma', \ell, \sigma \rangle \in \longrightarrow$, and $\sigma' \stackrel{\ell}{\not\longrightarrow}$ for $\neg\exists\sigma.\, \sigma' \xrightarrow{\ell} \sigma$. □

Since T is defined as a (total) function, each probabilistic state has exactly one outgoing transition. It can be shown that if *Prob*(Σ') contains only discrete probability spaces, PTSs are as expressive as the simple probabilistic automata of [23] and strictly more expressive than the class of reactive PTSs [17, 9].

Since our interest is to deal with time information using PTSs, the set of labels we will use is $\mathcal{L} = \mathbf{A} \times \mathbb{R}_{\geq 0}$, where $\mathbf{A}$ is a set of action names and $\mathbb{R}_{\geq 0}$ is the set of non-negative real numbers, which are intended to denote the (relative) time at which an action takes place. We usually denote $a(d)$ instead of (a, d) whenever $(a, d) \in \mathcal{L}$ and it means "action a occurs right after the system has been idle for d time units".

Probabilistic bisimulation. Probabilistic bisimulation was introduced in [17] for a class of PTSs dealing only with discrete probability spaces. This definition has been adapted in [9, 12, 23] for several variants of PTSs, all of them in a discrete probabilistic setting. Bisimulations have also been defined in settings where exponential distributions are involved [16, 15, 4]. [13] has defined bisimulation in a continuous setting and [22] used a coalgebraic approach for the general setting. In essence, our definition coincides with the one in [13].

Definition 2 Let $(\Sigma, \Sigma', \sigma_0, \mathcal{L}, T, \longrightarrow)$ be a PTS. We define the function $\mu : \Sigma \times \wp(\Sigma') \to [0,1]$ by $\mu(\sigma, S) \stackrel{\text{def}}{=}$ **if** $S \cap \Omega \in \mathcal{F}$ **then** $P(S \cap \Omega)$ **else** 0, provided that $T(\sigma) = (\Omega, \mathcal{F}, P)$.

Let R be an equivalence relation on $\Sigma \cup \Sigma'$ such that if $\sigma_1 R \sigma_2$ then either $\sigma_1, \sigma_2 \in \Sigma$ or $\sigma_1, \sigma_2 \in \Sigma'$. Let Σ'/R be the set of equivalence classes in Σ' induced by R. Then R is a *(probabilistic) bisimulation* if, whenever $\sigma_1 R \sigma_2$, for all $S \subseteq \Sigma'/R$ and $\ell \in \mathcal{L}$, the following transfer properties hold

1. $\mu(\sigma_1, \bigcup S) = \mu(\sigma_2, \bigcup S)$, if $\sigma_1, \sigma_2 \in \Sigma$; and
2. $\sigma_1 \stackrel{\ell}{\longrightarrow} \sigma_1'$ implies $\sigma_2 \stackrel{\ell}{\longrightarrow} \sigma_2'$ and $\sigma_1' R \sigma_2'$, for some $\sigma_2' \in \Sigma$, if $\sigma_1, \sigma_2 \in \Sigma'$.

Two states σ_1 and σ_2 are *(probabilistically) bisimilar*, notation $\sigma_1 \underline{\leftrightarrow} \sigma_2$, if there exists a probabilistic bisimulation R with $\sigma_1 R \sigma_2$. Two PTSs $\mathcal{T}_1$ and $\mathcal{T}_2$ are *bisimilar*, notation $\mathcal{T}_1 \underline{\leftrightarrow} \mathcal{T}_2$, if their respective initial states are bisimilar on the disjoint union of $\mathcal{T}_1$ and $\mathcal{T}_2$. □

It can be proven that $\underline{\leftrightarrow}$ is the largest probabilistic bisimulation, and hence, that it is an equivalence relation.

Although, the definition of probabilistic bisimulation coincides with the traditional definitions in the discrete case, e.g. [17, 12, 23], we remark a necessary difference. In the discrete case, instead of property 1. above, it suffices to insist that $\mu(\sigma_1, S) = \mu(\sigma_2, S)$ where $S \in \Sigma'/R$, i.e., S is an equivalence class instead of a set of equivalence classes. In our case, this would have been too weak due to the allowance of, for instance, continuous distribution function. For example, consider the PTSs $\mathcal{T}_i = (\{\sigma\}, \mathbb{R}, \sigma, \mathbb{R}, T_i, \longrightarrow)$, $i \in \{1, 2\}$, where $d \stackrel{d}{\longrightarrow} \sigma$, and $T_1(\sigma)$ and $T_2(\sigma)$ are the probability spaces for a uniform distribution on $[0,1]$ and $[1,2]$, respectively. According to Definition 2, $\mathcal{T}_1$ and $\mathcal{T}_2$ are not bisimilar, since they do not agree in their probabilities. However, the weaker property of the discrete case would have induced that the identity relation is a probabilistic bisimulation since the probability of a point in a continuous probability space is always zero.

3 THE STOCHASTIC AUTOMATON MODEL

In this section, we introduce a new automaton model that allows us to represent processes with stochastic information. The basic idea is borrowed from timed automata [2, 14] by combining it with ideas of discrete event systems, in particular GSMPs [10, 26]. Besides, we study two different semantic models for stochastic automata.

Stochastic Automata. We first enumerate all the ingredients of a stochastic automaton and then give an example to explain the intuition behind the definition.

Definition 3 A *stochastic automaton* is a structure $(\mathcal{S}, s_0, \mathcal{C}, \mathbf{A}, \longrightarrow, \kappa, F)$ where:

- $\mathcal{S}$ is a set of *locations* with $s_0 \in \mathcal{S}$ being the *initial location*.
- $\mathcal{C}$ is a set of *clocks*.
- $\mathbf{A}$ is a set of *actions*
- $\longrightarrow \subseteq \mathcal{S} \times (\mathbf{A} \times \wp_{\text{fin}}(\mathcal{C})) \times \mathcal{S}$ is the set of *edges*. We denote the edge $(s, a, C, s') \in \longrightarrow$ by $s \xrightarrow{a,C} s'$ and we say that C is its *trigger set*.
- $\kappa : \mathcal{S} \to \wp_{\text{fin}}(\mathcal{C})$ is the *clock setting function*.
- $F : \mathcal{C} \to (\mathbb{R} \to [0,1])$ assigns to each clock a *distribution function* such that $F(x)(t) = 0$ for $t < 0$; we write F_x instead of $F(x)$.

Notice that each clock $x \in \mathcal{C}$ is a random variable with distribution F_x. □

As in [7], the information of which clock should be set is related to the locations. Clocks are randomly set according to a certain associated distribution function and they count down. A clock expires if it has reached the value 0. The occurrence of an action is controlled by the expiration of clocks. Thus, whenever $s \xrightarrow{a,C} s'$ and the system is in location s, a happens as soon as all the clocks in the trigger set C have expired. Immediately afterwards all clocks in $\kappa(s')$ are randomly set according to their respective distributions.

Example 1 Figure 1 represents a switch that controls a light. In the picture, circles represent locations, variables enumerated in each location are the clocks that are to be set according to the function κ, and edges are represented by the arrows. The initial location is represented by a small ingoing arrow. The distribution function of each clock is given beside the picture.

The switch may be turned on at any time according to an exponential distribution with average of 30 minutes, even if the light is still on. It switches automatically off exactly 2 minutes after the most recent time the light was switched on. Since we considered that exactly 2 minutes must pass before the light is turned off, y is a random variable that takes value 2 with probability 1. Notice that we can easily change the system to consider that clock y is not

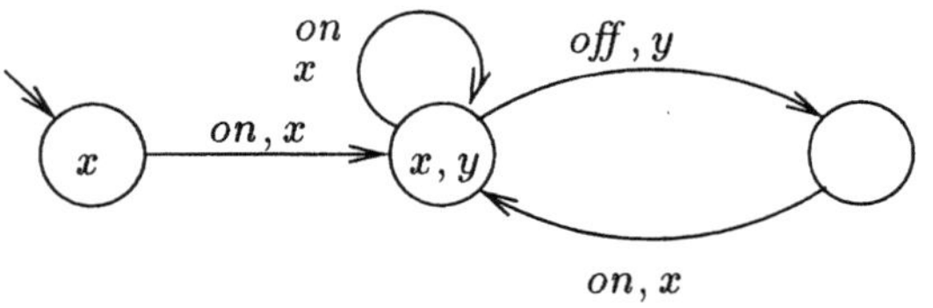

Figure 1 The switch

precise and has a drift of ϵ units of time. If, for instance, we assume that such a drift is uniformly distributed, then y would become a random variable with a uniform distribution in $[2-\epsilon, 2+\epsilon]$. □

Actual behaviour. In this subsection, we define the semantics of stochastic automata when it is regarded as a closed system. A *closed system* is a system which is considered complete by itself and no external interaction is needed. In this kind of system one not only models the components of the intended system but also the environment with which it interacts. In this way, the activity of the whole system can take place as soon as it becomes ready to be executed since there is no external agent that may delay its execution. That is, closed systems respond to the *maximal progress* property. We refer to this interpretation as the *actual behaviour*.

First, we introduce some background concepts, then we state which are the probabilistic spaces that we use, and finally we define the actual behaviour of stochastic automata.

A *valuation* is a function $v : \mathcal{C} \to \mathbb{R}$. Let $\mathcal{V}$ be the set of all valuations. If $d \in \mathbb{R}_{\geq 0}$, we define $v - d$ by $\forall x \in \mathcal{C}.\ (v-d)(x) \stackrel{\text{def}}{=} v(x) - d$. For simplicity, assume the set $\mathcal{C}$ of clock is totally ordered. Thus, if $C \subseteq \mathcal{C}$, we write $\overrightarrow{C}$ for the ordered form of C and $\overrightarrow{C}(i)$ for its i-th element. Let $C \subseteq \mathcal{C}$, $n = \#C$, and $\overrightarrow{D} \in \mathbb{R}^n$. We define $v[\overrightarrow{C} \leftarrow \overrightarrow{D}]$ by

$$v[\overrightarrow{C} \leftarrow \overrightarrow{D}](y) \stackrel{\text{def}}{=} \begin{cases} \overrightarrow{D}(i) & \text{if } y = \overrightarrow{C}(i), \text{ for some } i \in \{1, \ldots, n\} \\ v(y) & \text{otherwise} \end{cases}$$

Let $(\mathcal{S}, s_0, \mathcal{C}, \mathbf{A}, \longrightarrow, \kappa, F)$ be a stochastic automaton. Let s be a location in $\mathcal{S}$ and let $n = \#\kappa(s)$. Let v be a valuation in $\mathcal{V}$. Define $\mathcal{D}_v^s : \mathbb{R}^n \to \{s\} \times \mathcal{V} \times \{1\}$ by $\mathcal{D}_v^s(\overrightarrow{D}) \stackrel{\text{def}}{=} (s, v[\overrightarrow{\kappa(s)} \leftarrow \overrightarrow{D}], 1)$. Notice that $\mathcal{D}_v^s$ is injective. In the next definition we will use the probability space $\mathcal{R}(F_1, \ldots, F_n)$ decorated according to some $\mathcal{D}_v^s$.

Definition 4 Let $SA = (\mathcal{S}, s_0, \mathcal{C}, \mathbf{A}, \longrightarrow, \kappa, F)$ be a stochastic automaton. The *interpretation* (or the *actual behaviour*) of SA in a valuation v_0 is given by the PTS $I_{v_0}^A(SA) \stackrel{\text{def}}{=} ((\mathcal{S} \times \mathcal{V} \times \{0\}), (\mathcal{S} \times \mathcal{V} \times \{1\}), (s_0, v_0, 0), \mathbf{A} \times \mathbb{R}_{\geq 0}, T, \longrightarrow)$ with T and $\longrightarrow$ defined as follows

$$\textbf{Prob}\ \frac{\overrightarrow{\kappa(s)} = (x_1, \ldots, x_n)}{T(s, v, 0) \ = \ \mathcal{D}_v^s(\mathcal{R}(F_{x_1}, \ldots, F_{x_n}))}$$

$$\textbf{Act}\ \frac{s \xrightarrow{a,C} s' \qquad d \in \mathbb{R}_{\geq 0} \qquad \forall x \in C.\ (v-d)(x) \leq 0 \qquad \forall d' \in [0,d).\ \forall s \xrightarrow{b,C'}.\ \exists y \in C'.\ (v-d')(y) > 0}{(s,v,1) \xrightarrow{a(d)} (s',(v-d),0)}$$

We say that an edge $s \xrightarrow{a,C} s'$ is enabled in a valuation v if it induces a non-deterministic transition outgoing from $(s,v,1)$. In particular, notice that $s \xrightarrow{a,\emptyset} s'$ is enabled for any valuation v. □

Notice that, according to Definition 4, for each location s and valuation v there is exactly one probabilistic transition since $\mathcal{D}^s_v$ is injective. So, for any stochastic automaton SA and any valuation v_0, $I^A_{v_0}(SA)$ is indeed a PTS.

Rule **Prob** considers the setting of the clocks. Since the values of the clocks are assigned randomly, a probabilistic transition corresponds to this step. Notice that this definition relies on the definition of $\mathcal{D}^s_v$ on probability spaces. Rule **Act** explains the case of triggering an edge. So, for the occurrence of an action a at time d according to an edge $s \xrightarrow{a,C} s'$, we check that all the clocks in the trigger set C have already expired at time d. This part is considered by the satisfaction of the predicate $\forall x \in C.\ (v-d)(x) \leq 0$. Moreover, it should be the case that no edge was enabled before. That is, any edge must have an active (i.e. positive) clock at any valuation "previous" to $v-d$. In this way, the edge is forced to occur as soon as it becomes enabled. So, the maximal progress is checked by the formula $\forall d' \in [0,d).\ \forall s \xrightarrow{b,C'}.\ \exists y \in C'.\ (v-d')(y) > 0$. For the reader familiar with timed automata [2, 14], we may say that the first constraint corresponds to the guard of the edge $s \xrightarrow{a,C} s'$, and the second constraint is the invariant of location s.

Example 2. To understand the formal semantics, we consider a simple example. Figure 2 represents an alarm bell that rings randomly between 10 and 11 seconds according to a uniform distribution. We define clock x to be a random variable with a uniform distribution function F_x in the interval $[10,11]$. If s is the only location of the alarm bell, its PTS is given by

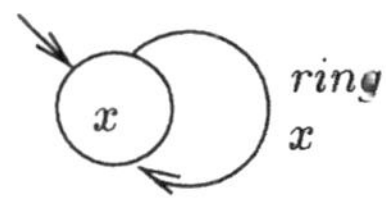

Figure 2 The alarm bell

$$\Sigma = \{(s, x \leftarrow\!\dashv d, 0) \mid d \in \mathbb{R}\} \qquad \Sigma' = \{(s, x \leftarrow\!\dashv d, 1) \mid d \in \mathbb{R}\}$$

$$T(s,v,0) = \mathcal{D}^s_v(\mathcal{R}(F_x)) \qquad (s, x := d, 1) \xrightarrow{ring(d)} (s, x := d, 0) \ \ (\text{if } d \geq 0)$$ □

We can extend the definition of probabilistic bisimulation to stochastic automata as follows.

Definition 5 Two stochastic automata SA_1 and SA_2 are *(probabilistically) bisimilar*, notation $SA_1 \leftrightarrow SA_2$, if, for every valuation v, their interpretations are bisimilar, i.e., $I^A_v(SA_1) \leftrightarrow I^A_v(SA_2)$. □

Potential behaviour. In this subsection, we define the behaviour of a stochastic automaton as an open system. An *open system* is a system that interacts with its environment. The environment can be a user or another system. Basically, an open system is a component of a larger system. When a stochastic automaton describes an open system, the semantics given in Definition 4 does not suffice. In an open system, an action that is enabled may not be executed until the environment is also ready to execute such an action. Therefore, an activity may not take place as soon as it is enabled. This kind of behaviour is appropriate to study compositionality. In fact, it turns out that probabilistic bisimilarity is not a congruence for some basic operations on stochastic automata, such as parallel composition. This has to do with the race condition on the branches of the stochastic automata. Fastest branches (i.e. branches which are enabled) may be disallowed or slowed down when the system is embedded in some context, and therefore, slower branches, which could not be executed in isolation, may become enabled in the composed stochastic automata. For a discussion of this phenomenon, we refer to Example 4.

Therefore, we need to consider not only the actual behaviour of a stochastic automaton, but also its *potential behaviour*. The potential behaviour is in principle the actual behaviour with a larger non-deterministic transition relation. A non-deterministic transition in the potential behaviour represents the fact that an edge is potentially executable at any time after it becomes enabled.

Definition 6 Let $SA = (\mathcal{S}, s_0, \mathcal{C}, \mathbf{A}, \twoheadrightarrow, \kappa, F)$ be a stochastic automaton. The *potential behaviour* of SA in a valuation v_0 is defined by the PTS $I^P_{v_0}(SA) \stackrel{\text{def}}{=} ((\mathcal{S} \times \mathcal{V} \times \{0\}), (\mathcal{S} \times \mathcal{V} \times \{1\}), (s_0, v_0, 0), \mathbf{A} \times \mathbb{R}_{\geq 0}, T, \longmapsto)$, where T is defined by rule **Prob** as in Definition 4 and $\longmapsto$ is defined as follows

$$\textbf{Pot}\ \frac{s \xrightarrow{a,C} s' \qquad d \in \mathbb{R}_{\geq 0} \qquad \forall x \in C.\ (v-d)(x) \leq 0}{(s, v, 1) \overset{a(d)}{\longmapsto} (s', (v-d), 0)}$$ □

The difference between the actual and the potential behaviour relies on rules **Act** and **Pot**. To be precise, **Pot** is the same as rule **Act** where the constraint of maximal progress has been omitted.

Definition 7 Two stochastic automata SA_1 and SA_2 are *potentially bisimilar*, notation $SA_1 \leftrightarrow_P SA_2$, if, for every valuation v, their potential behaviours are probabilistically bisimilar, i.e., $I^P_v(SA_1) \leftrightarrow I^P_v(SA_2)$. □

The following theorem states that it is always possible to recover the actual behaviour from the potential behaviour.

Theorem 8 *Let SA be a stochastic automaton and let $I^P_{v_0}(SA)$ and $I^A_{v_0}(SA)$ be its potential and actual behaviour in $v_0 \in \mathcal{V}$, respectively. The two following statements are equivalent*

1. $(s, v, 1) \overset{a(d)}{\longmapsto} (s', v', 0)$ *and for all* $d' \in [0, d)$, $b \in \mathbf{A}$, $(s, v, 1) \overset{b(d')}{\not\longmapsto}$

2. $(s, v, 1) \overset{a(d)}{\longrightarrow} (s', v', 0)$

As a consequence, we have that potential bisimulation is strictly finer than probabilistic bisimulation. That is, for two stochastic automata SA_1 *and* SA_2, $SA_1 \underline{\leftrightarrow}_P SA_2$ *implies* $SA_1 \underline{\leftrightarrow} SA_2$.

Structural bisimulation. Often, we can check if two stochastic automata are equivalent just by inspecting their structure, without the need to study their actual or potential behaviour. Thus, we define a stronger notion of equivalence which we call structural bisimulation. We also state that this relation is finer than potential bisimulation.

Definition 9 Let $(\mathcal{S}, s_0, \mathcal{C}, \mathbf{A}, \twoheadrightarrow, \kappa, F)$ be a stochastic automaton. A relation $R \subseteq \mathcal{S} \times \mathcal{S}$ is a *structural bisimulation* if R is symmetric and whenever $s_1 R s_2$, for all $a \in \mathbf{A}$, $C \subseteq \mathcal{C}$, the following transfer properties hold:

1. $s_1 \xrightarrow{a,C} s_1'$ implies $\exists s_2'.\ s_2 \xrightarrow{a,C} s_2'$ and $s_1' R s_2'$;
2. $\kappa(s_1) = \kappa(s_2)$

If R is a structural bisimulation such that $s_1 R s_2$, we denote $s_1 \underset{\sim}{\leftrightarrow} s_2$ and we say that s_1 and s_2 are structurally bisimilar. Two stochastic automata SA_1 and SA_2 are *structurally bisimilar*, notation $SA_1 \underset{\sim}{\leftrightarrow} SA_2$, if their respective initial locations are structurally bisimilar on the disjoint union of SA_1 and SA_2. □

Following standard results on bisimulation, we can prove that $\underset{\sim}{\leftrightarrow}$ is the largest structural bisimulation, and moreover, that it is an equivalence relation.

It is clear that two stochastic automata may be potentially bisimilar but not structurally bisimilar. Instead, structural bisimulation implies potential bisimulation, and hence probabilistic bisimulation, too.

Theorem 10 *Let* SA_1 *and* SA_2 *be two stochastic automata. If* $SA_1 \underset{\sim}{\leftrightarrow} SA_2$ *then* $SA_1 \underline{\leftrightarrow}_P SA_2$.

4 SPADES

In the following we introduce SPADES, denoted by ♠ and standing for *stochastic process algebra for discrete event simulation*. The methodology that we follow to define the syntax and the semantics is close to results in [7] where a process algebra for timed automata was introduced.

Syntax. Let $\mathbf{A}$ be a set of *actions*. Let $\mathcal{CN}$ be a set of clock names and $\mathcal{DF}$ a set of distribution functions. We define $\mathcal{C} \subseteq \mathcal{CN} \times \mathcal{DF}$ to be the set of clocks. We denote x_G for $(x, G) \in \mathcal{C}$. We define the distribution assignment function $F : \mathcal{C} \to (\mathrm{I\!R} \to [0, 1])$ by the second projection, i.e., $F(x_G) \overset{\mathrm{def}}{=} G$.

Definition 11 Let $\mathbf{V}$ be a set of *process variables*. The syntax of $\spadesuit$ is defined according to the following grammar:

$$p \ ::= \ \mathbf{stop} \ | \ a;p \ | \ C{\mapsto}p \ | \ p+p \ | \ \{\!|C|\!\}p \ | \ p||_A p \ | \ p|\!\!\lfloor_A p \ | \ p|_A p \ | \ p[f] \ | \ X$$

where $C \subseteq \mathcal{C}$ is finite, $a \in \mathbf{A}$, $A \subseteq \mathbf{A}$, $f : \mathbf{A} \to \mathbf{A}$, and $X \in \mathbf{V}$. A *recursive specification* E is a set of *recursive equations* having the form $X = p$ for each $X \in \mathbf{V}$, where $p \in \spadesuit$. Every recursive specification has a distinguished process variable called *root*. □

Process **stop** represents inaction; it is the process that cannot perform any action. The intended meaning of $a;p$ (named *(action-)prefixing*) is that action a is immediately enabled and once it is performed the behaviour of p is exhibit. $C{\mapsto}p$ is the *triggering condition*; process p becomes enabled as soon as all the clocks in C expire. $p + q$ is the *choice*; it behaves either as p or q, but not both. We remark that the passage of time does not resolve the choice if the process is regarded as an open system; if instead it is regarded as a closed system, the fastest process is the one to be executed. This last case is known as the race condition. The *clock setting operation* $\{\!|C|\!\}p$ sets the clocks in C according to their respective distribution function. We choose a LOTOS-like parallel composition. Thus, $p||_A q$ executes p and q in parallel, and they are synchronised by actions in A. We should remark that synchronisation may happen if both processes are ready to do it. We also introduce the operators $|\!\!\lfloor_A$ and $|_A$ (named *left* and *communication merge* respectively) in order to finitely axiomatise the parallel composition. Finally, the *renaming* operation $p[f]$ is a process that behaves like p except that actions are renamed by f.

Example 3 As a simple example, we give the specification of the switch described in Example 1.

$$\begin{aligned}
\mathit{Arrival} &= \{\!|x_G|\!\}\{x_G\}{\mapsto}\mathit{on}; \mathit{Arrival}\\
\mathit{Switch}_{\mathit{off}} &= \mathit{on}; \mathit{Switch}_{\mathit{on}}\\
\mathit{Switch}_{\mathit{on}} &= \mathit{on}; \mathit{Switch}_{\mathit{on}} + \{\!|y_K|\!\}\{y_K\}{\mapsto}\mathit{off}; \mathit{Switch}_{\mathit{off}}\\
\mathit{System} &= \mathit{Arrival} \,||_{\{\mathit{on}\}}\, \mathit{Switch}_{\mathit{off}}
\end{aligned}$$

In this case G is an exponential distribution with rate $\frac{1}{30}$ and K is the distribution function that gives probability 1 to the value 2. Process *Arrival* models the arrival of people which occurs exponentially distributed with average of 30 minutes. *Switch* models the switch itself which initially is *off*. Notice that the switch is always enabled to accept an "*on*" and hence no clock controls this activity on the switch part of the system. Process *System* describes the whole system, allowing people to turn on the switch, i.e., process *Arrival* and *Switch* should synchronise on the action *on*. □

In the sequel, we need the notion of free and bound clock variables. Let

Table 1 Stochastic automata for ♤ ($X = p \in E$)

$\kappa(\mathbf{stop}) = \emptyset$	$\kappa(\{\!\|C\|\!\}p) = C \cup \kappa(p)$	$\kappa(p+q) = \kappa(p) \cup \kappa(q)$
$\kappa(a;p) = \emptyset$	$\kappa(C \mapsto p) = \kappa(p)$	$\kappa(p\|\|_A q) = \kappa(p) \cup \kappa(q)$
	$\kappa(p[f]) = \kappa(p)$	$\kappa(p \lfloor\!\lfloor_A q) = \kappa(p) \cup \kappa(q)$
$\kappa(\overline{\mathsf{ck}}(p)) = \emptyset$	$\kappa(X) = \kappa(p)$	$\kappa(p\|_A q) = \kappa(p) \cup \kappa(q)$

$$a;p \xrightarrow{a,\emptyset} p \qquad \frac{p \xrightarrow{a,C} p'}{p+q \xrightarrow{a,C} p' \quad q+p \xrightarrow{a,C} p'} \qquad \frac{p \xrightarrow{a,C} p'}{p||_A q \xrightarrow{a,C} p'||_A \overline{\mathsf{ck}}(q) \quad q||_A p \xrightarrow{a,C} \overline{\mathsf{ck}}(q)||_A p' \quad p \lfloor\!\lfloor_A q \xrightarrow{a,C} p'||_A \overline{\mathsf{ck}}(q)}\ a \notin A$$

$$\frac{p \xrightarrow{a,C'} p'}{\{\!|C|\!\}p \xrightarrow{a,C'} p'}$$

$$\frac{p \xrightarrow{a,C'} p'}{C \mapsto p \xrightarrow{a,C \cup C'} p'} \qquad \frac{p \xrightarrow{a,C} p'}{p[f] \xrightarrow{f(a),C} p'[f]}$$

$$\frac{p \xrightarrow{a,C} p'}{X \xrightarrow{a,C} p'} \qquad \frac{p \xrightarrow{a,C} p'}{\overline{\mathsf{ck}}(p) \xrightarrow{a,C} p'} \qquad \frac{p \xrightarrow{a,C} p' \quad q \xrightarrow{a,C'} q'}{p||_A q \xrightarrow{a,C \cup C'} p'||_A q' \quad p|_A q \xrightarrow{a,C \cup C'} p'||_A q'}\ a \in A$$

$p \in$ ♤. A clock x is free in p if p has a subterm $C \mapsto q$ with $x \in C$ that does not appear in a context $\{\!|C'|\!\} \ldots$ with $x \in C'$. A clock x is bound in p if p has a subterm $\{\!|C|\!\}q$ such that $x \in C$. We denote by $fv(p)$ and $bv(p)$ the sets of free and bound clock variables respectively.

Semantics. As we already said, compositionality is a major drawback in many models for performance analysis, specially in those with the generality of stochastic automata. Instead, stochastic automata can be composed straightforwardly. In fact, we use stochastic automata to give semantics to ♤ in a structured operational (i.e., SOS) manner. In order to define the automaton associated to a parallel composition, we need to consider the additional operation $\overline{\mathsf{ck}}$. $\overline{\mathsf{ck}}(p)$ is a process that behaves like p except that no clock is set at the very beginning. We denote this extended language by ♤$^{\overline{\mathsf{ck}}}$. The sets of free and bounded variables for $\overline{\mathsf{ck}}(p)$ are defined by $fv(\overline{\mathsf{ck}}(p)) = fv(p) \cup \kappa(p)$ and $bv(\overline{\mathsf{ck}}(p)) = bv(p)$, where κ is defined in Table 1.

To associate a stochastic automaton to a given term, we need to define the different parts of the stochastic automaton. We start by defining the clock setting function κ and the set of edges $\longrightarrow$ as the least relations satisfying the rules in Table 1. However, not all the processes can have a straightforward stochastic automaton as a semantic interpretation. To do so, clock names must be considered with care as we see as follows. Consider the process

$$p \equiv \{\!|x_G|\!\}(a; \{x_G\} \mapsto (\{\!|x_G, y_H|\!\}\{y_H\} \mapsto b; \mathbf{stop})) \tag{1}$$

The second occurrence of x_G is intended to be bound to the outermost clock setting as shown by the grey arrow. Using the rules in Table 1, the following stochastic automaton would be obtained

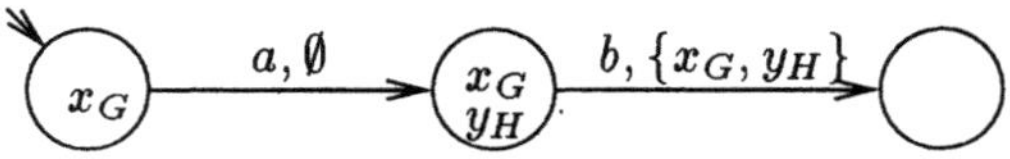

In this sense, x_G would be captured by the innermost clock setting as shown by the black arrow in (1). Therefore, we consider that clocks are different if they are set in different places, although they may have the same name. Clock capture may also occur in contexts with summations and parallel composition.

Capture of variables is a well known problem in languages with variables that can be solved by considering terms modulo α-congruence. It is indeed the solution that we adopt, although for recursive terms special care is needed. However, we would like to characterise processes which have conflict of variables since it is also relevant for the axiomatisation. In fact, we will see that the axiomatisation is sound and complete for structural bisimulation, and hence it becomes important that the scope and binding of clocks is correct since this relation considers clock names.

A first approach to characterise processes with conflict of variables could be purely syntactic. However, this notion turns out to be too strong. Although process p above is problematic, process $p||_{\{a\}}\mathbf{stop}$ does not introduce any problem since its associated stochastic automaton will not have any outgoing edge. In fact, it is evidently equivalent to $\{\!|x_G|\!\}\mathbf{stop}$.

Therefore, we need a dynamic characterisation of processes which do not have conflict of variables. A process p does not have *conflict of variables* if no clock is illegally captured, that is, for every path $p = p_0 \xrightarrow{a_1, C_1} p_1 \xrightarrow{a_2, C_2} p_2 \cdots p_{n-1} \xrightarrow{a_n, C_n} p_n$, for every subterm q of p_i, $i \in \{0, \ldots, n\}$, which is not in the scope of a prefix, the following conditions holds:

1. $q \equiv C \mapsto q'$ implies $C \cap \kappa(q') = \emptyset$
2. $q \equiv q' + q''$ implies $\kappa(q') \cap \kappa(q'') = fv(q') \cap \kappa(q'') = \kappa(q') \cap fv(q'') = \emptyset$
3. $q \equiv q'||_A q''$, $q' \lfloor\!\lfloor_A q''$, or $q'|_A q''$ implies $bv(q') \cap var(q'') = var(q') \cap bv(q'') = \emptyset$

Definition 12 Let p be a process without conflict of variables. The *stochastic automaton associated to* p is defined by $[\![p]\!] \stackrel{\text{def}}{=} (\spadesuit^{\overline{\mathsf{ck}}}, p, \mathcal{C}, \mathbf{A}, \longrightarrow, \kappa, F)$, where $\longrightarrow$ and κ are defined in Table 1, and $\mathcal{C}$, $\mathbf{A}$ and F are defined as for the syntax of $\spadesuit$. □

The reader is invited to check that the processes of the switch system defined in Example 3 do not have conflict of variables, and that the stochastic automaton associated to the process *System* is the one depicted in Figure 1 modulo the identification of $\overline{\mathsf{ck}}(\overline{\mathsf{ck}}(p))$ and $\overline{\mathsf{ck}}(p)$, for all p.

As we said, the restriction to processes which do not have conflict of variables is not an actual problem, since we can always properly rename clocks in any (guardedly defined) process to obtain another process which does not have conflict of variables. With "properly" we mean that the distribution function associated to the clock must be preserved. For instance, p can be α-converted into $\{\!|x_G|\!\}(a; \{x_G\} \mapsto (\{\!|z_G, y_H|\!\}\{y_H\} \mapsto b; \mathbf{stop}))$.

Relating stochastic automata and terms. In the following we study the connection between stochastic automata and recursive specifications. We show that guarded recursive specifications and finitely branching stochastic automata are equally expressive. In order to do so, we need to define the notion of guarded specification and finitely branching. A process variable is *guarded* if all its occurrences appear in a context of a prefix. A recursive specification E is *guarded* if $X = p \in E$ implies that all variables in p are guarded. A stochastic automaton is *finitely branching* if for every location s, its set of outgoing arrows $\{s \xrightarrow{a,C} s' \mid a \in \mathbf{A}, C \in \mathcal{C}, s' \in \mathcal{S}\}$ is finite. Now we can state:

Proposition 13 *Let E be a guarded recursive specification with root X. Assume E does not have conflict of variables. Then $[\![X]\!]$ is finitely branching.*

$\spadesuit$ has the property of expressing any (finitely branching) stochastic automaton. The proof of Theorem 14 follows closely the ideas of a similar theorem in [7].

Theorem 14 *For every finitely branching stochastic automaton SA there is a guarded recursive specification E with root X such that the reachable part of SA and the reachable part of $[\![X]\!]$ are isomorphic.*

Bisimulations in $\spadesuit$. We extend the notion of probabilistic bisimulation, potential bisimulation and structural bisimulation to $\spadesuit$ in the obvious way. Let $p, q \in \spadesuit$. We say that p and q are *probabilistically*, *potentially*, or *structurally bisimilar*, if their respective associated stochastic automata are. We use the notation $p \underline{\leftrightarrow}\, q$, $p \underline{\leftrightarrow}_P\, q$, and $p \underset{\sim}{\leftrightarrow} q$, respectively.

In Section 3, we have already anticipated that probabilistic bisimilarity is not a congruence. This is shown by the following example.

Example 4 *$\underline{\leftrightarrow}$ is not a congruence for parallel composition.* Processes $p_1 \equiv a;\mathbf{stop} + \{\!|x_G|\!\}\{x_G\}\mapsto b;\mathbf{stop}$ and $p_2 \equiv a;\mathbf{stop} + \{\!|x_G|\!\}\{x_G\}\mapsto c;\mathbf{stop}$ $(b \neq c)$ are probabilistically bisimilar if $G(0) = 0$, since in both cases, only the action a at time 0 can be performed. However, $p_1||_{\{a\}}\mathbf{stop}$ and $p_2||_{\{a\}}\mathbf{stop}$ are not bisimilar. In this context, the execution of action a is preempted since there is no possible synchronisation, and b or c may happen (at a certain time greater than 0). This example is depicted in Figure 3. The reader is invited to check that $\underline{\leftrightarrow}$ is neither a congruence for the triggering condition. □

This is precisely the kind of situations that occur when dealing with open systems, and hence they justify the introduction of potential bisimulation. The next theorem states that $\underline{\leftrightarrow}_P$ is a congruence for the operations in $\spadesuit$.

Theorem 15 *Let $p, q \in \spadesuit$ such that $p \underline{\leftrightarrow}_P\, q$. For any context* C[ ] *containing the operations* **stop**, *$a;$, $C\mapsto$, $\{\!|C|\!\}$, $+$, $||_A$, $\lfloor\!\lfloor_A$, $|_A$, or $[f]$, and such that* C[p] *and* C[q] *do not have conflict of variables, it holds that* C[p] $\underline{\leftrightarrow}_P$ C[q].

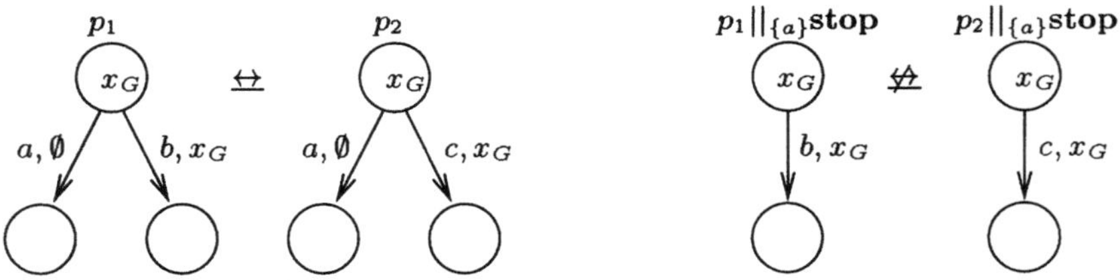

Figure 3 Bisimilarity is not a congruence

Besides, we have the result that structural bisimulation is a congruence for all the operations (including $\overline{\mathsf{ck}}$).

Theorem 16 *Let $p, q \in \spadesuit^{\overline{\mathsf{ck}}}$ such that $p \underset{\sim}{\leftrightarrow} q$. For any context* $\mathsf{C}[\,]$ *containing the operations* **stop**, *a;, $C\mapsto$, $\{\!|C|\!\}$, $+$, $||_A$, $\lfloor\!\lfloor_A$, $|_A$, $[f]$, or $\overline{\mathsf{ck}}$, it holds that* $\mathsf{C}[p] \underset{\sim}{\leftrightarrow} \mathsf{C}[q]$.

The proof of Theorem 15 is quite involved since it has to be done in a traditional way: a relation is given for each case and it is proven to be a potential bisimulation (up to $\underline{\leftrightarrow}_P$). Instead, the proof that $\underset{\sim}{\leftrightarrow}$ is a congruence uses the results of [3] since rules in Table 1 can be easily rewritten into *path* format.

Another important result that we would like to highlight is that proper renaming of variables preserves potential bisimulation. It is important indeed because it justifies the fact that we can always properly rename clocks to obtain processes without conflict of variables as we claimed before.

Structural axioms. In this paragraph, we give a set of axioms for $\spadesuit$. We study the so-called structural axioms. These axioms preserve structural bisimulation. We show that they allow to rewrite any (closed) term into a basic or normal form. Moreover, we show that parallel composition and renaming can be eliminated in favour of the basic operations **stop**, a;, $C\mapsto$, $\{\!|C|\!\}$ and $+$. When convenient, we consider terms modulo α-conversion.

Axioms in Table 2 can be explained as follows. The choice is commutative (**A1**) and associative (**A2**). Axiom **A3** states a kind of idempotency of $+$ and **A4** states that **stop** is the neutral element for $+$. Axioms **T1**–**T5** show the way in which triggering conditions can be simplified. **T3** defines how to reduce nested triggering conditions into only one. Axioms **T4** and **T5** say how to move clock settings and summations out of the scope of a guard. **S1** says that it is irrelevant to set an empty set of clocks. **S2** gathers all the clocks settings in only one operation and **S3** moves clocks settings out of the scope of a summation.

Axioms **R1**–**R5** define the renaming operation. The way in which they operate is more or less standard in process algebra.

Axioms **PC1** and **PC2** move clock settings out of the scope of the parallel composition. This is necessary because when expanding parallel composition

Table 2 Structural axioms for $\spadesuit$

A1	$p + q = q + p$	**R1**	$\mathbf{stop}[f] = \mathbf{stop}$
A2	$(p + q) + r = p + (q + r)$	**R2**	$(a; p)[f] = a; (p[f])$
A3	$a; p + a; p = a; p$	**R3**	$(C \mapsto p)[f] = C \mapsto p[f]$
A4	$p + \mathbf{stop} = p$	**R4**	$(\{\!\vert C \vert\!\} p)[f] = \{\!\vert C \vert\!\} p[f]$
T1	$C \mapsto \mathbf{stop} = \mathbf{stop}$	**R5**	$(p + q)[f] = p[f] + q[f]$
T2	$\emptyset \mapsto p = p$		
T3	$C \mapsto C' \mapsto p = C \cup C' \mapsto p$		
T4	$C \mapsto \{\!\vert C' \vert\!\} p = \{\!\vert C' \vert\!\} C \mapsto p$		if $C \cap C' = \emptyset$
T5	$C \mapsto (p + q) = C \mapsto p + C \mapsto q$		
S1	$\{\!\vert \emptyset \vert\!\} p = p$		
S2	$\{\!\vert C \vert\!\} \{\!\vert C' \vert\!\} p = \{\!\vert C \cup C' \vert\!\} p$		
S3	$\{\!\vert C \vert\!\} p + \{\!\vert C' \vert\!\} q = \{\!\vert C \cup C' \vert\!\} (p + q)$		if $C \cap fv(q) = C' \cap fv(p) = \emptyset$
PC1	$(\{\!\vert C \vert\!\} p) \vert\vert_A q = \{\!\vert C \vert\!\} (p \vert\vert_A q)$		if $C \cap var(q) = \emptyset$
PC2	$p \vert\vert_A (\{\!\vert C \vert\!\} q) = \{\!\vert C \vert\!\} (p \vert\vert_A q)$		if $C \cap var(p) = \emptyset$
PC3	$p \vert\vert_A q = p \lfloor\!\lfloor_A q + q \lfloor\!\lfloor_A p + p \vert_A q$		if $\mathsf{B}'(p) \wedge \mathsf{B}'(q)$
LM1	$\mathbf{stop} \lfloor\!\lfloor_A q = \mathbf{stop}$		if $\mathsf{B}'(q)$
LM2	$a; p \lfloor\!\lfloor_A q = \mathbf{stop}$		if $\mathsf{B}'(q) \wedge a \in A$
LM3	$a; p \lfloor\!\lfloor_A q = a; (p \vert\vert_A q)$		if $\mathsf{B}'(q) \wedge a \notin A$
LM4	$(C \mapsto p) \lfloor\!\lfloor_A q = C \mapsto (p \lfloor\!\lfloor_A q)$		
LM5	$(\{\!\vert C \vert\!\} p) \lfloor\!\lfloor_A q = \{\!\vert C \vert\!\} (p \lfloor\!\lfloor_A q)$		if $C \cap var(q) = \emptyset$
LM6	$p \lfloor\!\lfloor_A (\{\!\vert C \vert\!\} q) = \{\!\vert C \vert\!\} (p \lfloor\!\lfloor_A q)$		if $C \cap var(p) = \emptyset$
LM7	$(p + q) \lfloor\!\lfloor_A r = (p \lfloor\!\lfloor_A r) + (q \lfloor\!\lfloor_A r)$		if $\mathsf{B}'(r)$
CM1	$p \vert_A q = q \vert_A p$		
CM2	$\mathbf{stop} \vert_A \mathbf{stop} = \mathbf{stop}$		
CM3	$\mathbf{stop} \vert_A a; q = \mathbf{stop}$		
CM4	$a; p \vert_A b; q = \mathbf{stop}$		if $a \notin A$
CM5	$a; p \vert_A a; q = a; (p \vert\vert_A q)$		if $a \in A$
CM6	$(C \mapsto p) \vert_A q = C \mapsto (p \vert_A q)$		
CM7	$(\{\!\vert C \vert\!\} p) \vert_A q = \{\!\vert C \vert\!\} (p \vert_A q)$		if $C \cap var(q) = \emptyset$
CM8	$(p + q) \vert_A r = (p \vert_A r) + (q \vert_A r)$		if $\mathsf{B}'(r)$
UB1	$\mathsf{B}'(\mathbf{stop})$	**UB3** $\dfrac{\mathsf{B}'(p)}{\mathsf{B}'(C \mapsto p)}$	**UB4** $\dfrac{\mathsf{B}'(p) \quad \mathsf{B}'(q)}{\mathsf{B}'(p + q)}$
UB2	$\mathsf{B}'(a; p)$		

in terms of summations, we do not want to duplicate clocks. Duplicating clocks would transform processes without conflict of variables into (semantically different!) processes with conflict of variables. **PC3** decomposes the parallel composition in terms of the left merge and the communication merge provided no clock setting is wrongly duplicated. **LM1–LM7** and **CM1–CM8** define the left merge and the communication merge respectively. The predicate B' defined by the rules **UB1–UB4** encodes information about $\overline{\mathsf{ck}}$. In fact, for all guarded processes such that $\mathsf{B}'(p)$ can be proven using axioms **UB1–UB4**, it holds that $\overline{\mathsf{ck}}(p) \underline{\leftrightarrow} p$. We do not want to have $\overline{\mathsf{ck}}$ in our axiomatisation since it does not preserve $\underline{\leftrightarrow}_P$.

We observe that idempotency is not generally true in $\spadesuit$. Consider the process

$p \equiv \{\!|x_G|\!\}\{x_G\}\mapsto a; \textbf{stop}$ where G is uniform on $[0,2]$. The probability that a occurs in the interval $[0,1]$ in process p is $\frac{1}{2}$, while in process $p+p$ such probability is $\frac{3}{4}$. It follows that $p \not\underline{\leftrightarrow} p+p$ and so they are not related by finer bisimulations. Although axiom **A3** already states a notion of idempotency a more general property is $C\mapsto a;p = C\mapsto a;p + C\mapsto a;p$ which we call **A3'** and can be derived from the axioms **A3** and **T5**.

Axioms in Table 2 are sound for structural bisimulation. An immediate consequence is that they are also sound for potential and probabilistic bisimulation. Besides, it can be easily checked that the axioms preserve the property of non-conflict of variables. The side conditions in Table 2 are essential for this to hold.

Theorem 17 *Let $p, q \in \mathcal{Q}$ such that $p = q$ can be proved from axioms in Table 2. Then we have,*

1. *p does not have conflict of variables if and only if neither q does; and*
2. *if they do not have conflict of variables, then $p \underset{\sim}{\leftrightarrow} q$.*

An interesting property that is derived from these axioms is that every term can be expressed in a normal form.

Definition 18 Define the set $B \subseteq \mathcal{Q}$ of *basic terms* inductively as follows:

- $\textbf{stop} \in B'$
- $p \in B$, $C \in \wp_{\text{fin}}(\mathcal{C})$ and $a \in \mathbf{A} \implies C\mapsto a;p \in B'$
- $p, q \in B' \implies p+q \in B'$
- $p \in B'$ and $C \in \wp_{\text{fin}}(\mathcal{C}) \implies \{\!|C|\!\}p \in B$

$B' \subseteq \mathcal{Q}$ is the set of all terms whose clock settings are all within the scope of a prefix construction. (Notice that $p \in B'$ implies $\mathsf{B}'(p)$.) A basic term has the general form (modulo **A1**, **A2**, **A3'** and **A4**)

$$p \equiv \{\!|C|\!\}\left(\sum_{i\in I} C_i\mapsto a_i; p_i\right)$$

where each p_i is a basic term, and $\sum_{i\in I} q_i \stackrel{\text{def}}{=} q_1 + \cdots + q_n$ for $I = \{1,\ldots,n\}$. In particular, $\sum_{i\in\emptyset} q_i \stackrel{\text{def}}{=} \textbf{stop}$. □

Theorem 19 *Let $\mathcal{Q}^c$ ($\subseteq \mathcal{Q}$) be the set of all* finite *(or* closed*) terms, i.e., terms which do not contain process variables. For every term $p \in \mathcal{Q}^c$ there is a term $q \in B$ such that $p = q$ can be proven by means of the basic axioms and α-conversion.*

The set of axioms given in Table 2 is complete for structural bisimulation on the set $\mathcal{Q}^c$. Theorem 19 is essential for the proof of completeness. Since α-conversion does not imply structural bisimulation, we must ensure that it is not used in the proof of Theorem 19. To do so, it is enough to restrict to terms without conflict of variables because of Theorem 17.

Theorem 20 *Let $p, q \in \spadesuit^c$ be two terms without conflict of variables. Suppose $p = q$ can be derived from the axioms in Table 2 (but not α-conversion!). Then $p \underline{\leftrightarrow} q$.*

One of the reasons why many approaches to stochastic process algebras stick to only exponential distributions [16, 15, 4, ...] is that general distributions do not preserve Milner's expansion law in their models. In other cases, combining the expansion law with general distributions lead to infinite and sometimes quite complicated models [11, 13, 20]. In our case, the expansion law is inherent in the model and the way parallel composition is defined, and can be smoothly derived from the axioms as stated by the following theorem.

Theorem 21 (Expansion Law) *Let $p, q \in \spadesuit$ such that $p = \{\!|C|\!\}p'$ and $q = \{\!|C'|\!\}q'$ with $p' = \sum C_i \mapsto a_i; p_i$ and $q' = \sum C'_j \mapsto b_j; q_j$. Suppose $p||_A q$ does not have conflict of variables. From the axioms in Table 2 we can derive*

$$p||_A q \;=\; \{\!|C \cup C'|\!\} \Big(\textstyle\sum_{a_i \notin A} C_i \mapsto a_i; (p_i||_A q') \;+\; \sum_{b_j \notin A} C'_j \mapsto b_j; (p'||_A q_j) \;+\; \sum_{a_i = b_j \in A} (C_i \cup C'_j) \mapsto a_i; (p_i||_A q_j) \Big)$$

For clarity, we did not include the renaming operation. This, however, could be done straightforwardly.

Example 5 The reader is invited to check that, using the axioms, the process *System* of Example 3 can be re-written into the following expression.

$$\begin{aligned} System &= \{\!|x_G|\!\}\{x_G\} \mapsto on; Sys_{on} \\ Sys_{on} &= \{\!|x_G, y_K|\!\}(\{x_G\} \mapsto on; Sys_{on} + \{y_K\} \mapsto off; Sys_{off}) \\ Sys_{off} &= \{x_G\} \mapsto on; Sys_{on} \end{aligned}$$

Its associated stochastic automaton is indeed the one depicted in Figure 1. □

5 FURTHER DISCUSSIONS

Related work. Apart from the Markovian process algebras [16, 15, 4, ...], some general stochastic process algebras have been introduced.

TIPP [11] is the earliest approach to the general case. Its syntax has the integrated prefix $a_F; p$ which in $\spadesuit$ corresponds to $\{\!|x_F|\!\}\{x_F\} \mapsto a; p$. Its semantics is based on labelled transition systems in which transitions are decorated with the associated distribution function and, to keep track of the execution of parallel processes, a number that indicates how many times an action has not been chosen to execute. This number introduces infinite semantic objects, even for simple regular processes. [20] has followed a similar approach to give semantics to a stochastic extension of the π-calculus. In this case transitions are decorated with locality information to keep track which process performed it.

In [13], a process algebra for discrete event simulation is introduced. The concerns of randomly setting a timer, expiration of such a timer, and actual activity are splitted in a rather similar way to ours. The semantic model is similar to our PTSs but with explicit time transitions, and hence semantic objects are usually highly infinite. The process algebra includes an urgent and a delayable prefixing, so its interpretation combines both views of closed and open system.

[6] studies a semantic for a process algebra similar to TIPP in terms of a stochastic extension of event structures. This model seems to be more natural to deal with general distributions since activities that are not causally dependent (i.e. concurrent activity) are not related in the model, contrarily of what occurs in interleaving based models. However, recursive processes always have associated an infinite semantic object.

A general semi-Markovian process algebra based on EMPA [4] is discussed in [5]. Terms in this process algebra have semantics in an interleaving based model. Finiteness of the associated semantic object is kept in a reasonable way. As a price to pay, the way to give semantics is quite cumbersome and not only the transitions are decorated with many information (as for instance the locality of the occurrence of an action) but also the states.

Among the above enumerated stochastic process algebras, [13] is the closest to $\spadesuit$. As $\spadesuit$, [13] also allows non-determinism. In all the other cases (including the Markovian process algebras), choice is always solved either probabilistically or by the race condition. We also mention that none of [11, 20, 6, 5] discusses an axiomatic theory for their respective stochastic process algebras.

Conclusions and further work. We introduced new models to analyse stochastic and real-time systems. We discussed in depth a stochastic process algebra whose expressivity is richer than existing ones. We showed that this process algebra and its underlying semantic model, the stochastic automata, are equally expressive. We gave an axiomatisation and we showed that the expansion law can be straightforwardly derived from them. Besides, we have defined a general probabilistic transition system. We have used it as semantic model of the stochastic automata. In fact, we gave two different ways of assigning a PTS to a stochastic automaton, so we may understand systems either as closed or open.

It is worthwhile to notice that $\spadesuit$ is a conservative extension of the basic CCS (i.e. the sublanguage containing only prefixing, summation and stop) in both semantic and axiomatic sense. Besides, it can be proven that equivalences $\underline{\leftrightarrow}$, $\underline{\leftrightarrow}_P$, and $\underset{\sim}{\leftrightarrow}$ turn out to be the same in the non-stochastic sublanguage of $\spadesuit$, that is, the set of all the terms in which operations $\{\!|C|\!\}$ and $C\mapsto$ do not occur.

We should remark a couple of works we have already done regarding stochastic automata and discrete event simulation. The first is that the actual behaviour of stochastic automata leads to an algorithm for discrete event simulation. We use the notion of adversaries or schedulers [25, 23] to resolve non-deterministic choices. Since parallel composition of stochastic automata can be easily defined (actually, it is the one of $\spadesuit$), the simulation algorithm can compose the complete stochastic automaton on the fly, which reduces the state space explosion problem. Secondly, we already know that stochastic automata properly contain a wide class of GSMPs. We will report in detail about these works in the near future.

From the results reported in this paper and the observations just mentioned, we believe that our models are quite suitable to specify and analyse stochastic systems and real-time systems. But to go further in this direction many things have still to be done. First of all the axiomatisation for $\spadesuit$ is not sufficient as it is. Axioms for potential bisimulation as well as laws for probabilistic bisimulation have to be introduced. A clear example of this need is that terms p, and $\{\!|C|\!\}p$ are potentially bisimilar provided $C \cap fv(p) = \emptyset$. However, equality $p = \{\!|C|\!\}p$ cannot be proved from the axioms in Table 2, which is reasonable because p and $\{\!|C|\!\}p$ are not necessarily structurally bisimilar.

As we pointed out we have a method to simulate stochastic automata (and hence terms in $\spadesuit$). However, analytical methods are far more effective to study the correctness of a system. Usually errors are events with low probability, so the use of simulation may not guarantee that they are not present or that their probability is low enough to be considered. Model checking has proven to be a powerful tool to verify timed systems. Some early papers like [1] have shown the possibility of borrowing ideas from model checking on timed automata and applying them to stochastic systems. Our work will also address the use of model checking on stochastic automata. Besides, we will investigate on the possibility of borrowing from analytical methods already used in the performance analysis community, so it can be applied to study analytically the performance of systems modelled in $\spadesuit$.

REFERENCES

1. R. Alur, C. Courcoubetis, and D. Dill. Model-checking for probabilistic real-time systems. In J. Leach Albert, B. Monien, and M. Rodríguez, eds., *Proceedings* 18th *ICALP,* Madrid, *LNCS* 510, pp 113–126. Springer, 1991.
2. R. Alur and D. Dill. A theory of timed automata. *Theor. Comput. Sci.*, 126:183–235, 1994.
3. J.C.M. Baeten and C. Verhoef. A congruence theorem for structured operational semantics with predicates. In E. Best, ed., *Proceedings CONCUR 93,* Hildesheim, Germany, LNCS 715, pp 477–492. Springer, 1993.
4. M. Bernardo and R. Gorrieri. Extended Markovian process algebra. In U. Montanari and V. Sassone, eds., *Proceedings CONCUR 96,* Pisa, Italy, LNCS 1119, pp 314–330. Springer, 1996.
5. M. Bravetti, M. Bernardo, and R. Gorrieri. From EMPA to GSMPA: allowing for general distributions. In E. Brinksma and A. Nymeyer, eds., *Proceedings PAPM'97*, pp 17–33. University of Twente, June 1997.

6. E. Brinksma, J.-P. Katoen, R. Langerak, and D. Latella. A stochastic causality-based process algebra. *The Computer Journal*, 38(6):552–565, 1995.
7. P.R. D'Argenio and E. Brinksma. A calculus for timed automata (Extended abstract). In B. Jonsson and J. Parrow, eds., *Proceedings FTRTFT'96*, Uppsala, Sweden, LNCS 1135, pp 110–129. Springer, 1996.
8. P.R. D'Argenio, J.-P. Katoen, and E. Brinksma. An algebraic approach to the specification of stochastic systems. Technical Report CTIT-98-02. University of Twente, 1998.
9. R.J. van Glabbeek, S.A. Smolka, and B. Steffen. Reactive, generative, and stratified models of probabilistic processes. *Infor. & Comput.*, 121:59–80, 1995.
10. P.W. Glynn. A GSMP formalism for discrete event simulation. *Proceedings of the IEEE*, 77(1):14–23, 1989.
11. N. Götz, U. Herzog, and M.Rettelbach. TIPP - Introduction and application to protocol performance analysis. In H. König, ed., *Formale Beschreibungstechniken für verteilte Systeme*, FOKUS series. Saur Publishers, 1993.
12. H.A. Hansson and B. Jonsson. A calculus for communicating systems with time and probabilities. In *Proceedings 11th IEEE Real-Time Systems Symposium*, pp 278–287, Lake Buena Vista, Florida, December 1990.
13. P. Harrison and B. Strulo. Stochastic process algebra for discrete event simulation. In F. Bacelli, A. Jean-Marie, and I. Mitrani, eds., *Quantitative Methods in Parallel Systems*, Esprit Basic Research Series, pp 18–37. Springer, 1995.
14. T.A. Henzinger, X. Nicollin, J. Sifakis, and S. Yovine. Symbolic model checking for real-time systems. *Infor. & Comput.*, 111:193–244, 1994.
15. H. Hermanns and M.Rettelbach. Syntax, semantics, equivalences, and axioms for MTIPP. In *Proceedings PAPM'94*, pp 71–87. University of Erlangen, July 1994.
16. J. Hillston. *A Compositional Approach to Performance Modelling.* Distinguished Dissertation in Computer Science. Cambridge University Press, 1996.
17. K.G. Larsen and A. Skou. Bisimulation through probabilistic testing. *Infor. & Comput.*, 94:1–28, 1991.
18. R. Milner. *Communication and Concurrency.* Prentice-Hall International, 1989.
19. A. Pnueli and L.D. Zuck. Probabilistic verification. *Infor. & Comput.*, 103:1–29, 1993.
20. C. Priami. Stochastic π-calculus with general distributions. In [21], pp 41–57.
21. M. Ribaudo, ed. *Proceedings PAPM'96,* Torino, Italy. Università di Torino, 1996.
22. J.J.M.M. Rutten and E. de Vink. Bisimulation for probabilistic transition systems: a coalgebraic approach (extended abstract). In *Proceedings* 24th *ICALP,* Bologna, LNCS 1256, pp 460–470. Springer, 1997.
23. R. Segala and N. Lynch. Probabilistic simulations for probabilistic processes. *Nordic Journal of Computing*, 2(2):250–273, 1995.
24. A.N. Shiryaev. *Probability.* Springer, second edition, 1996.
25. M.Y. Vardi. Automatic verification of probabilistic concurrent finite state programs. In *Proceedings* 26th *FOCS,* Portland, pp 327–338. IEEE Comp. Soc. Press, 1985.
26. W. Whitt. Continuity of generalized semi-Markov processes. *Math. Oper. Res.*, 5:494–501, 1980.

BIOGRAPHY

Pedro R. D'Argenio graduated as Computing Analyst and Licentiate in Computer Science from the National University of La Plata, Argentina, in 1993 and 1994, respectively. Until 1995, he held research and teaching positions at the Department of Computer Science of the National University of La Plata. Since 1995, he is a Ph.D. student at the Department of Computer Science of the University of Twente, The Netherlands. His current research subjects include specification, verification, and validation of real-time, stochastic, and distributed systems as well as formal methods applied to performance analysis.

Joost-Pieter Katoen received his M.Sc. degree (with honours) and Ph.D. degree in Computer Science from the University of Twente, The Netherlands, in 1987 and 1996, respectively. From 1988 to 1990 he was a postgraduate student at the Eindhoven University of Technology, The Netherlands. He joined Philips Research Laboratories Eindhoven from 1990 to 1992. Since 1997, he is assistant professor at the Faculty of Computer Science of the University of Erlangen-Nürnberg. His current research interests include specification and verification of real-time and probabilistic systems, semantics, and performance analysis based on formal methods.

Ed Brinksma received his M.Sc. degree (cum laude) in Mathematics from the University of Groningen, The Netherlands, in 1982. In 1982 he joined the Department of Computer Science at the University of Twente as an assistant professor where he got his Ph.D. in Computer Science in 1988. In the period 1983-1989 he was the chairman of the committee of the International Organisation for Standardisation (ISO) that was responsible for the definition of the formal specification technique LOTOS. Since 1991, he is a full professor, occupying the chair in Formal Methods and Tools. His main research interest is the application of formal methods to the design and analysis of distributed systems. His current research topics include the application of formal methods to testing, the relation between formal methods and performance analysis, the application of correctness preserving transformations to realistic designs, and tool-oriented design of specification formalisms.

13
Refinement types for specification

E. Denney
LFCS, Department of Computer Science, University of Edinburgh
Kings Buildings, Edinburgh EH9 3JZ, Scotland
Tel. : +44 131 650 5151
Fax : +44 131 667 7209
Email : `ewd@dcs.ed.ac.uk`

Abstract
We develop a theory of program specification using the notion of *refinement type*. This provides a notion of structured specification, useful for verification and program development. We axiomatise the satisfaction of specifications by programs as a generalised typing relation and give rules for refining specifications. A per semantics based on Henkin models is given, for which the system is proven to be sound and complete.

Keywords
Specification, refinement, verification, type theory, Henkin models

1 INTRODUCTION

We address the question of what is a suitable notion of specification for a programming language, where the properties of interest can be expressed using some given program logic. In particular, we restrict our attention to those languages which can be studied using typed lambda calculi, that is, typed functional programming languages.

A number of possibilities can be considered. One is to say that a specification is a type in some expressive type theory. This is the approach taken by Luo (1991) for example. An integer square root function might be specified as the existential type $\exists f : \mathtt{nat} \to \mathtt{nat}\ .\ (f\ n)^2 = n \ \vee\ (f\ n)^2 + 1 = n$, where the logic is encoded in the type theory. The problem is that this only works for an intuitionistic logic. Classical logics are more common for specification, and cannot easily be encoded in type theories. Also, programming languages generally have a simple type system of their own, and this must somehow be related to the specification type theory.

Another possibility is to say that a specification is just a proposition of the program logic with a distinguished free variable. Our square root example would be the proposition $(f\ n)^2 = n \ \vee\ (f\ n)^2 + 1 = n$, where f is a free variable of type $\mathtt{nat} \to \mathtt{nat}$. This is the approach traditionally taken by the program refinement community, and Morgan (1994) describes a refinement calculus based on the use of first-order predicate logic.

Programming Concepts and Methods D. Gries, & W-P. de Roever (Eds.)

However, this approach has a number of shortcomings, which we illustrate with an example below. The main point is that for compositional verification and program development it is better to put more structure on specifications.

In this paper, we suggest a third possibility, a combination of the program logic with the type theory of the programming language known as *refinement types*. The notion of refinement type has been studied extensively in program analysis (under different names) and there are many different systems, depending on the area of interest. The general idea is to have two levels – an underlying level of program types, and a more expressive level of program properties, which are then treated like types. For us, this more expressive level will be the specifications. Hence we can exploit type-theoretic structure in our specifications, but do not need to do any encoding.

We describe a verification calculus based on the simply-typed lambda calculus with products ($\lambda^{\times\rightarrow}$) and some ground types such as `nat` and `bool`. The satisfaction of specifications by programs is axiomatised as a generalised typing relation. We do this by viewing specifications as refinements of an underlying type, expressed using the program logic. We use typed classical predicate logic as program logic here, and axiomatise an ordering on the refinement types, to be viewed as an increase in information, or refinement of specifications. We give a simple set-theoretic interpretation of the calculus. The main result of the paper is soundness and completeness with respect to this class of models.

In Section 2 we consider a simple example of specifying and verifying a program in order to motivate the features of our calculus. We then give the syntax and rules of the calculus in Section 3. In Section 4 we return to the example. Section 5 gives the semantics and proofs of soundness and completeness. Finally, we make some conclusions in Section 6.

Related Work

There have been a number of papers in the 'non-standard type system as program logic' paradigm. Nielson & Nielson (1988) and (Burn 1992) axiomatise consequence relations on properties as a form of refinement. Pfenning, who introduced the term "refinement type", used them to express properties of mini-ML programs (Freeman & Pfenning 1991).

There have been various approaches by type theorists to combining logic and types. Feferman's (1985) system of variable types extends $\lambda^{\times\rightarrow}$ with subset types, though equality does not depend on the type, as it does here. Refinement can be defined in the logic, and is not explicitly axiomatised. Other type-theoretic approaches include (Aspinall 1995, Aspinall & Compagnoni 1996), which differ from the present work in being concerned with subtyping type families. Dependency there is at the level of types themselves, whereas we only allow dependent structure at the refinement type level.

The deliverables approach (Burstall & McKinna 1992, McKinna 1992) is to consider a program paired with its proof of correctness. We are similarly motivated in wanting to structure specifications using program types, but differ in taking proof existence as more important than the proof itself – terms do not need an explicit witness to satisfy a refinement type. Our calculus could be regarded as an internal language for deliverables.

The work of Luo (1991) presents an encoding of specifications and 'specification morphisms' (corresponding to our terms) in an expressive type theory. Our work provides a more direct analysis of the concept of specification. The existential form of Martin-Löf's type theory with subset types in (Nordström, Petersson & Smith 1990) is similar. The work of Hayashi (1994) is also related.

The program refinement community has traditionally used unstructured specifications. For example, Morgan (1994) describes a refinement calculus based on the use of propositions of first order predicate logic.

2 EXAMPLE

Let us consider specifying division by 2 on the naturals and verifying that a program satisfies the specification. We will take the simply-typed lambda calculus and classical first-order predicate logic as simple programming and specification languages respectively. We will use an applied $\lambda^{\times\rightarrow}$ theory extended with a constant for iteration over the naturals, where `natiter` $z\ f\ n$ computes the n-th iterate $f^n(z)$. As a first approximation to specifications we use propositions with a distinguished free variable, which we write as $(x : \tau)P$ where τ is the type of the variable x in proposition P.

A program `div2` which implements division on the naturals is

$$\mathtt{div2} = \lambda n : \mathtt{nat}\ .\ \pi_1(\mathtt{div2}'\ n) : \mathtt{nat} \rightarrow \mathtt{nat}$$

where this uses the auxiliary function

$$\mathtt{div2}' = \mathtt{natiter}\ \langle 0,0\rangle\ (\lambda p : \mathtt{nat} \times \mathtt{nat}\ .\ \langle \pi_2 p, \pi_1 p + 1\rangle)$$

Now this can be specified as

$$\mathtt{div2\_spec} = (f : \mathtt{nat} \rightarrow \mathtt{nat})\ \forall n : \mathtt{nat}\ .\ n = 2 * f(n) \vee n = 2 * f(n) + 1$$

We want to axiomatise a satisfaction relation `sat` between programs (closed terms) and specifications, so that we can prove

$$\mathtt{div2\ sat\ div2\_spec}$$

One simple way of doing this is to say that t `sat` $(x : \tau)P$ is just taken to be a notation for a typing and a proposition, with the rule that t `sat` $(x : \tau)P$ when $t : \tau$ and $P[t/x]$. This example reduces then to proving

$$\forall n : \mathtt{nat}\ .\ n = 2 * \mathtt{div2}(n) \vee n = 2 * \mathtt{div2}(n) + 1$$

Now, our specification language is rather cumbersome as it stands, so let us introduce dependent products and functions as abbreviations

$$\Sigma_{x:(x:\sigma)P}(y : \tau)Q \quad \text{for} \quad (z : \sigma \times \tau)P[\pi_1 z/x] \wedge Q[\pi_1 z/x, \pi_2 z/y]$$

$$\Pi_{x:(x:\sigma)P}(y:\tau)Q \text{ for } (f:\sigma\to\tau)\forall x:\sigma\,.\,P\supset Q[fx/y]$$

The dependent function $\Pi_{x:(x:\sigma)P}(y:\tau)Q$ specifies some function which for all $x:\sigma$ such that P, returns a $y:\tau$ such that Q. This has combined the two quantifications in $(f:\sigma\to\tau)\forall x:\sigma\,.\,P\supset Q[fx/y]$, which we read as some $f:\sigma\to\tau$ such that for all $x:\sigma$, if P then $Q[fx/y]$. If we allow ourself the further abbreviation of viewing types as trivial specifications, so that for example, nat can stand for $(x:\texttt{nat})\texttt{true}$, then we can write our specification more compactly as

$$\texttt{div2\_spec} = \Pi_{n:\texttt{nat}}(m:\texttt{nat})n = 2*m \vee n = 2*m+1$$

Now, using our abbreviations, the following rule is admissible from our definition of sat

$$\frac{n:\texttt{nat}\vdash \pi_1(\texttt{div2}'\ n)\ \texttt{sat}\ (m:\texttt{nat})n = 2*m \vee n = 2*m+1}{\lambda n:\texttt{nat}.\pi_1(\texttt{div2}'\ n)\ \texttt{sat}\ \Pi_{n:\texttt{nat}}(m:\texttt{nat})n = 2*m \vee n = 2*m+1}$$

where we understand the sequent $n:\texttt{nat}\vdash t\ \texttt{sat}\ \phi$ to mean for all closed $t':\texttt{nat}$, $t[t'/n]\ \texttt{sat}\ \phi[t'/n]$. In general then, we want to consider satisfaction in an arbitrary context. Note the similarity to a typing rule. In fact, not only are Σ and Π useful structuring devices for specifications, they are also useful for proofs, as specifications of programs often tend to be most naturally expressed and proved in a 'shape' similar to the program.

For example, the program div2 is an abstraction and the specification div2_spec is of the form $\Pi_{x:\phi}\psi$. The rule directly reflects a natural proof that div2 satisfies div2_spec. Similarly, the auxiliary function div2′ has specification

$$\texttt{div2}'\texttt{\_spec} = \Pi_{n:\texttt{nat}}\Sigma_{(m:\texttt{nat})\texttt{n=2m}\vee\texttt{n=2m+1}}(m':\texttt{nat})m+m' = n$$

The proof of this, in turn, involves showing that a pair satisfies a product specification, and an abstraction satisfies a functional specification (as above). We also have to use induction to show that an iteration satisfies some specification parameterised on the naturals. We consider this example more fully in Section 4.

A significant benefit in writing specification in this more structured form is conceptual – it is preferable to structure specifications in such a way that it aids understanding of both specification and program. Then the task of comprehension need not be duplicated unnecessarily for specification and program. Also, separate checks of well-formedness (*i.e.* type-checking here) and correctness, will involve some duplication of effort, so it is better to combine types and correctness properties. Though we will not consider it here, in order to be the basis of a useful program development methodology, it helps for our specifications and proofs to reflect the structure of the programs. We do not throw away the original rule that t satisfies $(x:\tau)P$ when $t:\tau$ and $P[t/x]$, however, since not all specifications can be given in a structured form.

There is one final aspect of specifications which we must consider – equality. The kind of specifications with which we are concerned here are those which specify the input-output characteristics of programs. We are only interested in programs up to *extensional equality*. The alternative, in a type-theoretic setting, is to use an intensional equality and distinguish programs on the basis of syntactic form. This would be unnatural here however, so we view specifications as coming equipped with a *partial equivalence relation* (per), which acts as an equality. A per is a symmetric and transitive relation on the set of terms at the type, or equivalently, an equivalence relation on a subset of terms at the type.

For example, the specification $\Pi_{l:\mathtt{nonemptylist}}(n : \mathtt{nat})\mathtt{Min}(n, l)$ where the proposition $\mathtt{Min}(n, l)$ says that n is the minimum element in list l, is a refinement type over type $\mathtt{list} \to \mathtt{nat}$. We want to regard functions $f, f' : \mathtt{list} \to \mathtt{nat}$ as equal solutions of this specification if they give the same results for nonempty lists. Any program satisfying this specification must be defined on the empty list, but we are not interested in the value it takes there.

Now, we would attain some conceptual simplicity if specifications were to subsume types, satisfaction to subsume typing, and equality at a specification to subsume the usual equality at a type (which is often left implicit). For example, we use $(n : \mathtt{nat})\mathtt{true}$ in place of $\mathtt{nat}$, and $\Sigma_{n:(n:\mathtt{nat})\mathtt{true}}(b : \mathtt{bool})\mathtt{true}$ for $\mathtt{nat} \times \mathtt{bool}$. At this point, we must cease to regard $\Pi_{x:(x:\sigma)P}(y : \tau)Q$ as an abbreviation, since we want it to have a different equality from $(f : \sigma \to \tau)\forall x : \sigma \,.\, P \supset Q[fx/y]$. We believe it is misleading to regard specifications as types, though, and refer to the specifications of this idealised specification language as *refinement types*. Equality is given by a per over the underlying type.

A specification therefore, is a refinement type, and consists of a type τ, together with a per ϕ over τ. We take a program in this calculus to be an equivalence class of a per ϕ. The alternative would be to take a program as an element of the domain of a per, but this would be unnatural because we would then be distinguishing programs beyond extensional equality.

We use a notation for the equivalence classes of pers, by allowing refinement types on the variables in abstractions. For example, $\lambda n : \mathtt{even}.n$ is a class in the per $\mathtt{even} \to \mathtt{nat}$ but not $\mathtt{nat} \to \mathtt{nat}$, and $\lambda n : \mathtt{nat}.n$ is a class in both $\mathtt{even} \to \mathtt{nat}$ and $\mathtt{nat} \to \mathtt{nat}$. The equality $t =_\phi t'$ says that t and t' are the same equivalence class of per ϕ.

For refinement types ϕ and ϕ' over the same underlying type, we want to consider refinements $\phi \sqsubseteq \phi'$, to be though of semantically as per inclusion (*i.e.* equality at ϕ' implies equality at ϕ). We use the square $\sqsubseteq$ symbol to indicate an information ordering – the refinement of specifications. Note that this convention for refinement is the opposite direction to the usual subtyping relation.

3 THE CALCULUS

3.1 Syntax

The idea is that we construct a theory of refinement types on top of an underlying $\lambda^{\times\to}$ theory and a first-order logic theory. This is generated from a signature of types, constants and predicate symbols (in the underlying theory) and axioms (in the full theory). The well-formedness conditions on axioms will be explained in Section 3.3 below.

Definition 1 *A* signature *consists of a finite collection of ground types* γ*, n-ary constants k, each of which is assigned some sort* $\tau_1, \ldots, \tau_n \rightarrow \tau$*, and n-ary predicates F, which are assigned a sequence of types* $\tau_1, \ldots, \tau_n$*, indicated by* F : $\texttt{pred}\ \tau_1, \ldots, \tau_n$*. There are two forms of axiom. We write propositional axioms as* $Ax \triangleright \Gamma \vdash P$ *and require that* $\Gamma \vdash P\ \texttt{wf}$*. Axioms on the constants are given in the form* $Ax \triangleright \Gamma \vdash k : \phi_1, \ldots, \phi_n \rightarrow \psi$*, for constant k with sort* $\tau_1, \ldots, \tau_n \rightarrow \tau$*, and such that* $\Gamma \vdash \phi_i : \texttt{Ref}\ \tau_i$*,* $\Gamma \vdash \psi : \texttt{Ref}\ \tau$*.*

Note that the sorting $k : \tau \rightarrow \tau'$ and axiom $k : \phi \rightarrow \psi$ do not say that unary constant k is a well-formed term without the necessary number of arguments. For $t : \tau$, we have $k(t) : \tau'$, and if $t : \phi$ then $k(t) : \psi$.

Although we do not have arbitrary refinement types as primitive in a signature, we get much the same expressiveness using primitive predicate symbols. For example, with the ground type nat, we could have predicate even : pred nat, and then overload even for the refinement type $(n : \texttt{nat})\texttt{even}(n)$.

For ground type bool, we can have constants $\texttt{true} : \texttt{bool}, \texttt{false} : \texttt{bool}$ and $\texttt{cond}_\tau : \texttt{bool}, \tau, \tau \rightarrow \tau$, for each type τ. The axiom schema for conditionals can be given as $\texttt{cond}_\tau : P + P', (x : \phi)P \supset Q[x], (y : \phi)P' \supset Q[y] \rightarrow (z : \phi)Q[z]$, where $P + P'$ abbreviates $(b : \texttt{bool})b = \texttt{true} \supset P \wedge b = \texttt{false} \supset P'$.

The raw expressions of the language are given by a mutual recursion over refinement types, terms, propositions and contexts :

$$\phi ::= \mathbf{1} \mid \gamma \mid \Sigma_{x:\phi}\phi' \mid \Pi_{x:\phi}\phi' \mid (x : \phi)P$$

$$t ::= x \mid k(t_1, \ldots, t_n) \mid * \mid \langle t, t' \rangle \mid \lambda x : \phi.t \mid \pi_i(t) \mid tt'$$

$$P ::= \texttt{false} \mid P \supset P' \mid \forall x : \phi.P \mid F(t_1, \ldots, t_n) \mid t =_\phi t' \mid \phi \sqsubseteq \phi'$$

$$\Gamma ::= \langle\rangle \mid \Gamma, x : \phi \mid \Gamma, P$$

Conceptually, it is simpler not to distinguish types and refinement types as syntactic categories. Refinement types should be viewed as being refinements of underlying types, so for example, if ϕ is a refinement of (we will just say 'over') σ, and ψ is over τ, then $\Sigma_{x:\phi}\psi$ is over $\sigma \times \tau$. Formally however, types are just refinement types with no logical information, that is, not containing any propositions. We use σ and τ as metavariables for types.

There is a unique (up to equality) term $*$ of unit type $\mathbf{1}$. The meaning of the other refinement types in terms of satisfaction is that $\langle t, t' \rangle$ satisfies $\Sigma_{x:\phi}\psi$ when t satisfies ϕ and t' satisfies $\psi[t/x]$; term t satisfies $\Pi_{x:\phi}\psi$ when for every t' satisfying ϕ, tt' is well-formed and satisfies $\psi[t'/x]$; and t satisfies $(x : \phi)P$ when it satisfies ϕ and the proposition $P[t/x]$ holds.

We think of terms of the calculus as being simple specifications of terms in the underlying $\lambda^{\times\rightarrow}$. We will refer to terms of $\lambda^{\times\rightarrow}$ as *total* terms. Terms of the calculus uniquely specify total terms up to equality at some refinement type. Terms have their usual meaning in the lambda calculus, except that an abstraction $\lambda x : \phi.t$ should be thought of as a simple specification of terms $\lambda x : \sigma.t'$ such that for all t'' which satisfy ϕ, $t'[t''/x]$ satisfies $t[t''/x]$.

For example, $\lambda n : \texttt{even}.n$ specifies total terms of type $\texttt{nat} \rightarrow \texttt{nat}$ which are the identity on even arguments. The application $(\lambda x : \phi.t)t''$ is only well-formed for arguments t'' which satisfy ϕ so behaviour outwith ϕ is not constrained. Note that this means that although $\texttt{even} \rightarrow \texttt{even}$ is a refinement of the type $\texttt{nat} \rightarrow \texttt{nat}$, the term $\lambda n : \texttt{even}.n$ does not itself have type $\texttt{nat} \rightarrow \texttt{nat}$. Intuitively, we can say that a term t has refinement type ϕ if its behaviour 'at ϕ' is uniquely determined, that is, any two total terms which satisfy t are themselves equal at ϕ.

Remark 2 Our choice of first-order classical logic is only significant insofar as it is an example of what we might call an *extensional* logic. We make essential use of the fact that for all terms t, t' and propositions P, if t is extensionally equal to t' (which, in general, may coincide with the equality of the logic, if it has one, but otherwise can be defined as a logical relation), then $P[t/x]$ holds if and only if $P[t'/x]$ does. In other words, we require Leibniz and observational equality to coincide. It does not matter whether the logic is classical or intuitionistic.

This can be contrasted with, say, the use of an intensional logic such as the modal μ-calculus, where terms are viewed as transition systems through their reduction sequences.

3.2 Judgements

The judgements of the calculus are

$$\Gamma \vdash t : \phi \qquad\qquad \Gamma \vdash P$$

where the atomic propositions are $\Gamma \vdash t =_\phi t'$ and $\Gamma \vdash \phi \sqsubseteq \phi'$. Equality and refinement are not separate judgement classes from the other propositions. All judgements are made in a context Γ of variable assumptions $x : \phi$ and propositions P. There are also mutually dependent well-formedness judgements

$$\vdash \Gamma \ \texttt{wf} \qquad \Gamma \vdash \phi : \texttt{Ref}\ \tau \qquad \Gamma \vdash P\ \texttt{wf}$$

We say that a term t is well-formed in context Γ when there exists a refinement type ϕ such that $\Gamma \vdash t : \phi$. Note that ϕ need not be unique, though the underlying type is unique. We understand $\Gamma \vdash t : \phi$ to mean that for all the variables in the context Γ, if they satisfy the relevant refinement types, then the term t has refinement type ϕ. Sometimes we write $\Gamma \vdash t, t' : \phi$ for $\Gamma \vdash t : \phi$ and $\Gamma \vdash t : \phi'$.

The well-formedness judgement for refinement types, $\Gamma \vdash \phi : \texttt{Ref}\ \tau$, says that refinement type ϕ in context Γ is over the type τ. We abbreviate $\phi : \texttt{Ref}\ \tau$ as $\phi\ \texttt{wf}$ when the type τ is not significant.

3.3 Rules of the Calculus

Rather than give an exhaustive listing of all the rules of the calculus, we restrict the discussion to a subset of the rules and refer the interested reader to (Denney 1997) and (Denney 1998) for more details.

One distinctive feature of the calculus is the mutual dependencies of the different syntactic categories, and hence of the different judgement classes. Refinement types can contain propositions, which can contain terms, and these in turn can contain refinement types in the abstractions.

First we describe the well-formedness rules, starting with contexts. The empty context is well-formed, and there are two rules for extending an existing context.

$$\frac{\Gamma \vdash \phi \ \mathtt{wf}}{\vdash \Gamma, x : \phi \ \mathtt{wf}}\ x \notin \Gamma \qquad \frac{\Gamma \vdash P \ \mathtt{wf}}{\vdash \Gamma, P \ \mathtt{wf}}$$

The well-formedness rules for refinement types essentially involve stripping off the logic while checking that everything fits together correctly. For example,

$$\frac{\Gamma \vdash \phi : \mathtt{Ref}\ \sigma \quad \Gamma, x : \phi \vdash \psi : \mathtt{Ref}\ \tau}{\Gamma \vdash \Pi_{x:\phi}\psi : \mathtt{Ref}\ \sigma \to \tau} \qquad \frac{\Gamma \vdash \phi : \mathtt{Ref}\ \tau \quad \Gamma, x : \phi \vdash P \ \mathtt{wf}}{\Gamma \vdash (x : \phi)P : \mathtt{Ref}\ \tau}$$

There are checks on the well-formedness of the context for the base cases so as to ensure that all provable judgements are well-formed.

$$\frac{\vdash \Gamma \ \mathtt{wf}}{\Gamma \vdash \mathbf{1} : \mathtt{Ref}\ \mathbf{1}} \qquad \frac{\vdash \Gamma \ \mathtt{wf}}{\Gamma \vdash \gamma : \mathtt{Ref}\ \gamma}\ (\gamma \text{ ground type})$$

Similar conditions are made for the base cases of the other judgement classes.

It is straightforward to formulate well-formedness rules for propositions. We select two rules for discussion.

$$\frac{\Gamma \vdash t : \phi \quad \Gamma \vdash t' : \phi}{\Gamma \vdash t =_\phi t' \ \mathtt{wf}} \qquad \frac{\Gamma \vdash \phi : \mathtt{Ref}\ \tau \quad \Gamma \vdash \phi' : \mathtt{Ref}\ \tau}{\Gamma \vdash \phi \sqsubseteq \phi' \ \mathtt{wf}}$$

For $t =_\phi t'$ to be well-formed we require that t and t' both have refinement type ϕ. The appeal to refinement typing is why well-formedness involves logical reasoning, and this propagates through the well-formedness rules for the other syntactic categories. Similarly, the refinement $\phi \sqsubseteq \phi'$ is only well-formed when ϕ and ϕ' are over the same type.

The refinement typing rules are the natural generalisations of the usual typing rules for the simply-typed lambda calculus with products. For example, the introduction rules for abstractions and pairs are

$$\frac{\Gamma, x : \phi \vdash t : \psi}{\Gamma \vdash \lambda x : \phi . t : \Pi_{x:\phi}\psi} \qquad \frac{\Gamma \vdash t : \phi \quad \Gamma \vdash t' : \psi[t/x] \quad \Gamma, x : \phi \vdash \psi \ \mathtt{wf}}{\Gamma \vdash \langle t, t' \rangle : \Sigma_{x:\phi}\psi}$$

and the corresponding elimination rules are

$$\frac{\Gamma \vdash t : \Pi_{x:\phi}\psi \quad \Gamma \vdash t' : \phi}{\Gamma \vdash tt' : \psi[t'/x]} \qquad \frac{\Gamma \vdash t : \Sigma_{x:\phi}\psi}{\Gamma \vdash \pi_1(t) : \phi} \qquad \frac{\Gamma \vdash t : \Sigma_{x:\phi}\psi}{\Gamma \vdash \pi_2(t) : \psi[\pi_1(t)/x]}$$

Where the calculus differs from $\lambda^{\times\rightarrow}$ is in the logical reasoning which pervades the rules. This is evident in the rule for forming terms with a constant, where well-formedness uses a logical axiom

$$\frac{\Gamma \vdash t_i : \phi_i}{\Gamma \vdash k(t_1, \ldots, t_n) : \psi} \quad (Ax \rhd \Gamma \vdash k : \phi_1, \ldots, \phi_n \rightarrow \psi)$$

We have the obvious introduction rule for proving that a term inhabits a refinement type, and a weakening rule:

$$\frac{\Gamma \vdash t : \phi \quad \Gamma \vdash P[t/x]}{\Gamma \vdash t : (x : \phi)P} \qquad \frac{\Gamma \vdash t : \phi' \quad \Gamma \vdash \phi \sqsubseteq \phi'}{\Gamma \vdash t : \phi}$$

We do not include an elimination rule (allowing us to conclude that $t : \phi$ from $t : (x : \phi)P$) as primitive, since this follows from the weakening rule and the refinement rules which we give below.

One further rule is

$$\frac{\Gamma \vdash t =_{\phi} t'}{\Gamma \vdash t : \phi}$$

Inferring a refinement typing from an equality may seem strange, but it saves us a few rules. The reason for this is that in proving refinement typings and equalities we need to be able to combine assumptions on subterms. Since equalities are subscripted with a refinement type, the rule lets us use equality rules to prove a refinement typing. For example, the congruence rule for abstractions is

$$\frac{\Gamma \vdash \phi' \sqsubseteq \phi \quad \Gamma, x : \phi \vdash t =_{\psi} t'}{\Gamma \vdash \lambda x : \phi.t =_{\Pi_{x:\phi}\psi} \lambda x : \phi'.t'}$$

which lets us prove that $\lambda n : \mathtt{even}.n =_{\mathtt{even}\rightarrow\mathtt{even}} \lambda n : \mathtt{nat}.n$, and so we can infer that $\lambda n : \mathtt{nat}.n : \mathtt{even} \rightarrow \mathtt{even}$.

The η rules for abstractions and pairs have unconventional hypotheses, enabling us to combine logical and typing assumptions.

$$\frac{\Gamma, x : \phi \vdash tx : \psi}{\Gamma \vdash \lambda x : \phi.tx =_{\Pi_{x:\phi}\psi} t}\ x \notin t \qquad \frac{\Gamma \vdash \pi_1(t) : \phi \quad \Gamma \vdash \pi_2(t) : \psi[\pi_1(t)/x]}{\Gamma \vdash \langle \pi_1(t), \pi_2(t) \rangle =_{\Sigma_{x:\phi}\psi} t}$$

The usual hypothesis for the abstraction rule would be $\Gamma \vdash t : \Pi_{x:\phi}\psi$. The following example makes essential use of this rule.

$$\cfrac{\cfrac{\cfrac{\begin{array}{c} f : \mathtt{nat} \rightarrow \mathtt{nat}, \forall x : \mathtt{nat}.\mathtt{even}(fx), n : \mathtt{nat} \vdash fn : \mathtt{nat} \\ f : \mathtt{nat} \rightarrow \mathtt{nat}, \forall x : \mathtt{nat}.\mathtt{even}(fx), n : \mathtt{nat} \vdash \mathtt{even}(fn) \end{array}}{f : \mathtt{nat} \rightarrow \mathtt{nat}, \forall x : \mathtt{nat}.\mathtt{even}(fx), n : \mathtt{nat} \vdash fn : \mathtt{even}}}{f : \mathtt{nat} \rightarrow \mathtt{nat}, \forall x : \mathtt{nat}.\mathtt{even}(fx) \vdash f =_{\mathtt{nat}\rightarrow\mathtt{even}} \lambda n : \mathtt{nat}.fn}\ (\lambda\text{-}\eta\text{-EQ})}{f : \mathtt{nat} \rightarrow \mathtt{nat}, \forall x : \mathtt{nat}.\mathtt{even}(fx) \vdash f : \mathtt{nat} \rightarrow \mathtt{even}}$$

Similar examples can be given making use of the η rule for pairs.

The refinement rules are of two kinds – 'structural' and logical. The obvious structural rules are

$$\frac{\vdash \Gamma \ \texttt{wf}}{\Gamma \vdash \mathbf{1} \sqsubseteq \mathbf{1}} \qquad \frac{\Gamma \vdash \phi \sqsubseteq \phi' \quad \Gamma, x:\phi \vdash \psi \sqsubseteq \psi'}{\Gamma \vdash \Sigma_{x:\phi}\psi \sqsubseteq \Sigma_{x:\phi'}\psi'} \qquad \frac{\Gamma \vdash \phi' \sqsubseteq \phi \quad \Gamma, x:\phi \vdash \psi \sqsubseteq \psi'}{\Gamma \vdash \Pi_{x:\phi}\psi \sqsubseteq \Pi_{x:\phi'}\psi'}$$

The interesting rules, however, are for refinement involving propositions. We must say when an arbitrary refinement type is a refinement of a type with a proposition, and when it refines to one.

$$\frac{\Gamma \vdash \phi \sqsubseteq \psi \quad \Gamma, x:\psi \vdash P}{\Gamma \vdash (x:\phi)P \sqsubseteq \psi} \qquad \frac{\Gamma, x:\psi, Q \vdash x:\phi}{\Gamma \vdash \phi \sqsubseteq (x:\psi)Q}$$

The only other refinement rule is transitivity of refinement.

Finally, there are the rules of the logic. As the idea behind the calculus is that the logic should be orthogonal to the rules of the calculus, we do not list most of the (standard) rules of our example logic, typed classical first-order logic, but just indicate where refinement types are involved. One point is that the contexts are different from the usual formulation. This is made clear by the two introduction rules

$$\frac{\Gamma, P \vdash Q}{\Gamma \vdash P \supset Q} \qquad \frac{\Gamma, x:\phi \vdash P}{\Gamma \vdash \forall x:\phi.P}$$

We need a refinement typing for the $\forall$-elimination rule

$$\frac{\Gamma \vdash \forall x:\phi.P \quad \Gamma \vdash t:\phi}{\Gamma \vdash P[t/x]}$$

and refinement typings are also used to infer propositions with the rules

$$\frac{\Gamma \vdash t =_\phi t' \quad \Gamma, x:\phi \vdash P \ \texttt{wf} \quad \Gamma \vdash P[t/x]}{\Gamma \vdash P[t'/x]} \qquad \frac{\Gamma \vdash t:(x:\phi)P}{\Gamma \vdash P[t/x]}$$

4 DIVISION BY 2 REVISITED

As an illustration of how refinement types can provide a useful proof technique, we give the division by 2 example from the introduction again.

First, we give the inference rules for primitive and well-founded recursion over naturals, which combine the typing rules for recursion constants with the induction rules, into a single refinement typing. The sort is

$$\texttt{natrec} : \tau, (\texttt{nat} \to \tau \to \tau), \texttt{nat} \to \tau$$

and the axiom schemas are (for each ϕ)

$$\frac{\Gamma \vdash n:\texttt{nat} \quad \Gamma \vdash t:\phi[0] \quad \Gamma \vdash t' : \Pi_{n:\texttt{nat}}\phi[n] \to \phi[\texttt{succ}\ n]}{\Gamma \vdash \texttt{natrec}\ t\ t'\ n : \phi[n]}$$

$$\frac{\Gamma \vdash t:\phi[0] \quad \Gamma \vdash t' : \Pi_{n:\texttt{nat}}\phi[n] \to \phi[\texttt{succ}\ n]}{\Gamma \vdash \texttt{natrec}\ t\ t'\ 0 =_{\phi[0]} t}$$

$$\frac{\Gamma \vdash t : \phi[0] \quad \Gamma \vdash t' : \Pi_{n:\mathtt{nat}}\phi[n] \to \phi[\mathtt{succ}\ n]}{\Gamma \vdash \mathtt{natrec}\ t\ t'\ (\mathtt{succ}\ n) =_{\phi[\mathtt{succ}\ n]} t'\ n\ (\mathtt{natrec}\ t\ t'\ n)}$$

The axiom can also be expressed in the standard form of Definition 1. We define iteration from the more general recursion, as

$$\mathtt{natiter}\ t\ t'\ n = \mathtt{natrec}\ t\ (\lambda x : \mathtt{nat}.t')\ n$$

where $x \notin t'$.

The program is

$$\mathtt{div2} = \lambda n : \mathtt{nat}.\pi_1(\mathtt{div2'}\ n)$$

$$\mathtt{div2'} = \mathtt{natiter}\ \langle 0, 0\rangle\ (\lambda p : \mathtt{nat} \times \mathtt{nat}.\langle \pi_2 p, \pi_1 p + 1\rangle)$$

We prove that it satisfies the specification

$$\mathtt{div2} : \Pi_{n:\mathtt{nat}}(m : \mathtt{nat})n = 2m \vee n = 2m + 1$$

$$\mathtt{div2'} : \Pi_{n:\mathtt{nat}}\Sigma_{(m:\mathtt{nat})\mathtt{n=2m \vee n=2m+1}}(m' : \mathtt{nat})m + m' = n$$

In fact, there is little of interest in the main part of the proof. Since refinement types explicitly indicate the structure of the specification, this enables much of the proof to be carried out in a syntax-directed fashion. This would be useful for automation.

Write $\phi[n]$ as an abbreviation for $\Sigma_{m:(m:\mathtt{nat})n=2m \vee n=2m+1}(m' : \mathtt{nat})m + m' = n$.

$$\dfrac{\langle 0,0\rangle : \phi[0] \qquad \dfrac{\dfrac{\textit{see below}}{n : \mathtt{nat}, p : \phi[n] \vdash \langle \pi_2 p, \pi_1 p + 1\rangle : \phi[n+1]} \quad n : \mathtt{nat} \vdash \mathtt{nat} \times \mathtt{nat} \sqsubseteq \phi[n]}{n : \mathtt{nat} \vdash \lambda p : \mathtt{nat} \times \mathtt{nat}.\langle \pi_2 p, \pi_1 p + 1\rangle : \phi[n] \to \phi[n+1]}}{\dfrac{n : \mathtt{nat} \vdash \mathtt{natiter}\ \langle 0,0\rangle\ (\lambda p : \mathtt{nat} \times \mathtt{nat}.\langle \pi_2 p, \pi_1 p + 1\rangle)\ n\ :\ \Sigma_{(m:\mathtt{nat})\mathtt{n=2m \vee n=2m+1}}(m' : \mathtt{nat})m + m' = n}{\lambda n : \mathtt{nat}.\mathtt{natiter}\ \langle 0,0\rangle\ (\lambda p : \mathtt{nat} \times \mathtt{nat}.\langle \pi_2 p, \pi_1 p + 1\rangle)\ n\ :\ \Pi_{n:\mathtt{nat}}\Sigma_{(m:\mathtt{nat})\mathtt{n=2m \vee n=2m+1}}(m' : \mathtt{nat})m + m' = n}}$$

The proof continues with

$$\dfrac{\dfrac{n : \mathtt{nat}, n = 2\pi_1 p\ \vee\ n = 2\pi_1 p + 1, \pi_1 p + \pi_2 p = n \vdash n + 1 = 2\pi_2 p \vee n + 1 = 2\pi_2 p + 1}{n : \mathtt{nat}, p : \phi[n] \vdash n + 1 = 2\pi_2 p\ \vee\ n + 1 = 2\pi_2 p + 1}}{n : \mathtt{nat}, p : \phi[n] \vdash \pi_2 p : (m : \mathtt{nat})n + 1 = 2m \vee n + 1 = 2m + 1}$$

The remainder of the proof is arithmetic reasoning. In practice, we would use a theorem prover here.

5 MODELS

We give interpretations of the calculus in general models, known as *Henkin models* (Henkin 1950), with additional per structure. As is usual in concrete models of applied lambda calculi, we must consider such general models in order to get completeness. The per structure is to account for stratified equalities at different refinement types.

We define Henkin models in two stages. First, to each type σ (not just ground types) we ascribe the set A^σ, and to each constant $k : \tau_1, \ldots, \tau_n \to \tau$, an element $\mathtt{Const}(k)$ in the set $A^{\tau_1 \times \ldots \times \tau_n \to \tau}$. An applicative structure (with products) is a tuple

$$\langle \{A^\sigma\}, \{\mathtt{Proj}_1^{\sigma,\tau}\}, \{\mathtt{Proj}_2^{\sigma,\tau}\}, \{\mathtt{App}^{\sigma,\tau}\}, \mathtt{Const} \rangle$$

with families of projection and application maps. In addition, we require a function Pred which interprets predicates

$$\mathtt{Pred}(F) \subseteq A^{\tau_1 \times \ldots \times \tau_n}, \text{ for } F : \mathtt{pred}\, \tau_1, \ldots, \tau_n$$

Now, a Henkin Model is an applicative structure with two additional conditions, namely, that it is extensional, and that it satisfies the environment model condition. See (Mitchell 1996) for details. It is extensionality which allows us to interpret abstractions, pairs and the unit uniquely, up to equality in the appropriate per, and the environment model condition which gives enough elements in the model.

We do not have $A^{\sigma \times \tau} = A^\sigma \times A^\tau$ in general, but have an isomorphism mediated by the projection functions, $\mathtt{Proj}_1^{\sigma,\tau} : A^{\sigma \times \tau} \to A^\sigma$, and $\mathtt{Proj}_2^{\sigma,\tau} : A^{\sigma \times \tau} \to A^\tau$. In general, $A^{\sigma \to \tau}$ is embedded in $A^\sigma \to A^\tau$, but not equal.

A Henkin model models an applied theory when all constants and predicates are given an interpretation, and each axiom is true in the model, as defined below.

The idea is that refinement types over type σ are interpreted as pers over A^σ. Ground types are interpreted as the identity per over their set. It is easy to see that, in fact, all types are interpreted as identities.

Now, expressions are all interpreted in context, so we must first define environments g for context Γ, written $g \models \Gamma$, where g is a tuple of elements in the domains of the pers for the refinement types in Γ. We define this recursively with the interpretation of refinement types and propositions. For per R, we write $a \in R$ to mean $a\, R\, a$.

$$\langle\rangle \models \langle\rangle$$

$$\langle g, a\rangle \models \Gamma, x : \phi \text{ when } g \models \Gamma \text{ and } a \in [\![\Gamma \vdash \phi]\!](g)$$

$$g \models \Gamma, P \text{ when } g \models \Gamma \text{ and } g \in [\![\Gamma \vdash P]\!]$$

For $g, g' \models \Gamma$ we define equality of environments in the obvious way, as simultaneous equality of elements in the corresponding per, written $g\ [\![\Gamma]\!]\ g'$.

To avoid questions of coherence, we interpret raw terms*, and so raw propositions and refinement types too. The notation $\Gamma \vdash E$ indicates raw expression E in context Γ.

Now as mentioned above, refinement types are interpreted as pers over the associated type. The interpretation is given in Figure 1. The unit and ground types are interpreted as identities; the product and function refinement types are interpreted as the expected combination of pers, and $(x : \phi)P$ is interpreted as the restriction of ϕ to the elements for which P holds.

There is an apparent asymmetry in the definition of the product per for $\Sigma_{x:\phi}\psi$, but

---

*In fact, only well-structured terms are given an interpretation. For example, $(\lambda n : \mathbf{even}.n)*$ does not have a well-defined interpretation, but $(\lambda n : \mathbf{even}.n)3$ does, even though it is not syntactically well-formed.

$$a \, [\![\Gamma \vdash \mathbf{1}]\!](g) \, a' \iff a, a' \in A^{\mathbf{1}}$$

$$\frac{[\![\Gamma \vdash \phi]\!] = R \quad [\![\Gamma, x : \phi \vdash \psi]\!] = S}{a \, [\![\Gamma \vdash \Sigma_{x:\phi}\psi]\!](g) \, a' \iff \begin{array}{l} \mathtt{Proj}_1^{\sigma,\tau}(a) \; Rg \; \mathtt{Proj}_1^{\sigma,\tau}(a') \text{ and} \\ \mathtt{Proj}_2^{\sigma,\tau}(a) \; S\langle g, \mathtt{Proj}_1^{\sigma,\tau}(a)\rangle \; \mathtt{Proj}_2^{\sigma,\tau}(a') \end{array}}$$

$$\frac{[\![\Gamma \vdash \phi]\!] = R \quad [\![\Gamma, x : \phi \vdash \psi]\!] = S}{f \, [\![\Gamma \vdash \Pi_{x:\phi}\psi]\!](g) \, f' \iff \text{for all } a \; Rg \; a', \mathtt{App}(f, a) \; S\langle g, a\rangle \; \mathtt{App}(f', a')}$$

$$\frac{[\![\Gamma \vdash \phi]\!] = R \quad [\![\Gamma, x : \phi \vdash P]\!] = A}{a \, [\![\Gamma \vdash (x : \phi)P]\!](g) \, a' \iff a \; Rg \; a', \langle g, a\rangle \in A, \langle g, a'\rangle \in A}$$

$$a \, [\![\Gamma \vdash \gamma]\!](g) \, a' \iff a, a' \in A^{\gamma} \text{ and } a = a'$$

Figure 1 Interpretation of refinement types

in fact, if ϕ is a well-formed refinement type in context Γ, then the soundness result below states that if $g[\![\Gamma]\!]g'$ we have $[\![\Gamma \vdash \phi]\!](g) = [\![\Gamma \vdash \phi]\!](g')$.

The raw term in context $\Gamma \vdash t$ is interpreted in environment $g \models \Gamma$ as a subset (its 'total realizers') of A^{σ}. This is given in Figure 2. The idea is that terms are

$$\frac{[\![\Gamma \vdash \phi]\!] = R}{[\![\Gamma, x : \phi, \Gamma' \vdash x]\!]\langle g, a, g'\rangle = \{a' \mid a' \; Rg \; a\}}$$

$$\frac{[\![\Gamma \vdash t_i]\!] = m_i}{[\![\Gamma \vdash k(t_1, \ldots, t_n)]\!](g) = \{\mathtt{App}(\mathtt{Const}(k), \langle a_1, \ldots, a_n\rangle) \mid a_i \in m_i(g)\}}$$

$$[\![\Gamma \vdash *]\!](g) = A^{\mathbf{1}}$$

$$\frac{[\![\Gamma \vdash t]\!] = m \quad [\![\Gamma \vdash t']\!] = m'}{[\![\Gamma \vdash \langle t, t'\rangle]\!](g) = \{a \in A^{\sigma \times \tau} \mid \mathtt{Proj}_1^{\sigma,\tau}(a) \in mg, \mathtt{Proj}_2^{\sigma,\tau}(a) \in m'g\}}$$

$$\frac{[\![\Gamma, x : \phi \vdash t]\!] = m}{[\![\Gamma \vdash \lambda x : \phi.t]\!](g) = \{f \in A^{\sigma \to \tau} \mid \text{for all } a \in [\![\Gamma \vdash \phi]\!](g) \, . \, \mathtt{App}(f, a) \in m\langle g, a\rangle\}}$$

$$\frac{[\![\Gamma \vdash t]\!] = m}{[\![\Gamma \vdash \pi_1(t)]\!](g) = \{\mathtt{Proj}_1^{\sigma,\tau}(a) \mid a \in mg\}}$$

$$\frac{[\![\Gamma \vdash t]\!] = m}{[\![\Gamma \vdash \pi_2(t)]\!](g) = \{\mathtt{Proj}_2^{\sigma,\tau}(a) \mid a \in mg\}}$$

$$\frac{[\![\Gamma \vdash t]\!] = m \quad [\![\Gamma \vdash t']\!] = m'}{[\![\Gamma \vdash tt']\!](g) = \{\mathtt{App}(f, a) \mid f \in mg, a \in m'g\}}$$

Figure 2 Interpretation of terms

interpreted as morphisms of pers, that is, maps of equivalence classes, and so the interpretation of a variable is a map from an element to its equivalence class (in the relevant refinement type). It is because of the refinement type in abstractions that we interpret terms as sets rather than as single elements. For example, $\lambda n : \mathtt{even}.n$ is interpreted as the set of elements in $A^{\mathtt{nat}\to\mathtt{nat}}$ which are the identity for even arguments. In Figure 3 we give the interpretation of propositions. We interpret a raw proposition in context $\Gamma \vdash P$ as the set of environments $g \models \Gamma$ in which P holds.

$$[\![\Gamma \vdash \mathtt{false}]\!] = \emptyset$$

$$[\![\Gamma \vdash P \supset P']\!] = \{g \models \Gamma \mid g \notin [\![\Gamma \vdash P]\!] \text{ or } g \in [\![\Gamma \vdash P']\!]\}$$

$$[\![\Gamma \vdash \forall x : \phi.P]\!] = \{g \models \Gamma \mid \forall a \in [\![\Gamma \vdash \phi]\!](g) \,.\, \langle g, a\rangle \in [\![\Gamma, x : \phi \vdash P]\!]\}$$

$$\frac{[\![\Gamma \vdash t_i]\!] = m_i}{[\![\Gamma \vdash F(t_1, \ldots, t_n)]\!] = \{g \models \Gamma \mid \forall a_i \in m_i g \,.\, \langle a_1, \ldots, a_n\rangle \in \mathtt{Pred}(F)\}}$$

$$\frac{[\![\Gamma \vdash t]\!] = m \quad [\![\Gamma \vdash t']\!] = m' \quad [\![\Gamma \vdash \phi]\!] = R}{[\![\Gamma \vdash t =_\phi t']\!] = \{g \models \Gamma \mid \forall a \in mg \,.\, \forall a' \in m'g \,.\, a\, Rg\, a'\}}$$

$$\frac{[\![\Gamma \vdash \phi]\!] = R \quad [\![\Gamma \vdash \phi']\!] = R'}{[\![\Gamma \vdash \phi \sqsubseteq \phi']\!] = \{g \models \Gamma \mid Rg \supseteq R'g\}}$$

Figure 3 Interpretation of propositions

We may now say what the semantic analogues of the judgements are. Define $\Gamma \models t : \phi$ when (for all models $\mathcal{A}$) for all $g\ [\![\Gamma]\!]\ g'$, for all $a \in [\![\Gamma \vdash t]\!](g)$ and $a' \in [\![\Gamma \vdash t]\!](g')$, we have $a\ [\![\Gamma \vdash \phi]\!](g)\ a'$. In other words, the interpretation is unique up to the equality of the per. We say that $\Gamma \models P$ when $[\![\Gamma \vdash P]\!] = \{g \quad g \models \Gamma\}$. In particular, the refinement $\Gamma \models \phi \sqsubseteq \phi'$ is valid when for all $g \models \Gamma$, there is an inclusion of pers $[\![\Gamma \vdash \phi']\!](g) \subseteq [\![\Gamma \vdash \phi]\!](g)$. We define $\Gamma \models \phi\ \mathtt{wf}$ to mean : for all $g\ [\![\Gamma]\!]\ g'$, $[\![\Gamma \vdash \phi]\!](g) = [\![\Gamma \vdash \phi]\!](g')$, and $\Gamma \models P\ \mathtt{wf}$ to mean : for all $g\ [\![\Gamma]\!]\ g'$, $g \in [\![\Gamma \vdash P]\!] \iff g' \in [\![\Gamma \vdash P]\!]$.

5.1 Soundness and Completeness

Having given the meaning to the expressions of the calculus via an interpretation, we must verify that this respects the inference rules, that is, the calculus is sound with respect to the intended interpretation. A consequence of this is that since we can give nontrivial models the calculus is consistent.

Theorem 3 *(Soundness) If* $\Gamma \vdash t : \phi$ *then* $\Gamma \models t : \phi$*, if* $\Gamma \vdash \phi\ \mathtt{wf}$ *then* $\Gamma \models \phi\ \mathtt{wf}$*, if* $\Gamma \vdash P\ \mathtt{wf}$ *then* $\Gamma \models P\ \mathtt{wf}$*, and if* $\Gamma \vdash P$ *then* $\Gamma \models P$.

Proof: Simultaneous induction over all derivations. The soundness of β-reduction and $\forall$-elimination is by a substitution lemma. ∎

A more challenging question is whether the calculus is in any sense complete, that is, if a particular judgement holds in all the models (of the relevant signature) then it is provable. In fact, the calculus is also complete, with a couple of provisos. Firstly, due to the way in which well-formedness is combined with satisfying logical properties, we must assume that the judgement is well-formed. This is because it is possible for non well-formed terms to have a unique interpretation, and so, semantically, have a refinement type. For example, $(\lambda n : \texttt{even}.*)3$ is interpreted as the unique inhabitant of unit type, but cannot be typed in the system.

The second point arises with higher-order terms, and is due to the calculus requiring arguments to an abstraction to have the refinement type on the abstraction, but the model just needing equality of arguments at that refinement type to give equal results. For example, $\lambda f : \texttt{nat} \to \texttt{nat}.3$ has the refinement type $(\texttt{even} \to \texttt{nat}) \to \texttt{nat}$ in the model, but not in the calculus.

What we can show, however, is that if a term in context, $\Gamma \vdash t$, has refinement type ϕ in the model, then there exists a term t' which does have refinement type ϕ, such that $\Gamma \models t =_\phi t'$. We write this as $\Gamma \vdash t \sim \phi$.

Theorem 4 *(Completeness) For* $\Gamma \vdash P \ \texttt{wf}$*, if* $\Gamma \models P$ *then* $\Gamma \vdash P$*. For* $\Gamma \vdash \phi \ \texttt{wf}$*, if* $\Gamma \models t : \phi$ *then* $\Gamma \vdash t \sim \phi$*.*

Proof: Although we do not have minimal term models (due to having propositional assumptions), we can still use a term model construction to prove completeness, by using a slight generalisation of the standard 'consistency implies satisfiability' argument.

First we generalise consistency and satisfiability from sets of closed propositions to arbitrary contexts. Say that context Γ is *consistent*, when $\Gamma \nvdash \texttt{false}$, and *satisfiable*, when there exists a model $\mathcal{A}$ and environment g in $\mathcal{A}$ such that $g \models_{\mathcal{A}} \Gamma$. In the case that Γ is a context of closed propositions, these reduce to the usual definitions of consistency and satisfiability. Now we want to show that $\Gamma \models P \Rightarrow \Gamma \vdash P$, so suppose $\Gamma \nvdash P$. Then $\Gamma, \neg P$ is consistent and so, by assumption, is satisfiable. Hence $\Gamma \not\models P$.

Let Γ be a consistent context. We sketch the construction of a model $\mathcal{A}$ and environment $g \models_{\mathcal{A}} \Gamma$.

1. Let $A = \{P \mid \Gamma \vdash P \ \texttt{wf}\}$. Construct a maximal consistent Henkin theory Δ such that $\{P \mid \Gamma \vdash P\} \subseteq \Delta \subseteq A$.
   A *Henkin* theory* T, is a collection of sentences closed under derivation, such that if the proposition $\exists x : \phi.P$ is in T, then $P[t/x]$ is in T for some $t : \phi$.
   The construction of the Henkin theory involves adding constants $c_{\phi,P} : \tau$, and axioms $c_{\phi,P} : \phi$, $P[c_{\phi,P}]$, for each refinement type $\Gamma \vdash \phi : \texttt{Ref} \ \ \tau$, and propositions $\Gamma \vdash P \ \texttt{wf}$, for each $\exists x : \phi.P$ in T.

*These have nothing to do with Henkin models.

The existence of maximal consistent Henkin extensions follows using a standard argument from Zorn's Lemma. See (van Dalen 1994) for details. Note that for all $\Gamma \vdash P$ `wf` exactly one of P, $\neg P$ is in Δ.

2. Let Γ_∞ be a set of infinitely many declarations $x : \phi$ for each closed inhabited ϕ, *i.e.* for which there exists a t such that $\vdash t : \phi$. This is so that we can construct a model from open terms.
3. Define a family of logical equivalence relations, $R^\tau_\Delta(\_, \_)$ for each type τ, on open terms of $\lambda^{\times\to}$ with type τ, $\{t \mid \Gamma_\infty \vdash t : \tau\}$, as $R^\tau_\Delta(t, t') \iff \Delta_\infty \vdash t =_\tau t'$.
4. Define A^τ as the set of equivalence classes with respect to R of open terms in τ, and construct a Henkin model, $\mathcal{A}$, by interpreting constants syntactically. Interpret predicates $F : \mathtt{pred}\ \tau_1, \ldots, \tau_n$ as $\{[\langle t_1, \ldots, t_n \rangle] \mid F(t_1, \ldots, t_n) \in \Delta\}$.
5. The set Δ gives rise to an environment for Γ in $\mathcal{A}$. For every $x : \phi \in \Gamma$ there is a proposition $x =_{\phi'} t \in \Delta$, where t is closed, and ϕ' is a closed instantiation of ϕ. Define the corresponding element in the environment as $g_x = [u]^\tau$, where u is any total realizer of t (which must exist).
6. For $\Gamma \vdash P$ `wf`, prove that $g \in [\![\Gamma \vdash P]\!] \iff \Delta_\infty \vdash P \iff \Delta \vdash P$. To prove the first equivalence we directly characterise the interpretation of terms and refinement types in the term model, $\mathcal{A}$. The second equivalence is because for each $x : \phi \in \Gamma_\infty$, $x \notin P$ and ϕ is inhabited.

Hence $\mathcal{A}$ models Δ, and so it models Γ. ∎

Now since first-order logic, the simply-typed lambda calculus, and the refinement types calculus are all complete for the class of Henkin models, we have

Corollary 5 *The calculus is a conservative extension of $\lambda^{\times\to}$: If $\Gamma \vdash t =_\tau t'$ is a well-formed equation in $\lambda^{\times\to}$, then it is provable in $\lambda^{\times\to}$, if and only if it is provable in the calculus of refinement types.*

Corollary 6 *The calculus is a conservative extension of first-order logic : If $\Gamma \vdash P$ `wf` does not contain any refinement types, then it is provable in first-order logic, if and only if it is provable in the calculus of refinement types.*

The significance of these corollaries is that we are free to use the specification language for proving program equivalences and for reasoning about programs using the program logic, in the knowledge that it faithfully reflects the equality in the underlying programming language, and proofs in the program logic.

6 CONCLUSIONS

We have described the refinement type methodology of specification. This is a way of combining the type system of a programming language with a program logic to give a specification language. This is an alternative to approaches which rely on encoding a logic into an expressive type theory, and those which simply use a program logic.

The two-level nature of the calculus suggests the construction of a modular tool in which checking program correctness is a combination of type checking and theorem proving. The modularity would come from constructing a 'specification checker' from an existing theorem prover and a type checker, for the program logic and programming language respectively. Indeed, this is similar to what is done in the interactive proof development systems, Nuprl and PVS.

The calculus could provide a foundation for other specification based formalisms. In the proof that `div2` satisfied its specification we used the proof for `div2'`. There is an implicit element of refinement here. We envisage separate extensions to transformation and refinement calculi, and an embedding in a calculus of full program annotations.

Although we have given a refinement relation $\phi \sqsubseteq \phi'$ on specifications, this does not constitute a full *refinement calculus* (such as in (Morgan 1994)). The idea there is to internalise specifications into programs and consider a refinement relation on mixtures of specification and program. This is carried out in the author's forthcoming PhD thesis. The structure imposed on specifications would help to partially automate verification and derivation.

By extending the type system of $\lambda^{\times\rightarrow}$ to refinement types, we gain a simple notion of program annotation, where variables on abstractions are labelled with logical information. The ability to express information within a program context is useful. Program reasoning and manipulation often requires facts which are true at some local program point. For example, if it is known that variable n must be within certain bounds, then a programmer (or compiler) may be able to perform some partial evaluation or optimisation.

The ability to express equality at a refinement type is useful in program transformation. For example, we might want to transform a function of type $\mathtt{nat} \rightarrow \mathtt{nat}$, with the prescription "maintain value on evens, and improve on odds (in some way)". We can express (part of) this by saying that the terms are equal at the refinement type $\mathtt{even} \rightarrow \mathtt{nat}$.

This account of specifications which brings equality to the fore should be especially useful in data refinement, where it is natural to consider different equalities at the abstract and concrete types.

We believe that the principles outlined here are general enough to be applied to structures other than those traditionally studied – data flow diagrams for example. Since the logic is arbitrary (up to a point) we are not constrained by the type theory. It would be an interesting line of research to see how type-theoretic and semantic ideas could help there.

Acknowledgements

This work has benefited from discussions with my supervisors – Gordon Plotkin, John Power and Marcelo Fiore. Conversations with Alex Bunkenburg, Healfdene Goguen and James McKinna have also been useful. The presentation has been improved by numerous suggestions from the anonymous referees.

The author was supported by a postgraduate research studentship from the Engineering and Physical Sciences Research Council while carrying out this research.

REFERENCES

Aspinall, D. (1995) Subtyping with singleton types, *in* 'Proceedings of Computer Science Logic '94', Vol. 933 of *LNCS*.

Aspinall, D. & Compagnoni, A. (1996) Subtyping dependent types, *in* 'Proceedings of the eleventh IEEE Symposium on Logic in Computer Science'.

Burn, G. L. (1992) A logical framework for program analysis, *in* J. Launchbury & P. Sansom, eds, 'Proceedings of the 1992 Glasgow Functional Programming Workshop', Springer-Verlag Workshops in Computer Science series, pp. 30–42.

Burstall, R. & McKinna, J. (1992) Deliverables : A categorical approach to program development in type theory, *in* 'Mathematical Foundations of Computer Science : 18th International Symposium', Vol. 711 of *Lecture Notes in Computer Science*, pp. 32–67. An earlier version appeared as LFCS Technical Report ECS-LFCS-92-242.

Denney, E. (1997) Refining Refinement Types, *in* 'Informal Proceedings of Types Workshop on Subtyping, Inheritance and Modular Development of Proofs', University of Durham.

Denney, E. (1998) A General Theory of Program Refinement. PhD thesis Department of Computer Science, University of Edinburgh. Forthcoming.

Feferman, S. (1985) A theory of variable types, *in* 'Proceedings of the Fifth Latin American Symposium on Mathematical Logic', Vol. 19 of *Revista Colombiana de Matemáticas*.

Freeman, T. & Pfenning, F. (1991) Refinement types for ML, *in* 'Proceedings of the SIGPLAN'91 Symposium on Language Design and Implementation', ACM Press, pp. 268–277.

Hayashi, S. (1994) Logic of refinement types, *in* 'Types for Proofs and programs', Vol. 806 of *Lecture Notes in Computer Science*, Springer Verlag.

Henkin, L. (1950) Completeness in the theory of types. *Journal of Symbolic Logic* **15**(2), 81–91.

Luo, Z. (1991) Program specification and data refinement in type theory. LFCS Technical Report ECS-LFCS-90-131, Department of Computer Science, University of Edinburgh.

McKinna, J. (1992) Deliverables : A Categorical Approach to Program Development in Type Theory. PhD thesis, Department of Computer Science, University of Edinburgh.

Mitchell, J. (1996) *Foundations for Programming Languages*, Foundations of Computing Series, MIT Press.

Morgan, C. (1994) *Programming from Specifications*. Prentice Hall.

Nielson, H. & Nielson, F. (1988) Automatic binding time analysis for a typed λ-calculus, *in* 'Proceedings of the Fifteenth Annual ACM Symposium on Principles of Programming Languages'.

Nordström, B., Petersson, K. & Smith, J. M. (1990) *Programming in Martin-Löf's Type Theory*. Vol. 7 of *Monographs on Computer Science*, Oxford University Press.

van Dalen, D. (1994) *Logic and Structure*. Springer-Verlag.

BIOGRAPHY

Ewen Denney is a final year PhD student at the Laboratory for the Foundations of Computer Science in Edinburgh University, under the supervision of Professor Gordon Plotkin and Doctor Marcelo Fiore. His research is on the theory of program refinement, with an aim to characterising the logical and semantic structures involved. He holds a Masters Degree from Imperial College and a Bachelors from the University of Glasgow.

14

An extension of the program derivation format

A.J.M. van Gasteren and A. Bijlsma
Department of Mathematics and Computing Science, Eindhoven University of Technology
P.O. Box 513, 5600 MB Eindhoven, The Netherlands
telephone + 31-40-247-4317, fax + 31-40-245-1733
e-mail {netty, lexb}@win.tue.nl

Abstract

A convention is proposed for embedding program statements into the program derivation calculus, with the aim of simplifying the stepwise construction of programs.

Keywords

Program derivation, predicate calculus, data refinement

1 INTRODUCTION

In this paper we propose an extension to the proof format commonly used for calculational program derivation. This format, which was invented by W.H.J. Feijen, is becoming widely used in the computing community and has proved itself very useful for program derivation as well as the construction of mathematical proofs in general. In program derivation, it is usually employed together with the axiom of assignment to derive program fragments consisting of a single concurrent assignment in a fixed context. The extension is intended to facilitate the derivation of programs consisting of a sequence of assignments or procedure calls. To this end, we show how program statements may be successively embedded in an ongoing derivation, the intended result of which is the stepwise construction of the program in the course of the calculation.

2 REVIEW OF THE PROOF FORMAT

In the usual version of the proof format we find derivations like

$$
\begin{array}{ll}
 & P \\
\equiv & \{\text{explanation of } [P \equiv Q]\} \\
 & Q \\
\Leftarrow & \{\text{explanation of } [Q \Leftarrow R]\}
\end{array}
$$

Programming Concepts and Methods D. Gries, & W-P. de Roever (Eds.)

R ,

where P, Q, R denote predicates on a fixed space, and the brackets $[\ldots]$ denote universal quantification over that space, as in Dijkstra *et al.* (1990). From this we may draw the conclusion $[P \Leftarrow R]$. More generally, for any structures P, Q, R and relational binary operators $\oplus$ and $\otimes$ the derivation

$$
\begin{array}{ll}
& P \\
\oplus & \{\text{explanation of } [P \oplus Q]\} \\
& Q \\
\otimes & \{\text{explanation of } [Q \otimes R]\} \\
& R
\end{array}
$$

allows us to conclude $[P\ \ (\oplus)\circ(\otimes)\ \ R]$, where $(\oplus)\circ(\otimes)$ is the relational composition of binary relations $\oplus$ and $\otimes$. This conclusion is only useful if composition $(\oplus)\circ(\otimes)$ can be simplified, i.e. is equal to or implies a single familiar operator. Composition $(\Rightarrow)\circ(\Leftarrow)$, for instance, is decidedly not useful. The most commonly used compositions are composition with equality and continued compositions of a transitive operator:

$$
\begin{array}{lcll}
(=)\circ(\oplus) & = & (\oplus) & , \\
(\oplus)\circ(=) & = & (\oplus) & , \\
(\oplus)\circ(\oplus) & \Rightarrow & (\oplus) & \text{for transitive } \oplus \quad , \\
(\oplus)\circ(\oplus) & = & (\oplus) & \text{for transitive and reflexive } \oplus \quad .
\end{array}
$$

Here is a simplification that is perhaps less familiar: if we write $x =_m y$ for $x \bmod m = y \bmod m$, the derivation

$$
\begin{array}{ll}
& x \\
=_m & \{\text{explanation of } [x \bmod m = y \bmod m]\} \\
& y \\
=_n & \{\text{explanation of } [y \bmod n = z \bmod n]\} \\
& z
\end{array}
$$

admits the conclusion $[x \bmod (m \operatorname{gcd} n) = z \bmod (m \operatorname{gcd} n)]$. Another slightly unusual simplification is

$$(\not\equiv)\circ(\not\equiv) \;=\; (\equiv) \quad .$$

An example of its usefulness is the proof of Theorem 4 of Bijlsma *et al.* (1996).

3 DERIVATIONS CONTAINING PROGRAM STATEMENTS

For structure transformer f and relational binary operator $\oplus$, we propose to admit into program derivations steps like

$$\begin{array}{ll} & P \\ \oplus & \lhd f \rhd \\ & \quad \{\text{explanation of } [f.P \oplus Q]\} \\ & Q \end{array}$$

which, as the hint suggests, will signify the validity of $[f.P \oplus Q]$. We propose to pronounce the above step, in the case where $\oplus$ is $\Leftarrow$, as "P follows by f from Q", and similarly in other cases. As to the combination of such steps,

$$\begin{array}{ll} & P \\ \oplus & \lhd f \rhd \\ & \quad \{\text{explanation of } [f.P \oplus Q]\} \\ & Q \\ \otimes & \lhd g \rhd \\ & \quad \{\text{explanation of } [g.Q \otimes R]\} \\ & R \end{array}$$

admits only the conclusion $[f.P \oplus Q] \;\wedge\; [g.Q \otimes R]$, which cannot be simplified any further without knowledge of the properties of the operators and structure transformers involved. However, if the operators are $\equiv$, it follows that $[g.(f.P) \equiv R]$; if the operators are $\Leftarrow$ and g is monotonic, it follows that $[g.(f.P) \Leftarrow R]$.

In this paper, we limit ourselves to a special case where the insertion of structure transformers yields particularly useful conclusions. From now on f will be a particular predicate transformer, namely the weakest precondition of a program statement S. For this particular purpose, we prefer to write $\lhd\; S \;\rhd$ rather than $\lhd\; wp.S \;\rhd$. As promised in the Introduction, this allows us to write derivations like

$$\begin{array}{ll} & P \\ \Leftarrow & \lhd S \rhd \\ & \quad \{\text{explanation of } [wp.S.P \Leftarrow Q]\} \\ & Q \\ \equiv & \lhd T \rhd \\ & \quad \{\text{explanation of } [wp.T.Q \equiv R]\} \\ & R \;\;, \end{array}$$

and draw the conclusion

$$\{R\} \;\; T;\; S \;\; \{P\} \;\; .$$

Observe that the statements of the program are discovered consecutively in the course of a single derivation. Because

$$\begin{array}{ll} & P \\ \Leftarrow & \quad \{\text{explanation of } [P \Leftarrow Q]\} \\ & Q \end{array}$$

is equivalent to

$$\begin{array}{ll} & P \\ \Leftarrow & \lhd\, skip \,\rhd \\ & \quad \{\text{explanation of } [P \Leftarrow Q]\} \\ & Q \ , \end{array}$$

steps introducing a program statement may be freely intermixed with classical steps expressing a strengthening or an equivalence.

Example 1 The task is to write a program that cyclically rotates the values of integer variables x, y, z and uses neither auxiliary variables nor multiple assignments. The analogous program with two variables occurs in many textbooks of programming (e.g. Dijkstra *et al.* (1984)) as an example of how to use the semantics of assignment, but it is always given as a task for a posteriori verification, never derived. The specification of the problem is

$$\begin{array}{l} \{true\} \\ rot.x.y.z \\ \{x = y_\bullet \ \wedge \ y = z_\bullet \ \wedge \ z = x_\bullet\} \ , \end{array}$$

where we have followed the convention of denoting the original value of x by $x_\bullet$ (pronounce 'x old'). (This can be seen as an application of the traditional 'specification variable' or 'logical constant' approach where the precondition is implicitly extended with terms like $x = x_\bullet$.)

Without introducing statements into derivations there is really no good way to tackle this. With statements, however, we may derive

$$\begin{array}{ll} & x = y_\bullet \ \wedge \ y = z_\bullet \ \wedge \ z = x_\bullet \\ \equiv & \lhd\, x := x + y + z \,\rhd \\ & \quad \{\text{to bring } y \text{ and } y_\bullet \text{ together in a single conjunct}\} \\ & x + y + z = y_\bullet \ \wedge \ y = z_\bullet \ \wedge \ z = x_\bullet \\ \equiv & \lhd\, y := -x + y - z \,\rhd \\ & \quad \{\text{to create a term } y = y_\bullet\} \\ & y = y_\bullet \ \wedge \ -x + y - z = z_\bullet \ \wedge \ z = x_\bullet \\ \equiv & \lhd\, z := -x + y - z \,\rhd \\ & \quad \{\text{to create a term } z = z_\bullet\} \end{array}$$

$$
\begin{array}{ll}
& y = y_\bullet \ \wedge\ z = z_\bullet \ \wedge\ -x + y - z = x_\bullet \\
\equiv & \quad \triangleleft\, x := -x + y - z \,\triangleright \\
& \qquad \{\text{to create a term } x = x_\bullet\} \\
& y = y_\bullet \ \wedge\ z = z_\bullet \ \wedge\ x = x_\bullet \quad .
\end{array}
$$

(Note that the first step in this derivation is rather arbitrary: it should satisfy the criteria that it introduces y into the first conjunct and does not remove x from it, but apart from these we have a lot of choice. After the first step, however, there is no more choice and the calculation is guided entirely by the wish to create the conjuncts of the precondition one by one.)

We conclude that the specification is satisfied by the program

$$
\begin{array}{l}
\quad \{true\} \\
\quad x := -x + y - z \\
;\, z := -x + y - z \\
;\, y := -x + y - z \\
;\, x := x + y + z \\
\quad \{x = y_\bullet \ \wedge\ y = x_\bullet \ \wedge\ z = x_\bullet\} \quad .
\end{array}
$$

□

4 DERIVATIONS CONTAINING COERCION STATEMENTS

For every predicate B, a program statement S is defined by the condition that, for every predicate R,

$$[wp.S.R \ \equiv\ (R \ \Leftarrow\ B)].$$

Such a statement S is called a *coercion statement* in Morgan (1990). We shall denote the coercion statement corresponding to a boolean expression B by B as well, as no confusion threatens. The coercion statement behaves like **magic** in case $\neg B$ holds, and hence it is not implementable; its value lies in the fact that Hoare triples like

$$\{P\}\ \ B;\ S\ \ \{Q\}$$

and

$$\{P\}\ \ \neg B;\ T\ \ \{Q\}$$

can be combined into

$$\{P\}$$

$$
\begin{array}{l}
\textbf{if}\ B \rightarrow\ \ S \\
[\!]\ \neg B \rightarrow T \\
\textbf{fi} \\
\{Q\}\ .
\end{array}
$$

We shall see several cases of this use of coercion statements to produce selection statements in the next sections. In the present section, however, we concentrate on derivations that contain *only* coercion statements, i.e. no statements of other kinds. It will be seen that these can be used as a way to introduce local hypotheses into proofs that may have nothing to do with programming at all.

An important ingredient of natural deduction systems is their ability to introduce local hypotheses into a proof. Equational reasoning, as commonly understood, lacks a facility for doing this – possibly the most important cause of the continued popularity of otherwise awkward and unwieldy proof systems based on natural deduction.

Consider a proof step where a coercion statement B is introduced, say

$$
\begin{array}{ll}
 & P \\
\Leftarrow & \lhd B \rhd \\
 & \quad \{\text{explanation of } [(P \Leftarrow B) \Leftarrow Q]\} \\
 & Q\ .
\end{array}
$$

Here the hint can be simplified to $[P \Leftarrow B \wedge Q]$. As to the composition of such steps, observe that

$$
\begin{array}{ll}
 & P \\
\Leftarrow & \lhd B \rhd \\
 & \quad \{\text{explanation of } [P \Leftarrow B \wedge Q]\} \\
 & Q \\
\Leftarrow & \lhd C \rhd \\
 & \quad \{\text{explanation of } [Q \Leftarrow C \wedge R]\} \\
 & R
\end{array}
$$

admits conclusion

$$[P \Leftarrow B \wedge C \wedge R]\ .$$

Using this technique to prove an implication gives us the opportunity to choose among several different calculations that differ in the way the antecedent is distributed over the hints. Conversely, to draw a conclusion from such a derivation, one has to gather the conjuncts of the antecedent from the proof steps in which a hypothesis was introduced. This is made easy by the use of the conspicuous symbols $\lhd \ldots \rhd$.

Remark This method of introducing hypotheses into a transformational proof has aims similar to the generalized window inference proposed by Grundy (1996); however, our method requires much less of a departure from normal practice. Some other authors, e.g. Gries *et al.* (1993, sec. 4.2), use a notation like

$$\begin{array}{ll} & P \\ \equiv & \qquad \{\textbf{Assumption } X\} \\ & Q \ , \end{array}$$

which requires the validity of

$$[(P \equiv Q) \ \Leftarrow \ X] \ .$$

This is not the same as a step of the form

$$\begin{array}{ll} & P \\ \equiv & \lhd X \rhd \\ & \qquad \{\text{explanation}\} \\ & Q \end{array}$$

which requires the stronger

$$[(P \Leftarrow X) \ \equiv \ Q] \ .$$

This stronger property has the advantage that Q is precisely the weakest precondition of the program obtained: there is no 'slack' in the calculation. If, however, the operator is a consequence ($\Leftarrow$) rather than an equivalence ($\equiv$), the proof obligations in both styles coincide.
□

When using coercion statements in combination with other statements, one must be careful to remember that sequential composition is not commutative. For instance, a calculation like

$$\begin{array}{ll} & \mathit{false} \\ \equiv & \lhd b \rhd \\ & \qquad \{(b \Rightarrow \mathit{false}) \ \equiv \ \neg b\} \\ & \neg b \\ \equiv & \lhd b := \neg b \rhd \\ & \qquad \{\text{axiom of assignment}\} \\ & b \end{array}$$

does *not* imply the validity of

$$\{b\} \ \ b := \neg b \ \ \{\mathit{false}\} \ .$$

One situation in which the successive introduction of coercions is particularly useful is in the invention of the right way to strengthen the invariant of a repetition. This is illustrated in the following example*

Example 2 Given is an integer array $a[0\,..\,N)$, where $N \geq 0$. We are to determine the number of unordered pairs of distinct indices whose array values have a nonnegative product. Formally, we are to establish the postcondition

$$r = \langle \# p, q : 0 \leq p < q < N : a.p * a.q \geq 0 \rangle \quad .$$

For our first approximation, we replace a constant by a variable and obtain invariants

$$\begin{array}{lll} P0 & : & 0 \leq n \leq N \quad , \\ P1 & : & r = \langle \# p, q : 0 \leq p < q < n : a.p * a.q \geq 0 \rangle \quad , \end{array}$$

which is initialized by $n, r := 0, 0$. In order to decide how we can maintain $P1$ under $n := n + 1$, we calculate as follows:

$$\begin{array}{ll}
 & P1 \\
\equiv & \quad \triangleleft\, n := n+1 \,\triangleright \\
 & \qquad \{\text{for progress}\} \\
 & r = \langle \# p, q : 0 \leq p < q < n+1 : a.p * a.q \geq 0 \rangle \\
\equiv & \quad \triangleleft\, r := r' \,\triangleright \\
 & \qquad \{\text{to reestablish } P1\} \\
 & r' = \langle \# p, q : 0 \leq p < q < n+1 : a.p * a.q \geq 0 \rangle \\
\Leftarrow & \quad \triangleleft\, P0 \;\wedge\; n \neq N \,\triangleright \\
 & \qquad \{\text{split off } q = n\} \\
 & r' = \langle \# p, q : 0 \leq p < q < n : a.p * a.q \geq 0 \rangle + \langle \# p : 0 \leq p < n : a.p * a.n \geq 0 \rangle \\
\Leftarrow & \quad \triangleleft\, P1 \,\triangleright \\
 & \qquad \{\text{we now start leaving out the domain } 0 \leq p < n\} \\
 & r' = r + \langle \# p :: a.p * a.n \geq 0 \rangle \\
\equiv & \qquad \{\text{case analysis}\} \\
 & (a.n > 0 \;\wedge\; r' = r + \langle \# p :: a.p \geq 0 \rangle) \\
 & \vee\; (a.n = 0 \;\wedge\; r' = r + n) \\
 & \vee\; (a.n < 0 \;\wedge\; r' = r + \langle \# p :: a.p \leq 0 \rangle) \\
\Leftarrow & \quad \triangleleft\, s = \langle \# p :: a.p \geq 0 \rangle \;\wedge\; t = \langle \# p :: a.p \leq 0 \rangle \,\triangleright \\
 & \qquad \{\} \\
 & (a.n > 0 \;\wedge\; r' = r + s) \;\vee\; (a.n = 0 \;\wedge\; r' = r + n) \;\vee\; (a.n < 0 \;\wedge\; r' = r + t) \quad .
\end{array}$$

The predicate following the final $\Leftarrow$ is a good candidate for a strengthening of the invariant; notice that this predicate forms a context for the above calculation as a whole,

---

*The example given is, in fact, exercise 4.3.3 of Kaldewaij (1990).

but is produced by the calculation itself, making it impractical to insist upon stating such conditions in advance.
□

5 DERIVATIONS CONTAINING METHOD CALLS

In object-oriented programs, one uses abstract classes or interfaces that are essentially abstract data types whose implementation is not statically known. The only way to derive programs using such interfaces is by agreeing on a specification that future implementers must respect. There are several ways to specify a class; here we follow Morgan (1990) in associating with every object one or more *thought variables*, taken from some mathematically tractable domain, and specifying the methods in the interface by pre- and postconditions expressed in the thought variables. The relation of these abstract specifications to the implementing code is that the latter must be a *data refinement* of the former.

Example 3 Consider the abstract data type queue, given by the following interface. An object q of type queue is described by a thought variable $q.s$ denoting a finite list of values of some component type. For a queue q, boolean function $q.empty$ is specified in terms of $q.s$ by

$$q.empty \;\equiv\; q.s = [\,] \enspace .$$

Function $q.head$, returning a value of the component type, is specified by

$$q.s \neq [\,] \;\Rightarrow\; q.head = hd.(q.s) \enspace ,$$

where hd denotes the standard list-processing function that, when applied to a nonempty list, returns the value of its first term. Procedure call $q.add(a)$ can be specified by a Hoare triple

$$\{true\} \;\; q.add(a) \;\; \{q.s = q.s_{\bullet}{+\!\!+}[a]\} \enspace ,$$

but it is more convenient, and semantically equivalent, to think of it as an assignment to the abstract variable

$$q.s := q.s{+\!\!+}[a] \enspace .$$

It is often the case that procedure calls can be viewed as abstract assignments; for nondeterministic specifications, however, this point of view presents difficulties and we need the power of a general procedure call proof rule (e.g. Bijlsma *et al.* (1989)). Finally, procedure call $q.remove$ can be specified by a Hoare triple

$$\{q.s \neq [\,]\}\ \ q.remove\ \ \{q.s = tl.(q.s_\bullet)\}$$

or by the abstract assignment

$$q.s := tl.(q.s)$$

where tl is the standard list-processing function that applies to a nonempty list and returns that list minus its first term. Because tl is a partial function, the weakest precondition of the abstract assignment contains a conjunct $q.s \neq [\,]$.

The problem we now address is how to merge two given ascending queues into a single one. Formally, this may be specified by

$$\begin{array}{l} \{asc.(p.s)\ \wedge\ asc.(q.s)\} \\ merge.p.q.r \\ \{R:\quad r.s = sort.(p.s_\bullet +\!\!+ q.s_\bullet)\}\ \ . \end{array}$$

We achieve our purpose by a repetition with a tail invariant, viz.

$$P0:\quad sort.(p.s_\bullet +\!\!+ q.s_\bullet) = r.s +\!\!+ sort.(p.s +\!\!+ q.s)\ \ .$$

The choice of $P0$ is guided by the considerations that, first, $P0$ is easy to establish since

$$p.s = p.s_\bullet\ \wedge\ q.s = q.s_\bullet\ \Rightarrow\ (r.s := [\,]).P0\ \ ,$$

and, secondly, $P0$ helps to attain the required postcondition since

$$P0\ \wedge\ p.s +\!\!+ q.s = [\,]\ \Rightarrow\ R\ \ .$$

As a further constraint on the design, we decide to add the precondition as an invariant, viz.

$$P1:\quad asc.(p.s)\ \wedge\ asc.(q.s)\ \ .$$

The rationale behind this is that, the given queues being already sorted, it would be a waste not to exploit this fact. Progress will consist in extending r until it is as long as $p.s_\bullet +\!\!+ q.s_\bullet$ under invariance of $P0..1$. We calculate as follows:

$$\begin{array}{ll} & P0 \\ \equiv & \{\text{definition of } P0\} \end{array}$$

$sort.(p.s_\bullet +\!\!+ q.s_\bullet) = r.s +\!\!+\ sort.(p.s +\!\!+ q.s)$

$\equiv \quad \lhd\ r.add(a)\ \rhd$

{for progress}

$sort.(p.s_\bullet +\!\!+ q.s_\bullet) = r.s +\!\!+ [a] +\!\!+ sort.(p.s +\!\!+ q.s)$

$\Leftarrow$ {property of *sort*, see (1) below}

$sort.(p.s_\bullet +\!\!+ q.s_\bullet) = r.s +\!\!+ sort.([a] +\!\!+ p.s +\!\!+ q.s) \ \wedge\ a = min.([a] +\!\!+ p.s +\!\!+ q.s)$

$\equiv \quad \lhd\ p.remove\ \rhd$

{preparing to get rid of $[a]$}

$sort.(p.s_\bullet +\!\!+ q.s_\bullet) = r.s +\!\!+ sort.([a] +\!\!+ tl.(p.s) +\!\!+ q.s)$

$\wedge\ a = min.([a] +\!\!+ tl.(p.s) +\!\!+ q.s) \ \wedge\ p.s \neq [\,]$

$\Leftarrow$ {to combine $[a]$ with $tl.(p.s)$, heading for $P0$}

$sort.(p.s_\bullet +\!\!+ q.s_\bullet) = r.s +\!\!+ sort.(p.s +\!\!+ q.s)$

$\wedge\ a = min.(p.s +\!\!+ q.s) \ \wedge\ p.s \neq [\,] \ \wedge\ hd.(p.s) = a$

$\equiv$ {definition of $P0$}

$P0 \ \wedge\ a = min.(p.s +\!\!+ q.s) \ \wedge\ p.s \neq [\,] \ \wedge\ hd.(p.s) = a$

$\equiv$ {property of *min*, see (3) below}

$P0 \ \wedge\ a = min.(p.s) \downarrow min.(q.s) \ \wedge\ p.s \neq [\,] \ \wedge\ hd.(p.s) = a$

$\Leftarrow$ {property of *min*, see (2) below}

$P0..1 \ \wedge\ a = a \downarrow b \ \wedge\ p.s \neq [\,] \ \wedge\ hd.(p.s) = a \ \wedge\ q.s \neq [\,] \ \wedge\ hd\ (q.s) = b$

$\equiv$ {property of $\downarrow$}

$P0..1 \ \wedge\ a \leq b \ \wedge\ p.s \neq [\,] \ \wedge\ hd.(p.s) = a \ \wedge\ q.s \neq [\,] \ \wedge\ hd.(q.s) = b$

$\Leftarrow \quad \lhd\ a \leq b\ \rhd$

{can be checked in constant time}

$P0..1 \ \wedge\ p.s \neq [\,] \ \wedge\ hd.(p.s) = a \ \wedge\ q.s \neq [\,] \ \wedge\ hd.(q.s) = b$

$\Leftarrow \quad \lhd\ a, b := p.head,\ q.head\ \rhd$

{}

$P0..1 \ \wedge\ p.s \neq [\,] \ \wedge\ q.s \neq [\,]$.

Thus we have proved

$\{P0..1 \ \wedge\ p.s \neq [\,] \ \wedge\ q.s \neq [\,]\}$
$a, b := p.head,\ q.head$
$;\ a \leq b$
$;\ p.remove$
$;\ r.add(a)$
$\{P0..1\}$.

By symmetry, this gives

$\{P0..1 \ \wedge\ p.s \neq [\,] \ \wedge\ q.s \neq [\,]\}$
$a, b := p.head,\ q.head$
; **if** $a \leq b \ \rightarrow\ p.remove;\ \ r.add(a)$
$[\!]\ b \leq a \ \rightarrow\ q.remove;\ \ r.add(b)$
fi

$$\{P0..1\} \ .$$

This is the heart of the merge algorithm. The only ingredient still missing, the case where one of the queues has become empty, is treated the same way. In the derivation, some elementary properties of list calculus were used. These are

$$sort.([\alpha]{+\!\!+}\sigma) = [\alpha]{+\!\!+}sort.\sigma \quad \equiv \quad \alpha = min.([\alpha]{+\!\!+}\sigma) \ , \tag{1}$$

$$\sigma \neq [\,] \wedge asc.(\sigma) \quad \Rightarrow \quad hd.\sigma = min.\sigma \ , \tag{2}$$

$$min.(\sigma{+\!\!+}\tau) \quad = \quad min.\sigma \downarrow min.\tau \ . \tag{3}$$

□

6 APPLICATION: SIMULATING FILE OPERATIONS

6.1 Specification of the ISO Pascal file type

In this section, we apply the techniques developed earlier in the context of a realistic example. Indeed, we have chosen an example that is well-known to anyone who has ever struggled to convert programs involving ISO Pascal file operations to some nonstandard Pascal version – an experience by now familiar to a sizable proportion of the earth's population. In order to derive a solution to this problem, we regard ISO Pascal files as an abstract data type, disregarding the fact that Pascal compilers will not support this. We specify this abstract data type by giving a *model*, i.e. we define a number of thought variables of mathematically well-understood types in terms of which the operations on ISO Pascal files can be described. Let a component type T be given. Our model consists of four thought variables, namely

$P : T^*$	(the file prefix, consisting of the items already read)
$S : T^*$	(the file suffix, consisting of the items not yet read)
$Q : \{in, out\}$	(whether the file is opened for input or for output)
$B : T \cup \{\bot\}$	(the file buffer)

The values of these four variables are not quite independent: they are linked by the *type invariant*

$$Q = out \ \Rightarrow \ S = [\,] \ . \tag{4}$$

The value $\bot$ (pronounced 'bottom') is added because the ISO Pascal standard sometimes requires the buffer to become undefined.

The abstract data type for ISO Pascal files is defined by listing its operations and specifying these by pre- and postconditions in terms of the four variables P, S, Q, B.

Here we shall concentrate on specifying and implementing a single operation, *Reset*. Readers wishing to see the specification and implementation of the full ISO Pascal type may consult Bijlsma (1997). The specification of *Reset* reads as follows:

pre: *true*
post: $P = [\,] \wedge S = P_\bullet {+\!\!+} S_\bullet \wedge Q = in \wedge B = Hd.S$

Function *Hd* is similar to, but slightly more general than, the function *hd* usually provided in functional programming languages. It is defined inductively by

$$\begin{aligned} Hd.[\,] &= \perp \\ Hd.([a]{+\!\!+}as) &= a \end{aligned}$$

The proof obligation that this specification is compatible with type invariant (4) is left to the reader.

6.2 Specification of a simple file type

In this section, we specify a simpler file type that can be regarded as a greatest common divisor of several commercial implementations of Pascal. Here the model consists of only two variables, namely

$p : T^*$ (the file prefix, consisting of the items already read)
$s : T^*$ (the file suffix, consisting of the items not yet read)

In the same notation as the previous section, the relevant operations can be specified as follows:

reset pre: *true*
post: $p = [\,] \wedge s = p_\bullet {+\!\!+} s_\bullet$

$read(x)$ pre: $s \neq [\,]$
post: $p = p_\bullet {+\!\!+} [Hd.s_\bullet] \wedge s = Tl.s_\bullet \wedge x = Hd.s_\bullet$

eof pre: *true*
ret: $s = [\,]$

However, we are not yet quite satisfied with this form. The reason is that specifying a relation by means of a precondition/postcondition pair is the easiest way if we are asked to *implement* that relation; however, if we are to *use* the procedure described by a relation as a given building block to be used in programming some higher-level module, it is far more convenient to have the specification in a predicate-transformer form. This is why, traditionally, programming exercises are specified by a pair of predicates, while programming constructs are specified by a predicate transformer. Now in a state space with coordinate vectors x, y, any specification of the form

pre: $def.E$
post: $x = x_\bullet \ \wedge \ y = E_\bullet$

has the same weakest precondition as, hence can be identified with, the assignment $y := E$.

Therefore we may reformulate our specification as follows:

$$reset \quad = \quad p, s := [\,], p{+\!\!+}s \tag{5}$$

$$read(x) \quad = \quad \{s \neq [\,]\};\ \ p, s, x := p{+\!\!+}[Hd.s],\ Tl.s,\ Hd.s \tag{6}$$

$$eof \quad \equiv \quad s = [\,] \tag{7}$$

The statement $\{s \neq [\,]\}$ is a so-called assertion statement, whose semantics is defined by

$$wp.\{Q\}.R \ \equiv \ Q \wedge R \ .$$

In other words, assertion statement $\{Q\}$ behaves like *skip* when boolean condition Q is satisfied, and aborts otherwise. See Morgan (1990), Morris (1989) for further discussion. This is not to be confused with the coercion statement introduced in an earlier section, whose semantics is defined by

$$wp.Q.R \ \equiv \ (Q \Rightarrow R) \ .$$

6.3 Derivation of the implementation code

It is our goal to implement the specification of the ISO file operations in terms of the simpler operations of the previous section. Now the theory of data refinement (Morgan 1990) (Morgan *et al.* 1990) (Morris 1989) states that data refining an abstract specification

pre: U, post: V

is achieved by choosing an *abstraction invariant* A linking the abstract variables a and the concrete variables c, and then constructing code S that does not mention a and satisfies

$$\{\langle \exists a :: U \wedge A \rangle\} \quad S \quad \{\langle \exists a :: V \wedge A \rangle\} \quad . \tag{8}$$

As a practical observation, we prefer to work without the quantifiers and just construct some code S satisfying

$$\{U \wedge A\} \quad S \quad \{V \wedge A\} \quad ,$$

where S may mention a but only as a *ghost variable*, that is to say that in S, the variables from a may not occur in statements that change the value of any other variables. If we have constructed an S satisfying these restrictions, it can be turned into a program fragment satisfying (8) by simply leaving out all statements that mention a. For the problem at hand, we take as concrete variables the sequences p and s from the preceding section, augmented by the following variables:

d, e :	*Boolean*
f, g :	T

Now we propose the following abstraction invariant:

$A0$:	$d \Rightarrow P = p \wedge S = s = [\,]$
$A1$:	$\neg d \Rightarrow p = P{+\!\!+}[f] \wedge S = [f]{+\!\!+}s$
$A2$:	$e \Rightarrow B = g$
$A3$:	$\neg e \Rightarrow B = \bot$

We shall use A as an abbreviation for $A0 \wedge A1 \wedge A2 \wedge A3$. The heuristics behind the choice of A are as follows: in the first place, in our simple file type there is no equivalent of the file buffer B. In order to simulate B, we introduce variable g. We assume that value $\bot$ is not actually implemented, so we simulate that by letting g be of type T rather than $T \cup \{\bot\}$, and letting $\neg e$ signal* when B should have the value $\bot$. Now a straightforward simulation would simulate P and S by p and s respectively, but the difficulty with this is that the semantics of *Reset* requires setting the file buffer to the first unread element. Our simple file system affords no knowledge of unread elements, so the only recourse is reading one extra element and preserving its value in f. This strategy implies *eof* may become true one step sooner than its ISO file analogue *Eof*, so we add another boolean d to simulate *Eof*.

*Actually, it turns out that e is superfluous, as we shall see at the end of this section. It is not necessary to observe this at the present stage of development.

Observe that A nowhere mentions Q, so the abstract state is not determined by the concrete state. Therefore this abstraction invariant cannot be replaced by the better-known technique of abstraction *functions*.

Now we are ready to derive the implementation of the ISO file operation *Reset*. Let R denote the postcondition given for *Reset*, i.e.

$$R: \quad P = [\,] \wedge S = P_\bullet +\!\!+ S_\bullet \wedge Q = in \wedge B = Hd.S \ .$$

Code is derived separately for postconditions $R \wedge S=[\,]$ and $R \wedge S\neq[\,]$, as we are more or less forced to do on account of the shape of $A0$ and $A1$. As both derivations are similar, we give only the derivation for the case $R \wedge S \neq [\,]$ and refer the reader to Bijlsma (1997) for the other case.

$$
\begin{array}{ll}
 & R \wedge S \neq [\,] \wedge A \\
\equiv & \quad \{\text{definitions of } R,\ A, \text{ and } Hd\} \\
 & P = [\,] \wedge p = [f] \wedge S = [f]+\!\!+s = P_\bullet +\!\!+ S_\bullet \wedge \neg d \wedge Q = in \wedge e \wedge B = f = \\
\equiv & \lhd\ P, S, Q, B := [\,], [f]+\!\!+s, in, f\ \rhd \\
 & \quad \{\text{eliminate abstract variables by explicit assignment}\} \\
 & p = [f] \wedge [f]+\!\!+s = P_\bullet +\!\!+ S_\bullet \wedge \neg d \wedge e \wedge f = g \\
\equiv & \lhd\ d, e, g := false, true, f\ \rhd \\
 & \quad \{\text{eliminate booleans and pseudo-buffer } g \text{ by explicit assignment}\} \\
 & p = [f] \wedge [f]+\!\!+s = P_\bullet +\!\!+ S_\bullet \\
\equiv & \lhd\ read(f)\ \rhd \\
 & \quad \{\text{applying (6) eliminates } f\} \\
 & s \neq [\,] \wedge p = [\,] \wedge s = P_\bullet +\!\!+ S_\bullet \\
\equiv & \lhd\ \neg eof\ \rhd \\
 & \quad \{\text{applying (7) moves } s \text{ to antecedent}\} \\
 & s \neq [\,] \Rightarrow p = [\,] \wedge s = P_\bullet +\!\!+ S_\bullet \\
\Leftarrow & \quad \{\text{just predicate calculus... we're lucky if we get away with this strenghtening}\} \\
 & p = [\,] \wedge s = P_\bullet +\!\!+ S_\bullet \\
\equiv & \lhd\ reset\ \rhd \\
 & \quad \{\text{applying (5) gives a formally weaker single identity}\} \\
 & p+\!\!+s = P_\bullet +\!\!+ S_\bullet \\
\Leftarrow & \quad \{\text{separating initial values}\} \\
 & p+\!\!+s = P+\!\!+S \wedge P = P_\bullet \wedge S = S_\bullet \\
\Leftarrow & \quad \{\text{definition of } A0 \text{ and } A1\} \\
 & A \wedge P = P_\bullet \wedge S = S_\bullet \ ,
\end{array}
$$

which gives

$\{A\}$
reset
; $\neg$*eof*
; *read*(f)

$$
\begin{array}{l}
;\ d, e, g := \mathit{false}, \mathit{true}, f \\
;\ P, S, Q, B; = [\,], [f]{+\!\!+}s, \mathit{in}, f \\
\quad \{R \wedge S \neq [\,] \wedge A\} \ .
\end{array}
$$

Combining this with the result for the other case gives

$$
\begin{array}{lll}
\{A\} & & \\
\mathit{reset} & & \\
;\ \mathbf{if}\ \mathit{eof} \rightarrow & & d, e := \mathit{true}, \mathit{false} \\
 & ; & P, S, Q, B := [\,], [\,], \mathit{in}, \bot \\
[\!]\ \neg \mathit{eof} \rightarrow & & \mathit{read}(f) \\
 & ; & d, e, g := \mathit{false}, \mathit{true}, f \\
 & ; & P, S, Q, B := [\,], [f]{+\!\!+}s, \mathit{in}, f \\
\mathbf{fi} & & \\
\{R \wedge A\} \ , & &
\end{array}
$$

in which no miraculous coercion statements occur any more. Finally, by omitting the abstract ghost variables, we get

$$
\begin{array}{lll}
\mathit{reset} & & \\
;\ \mathbf{if}\ \mathit{eof} \rightarrow & & e := \mathit{false} \\
[\!]\ \neg \mathit{eof} \rightarrow & & \mathit{read}(f) \\
 & ; & d, e, g := \mathit{false}, \mathit{true}, f \\
\mathbf{fi} \ , & &
\end{array}
$$

and this is the code for *Reset* that our derivation produces.

Observing the code we have produced, it may strike us that variable e is inspected neither in *Reset* nor in any of the other operations that have not been reproduced here. Therefore e too can be regarded as a ghost variable and left out. With sufficient foresight, we might have seen this already in the specifications of the ISO operations: none of these require the definedness of the file buffer to be tested. From this observation, we might then have decided to replace $A2$ and $A3$ by the weaker

$$B = g \vee B = \bot \ .$$

Leaving out e produces the final version of our implementation:

$$
\begin{array}{lll}
\mathit{reset} & & \\
;\ \mathbf{if}\ \mathit{eof} \rightarrow & & \mathit{skip} \\
[\!]\ \neg \mathit{eof} \rightarrow & & \mathit{read}(f) \\
 & ; & d, g := \mathit{false}, f \\
\mathbf{fi} & &
\end{array}
$$

7 CONCLUSION

The extension we propose in this paper has been demonstrated to be practically useful in situations where either hypotheses or program statements are discovered one at a time as the calculation progresses, since it does away with the need to restart the calculation in a slightly different context every time such an ingredient is produced. Thus, it serves to make Dijkstra-style program derivation feasible for a wider class of programming problems.

REFERENCES

Bijlsma, A. (1997) Simulating file operations: an exercise in calculational data refinement. Memorandum AB66, Eindhoven University of Technology, 1997. Available from `http://www.win.tue.nl/inf/staf/secties/st/pm/lexb/ab66.ps`

Bijlsma, A., Matthews, P.A., and Wiltink, J.G. (1989) A sharp proof rule for procedures in *wp* semantics. *Acta Inf.* **26**, 409–419.

Bijlsma, A. and Scholten, C.S. (1996) Point-free substitution. *Sci. Comput. Prog.* **27**, 205–214.

Dijkstra, E.W. and Feijen, W.H.J. (1984) *Een methode van programmeren*. Academic Service, The Hague. English translation (1988) *A method of programming*. Addison-Wesley, Reading (Mass.).

Dijkstra, E.W. and Scholten, C.S. (1990) *Predicate calculus and program semantics*. Springer-Verlag, New York.

Gries, D. and Schneider, F.B. (1993) *A logical approach to discrete math*. Springer-Verlag, New York.

Grundy, J. (1996) Transformational hierarchical reasoning. *Comput. J.* **39**, 291–302.

Kaldewaij, A. (1990) *Programming: the derivation of algorithms*. Prentice-Hall International, London.

Morgan, C.C. (1990) *Programming from specifications*. Prentice-Hall International, London.

Morgan, C.C. and Gardiner, P.H.B. (1990) Data refinement by calculation. *Acta Inf.* **27**, 481–503.

Morris, J.M. (1989) Laws of data refinement. *Acta Inf.* **26**, 287–308.

8 BIOGRAPHY

A.J.M. van Gasteren received a master's degree in mathematics, supervised by Edsger W. Dijkstra.

In 1981 she joined Dijkstra's group as a BP Venture Research Fellow, investigating the orderly presentation and design of programs and proofs. As a result of this work, she received a PhD from Eindhoven University of Technology in 1988.

Since then she has taught and investigated programming methodology, getting more and more interested and involved in the use of calculational methods. A main driving force of her work is the quest for ways and methods to achieve clarity of thought and economy of expression.

A. Bijlsma studied number theory with H. Jager (Amsterdam), P.L. Cijsouw (Eindhoven), and M. Waldschmidt (Paris). In 1978 he received a PhD from the University of Amsterdam.

In 1983 he shifted his attention to computing. At Eindhoven University of Technology, he has since worked in the groups of M. Rem, A. Kaldewaij, and R.C. Backhouse. His research interest focuses on the interplay between programming language constructs and program construction style, in particular with respect to object-oriented design.

15
Deadlines are termination

I. J. Hayes
Department of Computer Science and Electrical Engineering, and Software Verification Research Centre, The University of Queensland Brisbane, 4072, Australia (ianh@csee.uq.edu.au).

M. Utting
Department of Computer Science, School of Computing and Mathematical Sciences, The University of Waikato
Private Bag 3105, Hamilton, New Zealand (marku@cs.waikato.ac.nz).

Abstract

We have recently extended the sequential refinement calculus to handle real-time programs. A novel deadline command allows execution time limits to be expressed in a high-level language. The calculus allows refinement steps that separate timing constraints from non-timing requirements. Rules are provided for handling timing constraints, but the refinement of components implementing non-timing requirements is essentially the same as in the standard refinement calculus.

In this paper, we present a new refinement rule for loops that does not require a variant for termination, but uses a deadline command instead. To illustrate the calculus and the new loop introduction rule, we present an example refinement of a program that calculates the size of a kiwifruit from the time it takes to pass through a light beam.

Keywords

Real-time, refinement, deadlines, termination

1 INTRODUCTION

Formal correctness techniques for real-time programs are less well-developed than those for non-real-time programs, yet the need for them is certainly no less, given that many safety-critical embedded systems involve real-time requirements.

Our goal is to provide a method for the stepwise refinement of sequential, real-time programs from real-time specifications. We follow the refinement calculus approach (Back 1980, Morgan 1994) of devising a wide-spectrum language that encompasses both real-time programs and real-time specifications, and the spectrum in between. To meet this goal, we have found it desirable to:

- use a specification notation which represents variables as traces (functions over

Programming Concepts and Methods D. Gries, & W-P. de Roever (Eds.)

time (real numbers)), so that timing requirements can be expressed, including properties of variables whose values change over time.

- distinguish between external inputs, that are not under the direct control of the program, and external outputs and local variables that are.
- add a **deadline** command to our high-level programming language to allow timing requirements to be recorded during development.
- delay the discharging of timing requirements (e.g., **deadline** commands) until after compilation, when the detailed properties of the target machine can be taken into account.

In a previous paper (Hayes & Utting 1997*a*), we developed a calculus for refining an individual real-time process to sequential code. That work was based on the foundations developed by Utting & Fidge (1996), but extended them by introducing a deadline command, which greatly simplifies the treatment of timing constraints. Section 2 gives an overview of this calculus, its real-time, wide-spectrum language and the mechanism for dealing with real-time constraints in the target code. The motivation for our work comes from the real-time refinement calculus of Mahony (1992), which allows not only the specification of real-time systems, but the refinement of a specification into a set of truly parallel processes. Our work complements Mahony's by allowing individual processes to be refined to sequential code.

In this paper, we use the calculus to develop a program that calculates the size of a single kiwifruit from the time it takes to pass through a light beam. Section 3 specifies the requirements, and Sections 4 and 5 show how they can be refined into a real-time program. The timing analysis of the program is discussed in Section 6.

The example illustrates the main features and difficulties of the calculus. In order to develop the obvious program for the task, we needed to develop a novel loop introduction law, that does not require a variant for termination, but uses a fixed time deadline instead.

2 THE SEQUENTIAL REAL-TIME REFINEMENT CALCULUS

An obvious difference between our calculus and the standard refinement calculus is that our calculus has a special variable, τ, that represents the *current time*. Each command advances τ to reflect the passage of time.

We distinguish between three types of variables: external inputs, external outputs and local variables. Input variables correspond to input device registers. They are not under the control of the program, but may be read via a special command. Output variables correspond to output device registers. They are under the control of the program, but differ from local variables in that changes to output variables are externally visible. We write real-time specification commands as $\star\, \vec{v}\colon \left[A\ ,\ E\right]$, where

- $\vec{v}$ is a list of variables that may be modified by the command. These variables must be a subset of the outputs and local variables of the program, (variables that correspond to external inputs are read-only). Since τ is modified by almost every command, it is implicitly in the frame of every command and is not explicitly included in the frame.

- A is a predicate that gives the *assumptions* the command may make about the variables. Within A, τ refers to the time that the command starts execution, but A may also explicitly reference the value of variables at other times.
- E is a predicate that gives the *effect* that the command is to achieve by modifying the variables in the frame. Within E, τ_0 and τ refer to the time that the command starts and finishes execution, respectively.

A key change from the standard refinement calculus is our treatment of variables; they are modelled as functions from time to their value at that time. This allows a real-time specification command to constrain not only the final value of variables, but also their values at other times. Given a variable v, its value at time t is written as $v(t)$. However, to recover the *look and feel* of the standard refinement calculus, we follow the convention that an unindexed variable v in a predicate means $v(\tau)$, and v_0 means $v(\tau_0)$. The semantics of the specification command are given in Appendix 1.

The basic refinement rules from the standard refinement calculus carry over into our calculus (Hayes & Utting 1997*b*), although some have additional side-conditions to restrict the times at which predicates refer to variables (these side-conditions are satisfied trivially for untimed predicates that use the v and v_0 convention described above). We use an extended target language that includes several real-time commands, such as:

- **gettime**$(x) \overset{\text{def}}{=} \star x\!: \left[\text{true}\,,\, x \in [\tau_0 \ldots \tau]\right]$.
  This puts a timestamp (an approximation to τ) into the variable x. The notation $[\tau_0 \ldots \tau]$ stands for the closed interval from the start time of the command, τ_0, to the finish time, τ.
- **read**$(e, x) \overset{\text{def}}{=} \star x\!: \left[\text{true}\,,\, x \in e(\!|\, [\tau_0 \ldots \tau] \,|\!)\right]$.
  This copies a snapshot of an external input e into the local variable x. The notation $e(\!|\, [\tau_0 \ldots \tau] \,|\!)$ stands for the set of values of the input variable e over the time interval $[\tau_0 \ldots \tau]$.
- **delay until** $D \overset{\text{def}}{=} \star\!: \left[\text{true}\,,\, \tau \geq D\right]$.
  This is similar to the delay-until command in many programming languages. The delay command finishes execution at or after the (absolute) time D.
- **deadline** $D \overset{\text{def}}{=} \star\!: \left[\text{true}\,,\, \tau_0 = \tau \wedge \tau \leq D\right]$.
  The **deadline** command is novel to our approach and allows timing constraints to be expressed abstractly in the extended programming language (Hayes & Utting 1997*a*). It takes no time and must terminate at or before time D. Hence, it requires the preceding portion of the program to be complete by time D.
- **idle** $\overset{\text{def}}{=} \star\!: \left[\text{true}\,,\, \tau_0 \leq \tau\right]$.
  The **idle** command may take time but does not change any variables. Note that external inputs may change during the time it takes to execute.

The presence of deadline commands means that a separate program analysis is required to guarantee that the deadlines will be met by the machine code generated for the program by a compiler. If the program analysis cannot guarantee that a deadline will be met, the program is rejected. Note that it is important to analyse timing *after* compilation, because no analysis of the higher-level program can take into account low-level aspects such as register allocation and code optimisation within a compiler, or instruction pipelining and cache memories within processors, which together can significantly affect the timing characteristics of a program.

3 ON MEASURING THE SIZE OF A KIWIFRUIT

Imagine that a single kiwifruit is moving along on a conveyor belt and goes through a light beam sensor that is connected into an embedded microcomputer. A program on the microcomputer polls the boolean *sensor* status and uses a real-time clock to determine the approximate start and end times of when the light beam is broken. When the kiwifruit breaks the light beam the *sensor* rises (to true) and after the kiwifruit passes the light beam is re-established and the *sensor* falls (to false). From those times, and the known speed of the conveyor belt, the size of the kiwifruit can be computed.

The following declarations define the environment in which our program will be used. As well as documenting the type of variables representing physical quantities, we also document their units (Hayes & Mahony 1995). Variables of type `time` are in units of nanoseconds.

const $speed \stackrel{\text{def}}{=} 10\,\text{m/s}$ -- The speed of the conveyor belt
const $react \stackrel{\text{def}}{=} 100\,\mu\text{s}$ -- Desired reaction time after the kiwifruit passes

The *sensor* is an external input to the program. It is derived from the light beam detecting hardware. Its value over time is not under the control of the program, but the program does make assumptions about the behaviour of the input sensor.

input $sensor : \mathbb{B}$
var $size : \mathbb{N}\,\text{nm}$ -- Returned size of the kiwifruit in nanometres

The logical constants *rises* and *falls* are introduced solely for specification purposes. They denote, respectively, the exact time at which the sensor rises and falls. Logical constants may not be used in the final program, except in assertions and deadlines.

con *rises*, *falls* : `time`
const $minsep \stackrel{\text{def}}{=} 1\,\text{ms}$ -- Minimum separation between *rises* and *falls*
-- Corresponds to length of 10 mm

The program may assume that the rise time precedes the fall time by *minsep*.

$$\star\,\{rises + minsep \leq falls\} \tag{1}$$

Because (1) does not refer to any variables modified by the program, it may be assumed to hold throughout the program. To avoid cluttering the specification and the refinement below, we state (1) once here and assume it where needed. Logically it could be conjoined to the assumption of the specification (2) below and passed through the refinement as necessary. The sensor detects (is true) when the light beam is interrupted by the passing kiwifruit.

$$SENSOR(\tau) \stackrel{\mathrm{def}}{=} (\forall t : [\tau \ldots falls + react] \bullet sensor(t) = \mathrm{true} \Leftrightarrow t \in [rises \ldots falls])$$

The top level specification is:

$$\star\, size\colon \begin{bmatrix} \tau \le rises & \tau \le falls + react \\ SENSOR(\tau) & \text{'}\, size \in speed * (falls - rises) \pm 1\,\mathrm{mm} \end{bmatrix} \qquad (2)$$

4 REFINEMENT OF THE KIWIFRUIT SIZER

Appendix 1 provides a summary of refinement laws used within this paper.

As a first refinement step, it is useful to separate out the initial time assumption, $\tau \le rises$, and the final deadline requirement, $\tau \le falls + react$, so that we may concentrate on implementing the remaining functionality.

(2)

$\sqsubseteq$ Law 6 (separate assumption); Law 10 (separate deadline)

$\star \{\tau \le rises\}$;

$\star\, size\colon [SENSOR(\tau)\ ,\ size \in speed * (falls - rises) \pm 1\,\mathrm{mm}]$; (3)

deadline *falls* + *react*

The assertion and deadline become part of the final program, and we are left to refine the specification command (3).

The next refinement step is obvious – we want to split the program into three parts: the first two will determine the rise and fall times and the third part computes the size output. We introduce a constant *err* as an error bound on the time to detect the change in the sensor. We leave the actual value of *err* to be determined later, but at this stage we require that it is less than both *minsep* and *react*, so that the sensor is stable for at least a period of *err* after it changes.

$$\mathbf{const}\ err \in \{t : \mathtt{time} \mid t \le minsep \wedge t \le react\} \qquad (4)$$

Local variables *riset* and *fallt* are used to communicate the approximations to the rise and fall times between the parts. When introducing a local variable one cannot assume that the allocation and deallocation of the local variable take no time. Hence, an assumption that held immediately before the allocation of a local variable, may not hold immediately after the allocation. However, during the allocation of a new variable the other program variables (not including the external inputs) are stable and time can only increase. A predicate that remains true under these circumstances is referred to as being *idle-stable*. It is invariant over the execution of an **idle** command. The predicate $SENSOR(\tau)$ is idle-stable. It states a property that holds at every instant of time from τ up to $falls + react$. Hence, $SENSOR(x)$ also holds for all values of x later than τ.

The time taken for the allocation and deallocation of variables may also affect the effect of a specification command. In (3) the effect only refers to constants and the program variable *size*. Because *size* is stable during the deallocation of the variables, the effect will still be true after the deallocation. Note that we follow Morgan's (1994) convention of using a $\lhd$ symbol to mark the specification statement that is refined next – the context of that statement becomes the context of the next refinement.

(3)

$\sqsubseteq$ Law 11 (introduce variable)

$[\![$**var** $riset, fallt$: `time`;

$\quad \star\, size, riset, fallt$: $[SENSOR(\tau)\ ,\ size \in speed * (falls - rises) \pm 1\,\text{mm}] \qquad \lhd$

$]\!]$

$\sqsubseteq$ Law 9 (simple sequential composition) $\times$ 2; Law 5 (remove from frame) $\times$ 3

$$\star\, riset: \left[SENSOR(\tau)\ ,\ \begin{matrix} SENSOR(\tau) \\ riset \in [rises \ldots rises + err]\end{matrix}\right]; \tag{5}$$

$$\star\, fallt: \left[\begin{matrix} SENSOR(\tau) \\ riset \in [rises \ldots rises + err]\end{matrix}\ ,\ \begin{matrix} riset \in [rises \ldots rises + err] \\ fallt \in [falls \ldots falls + err]\end{matrix}\right]; \tag{6}$$

$$\star\, size: \left[\begin{matrix} riset \in [rises \ldots rises + err] \\ fallt \in [falls \ldots falls + err]\end{matrix}\ ,\ size \in speed * (falls - rises) \pm 1\,\text{mm}\right] \tag{7}$$

The refinement of (5) is more interesting. The goal is to determine the time at which the light beam sensor rises. Our first step is to massage the specification to reflect this more specific goal. Firstly, the effect $SENSOR(\tau)$ is immediate from the assumption because $SENSOR(\tau)$ is an idle-stable predicate that does not refer to the variable in the frame, *riset*. Secondly, we weaken the assumption so that we only consider the rising phase of the signal.

(5)

$\sqsubseteq$ Law 4 (strengthen effect); Law 3 (weaken assumption)

$$\star\, riset: \left[\begin{matrix} \forall\, t : [\tau \ldots rises + err] \bullet \\ \quad sensor(t) = \text{true} \Leftrightarrow rises \le t\end{matrix}\ ,\ riset \in [rises \ldots rises + err]\right] \tag{8}$$

We make use of the following definition which is written to allow detection of either a rising edge (the new sensor value we are required to detect, *srqd*, is true), or a falling edge change ($srqd$ = false).

$$CHNG(chngs, srqd) \ \stackrel{\text{def}}{=}\ \forall\, t : [\tau \ldots chngs + err] \bullet sensor(t) = srqd \Leftrightarrow chngs \le t$$

To refine the detection of the rise of the sensor, we make use of a procedure, *detect_chng*. The first step is a refinement equivalence ($\sqsubseteq\!\!\sqsupseteq$).

(8)

$\sqsubseteq\!\!\sqsupseteq \star\, riset\!: \left[CHNG(rises, \text{true})\ ,\ riset \in [rises \ldots rises + err] \right]$

$\sqsubseteq$ parametrized procedure

$detect\_chng(rises, \text{true}, riset)$

The procedure *detect_chng* can be used to detect either a rising or falling edge of the sensor value depending on the parameter *srqd*, which is the required new value of the sensor.

$$\textbf{proc}\ detect\_chng(\textbf{con}\ chngs : \texttt{time};\ \textbf{value}\ srqd : \mathbb{B};\ \textbf{result}\ chngt : \texttt{time}) \stackrel{\text{def}}{=}$$
$$\star\, chngt\!: \left[CHNG(chngs, srqd)\ ,\ chngt \in [chngs \ldots chngs + err] \right] \qquad (9)$$

Before giving a refinement of *detect_chng* (Section 5) we complete the refinement of the program. Detecting the falling edge also makes use of the procedure *detect_chng*.

(6)

$\sqsubseteq$ Law 4 (strengthen effect); Law 3 (weaken assumption)

$\star\, fallt\!: \left[CHNG(falls, \text{false})\ ,\ fallt \in [falls \ldots falls + err] \right]$

$\sqsubseteq detect\_chng(falls, \text{false}, fallt)$

Once both the rise time and the fall time have been determined, the size of the kiwifruit can be calculated.

(7)

$\sqsubseteq$ Law 7 (assignment)

$size := speed * (fallt - riset)$

The units of the right side expression are $(\text{m}/\text{s}) * \text{ns} = \text{nm}$, which matches the units of *size*. The proof obligation for the last step is

$$
\begin{aligned}
& speed * (fallt - riset) \in speed * (falls - rises) \pm 1\,\text{mm} \\
\equiv\ & fallt - riset \in (falls - rises) \pm (1\,\text{mm}/speed) \\
\Leftarrow\ & \text{from the assumptions on } riset \text{ and } fallt \\
& [falls - (rises + err) \ldots (falls + err) - rises] \subseteq (falls - rises) \pm (1\,\text{mm}/speed) \\
\equiv\ & (falls - rises) \pm err \subseteq (falls - rises) \pm (1\,\text{mm}/speed) \\
\equiv\ & err \leq (1\,\text{mm}/speed) \\
\equiv\ & err \leq 100\,\mu\text{s}
\end{aligned}
$$

5 REFINEMENT OF DETECTION OF A SENSOR CHANGE

The following code is the implementation of *detect_chng* (the refinement to this code follows shortly). Note that this code is similar to what a programmer would write for this task, except that *deadline* commands have been added to make the timing requirements of the program explicit.

```
proc detect_chng(con chngs : time; value srqd : 𝔹; result chngt : time) ⊑
|[var sens : 𝔹 ;
    read(sensor, sens) ;
    deadline chngs + err ;
    ⋆do sens ≠ srqd →
        read(sensor, sens) ;
        deadline chngs + err
    od ;
    gettime(chngt) ;
    deadline chngs + err
]|
```

Aside: The above code corresponds to what is usually referred to as busy waiting. In the current context we are assuming a single sequential process, and hence busy waiting is acceptable. It would also be acceptable to include a (sampling) delay in the above code, provided the delay time is sufficiently short to allow the program to meet its deadlines. We have not done so here.

The final deadline ensures that the captured change time is within its allowable error bounds. Given the last deadline, the first two deadlines seem redundant, but they are essential for the correct operation of the program. The final deadline command will not be reached by the program if the loop does not terminate, and if the deadline is not reached, it does not have to be met. Consider the case where we want to detect the rise of the sensor. Without the first deadline the initial code could take so long that the first read command completely misses the period when the sensor is true. (This is unlikely in practice, but not excluded by the meanings we have given to the programming constructs.) If the first read completely misses the sensor when it is raised, then the loop will not be guaranteed to terminate because our assumptions only guarantee one period when the sensor is raised. Hence the final deadline may never be reached. The deadline within the loop has a similar purpose. It guarantees that the body of the loop will not take so long that the read of the sensor misses the raised period of the sensor. Again, if the raised period were missed the loop would not be guaranteed to terminate, and the final deadline would not be reached. As we shall see shortly, the refinement process needs to introduce the deadlines in order to guarantee that the specification will be met. In addition, the deadline within the loop is also used to guarantee its termination.

Before continuing, we invite the reader to informally analyse this code (e.g., unroll the loop once or twice) to determine the longest path through the code that can be executed from time *chngs* to the **gettime** command. Note how the analysis depends on consequences of $CHNG(chngs, srqd)$, such as the shape of the *sensor* waveform. Our real-time calculus enables us to make these implicit timing assumptions and invariants explicit, so that we can provide an invariant for the loop and so that the timing analysis phase has a manageable task. With these goals in mind, it turns out (after several attempts!) that a suitable loop invariant is:

$$INV \stackrel{\text{def}}{=} CHNG(chngs, srqd) \wedge (sens = srqd \Rightarrow chngs \leq \tau)$$

The first step is to introduce a local variable, *sens*, that is used to capture the sensor's values.

(9)

$\sqsubseteq$ Law 11 (introduce variable)

$[\![$**var** $sens : \mathbb{B};$

$\quad \star\, chngt, sens\colon \left[CHNG(chngs, srqd)\ .\ chngt \in [chngs \ldots chngs + err]\right]$ (10)

$]\!]$

Next we set up a loop that searches for the change of the sensor and then we capture the time. The introduction of the loop makes use of the following law, that does not have a conventional variant to show termination. Our semantics of the loop guarantees that each iteration takes a minimum amount of time, due for example to loop overheads and guard evaluation. Termination is guaranteed by the fact that time increases by at least that minimum amount on each iteration, and every iteration of the body of the loop is bounded by the same constant time limit. The time limit, L, is required to be frame-stable with respect to the frame, $\vec{x}$, of the loop. That guarantees that L will remain invariant (stable) during the execution of the loop. If L does not refer to variables in the frame, or τ, or external inputs, then it is frame-stable.

Law 1 (iteration with deadline) *Given an idle-stable invariant property, INV, a deadline expression L, which is frame-stable with respect to the frame $\vec{x}$, and an idle-stable expression G, where none of G, L and INV contain references to τ_0 or zero-subscripted variables,*

$$\star\vec{x}\colon \left[INV \wedge \tau \leq L, \neg\, G \wedge INV\right] \sqsubseteq \star\mathbf{do}\ G \rightarrow \star\vec{x}\colon \left[G \wedge INV, INV \wedge \tau \leq L\right]\ \mathbf{od}$$

The semantics of loops and the proof of this law are contained in Appendix 2. Before introducing the loop, we separate the initialisation, loop, and final capture of the change time.

(10)

$\sqsubseteq$ Law 9 (simple sequential composition) $\times$ 2; Law 5 (remove from frame) $\times$ 3

$\star\, sens\colon \left[CHNG(chngs, srqd)\ .\ INV \wedge \tau \leq chngs + err\right];$ (11)

$\star\, sens\colon \left[INV \wedge \tau \leq chngs + err\ ,\ INV \wedge sens = srqd\right];$ (12)

$\star\, chngt\colon \left[INV \wedge sens = srqd\ ,\ chngt \in [chngs \ldots chngs + err]\right]$ (13)

The initialisation establishes the loop invariant. In the second refinement step below, because of the assumption, if the value sensed is equal to *srqd* then the completion time of the command must be after *chngs*. If the sensed value is not equal to *srqd* the completion time may be either before or after *chngs*, but that does not matter.

(11)

$\sqsubseteq$ Law 4 (strengthen effect)

$$\star\, sens\colon \begin{bmatrix} \forall t : [\tau \ldots chngs + err] \bullet & sens = srqd \Rightarrow chngs \leq \tau \\ \quad sensor(t) = srqd \Leftrightarrow chngs \leq t \text{ '} & \tau \leq chngs + err \end{bmatrix}$$

$\sqsubseteq$ Law 4 (strengthen effect)

$$\star\, sens\colon \begin{bmatrix} \forall t : [\tau \ldots chngs + err] \bullet & sens \in sensor(\!|\, [\tau_0 \ldots \tau] \,|\!) \\ \quad sensor(t) = srqd \Leftrightarrow chngs \leq t \text{ '} & \tau \leq chngs + err \end{bmatrix}$$

$\sqsubseteq$ Law 3 (weaken assumption); Law 10 (separate deadline); Definition of read

read(*sensor*, *sens*) ; **deadline** *chngs* + *err*

Now we can introduce the loop.

(12)

$\sqsubseteq$ Law 1 (iteration with deadline)

$\star$ **do** $sens \neq sqrd \rightarrow$

$\quad\star\, sens\colon [sens \neq srqd \wedge INV \text{ , } INV \wedge \tau \leq chngs + err]$ $\triangleleft$

od

$\sqsubseteq$ Law 3 (weaken assumption)

$\star\, sens\colon [CHNG(chngs, srqd) \text{ , } INV \wedge \tau \leq chngs + err]$

$\sqsubseteq$ as for the refinement of (11)

read(*sensor*, *sens*) ; **deadline** *chngs* + *err*

On termination the change of the sensor has been detected. It only remains to capture the current time, before the allowed error bound.

(13)

$\sqsubseteq$ Law 3 (weaken assumption)

$\star\, chngt\colon [chngs \leq \tau \text{ , } chngt \in [chngs \ldots chngs + err]]$

$\sqsubseteq$ Law 4 (strengthen effect)

$\star\, chngt\colon [chngs \leq \tau \text{ , } chngt \in [\tau_0 \ldots \tau] \wedge \tau \leq chngs + err]$

$\sqsubseteq$ Law 10 (separate deadline); Law 3 (weaken assumption); Definition of gettime

gettime(*chngt*) ; **deadline** *chngs* + *err*

The final program, with the procedure *detect_chng* inlined is shown in Figure 1.

6 TIMING ANALYSIS

The final phase is to determine the time constraints on paths through the code in order to guarantee that all deadlines will be met. For each deadline command we

```
A : ⋆ {τ ≤ rises} ;
  ⟦var riset, fallt : time;
     ⟦var sens : 𝔹;
         read(sensor, sens);
      B : deadline rises + err;
         ⋆ do invariant CHNG(rises, true) ∧ (sens = true ⇒ rises ≤ τ)
         sens ≠ true →
               read(sensor, sens);
            C : deadline rises + err
         od ;
         gettime riset;
      D : deadline rises + err
     ⟧;
     ⟦var sens : 𝔹;
         read(sensor, sens);
      E : deadline falls + err;
         ⋆ do invariant CHNG(falls, false) ∧ (sens = false ⇒ falls ≤ τ)
         sens ≠ false →
               read(sensor, sens);
            F : deadline falls + err
         od ;
         gettime fallt;
      G : deadline falls + err
     ⟧;
     size := speed ∗ (fallt − riset)
  ⟧;
H : deadline falls + react
```

Figure 1 Final program with the procedure inlined.

consider the paths through the program that terminate at the deadline. For each such path we need to determine a time constraint on the execution time of the path that guarantees that the deadline will be met. Grundon, Hayes & Fidge (1998) have formalised the details of timing path analysis, but here we present a brief overview of the process for the program in Figure 1.

The first path we consider is A–B, which has a start time before* *rises* and must

*To simplify presentation, 'before' is taken to mean 'no later than' throughout this section.

complete before $rises + err$. That gives a time constraint for the path of err. Both path A–C, which enters the loop on the first iteration, and path A–D, which does not enter the loop at all, have the same constraint of err.

The path starting at A that enters the loop for the first iteration is not the only path that ends at C. The other possibilities come from the repetition of the loop. These paths require some intricate reasoning to determine suitable time constraints. Our goal is to determine timing constraints on paths through the code that guarantee that the deadline at point C is reached before its deadline of $rises + err$. Because the deadline is within the loop body, we know on entry to the loop that $sens$ is false, which implies that the previous read must have commenced before time $rises$. Hence our constraint is that the path from the previous read, around the loop through the current read, and finishing at the deadline at C, must take time less than $rises + err - rises = err$.

There are paths from D to E, F and G. All start no later than $rises + err$ and must complete before $falls + err$. That gives them a time constraint of $falls - rises$. However, we are guaranteed by (1) that $falls - rises \geq minsep$, and hence we can use $minsep$ as our time constraint.

The remainder of the paths for calculating the fall time of the sensor are similar to those for calculating the rise. We do not discuss them in detail here.

The final path that we consider is G–H. It has a start time before $falls + err$ and must complete before $falls + react$. This gives a time constraint of $react - err$. The specification gives $react$ as $100\,\mu s$, and our refinement requires that $err \leq 100\,\mu s$. The constant err appears in the constraints of many paths. It can be chosen up to the limit of $100\,\mu s$ so that the paths can meet their timing constraints.

Provided we can show that the machine code generated for each of the above paths satisfies the corresponding time constraint, then we can guarantee all deadlines will be met. There has been considerable research in the real-time community on timing analysis of such machine code sequences (Lim et al. 1995).

7 CONCLUSIONS

The main advantage of the sequential real-time refinement calculus presented here is that, to developers, it appears to be a straightforward extension of the standard refinement calculus. Although it has a different underlying semantics, most of the standard refinement laws carry over, and the real-time extended programming language is a superset of the standard target language. In practice, a development in the real-time calculus is similar to standard refinement calculus development, but with the addition of steps to separate out timing constraints and refine them into real-time language constructs.

However, even with this strong connection to the standard calculus, our experience so far suggests that programs that rely heavily on timing behaviour for their correctness are quite challenging to develop in our calculus. Finding loop invariants and sequential composition intermediate predicates seems more difficult than in the standard calculus. We suspect that this is partly because we have had more experience with the standard calculus, and partly because real-time programming is intrinsically difficult. Certainly the timing analysis phase is an additional requirement with its own intricacies. Anyway, it is exciting to have a calculus that allows the subtle aspects of real-time programs to be formally proved, just as the standard calculus "dots the i's and crosses the t's" of ordinary sequential programming.

REFERENCES

Back, R.-J. (1980) Correctness preserving program refinements: Proof theory and applications. Tract 131, Mathematisch Centrum, Amsterdam.

Grundon, S., Hayes, I. J. & Fidge, C. J. (1998) Timing constraint analysis, *in* C. McDonald, ed., 'Computer Science '98: Proc. 21st Australasian Computer Science Conf. (ACSC'98), Perth, 4–6 Feb.', Springer-Verlag, pp. 575–586.

Hayes, I. J. & Mahony, B. P. (1995) 'Using units of measurement in formal specifications'. *Formal Aspects of Computing* 7(3), 329–347.

Hayes, I. & Utting, M. (1997*a*) Coercing real-time refinement: A transmitter, *in* D. J. Duke & A. S. Evans, eds, 'BCS-FACS Northern Formal Methods Workshop', Electronic Workshops in Computing, Springer Verlag. URL http://www.springer.co.uk/ewic/workshops/NFM96/.

Hayes, I. & Utting, M. (1997*b*) A sequential real-time refinement calculus. Technical Report UQ-SVRC-97-33, Software Verification Research Centre, The University of Queensland, URL http://svrc.it.uq.edu.au.

Lim, S.-S., Bae, Y. H., Jang, G. T., Rhee, B.-D., Min, S. L., Park, C. Y., Shin, H., Park, K., Moon, S.-M. & Kim, C. S. (1995) 'An accurate worst case timing analysis for RISC processors'. *IEEE Trans. on Software Eng.* **21**(7), 593–604.

Mahony, B. P. (1992) The Specification and Refinement of Timed Processes. PhD thesis, Department of Computer Science, The University of Queensland.

Morgan, C. (1994) *Programming from Specifications.* second edn, Prentice Hall.

Utting, M. & Fidge, C. (1996) A real-time refinement calculus that changes only time, *in* He Jifeng, ed., 'Proc. 7th BCS/FACS Refinement Workshop', Electronic Workshops in Computing, Springer. URL http://www.springer.co.uk/eWiC/Workshops/7RW.html.

Utting, M. & Fidge, C. J. (1997) Refinement of infeasible real-time programs, *in* 'Proc. Formal Methods Pacific '97', Discrete Mathematics and Theoretical Computer Science, Springer, Wellington, New Zealand, pp. 243–262.

APPENDIX 1 LAWS FOR LANGUAGE CONSTRUCTS

The following laws are extracted from an earlier paper (Hayes & Utting 1997*b*) that gives the semantics of the real-time language constructs, as well as a more comprehensive set of laws.

Unindexed variables in predicates and expressions In a predicate, unindexed variables of the form v stand for $v(\tau)$, and variables of the form v_0 stand for $v(\tau_0)$. We introduce the notation $R @ (\tau_0, \tau)$ to stand for the predicate R with every unindexed occurrence of a variable, v, replaced by $v(\tau)$ and every occurrence of v_0 replaced by $v(\tau_0)$. Note that R may contain explicit indexed references to variables at times other than τ; these are not affected by the '@' operator. The operator '@' has a lower precedence than all the normal logical operators, but a higher precedence than '$\equiv$' and '$\Rrightarrow$'. For predicates, such as assumptions, that do not contain any zero-subscripted variables, we use the notation $P @ \tau$. If there are no occurrences of τ_0 or zero-subscripted variables in P then $P @ (\tau_0, \tau) \equiv P @ \tau$. The operator '@' distributes over logical operators.

Specifications The assumptions of a specification command determine the range of possible values of variables over time, as well as the start time of the command. The effect further constrains the values of variables over time, as well as constraining the finish time of the command. Program variables (local variables and outputs) not in the frame of a specification are stable over its execution. Given a variable, v, and a set of times, S,

$$stable(v, S) \stackrel{\text{def}}{=} (\forall\, t, u : S \bullet v(t) = v(u))$$

The meaning of a specification command is given with respect to a given environment, where an environment just records the variables (inputs, outputs and local variables) that are in scope. We use ρ to stand for an environment, and $\hat{\rho}$ to stand for the program variables (outputs and local variables) within ρ. The meaning function, $\mathcal{M}_\rho$, gives the meaning of a real-time construct in environment ρ in terms of a predicate transformer determined by a standard refinement calculus construct.

Definition 2 (specification) *A specification command, $\star\vec{x}\colon [P, R]$, is well formed in an environment, ρ, provided (i) the frame, $\vec{x}$, is a vector of program variables (outputs and local variables), (ii) P is a predicate involving the variables in the environment plus τ, and (iii) R is a predicate involving variables in the environment plus τ_0, τ and zero-subscripted versions of variables in the environment. The meaning of a well-formed specification command is given by the following*

$$\mathcal{M}_\rho\,(\star\vec{x}\colon [P, R]) \stackrel{\text{def}}{=} \tau\colon [P @ \tau,\ R @ (\tau_0, \tau) \wedge \tau_0 \leq \tau \wedge stable(\hat{\rho} \setminus \vec{x}, [\tau_0 \ldots \tau])]$$

where $\hat{\rho} \setminus \vec{x}$ stands for the program variables, $\hat{\rho}$, with any elements in the frame $\vec{x}$ removed.

Note that τ, unlike other variables, is not itself a function of time. The frame, $\vec{x}$, of the real-time command does not appear in the frame of the equivalent standard command. Instead, those program variables that are not in the frame are constrained to be stable for its duration, and the program variables in the frame are only constrained by the effect of the specification, R. In the assumption and effect of a specification command it is permissible to include both explicitly indexed references and unindexed references to the same variable. For more details on the encoding of real-time specifications the reader is referred to Utting & Fidge (1997).

The refinement rules for weakening an assumption and strengthening an effect carry over to the real-time refinement calculus.

Law 3 (weaken assumption) *Provided* $P \mathbin{@} \tau \Rrightarrow P' \mathbin{@} \tau$,

$$\star\vec{x}\colon [P, R] \sqsubseteq \star\vec{x}\colon [P', R] \,.$$

When applying this law we can use the fact that from $P \Rrightarrow P'$ one can deduce that $P \mathbin{@} \tau \Rrightarrow P' \mathbin{@} \tau$. That gives a special case of the law for dealing with properties that are not time dependent.

Law 4 (strengthen effect) *Given an environment, ρ, provided*

$$(P \mathbin{@} \tau_0) \wedge (R' \mathbin{@} (\tau_0, \tau)) \wedge \tau_0 \le \tau \wedge stable(\hat{\rho} \setminus \vec{x}, [\tau_0 \ldots \tau]) \Rrightarrow R \mathbin{@} (\tau_0, \tau)$$

then

$$\star\vec{x}\colon [P, R] \sqsubseteq \star\vec{x}\colon [P, R']$$

where $\hat{\rho} \setminus \vec{x}$ stands for the program variables (local variables and outputs) of the environment ρ, minus the variables in the frame, $\vec{x}$.

In the case where the properties are not time dependent, a special case of the proviso is, $P_0 \wedge R' \Rrightarrow R$, where P_0 stands for the predicate P with all occurrences of τ replaced by τ_0, and all unindexed occurrences of every variable, v, that is in the frame or is an external input, replaced by v_0.

Law 5 (remove from frame) *Given disjoint vectors of program variables, $\vec{x}$ and $\vec{v}$,*

$$\star\vec{x}, \vec{v}\colon [P, R] \sqsubseteq \star\vec{v}\colon [P, R]$$

Assertions Assertions may state assumptions about the variables at the point at which they occur. Hence in an assertion, $\star\{A\}$, an unindexed reference to a variable, v, is interpreted as $v(\tau)$. Assertions can also state assumptions about the value of variables at other times by using explicit indices. Assertions take no time, and hence there is no need for τ_0 or zero-subscripted variables, within assertions.

Law 6 (separate assumption)

$$\star\vec{x}\colon [U \wedge P, R] \sqsubseteq \star\{U\}\,;\ \star\vec{x}\colon [P, R]$$

Assignment As the evaluation of the expressions in an assignment takes time, we require that the expressions in assignments are idle-stable (time-independent).

Law 7 (assignment) *Given an environment, ρ, a frame, $\vec{x}$, such that $\vec{x}$ is contained in the program variables, $\hat{\rho}$, and a vector, $\vec{D}$, of idle-stable expressions, provided*

$$(P @ \tau_0) \wedge (\vec{x} @ \tau) = (\vec{D} @ \tau_0) \wedge \tau_0 \le \tau \wedge stable(\hat{\rho} \setminus \vec{x}, [\tau_0 \dots \tau]) \Rrightarrow R @ (\tau_0, \tau)$$

then

$$\star\vec{x}\colon [P, R] \sqsubseteq \vec{x} := \vec{D}.$$

If the properties do not involve time then the following special case of the proviso can be used: $P_0 \wedge \vec{x} = \vec{D}_0 \Rrightarrow R$.

Logical constants Note that logical constants are not implicit functions of time.

Law 8 (logical constant) *Provided* $(\exists\, u : T \bullet P @ \tau)$ *and u does not occur in C or the variables in the environment,*

$$C \sqsubseteq |[\ \mathbf{con}\ u : T \bullet \star\{P\}\ ;\ C\ ]|$$

Refinement to a sequential composition The refinement of a specification command to a sequential composition of specification commands follows the same approach as in the standard refinement calculus. One must devise an intermediate predicate Q that holds on termination of the first component, and hence also for the assumption of the second component. Because we have assumed that there is no time delay between the execution of the two commands, τ in the effect of the first component refers to the same time as τ in the assumptions of the second component.

Law 9 (simple sequential composition) *Provided Q and R do not involve τ_0 or zero-subscripted variables,*

$$\star\vec{x}\colon [P, R] \sqsubseteq \star\vec{x}\colon [P, Q]\ ;\ \star\vec{x}\colon [Q, R]$$

A timing deadline in the effect of a specification command may be separated out into a deadline command.

Law 10 (separate deadline) *Provided D is a time-valued expression, which may include references to logical constants but no references to τ_0 or zero-subscripted variables,*

$$\star\vec{x}\colon [P, R \wedge \tau \le D] \sqsubseteq \star\vec{x}\colon [P, R]\ ;\ \mathbf{deadline}\ D$$

Local variables The definition of a local variable block in the real-time language involves expanding the environment for the command within the block. The allocation and deallocation of local variables may take time. Hence we need stability requirements on the assumption and effect in the variable introduction law.

Law 11 (introduce variable) *Given an environment, ρ, such that v does not occur in the variables of ρ (and hence does not occur free within P or R or in $\vec{x}$), provided T is nonempty, P is idle-stable and R is both pre- and post-idle-stable, then*

$$\star\vec{x}\colon [P, R] \sqsubseteq |[\ \textbf{var}\ v : T \bullet \star v, \vec{x}\colon [P, R]\ ]|$$

A predicate R is pre-idle-stable (post-idle-stable) if when R is used as an effect of a specification command, the specification command can be prefixed (postfixed) by an idle command and the result is a refinement of the original specification command (Hayes & Utting 1997*b*).

APPENDIX 2 ITERATION

We distinguish between the real-time iteration command ($\star$**do**) and the standard iteration command (**do**) within this section and use the latter in the definition of the former as a way of reusing its predicate transformer.

The guard of an iteration is required to be idle-stable so that it is stable during its evaluation. To account for the delay to evaluate the guard an idle command with a minimum execution time ($d1$) is used,

$$\textbf{idle}_{\geq d1} \stackrel{\text{def}}{=} \star\colon [\mathsf{true}\ , \tau - \tau_0 \geq d1]$$

and to account for exiting the loop, an idle command with a maximum execution time ($d2$) is used,

$$\textbf{idle}_{\leq d2} \stackrel{\text{def}}{=} \star\colon [\mathsf{true}\ , \tau - \tau_0 \leq d2]$$

Of course, both $d1$ and $d2$ are dependent on the implementation, but our definition does not rely on the particular values of these, just that such constants exist. To allow for the case when the guard is initially false, an **idle** is added after the loop to allow the loop to take some time in this case.

Definition 12 (iteration) *Given an environment, ρ, and an idle-stable expression, G, which does not contain references to τ_0 or zero-subscripted variables,*

$$\begin{array}{l} \mathcal{M}_\rho(\star\textbf{do}\ G \rightarrow C\ \textbf{od}) \stackrel{\text{def}}{=} \\ \quad [\![d1, d2 : Time \mid d1 > 0 \wedge d2 > 0 \bullet \\ \qquad \textbf{do}\ G\,@\,\tau \rightarrow \mathcal{M}_\rho(\textbf{idle}_{\geq d1};\ C\colon \textbf{idle}_{\leq d2})\ \textbf{od} \circ \mathcal{M}_\rho(\textbf{idle}) \end{array}$$

where '$[\![$' is generalised nondeterministic choice and '$\circ$' is standard sequential composition.

The following loop introduction rule does not make use of a conventional variant to show termination. Instead it makes use of a fixed deadline that does not change during the execution of the loop. When combined with the inevitable progress of time due to execution of the loop, this has the same effect as a variant.

Law 13 (iteration timing with deadline) *Given an idle-stable invariant property, INV, a deadline expression, L, which is frame-stable with respect to the frame $\vec{x}$, idle-stable expressions G and D, and an environment, ρ, where none of G, D, L and INV contain references to τ_0 or zero-subscripted variables,*

$$\star\vec{x}\colon [INV \wedge D = \tau \leq L, \neg\, G \wedge INV']$$
$$\sqsubseteq \star\mathbf{do}\ G \rightarrow \star\vec{x}\colon [G \wedge INV', INV' \wedge \tau \leq L]\ \mathbf{od}$$

where $INV' \stackrel{\text{def}}{=} INV \wedge D \leq \tau \wedge stable(\hat{\rho} \setminus \vec{x}, [D \ldots \tau])$.

Proof Our first step is to introduce the **idle** command at the end of Definition 12 (iteration). The introduction relies on $\neg\, G \wedge INV'$ being post-idle-stable.

$$\star\vec{x}\colon [INV \wedge D = \tau \leq L, \neg\, G \wedge INV']$$
$\sqsubseteq$ Law 9 (simple sequential composition); Definition of idle
$$\star\vec{x}\colon [INV \wedge D = \tau \leq L, \neg\, G \wedge INV']\,;\ \mathbf{idle}$$

We now proceed to refine the first component using the standard refinement calculus laws. To emphasise this we use the s-subscripted '$\sqsubseteq_s$' to stand for refinement in the standard calculus.

$$\mathcal{M}_\rho\,(\star\vec{x}\colon [INV \wedge D = \tau \leq L, \neg\, G \wedge INV'])$$
$\sqsubseteq_s$ Definition 2 (specification)
$$\tau\colon [INV \wedge D = \tau \leq L \mathbin{@} \tau, \neg\, G \wedge INV' \mathbin{@} (\tau_0, \tau) \wedge \tau_0 \leq \tau \wedge stable(\hat{\rho} \setminus \vec{x}, [\tau_0 \ldots \tau])]$$
$\sqsubseteq_s$ definition of INV'; strengthen postcondition; weaken precondition; choice
$$[\!] \; d1, d2 : Time \mid d1 > 0 \wedge d2 > 0 \bullet$$
$$\tau\colon [INV' \wedge \tau \leq L + d2 \mathbin{@} \tau, \neg\, G \wedge INV' \wedge \tau \leq L + d2 \mathbin{@} \tau] \qquad \lhd$$
$\sqsubseteq_s$ Standard iteration with variant $\left\lfloor \frac{L+d2-\tau}{d1} \right\rfloor$

do $G \mathbin{@} \tau \rightarrow$
$$\tau\colon \left[G \wedge INV' \wedge \tau \leq L + d2 \mathbin{@} \tau,\ \begin{array}{l} INV' \wedge \tau \leq L + d2 \mathbin{@} \tau \wedge \\ \left\lfloor \frac{L+d2-\tau}{d1} \right\rfloor < \left\lfloor \frac{L+d2-\tau_0}{d1} \right\rfloor \end{array} \right]$$
od

$\sqsubseteq_s$ definition of INV'; weaken precondition; strengthen with $\tau_0 \leq \tau$

do $G \mathbin{@} \tau \rightarrow$
$$\tau\colon \left[G \wedge INV' \mathbin{@} \tau,\ \begin{array}{l} INV' \wedge \tau_0 + d1 \leq \tau \leq L + d2 \mathbin{@} (\tau_0, \tau) \\ \tau_0 \leq \tau \wedge stable(\hat{\rho} \setminus \vec{x}, [\tau_0 \ldots \tau]) \end{array} \right]$$
od

$\sqsupseteq_s$ Definition 2 (specification)

do $G \mathbin{@} \tau \rightarrow \mathcal{M}_\rho\,(\star\vec{x}\colon [G \wedge INV', INV' \wedge \tau_0 + d1 \leq \tau \leq L + d2])$ **od**

We now concentrate on the body of the loop. The following step relies on the fact that $G \wedge INV'$ is idle-stable, and that INV' is both pre- and post-idle-stable.

$$\star\vec{x}\colon [G \wedge INV', INV' \wedge \tau_0 + d1 \leq \tau \leq L + d2]$$

$\sqsubseteq$ Law 9 (simple sequential composition) $\times$ 2; Definitions of idles
$\mathbf{idle}_{\geq d1};\ \star\vec{x}\colon [G \wedge INV', INV' \wedge \tau \leq L]\ ;\ \mathbf{idle}_{\leq d2}$

Combining the above together we get,

$$
\begin{array}{l}
[\!] \; d1, d2 : Time \mid d1 > 0 \wedge d2 > 0 \bullet \\
\qquad \mathbf{do}\ G @ \tau \rightarrow \mathcal{M}_{\rho}\,(\mathbf{idle}_{\geq d1};\ \star\vec{x}\colon [G \wedge INV', INV' \wedge \tau \leq L]\ ;\ \mathbf{idle}_{\leq d2}) \\
\qquad \mathbf{od} \circ \mathcal{M}_{\rho}\,(\mathbf{idle})
\end{array}
$$

$\sqsubseteq_s$ Definition 12 (iteration)
$\mathcal{M}_{\rho}\,(\star\mathbf{do}\ G \rightarrow \star\vec{x}\colon [G \wedge INV', INV' \wedge \tau \leq L]\ \mathbf{od})$

□

A simpler rule for iteration does not involve all timing aspects.

Law 1 (iteration with deadline) *Given an idle-stable invariant property, INV, a deadline expression L, which is frame-stable with respect to the frame $\vec{x}$, and an idle-stable expression G, where none of G, L and INV contain references to τ_0 or zero-subscripted variables,*

$$\star\vec{x}\colon [INV \wedge \tau \leq L, \neg\, G \wedge INV] \sqsubseteq \star\mathbf{do}\ G \rightarrow \star\vec{x}\colon [G \wedge INV, INV \wedge \tau \leq L]\ \mathbf{od}$$

Proof We let $INV' \stackrel{\text{def}}{=} INV \wedge D \leq \tau \wedge stable(\hat{\rho} \setminus \vec{x}, [D \ldots \tau])$, where D is fresh, and make use of Law 13 (iteration timing with deadline).

$\star\vec{x}\colon [INV \wedge \tau \leq L, \neg\, G \wedge INV]$
$\sqsubseteq$ Law 8 (logical constant); Law 6 (separate assumption); Law 4 (strengthen effect)
$|[\ \mathbf{con}\, D : Time \bullet \star\vec{x}\colon [INV \wedge D = \tau \leq L, \neg\, G \wedge INV']\ ]|$
$\sqsubseteq$ Law 13 (iteration timing with deadline)
$|[\ \mathbf{con}\, D : Time \bullet \star\mathbf{do}\ G \rightarrow \star\vec{x}\colon [G \wedge INV', INV' \wedge \tau \leq L]\ \mathbf{od}\ ]|$
$\sqsubseteq$ Equivalent effect by Law 4 (strengthen effect); Law 3 (weaken assumption)
$|[\ \mathbf{con}\, D : Time \bullet \star\mathbf{do}\ G \rightarrow \star\vec{x}\colon [G \wedge INV, INV \wedge \tau \leq L]\ \mathbf{od}\ ]|$
$\sqsubseteq$ Law 8 (logical constant)
$\star\mathbf{do}\ G \rightarrow \star\vec{x}\colon [G \wedge INV, INV \wedge \tau \leq L]\ \mathbf{od}$

□

BIOGRAPHIES

Ian Hayes received his PhD from the University of New South Wales, Australia in 1983. He has been on the academic staff of the University of Queensland since 1985, and is an associated academic of the Software Verification Research Centre there.

Mark Utting received his PhD from the University of New South Wales in 1992. He then worked at the Software Verification Research Centre in Brisbane, developing the Ergo theorem prover and this real-time refinement calculus. In late 1996 he became a lecturer at Waikato University, and is now enjoying teaching programming languages and formal methods there. He is married to Lynda and they have four young children and a cat.

16

The design of a linearization of a concurrent data object

W.H. Hesselink
Dept. of Mathematics and Computing Science, University of Groningen
Postbox 800, 9700 AV Groningen, The Netherlands
Web site: `http://www.cs.rug.nl/~wim`
email: `wim@cs.rug.nl`, *fax +31.50.3633800*

Abstract

A design is presented for fault tolerant linearization of a concurrent data object in shared memory. Server processes may stop and restart functioning without notification, but always at least one member of each family of server processes makes progress. Then every client process that makes progress gets its transactions done within bounded delay.

Invariants are used to prove the safety properties. The processes are tightly coupled but the separation into client processes and some families of server processes enables modularity in the design. Preservation of the invariants is proved by means of the theorem prover Nqthm of Boyer and Moore.

Keywords

Linearization, shared memory, concurrent data object, fault tolerance, memory management, client server architecture, theorem proving

1 INTRODUCTION

A concurrent data object is a data structure shared by concurrent processes. It has a number of client processes that send invocations to the data object and receive corresponding responses. Logically, the object behaves as if the invocations are processed in some sequential order. This requirement is formalized in the concept of linearizability, see (Herlihy *et al.* 1990). Linearizability can be achieved by temporarily blocking some processes, but this has the disadvantage that, if a blocking process is delayed or stopped, other processes are delayed or stopped as well.

In a waitfree data object, cf. (Herlihy 1991), every process completes its invocation in a bounded number of atomic actions, regardless of the actions and execution speeds of the other processes. A waitfree data object is fault tolerant in the sense that, if some process stops executing, the invocations of other processes are not affected. For an object to be waitfree, every client

Programming Concepts and Methods D. Gries, & W-P. de Roever (Eds.)

must be able to treat its own invocations, since all other processes are allowed to fail. Waitfreedom is thus a clean but rigid concept. In particular, it does not allow us to delegate subtasks to separate processes. With the aim of fault tolerance and separation of concerns, it is therefore better to require progress under somewhat stronger assumptions on the distribution of failures.

We use the term bounded delay to express the assumption that *the tasks of the system are distributed over a number of families of related processes,* and the requirement that *progress is guaranteed if, and only if, each of these families contains at least one active process.* There is no requirement that an inactive process remains inactive, but if it becomes active again, it restarts at the point where it stopped and with all its previous information.

The stronger fault model allows us to delegate subtasks to separate processes. The resulting separation of concerns leads to much greater elegance and ease of design. Of course, the delegation destroys waitfreedom but the resulting design is much more flexible. It can be tuned to the requirements of the specific situation. Finally, the design can easily be converted into a waitfree implementation: enlarge every client process to a package that also contains one member of each family of server processes, and then schedule the processes in the package in a round robin fashion.

Inspired by (Herlihy 1991), we presented in (Hesselink 1995) a waitfree implementation of an arbitrary concurrent data object in shared memory. Here we present a related design of a linearization with bounded delay of such a data object. We eliminate the assumptions of safe registers and determinacy of the object. We make slightly stronger assumptions on the consensus registers (see Section 2), in order to improve the space and time complexity.

Overview of the paper

In Section 2 we present the general setting: the shared variable model with interleaving semantics, the atomic instructions used, the concepts of invariants and bounded delay, and the aspects of theorem prover assistance. Section 3 contains the formalization of the safety requirements. In Section 4 we present a version of the design without memory management and without proofs.

We then enter the central stage of the design with the verification that the informally motivated design up to this point meets its specification. Indeed, in the Sections 5, 6, 7, we prove centralized safety of this design, i.e., preservation of the first main invariant under the three families of processes Client, Linearizer, and Applier. Section 8 contains the proof of the second main invariant, which expresses that the client processes are served correctly. Section 9 contains the proof of the regularity requirements for read–write variables of larger values.

The Sections 5 up to 8 are enough to indicate our ways to find and preserve invariants. An important issue of the design, however, is that it should work in bounded memory. We therefore have to implement memory management.

Here we use the same methods as above, but, since we do not want to stretch the readers' patience unduly, we start skipping most of the details.

In Section 10, we extend the processes Client, Linearizer, Applier in such a way that efficient distributed garbage collection is possible. We then give the two garbage collecting programs Collector and Distributor for the spaces of addresses and locations. Section 11 contains the initialization. Section 12 contains concluding remarks.

We present around fifty invariants for the design without memory management and skip the eighty invariants for memory management. The reader is not expected to verify that the invariants presented are indeed preserved. We have used a theorem prover for that purpose. Rather, the reader may concentrate on how the invariants are found, and whether they are conceivable and serve some purpose.

2 THE MODEL AND THE REPERTOIRE

Concurrent data objects are reactive systems: they maintain an ongoing interaction with the environment, which is represented by the client processes.

The model of concurrency is as follows. There is a set of processes that communicate by means of shared variables. Every process also has private variables. The (global) state of the system consists of the values of all variables, the instruction pointers included. A step of the system is a transition between states in which one process executes its current instruction. An execution sequence is a sequence of steps. A state is called reachable iff it occurs in an execution sequence that starts in an initial state.

It follows that a single instruction is always treated as atomic. Certain instructions, like read or write instructions of large values, however, are regarded as taking time. This point is formalized as follows. If the current instruction of one process is to write a large value at address v, it is forbidden that the current instruction of another process is to read or write at address v. This is an additional proof obligation. We come back to it in Section 9.

It has been shown in (Herlihy 1991) that atomic read–write registers are not sufficient to construct arbitrary data objects, but that such objects can be constructed if one also allows so–called consensus registers, cf. (Fischer *et al.* 1985, Herlihy 1991).

A consensus register is a shared variable, say $\mathtt{x}$, with atomic actions $u := \mathtt{x}$ and $\mathtt{x} := 0$, and an atomic setting actions

$$\langle \ \mathbf{if}\ \mathtt{x} = 0\ \ \mathbf{then}\ \ \mathtt{x} := u\ \ \mathbf{fi}\ \rangle$$

where 0 is some constant and u is a private variable.

For the sake of efficiency, we also use a somewhat stronger version of consensus. A shared variable $\mathtt{x}$ is called a strong consensus object if the atomic setting action also sets a "status bit", say b, to indicate whether the setting action has been performed. Since atomic operations can always be combined with actions on private variables, we can replace the action on b by other private actions, see the instructions 60, 77, 91, 95 in Section 10.

We also use compare and swap registers. A shared variable $\mathtt{x}$ is called a compare and swap register if it allows instructions of the form

$$\langle\ \textbf{if}\ \mathtt{x} = u\ \ \textbf{then}\ \ \mathtt{x} := v\ \ \textbf{fi}\ \rangle$$

where u and v are private variables of the same type as $\mathtt{x}$.

For the purpose of efficient garbage collection, we also use counter variables, which allow an atomic test for equality with zero and can be atomically incremented and decremented.

Certain variables do not belong to the algorithm proper, but only serve in the proof (and possibly the specification) of the algorithm. Such variables are called ghost variables, or auxiliary variables (Owicki *et al.* 1976) (3.6), or also history variables. The values of these variables may not influence the flow of control or values of the proper variables. Assignments to ghost variables can be combined atomically with other instructions.

Invariants and bounded delay

For us a predicate is a boolean function on the global state. A predicate is called invariant iff it holds in all reachable states. It is called stable (or inductive) iff it is preserved by every transition. Clearly, a stable predicate that holds initially is an invariant, and every predicate implied by an invariant is an invariant. Thus, the standard way to prove that a predicate P is invariant is to find a stable predicate Q that holds initially and that implies P.

In practice, invariants are obtained in the following way. Let us write $P \triangleright Q$ to denote that every transition that starts in a state where P holds terminates in a state where Q holds (all transitions terminate). Now, let $(i :: P_i)$ be a family of predicates that all hold initially. Let R be the conjunction of all P_i. Assume that $R \triangleright P_i$ holds for all i. Then predicate R is stable, holds initially, and implies all P_i. Therefore each P_i is an invariant. In such a construction, the predicates P_i are called the ***constituent*** invariants, while other predicates implied by R are called ***derived*** invariants.

In (Bjørner *et al.* 1997, Manna *et al.* 1994) a more or less dual approach is advocated: there the global invariant is regarded as a disjunction of predicates. We do not know whether that approach could be used in our algorithm.

If a concurrent system has more than one process, there are execution sequences in which not all processes act. Usually one disallows such execution sequences by requiring some form of justness or fairness, cf. (Manna *et al.* 1994). For this purpose, we use a finitary form of fairness which is called ***bounded delay*** and in which progress is specified for families of processes.

It is formalized as follows. A history of the system is a finite nonempty sequence of pairs (x_i, q_i), such that each x_i is a global state and q_i is a process name, and that, for each state x_i except the last one, the current instruction of q_i can transform x_i into x_{i+1}. The corresponding sequence of processes is called the schedule of the history.

A schedule is called a *round* for client process p iff it contains p and at least one member of each family of server processes (at least once). The schedule is said to be k–fair for client p iff it is a concatenation of k rounds for p. Client p is said to be served with delay $\leq k$ iff every history k–fair for p contains at least one completion of a transaction of p. We define *bounded delay for all client processes* as the existence of a number k, such that every client is served with delay $\leq k$.

By this definition, bounded delay implies progress for every active client as long as each family of server processes contains at least one active member. Actually, in this paper we do not prove bounded delay but we present a design in which further choices can lead to bounded delay, cf. (Hesselink 1998).

Computer aided design

We use the general purpose theorem prover Nqthm to verify whether predicates are invariant under the step relation. Since our processes can make many different steps, even the effect of steps on variables requires verification. Since we have many predicates and many variables, automation of the verification is essential. The automation does not directly generate invariants, but whenever the prover is not able to prove invariance of some predicate, its failing final proof obligation often suggests a useful auxiliary invariant. The method to use Nqthm is described in more detail in (Hesselink 1996). The present paper seems to indicate that the method scales. The `event` files for our proofs have a length of about 9000 lines. They can be inspected at our Web site. During the design, we often had to modify the list of invariants or the list of instructions. To ease consistent modification in large text files, we have given the constituent invariants names of the form (Xqn) where n is a number smaller than the *pc* values used.

The computer aided verification in (Sipma *et al.* 1996) seems to require less user interaction. On the other hand, the example shown in (Sipma *et al.* 1996) is very small in comparison with the system described below.

3 CONCURRENT DATA OBJECTS IN SHARED MEMORY

A data object has an internal state x which is modified by means of invocations u. So, formally, it is a tuple $\langle X, x_0, U, R\rangle$ where X is the state space of the data object, $x_0 \in X$ is the initial state, U is the input space (the set of invocations), and $R \subseteq X \times U \times X$ is the transition relation. If the object is invoked in state x with invocation u, it may go into state y iff $\langle x, u, y\rangle \in R$.

In (Hesselink 1995), we used a model in which the data object gives output at every invocation. Here, we just assume that the whole new state of the object is the output. This simplification makes no difference for the algorithmic aspects.

Just as in (Hesselink 1995), we assume that relation R is total, i.e., for every pair $\langle x, u\rangle$ there exists y with $\langle x, u, y\rangle \in R$. The new state y need not be unique, however, as was needed before.

We assume that there are a number of concurrent processes that have private variables and that communicate by means of shared variables. The data object resides in this shared data space. It is passive, and all its actions are performed by processes.

The concurrent data object $\langle X, x_0, U, R\rangle$ consists of a procedure that, conceptually, acts on one shared program variable $\mathtt{x}$ of type X and that could be specified by

$$\begin{array}{l}\textbf{proc}\ \textit{apply}\ (\textbf{in}\ p : \textit{process}, u : U;\ \textbf{out}\ y : X) \\ \quad \{\ \textbf{pre}\ \mathtt{x} = w,\ \ \textbf{post}\ \mathtt{x} = y\ \wedge\ \langle w, u, y\rangle \in R\ \}\end{array}$$

for every value $w \in X$. A client process p calls procedure *apply* in the form $\textit{apply}(p, u, y)$ for the treatment of invocation u to obtain the new state y. So, p and u are input parameters and y is a result parameter. All clients may call *apply* concurrently and repeatedly.

The aim is to construct a distributed implementation of *apply* by means of a given sequential implementation of procedure

$$\begin{array}{l}\textbf{proc}\ \textit{locapply}\ (\textbf{in}\ u : U, w : X;\ \textbf{out}\ y : X) \\ \quad \{\ \ \textbf{post}\ \langle w, u, y\rangle \in R\ \}\end{array}$$

This procedure can be used by the processes, provided that concurrent reading and writing of variables of types U and X is avoided. More precisely, we assume that such variables reside in regular registers, see Section 9.

We formalize linearization in the following way, cf. (Hesselink 1995). For each client p, we define $\beta.p$ to be the list of consecutive pairs $\langle u, y\rangle$ of invocations and results of p. For a list β and element w, let $w : \beta$ be the list obtained by prefixing list β with w. Conceptually, each client executes the infinite loop

$$*\ [\ u := \textit{arbitrary}\ ;\quad \textit{apply}\ (\textit{self}, u, y)\ ;\quad \beta :=\ \langle u, y\rangle : \beta\ ]\ .$$

We represent the logical history of the *object* by an ordered list σ of triples $\langle p, u, y\rangle \in P \times U \times X$, where P is the set of clients. The occurrence of $\langle p, u, y\rangle$ means that process p has performed an invocation u with resulting state y. Let ε be the empty list. In order to relate σ to β, we define $\sigma|p$ to be list of pairs given by $\varepsilon|p = \varepsilon$, and

$$(\langle q, u, y\rangle : \sigma)|p \quad = \quad \textbf{if}\ p = q\ \textbf{then}\ \langle u, y\rangle : (\sigma|p)\ \textbf{else}\ \sigma|p\ \textbf{fi}\ .$$

List σ is said to be acceptable iff it corresponds to a legal sequential history of the object. This is formalized in predicate *acc*, defined by $\textit{acc}.\varepsilon = \textit{true}$ and

$$\textit{acc}.(\langle p, u, y\rangle : \sigma) \quad = \quad \textit{acc}.\sigma \quad \wedge \quad \langle \textit{stafi}.\sigma, u, y\rangle \in R$$

where *stafi*.σ is the last state of history σ, defined by *stafi*.$\varepsilon = x_0$ and *stafi*.$(\langle p, u, y\rangle : \sigma) = y$.

The data object is said to be ***linearizing*** iff one can construct a ghost variable σ with initially $\sigma = \varepsilon$, that for every execution satisfies the invariants

(Lin0) $acc.\sigma$;
(Lin1) $\beta.q = \sigma|q$ for every $q \in P$, whenever client q is not in *apply*.

4 A LINEARIZING DESIGN

We model the repeated calls of procedure *apply* by means of a number of looping sequential processes. We use an instruction pointer *pc* for each process and we number the atomic commands. In this section we propose three families of processes, as yet without proof. Compare (Herlihy 1991, Hesselink 1995).

We use two regions of shared memory, one for the invocation values $u : U$, and one for the state values $x : X$. The pointers into these regions are called *addresses* and *locations*, respectively. In both cases we use the value 0 as the *nil* address; nothing is stored there.

The following shared variables occur: *iloc.p* is the shared address of the current invocation of process p, and *inv.i* is the invocation stored at address i. The boolean *tolin.i* is a flag to indicate that the invocation at i is ready to be included in the linearization. Variable *post.i* gets the location of the new state corresponding to the invocation stored at i, and *sta.u* is the state located at u. We use *own.i* as a ghost variable to indicate the owner of an invocation address. The variables *iloc.i* and *own.i* will get nonzero values in collector processes, to be treated later. For the moment we only reset these variables.

Every client process executes the program Client. It has the private variables u for its current invocation, i and *sl* as copies of shared information, and the ghost variable β mentioned above. The elementary commands are numbered from 20 to enable easier modification. Notice that an invoking client q waits at command 21 until *iloc.q* is nonzero, and that it waits at 24 until *post.i* is nonzero. The private variable i is used to avoid that a single instruction has to access more than one shared variable. The result of the invocation is obtained in the read action 25.

Client
20 $u :=$ *arbitrary* ;
21 $i :=$ *iloc.self* ; **if** $i = 0$ **then goto** 21 **fi** ;
22 *inv.i* $:= u$;
23 *tolin.i* $:=$ *true* ;
24 *sl* $:=$ *post.i* ; **if** *sl* $= 0$ **then goto** 24 **fi** ;
25 $\beta := \langle u, sta.sl\rangle : \beta$;
26 *iloc.self* $:= 0$; *own.i* $:= 0$; **goto** 20 .

We introduce a family Linearizer of server processes for the linearization of the invocations. Ignoring all questions of fairness, each linearizer process chooses an arbitrary client and tries to linearize its invocation. We form a linked list with the shared variable *nx* as a forward pointer. Linearization of an address z means the inclusion of z at the head of this list. The shared variable *invHead* points to the address most recently linearized. The linearizer processes use a private variables s for processes, and y and z for addresses.

```
Linearizer
30        choose  s ∈ Client ;
31        y := invHead ;
32        z := iloc.s ;
33        if ¬tolin.z  then goto 38 fi ;
34        if  nx.y = 0  then  nx.y := z  fi ;
35        z := nx.y ;
36        tolin.z := false ;
37        if  invHead = y  then  invHead := z  fi ;
38        goto 30 .
```

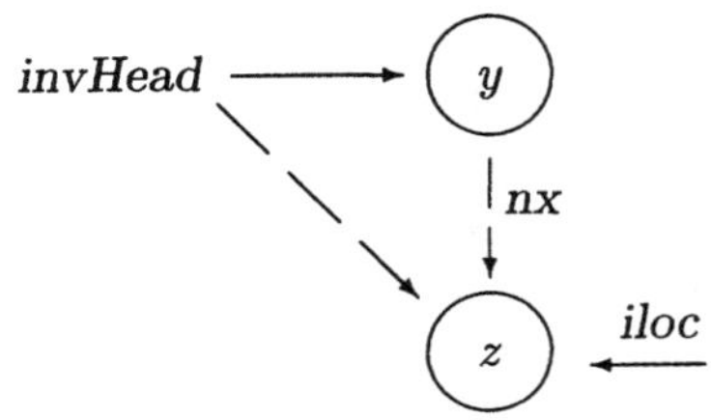

The atomic commands 34 and 37 show that the shared variable *nx.y* is a consensus register and that *invHead* is a compare and swap register.

We introduce a family Applier of server processes that concurrently compute and store the results of procedure *locapply* for relevant invocations. We use an array *staloc* of locations for new states. The situation of Applier is sketched in the following diagram.

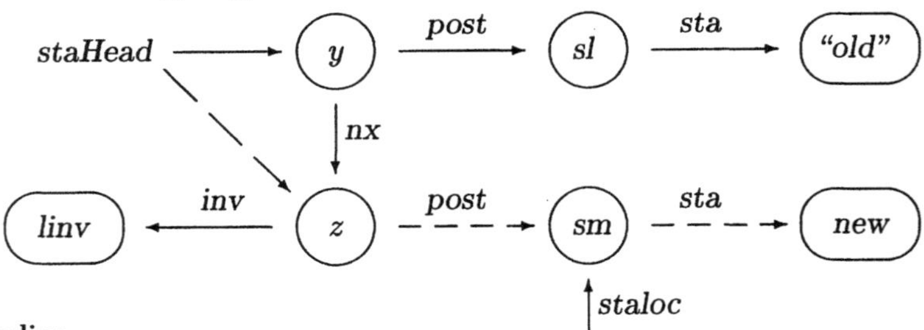


```
Applier
45        sm := staloc.self ;   if  sm = 0  then goto 45  fi ;
46        y := staHead ;
47        z := nx.y ;   if  z = 0  then goto 46 fi ;
48        linv := inv.z ;
49        sl := post.y ;
50        locapply(linv, sta.sl, new) ;
51        sta.sm := new ;
52        if  post.z = 0  then
              post.z := sm ;   σ := ⟨own.z, linv, new⟩ : σ  fi ;
53        if  staHead = y  then  staHead := z  fi ;
```

```
54        if post.z ≠ sm then goto 56 fi ;
55        staloc.self := 0 ;
56        goto 45 .
```

An applier first waits until a free location *sm* is obtained. Then y becomes the address of the invocation most recently treated, and z becomes the address of the next invocation. The applier waits if there is no next invocation. Then *linv* gets the value of the new invocation and *sl* becomes the location of the (presumed) most recent state. Procedure *locapply* yields a candidate for the new state, which is then stored at *sm*. Lines 52, 53 of Applier can be compared with line 37 of Client. The assignment to *post.z* is accompanied by an update of the ghost variable σ. This update must occur in command 52, since command 52 makes the new result available to the invoking process, see command 24 of Client. In 55, the location *staloc.self* is released, if necessary.

5 LINEARIZATION UNDER APPLIER

Up to this point nothing formal has been done. We have presented code for three families of processes, accompanied by informal arguments, as inspired by our previous experience in waitfree linearization. We now come to the central question: how to prove formally that the code satisfies the specification, i.e., the two invariants (Lin0) and (Lin1)?

We proceed as follows. We start with the invariants (Lin0) and (Lin1) of the specification, and analyse how these invariants can be invalidated. We then postulate new invariants as weak as possible to preserve the invariants. We analyse the new invariants in the same way, etc. The theorem prover is the central tool of the analysis: we submit invariants to the prover and see at which points additional arguments are needed.

We thus use the proof obligation (Lin0) as our first invariant:

(Aq0) $\quad acc.\sigma$.

Let us first prove that predicate (Aq0) is preserved by all actions of applier processes. In the course of this proof we postulate other invariants that must also be preserved by all applier actions. For the moment we ignore actions of client and linearizer processes.

First some terminology. A predicate Q is said not to be threatened by action m iff, for every global state that satisfies Q, the action of any process p with $pc.p = m$ preserves Q. If Q is threatened by action m, we need an additional invariant in the precondition to guarantee that Q is not falsified at m. Usually, the theorem prover is able to prove preservation of an invariant at all points where it is not threatened. Of course, the prover always fails where the invariant is threatened. It is our experience that it saves user time to anticipate most of the threats and prepare the remedies beforehand. For a private variable v, we write $v.p$ to denote the value of variable v of process p. We write $pc.p$ to denote the instruction pointer of process p.

The invariant (Aq0) is threatened only by the update of σ in command 52. In order to prove that (Aq0) is preserved at 52, it suffices to postulate the invariants

$$\begin{array}{ll} \text{(Aq1)} & 50 < pc.q \leq 52 \;\Rightarrow\; \langle sta.(sl.q), linv.q, new.q\rangle \in R \;; \\ \text{(Drv0)} & pc.q = 52 \;\wedge\; post.(z.q) = 0 \;\Rightarrow\; sta.(sl.q) = stafi.\sigma \;. \end{array}$$

Remark. Many of our invariants are of the form $b < pc.q \leq e \Rightarrow X$. We use intervals open to the left, since the command at b usually verifies X or makes it true, while the command at e is allowed to make X false. □

We decide to let predicate (Drv0) be a derived invariant. In order to get (Drv0), we postulate the new constituent invariants

$$\begin{array}{ll} \text{(Aq2)} & 47 < pc.q \leq 56 \;\Rightarrow\; z.q = nx.(y.q) \;; \\ \text{(Aq3)} & 49 < pc.q \leq 56 \;\Rightarrow\; sl.q = post.(y.q) \;; \\ \text{(Aq4)} & 46 < pc.q \leq 52 \;\wedge\; post.(nx.(y.q)) = 0 \;\Rightarrow\; y.q = staHead \;; \\ \text{(Aq5)} & stafi.\sigma \;=\; \textbf{if}\; post.(nx.staHead) = 0 \;\textbf{then}\; sta.(post.staHead) \\ & \qquad\qquad \textbf{else}\; sta.(post.(nx.staHead)) \;\textbf{fi}\;. \end{array}$$

Indeed, it is easy to verify that these four predicates together imply (Drv0).

Now we have to prove the invariance of (Aq1) through (Aq5) under applier processes. The invariance of (Aq1) is rather easy. First note that (Aq1) is preserved when process q itself executes command 50 because of the specification of procedure *locapply*. It follows that, since *linv*, *sl*, and *new* are private variables, (Aq1) is threatened only when some process p executes 51 with $sm.p = sl.q$. This is a question of the avoidance of interference. Indeed, preservation of (Aq1) at 51 follows from (Aq3) together with the new postulate

$$\text{(Ia0)} \qquad 45 < pc.q \leq 52 \;\Rightarrow\; sm.q \neq post.k \;.$$

Here k stands for an arbitrary address, possibly 0. Indeed all invariants are universally quantified over processes q (and r) and addresses k (and m).

We treat (Ia0) as a derived invariant, which is implied by the new postulates

$$\begin{array}{ll} \text{(Aq6)} & 45 < pc.q \leq 57 \;\Rightarrow\; sm.q \neq 0 \;; \\ \text{(Aq7)} & 45 < pc.q \leq 55 \;\Rightarrow\; sm.q = staloc.q \;; \\ \text{(Aq8)} & staloc.q = post.k \neq 0 \;\Rightarrow\; pc.q \in \{53, 54\} \;. \end{array}$$

Here we allow pc values that do not yet occur. These pc values will occur later, and we want to avoid unnecessary modifications of the invariants as much as possible. Of course we have to replay the mechanical proof for every modification of the algorithm.

Predicate (Aq2) is not threatened by applier processes. Predicate (Aq3) is threatened only at 52. It is preserved at 52 if we postulate

(Aq9) $\quad 46 < pc.q \leq 56 \quad \Rightarrow \quad post.(y.q) \neq 0$.

Predicate (Aq4) is preserved at 53 because of (Aq2) and the new postulate

(Aq10) $\quad 52 < pc.q \leq 56 \quad \Rightarrow \quad post.(z.q) \neq 0$.

Predicate (Aq5) is preserved at 51 because of (Ia0). It is preserved at 52 and 53 because of (Aq2), (Aq4), (Aq6), (Aq10), and the new postulates

(Aq11) $\quad pc.q = 52 \quad \Rightarrow \quad new.q = sta.(sm.q)$;
(Aq12) $\quad post.(nx.(nx.staHead)) = 0$.

The predicates (Aq6) and (Aq7) are not threatened. The predicates (Aq8) and (Aq9) are preserved because of (Aq7) and the new postulates

(Bq0) $\quad staloc.q = staloc.r \neq 0 \quad \Rightarrow \quad q = r$;
(Bq1) $\quad staloc.q = post.k \neq 0 \quad \Rightarrow \quad z.q = k$;
(Bq2) $\quad post.staHead \neq 0$.

Predicate (Aq10) is preserved because of (Aq6), used at 52. Preservation of (Aq11) only requires (at 51) the new predicate

(Ia2) $\quad 45 < pc.q \leq 54 \quad \wedge \quad 45 < pc.r \leq 54 \quad \wedge \quad sm.q = sm.r \quad \Rightarrow \quad q = r$.

This predicate follows from (Aq6), (Aq7), and (Bq0). Predicate (Aq12) is preserved because of (Aq2), (Aq4), and the new postulates

(Bq3) $\quad 47 < pc.q \leq 56 \quad \Rightarrow \quad z.q \neq 0$;
(Bq4) $\quad nx.k = k \quad \Rightarrow \quad k = 0$;
(Bq5) $\quad post.k = 0 \quad \Rightarrow \quad post.(nx.k) = 0$.

For preservation of (Bq5) we also need the postulate

(Bq6) $\quad nx.k = nx.m \neq 0 \quad \Rightarrow \quad k = m$.

Using all current invariants, one can prove preservation of (Bq0) up to (Bq6).

Remarks. The choice of invariants constrains later stages of the design. Some invariants are more or less forced, like (Aq1). The choice of (Aq2) is not forced, however, and will preclude the garbage collector to reset $nx.k := 0$ while $k = y.q$. It is conceivable that this invariant can be avoided. The invariants (Bq5) and (Bq6) also impose considerable constraints on garbage collection.

As an alternative for (Aq12) and (Bq5), one may introduce nx^k for repeated application of nx and then postulate that $post.(nx^k.staHead) = 0$ for every $k \geq 2$. We avoid this since mechanical verification of such an invariant requires much user assistence. □

6 PRESERVATION UNDER THE ACTIONS OF LINEARIZER

We now have to ensure that the invariants postulated in the previous section are also preserved by the action of linearizer and client processes. We first treat linearizers.

It is easy to see that the invariants of the families (Aq) and (Bq) can only be threatened by the commands 32, 34 and 35. Indeed, predicate (Aq2) is threatened at 34, and preserved because of (Bq3). The predicates (Aq4) and (Aq5) are threatened by 34 and preserved if we postulate

(Cq0) $post.0 = 0$;
(Cq1) $pc.q = 34 \ \wedge \ nx.(y.q) = 0 \ \Rightarrow \ post.(z.q) = 0$.

The invariants (Aq6), (Aq7), (Aq8), (Aq9), (Aq10), (Aq11), (Bq0), (Bq2), (Bq3) need no new arguments. Predicate (Aq12) is preserved because of (Bq5) and (Cq1). Predicate (Bq1) is preserved at 32 and 35 because of (Aq8). Predicate (Bq4) is threatened at 34, and preserved because of the new postulates

(Cq2) $31 < pc.q \leq 37 \ \wedge \ nx.(y.q) = 0 \ \Rightarrow \ y.q = invHead$;
(Cq3) $pc.q = 34 \ \wedge \ nx.(y.q) = 0 \ \Rightarrow \ tolin.(z.q)$;
(Cq4) $\neg tolin.invHead$.

Predicate (Bq5) is preserved at 34 because of (Cq1). Predicate (Bq6) is threatened at 34, and preserved because of (Cq2), (Cq3), and the new postulate

(Cq5) $tolin.(nx.k) \ \Rightarrow \ invHead = k$.

Now the new postulates must also be proved to be invariant, also under actions of applier processes. Preservation of (Cq0) only requires (Bq3), which is used at 52. Preservation of (Cq1) at 52 follows from (Aq2), (Bq3), (Cq2), (Cq3), and (Cq5). Preservation of (Cq1) at 33 follows (with $k = z.q$) from the new postulate

(Cq6) $tolin.k \ \Rightarrow \ post.k = 0 \ \vee \ nx.invHead = k$.

Preservation of (Cq2) follows from the new postulates

(Cq7) $34 < pc.q \leq 37 \quad \Rightarrow \quad nx.(y.q) \neq 0$;
(Cq8) $35 < pc.q \leq 37 \quad \Rightarrow \quad nx.(y.q) = z.q$.

For preservation of (Cq6) at 37 and (Cq7) at 34, we postulate

(Cq9) $pc.q = 37 \quad \Rightarrow \quad \neg tolin.(z.q)$;
(Cq10) $\neg tolin.0$.

For preservation of (Cq8) at 34 we need (Cq7). Preservation of (Cq9) and (Cq10) under Linearizer and Applier is trivial.

Remark. Invariant (Cq6) came as a surprize. We had expected $tolin.k \Rightarrow post.k = 0$, but that predicate is too strong and can be falsified at command 52. □

7 PRESERVATION UNDER CLIENT

We turn to the actions of client processes. The only threat of Client to the above invariants is the modification of *tolin.i* in 23, and this is only a threat for the invariants (Cq4), (Cq5), (Cq6), (Cq9), and (Cq10). In order to preserve (Cq4) and (Cq5) under action 23, we postulate

(Dq0) $21 < pc.q \leq 26 \quad \Rightarrow \quad iloc.q = i.q$;
(Dq1) $18 < pc.q \leq 23 \quad \Rightarrow \quad iloc.q \neq invHead$;
(Ia1) $21 < pc.q \leq 23 \quad \Rightarrow \quad i.q \neq nx.k$.

Predicate (Ia1) follows from (Dq0) and the new postulates

(Dq2) $18 < pc.q \leq 23 \ \wedge \ iloc.q = nx.k \quad \Rightarrow \quad iloc.q = 0$;
(Dq3) $21 < pc.q \leq 26 \quad \Rightarrow \quad i.q \neq 0$.

Predicate (Cq6) is preserved at 23 because of (Dq0) and the new postulate

(Dq4) $18 < pc.q \leq 23 \quad \Rightarrow \quad post.(iloc.q) = 0$.

Predicate (Cq9) is preserved at 23 because of (Cq8) and (Ia1). Preservation of (Cq10) follows from (Dq3).

In order to preserve (Dq1) and (Dq2), we postulate

(Dq5) $invHead \neq 0$;
(Dq6) $18 < pc.q \leq 23 \quad \Rightarrow \quad \neg tolin.(iloc.q)$.

Now one can prove the invariance of (Dq0) up to (Dq5). Predicate (Dq6) also needs the new postulate

(Ia3) $\quad iloc.q = iloc.r \neq 0 \quad \Rightarrow \quad q = r$,

which will follow from a postulate in the next section. This concludes the proof of invariance of (Aq0), i.e., proof obligation (Lin0).

8 THE TREATMENT OF THE CLIENT PROCESSES

We now turn to proof obligation (Lin1), i.e., $\beta.q = \sigma|q$ for every $q \in P$ whenever client q is not in *apply*. This expresses that the client processes are served correctly. We formalize and strengthen proof obligation (Lin1) to

(Eq0) $\quad \beta.q \;=\; \textbf{if}\;\; post.(iloc.q) = 0 \;\;\vee\;\; pc.q = 26 \;\; \textbf{then}\;\; \sigma|q \;\;\textbf{else}\;\; tail.(\sigma|q)\;\; \textbf{fi}$.

Predicate (Eq0) is clearly threatened when some process executes command 52. In this command we use the ghost variable *own.z* to indicate the owner of the invocation at address z. To formalize ownership, we postulate

(Eq1) $\quad own.k = 0 \;\;\vee\;\; iloc.(own.k) = k$;
(Eq2) $\quad iloc.q = 0 \;\;\vee\;\; own.(iloc.q) = q$.

Notice that (Ia3) follows from (Eq2).

We now come at a tricky point. By convention, we disallow process number 0. So a client with number 0 does not exist. Yet we want (Eq0) to hold for $q = 0$, since $\beta.0 = \sigma|0$ together with $\beta.0 = \varepsilon$ expresses that no ownerless invocations have been treated. Moreover, $own.k = 0$ must be allowed, just like $iloc.q = 0$. Therefore, in (Lin1), we take $P = \{0\} \cup Client$ and postulate the typing invariant $own.k \in P$.

For preservation of (Eq0) at 52, we postulate

(Drv1) $\quad pc.q = 52 \;\;\wedge\;\; post.(z.q) = 0 \;\;\wedge\;\; r = own.(z.q) \;\; \Rightarrow \;\; r \neq 0 \;\;\wedge\;\; z.q = iloc.r \;\;\wedge\;\; pc.r \neq 26$.

Preservation of (Eq0) at 52 follows from (Aq6), (Bq3), (Eq2), and (Drv1). Predicate (Eq0) is further threatened only when process q itself executes commands 25 or 26. Preservation at 26 follows from (Cq0). Preservation at 25 follows from the new postulates

(Eq3) $\quad 24 < pc.q \leq 26 \;\;\Rightarrow\;\; post.(iloc.q) \neq 0$;
(Drv2) $\quad pc.q = 25 \;\;\Rightarrow\;\; head.(\sigma|q) = \langle q, u.q, sta.(sl.q)\rangle$.

The predicates (Drv1) and (Drv2) follow from (Aq2), (Bq3), (Dq2), (Eq1), (Eq3), and the new postulates

(Eq4) $post.(nx.k) = 0 \quad \wedge \quad own.(nx.k) = 0 \quad \Rightarrow \quad nx.k = 0$;
(Eq5) $post.(iloc.q) \neq 0 \;\Rightarrow\; head.(\sigma|q) = \langle q, u.q, sta.(post.(iloc.q))\rangle$;
(Eq6) $pc.q = 25 \quad \Rightarrow \quad sl.q = post.(iloc.q)$.

We turn to the preservation of (Eq1) through (Eq6). The predicates (Eq1), (Eq2), (Eq3) need no new arguments. To preserve (Eq4) at 34 and (Eq5) at 52, we postulate

(Eq7) $post.k = 0 \quad \wedge \quad own.k = 0 \quad \Rightarrow \quad \neg tolin.k$;
(Eq8) $48 < pc.q \leq 52 \quad \Rightarrow \quad linv.q = inv.(z.q)$;
(Eq9) $q \in Client \quad \Rightarrow \quad 18 < pc.q \leq 22 \quad \vee \quad u.q = inv.(iloc.q)$.

We need no new postulates to prove preservation of (Eq6) up to (Eq9). This concludes the treatment of proof obligation (Lin1).

Remark. We could have chosen to strengthen (Eq4) and (Eq7) to $post.k = 0 \Rightarrow own.k \neq 0$, but then $post.k := 0$ must be done by Client, so that garbage collection may be hampered by "old" pointers $post.k \neq 0$. □

9 REGULAR REGISTERS

As announced above the invocation and state values of the object need not be so small that they can be put into an atomic register, i.e., one that allows concurrent reading and writing. A register is called *regular* if concurrent reading is allowed, but whenever a process is writing the register no other process is allowed to read or write the register.

We assume that the elements of the arrays *inv* and *sta* are regular registers. So, we have the proof obligations to show that, whenever some process, say q, is writing $inv.k$ or $sta.k$, no other process, say r, is writing or reading at that address or location. This amounts to the regularity requirements

(rg0) $q \neq r \quad \wedge \quad pc.q = 22 \quad \wedge \quad pc.r = 22 \quad \Rightarrow \quad i.q \neq i.r$;
(rg1) $pc.q = 22 \quad \wedge \quad pc.r = 48 \quad \Rightarrow \quad i.q \neq z.r$;
(rg2) $q \neq r \quad \wedge \quad pc.q = 51 \quad \wedge \quad pc.r = 51 \quad \Rightarrow \quad sm.q \neq sm.r$;
(rg3) $pc.q = 51 \quad \wedge \quad pc.r = 25 \quad \Rightarrow \quad sm.q \neq sl.r$;
(rg4) $pc.q = 51 \quad \wedge \quad pc.r = 50 \quad \Rightarrow \quad sm.q \neq sl.r$.

These regularity requirements are all implied by the above invariants, in particular by (Ia0) up to (Ia3), and (Aq2), (Aq3), (Dq0), (Dq3), (Eq6).

10 GARBAGE COLLECTION

In view of space limitations we now lower the levels of formality and completeness considerably. So, for the remainder of the design we omit most of the invariants and proofs. The details can be found on our Web site.

For the sake of efficiency, we provide every address with sufficient information for a collector process to decide that the address is free for recycling, without sweeps over lists of processes or addresses. This information will consist of a number (*cnt*) and five essentially boolean flags.

The first requirement of progress is that an interested client p gets an address $i = iloc.p \neq 0$. For this purpose we use a command of the form

$$\textbf{if}\ \ iloc.sg = 0\ \ \textbf{then}\ \ iloc.sg := yg\ ;\quad own.yg := sg\ \ \textbf{fi}.$$

So we need to find addresses *yg* that can be used in this command. The theorem prover has been used to find the conditions on *yg* needed.

In order to avoid that the address y of a linearizer or applier process is recycled prematurely, an address k gets a counter for the number of such processes q with $y.q = k$. So we redefine

```
Linearizer
28        choose  s ∈ Client ;
29        y := invHead ;
30        cnt.y := cnt.y + 1 ;
31        if  y ≠ invHead  then goto 38 fi ;
32 ... 37 Instructions as before ;
38        cnt.y := cnt.y − 1 ;   goto 28 .
```

The test of $y \neq invHead$ in command 31 serves to handle the case that a collector grabs the address while a delayed linearizer is about to increment the counter from 0 to 1. A similar modification is made in Applier below.

In order to avoid that the address of a linearized invocation that has not yet been treated, is recycled prematurely, the addresses get boolean flags *usob* ("in use for the object") with the invariants that *usob* holds for the addresses *invHead* and *nx.invHead*, and for all addresses k where $post.k = 0$ holds. The flags are lowered at command 56. We thus redefine

```
Applier
43        sm := staloc.self ;   if  sm = 0  then goto 43  fi ;
44        y := staHead ;
45        cnt.y := cnt.y + 1 ;
46        if  y ≠ staHead  then goto 57 fi ;
47        z := nx.y ;   if  z = 0  then goto 56 fi ;
48 ... 55 Instructions as before ;
56        usob.y := false ;
57        cnt.y := cnt.y − 1 ;   goto 43 .
```

In the invariants (Ia0), (Aq6), and (Aq7), the starting point 45 of the ranges must now be replaced by 43. We can then replay the old proofs on the theorem prover. Note that extension at the end of the ranges was anticipated.

It is easy to see that the counters indeed count, i.e., that *cnt.k* always equals the number of processes q with $y.q = k$, and $pc.q$ either in (30 . . 38] or in (45 . . 57]. This is one of the harder invariants to prove with a theorem prover.

We also have to avoid recycling the address of the result of a delayed client. The test $own.k = 0$ would serve for this purpose. Since we want to treat *own* as a ghost variable, however, we give each address a flag *isil* (this stands for *is iloc*) with the intention that $own.k \neq 0$ implies *isil.k*. The idea is to set *isil.i* to *false* after command 26, but we do it at 19, as was anticipated in the invariants (Dq2), (Dq4), etc. Thus, program Client is modified as follows.

```
Client
19         isil.i := false ;
20 ... 25  Instructions as before ;
26         iloc.self := 0 ;   own.i := 0 ;   goto 19 .
```

Collector processes

The collector processes have to inspect addresses and make these available to the clients. For each separate address, they must work under mutual exclusion. For this purpose we use a strong consensus object *down*.

We introduce a flag *open* to mark addresses ready for recycling and not yet used. This flag is raised at 78 and lowered at 75 just before recycling is attempted. We thus arrive at the following form of garbage collection

```
Collector
59         choose yg ∈ Address ;
60         if down.yg = 0 then down.yg := 1 else goto 59 fi ;
61         if open.yg then goto 75 fi ;
62         if usob.yg then goto 79 fi ;
63         if cnt.yg ≠ 0 then goto 79 fi ;
64         zg := nx.yg ; { decouple zg }
65         nx.yg := 0 ;
66         isnx.zg := false ;
67         if isil.yg then goto 79 fi ;
68         if isnx.yg then goto 79 fi ;
69         usob.yg := true ;
70         ug := post.yg ; { decouple ug }
71         post.yg := 0 ;
72         occ.ug := false ;
73         isil.yg := true ;
74         isnx.yg := true ;
75         open.yg := false ;
```

```
76        choose  sg ∈ Client ;
77        if  iloc.sg = 0  then  { recycle yg }
              iloc.sg := yg ;   own.yg := sg ;   goto 79 fi ;
78        open.yg := true ;
79        down.yg := 0 ;   goto 59 .
```

We use a flag *isnx* at each address to record that it does not occur as *nx* of another address. After the tests in 61, 62, and 63, we let the successor of *yg* be decoupled and set its *isnx* to false. This form of garbage collection is possible because of (Bq6). After two subsequent tests the location of *yg* is decoupled, and this is recorded by lowering flag *occ*.

The order of the commands is critical. In particular, command 62 must come before the others, and 63 must be the next. The tests 67 and 68 must come before commands 69 through 74. It is good for progress that the tests 67 and 68 come after the decoupling of *nx.yg*.

Distributing locations

We finally introduce processes to distribute locations, i.e., to give *staloc* adequate nonzero values. The procedure is similar as for invocation addresses, but simpler since some work has been done in Collector. We use a shared variable *lock* to avoid that the same location is distributed by different distributors at the same time. We use the flags *occ*, which were introduced above to indicate that a location is occupied. In this way, we arrive at

```
Distributor
90        choose  ug ∈ Location ;
91        if  lock.ug = 0  then  lock.ug := 1  else goto 90 fi ;
92        if  occ.ug  then goto 96 fi ;
93        occ.ug := true ;
94        choose  sg ∈ Applier ;
95        if  staloc.sg = 0  then  staloc.sg := ug  else goto 94 fi ;
96        lock.ug := 0 ;   goto 90 .
```

11 THE INITIAL STATE

The system we have developed is a reactive system, which is supposed never to terminate. Yet, after building it, one must be able to start it. We therefore now describe the initial state. All invariants are implied by the following predicate.

$$
\begin{aligned}
& \sigma = \varepsilon \quad \wedge \quad staHead = invHead \neq 0 \quad \wedge \quad post.staHead \neq 0 \\
\wedge \quad & sta.(post.staHead) = x_0 \quad \wedge \quad occ.(post.staHead) \\
\wedge \quad & \neg open.staHead \quad \wedge \quad \neg isnx.staHead \quad \wedge \quad \neg isil.staHead \\
\wedge \quad & post.0 = 0 \quad \wedge \quad \neg open.0 \quad \wedge \quad \beta.0 = \varepsilon \quad \wedge \quad iloc.0 = 0
\end{aligned}
$$

$$
\begin{aligned}
\wedge \quad & (\forall\, k :: nx.k = 0 \;\wedge\; own.k = 0 \;\wedge\; cnt.k = 0 \;\wedge\; usob.k \;\wedge\; \neg tolin.k) \\
\wedge \quad & (\forall\, k : k \neq 0 \;\wedge\; k \neq staHead : post.k = 0 \;\wedge\; open.k \;\wedge\; isnx.k \;\wedge\; isil.k) \\
\wedge \quad & (\forall\, q :: \beta.q = \varepsilon \;\wedge\; iloc.q = 0 \;\wedge\; staloc.q = 0 \\
& \quad \wedge\; pc.q \in \{20, 28, 43, 59, 90\} \;\wedge\; (q \in Client \Rightarrow pc.q = 20)\,).
\end{aligned}
$$

12 CONCLUDING REMARKS

We have constructed a concurrent system for linearization of an arbitrary data object under a form of fault tolerance. The memory requirements are linear in the number of processes. We would not have been able to conclude the design without a powerful theorem prover to verify the invariants. The design has 61 atomic instructions in tightly coupled concurrency. Although we had previous experience with similar algorithms, we started from scratch and essentially concluded it within ten weeks. This indicates that the method of (Hesselink 1996) scales to intricate distributed algorithms of moderate size.

REFERENCES

Bjøerner, N., Browne, A. and Manna, Z. (1997) Automatic generation of invariants and intermediate assertions. Theor.Comp.Science **173**, 49–87.

Boyer, R.S. and Moore J S. (1988) A Computational Logic Handbook. Academic Press, Boston etc.

Fischer, M.J., Lynch, N.A. and Paterson, M.S. (1985) Impossibility of distributed consensus with one faulty process. J. ACM **32**, 374–382.

Herlihy, M.P. (1991) Wait–free synchronization. ACM Trans. on Program. Languages and Systems **13**, 124–149.

Herlihy, M.P. and Wing, J. (1990) Linearizability: a correctness condition for concurrent objects. ACM Trans Program Lang Syst **12**, 463–492.

Hesselink, W.H. (1995) Wait–free linearization with a mechanical proof. Distr. Comput. **9**, 21–36.

Hesselink, W.H. (1996) NQTHM proving sequential programs. Computing Science Reports CS-R9605, Groningen. See also our Web site.

Hesselink, W.H. (1998) A formal proof of fault tolerant progress. In preparation.

Manna, Z. and Pnueli, A. (1994) Temporal verification diagrams. In *Proc. Int. Symp. on Theoretical Aspects of Computer Software*. LNCS 789. Springer, pp. 726–765.

Owicki, S. and Gries, D. (1976) An axiomatic proof technique for parallel programs. Acta Informatica **6**, 319–340.

Sipma, H.B., Uribe, T.E. and Manna, Z. (1996) Deductive model checking. In *Proc. 8th Intl. Conference on Computer Aided Verification*. LNCS 1102, Springer, pp. 208–219.

BIOGRAPHY

Wim. H. Hesselink received his PhD in mathematics from the University of Utrecht in 1975. After ten years of research in algebraic groups and Lie algebras, he turned to computing science. His research interests include predicate transformation semantics of recursive procedures with nondeterminacy of various flavours, distributed programming, design and correctness of algorithms, and the use of mechanical theorem provers. He is a professor at Groningen University since 1994. He now just concluded a term as Chairman of the Department of Computing Science.

17

Final semantics for the π-calculus*

F. Honsell, M. Lenisa
Università di Udine
Via delle Scienze 208, Udine, Italy. {honsell,lenisa}@dimi.uniud.it

U. Montanari, M. Pistore
Università di Pisa
Corso Italia 40, Pisa, Italy. {ugo,pistore}@di.unipi.it

Abstract

In this paper we discuss *final semantics* for the π-calculus, a process algebra which models systems that can dynamically change the topology of the channels. We show that the final semantics paradigm, originated by Aczel and Rutten for CCS-like languages, can be successfully applied also here. This is achieved by suitably generalizing the standard techniques so as to accommodate the mechanism of *name creation* and the behaviour of the binding operators peculiar to the π-calculus. As a preliminary step, we give a *higher order* presentation of the π-calculus using as metalanguage LF, a *logical framework* based on typed λ-calculus. Such a presentation highlights the nature of the binding operators and elucidates the rôle of free and bound channels. The final semantics is defined making use of this higher order presentation, within a category of *hypersets*.

Keywords

Semantics, process calculi, coalgebras, logical frameworks, hypersets

1 INTRODUCTION

The π-calculus [12, 11] is a process algebra which models communicating systems that can dynamically change the topology of the channels. This is obtained by allowing (channel) names to appear as values in communications. The possibility of reconfiguring process adjacency gives to the π-calculus a richer expressive power than CCS: for instance, π-calculus can be used to model object oriented languages, and higher-order communications can be encoded in it.

*Research supported in part by CNR Integrated Project *Metodi e Strumenti per la Progettazione e la Verifica di Sistemi Eterogenei Connessi mediante Reti di Comunicazione* and Esprit Working Groups *CONFER2* and *TYPES*.

Programming Concepts and Methods D. Gries, & W-P. de Roever (Eds.)

However, this possibility of communicating names, and hence of dynamically modifying the scope of local names, leads to new problems when one tries to extend to the π-calculus the techniques which have been developed for CCS-like languages. In this paper we address the problem of extending to the π-calculus the *final-semantics* approach originally introduced by Aczel, Rutten and Turi [2, 15, 14] for CCS-like languages and further generalized to λ-calculus [8] and higher order concurrent imperative languages [9].

The gist of the *final semantics paradigm* [2] is to view the *interpretation* function from *syntax* to *semantics* as a *final* mapping in a suitable category. To this end the semantics has to be construed as a *terminal coalgebra* for a suitable functor F and the syntax has to be cast in the form of an F-coalgebra. In a sense, this approach is driven by the operational semantics of the language, because it is the semantics which determines the structure of the functor F. This is dual to the syntax-driven approach of *initial semantics*, where syntax is construed as an initial F-algebra and the semantics is defined as an F-algebra. As Rutten [14] has clearly explained, the duality between final semantics and initial semantics can be pushed very far and it is rather fruitful. By way of example we just mention a few intriguing correspondences: *congruences* are dual to *bisimulations*, so that *induction* (i.e. identity is the least congruence) is dual to *coinduction* (i.e. identity is the largest bisimulation); *inductively defined* functions (i.e. unique maps out of the initial algebra) are dual to *coiterative* functions (i.e. unique maps into the final algebra).

More specifically, the final semantics paradigm consists in representing the operational semantics of a programming language as a *syntactical F-coalgebra*, for a suitable functor F, in such a way that the appropriate behavioral equivalence (e.g. bisimilarity) can be characterized as the equivalence induced on terms (processes) by the unique morphism from the syntactical coalgebra to the *final F-coalgebra*. Final semantics is a fruitful way of understanding the correspondence between syntax and operational semantics. First of all, it naturally validates *coinductive* proof techniques for establishing behavioral equivalences, as well as other properties, and it immediately allows to define semantical operators by *corecursion*. But more than this, it allows to phrase such proofs by coinduction in a more principled and uniform way using the notion of F-coalgebra (see Section 6). And furthermore, it allows to view corecursion and coinduction as two aspects of the same phenomenon.

In order to extend the final semantics approach to the π-calculus, we have found it convenient to give first a *higher order* presentation of it, using as metalanguage a logical framework based on typed λ-calculus, such as the Edinburgh Logical Framework *LF* [7]. This *LF* presentation provides useful insights into the nature of the various binding operators of the π-calculus, thus allowing to focus on the uses of free and bound names. Capitalizing on this, one can overcome many of those problematic aspects of the π-calculus, which do not allow for a direct reuse of the techniques in [2, 15]. The proposed presentation-encoding of the π-calculus can be proved to be *faithful* to the original system using standard techniques. It can be viewed also as the specification of a *derivation editor* for the π-calculus, in any of the various computer assisted proof development environments based on constructive type theory such as *Coq* [3].

Utilizing the LF presentation, coalgebras are defined for the *strong* and for the *weak* semantics of the π-calculus. Strong and weak *late* bisimilarities are the equivalences induced by finality on the two coalgebras. In this paper we consider only the late semantics, but our techniques can be easily extended to the *early* [13] and *open* [16] semantics, see [10] for details. At the price of a slight complication, one can deal also with strong and weak *congruences*; we illustrate only the first case.

We give the final semantics within a category $Class^*$ [2, 15] of classes of hypersets, i.e. non-wellfounded sets satisfying the antifoundation axiom X_1 of [6] (aka AFA [1]), which asserts that the Universe of sets is a final-coalgebra for the functor $\mathcal{P}(\ )$. We use this setting because it is rather natural and moreover, as is the case for CCS [2], it seems that a set-theoretic setting is essential in dealing with the non-continuous character of weak semantics. Of course one could also work in the category of wellfounded sets Set, explaining away non-wellfounded sets at the price of some extra-coding and replacing identity with isomorphism.

Two versions of denotational semantics have been recently defined for the π-calculus in [17] and [5]. However, these approaches just work for *strong* semantics, and, as far as we know, no denotational semantics have been defined for the *weak* case. From this perspective, the final characterization of the weak semantics is particularly interesting.

The paper is organized as follows. In Section 2 we review the standard syntax and operational semantics of the π-calculus; in Section 3 we show how a convenient presentation of the operational semantics of the π-calculus can be given using LF as metalanguage. In Section 4 we present the definitions of strong and weak late bisimulations, and of late strong congruence In Section 5 final characterizations of these semantics are obtained. Applications are discussed in Section 6. Concluding remarks appear in Section 7.

2 THE π-CALCULUS

In this section we review the ordinary syntax and operational semantics of (late, monadic) π-calculus. More details can be found in [12, 11].

Given an infinite set $\mathcal{N}$ of *names*, ranged over by $x, y, z \ldots$, the π-calculus *processes*, denoted by $p, q, r \ldots$, are defined by the syntax:

$$p ::= 0 \mid \tau.p \mid x(y).p \mid \bar{x}y.p \mid p|q \mid p{+}q \mid !p \mid (\nu x)p \mid [x{=}y]p.$$

The occurrences of y in $x(y).p$ and $(\nu y)p$ are bound; *free names*, $fn(p)$, are defined as usual. If $\sigma : \mathcal{N} \to \mathcal{N}$, we denote with $p\sigma$ the process p whose free names have been replaced according to substitution σ (possibly with α-

Table 1 Late operational semantics

$$TAU : \tau.p \xrightarrow{\tau} p \qquad OUT : \bar{x}y.p \xrightarrow{\bar{x}y} p \qquad IN : x(y).p \xrightarrow{x(y)} p$$

$$SUM^l : \frac{p \xrightarrow{\alpha} p'}{p+q \xrightarrow{\alpha} p'} \qquad PAR^l : \frac{p \xrightarrow{\alpha} p'}{p|q \xrightarrow{\alpha} p'|q} \text{ if } bn(\alpha) \cap fn(q) = \emptyset$$

$$COM^l : \frac{p \xrightarrow{\bar{x}y} p' \quad q \xrightarrow{x(z)} q'}{p|q \xrightarrow{\tau} p'|q'\{y/z\}} \qquad CLOSE^l : \frac{p \xrightarrow{\bar{x}(y)} p' \quad q \xrightarrow{x(y)} q'}{p|q \xrightarrow{\tau} (\nu y)(p'|q')}$$

$$RES : \frac{p \xrightarrow{\alpha} p'}{(\nu x)p \xrightarrow{\alpha} (\nu x)p'} \text{ if } x \notin n(\alpha) \qquad OPEN : \frac{p \xrightarrow{\bar{x}y} p'}{(\nu y)p \xrightarrow{\bar{x}(y)} p'} \text{ if } x \neq y$$

$$BANG : \frac{p|!p \xrightarrow{\alpha} p'}{!p \xrightarrow{\alpha} p'} \qquad COND : \frac{p \xrightarrow{\alpha} p'}{[x=x]p \xrightarrow{\alpha} p'}$$

$$EQ : \frac{p \equiv p' \quad p' \xrightarrow{\alpha} q' \quad q' \equiv q}{p \xrightarrow{\alpha} q}$$

conversions to avoid name clashing); we denote with $\{y_1/x_1 \cdots y_n/x_n\}$ the substitution that maps x_i into y_i for $i = 1, \ldots, n$, and which is the identity on the other names. Processes which differ by α-conversion, $\equiv$, are identified.

The *actions* that a process can perform, ranged over by α, are defined by the following syntax:

$$\alpha ::= \tau \mid x(z) \mid \bar{x}y \mid \bar{x}(z).$$

Names x and y are *free names* of α, $(fn(\alpha))$, whereas z is a *bound name* $(bn(\alpha))$; moreover $n(\alpha) = fn(\alpha) \cup bn(\alpha)$. The transitions for the *late operational semantics* are defined by the rules of Table 1 (rules SUM^r, PAR^r, COM^r and $CLOSE^r$ have been omitted).

In transition $p \xrightarrow{x(y)} p'$ (resp. $p \xrightarrow{\bar{x}(y)} p'$), name y represents a reference in p' for the place where the received name of the input will go (resp. where the private name which is emitted occurs). Since y is a reference, it has to be a *fresh* name, i.e., a name which is different from all the other names of p'. The side-conditions which appear in the rules PAR and $OPEN$ are required to enforce this. These transitions are called *bound transitions* (in contrast, τ- and $\bar{x}y$-transitions are called *free transitions*).

3 AN *LF* ENCODING OF THE π-CALCULUS

In this section we reformulate the syntax and the operational semantics of the π-calculus using as metalanguage the Edinburgh Logical Framework *LF* [7]. Logical Frameworks are general *specification languages* for formal systems where one can express uniformly all the features and aspects of an arbitrary system, e.g.: syntactic categories, variables, syntactic constructors, binding operators, substitution mechanisms, judgements, rules, derivations, etc. Encodings in Logical Frameworks readily provide "derivation editors" for the "object logic", given an editor for the metalanguage.

LF is based on a dependent typed λ-calculus and it exploits the well known "judgements (formulæ) as types", "proofs (derivations) as λ-terms" paradigm. LF allows also a smooth treatment of binding operators in terms of *higher order syntax* à la Church. More specifically, LF is a system for deriving typing assertions of the shape $\Gamma \vdash P : Q$, whose intended meaning is "in the environment Γ, P is classified by Q". Three kinds of entities are involved, i.e. *terms* (ranged over by M, N), *types* and *typed valued functions* (ranged over by A, B), and *kinds* (ranged over by K). Types are used to classify terms, and kinds are used to classify types and typed valued functions. These entities are defined by the following abstract syntax:

$$\begin{array}{lcl} M & ::= & x \mid MN \mid \lambda x : A.M \\ A & ::= & X \mid AM \mid \Pi_{x:A}.B \mid \lambda x : A.B \\ K & ::= & Type \mid \Pi_{x:A}.K. \end{array}$$

Π is the *dependent type* constructor. Intuitively $\Pi_{x:A}.B(x)$ denotes the type of those functions, f, whose domain is A and whose values belong to a codomain *depending* on the input, i.e. $f(a) \in B(a)$, for all $a \in A$. Hence, in LF, $A \to B$ is just notation abbreviating $\Pi_{x:A}.B$, when x does not occur free in B ($x \notin FV(B)$). In the "propositions-as-types" analogy the dependent product type $\Pi_{x:A}.B(x)$ represents the proposition $\forall x : A.\ B(x)$.

Environments are lists of pairs consisting of a variable and its type or kind.

The LF specification of a formal system is given by a particular environment, called *signature*, determined according to the following methodology. The *syntactic categories* of the abstract syntax language are encoded as type-variables, *syntactic constructors* are encoded as term-variables of the appropriate type, *judgements* are encoded as variables of "typed-valued function" kind, and *rules* are encoded as term-variables of the appropriate types. Hence, derivations of a given assertion are represented as terms of the type corresponding to the assertion in question, so that *checking* the correctness of a derivation amounts just to *type-checking*. Thus, *derivability* of an assertion corresponds to the *inhabitation* of the type corresponding to that assertion, i.e. the derivability of a term of that type.

Metalanguage variables play also the rôle of "object logic" variables so that *schemata* are represented as λ-abstractions and *instantiation* amounts to β-reduction. Hence *binding operators* are encoded as *higher order* variables, being viewed as ranging over schemata.

3.1 The LF-signature Σ_π of the π-calculus

The **syntactic categories** for names, labels and processes are encoded by the following types:

$$\begin{array}{lcl} name & : & Type \\ label & : & Type \\ proc & : & Type \end{array}$$

Syntactic constructors are defined for labels and processes. Functional types are used for constructors, e.g: the constructor *out* for output requires two names to generate a label and so it is represented by assigning to *out* type $name \rightarrow name \rightarrow label$.

- Constructors for *label*:

$$\begin{array}{lcl} \tau & : & label \\ in & : & name \rightarrow name \rightarrow label \\ out & : & name \rightarrow name \rightarrow label \end{array}$$

- Constructors for *proc*:

$$\begin{array}{lcl} 0 & : & proc \\ \tau_{pref} & : & proc \rightarrow proc \\ in_{pref} & : & name \rightarrow (name \rightarrow proc) \rightarrow proc \\ out_{pref} & : & name \rightarrow name \rightarrow proc \rightarrow proc \\ \mid & : & proc \rightarrow proc \rightarrow proc \\ + & : & proc \rightarrow proc \rightarrow proc \\ ! & : & proc \rightarrow proc \\ \nu & : & (name \rightarrow proc) \rightarrow proc \\ [\,=\,] & : & name \rightarrow name \rightarrow proc \rightarrow proc \end{array}$$

Notice that labels are defined only for free transitions: we will see below how bound transitions, such as bound output, are represented by giving a higher order type to the corresponding transition judgment. We shall freely pretty-print $in(x, y)$ as xy and $out(x, y)$ as $\bar{x}y$.

Notice also how π-calculus binders are expressed in LF making use of suitable abstractions. E.g.: in the case of the input prefix, in order to obtain a process, a name (the channel for the input) and an abstraction (i.e., a function from names to processes) are required. Similarly, restrictions are encoded using abstractions. This is the core of higher order syntax.

It is easy to define a translation function $\mathbf{t}$ from π-calculus processes, as defined in Section 2, to elements of type *proc*. Most of the π-calculus constructors are translated in the obvious way, but for input prefix and restrictions:

$$\mathbf{t}(x(y).p) = in_{pref}(x, \lambda y : name.\ \mathbf{t}(p)) \qquad \mathbf{t}((\nu y)p) = \nu(\lambda y : name.\ \mathbf{t}(p)).$$

Accordingly, π-calculus processes will be often pretty-printed, following the notation of Section 2.

The **judgments** we introduce are the following:

$$\begin{array}{lcl} \longmapsto & : & proc \rightarrow label \rightarrow proc \rightarrow Type \\ \longmapsto\!\!\!\!\rightarrow & : & proc \rightarrow (name \rightarrow label) \rightarrow (name \rightarrow proc) \rightarrow Type \end{array}$$

Table 2 LF rules

TAU	$: \Pi_{p:proc}.\ \tau.p \stackrel{\tau}{\longmapsto} p$
OUT	$: \Pi_{p:proc}\Pi_{x,y:name}.\ \bar{x}y.p \stackrel{\bar{x}y}{\longmapsto} p$
IN	$: \Pi_{p:name\to proc}\Pi_{x:name}.\ in_{pref}(x,p) \stackrel{\lambda z:name.xz}{\longmapsto\!\!\!\!\twoheadrightarrow} p$
SUM^l_f	$: \Pi_{p,q,r:proc}\Pi_{\alpha:label}.\ p \stackrel{\alpha}{\longmapsto} r \to (p+q) \stackrel{\alpha}{\longmapsto} r$
SUM^l_b	$: \Pi_{p,q:proc}\Pi_{r:name\to proc}\Pi_{\alpha:name\to label}.\ p \stackrel{\alpha}{\longmapsto\!\!\!\!\twoheadrightarrow} r \to (p+q) \stackrel{\alpha}{\longmapsto\!\!\!\!\twoheadrightarrow} r$
PAR^l_f	$: \Pi_{p,q,r:proc}\Pi_{\alpha:label}.\ p \stackrel{\alpha}{\longmapsto} r \to (p\vert q) \stackrel{\alpha}{\longmapsto} (r\vert q)$
PAR^l_b	$: \Pi_{p,q:proc}\Pi_{r:name\to proc}\Pi_{\alpha:name\to label}.\ p \stackrel{\alpha}{\longmapsto\!\!\!\!\twoheadrightarrow} r \to$ $(p\vert q) \stackrel{\alpha}{\longmapsto\!\!\!\!\twoheadrightarrow} (\lambda x : name.\ (rx\vert q))$
COM^l	$: \Pi_{p,q,r:proc}\Pi_{s:name\to proc}\Pi_{x,y:name}.\ p \stackrel{\bar{x}y}{\longmapsto} r \to$ $q \stackrel{\lambda z:name.xz}{\longmapsto\!\!\!\!\twoheadrightarrow} s \to (p\vert q) \stackrel{\tau}{\longmapsto} (r\vert sy)$
RES_f	$: \Pi_{p,q:name\to proc}\Pi_{\alpha:label}.(\Pi_{x:name}.px \stackrel{\alpha}{\longmapsto} qx) \to \nu(p) \stackrel{\alpha}{\longmapsto} \nu(q)$
RES_b	$: \Pi_{p:name\to proc}\Pi_{q:name\to name\to proc}\Pi_{\alpha:name\to label}.$ $(\Pi_{x:name}.\ px \stackrel{\alpha}{\longmapsto\!\!\!\!\twoheadrightarrow} \lambda z : name.\ qzx) \to$ $\nu(p) \stackrel{\alpha}{\longmapsto\!\!\!\!\twoheadrightarrow} \lambda z : name.\ \nu(qz)$
$OPEN$	$: \Pi_{p,q:name\to proc}\Pi_{x:name}.$ $(\Pi_{y:name}.\ py \stackrel{\bar{x}y}{\longmapsto} qy) \to \nu(p) \stackrel{\lambda z:name.\ \bar{x}z}{\longmapsto\!\!\!\!\twoheadrightarrow} q$
$CLOSE^l$	$: \Pi_{p,q:proc}\Pi_{r,s:name\to proc}\Pi_{x:name}.\ p \stackrel{\lambda z:name.\ \bar{x}z}{\longmapsto\!\!\!\!\twoheadrightarrow} r \to$ $q \stackrel{\lambda z:name.\ xz}{\longmapsto\!\!\!\!\twoheadrightarrow} s \to (p\vert q) \stackrel{\tau}{\longmapsto} \nu(\lambda z : name.\ (rz\vert sz))$
$BANG_f$	$: \Pi_{p,q:proc}\Pi_{\alpha:label}.\ p\vert !p \stackrel{\alpha}{\longmapsto} q \to !p \stackrel{\alpha}{\longmapsto} q$
$BANG_b$	$: \Pi_{p:proc}\Pi_{q:name\to proc}\Pi_{\alpha:name\to label}.\ p\vert !p \stackrel{\alpha}{\longmapsto\!\!\!\!\twoheadrightarrow} q \to !p \stackrel{\alpha}{\longmapsto\!\!\!\!\twoheadrightarrow} q$
$COND_f$	$: \Pi_{p,q:proc}\Pi_{\alpha:label}\Pi_{x:name}.\ p \stackrel{\alpha}{\longmapsto} q \to [x=x]p \stackrel{\alpha}{\longmapsto} q$
$COND_b$	$: \Pi_{p:proc}\Pi_{q:name\to proc}\Pi_{\alpha:name\to label}\Pi_{x:name}.$ $p \stackrel{\alpha}{\longmapsto\!\!\!\!\twoheadrightarrow} q \to [x=x]p \stackrel{\alpha}{\longmapsto\!\!\!\!\twoheadrightarrow} q$

Judgment $\longmapsto$ is used to encode the free transition assertion. Its meaning should be clear. We will often write $p \stackrel{\alpha}{\longmapsto} p'$ instead of $\longmapsto\ p\,\alpha\,p'$. Judgment $\longmapsto\!\!\!\!\twoheadrightarrow$ is used to encode bound transitions. We will write $p \stackrel{\alpha}{\longmapsto\!\!\!\!\twoheadrightarrow} p'$ instead of $\longmapsto\!\!\!\!\twoheadrightarrow (p, \alpha, p')$. In this case, both the label and the target are abstractions (of a *label* and of a *proc* respectively).

Rules for $\longmapsto$ and $\longmapsto\!\!\!\!\twoheadrightarrow$ appear in Table 2 (rules SUM^r_f, SUM^r_b, PAR^r_f, PAR^r_b, COM^r and $CLOSE^r$ have been omitted). Notice that some of the rules of Table 1 have two counterparts, according to whether they refer to free or bound transitions. Some comments on the rules of Table 2 are in order.

- No explicit axiomatization of α-conversion is needed. Since the π-calculus binders are explained in terms of abstractions, α-conversion is delegated to the metalanguage and hence it is for free.
- In rule IN, both the label and the target process are abstractions; the idea is that, when an input occurs, the target is applied to the effectively received name, so that this name replaces all the occurrences of the placeholder in the target process. This happens, for instance, in rule COM: in this case, the target s of the input transition is applied to the name y, which is the message of the output transition.
- Consider now rules RES: in Table 1 these rules have a side-condition; namely a transition of p with label α can be performed also by $(\nu x)p$ *provided* x does not appear among the names of α. This side-condition is expressed in the LF encoding by requiring that the process px perform the transition independently from the name x, which is chosen to instantiate abstraction p. In this way, the variable x, being bound, behaves as "generic" hence different from all the names in α.
- Rule $OPEN$ is similar; in this case, however, according to Table 1, the value of the free output has to coincide with the name of the restriction. The free output becomes a bound output, so the restriction is removed in the target state, which then becomes an abstraction.
- In rule $CLOSE$ an input and a bound output are synchronized. In this case, the fact that the values of the two transitions should be identified is obtained by combining the target processes $\lambda z : name.\ rz$ and $\lambda z : name.\ sz$ into $\lambda z : name.\ (rz|sz)$.

The operational semantics we have presented here has some advantages w.r.t. the ordinary one, deriving from the usage of functions to model bound transitions. First of all, one can eliminate those explicit side-conditions, which are needed in the ordinary semantics to enforce that the bound names be fresh, so as to avoid name clashing. In the LF presentation, the side conditions are implicit in the higher-order nature of the type encoding the rule. Bound names remain *bound* also when the transition is performed, since abstractions are used for the label and for the target process. As we will see, the names which have been abstracted in the targets of bound transitions will be instantiated in the definition of bisimulation. Another advantage is that name substitution is not required in the operational semantics (and in the definition of bisimulation): function applications are sufficient to represent all the required forms of name instantiation.

Let Σ_π denote the list of variable declarations introduced above. The signature Σ_π is the LF presentation of the π-calculus. Throughout this paper we shall assume that we have an infinite supply of different variables of type $name$, standing for the names in $\mathcal{N}$, and we shall work, even without explicit mention, in the environment Γ_π defined as follows: $\Gamma_\pi \cong \Sigma_\pi \cup \{x_i : name\}_{i\in\mathbf{N}}$. We shall denote with the name of the type (i.e. $name$, $label$, $proc$) the collection of all canonical (normal) well-typed terms of that type, derivable in the context Γ_π. Moreover, for $a \subseteq name$, we shall denote with $label_a$ the subset of $label$, consisting only of normal forms whose free variables appear in a.

In view of the remarks above, the set $fn(p)$ of free names of $p \in proc$ is therefore simply the set of *free variables* of type $name$, occurring in the canonical (normal) form of p.

It is possible to establish a precise correspondence between LF judgements derivable in the environment Γ_π and the corresponding concepts phrased in terms of the system in Section 2. This takes the form of an *Adequacy Theorem* for the encoding. Here, we do this just for transitions. The proof of the following proposition is by induction on the structure of derivations (only if part) and on the structure of *normal forms* (if part).

Proposition 3.1.1 (adequacy) *Let p, q be π-calculus processes and x, y be names in Γ_π; then:*

- $p \xrightarrow{\tau} q \iff$ *the type* $p \stackrel{\tau}{\longmapsto} q$ *is inhabited in* Γ_π.
- $p \xrightarrow{\bar{x}y} q \iff$ *the type* $p \stackrel{\bar{x}y}{\longmapsto} q$ *is inhabited in* Γ_π.
- $p \xrightarrow{x(y)} q \iff$ *the type* $p \stackrel{\lambda y:name.\ xy}{\longmapsto\!\!\!\!\rightarrow} \lambda y : name.\ q$ *is inhabited in* Γ_π.
- $p \xrightarrow{\bar{x}(y)} q \iff$ *the type* $p \stackrel{\lambda y:name.\ \bar{x}y}{\longmapsto\!\!\!\!\rightarrow} \lambda y : name.\ q$ *is inhabited in* Γ_π.

4 LATE BISIMULATION

Here we present the definition of late strong bisimulation making use of the LF presentation of the π-calculus, Σ_π. Using Proposition 3.1.1, one can show that it is equivalent to that in [12].

Definition 4.0.1 (late strong bisimulation) *A symmetric relation $\mathcal{R} \subseteq proc \times proc$ is a* late strong bisimulation *if and only if, $\forall p, q : proc$, whenever $p\, \mathcal{R}\, q$:*

- $\forall \alpha : label.\ \forall r : proc.\ p \stackrel{\alpha}{\longmapsto} r \to (\exists s : proc.\ q \stackrel{\alpha}{\longmapsto} s \wedge r\, \mathcal{R}\, s)$,
- $\forall x : name.\ \forall r : name \to proc.\ p \stackrel{\lambda z:name.\bar{x}z}{\longmapsto\!\!\!\!\rightarrow} r \to$
  $(\exists s : name \to proc.\ q \stackrel{\lambda z:name.\bar{x}z}{\longmapsto\!\!\!\!\rightarrow} s \wedge \forall y : name.\ (y \notin fn(r), fn(s) \to$
  $ry\, \mathcal{R}\, sy))$, *and*
- $\forall x : name.\ \forall r : name \to proc.\ p \stackrel{\lambda z:name.xz}{\longmapsto\!\!\!\!\rightarrow} r \to$
  $(\exists s : name \to proc.\ q \stackrel{\lambda z:name.xz}{\longmapsto\!\!\!\!\rightarrow} s \wedge \forall y : name.\ ry\, \mathcal{R}\, sy)$.

Let $p, q : proc$; p is late strongly bisimilar *to q if there exists a late strong bisimulation $\mathcal{R} \subseteq proc \times proc$ such that $p\, \mathcal{R}\, q$. The union of all late strong bisimulations (denoted by $\sim$) is a late strong bisimulation itself, called* late strong bisimilarity.

It is well known that late strong bisimularity is not a congruence with respect to *input prefix*. The largest congruence included in late bisimilarity can be obtained by allowing to instantiate the names in the processes to be compared, before starting to match their transitions.

Definition 4.0.2 (late strong congruence) *Two processes $p, q \in proc$ are* late strong congruent, *written $p \sim^c q$, if $p\sigma \sim q\sigma$ for all substitutions σ.*

Now we give the *LF* representation of *late weak bisimilarity.* First, we encode the notion of weak transition, by extending the *LF* signature Σ_π with seven new variable declarations, corresponding to two new judgments and five new rules:

$$\begin{array}{ll}
\Longmapsto & : \ proc \to label \to proc \to Type \\
\Longmapsto\!\!\!\!\to & : \ proc \to (name \to label) \to (name \to proc) \to Type \\
weak1_\tau & : \Pi_{p:proc}.\ p \overset{\tau}{\Longmapsto} p \\
weak2_\tau & : \Pi_{p,q,r:proc}.\ p \overset{\tau}{\Longmapsto} q \to q \overset{\tau}{\longmapsto} r \to p \overset{\tau}{\Longmapsto} r \\
weak_{out} & : \Pi_{p,q,r,s:proc}\Pi_{x,y:name}.\ p \overset{\tau}{\Longmapsto} q \to q \overset{\bar{x}y}{\longmapsto} r \to \\
& \qquad r \overset{\tau}{\Longmapsto} s \to p \overset{\bar{x}y}{\Longmapsto} s \\
weak_{in} & : \Pi_{p,q:proc}\Pi_{r:name\to proc}\Pi_{x:name}.\ p \overset{\tau}{\Longmapsto} q \to \\
& \qquad q \overset{\lambda z:name.xz}{\longmapsto\!\!\!\to} r \to p \overset{\lambda z:name.xz}{\Longmapsto\!\!\!\to} r \\
weak_{bout} & : \Pi_{p,q:proc}\Pi_{r,s:name\to proc}\Pi_{x:name}.\ p \overset{\tau}{\Longmapsto} q \to \\
& \qquad q \overset{\lambda z:name.\bar{x}z}{\longmapsto\!\!\!\to} r \to (\Pi_{z:name}.rz \overset{\tau}{\Longmapsto} sz) \to p \overset{\lambda z:name.\bar{x}z}{\Longmapsto\!\!\!\to} s
\end{array}$$

Notice that, in the case of weak input transitions, no τ-actions are allowed after the visible transitions. This is standard for the weak semantics of late π-calculus.

Definition 4.0.3 (late weak bisimulation) *A symmetric relation $\mathcal{R} \subseteq proc \times proc$ is a* late weak bisimulation *if and only if, whenever $p\,\mathcal{R}\,q$ then:*

- $\forall \alpha : label.\ \forall r : proc.\ p \overset{\alpha}{\Longmapsto} r \to (\exists s : proc.\ q \overset{\alpha}{\Longmapsto} s \wedge r\,\mathcal{R}\,s)$,
- $\forall x : name.\ \forall r : name \to proc.\ p \overset{\lambda z:name.\bar{x}z}{\Longmapsto\!\!\!\to} r \to$
  $(\exists s : name \to proc.\ q \overset{\lambda z:name.\bar{x}z}{\Longmapsto\!\!\!\to} s \wedge \forall y : name.\ (y \notin fn(r), fn(s)) \to$
  $ry\,\mathcal{R}\,sy))$ *, and*
- $\forall x : name.\ \forall r : name \to proc.\ p \overset{\lambda z:name.xz}{\Longmapsto\!\!\!\to} r \to$
  $(\exists s : name \to proc.\ q \overset{\lambda z:name.xz}{\Longmapsto\!\!\!\to} s \wedge \forall y : name\ ry\,\mathcal{R}\,sy)$.

Let $p, q : proc$. Then p is late weak bisimilar *to q if there exists a late weak bisimulation $\mathcal{R} \subseteq proc \times proc$ such that $p\,\mathcal{R}\,q$. The union of all late weak bisimulations (denoted by $\approx$) is a late weak bisimulation itself, called* late weak bisimilarity.

Sometimes an alternative characterization of weak bisimulation is used, in which strong transitions are used for the first process. The two definitions are equivalent. We give the version with weak transitions for both processes, since it can be captured more easily in the final approach.

5 FINAL SEMANTICS

In this section we show how to re-obtain by finality the notions of strong and weak bisimilarity defined in the previous section.

5.1 The final approach

We work in $Class^*$, the category whose objects are the classes of the Universe of $ZF_0^-(U)X_1$ and whose arrows are the functional classes. The theory $ZF_0^-(U)X_1$ is a theory of hypersets with atoms, i.e. a Zermelo-Frænkel-like set theory where the Axiom of Extensionality has been weakened so as to allow for a class U of atoms, and where the axiom of Foundation has been replaced by the *Antifoundation Axiom* X_1 of [6] (also known as AFA [1]). As was originally shown by Aczel ([1]), a large class of endofunctors $F : Class^* \to Class^*$ admit *final F-coalgebras* of the form $(\bar{X}_F, \iota_{\bar{X}_F})$, where $\iota_{\bar{X}_F}$ is the *identity*. Recall that an F-coalgebra morphism $h : (A, f) \to (B, g)$ amounts to a function $h : A \to B$, such that $g \circ h = F(h) \circ f$.

According to the final semantics approach (see [1, 2, 15, 9]), the operational semantics of a language is represented as an *F-coalgebra* for a suitable functor F, i.e. as a pair (A, f) such that $f : A \to F(A)$. If the functor is "well-behaved", then there exists a *final F-coalgebra* in $Class^*$, i.e. $(\bar{X}_F, \iota_{\bar{X}_F})$. Moreover, the unique arrow $\mathcal{M}_F : (A, f) \to (\bar{X}_F, \iota_{\bar{X}_F})$, induces an equivalence on A which can be characterized as the union of all *F-bisimulations* on (A, f). An F-bisimulation on (A, f) is the categorical counterpart of the ordinary notion of bisimulation. It is a relation $R \subseteq A \times A$ for which there exists an arrow $\gamma : R \to F(R)$, such that the projections π_1, π_2 can be lifted to F-coalgebra morphisms from (R, γ) to (A, f).

In the case of CCS-like languages, the appropriate functor is $F_{ord}(X) = \mathcal{P}(Label \times X)$. Then the syntactical F-coalgebra which embodies the operational semantics is $(Proc, f_{ord})$, where: $f_{ord}(p) = \{(\alpha, q) \mid p \xrightarrow{\alpha} q\}$. The equivalence captured by the unique morphism is the CCS bisimilarity corresponding to the operational semantics given by $\xrightarrow{\alpha}$. We will see that the functor (and the syntactical coalgebra) are more complex in the case of π-calculus.

5.2 Final description of late strong bisimilarity

In defining the functor F, and the syntactical F-coalgebra, for the strong late semantics of the π-calculus, we cannot re-use directly the standard functor F_{ord} described above. In fact, in the definition of late bisimulation, when two bound outputs are compared, we require that the names which are used to instantiate the placeholder in the pair of target processes are fresh for both processes (conditions $y \notin fn(r), fn(s)$ in Definitions 4.0.1 and 4.0.3). This is unproblematic when dealing with pairs of processes. In the co-algebraic approach, however, the arrow f, corresponding to the syntactical coalgebra, should describe the transitions of each process independently from its possible partners. One cannot use simply, as names for the bound outputs of p, the names which do not appear in p, otherwise equivalent processes with different sets of free names would give rise to different sets of transitions, and hence would receive different final semantics.

The solution we propose consists in associating to processes sets of names (of possible partners). We work with pairs of the form (a,p), where p is a process and $a \in \mathcal{P}_{fin}(name)$ is an estimate of the finite set of free names currently available for interaction: i.e., $fn(p) \subseteq a$. When two processes p and q are compared, it is sufficient to choose $a \in \mathcal{P}_{fin}(name)$ so that $fn(p), fn(q) \subseteq a$ and to compare (a,p) and (a,q). This idea of associating the set of free names to a π-calculus process has been used also in [4] to obtain a characterization of π-calculus based on ordinary transition systems and bisimulations.

In the sequel we fix a function $e : \mathcal{P}_{fin}(name) \to name$ such that, for all $a \subseteq name$, the value x_a of e on a is not in a. We shall denote by a^+ the finite set of names $a \cup \{x_a\}$.

Throughout this paper, we shall introduce functors and refer to their final coalgebras, without explicit proofs that they are indeed functors having final coalgebras. Using standard facts and the theorems in [15], one can always see immediately that this is the case.

Definition 5.2.1 *Let $F : Class^* \to Class^*$ be the functor:*

$$F(X) = \bigcup_{a \in \mathcal{P}_{fin}(name)} \{a\} \times (\mathcal{P}_{fin}((label_{a^+} \times X) \cup (label_{a^+} \times X)^{a^+}) \cup \{\bot\}).$$

The definition of F on arrows is canonical.

Proposition 5.2.1 *The functor F has a final coalgebra: $(\bar{X}_F, \iota_{\bar{X}_F})$.*

Definition 5.2.2 *Let $(\mathcal{P}_{fin}(name) \times proc, f)$ be the F-coalgebra defined as follows:*

$$f(a,p) = \begin{cases} (a, \{(\alpha,(a,q)) \mid p \overset{\alpha}{\longmapsto} q\} \cup \\ \quad \{(\bar{y}x_a,(a^+,qx_a)) \mid p \overset{\lambda z:name.\ \bar{y}z}{\longmapsto\!\!\!\!\rightarrow} q\} \cup \\ \quad \{\lambda x \in a^+. \\ \qquad if\ x \in a\ then\ (yx,(a,qx)) \\ \qquad else\ (yx_a,(a^+,qx_a) \mid p \overset{\lambda z:name.\ yz}{\longmapsto\!\!\!\!\rightarrow} q\}) & if\ fn(p) \subseteq a \\ (a, \bot) & if\ fn(p) \not\subseteq a \end{cases}$$

According to the definition of the functor F, the function f associates to each pair $(a,p) \in \mathcal{P}_{fin}(name) \times proc$ a pair (a,U). The component U is $\bot$, whenever a is not a correct estimate of the free names of p. Otherwise, $U \subseteq (label_{a^+} \times X) \cup (label_{a^+} \times X)^{a^+}$ represents the transitions that the process

p can perform. In the case of τ-actions, output, and bounded output, U is a subset of $\mathcal{P}_{fin}(name) \times proc$. In the case of input transitions, U is a function defined on a suitable finite set of names. This is arranged in such a way that all the names in a and the fresh name x_a are used as possible input values. In the case of bound output transitions, just name x_a is used. A single name, namely x_a, is chosen when a fresh name is required in a bound transition. This is not restrictive, since a single fresh name is sufficient for checking bisimulation equivalence. In this way, moreover, the function f maps each process (a, p) to a finite set U.

The following theorem is the main result of the paper: two π-calculus processes are equivalent according to Definition 4.0.1 if and only if they are equivalent according to the co-algebraic approach.

Theorem 5.2.1 *Let $p, q \in proc$ be such that $fn(p), fn(q) \subseteq a$. Then $p \sim q$ if and only if there exists an F-bisimulation, $\mathcal{R}$, on the coalgebra $(\mathcal{P}_{fin}(name) \times proc, f)$ such that $(a,p)\mathcal{R}(a,q)$.*

The proof of this theorem is based on the following lemma, which characterizes F-bisimulations. Notice that any *categorical bisimulation*, such as the F-bisimulation above, is symmetric by definition.

Lemma 5.2.1 *An F-bisimulation on the F-coalgebra $(\mathcal{P}_{fin}(name) \times proc, f)$ is a symmetric relation $\mathcal{R} \subseteq (\mathcal{P}_{fin}(name) \times proc) \times (\mathcal{P}_{fin}(name) \times proc)$, such that $(a,p)\mathcal{R}(a',q)$ implies $a = a'$ and one of the two conditions:*

- $fn(p) \not\subseteq a \ \wedge \ fn(q) \not\subseteq a,$
- $fn(p) \subseteq a \ \wedge \ fn(q) \subseteq a \ \wedge$
  $[\forall \alpha : label.\ \forall r : proc.\ p \overset{\alpha}{\longmapsto} r \to (\exists s : proc.\ q \overset{\alpha}{\longmapsto} s \wedge (a,r)\mathcal{R}(a,s))] \ \wedge$
  $[\forall x : name.\ \forall r : name \to proc.\ p \overset{\lambda z:name.xz}{\longmapsto\!\!\!\!\!\rightarrow} r \to$
  $(\exists s : name \to proc.\ q \overset{\lambda z:name.xz}{\longmapsto\!\!\!\!\!\rightarrow} s \wedge \ \forall x \in a.\ (a, rx)\mathcal{R}(a, sx))] \ \wedge$
  $[\forall \alpha : name \to label.\ \forall r : name \to proc.\ p \overset{\alpha}{\longmapsto\!\!\!\!\!\rightarrow} r \to$
  $(\exists s : name \to proc.\ q \overset{\alpha}{\longmapsto\!\!\!\!\!\rightarrow} s \wedge \ (a^+, rx_a)\mathcal{R}(a^+, sx_a))]$.

The following proposition characterizes F-bisimilarity by finality, and, by Theorem 5.2.1, also bisimilarity on π-calculus processes.

Proposition 5.2.2 *The equivalence induced by the unique morphism $\mathcal{M}_F : (\mathcal{P}_{fin}(name) \times proc, f) \to (\bar{X}_F, \iota_{\bar{X}_F})$ coincides with the union of all F-bisimulations, $\sim_F^{(\mathcal{P}_{fin}(name)\times proc, f)}$, on the F-coalgebra $(\mathcal{P}_{fin}(name) \times proc, f)$.*

5.3 Alternative semantics

The functor F of Definition 5.2.1 is by no means the unique possible. Many other kinds of functors can be used just as well to provide a final account of strong bisimilarity. We chose such an F because we feel that it is simple and yet perspicuous.

By way of example we shall present an interesting alternative, which eliminates, at the price of an increase in complexity, the somewhat unpleasant fact that F yields only indirectly the semantics of a process. We use the notation of definitions 5.2.1 and 5.2.2.

Definition 5.3.1 *Let $G : Class^* \to Class^*$ be the functor:*

$$G(X) = [F(\mathcal{P}_{fin}(name) \times X)^{\mathcal{P}_{fin}(name)}]_{/\simeq}$$

where $[F(\mathcal{P}_{fin}(name) \times X)^{\mathcal{P}_{fin}(name)}]_{/\simeq}$ denotes the set of equivalence classes of elements of $F(\mathcal{P}_{fin}(name) \times X)^{\mathcal{P}_{fin}(name)}$ modulo the equivalence:

$$g \simeq g' \iff \exists a \in \mathcal{P}_{fin}(name).\ \forall b \in \mathcal{P}_{fin}(name).\ a \subseteq b \Longrightarrow g(b) = g'(b).$$

The definition of G on arrows is canonical.

Definition 5.3.2 *Let $(proc, g)$ be the G-coalgebra defined as follows:*

$$g(p) = [\lambda a \in \mathcal{P}_{fin}(name).(a, f(a,p))]_{\simeq}.$$

Using standard arguments, one can show that the functor G is well-behaved and that the following proposition holds.

Proposition 5.3.1 *Let $p, q \in proc$. Then*

$$\mathcal{M}_G(p) = \mathcal{M}_G(q) \iff \exists a \in \mathcal{P}_{fin}(name).\ \mathcal{M}_F((a,p)) = \mathcal{M}_F((a,q)).$$

5.4 Final description of late strong congruence

The difficulty in capturing by finality late strong congruence (see Definition 4.0.2) lies in the fact that substitutions of names are applied only to the starting pair of processes. But according to the final semantics paradigm, any functor has to act uniformly on all the processes; and so there is no natural notion of "initial pair". At the price of a little awkwardness, however, we can proceed as follows. We split the type of names into two infinite subsets, e.g $name_{even}$ consisting of those names with an *even* index and $name_{odd}$, consisting of those names with an *odd* index. We assume that initial π-calculus processes have only names in $name_{odd}$. By considering processes only "up to" substitutions of the form $\sigma : name \to name_{even}$, which are *injective* on $name_{even}$, we can then sidestep the problem given by the absence of an "initial pair". An adequate, uniform definition of a functor F_{lc} can then be defined, whose largest F_{lc}-bisimulation can be shown to be the required congruence.

More specifically, we proceed as follows. First of all we assume that for all $a \in \mathcal{P}_{fin}(name)$, $x_a \in name_{even}$. Let:

$$\mathcal{S} = \{\sigma : name \to name_{even} \mid \sigma \text{ injective on } name_{even}\}.$$

Definition 5.4.1 *Let $F_{lc} : Class^* \to Class^*$ be the functor:*

$$F_{lc}(X) = \{\bot\} \cup (\bigcup_{a \in \mathcal{P}_{fin}(name)} \{a\} \times \mathcal{P}_{fin}((label_{a^+} \times X) \cup (label_{a^+} \times X)^{a^+}))^{\mathcal{S}}.$$

The definition of F_{lc} on arrows is canonical.

The following proposition is straightforward.

Proposition 5.4.1 *The functor F_{lc} has a final coalgebra $(\bar{X}_{F_{lc}}, \iota_{\bar{X}_{F_{lc}}})$.*

Definition 5.4.2 *Let $(\mathcal{P}_{fin}(name) \times proc, f_{lc})$ be the F_{lc}-coalgebra:*

$$f_{lc}(a,p) = \begin{cases} \bot & \text{if } fn(p) \not\subseteq a \\ \lambda\sigma \in \mathcal{S}.\ f(\sigma^*(a), p\sigma) & \text{if } fn(p) \subseteq a \end{cases}$$

where $\sigma^*(a) = \{\sigma(x) \mid x \in a\}$.

Finally we have the following proposition, whose proof is standard

Proposition 5.4.2 *Let $p, q \in proc$ such that $fn(p), fn(q) \subseteq (a \cap name_{odd})$. Then $p \sim^c q$ if and only if $\mathcal{M}_{F_{lc}}((a,p)) = \mathcal{M}_{F_{lc}}((a,q))$.*

5.5 Final description of late weak bisimilarity

Weak bisimulations differ from strong bisimulations only in that *weak transitions* are used instead of strong transitions. Contrary to what happens in other semantical settings based on the notion of *continuity* (e.g. domain theory or complete metric spaces), this is not at all problematic in our purely set-theoretical setting. We can easily obtain also in the weak context all the results we have for strong bisimulation. We only need to modify slightly the functor F of Definition 5.2.1 and the coalgebra of Definition 5.2.2, taking into account the fact that weak processes can be infinitely branching.

Definition 5.5.1 *Let $F_w : Class^* \to Class^*$ be the functor:*

$$F_w(X) = \bigcup_{a \in \mathcal{P}_{fin}(name)} \{a\} \times (\mathcal{P}_{<2^{\aleph_0}}((label_{a^+} \times X) \cup (label_{a^+} \times X)^{a^+}) \cup \{\bot\}).$$

The definition of F_w on arrows is canonical.

Definition 5.5.2 *Let $(\mathcal{P}_{fin}(name) \times proc, f_w)$ be the F_w-coalgebra:*

$$f_w(a,p) = \begin{cases} (a,\ \{(\alpha,(a,q)) \mid p \overset{\alpha}{\Longmapsto} q\} \cup \\ \quad \{(\bar{y}x_a,(a^+,qx_a)) \mid p \overset{\lambda z:name.\ \bar{y}z}{\Longmapsto} q\} \cup \\ \quad \{\lambda x \in a^+. \\ \qquad \textit{if } x \in a \textit{ then } (yx,(a,qx)) \\ \qquad \textit{else } (yx_a,(a^+,qx_a) \mid p \overset{\lambda z:name.\ yz}{\Longmapsto} q\}) & \textit{if } fn(p) \subseteq a \\ (a,\ \bot) & \textit{if } fn(p) \not\subseteq a \end{cases}$$

Theorem 5.5.1 *Let $p, q \in proc$ be such that $fn(p), fn(q) \subseteq a$. Then $p \approx q$ if and only if there exists an F_w-bisimulation on the F_w-coalgebra $(\mathcal{P}_{fin}(name) \times proc, f_w)$ such that $(a,p)\mathcal{R}(a,q)$.*

Proposition 5.5.1 *The equivalence induced by the unique morphism $\mathcal{M}^{w}_{F_w}$: $(\mathcal{P}_{fin}(name) \times proc, f_w) \to (\bar{X}_{F_w}, \iota_{\bar{X}_{F_w}})$ coincides with the union of all F_w-bisimulations, $\sim_{F_w}^{(\mathcal{P}_{fin}(name)\times proc, f_w)}$, on the coalgebra $(\mathcal{P}_{fin}(name) \times proc, f_w)$.*

6 APPLICATIONS

As an application of the final semantics apparatus, that we have erected so far, we give a semantical proof of the law $p|q \sim q|p$. Of course this proof ultimately corresponds to the usual proof by coinduction, but the machinery of final semantics allows to express it in a more structured way. In our setting this amounts to showing that $\forall a \in \mathcal{P}_{fin}(name).\ \mathcal{M}_F(\langle a, p|q\rangle) = \mathcal{M}_F(\langle a, q|p\rangle)$. To this end, because of the particular nature of the π-calculus, we will have to show more in general that

$$\begin{aligned}\forall a \in \mathcal{P}_{fin}(name).\quad & \mathcal{M}_F(\langle a, \nu(\lambda z_1.(\cdots \nu(\lambda z_n.\ pz_1 \cdots z_n | qz_1 \cdots z_n)\cdots))\rangle) = \\ & \mathcal{M}_F(\langle a, \nu(\lambda z_1.(\cdots \nu(\lambda z_n.\ qz_1 \cdots z_n | pz_1 \cdots z_n)\cdots))\rangle)\end{aligned}$$

holds for all naturals $n \in \mathbf{N}$ and $p, q \in name^n \to proc$, where $name^0 \to proc = proc$ and $name^{n+1} \to proc = (name^n \to proc)^{name}$. In the case $n = 0$ this reduces to $\forall a \in \mathcal{P}_{fin}(name).\ \mathcal{M}_F(\langle a, p|q\rangle) = \mathcal{M}_F(\langle a, q|p\rangle)$.

We will achieve our goal exploiting the finality of (X_F, ι_F) among F-coalgebras. First we introduce a suitable F-coalgebra (B, β), and two functions $g_1, g_2 : B \to \mathcal{P}_{fin}(name) \times proc$, such that for suitable elements $u_{a,n,p,q}$ in B, $g_1(u_{a,n,p,q}) = \langle a, \nu(\lambda z_1.(\cdots \nu(\lambda z_n.\ pz_1 \cdots z_n | qz_1 \cdots z_n)\cdots))\rangle$ while $g_2(u_{a,n,p,q}) = \langle a, \nu(\lambda z_1.(\cdots \nu(\lambda z_n.\ qz_1 \cdots z_n | pz_1 \cdots z_n)\cdots))\rangle$.

We show then that both $\mathcal{M}_F \circ g_1$ and $\mathcal{M}_F \circ g_2$ are F-coalgebra morphisms from (B, β) to the final F-coalgebra (X_F, ι_F). Therefore they coincide by finality.

Here are the details. Let:

$$\begin{aligned}&B = \mathcal{P}_{fin}(name) \times (\textstyle\bigcup_{n\in\mathbf{N}}\{n\} \times (name^n \to proc) \times (name^n \to proc));\\ &g_1(\langle a, \langle n, p, q\rangle\rangle) = \langle a, \nu(\lambda z_1(\cdots \nu(\lambda z_n.\ pz_1 \cdots z_n | qz_1 \cdots z_n)\cdots))\rangle;\\ &g_2(\langle a, \langle n, p, q\rangle\rangle) = \langle a, \nu(\lambda z_1(\cdots \nu(\lambda z_n.\ qz_1 \cdots z_n | pz_1 \cdots z_n)\cdots))\rangle.\end{aligned}$$

The definition of β is rather involved, since it has to take into account the different kinds of transitions:

$$\beta(\langle a, \langle n, p, q\rangle\rangle) = \begin{cases} \langle a, \bot\rangle & \text{if } fn(p), fn(q) \not\subseteq a \\ \langle a, A_{par} \cup A_{open} \cup A_{close}\rangle & \text{if } fn(p), fn(q) \subseteq a \end{cases}$$

where:

$$\begin{aligned}A_{par} \quad = \quad & \{\langle \alpha, \langle a, \langle n, r, s\rangle\rangle\rangle \mid \\ & \quad \nu(\lambda z_1.(\cdots \nu(\lambda z_n.\ pz_1 \cdots z_n | qz_1 \cdots z_n)\cdots)) \stackrel{\alpha}{\longmapsto} \\ & \quad \nu(\lambda z_1.(\cdots \nu(\lambda z_n.\ rz_1 \cdots z_n | sz_1 \cdots z_n)\cdots))\} \\ \cup \quad & \{\langle \bar{y}x_a, \langle a^+, \langle n, rx_a, sx_a\rangle\rangle\rangle \mid \end{aligned}$$

$$
\begin{array}{lll}
 & & \nu(\lambda z_1.(\cdots\nu(\lambda z_n.\ pz_1\cdots z_n|qz_1\cdots z_n)\cdots)) \overset{\lambda x.\bar{y}x}{\longmapsto\!\!\!\!\rightarrow} \\
 & & \lambda x.\nu(\lambda z_1.(\cdots\nu(\lambda z_n.\ rxz_1\cdots z_n|sxz_1\cdots z_n)\cdots))\} \\
 & \cup & \{\lambda x\in a^+.\ \text{if } x\in a \text{ then } \langle yx,\langle a,\langle n,rx,sx\rangle\rangle\rangle \\
 & & \text{else } \langle yx_a,\langle a^+,\langle n,rx_a,sx_a\rangle\rangle\rangle \mid \\
 & & \nu(\lambda z_1.(\cdots\nu(\lambda z_n.\ pz_1\cdots z_n|qz_1\cdots z_n)\cdots)) \overset{\lambda x.yx}{\longmapsto\!\!\!\!\rightarrow} \\
 & & \lambda x.\nu(\lambda z_1.(\cdots\nu(\lambda z_n.\ rxz_1\cdots z_n|sxz_1\cdots z_n)\cdots))\}, \\
A_{open} & = & \{\langle \bar{y}x_a,\langle a^+,\langle n-1,rx_a,sx_a\rangle\rangle\rangle \mid \\
 & & \nu(\lambda z_1.(\cdots\nu(\lambda z_n.\ pz_1\cdots z_n|qz_1\cdots z_n)\cdots)) \overset{\lambda x:name.\ \bar{y}x}{\longmapsto\!\!\!\!\rightarrow} \\
 & & \quad \lambda x.\nu(\lambda z_1.(\cdots\nu(\lambda z_{n-1}.\ rxz_1\cdots z_{n-1}|sxz_1\cdots z_{n-1})\cdots))\}, \\
A_{close} & = & \{\langle \tau,\langle a,\langle n+1,r,s\rangle\rangle\rangle \mid \\
 & & \nu(\lambda z_1.(\cdots\nu(\lambda z_n.\ pz_1\cdots z_n|qz_1\cdots z_n)\cdots)) \overset{\tau}{\longmapsto} \\
 & & \quad \nu(\lambda z_1.(\cdots\nu(\lambda z_n.\nu(\lambda x.\ rz_1\cdots z_nx|sz_1\cdots z_nx))\cdots))\}.
\end{array}
$$

It is interesting to point out that the categorical methodology used above, i.e. defining suitable coalgebras and exploiting uniqueness of the final morphism, can be uniformly applied to other coinductive proofs of properties of processes. This methodology is also quite general. For instance it could be used to define coinductively a semantical operator of parallel composition.

7 CONCLUDING REMARKS

In this paper we have given a higher order presentation of the π-calculus and its operational semantics, using *LF* as metalanguage. This has allowed us to do away with α-conversion, and any explicit mentioning in rules of side-conditions enforcing freshness of names. Building on this operational semantics, we have equipped the π-calculus with a final semantics in both the strong and the weak context. We have presented only late bisimulation, since it is easy to extend the above results to ***early*** [13] and to ***open*** [16] bisimulations, see [10] for more details.

One can reasonably question as to how crucial the *LF* encoding is for the purposes of the paper. Probably, more investigation is needed to give a definitive answer. In principle, being a general metalanguage, which usually provides adequate representations of object languages, *LF* could be explained away. We feel however, that in this context, *LF* helps in separating concerns and it greatly simplifies the treatment of binding operators and bound variables.

We did not deal with the mismatch operator, $[\ \neq\ ]$. We could have easily done so at the price of an increase in the complexity of the *LF* encoding of the π-calculus. In fact, in order to produce an adequate encoding of the mismatch operator, it is not enough to add an explicit judgement to express ***name diversity*** and the rule for mismatch. Because of technical reasons, we need to modify also all rules in Table 2 which have a premise with a locally bound name. The fact that such a name is different from all the ones which can possibly occur in the global parameters has to be explicitly asserted. Perhaps this increase in complexity is an indication that such an operator has not as an immediate semantics as the others.

Rather problematic was the extension of the theory to obtain final characterizations of the various bisimulation congruences. In fact, neither strong nor weak late bisimulations are congruences. We have presented a possible solution for dealing with late strong congruence. In the case of weak late congruence, besides the problem of instantiating the names in the initial pair of processes, the usual problem due to τ-actions and summation also occurs. This second issue can be easily solved since we are working in a hyperset setting, using the technique proposed in [2] for CCS.

We have utilized the category $Class^*$ throughout our paper for uniformity with [2, 15]; but clearly much smaller categories are sufficient to carry out our constructions. For instance, we could have used the category of ***sets of hereditarily finite hypersets***, in dealing with strong late bisimilarity, and the category of ***sets of hereditarily countable hypersets***, in dealing with weak late bisimilarity. As a side remark related to the latter case, let us point out again, that it is the low mathematical overhead of our approach, that allows us to deal smoothly with arbitrary countably branching weak processes. Contrary to what happens in mathematically more constrained semantical settings, we do not need to worry about closedness or compactness of denotations.

A more thorough comparison of the final semantics for π-calculus presented here and the initial semantics presented in [5, 17] is called for, especially with respect to the metalanguage used in representing the language.

REFERENCES

[1] P.Aczel. Non-wellfounded sets. Number 14, Lecture Notes CSLI, 1988.

[2] P.Aczel. Final universes of processes. LNCS 802. Springer, 1993.

[3] C.Cornes *et al.* The Coq proof assistant reference manual. Version 5.10. INRIA, Rocquencourt, 1995.

[4] G.-L.Ferrari, U.Montanari, P.Quaglia. The weak late π-calculus semantics as observation equivalence. LNCS 962. Springer, 1995.

[5] M.Fiore, E.Moggi, D.Sangiorgi. A fully-abstract model for the π-calculus. In *LICS'96*, IEEE, 1996.

[6] M.Forti and F.Honsell. Set theory with free construction principles. Annali Scuola Normale Sup. Pisa, Cl. Sci., (IV), 10:493–522, 1983.

[7] R.Harper, F.Honsell, G.Plotkin. A framework for defining logics. *JACM*, 40(1):143–184, 1993.

[8] F.Honsell and M.Lenisa. Final semantics for untyped λ-calculus. In *TLCA'95*, LNCS 902, Springer, 1995.

[9] M.Lenisa. Final semantics for a higher order concurrent language. In *CAAP'96*, LNCS 1059, Springer, 1996.

[10] M.Lenisa. *Themes in final semantics*. PhD Thesis, Pisa, 1996.

[11] R.Milner. The polyadic π-calculus: a tutorial. In *Logic and Algebra of Specification*, NATO ASI Series F, Vol. 94. Springer, 1993.

[12] R.Milner, J.Parrow, D.Walker. A calculus of mobile processes. *Inf. and Comp.*, 100:1–77, 1992.

[13] R.Milner, J.Parrow, D.Walker. Modal logic for mobile processes. *Th. Comp. Sci.*, 114:149–171, 1993.

[14] J.J.M.M.Rutten. Universal coalgebra: a theory of systems. CWI Techical Report CS-R9652, 1996.

[15] J.J.M.M.Rutten and D.Turi. On the foundations of final semantics. In *REX'92*, LNCS 666. Springer, 1993.

[16] D.Sangiorgi. A theory of bisimulation for the π-calculus. In *CONCUR'93*, LNCS 715. Springer, 1993.

[17] I.Stark. A fully abstract domain model for the π-calculus. In *Proc. LICS'96*, IEEE Press, 1996.

BIOGRAPHY

Furio Honsell is Full Professor in Foundations of Computer Science at the University of Udine (Italy) since 1990. He has received a degree in Mathematics from the Scuola Normale Superiore in Pisa (Italy) in 1980. He has held research positions at the Computer Science Departments of the Universities of Torino and Edinburgh. His main areas of interest are in the Foundations of Mathematics and Computer Science as well as in Computer Assisted Formal Reasoning.

Marina Lenisa has received her PhD in Computer Science in 1998 at the Pisa-Udine Universities Consortium. Her main areas of interest are in Semantics and Formal Methods in Computer Science.

Ugo Montanari is Full Professor in Foundation of Computer Science at the University of Pisa (Italy) since 1976. He received a degree in Electronic Engineering from the Politecnico di Milano (Italy) in 1966. He took sabbatical leaves of absence in 1987 and 1997 at SRI Int., Menlo Park (USA). His main areas of interest are Semantics of Concurrency, Constraint Programming and Formal Methods.

Marco Pistore is currently doing his PhD in Computer Science at the University of Pisa (Italy). His main areas of interest are in Theory of Concurrency and in Formal Methods in Verification.

18

Comparing CTL and PCTL on Labeled Markov Chains

M.R.A. Huth
Department of Computing and Information Sciences
Kansas State University, Manhattan, KS66506, USA; phone: +1-785-532-6350; fax: +1-785-532-7353; email: huth@cis.ksu.edu

M.Z. Kwiatkowska
School of Computer Science, University of Birmingham
Edgbaston, B15 2TT, United Kingdom; phone: +44-121-414-7264; fax: +44-121-414-4281; email: mzk@cs.bham.ac.uk

Abstract

We interpret modal mu-calculus formulas in a non-standard way as expectations over labeled Markov chains. In this semantics fixed-points are computed in an iterative incremental/decremental fashion. This provides the foundation for a symbolic model checking algorithm for CTL over labeled Markov chains using Multi-Terminal Binary Decision Diagrams, where expectations of `until`-formulas are calculated via suitable fixed-point approximations. We compare this non-standard semantics of CTL to the standard one for the probabilistic logic PCTL by specifying a translation $\phi \mapsto \phi^b$ of the positive existential fragment CTL$^+$ of CTL into PCTL, where PCTL probability thresholds are supplied by the non-standard semantics. Finally, we show soundness of our non-standard semantics of CTL$^+$ with respect to the one for PCTL in the following sense: if our semantics computes a positive evidence for ϕ at state s then s satisfies the translated PCTL formula ϕ^b.

Keywords

Labeled Markov Chains, Probabilistic Verification, Fuzzy Logic, CTL, PCTL.

1 INTRODUCTION

Probabilistic logics have proved successful in the specification and verification of systems that exhibit uncertainty. The behavior of such systems is typically governed by a known probability distribution; for example, randomized algorithms toss fair coins before making choices, and communication protocols must be designed so that the loss of messages in the medium is tolerated up to some appropriately small probability. With the advent of randomization, which ensures that many problems in distributed systems have efficient

Programming Concepts and Methods D. Gries, & W-P. de Roever (Eds.)

solutions albeit at a cost of probabilistically complex scenarios developing during execution, it has become necessary to develop formalisms in which the probability of some event happening in the course of execution can be assessed and, whenever possible, calculated automatically and efficiently by means of a model checking tool. The importance of probabilistic verification lies in the fact that it can provide guarantees that the specifications hold with satisfactory probability in cases when conventional model checking fails, for example, when exhaustive search is not feasible due to the size of the system, or when checking 'soft deadlines' in real-time systems, i.e. properties such as 'the system will respond within time t with probability 0.99'.

Established work on probabilistic temporal logics e.g. [25, 13, 12, 3, 23, 10] (and also modal logics, for example a probabilistic extension of Hennessy-Milner logic called PML [19]) uses probability thresholds for truth in the syntax of an underlying language of logic such as CTL [7]. This was achieved by H. Hansson and B. Jonsson by extending the models to variants of Markov chains, which involves adding probabilities to the transitions, and the addition of probabilistic operators $[\cdot]_{>p}$ to form the logic PCTL [13, 12]; then for a path formula ϕ the probabilistic formula $[\phi]_{>p}$ is satisfied in the given state if the probability of the set of paths starting in this state on which ϕ holds is *at least* p for some real number p in the unit interval. Model checking algorithms based on computing the probability and then comparing it against the threshold have been formulated for such systems (and also their extensions to allow concurrency or non-determinism), see e.g. [25, 10, 13, 3, 2]. Their complexity, however, is high, and so efficient techniques, such as symbolic model checking proposed in [1] or approximative reasoning, are sought for.

A more recent alternative to the above is to re-interpret the conventional logics in terms of *expectations*, see [20, 14]; see [16, 18] for a much earlier source of similar ideas. This involves assigning to formulas a map from states to the unit interval instead of the usual truth values, with the value at a given state representing (an estimate of) *the probability* of the formula being true in this state as calculated in the underlying Markov chain model.

This paper draws its main motivation from trying to understand the two seemingly opposing semantic approaches mentioned above when interpreted over labeled Markov chains: the threshold view as espoused by PCTL [13, 12] versus the logic CTL with the non-standard expectations semantics extracted from the quantitative mu-calculus semantics of [14]. If we think of such logics as providing a foundation for probabilistic methods in verification then a number of observations can be made about the threshold approach to probabilistic semantics:

1. The user might have to guess a threshold and the reply will be 'yes' or 'no'; thus, repeated checks are necessary to find out the critical region where 'yes' answers turn into 'no' replies and vice versa; in safety-critical applications this objection might be weak since one could argue that thresholds ought to be extremely close to 1 anyway. But, if we think of typical measures in

performance analysis, like the utilization of some resource, we would have to rely on probabilities, or percentages, anywhere in between 0 and 1. Finding critical regions of thresholds would then be non-trivial.

2. There is no compelling argument for considering only global thresholds: the level of safety required or the performance with respect to some measure is typically a function of the state being considered and leads to probabilistic logics where one considers *vectors of thresholds*.

3. Some methods for computing the probabilities of path formulas $\phi_1 \mathbf{U} \phi_2$ are non-incremental: this is in contrast to e.g. our non-standard semantics of CTL, presented in this paper, which computes fixed-points *incrementally* by iterating the meaning of the underlying recursion, and so the finite approximations of least/greatest fixed-points increase/decrease the information computed so far, thus allowing to compute approximate solutions to precise analytical probabilities.

4. The threshold approach is most sensitive to numerical errors close to the threshold region: thresholds are dis-continuous cut-off points.

5. If models are still in the design phase one might have very little intuition about the actual performance of such systems with respect to various (probabilistic) performance measures; thus, having to begin with any 'random' threshold seems unacceptable if probabilistic logics should become an active part in the design of stochastic systems.

Clearly, an alternative to threshold semantics would have to render replies which are of a *quantitative* rather than a qualitative kind. In this paper we demonstrate that if we drop thresholds altogether from PCTL following [20, 14] then we are essentially looking at the ordinary temporal logic CTL but now CTL formulas are no longer interpreted as predicates (subsets of states) but as functions $[\![\phi]\!]: S \to [0,1]$ from states into the unit interval $[0,1]$, termed 'expectations' in [20]. The difficulty and weakness of such semantics lies in their interpretation of the logical conjunction and disjunction to the effect that $[\![\phi]\!]\ s$ is no longer an exact probability but a 'sound' estimate thereof.

The main effort of the work presented here consists of establishing a firm link between these two semantic paradigms. Thus, one really ought to see these approaches as being *complementary* rather than conflicting. Based on [9, 8, 1] we also develop a symbolic model checking algorithm for our non-standard interpretation of the modal mu-calculus fragment of alternation depth ≤ 1.

2 THE MODAL MU-CALCULUS ON FINITE MARKOV CHAINS

A finite Markov chain [15] is a pair $(S, \mathbf{P})$, where S is a finite set of n states and $\mathbf{P} = (\mathbf{P}(s,s'))$ is a $n \times n$-matrix of entries in $[0,1]$ such that $\mathbf{P}(s,s')$ is the probability of the state transition $s \to s'$. Of course, we require that $\sum_{s' \in S} \mathbf{P}(s,s') = 1$ for all $s \in S$. Our approach allows us to analyze systems where this sum is strictly less than one (= sub-stochastic matrix), in which case we interpret the difference of $\sum_{s' \in S} \mathbf{P}(s,s')$ to 1 as the probability of the system deadlocking in state s. We could also have considered *families* of such sub-stochastic matrices $\mathbf{P}_a$ indexed by actions $a \in \mathsf{Act}$. However, we prefer the simpler presentation based on a single action $*$ for the purpose of illustration. Given sets C of constants and Var of variables such that Var is countable we then obtain a version of Kozen's modal mu-calculus $\mu\mathtt{M}$ [17] by considering the following grammar:

$$\phi ::= \mathtt{tt} \mid \mathtt{ff} \mid c_i \mid \neg\phi \mid \phi \wedge \phi \mid \phi \vee \phi \mid \langle * \rangle \phi \mid [*]\phi \mid x \mid \mu x.\phi \mid \nu x.\phi$$

with $c_i \in \mathsf{C}$ and $x \in \mathsf{Var}$ and where recursion $\mu x.\phi$ and $\nu x.\phi$ is confined to formally monotone ϕ. We also consider the *positive* fragment of the modal mu-calculus $\mu\mathtt{M}^+$ by dropping the clause for $\neg\phi$ and for $\nu x.\phi$. Given a finite Markov chain $(S, \mathbf{P})$ we may interpret any $\phi \in \mu\mathtt{M}$ in the following way: the meaning $[\![\phi]\!]$ maps an environment ρ to a function $[\![\phi]\!]\rho \colon S \to [0,1]$; thus, ρ is of type $\mathsf{Var} \to S \to [0,1]$. Since S is assumed to have n elements we may think of any $f \colon S \to [0,1]$ as a vector $\mathbf{q} \in [0,1]^n$. Thus, we may now express our semantics, given already in [14], as a transformation of vectors:

$$
\begin{array}{ll}
[\![\mathtt{tt}]\!]\rho\,\mathbf{q} = \mathbf{1} & [\![\mathtt{ff}]\!]\rho\,\mathbf{q} = \mathbf{0} \\
[\![c_i]\!]\rho\,\mathbf{q} = \mathbf{c_i} & [\![\neg\phi]\!]\rho\,\mathbf{q} = \mathbf{1} - ([\![\phi]\!]\rho\,\mathbf{q}) \\
[\![\phi_1 \wedge \phi_2]\!]\rho\,\mathbf{q} = \max(\mathbf{0}, [\![\phi_1]\!]\rho\,\mathbf{q} + [\![\phi_2]\!]\rho\,\mathbf{q} - \mathbf{1}) & [\![\phi_1 \vee \phi_2]\!]\rho = [\![\neg(\neg\phi_1 \wedge \neg\phi_2)]\!]\rho \\
[\![\langle * \rangle\phi]\!]\rho\,\mathbf{q} = \mathbf{P} \cdot ([\![\phi]\!]\rho\,\mathbf{q}) & [\![[*]\phi]\!]\rho = [\![\neg\langle * \rangle\neg\phi]\!]\rho \\
[\![\mu x.\phi]\!]\rho = \mathsf{fix}\,\mathbf{F}_{[\phi,x]} & [\![\nu x.\phi]\!]\rho = \mathsf{FIX}\,\mathbf{F}_{[\phi,x]}
\end{array}
$$

where $\mathbf{P} \cdot \mathbf{q}$ is the usual multiplication of the matrix $\mathbf{P}$ with the vector $\mathbf{q}$; $\mathbf{0}$ is the zero vector and $\mathbf{1}$ is the vector $(1, 1, \ldots, 1)$. Furthermore, $\mathbf{F}_{[\phi,x]} \colon (S \to [0,1]) \to (S \to [0,1])$ is the monotone function defined by $\mathbf{F}_{[\phi,x]}\, f = [\![\phi]\!]\rho[x \mapsto f]$ and $\mathsf{fix}\,\mathbf{F}_{[\phi,x]}$ is the least, $\mathsf{FIX}\,\mathbf{F}_{[\phi,x]}$ the greatest fixed-point of $\mathbf{F}_{[\phi,x]}$. Finally, for the motivation of this semantics for $\wedge$ see [14] (this idea was taken from [24]); in summary, our semantics of conjunction guarantees that we never compute meanings $[\![\phi_1 \wedge \phi_2]\!]s$ which are greater than the value $\mu_s(\phi_1 \wedge \phi_2)$ where μ_s is *any* probability measure on the Borel algebra generated by the lattice of predicates of Kozen's standard interpretation of $\mu\mathtt{M}$. Note that the meaning of c_i can be any (fixed) function $f_{c_i} \colon S \to [0,1]$. In particular, if the image of f_{c_i} is in $\{0,1\}$ for all $c_i \in \mathsf{C}$ then we obtain ordinary *labeled* Markov chains $(S, \mathbf{P}, L)$ where $L(s) = \{c_i \in \mathsf{C} \mid f_{c_i}(s) = 1\}$ with $L \colon S \to \mathcal{P}(\mathsf{C})$. We shall abbreviate $\max(0, a + b - 1)$ by $0 \vee (a + b - 1)$, and likewise its dual $\min(1, a + b)$ by $1 \wedge (a + b)$.

3 MODEL CHECKING $\mu\mathtt{M}_{\leq 1}$ ON FINITE MARKOV CHAINS

We now derive an algorithm for model checking modal mu-calculus formulas ϕ without nested fixed-points [4] based on the semantics defined in the previous section. For that purpose we consider a fragment of the modal mu-calculus, where we restrict the clauses $\mu x.\phi$ and $\nu x.\phi$ to those ϕ which have at most x as a free variable. We call that fragment $\mu\mathtt{M}_{\leq 1}$ (alternation depth ≤ 1 in [11]).

Proposition 1 *Let $\sigma x.\phi$ be in $\mu\mathtt{M}_{\leq 1}$, where $\sigma \in \{\mu, \nu\}$. The function $\mathbf{F}_{[\phi,x]}$, of type $(S \to [0,1]) \to (S \to [0,1])$, defined above is continuous as a map from $\mathbf{R}^n \to \mathbf{R}^n$ in the Euclidean topology. This is also true for other interpretations of conjunction and disjunction which are continuous in the Euclidean topology, e.g. if conjunction is interpreted as minimum or multiplication.*

Proof: We prove the statement above by showing that all functions $\mathbf{F}_{[\psi,x]}$ are continuous where ψ is a subformula of ϕ; this argument proceeds in a bottom-up fashion on the parse tree of ϕ:

First, if $\psi \equiv x$ then $\mathbf{F}_{[\psi,x]}$ is the identity function which is continuous. Second, if x is not free in ψ then $\mathbf{F}_{[\psi,x]}$ is constant, and therefore continuous, for $[\![\psi]\!]\rho = [\![\psi]\!]\rho'$ if ρ and ρ' agree on ψ's free variables.

Third, if $\psi \equiv \neg\psi_1$ then $\mathbf{F}_{[\neg\psi_1,x]}(\mathbf{q}) = \mathbf{1} - \mathbf{F}_{[\psi_1,x]}(\mathbf{q})$ from which we infer that $\mathbf{F}_{[\neg\psi_1,x]}$ is continuous since vector subtraction is continuous.

Fourth, if $\psi = \langle * \rangle\psi_1$ then by construction and by the semantics of $\langle * \rangle$ we get $\mathbf{F}_{[\langle * \rangle\psi_1,x]}(\mathbf{q}) = \mathbf{P} \cdot (\mathbf{F}_{[\psi_1,x]}\,\mathbf{q})$; since $\mathbf{F}_{[\psi_1,x]}$ and matrix multiplication are continuous we infer that $\mathbf{F}_{[\langle * \rangle\psi_1,x]}$ is continuous as well.

Fifth, if $\psi = [*]\psi_1$ then by construction and by the semantics of $[*]$ we get $\mathbf{F}_{[[*]\psi_1,x]}(\mathbf{q}) = (\mathbf{1} - \mathbf{P} \cdot \mathbf{1}) + \mathbf{F}_{[\langle * \rangle\psi_1,x]}(\mathbf{q})$. Since $\mathbf{F}_{[\langle * \rangle\psi_1,x]}$ and the addition with a constant vector are continuous, we see that $\mathbf{F}_{[[*]\psi_1,x]}$ is continuous, too; note that $\mathbf{1} - \mathbf{P} \cdot \mathbf{1} = \mathbf{0}$ if P is a stochastic matrix, i.e. if the process modeled by $(S, \mathbf{P})$ is free of divergence, so in that case the semantics of $\langle * \rangle$ and $[*]$ coincide.

Sixth, if $\psi \equiv \psi_1 \wedge \psi_2$ we have $\mathbf{F}_{[\psi_1 \wedge \phi_2,x]}(\mathbf{q}) = \mathbf{0} \vee (\mathbf{F}_{[\psi_1,x]}(\mathbf{q}) + \mathbf{F}_{[\psi_2,x]}(\mathbf{q}) - \mathbf{1})$ from which we can infer the continuity of $\mathbf{F}_{[\psi_1 \wedge \phi_2,x]}$ since $\mathbf{F}_{[\psi_1,x]}$, $\mathbf{F}_{[\psi_2,x]}$, $-$ and $\vee$ are continuous on $\mathbf{R}^n$.

Seventh, if $\psi \equiv \psi_1 \vee \psi_2$ then this is similar to the previous case, for $\mathbf{F}_{[\psi_1 \vee \phi_2,x]}(\mathbf{q}) = \mathbf{1} \wedge (\mathbf{F}_{[\psi_1,x]}(\mathbf{q}) + \mathbf{F}_{[\psi_2,x]}(\mathbf{q}))$.

Finally, note that this concludes all possible cases since ϕ has at most x as a free variable; thus, alternation depth ≤ 1 excludes the cases $\psi \equiv \mu y.\psi_1$ and $\psi \equiv \nu y.\psi_1$, where y is free in ψ_1. End of Proof.

We can exploit the fact that all functions $\mathbf{F}_{[\phi,x]}$ are continuous maps to guarantee that fixed-point iterations on the infinite domain $S \to [0,1]$ reach a fixed-point at ω. This is a non-trivial result since it can not necessarily be inferred from the standard facts about the continuity of $\mathsf{fix}\colon (S \to [0,1]) \to (S \to [0,1])$ since the semantics of subformulas $\nu x.\eta$, via FIX, might give rise to meanings which are not Scott-continuous.

Proposition 2 *Let $\mu x.\phi$ be in $\mu\mathsf{M}_{\leq 1}$. Then $\bigvee_{0\leq m<\omega} \mathbf{F}_{[\phi,x]}{}^m \mathbf{0}$ is the least fixed-point of $\mathbf{F}_{[\phi,x]}$. Dually, if $\nu x.\phi$ is in $\mu\mathsf{M}_{\leq 1}$ then $\bigwedge_{0\leq m<\omega} \mathbf{F}_{[\phi,x]}{}^m \mathbf{1}$ is the greatest fixed-point of $\mathbf{F}_{[\phi,x]}$. In fact, the above holds for all monotone interpretations of conjunction and disjunction which are continuous in the Euclidean topology.*

Proof: The argument is, in spirit, the same as the usual one for least fixed-points of Scott-continuous functions. However, we need to adapt this argument since the function $\mathbf{F}_{[\phi,x]}$ is not Scott-continuous in general. But directed suprema and filtered infima in $[0,1]^n$ are pointwise, so we see that the supremum and the infimum in $S \to [0,1]$ are also limits in the Euclidean topology. Thus, we infer that $\mathbf{F}_{[\phi,x]}(\bigvee_{0\leq n<\omega} \mathbf{F}_{[\phi,x]}{}^n \mathbf{0}) = \mathbf{F}_{[\phi,x]}(\lim_{0\leq n<\omega} \mathbf{F}_{[\phi,x]}{}^n \mathbf{0}) = \lim_{0\leq n<\omega} \mathbf{F}_{[\phi,x]}{}^{n+1} \mathbf{0} = \bigvee_{1\leq n<\omega} \mathbf{F}_{[\phi,x]}{}^n \mathbf{0} = \bigvee_{0\leq n<\omega} \mathbf{F}_{[\phi,x]}{}^n \mathbf{0}$ as $\mathbf{F}_{[\phi,x]}$ is monotone and continuous in the Euclidean topology. The argument for the greatest fixed-point is dual to this one. End of Proof.

We use a simple example of a probabilistic protocol to demonstrate our approach. For simplicity we merely consider the states of the protocol pertaining to the transmission of one message only. Initially (state s_1), the protocol will *send* the message to the medium. The *medium* (state s_2) will attempt to transmit the message to the *receiver* (state s_3), which is possible with probability 0.75; with probability 0.25 the message will get *lost* (state s_4). Upon receiving the message, the receiver will attempt to *acknowledge* it. If the acknowledgment is received intact, which is possible with probability 0.9 then the message is *delivered* (state s_5) and the protocol terminates; failure to receive acknowledgment causes the protocol to resend the message again (return to state s_1). Again, for simplicity we shall assume an unbounded number of retries. The example can be easily extended to cater for a bounded number of retries. To model a distributed protocol it may be necessary to go beyond Markov chains.

The diagram below represents the protocol.

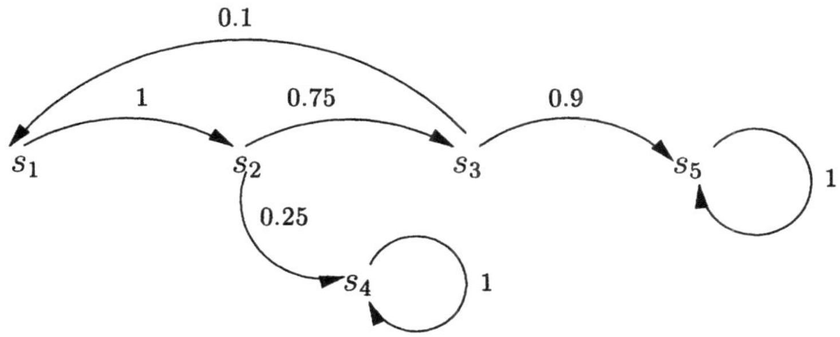

The Markov chain matrix for the above protocol is given below.

$$\begin{pmatrix} 0 & 1 & 0 & 0 & 0 \\ 0 & 0 & 0.75 & 0.25 & 0 \\ 0.1 & 0 & 0 & 0 & 0.9 \\ 0 & 0 & 0 & 1 & 0 \\ 0 & 0 & 0 & 0 & 1 \end{pmatrix}$$

The property we would like to calculate is: *what is the probability of delivering the message?* This can be expressed as $\mu x.(c_{delv} \vee \langle * \rangle x)$, where $c_{delv} = (0,0,0,0,1)$; in other words, $c_{delv} = \mathtt{tt}$ at the state s_5 and $\mathtt{ff}$ at all other states. The successive iterations starting from $(0,0,0,0,0)$ produce:

$$\begin{pmatrix} 0 \\ 0 \\ 0 \\ 0 \\ 1 \end{pmatrix}, \begin{pmatrix} 0 \\ 0 \\ 0.9 \\ 0 \\ 1 \end{pmatrix}, \begin{pmatrix} 0 \\ 0.675 \\ 0.9 \\ 0 \\ 1 \end{pmatrix}, \begin{pmatrix} 0.675 \\ 0.675 \\ 0.9 \\ 0 \\ 1 \end{pmatrix}, \begin{pmatrix} 0.675 \\ 0.675 \\ 0.9675 \\ 0 \\ 1 \end{pmatrix}, \begin{pmatrix} 0.675 \\ 0.725625 \\ 0.9675 \\ 0 \\ 1 \end{pmatrix},$$

$$\begin{pmatrix} 0.725625 \\ 0.725625 \\ 0.9675 \\ 0 \\ 1 \end{pmatrix}, \begin{pmatrix} 0.725625 \\ 0.725625 \\ 0.9725625 \\ 0 \\ 1 \end{pmatrix}, \begin{pmatrix} 0.725625 \\ 0.7294218 \\ 0.9725625 \\ 0 \\ 1 \end{pmatrix}, \begin{pmatrix} 0.7294218 \\ 0.7294218 \\ 0.9725625 \\ 0 \\ 1 \end{pmatrix}, \ldots$$

Thus, the probability of the message being eventually delivered is at least 0.729 (up to 3 significant digits, which one further iteration would reveal); this follows from Corollary 1 in Section 5.

4 SYMBOLIC PROBABILISTIC MODEL CHECKING FOR $\mu\mathtt{M}_{\leq 1}$

We now present a symbolic model checking algorithm for all closed $\phi \in \mu\mathtt{M}_{\leq 1}$ which computes expectations of formulas for a given labeled Markov chain without constructing the state space explicitly. This algorithm represents $[\![\phi]\!]$ symbolically as a Multi-Terminal Binary Decision Diagram; for more details on symbolic model checking with Multi-Terminal Binary Decision Diagrams (MTBDDs) we refer the reader to [9, 8, 1].

Binary-Decision-Diagram-based model checking [21] has proved effective in practice: it tackles the state explosion problem by providing a symbolic representation for the state space. With MTBDDs one can extend existing automatic verification tools to cater for quantitative information contained in the models such as probability [1]. The MTBBD representation is compact and no less efficient than sparse matrix techniques [8].

Given a closed formula $\phi \in \mu\mathsf{M}_{\leq 1}$ the basic idea is to represent the function $[\![\phi]\!]: S \rightarrow [0,1]$ symbolically by a Multi-Terminal Binary Decision Diagram $\mathcal{M}[\phi]$. We define this MTBDD by structural induction on ϕ. However, we will only compute *approximate* results for fixed-points $\phi \equiv \sigma x.\psi$ since we cannot iterate $\mathbf{F}_{[\psi,x]}$ forever. We use a function $\mathsf{ITERATE}(A, Q, E)$ which requires its first argument A to represent a map from $\mathbf{R}^n$ to $\mathbf{R}^n$, Q to represent an element of $\mathbf{R}^n$, and E a real number $\varepsilon > 0$. The code for this function is similar to that of fixed-point approximation for the Boolean symbolic model checking algorithm [5] except that we enforce termination w.r.t. ε as follows: $\mathsf{ITERATE}(A, Q, E)$ returns the MTBDD which represents the vector $A^{m+1}Q$ where m is the least natural number such that $\sum_{i=1}^{n} |(A^{m+1}Q)_i - (A^m Q)_i| < \varepsilon$. Naturally, termination criteria other than the above are conceivable.

The model checking algorithm will, of course, need to work with the MTBDD representation of the $n \times n$ probability transition matrix $\mathbf{P}$. For $k = \lceil \log n \rceil$ we may identify the $2^k \times 2^k$ matrix $\mathbf{P}$ with the function $f : \{0,1\}^{2k} \rightarrow [0,1]$ where $f(x_1, y_1, \ldots, x_k, y_k)$ is the value of $\mathbf{P}$ in the $(i+1)$-th row and $(j+1)$-th column and $i = \sum_{u=1}^{k} x_u \cdot 2^{k-u}$, $j = \sum_{v=1}^{k} y_v \cdot 2^{k-v}$. Thus, $\mathbf{P}$ can be identified with a MTBDD P over $(x_1, y_1, \ldots, x_k, y_k)$. Similarly, each vector $\mathbf{q}$ with 2^k arguments can be identified with the MTBDD q over $(x_1, \ldots, x_k)$ for the function $F : \{0,1\}^n \rightarrow [0,1]$ where $F(x_1, \ldots, x_n)$ is the $(i+1)$-th argument of $\mathbf{q}$ and where i is as above. The remaining operators needed for the algorithm, both from [8], are: $\mathsf{MV\_MULTI}(\mathsf{P}, \mathsf{q})$ (matrix-by-vector multiplication), and $\mathsf{APPLY}(\cdot)$ (elementwise application of the binary operator *op* on real numbers, such as addition, to two MTBDDs).

Let ϕ be a closed formula in $\mu\mathsf{M}_{\leq 1}$ and $(S, \mathbf{P}, L)$ a labeled Markov chain. We assume that constants c_i can only take values in $\{0,1\}$ and that there are 'enough' of them so that we can identify each state s with the Boolean vector $(x_1, x_2, ..., x_n)$ where $x_i = 1$ iff $c_i \in L(s)$ (an extension to arbitrary functions is straightforward). We define an MTBDD over the variables $\overline{x} = (x_1, x_2, ..., x_n)$ by structural induction on ϕ:

1. $\mathcal{M}[\mathtt{tt}] = \mathtt{TRUE}$, the (unique) MTBDD representing the constant function 1 which consists of a terminal vertex labeled with value 1,
2. $\mathcal{M}[\mathtt{ff}] = \mathtt{FALSE}$, the (unique) MTBDD representing the constant function 0 which consists of a terminal vertex labeled with value 0,
3. $\mathcal{M}[c_i] = \lambda\overline{x}.[x_i]$, the (unique) MTBDD representing the function $f(\overline{x}) = x_i$, i.e. the MTBDD with one nonterminal vertex labeled with x_i and two terminal vertices, the left labeled with value 0 and right with value 1,
4. $\mathcal{M}[\neg\phi] = \mathsf{APPLY}(\mathtt{TRUE}, \mathcal{M}[\phi], -)$, the MTBDD obtained from applying the operator $(1 - \cdot)$ to the MTBDD for ϕ,
5. $\mathcal{M}[\phi_1 \wedge \phi_2]$ is the MTBDD obtained by applying our conjunction semantics to the MTBDDs for ϕ_1 and ϕ_2, where $\mathtt{FALSE}$ is the MTBDD representing the constant function 0: $\mathsf{APPLY}(\mathsf{APPLY}(\mathsf{APPLY}(\mathcal{M}[\phi_1], \mathcal{M}[\phi_2], \cdot + \cdot), \mathtt{TRUE}, \cdot - \cdot), \mathtt{FALSE}, \max)$,
6. $\mathcal{M}[\phi_1 \vee \phi_2] = \mathsf{APPLY}(\mathsf{APPLY}(\mathcal{M}[\phi_1], \mathcal{M}[\phi_2], \cdot + \cdot), \mathtt{TRUE}, \min)$ is ob-

tained similarly to the above except that the operation is our semantic disjunction: $\min(1, \cdot + \cdot)$,

7. $\mathcal{M}[\langle * \rangle \phi] = \mathsf{MV\_MULTI}(\mathtt{P}, \mathcal{M}[\phi])$, the MTBDD obtained as a result of a call to the matrix-by-vector multiplication operation with the MTBDD P representing the Markov transition probability matrix and the MTBDD for ϕ passed as arguments,

8. $\mathcal{M}[[*]\phi] = \mathcal{M}[\neg\langle * \rangle \neg\phi]$, the MTBDD for the form equivalent to $[*]\phi$,

9. $\mathcal{M}[\mu x.\phi] = \mathsf{ITERATE}(\mathcal{F}_{[\phi,x]}, \mathtt{FALSE}, \mathtt{EPSILON})$, the MTBDD obtained as a result of a call to the fixed-point iteration algorithm with the MTBDDs for $\mathcal{F}_{[\phi,x]}$ and FALSE passed as arguments,

10. $\mathcal{M}[\nu x.\phi] = \mathsf{ITERATE}(\mathcal{F}_{[\phi,x]}, \mathtt{TRUE}, \mathtt{EPSILON})$, similar to the above except that the iteration computes a decreasing sequence of approximations starting with 1.

We should stress that the last clause is actually computing ***upper*** bounds. This points out the fundamental weakness of our results as presented here. One needs to develop a suitable semantic framework which allows the simultaneous consideration of lower and upper bounds, and then clarify how negation and greatest fixed point act thereon.

The symbol P above is the MTBDD representing $\mathbf{P}$ and EPSILON represents some $\varepsilon > 0$. Of course, this requires that we give symbolic representations $\mathcal{F}_{[\phi,x]}$ of the continuous functions $\mathbf{F}_{[\phi,x]}$ as MTBDDs; such a definition simply copies the constructive argument of Proposition 1:

$$
\begin{aligned}
\mathcal{F}_{[x,x]} &= \mathtt{I}, \text{ the MTBDD representing the identity matrix,} \\
\mathcal{F}_{[\psi,x]} &= \lambda\bar{x}.\mathcal{M}[\psi] \text{ if } x \text{ is not free in } \psi, \\
\mathcal{F}_{[\neg\psi,x]} &= \lambda\bar{x}.\mathsf{APPLY}(\mathtt{TRUE}, \mathcal{F}_{[\psi,x]}\,\bar{x},\ -\ ), \\
\mathcal{F}_{[\langle * \rangle\psi,x]} &= \lambda\bar{x}.\mathsf{MV\_MULTI}(\mathtt{P}, \mathcal{F}_{[\psi,x]}\,\bar{x}), \\
\mathcal{F}_{[[*]\psi,x]} &= \lambda\bar{x}.\mathsf{APPLY}(\mathsf{APPLY}(\mathtt{TRUE}, \mathsf{MV\_MULTI}(\mathtt{P}, \mathtt{TRUE}),\ -\ ), \\
&\qquad \mathsf{MV\_MULTI}(\mathtt{P}, \mathcal{F}_{[\psi,x]}\,\bar{x}),\ +\ ), \\
\mathcal{F}_{[\psi_1 \wedge \psi_2,x]} &= \lambda\bar{x}.\mathsf{APPLY}(\mathtt{FALSE}, \\
&\qquad \mathsf{APPLY}(\mathsf{APPLY}(\mathcal{F}_{[\psi_1,x]}\,\bar{x}, \mathcal{F}_{[\psi_2,x]}\,\bar{x},\ +\ ), \mathtt{TRUE},\ -\ ), \max), \\
\mathcal{F}_{[\psi_1 \vee \psi_2,x]} &= \lambda\bar{x}.\mathsf{APPLY}(\mathsf{APPLY}(\mathcal{F}_{[\psi_1,x]}\,\bar{x}, \mathcal{F}_{[\psi_2,x]}\,\bar{x},\ +\ ), \min).
\end{aligned}
$$

5 COMPARING CTL TO PCTL

The semantics of the modal mu-calculus given above for finite labeled Markov chains is ***fuzzy*** [27] in its interpretation of the logical connectives $\wedge$ and $\vee$; yet, it also employs ***probabilistic*** meaning as in the weighted average for the modalities $\langle * \rangle$ and $[*]$. This unusual combination warrants a comparison with purely probabilistic semantics which we now develop. First of all, we saw that our semantics identifies $\langle * \rangle$ and $[*]$ if the matrix $\mathbf{P}$ of the underlying model is stochastic which we assume throughout this section. This leads to a simplified grammar for CTL viewed as a subset of $\mu M_{\leq 1}$ [4, 21]: $\mathbf{AX}\phi$ and $\mathbf{EX}\phi$ correspond to $\langle * \rangle \phi$, $\mathbf{A}(\phi_1 \mathbf{U}\, \phi_2)$ and $\mathbf{E}(\phi_1 \mathbf{U}\, \phi_2)$ translate to $\mu x.\phi_2 \vee (\phi_1 \wedge \langle * \rangle x)$, and $\mathbf{AG}\phi$ and $\mathbf{EG}\phi$ turn into $\nu x.\phi \wedge \langle * \rangle x$.

Based on our semantics for finite Markov chains we may therefore reduce the image of CTL in $\mu M_{\leq 1}$ to the following, *semantically driven*, grammar:

$$\phi ::= \mathtt{tt} \mid \mathtt{ff} \mid c_i \mid \neg\phi \mid \phi_1 \wedge \phi_2 \mid \phi_1 \vee \phi_2 \mid \mathbf{EX}\phi \mid \mathbf{E}(\phi_1 \mathbf{U} \phi_2) \mid \mathbf{EG}\phi$$

where $c_i \in C$. A straightforward mathematical induction shows that any closed ϕ generated by this grammar is of alternation depth ≤ 1. Of course, not every closed $\phi \in \mu M_{\leq 1}$ is generated by the grammar above; e.g. the formula $\nu x.\psi \wedge \langle * \rangle \langle * \rangle x$ which qualitatively expresses the property that ψ occurs every other time cannot be specified in CTL [26]. Note that the grammar above still has some redundancy in the presence of negation, but we intend to have separate clauses for $\vee$ and $\wedge$ as well as for tt and ff since we intend to show results for the fragment of CTL without the clauses $\neg\phi$ and $\mathbf{EG}\phi$; we denote the resulting fragment of CTL by CTL$^+$.

5.1 Translating CTL$^+$ into PCTL

We now introduce the syntax and semantics of PCTL [13, 12] interpreted over labeled Markov chains. Let $(S, \mathbf{P}, L)$ be a labeled Markov chain. A *path* in such a chain is a nonempty (finite or infinite) sequence $\pi = s_0 s_1 s_2, \ldots$ where $s_i \in S$ and $\mathbf{P}(s_{i-1}, s_i) > 0$ for $i = 1, 2, \ldots$. We denote by $\mathsf{Path}_\omega(s)$ the set of all infinite paths starting in the state s and endow $\mathsf{Path}_\omega(s)$ with a σ-algebra structure by taking the smallest σ-algebra on $\mathsf{Path}_\omega(s)$ which contains the basic cylinders $\{\pi \in \mathsf{Path}_\omega(s) \mid u \text{ is a prefix of } \pi\}$ for finite paths u starting in s. Each such basic cylinder corresponds to the event of executing the finite path u. The probability measure *Prob* on the σ-algebra is the unique measure with $Prob\{\, \pi \in \mathsf{Path}_\omega(s) \mid u \text{ is a prefix of } \pi \,\} = \mathbf{P}(u)$ where $\mathbf{P}(s_0 s_1 \ldots s_k) = \mathbf{P}(s_0, s_1) \cdot \mathbf{P}(s_1, s_2) \cdot \ldots \cdot \mathbf{P}(s_{k-1}, s_k)$ [25].

PCTL [13], the aforementioned probabilistic extension of CTL, contains atomic propositions and the operators next-step $\mathbf{X}$ and until $\mathbf{U}$ decorated with probabilities (we omit the bounded `until` to simplify the presentation). Formally, the syntax of PCTL is as follows:

$$\phi \quad ::= \quad \mathtt{tt} \mid c_i \mid \phi_1 \wedge \phi_2 \mid \neg\phi \mid [\, \mathbf{X}\, \phi\,]_{\sqsupseteq p} \mid [\, \phi_1 \mathbf{U} \phi_2\,]_{\sqsupseteq p}$$

where c_i is an atomic proposition, $p \in [0, 1]$, $\sqsupseteq$ is either $\geq$ or $>$. The satisfaction relation $\models \subseteq S \times$ PCTL for state formulas is given as usual:

$s \models \mathtt{tt}$ for all $s \in S$	$s \models c_i$ iff $c_i \in L(s)$
$s \models \phi_1 \wedge \phi_2$ iff $s \models \phi_i$ for $i = 1, 2$	$s \models \neg\phi$ iff $s \not\models \phi$

In contrast, probabilistic formulas $[\mathbf{X}\,\phi]_{\sqsupseteq p}$ or $[\phi_1 \mathbf{U}\ \phi_2]_{\sqsupseteq p}$, where ϕ, ϕ_1, ϕ_2 are PCTL formulas, are interpreted with the help of the probability measure *Prob* over the σ- algebra of the infinite paths of the labeled Markov chain:

$$s \models [\mathbf{X}\,\phi]_{\sqsupseteq p} \text{ iff } Prob\{\pi \in \mathsf{Path}_\omega(s) \mid \pi \models \mathbf{X}\ \phi\} \sqsupseteq p$$
$$s \models [\phi_1 \mathbf{U}\,\phi_2]_{\sqsupseteq p} \text{ iff } Prob\{\pi \in \mathsf{Path}_\omega(s) \mid \pi \models \phi_1 \mathbf{U}\,\phi_2\} \sqsupseteq p$$

where $\pi \models \mathbf{X}\,\phi$ iff the first state of π satisfies ϕ, and $\pi \models \phi_1 \mathbf{U}\phi_2$ iff there exists $k \geq 0$ such that ϕ_1 is satisfied at all states of π up to and including $k-1$ and ϕ_2 is satisfied at k. The operators of disjunction and implication can be derived. One can also derive probabilistic analogues of the linear operators 'eventually' and 'always'; these are weaker than their classical linear counterparts since events that happen with probability 1 are not necessarily always guaranteed to happen.

Given a formula $\phi \in \text{CTL}^+$ we translate it into a formula $\phi^\flat \in \text{PCTL}$ such that the annotated probability thresholds in $\phi^\flat$ are the corresponding quantitative evidences computed by our semantics. We then show that $[\![\phi]\!]s > 0$ implies $s \models \phi^\flat$. In order to unfold this argument in the sharpest sense possible we slightly generalize PCTL: if ψ is a path formula and $\psi_{\sqsupseteq p}$ is an ordinary PCTL formula with $p \in [0,1]$ we now also allow $\psi_{\sqsupseteq \mathbf{p}}$ to be a formula of PCTL where $\mathbf{p}$ is a *vector of thresholds* and therefore in $[0,1]^n$. Of course, this only makes sense for models $(S, \mathbf{P}, L)$ with a fixed number n of states. It should also be noted that this translation is dependent on a fixed model since we use the non-standard semantics of this model to compute thresholds needed for the translated formulas, but these constraints are not crucial since our objective is to implement model checking algorithms which work on concrete labeled Markov chains.

Since we generalized thresholds to *vectors of thresholds* we have to give a semantics to those extensions. This works as expected, e.g. $s \models [\phi_1 \mathbf{U}\,\phi_2]_{\sqsupseteq \mathbf{p}}$ iff $Prob\{\pi \in \mathsf{Path}_\omega(s) \mid \pi \models \phi_1 \mathbf{U}\,\phi_2\} \sqsupseteq p_s$ where $\mathbf{p} = (p_s)_{s \in S}$. This generalization is not necessary since we could use the minimum of all the quantitative evidences $[\![\phi]\!]s$, $s \in S$, as a threshold p for the usual PCTL formulas, but a vector semantics for PCTL makes our semantic comparison tighter.

Fixing a model $(S, \mathbf{P}, L)$, we translate closed expressions of CTL^+ into PCTL based on our semantics. The translation is a map ${}^\flat : \text{CTL}^+ \to \text{PCTL}$ defined by structural induction on ϕ:

$$\mathtt{tt}^\flat = \mathtt{tt} \qquad \mathtt{ff}^\flat = \mathtt{ff}$$
$$c_i^\flat = c_i \qquad (\phi_1 \wedge \phi_2)^\flat = \phi_1^\flat \wedge \phi_2^\flat$$
$$(\phi_1 \vee \phi_2)^\flat = \neg(\neg(\phi_1^\flat) \wedge \neg(\phi_2^\flat)) \qquad (\mathbf{EX}\,\phi)^\flat = [\mathbf{X}\,(\phi^\flat)]_{\geq \mathbf{p}}$$
$$(\mathbf{E}(\phi_1 \mathbf{U} \phi_2))^\flat = [(\phi_1^\flat)\mathbf{U}\,(\phi_2^\flat)]_{\geq \mathbf{q}}$$

where $\mathbf{p} = [\![\langle * \rangle \phi]\!]$ and $\mathbf{q} = [\![\mu x.\phi_2 \vee (\phi_1 \wedge \langle * \rangle x)]\!]$.

5.2 SOUNDNESS OF OUR TRANSLATION

Definition 1 *For closed* $\phi \in \mu\mathtt{M}$ *let* $\mathsf{Pos}(\phi)$ *be the set of all* $s \in S$ *such that* $[\![\phi]\!]s > 0$. *Given* $\eta \in PCTL$, *let* $\mathsf{Sat}(\eta)$ *denote the set of all* $s \in S$ *such that* $s \models \eta$.

The role of $\mathsf{Pos}(\cdot)$ is that it mediates between the unit interval $[0,1]$ and the domain of truth values in that we identify 0 with FALSE and any positive value with TRUE if the root of the formula is tt, ff, c_i, $\wedge$, or $\vee$.

Theorem 1 *We assume that* CTL^+ *and PCTL have the same interpretation of the constants* $c_i \in C$ *for a fixed model* $(S, \mathbf{P}, L)$. *Then for all* $\phi \in CTL^+$ *we have* $\mathsf{Pos}(\phi) \subseteq \mathsf{Sat}(\phi^\flat)$.

Proof: We use mathematical induction on the lexicographical ordering of fixed-point depth and rank of ϕ. That way we may reason by ordinary structural induction, but for the case of recursion where we use syntactic approximations. We implicitly identify CTL$^+$ formulas with their equivalent translations into $\mu\mathtt{M}_{\leq 1}$.

The cases $\phi \equiv \mathtt{tt}$ and $\phi \equiv \mathtt{ff}$ are clear and the case $\phi \equiv c_i$ follows from our assumption. If $\phi \equiv \phi_1 \wedge \phi_2$ then

$$\begin{aligned}
\mathsf{Pos}(\phi_1 \wedge \phi_2) &= \{s \in S \mid 0 \vee ([\![\phi_1]\!]s + [\![\phi_2]\!]s - 1) > 0\} && (1)\\
&\subseteq \{s \in S \mid [\![\phi_1]\!]s > 0 \text{ and } [\![\phi_2]\!]s > 0\} \quad \text{since } [\![\phi_i]\!]s \in [0,1]\\
&= \mathsf{Pos}(\phi_1) \cap \mathsf{Pos}(\phi_2)\\
&\subseteq \mathsf{Sat}(\phi_1^\flat) \cap \mathsf{Sat}(\phi_2^\flat) \quad \text{by induction}\\
&= \mathsf{Sat}(\phi_1^\flat \wedge \phi_2^\flat) \quad \text{by the semantics of PCTL}\\
&= \mathsf{Sat}((\phi_1 \wedge \phi_2)^\flat) \quad \text{by def. of } {}^\flat.
\end{aligned}$$

Dually, if $\phi \equiv \phi_1 \vee \phi_2$ then

$$\begin{aligned}
\mathsf{Pos}(\phi_1 \vee \phi_2) &= \{s \in S \mid 1 \wedge ([\![\phi_1]\!]s + [\![\phi_2]\!]s) > 0\} && (2)\\
&\subseteq \{s \in S \mid [\![\phi_1]\!]s > 0 \text{ or } [\![\phi_2]\!]s > 0\} \quad \text{since } [\![\phi_i]\!]s \in [0,1]\\
&= \mathsf{Pos}(\phi_1) \cup \mathsf{Pos}(\phi_2)\\
&\subseteq \mathsf{Sat}(\phi_1^\flat) \cup \mathsf{Sat}(\phi_2^\flat) \quad \text{by induction}\\
&= \mathsf{Sat}(\phi_1^\flat \vee \phi_2^\flat) \quad \text{by the semantics of PCTL}\\
&= \mathsf{Sat}((\phi_1 \vee \phi_2)^\flat) \quad \text{by def. of } {}^\flat.
\end{aligned}$$

As for the modalities, if $\phi \equiv \langle * \rangle \psi$ then

$$\mathsf{Pos}(\langle * \rangle \psi) = \{s \in S \mid \sum_{s' \in S} \mathbf{P}(s,s') \cdot ([\![\psi]\!]s') > 0\}. \quad (3)$$

So let $s \in \mathsf{Pos}(\langle * \rangle \psi)$ be given. We need to show that $s \in \mathsf{Sat}([\mathbf{X}\,(\psi^\flat)]_{\geq \mathbf{p}})$ where $\mathbf{p} = [\![\langle * \rangle \psi]\!]$. Thus, we need to demonstrate the inequality $[\![\langle * \rangle \psi]\!] s \leq \sum_{s' \in \mathsf{Sat}(\psi^\flat)} \mathbf{P}(s, s')$. We compute

$$\begin{aligned} [\![\langle * \rangle \psi]\!] s &= \sum_{s' \in S} \mathbf{P}(s, s') \cdot [\![\psi]\!] s' && (4) \\ &= \sum_{s' \in \mathsf{Pos}(\psi)} \mathbf{P}(s, s') \cdot [\![\psi]\!] s' \quad \text{as } [\![\psi]\!] s' \in [0,1], \\ &\leq \sum_{s' \in \mathsf{Sat}(\psi^\flat)} \mathbf{P}(s, s') \cdot [\![\psi]\!] s' \quad \text{by ind.} \\ &\leq \sum_{s' \in \mathsf{Sat}(\psi^\flat)} \mathbf{P}(s, s') \quad \text{as } [\![\psi]\!] s' \in [0,1]. \end{aligned}$$

Finally, if $\phi \equiv \mu x.\phi_2 \vee (\phi_1 \wedge \langle * \rangle x)$ we define syntactic approximations [4] η_m for all $0 \leq m < \omega$ such that

$$[\![\phi]\!] = \bigvee_{0 \leq m < \omega} [\![\eta_m]\!]. \tag{5}$$

We set

$$\begin{aligned} \eta_0 &= \mathbf{ff} && (6) \\ \eta_{m+1} &= \phi_2 \vee (\phi_1 \wedge \langle * \rangle \eta_m) \quad \text{for all } m \geq 0. \end{aligned}$$

Note that equation (5) holds since all semantic operations in our interpretation of CTL$^+$ are continuous and since we only compute least fixed-points thereof. Suppose that $[\![\mu x.\phi_2 \vee (\phi_1 \wedge \langle * \rangle x)]\!]\, s > 0$. We have to show that $s \models [\phi_1^\flat \mathbf{U}\, \phi_2^\flat]_{\geq \mathbf{p}}$, where $\mathbf{p} = [\![\mu x.\phi_2 \vee (\phi_1 \wedge \langle * \rangle x)]\!]$. If we set

$$q_s = \mathit{Prob}\{\pi \in \mathsf{Path}_\omega(s) \mid \pi \models \phi_1^\flat \mathbf{U}\, \phi_2^\flat\} \tag{7}$$

then we simply have to show that $p_s \leq q_s$. By equation (5), we know that $p_s = \bigvee_{0 \leq m \leq \omega} [\![\eta_m]\!] s$ and therefore it suffices to show that $[\![\eta_m]\!] s \leq q_s$ for all $0 \leq m < \omega$. For $m = 0$ this is true since $[\![\eta_0]\!] s = 0 \leq q_s$. Assuming that $[\![\eta_m]\!] s \leq q_s$ holds for m (and *all* $s \in S$!) we now demonstrate its validity for $m + 1$. We compute

$$\begin{aligned} [\![\eta_{m+1}]\!] s &= [\![\phi_2 \vee (\phi_1 \wedge \langle * \rangle \eta_m)]\!] s && (8) \\ &= 1 \wedge ([\![\phi_2]\!] s + [0 \vee ([\![\phi_1]\!] s + [\![\langle * \rangle \eta_m]\!] s - 1)]), \end{aligned}$$

for which we can safely assume that it be positive; otherwise, there is nothing to show. Thus, $[\![\phi_2]\!] s$ or $[\![\phi_1]\!] s + [\![\langle * \rangle \eta_m]\!] s - 1$ is positive. In the first case we may use our global induction hypothesis to infer that $s \models \phi_2^\flat$ which gives us $q_s = 1$ and so $[\![\eta_{m+1}]\!]s \leq q_s$ is clear. In the second case we may therefore assume

$$\begin{aligned} s &\not\models \phi_2^\flat \\ [\![\phi_2]\!]s &= 0 \\ [\![\phi_1]\!]s + [\![\langle * \rangle \eta_m]\!]s - 1 &> 0. \end{aligned} \tag{9}$$

Since $[\![\phi_1]\!]s + [\![\langle * \rangle \eta_m]\!]s - 1$ is positive we conclude that $[\![\phi_1]\!]s$ must be positive. Using our global induction hypothesis we infer that

$$s \models \phi_1^\flat. \tag{10}$$

Using (9) we can continue to unfold equation (8) as

$$\begin{aligned} [\![\eta_{m+1}]\!]s &= 1 \wedge ([\![\phi_2]\!]s + [0 \vee ([\![\phi_1]\!]s + [\![\langle * \rangle \eta_m]\!]s - 1)]) \\ &= 1 \wedge (0 + [0 \vee ([\![\phi_1]\!]s + [\![\langle * \rangle \eta_m]\!]s - 1)]) \\ &= 1 \wedge ([\![\phi_1]\!]s + [\![\langle * \rangle \eta_m]\!]s - 1) \\ &= [\![\phi_1]\!]s + [\![\langle * \rangle \eta_m]\!]s - 1 \\ &= ([\![\phi_1]\!]s - 1) + \sum_{s' \in S} \mathbf{P}(s, s') \cdot [\![\eta_m]\!]s' \\ &\leq (1 - 1) + \sum_{s' \in S} \mathbf{P}(s, s') \cdot [\![\eta_m]\!]s' \\ &\leq \sum_{s' \in S} \mathbf{P}(s, s') \cdot q_{s'} \qquad \text{by ind. hyp.} \\ &= q_s \qquad \text{as } s \models \phi_1^\flat \wedge \neg\phi_2^\flat \text{ by (9) and (10).} \end{aligned} \tag{11}$$

End of Proof.

We should stress that this particular result remains valid for a range of interpretations of conjunction and disjunction as long as such interpretations are monotone, continuous, and satisfy $\mathsf{Pos}(\phi_1 \wedge \phi_2) \subseteq \mathsf{Pos}(\phi_1) \cap \mathsf{Pos}(\phi_2)$ as well as $\mathsf{Pos}(\phi_1 \vee \phi_2) \subseteq \mathsf{Pos}(\phi_1) \cup \mathsf{Pos}(\phi_2)$. For example, one might interpret $\wedge$ as minimum and $\vee$ as maximum which, incidentally, renders bigger thresholds for conjunction in general as $0 \vee (x + y - 1) \leq x \wedge y$ for all $x, y \in [0, 1]$. As for disjunction, we obtain $x \vee y \leq (x + y) \wedge 1$ for all $x, y \in [0, 1]$. Thus, the choice of maximum results in smaller thresholds, so there appears to be a trade-off between conjunction and disjunction in the improvement of lower bounds of probabilities. Again, one needs a clean way of simultaneously expressing lower and upper bound information to avoid this problem.

Corollary 1 *The soundness of our interpretation of CTL^+ in PCTL remains* *valid if we prematurely terminate fixed-point iterations in our model-checking algorithms.*

The last insight, which is true since 'being a lower bound' is a transitive property, is most important from a practical point of view. One may wonder why our fuzzy interpretation of $\wedge$ and $\vee$ worked. This is most likely due to that fact that path formulas in CTL are not allowed to contain logical connectives nor those of certain temporal operators. Thus, our approach will be challenged if one desires to extend it to CTL* or all of $\mu M_{\leq 1}$. Nonetheless, the significance of Theorem 1 is that it provides a semantic bridge between two opposing views of quantitative model checking for labeled Markov chains as explained below.

First, our semantics endorses computations of quantitative evidence employing only one conceptual level, namely, *compositional* meaning in $S \to [0,1]$; this leads to a direct computational engine which need not be concerned with guessing informative thresholds for big systems and which computes evidence in an incremental way. The price being paid is the fuzzy interpretation of disjunction and conjunction by not addressing potential issues of conditional probabilities, so we might not compute precise probabilities although the considered property might induce a measurable set. However, Theorem 1 above can be seen as proving soundness of our semantics with respect to the one for PCTL. In particular, one can take the numbers computed for a CTL formula ϕ as a first safe guess of what will turn out to be 'true' probabilistically. Thus, one might want to check ϕ^b with appropriately higher thresholds than those computed for ϕ.

Second, the semantics for PCTL necessitates two conceptual levels: the usual qualitative semantics for formulas of CTL (including the usual interpretation of path formulas $\mathbf{X}\,\phi$ and $\phi_1 \mathbf{U}\, \phi_2$), and the computation of a probability for path formulas in a given state s. These distinct levels of analysis are linked via the annotation of thresholds to path formulas. The advantage lies in precise probabilistic results but it is not clear whether the framework of probability spaces can be applied in this manner for arbitrary $\phi \in \mu M_{\leq 1}$ or for formulas with even higher alternation depths; this approach is also not continuous with respect to small changes in $\mathbf{P}$, the matrix of transition probabilities, for small changes of $\mathbf{P}(s, s')$ can change the Boolean truth value of a formula $\psi_{\sqsupseteq \mathbf{p}}$ at state s. As such it is quite sensitive to numerical errors. Incidentally, one could improve the symbolic model checking algorithm for PCTL in [1] by allowing *vectors of thresholds* and by overwriting thresholds on-the-fly that have been specified by the user in certain cases. For example, if the user would like to check $s \models [\phi_1 \mathbf{U} \phi_2]_{\geq \mathbf{p}}$ and if the probability of $\phi_1 \mathbf{U} \phi_2$ at s is greater than $\mathbf{p}_s$, then the check is not only successful, but it is also verifying the *stronger* check where we replace the threshold $\mathbf{p}_s$ by that very probability.

It should be noted that our fuzzy semantics of conjunction and disjunction *penalizes* the repeated check of the same property at the same syntactic level within a given formula, for such interpretations are not idempotent: we have $\min(0.5 + 0.5 - 1, 0) = 0$.

6 INFINITE LABELED MARKOV CHAINS

In this section we consider labeled Markov chains $(S, \mathbf{P}, L)$ such that S is countable where we demand that the infinite sums $\sum_{s' \in S} \mathbf{P}(s, s')$ have limit 1 for all $s \in S$ (this generalizes to uncountable state sets by means of integration). Countably infinite state sets suffice to show that fixed-point iterations for Kozen's standard interpretation of the modal mu-calculus may have to go beyond ω in order to reach their semantic invariants; see e.g. [4, pg. 20] for such an example within $\mu\mathtt{M}_{\leq 1}$. Yet, there is a significant difference between qualitative and quantitative fixed-points which guarantees that fixed-points in our semantics are always attained at the ordinal level ω for any fixed-point formula in $\mu\mathtt{M}_{\leq 1}$ even if the underlying state set is countably infinite: computing the meaning of $\mu x.\phi$ we can ask the questions '$1 = \bigvee_{0 \leq m \leq \omega} (\mathbf{F}_{[\phi,x]}{}^m\, \mathbf{0})\, s$?' and '$s \in \bigcup_{0 \leq m \leq \omega} \mathbf{G}_{[\phi,x]}{}^m\, \emptyset$?', where $\mathbf{G}_{[\phi,x]}$ is the function whose least fixed-point determines the meaning of $\mu x.\phi$ in Kozen's standard interpretation. The crucial difference is that s is an element of $\bigcup_{0 \leq m \leq \omega} \mathbf{G}_{[\phi,x]}{}^m\, \emptyset$ only if it is already a member in one of the finite unwindings $\mathbf{G}_{[\phi,x]}{}^m\, \emptyset$, whereas 1's being equal to $\bigvee_{0 \leq m \leq \omega} (\mathbf{F}_{[\phi,x]}{}^m\, \mathbf{0})\, s$ does not necessitate any of the numbers $(\mathbf{F}_{[\phi,x]}{}^m\, \mathbf{0})\, s$ to be 1; the powerset lattice $\mathcal{P}(S)$ is algebraic whereas the lattice $S \to [0, 1]$ is 'only' continuous.

Recall that we proved that fixed-points of our semantics are reached at ω for all formulas of $\mu\mathtt{M}_{\leq 1}$ provided that S is finite. The arguments put forward in that proof essentially transfer to the case where S is countable. We simply endow $\mathbf{R}^\infty$ with the topology of pointwise convergence and note that this topology satisfies the following: the componentwise addition or subtraction of vectors in $\mathbf{R}^\infty$ is continuous, the componentwise operations $\mathbf{q} \mapsto 0 \vee \mathbf{q} \colon \mathbf{R}^\infty \to \mathbf{R}^\infty$ and $\mathbf{q} \mapsto 1 \wedge \mathbf{q} \colon \mathbf{R}^\infty \to \mathbf{R}^\infty$ are continuous, constant vectors give rise to continuous functions $\mathbf{R}^\infty \to \mathbf{R}^\infty$, and directed suprema and filtered infima are topological limits. The only fact we still require is that $(x_s)_{s \in S} \mapsto (\sum_{s' \in S} \mathbf{P}(s, s') \cdot x_{s'})_{s \in S} \colon \mathbf{R}^\infty \to \mathbf{R}^\infty$ be continuous, but this follows from basis facts on absolute convergence of real sums and the fact that $\mathbf{P}$ is a bounded linear operator on a Banach space.

Corollary 2 *Proposition 1 and Theorem 1 generalize to countable state sets.*

7 SUMMARY AND OUTLOOK

This paper is part of an effort to develop the *quantitative* model checking paradigm proposed in [14], where one requires quantities as answers to checks, such as performance or reliability measures, instead of simply 'yes' or 'no' answers. We have derived a symbolic model checking algorithm for the modal mu-calculus (without nested fixed points) re-interpreted in terms of expectations, also considered in [20]. Such algorithms form the basis of software tools supporting automatic and semi-automatic checks of programs containing quantitative information in the form of probability and time. The methods proposed here should avoid the state explosion problem in various important application domains by relying on a cogent representation of Markov transition probability matrices as MTBDDs introduced in [9, 1, 6]. The fixed-points can be reached in ω steps by successive approximation, which in practice means that the desired expectations can be computed to within a given $\varepsilon > 0$ in finitely many steps.

The expectations computed by the algorithm are not exact probabilities but lower bounds only; while exact probabilities might be preferable, the corresponding algorithms for satisfiability checking are complex (i.e. exponential in the size of the formula and polynomial in the size of the system for the case of Markov chains [10]), and so in such cases our algorithm provides a more efficient albeit coarser alternative. We can state that, in the case of positive CTL, the expectations semantics is probabilistically sound, in the sense that if the expectation p computed for a positive CTL formula is positive then the corresponding PCTL is also satisfied w.r.t. the threshold p. It would be worthwhile to extend this result to the full CTL and more expressive logics, such as CTL*, and models, for example concurrent Markov chains [25] or probabilistic systems which also exhibit non-determinism [3, 2], but it is not clear how this can be done without suitably extending the framework. Moreover, we would like to know whether Theorem 1 would go through for a framework *with* non-determinism, as in [22]. Most importantly, we need to find out whether there are any sensible ways of handling νx and $\neg$ within a semantics that approximates actual probabilities. Finally, we should point out that our semantic framework cuts across the usual classification of branching time versus linear time temporal logics. Our semantics of CTL has the feel of linear time temporal logic as the two quantifiers collapse into one notion, but it also contains branching aspects in the meaning of the modalities.

8 ACKNOWLEDGMENTS

We would like to thank all the anonymous referees for their constructive criticism.

REFERENCES

[1] C. Baier, E.M. Clarke, V. Hartonas-Garmhausen, M.Z. Kwiatkowska, and M.D. Ryan. Symbolic model checking for probabilistic processes. In *Pro-*

ceedings, 24th ICALP, volume 1256 of *Lecture Notes in Computer Science*, pages 430–440. Springer-Verlag, 1997.

[2] C. Baier and M.Z. Kwiatkowska. Model checking for a probabilistic branching time logic with fairness. Accepted for *Distributed Computing* subject to revisions. Also available as Technical Report CSR-96-12.

[3] A. Bianco and L. de Alfaro. Model checking of probabilistic and nondeterministic systems. In *Proceedings, FST&TCS*, volume 1026 of *Lecture Notes in Computer Science*, pages 499–513. Springer-Verlag, 1995.

[4] J. C. Bradfield. *Verifying Temporal Properties Of Systems*. Birkhaeuser, Boston, Mass., 1991.

[5] J. R. Burch, E. M. Clarke, D. L. Dill K. L. McMillan, and J. Hwang. Symbolic model checking: 10^{20} states and beyond. *Information and Computation*, 98(2):142–170, 1992.

[6] S.V. Campos, E.M. Clarke, W.Marrero, and M. Minea. Verus: a tool for quantitative analysis of finite-state real-time systems. In *Proc. Workshop on Languages, Compilers and Tools for Real-Time Systems*, 1995.

[7] E. M. Clarke and E. M. Emerson. Synthesis of synchronization skeletons for branching time temporal logic. In D. Kozen, editor, *Proc. Logic of Programs*, number 131 in LNCS. Springer Verlag, 1981.

[8] E.M. Clarke, M. Fujita, P.C. McGeer, J.Yang, and X. Zhao. Multi-terminal binary decision diagrams: an efficient data structure for matrix representation. In *IWLS'93: International Workshop on Logic Synthesis, Tahoe City*, May 1993.

[9] E.M. Clarke, K. L. McMillan, X. Zhao, M. Fujita, and J.Yang. Spectral transforms for large boolean functions with applications to technology mapping. In *30th ACM/IEEE Design Automation Conference*, pages 54–60. ACM/IEEE, ACM, 1993.

[10] C. Courcoubetis and M. Yannakakis. The complexity of probabilistic verification. *Journal of the ACM*, 42(4):857–907, 1995.

[11] E. A. Emerson and C.-L. Lei. Efficient model checking in fragments of the propositional mu-calculus. Annual IEEE Symposium on Logic in Computer Science, pages 267–279. IEEE Computer Society Press, 1986.

[12] H. Hansson. *Time and Probability in Formal Design of Distributed Systems*. Elsevier, 1994.

[13] H. Hansson and B. Jonsson. A logic for reasoning about time and probability. *Formal Aspects of Computing*, 6:512–535, 1994.

[14] M.R.A. Huth and M.Z. Kwiatkowska. Quantitative analysis and model checking. Annual IEEE Symposium on Logic in Computer Science, pages 111–122. IEEE Computer Society Press, June 1997.

[15] J.G. Kemeny and J.L. Snell. *Finite Markov Chains*. Van Nostrand, 1960.

[16] D. Kozen. A probabilistic PDL. In *15th Annual ACM Symposium on Theory of Computing*, pages 291–297, 1983.

[17] D. Kozen. Results on the propositional mu-calculus. *Theoretical Computer Science*, 27:333–354, 1983.

[18] D. Kozen. A probabilistic PDL. *JCSS*, 30(2):162–178, 1985.

[19] K. G. Larsen and A. Skou. Bisimulation through probabilistic testing. *Information and Computation*, 94(1):1–28, September 1991.

[20] A. McIver and C. Morgan. A probabilistic temporal calculus based on expec-

tations. In *Proceedings, Formal Methods Pacific'97*. Springer-Verlag, 1997. Also available as Technical Report PRG-TR-13-97.

[21] K. L. McMillan. *Symbolic Model Checking*. Kluwer Academic Publishers, 1993.

[22] C. Morgan and A. McIver. An expectation-transformer model for probabilistic temporal logic. Technical report, Computing Laboratory, Oxford University, April 1997. Draft. Personal Communication.

[23] R. Segala and N. Lynch. Probabilistic simulations for probabilistic processes. In *Proceedings, CONCUR*, volume 836 of *Lecture Notes in Computer Science*, pages 481–496. Springer-Verlag, 1994.

[24] K. Seidel, C. Morgan, and A. McIver. An introduction to probabilistic predicate transformers. Technical Report PRG-TR-6-96, Oxford University Computing Laboratory, 1996.

[25] M. Vardi. Automatic verification of probabilistic concurrent finite-state programs. In *Proc. FOCS'85*, pages 327–338. IEEE, 1985.

[26] P. Wolper. Temporal logic can be more expressive. Proc. of the 22nd Annual ACM Symposium on Foundations of Computer Science, pages 340–348, 1981.

[27] L. A. Zadeh. Fuzzy Sets. *Information and Control*, 8:338–353, 1965.

BIOGRAPHY

Michael Huth studied mathematics and computer science at the TU Darmstadt in Germany. In 1991 he received his Ph.D. from Tulane University of Louisiana. From 1991 to 1996 he took on post-doctoral fellowships at Kansas State University, Manhattan; Imperial College, London; TU Darmstadt, Darmstadt; and at the University of Birmingham in the United Kingdom. He is currently an assistant professor and a member of the programming languages group at Kansas State University. His interests range from the mathematical foundations of semantics, computational logic, language design and analysis, formal verification of concurrent systems, to the social impact of modern information technologies.

Marta Kwiatkowska graduated in computer science from the Jagiellonian University, Kraków, Poland. She moved to England in 1984, where she took up a lectureship at the University of Leicester and obtained her Ph.D. She held visiting positions at CWI, Amsterdam, and Imperial College, London, and has a wide network of international collaborators. Since 1994 she has been a member of the Theory of Computation group at the University of Birmingham. Her interests are in semantics for concurrency, infinite behaviour and fairness, and more recently probabilistic modelling and verification.

19
Reactive Functional Programming*

R. B. Kieburtz
Oregon Graduate Institute of Science & Technology
P.O. Box 91000, Portland, OR 97291-1000 USA `dick@cse.ogi.edu`

Abstract

Reactive systems respond to concurrent, possibly unsynchronized streams of input events. Programming reactive systems is challenging without language support for event-triggered actions. It is even more challenging to reason about reactive systems. This paper explores a new conceptual basis for applying functional programming techniques to the design and formal verification of reactive systems. The mathematical foundation for this approach is based upon signature coalgebras and derived proof rules for coinduction. The concepts are illustrated with an example that has been used with the language *Esterel*.

Keywords

Reactive systems, programming languages, coalgebras, coinduction, verification

1 INTRODUCTION

Reactive systems are characterized by sequences of history-determined reactions to external events. It is known that a non-strict functional programming language can provide a suitable linguistic vehicle for programming reactive systems because streams, modeling temporal sequences of values, can be represented. It is necessary to represent more than streams, however. Current reactive programming languages, such as *Esterel*, *Lustre*, *Signal* and *Statecharts* provide implicit or explicit representations of state, iterative control structures, and parallel threads of activity. Use of these languages has advanced the state of the art of designing reactive systems, however, it is not easy to reason about their properties. For ease of reasoning, we should like to have a sound programming logic that is expressive over the terms of the programming language. A principal motivation for this research is to develop in tandem a programming notation well suited to specifying reactive systems, and an associated programming logic.

The control structure needed for reactive programs is inherently iterative, not recursive. The data of interest are infinitary sequences or trees of states, representing the evolution of systems that may never terminate. We have searched for an underlying mathematical structure to model reactive systems. The structure we have found most useful is that of coalgebras, which unfortunately, are not very well understood by most functional programmers.

---

*The research reported in this paper was supported by the USAF Materiel Command.

Programming Concepts and Methods D. Gries, & W-P. de Roever (Eds.)

Section 2 of the paper introduces the notation and concepts of programming with coalgebras. Section 3 illustrates application of the concepts to formulate a non-trivial example that has previously appeared in the literature. This example is used to illustrate one of the main points of the paper: that a coalgebra provides structure for verification of properties as well for an algorithm. Section 4 presents brief conclusions.

1.1 Iterative functional programming

In the past, several researchers have observed that programming with terminating recursion schemes is algebraic in nature [7, 8, 4, 13, 23, 22]. Results of this body of research include (1) the discovery that recursion over typed data structures has a logical counterpart in structural induction and (2) that the recursion patterns can be captured in higher-order, type-parametric (also called *polytypic*) combinators, embedded in a strict functional programming language. There is a dual to algebraic programming and it leads to another style of functional programming, which is the topic of this paper.

Process-oriented programs are iterative. They are controlled by tests of their partial results, driven by external events rather than by the interpretation of data, and are naturally modeled by coalgebras. Because control is derived to meet external demand rather than induced by the structure of arguments, a non-strict evaluation mechanism is needed. The rules of coinduction induced by codatatypes are logical duals of the familiar rules of structural induction that are induced by datatype definitions. Dual to the recursive structure of algebraic programs is the iterative structure of coalgebraic programs, which can be made manifest by embedding a set of type-parametric combinators in a non-strict programming language.

Examples of iterative algorithms are common. They include linear and tree-structured searching, shift-reduce parsing, and both synchronous and asynchronous reactive systems. Before looking at examples, including proof rules, let's introduce a formalism for expressing coalgebraic programs. The notation presented in this paper is taken from *DUALITY*, which is an experimental, functional language based upon algebras and coalgebras as its fundamental computational structures. In this paper we shall deal only with the coalgebraic part. An early version of this language has been implemented and is described in a technical report [21].

This is by no means the first time that the concepts of iterative control and synchronous data flow (i.e. streams) have been embedded into a programming notation. These concepts were the basis for the language *Lucid* [2], and earlier, in Kahn-McQueen networks [20]. These early language developments led directly to *Lustre* [15], a language that has found considerable use for programming reactive systems. Synchronous data flow techniques have been further generalized [9] to networks of higher-order typed entities.

2 COVARIETIES OF COALGEBRAS

A covariety is a class of coalgebras with a common signature. The archetypical example is the covariety of stream coalgebras, whose signature is:

cosig *Stream*(a)\{**type** c; str/c : \{$\$shd : a,\ \$stl : c$\}\};

Here *Stream* is the name of the covariety and *str* is the name of its single sort, analogous to a type constructor. It is redundant to name both the covariety and its single sort, but later we shall see an example that requires a multi-sorted signature.

Each *Stream*-coalgebra has a type parameter, a, a carrier type, c, and two projectors (some authors call these *destructors*) identified by the symbols *$shd* and *$stl*. Each projector is a total function whose domain is the carrier and whose codomain is indicated by the typing given in the signature. A signature of projectors can be thought of as a generalized record declaration. Binding a type for the carrier and typed functions for the projectors defines a specific coalgebra parameterized by the type variable, a.

Every covariety defined in this way contains a final coalgebra which is unique up to isomorphism [18]. Call the carrier of the final *Stream*-coalgebra $str(a)$ and call its projectors *Shd* and *Stl*. The finality condition implies that given any coalgebra of the variety *Stream*, with bindings $\{c := t,\ \$shd := f,\ \$stl := g\}$, there is an assignment of the type parameter, $a := t'$, and a unique mapping, $h : t \rightarrow str(t')$, satisfying the homomorphism condition:

$$Stl \circ h = h \circ g$$
$$Shd \circ h = f$$

The significance of the final coalgebra is that any *Stream*-coalgebra may be represented as an infinite sequence of values. Because of this property, a stream is often identified with an infinite list. While that is certainly one way to encode a stream as data, it is by no means the only way. If we accept that a stream is *codata*, then encoding it as data seems unnecessary. A codata object is defined with methods for observing it, rather than with constructors for building its representation. Other examples of codata are found in the *intensions* of *Lucid*, which denote suspended, iterative computations, rather than values.

Every stream is infinite; that is, it is meaningful to iterate the projection operator *Stl* on a stream arbitrarily many times, even though there is no way to witness the entire stream at once. A stream provides a good model for an incrementally readable input file. The projection *Shd* yields the value of the first element of a stream, just as a *get* operation on an open file produces a value from it. The projection *Stl* yields the rest of a stream, but it is not manifested until projections of it are taken. The situation is familiar in non-strict functional languages.

There are infinitely many access paths to elements of a stream. A path is expressed by a well-typed composition of the projectors *Shd* and *Stl*, i.e. $Shd \circ \underbrace{Stl \circ \cdots \circ Stl}_{i \text{ times}}$, for $i \geq 0$.

2.1 Generators of codata

We say that the carrier of a final coalgebra is a type of codata, meaning that data values can be gotten from it by projection. Data and codata are distinguished by the type system of *DUALITY*. When a sort of a covariety is used as a type constructor, it designates a type of codata.

If $T(a)$ is a covariety and t is a sort symbol of the signature T, a generator of sort t is a function with a type $c \to t(a)$, where the codomain is a type of codata. To determine a generator, we must specify a coalgebra by naming a covariety, a type for the carrier and bindings of functions for the projectors. Coalgebras are first-class objects of *DUALITY*.

Example 21 : Integer sequences
Declare a *Stream* coalgebra by:

$$\textbf{coalgebra}\ intseq \doteq Stream\{c := int;\ \$shd := id,\ \$stl := add1\}$$

where $add1 \doteq \lambda n.\, n+1$. To obtain an expression of type $str(int)$, we can apply the *DUALITY* combinator, $gen[str]$, to the coalgebra specification, creating a generator for this type,

$$gen[str]\, intseq\ :\ int \to str(int)$$

The combinator $gen[str]$ is an instance of a higher-order combinator, *gen*, specialized to the sort *str* of the covariety *Stream*. The higher-order combinators in *DUALITY* substitute for the recursion operator found in conventional functional languages. The generator $h \doteq gen[str]\, intseq$ is the unique map taking the coalgebra *intseq* to a final *Stream* coalgebra. The homomorphism condition it satisfies is expressed by the pair of equations:

$$Shd \circ h = id_{int}$$
$$Stl \circ h = h \circ add1$$

□

Other applications of *Stream* coalgebra generators define pseudo-random number sequences, sequences of unique identifiers and other enumerated sets.

(a) A proof rule for stream generators

All functional programmers are familiar with proof rules based upon induction. Somewhat less familiar is the dual rule of coinduction. The possible observations of a codata object are enumerable composites of a finite basis of primitive witness functions. The coinduction principle is that the finitely observable properties of an object completely characterize it, even if the object is infinitary [1, 24, 26, 18, 12]. Expositions of coinduction are given by Paulson [25], Gordon [14], Jacobs and Rutten [19].

To define a proof rule for a stream of elements of type a, generated from a carrier of type t, let P be a two-place, typed predicate symbol whose arguments range over t and a, respectively. We prefer a two-place predicate because it can express the input-output relation of a function. Coinduction extends the domain of the relation to infinitary objects. A proof rule for a stream of elements is:

$$\frac{\begin{array}{l} x_0 \,:\, t \\ f \,:\, t \rightarrow a \\ g \,:\, t \rightarrow t. \qquad \forall x \,:\, t.\, P(x_0, x) \Rightarrow P(x_0, g\, x) \end{array}}{P(x_0,\, x_0) \Rightarrow \Box P(x_0,\, gen[str]\{c := t;\ \$shd := f,\ \$stl := g\}\ x_0)}$$

We have used a linear temporal operator, $\Box$ (read as *always*), as a quantifier on the predicate P in the consequent of the rule to express that the proposition $P(x_0, x)$ is asserted for every element, x, of the generated stream.

2.2 Coalgebra homomorphisms define iteration schemes

A compelling reason to consider coalgebras is that *coalgebra homomorphisms*, i.e. the structure-preserving maps between coalgebras of a given covariety, conform directly to an iteration scheme for computation. Thus coalgebras afford a mechanism to prescribe a specific control structure for computation and to communicate this structure to program analysis and translation software.

For the covariety *Stream*, the related iteration scheme is linear search. For more complex covarieties, the iteration schemes are more specialized, including algorithm schemes such as binary search and shift-reduce parsing.

A coalgebra homomorphism is composed of two parts: a coalgebra specification, such as *intseq* in Example 21, and a *control* that selects among the projectors of the coalgebra. The body of a control has the form of a conditional or a case expression. A control and a coalgebra specification are combined by a *DUALITY* combinator, *cohom*, suitably specialized to a sort of the covariety.

This forms a limit of the specified coalgebra, determined by the control. It is, of course, necessary to confirm that such limits exist, in each case.

Example 22 : Sequential search
We shall define a generic sequential search function, give a necessary and sufficient condition for its termination, and give a hypothetical rule of logic to conclude a property of a search. Let a be a type, $p : a \to bool$ and $r : a \to a$. Define a sequential search combinator, *while*, by

$$\begin{aligned} while(p, r) \doteq\ & cohom[str]Stream\ \{c := a;\ \$shd := id_a,\ \$stl := r\} \\ & \quad (\lambda x.\ \textbf{let}\ u = \$shd\, x\ \textbf{in} \\ & \qquad \textbf{if}\ \neg p\, u\ \textbf{then}\ u\ \textbf{else}\ \$stl\, x) \end{aligned}$$

The control is expressed as a lambda abstraction enclosed in parentheses. The expressions on the arms of a conditional (or case expression) that forms the return expression of the control must be applications of projectors of the coalgebraic variety, or as in this example, identifiers bound to such applications in a local definition. A control expression should not be confused with a function declaration; in particular, the types of the expressions on the arms of a conditional or case are not all of a common type.

A function composed with *cohom*[*str*] satisfies a set of conditional equations such as the ones given below for the sequential search combinator:

$$\begin{aligned} p\,x = tt &\ \Rightarrow\ while(p, r)\, x = while(p, r)\ (r\ x) \\ p\,x = f\!f &\ \Rightarrow\ while(p, r)\, x = id_a\ x \end{aligned}$$

The right-hand sides of the equations are formed by substitution into the control expression. The bindings of the projectors *$shd* and *$stl* are taken from the coalgebra declaration, and in addition, the defined combinator is recursively applied to every projector expression whose codomain type has been specified to be the carrier. In this example, the declaration $\$stl : c$ in the signature dictates that $while(p, r)$ is applied to $(r\ x)$, gotten from the binding of *$stl*. It is not misleading to imagine the combinator expressions of *DUALITY* translated in this way into recursive function definitions in a conventional language. However, the patterns of recursion so obtained are rigidly constrained to tail recursion.

Of course, it is useful to have a more compact declaration for such a useful combinator as *while*(_, _) and it is often made a language primitive. We have used it here as the simplest illustration of coalgebraic program construction with explicit control. Before leaving the example, we call the reader's attention to another aspect of the coalgebraic declaration. The declarations of data transformation and control are separated; each is a first-class entity in *DUALITY*. The data transformation is fully specified by the coalgebra, which could be used in other declarations with a different control. The control specification could be used with other *Stream* coalgebras.

3 FINITE-STATE REACTIVE SYSTEMS

Finite-state systems are naturally modeled by multi-sorted coalgebras. The states of a system correspond to sorts of a coalgebra; the carrier in each sort is comprised of the state variables, and the projectors in each sort are the possible transitions from the state that corresponds to the sort. Traditional functional programming languages have not been easy to use in describing reactive systems because the sequences of possible reactions often seem to require complex mutual recursion for their specification. Formulating a reactive system as a coalgebra is more natural because the use of multiple sorts provides a detailed structure for the specification.

We shall illustrate the technique with an example of a synchronous reactive system previously used to illustrate programming in *Esterel* [3].

Example 31 : The Reflex game
The Reflex game is a coin-operated machine on which a player measures the time constant of her reflexes. After depositing a coin to start the game, she can depress a Ready button to signify that she is prepared to start a trial. When she receives a Go signal from the machine, she depresses a Stop button as quickly as she can. The machine times her response in several trials, then displays the average response time. There are several illegal moves that must be accounted for. If the Stop button is depressed after the player is ready but before Go has been signaled, this action is interpreted as cheating and terminates the game. If either the Ready or the Stop button is depressed when it is not expected, a warning bell sounds, but the game is not interrupted. A coin drop always restarts the game, even when this event occurs during the progress of a previous game.

The game also depends upon timing signals emitted by a clock. Clock ticks must be counted to measure the player's latency. Also, the Go signal is emitted after a randomly determined number of clock ticks following depression of the Ready button by the player. And if a player fails to respond within a predetermined interval when a response is expected, the game times out.

The events that the machine must react to are a coin drop, depression of the Ready and Stop buttons, and ticks of the clock. We assume that these events never occur exactly simultaneously, or that they can be separated in a sequence.

Analysis of the Reflex game shows that the machine can be described as having five major states:

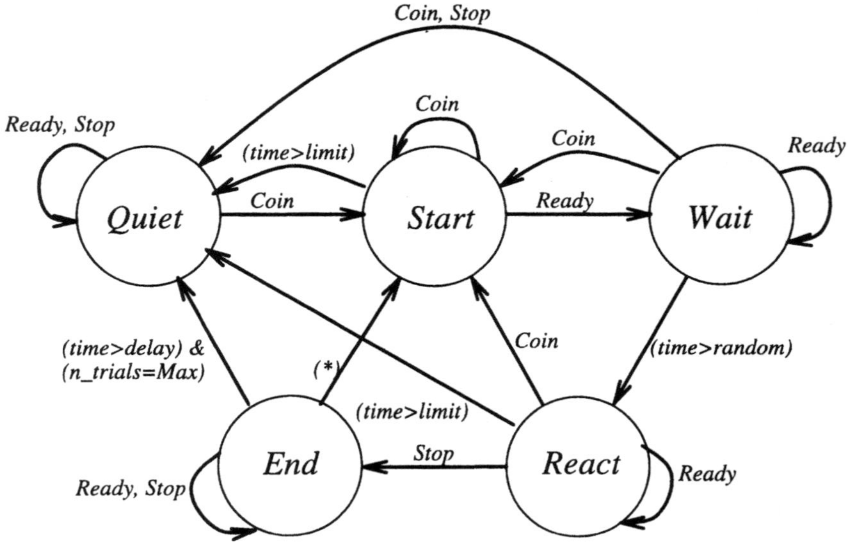

* Coin, (time>delay) & (n_trials<Max)

Figure 1—Major states of the Reflex game

quiet, when no game is in progress,
start, when awaiting a Ready event to start a trial,
wait, when the player is awaiting a Go signal from the machine,
react, when he machine awaits a Stop event,
end, when the machine pauses to display the response time of the player.

The machine responds to events differently in each of these five states. Some of the responses are transitions from one state to another. Figure 1 is a state transition diagram for the reflex game machine.

In the solution of this problem as an *Esterel* program, the states of the game are not manifest but are implicit in the control. The control consists of a nested loop structure, triggered by events, that takes the machine through the possible sequences of state transitions. Although *Esterel* provides intuitive syntax for coding even-driven nested loop structures, it is still challenging to get them right. This represents the state-of-the-art in programming reactive systems.

The Reflex game can be modeled by a multi-sorted coalgebra. We associate a separate sort with each of the major states of the game. In each of these states, we identify the possible transitions and name them. The reactions in each state become the projectors of the corresponding sort. The codomain type of each projector is the carrier that corresponds to the game state to which the transition leads. No explicit recursion or iteration is involved in programming the game in this way.

The output of the Reflex game will be modeled as a sequence of states. A state will include state variables and output signals produced by a transition. However, these are details that will appear in a coalgebra for the game. None of these details are manifested in a covariety. A signature for the covariety is:

cosig *Reflex*(*a*) {**type** *q*, *s*, *w*, *r*, *t*;
  quiet/q : {*$coin* : *s*, *$noop* : *q*},
  start/s : {*$reveal*: *a*, *$ready*: *w*, *$renew*: *s*, *$warn*: *s*, *$timeout*: *q*, *$tick*: *s*},
  wait/w : {*$reveal* : *a*, *$renew* : *s*, *$warn* : *w*, *$abort* : *q*, *$tick* : *w*, *$go* : *r*},
  react/r : {*$reveal*: *a*, *$react*: *t*, *$renew*: *s*, *$warn*: *r*, *$tick*: *r*, *$timeout*: *q*},
  end/t : {*$reveal* : *a*, *$warn* : *t*, *$renew* : *s*, *$tick* : *t*, *$tock* : *s*, *$finish* : *q*}}

The projectors *$reveal* do not correspond to state transitions of the game, but are instead actual projections of the machine state.

The game is specified in terms of a *Reflex*-coalgebra, binding data transformation functions associated with state transitions to each of the projector symbols. To determine all trajectories of play, we shall generate a game tree, which will be codata, of course. To simulate a game, we shall interpret a sequence of externally caused events (coin drops, clock ticks and button pushes) as control for the projectors in each state.

Minor states of the game are determined by the values of three integer-valued state components. These are packaged as fields of a record type,

record *State*{*time*, *total_time*, *trial_number* : *int*};

Further, there are signals delivered to the actuators that implement the machine. These unvalued signals can be represented by a set of elements of an enumerated type,

type *Signals* = **set of** [*game_over_on* | *game_over_off* | *go_on* | *go_off* |
    tilt_on | *tilt_off* | *ring_bell* | *bump_random*];

There is one integer-valued signal which sends values to the display. The state components and the signals are conveniently packaged as fields of a record type. We declare

record *Game*{*state* : *State*; *sigs* : *Signals*; *display* : *int*};

It is convenient to define a pair of constants of type *Game*,

def *initial_game* = {*state* := {*time* := 0; *total_time* := 0; *trial_number* := 0};
    sigs := [*game_over_off*, *go_off*, *tilt_off*];
    display := 0};
def *tilt_game* = {{*state* := {*time* := 0; *total_time* := 0; *trial_number* := 0};
    sigs := [*game_over_on*, *go_off*, *tilt_on*];
    display := 0};

There are also three integer constants, *Time_limit*, *Delay* and *Max_trials*, and a stream, *random*, which is a randomly generated sequence of positive integers of bounded size, supplied by the machine. As a notational abbreviation, let $R \oplus \{X := e\}$ denote the record whose fields have the values of the corresponding fields in the record R, except for field X, which has the value of e.

The next task is to define a coalgebra by specifying the projectors of each sort. These correspond to the possible transitions from each state.

$$
\begin{array}{l}
\mathit{reflex} \doteq \textbf{coalgebra}\ \mathit{Reflex}\ \{q, s, w, r, t := \mathit{state};\\
\quad \mathit{quiet} : \{\$\mathit{coin} := \lambda s.\ \mathit{initial\_game},\\
\qquad \$\mathit{noop} := \mathit{id}_{\mathit{Game}}\},\\
\quad \mathit{start} : \{\$\mathit{reveal} := \lambda s.\ s.\mathit{state},\\
\qquad \$\mathit{ready} := \lambda s.\ s \oplus \{\mathit{state} \oplus \{\mathit{time} := 0\},\\
\qquad\qquad \mathit{sigs} := [\mathit{bump\_random}]\},\\
\qquad \$\mathit{renew} := \lambda s.\ \mathit{initial\_game},\\
\qquad \$\mathit{warn} := \lambda s.\ s \oplus \{\mathit{sigs} := [\mathit{ring\_bell}]\},\\
\qquad \$\mathit{timeout} := \lambda s.\ \mathit{tilt\_game},\\
\qquad \$\mathit{tick} := \lambda s.\ s \oplus \{\mathit{state} \oplus \{\mathit{time} := s.\mathit{state}.\mathit{time} + 1\}\}\},\\
\quad \mathit{wait} : \{\$\mathit{reveal} := \lambda s.\ s.\mathit{state},\\
\qquad \$\mathit{renew} := \lambda s.\ \mathit{initial\_game},\\
\qquad \$\mathit{warn} := \lambda s.\ s \oplus \{\mathit{sigs} := [\mathit{ring\_bell}]\},\\
\qquad \$\mathit{abort} := \lambda s.\ \mathit{tilt\_game},\\
\qquad \$\mathit{tick} := \lambda s.\ s \oplus \{\mathit{state} \oplus \{\mathit{time} := s.\mathit{state}.\mathit{time} + 1\}\},\\
\qquad \$\mathit{go} := \lambda s.\ s \oplus \{\mathit{state} \oplus \{\mathit{time} := 0\};\ \mathit{sigs} := [\mathit{go\_on}]\}\},\\
\\
\quad \mathit{react} : \{\$\mathit{reveal} := \lambda s.\ s.\mathit{state},\\
\qquad \$\mathit{react} := \lambda s.\ \{\mathit{state} := \{\mathit{time} := 0;\\
\qquad\qquad \mathit{total\_time} := s.\mathit{state}.\mathit{total\_time} + s.\mathit{state}.\mathit{time};\\
\qquad\qquad \mathit{trial\_number} := s.\mathit{state}.\mathit{trial\_number} + 1\};\\
\qquad\qquad \mathit{sigs} := [\mathit{go\_off}];\ \mathit{display} := s.\mathit{state}.\mathit{time}\},\\
\qquad \$\mathit{renew} := \lambda s.\ \mathit{initial\_game},\\
\qquad \$\mathit{warn} := \lambda s.\ s \oplus \{\mathit{sigs} := [\mathit{ring\_bell}]\},\\
\qquad \$\mathit{tick} := \lambda s.\ s \oplus \{\mathit{state} \oplus \{\mathit{time} := s.\mathit{state}.\mathit{time} + 1\}\},\\
\qquad \$\mathit{timeout} := \lambda s.\ \mathit{tilt\_game}\},\\
\quad \mathit{end} : \{\$\mathit{reveal} := \lambda s.\ s.\mathit{state},\\
\qquad \$\mathit{renew} := \lambda s.\ \mathit{initial\_game},\\
\qquad \$\mathit{warn} := \lambda s.\ s \oplus \{\mathit{sigs} := [\mathit{ring\_bell}]\},\\
\qquad \$\mathit{tick} := \lambda s.\ s \oplus \{\mathit{state} \oplus \{\mathit{time} := s.\mathit{state}.\mathit{time} + 1\}\},\\
\qquad \$\mathit{tock} := \lambda s.\ \{\mathit{state} := \{\mathit{time} := 0\},\\
\qquad\qquad \mathit{display} := 0\},\\
\qquad \$\mathit{finish} := \lambda s.\ s \oplus \{\mathit{sigs} := [\mathit{game\_over\_on}];\\
\qquad\qquad \mathit{display} := s.\mathit{state}.\mathit{total\_time} / \mathit{Max\_trials}\}\}\}
\end{array}
$$

A generator composed from this coalgebra, for instance, $\mathit{gen}[\mathit{quiet}]\ \mathit{reflex} : \mathit{Game} \rightarrow \mathit{quiet}$ generates, in response to demand, an infinite game tree rooted on the quiescent game state. Paths in this game tree incorporate all major-state transitions allowed by the rules of the game and in addition, some that are not allowed, because transitions in the game tree are unconstrained by conditions on the state variables that govern the progress of an actual game (i.e. the rules of the game).

To obtain a function that accurately simulates the game, the coalgebra must be composed with a control that responds to input events and reads state variables to determine a game path. The control is defined as a cluster of five expressions, one for each sort, as the game's response to events depends upon the major state that it occupies.

Since the final result is a stream of game states, the body of each component of the control has the form of a *Stream*-generator. The *$shd* projector defined in each game state translates each of the possible input events into a state transition event. In some cases, the translation is conditioned by the elapsed time recorded in a game state. Here is a definition of the control:

```
def transition ≐
  (quiet: (λs. gen[str] Stream{c := str(event);
                        $shd := λes. let e = Shd es in
                                     case e of
                                         Coin ⇒ $coin s
                                       | Ready ⇒ $noop s
                                       | Stop ⇒ $noop s
                                       | Tick ⇒ $noop s
                                     end
                        $stl := Stl}),
  start: (λs. gen[str] Stream{c := str(event);
                        $shd := λes. let e = Shd es in
                                     case e of
                                         Coin ⇒ $renew s
                                       | Ready ⇒ $ready s
                                       | Stop ⇒ $warn s
                                       | Tick ⇒ let v = $reveal s in
                                                if v.time < Time_limit then $tick s
                                                else $timeout s
                                     end
                        $stl := Stl}),
  wait: (λs. gen[str] Stream{c := str(event);
                        $shd := λes. let e = Shd es in
                                     case e of
                                         Coin ⇒ $renew s
                                       | Ready ⇒ $warn s
                                       | Stop ⇒ $abort s
                                       | Tick ⇒ let v = $reveal s in
                                                if v.time < random then $tick s
                                                else $go s
                                     end
                        $stl := Stl}),
```

$$
\begin{array}{l}
react : (\lambda s.\ gen[str]\ Stream\{c := str(event);\\
\qquad \$shd := \lambda es.\ \mathbf{let}\ e = Shd\ es\ \mathbf{in}\\
\qquad\qquad \mathbf{case}\ e\ \mathbf{of}\\
\qquad\qquad\quad Coin \Rightarrow \$renew\ s\\
\qquad\qquad \mid\ Ready \Rightarrow \$warn\ s\\
\qquad\qquad \mid\ Stop \Rightarrow \$react\ s\\
\qquad\qquad \mid\ Tick \Rightarrow \mathbf{let}\ v = \$reveal\ s\ \mathbf{in}\\
\qquad\qquad\qquad\quad \mathbf{if}\ v.time < Time\_limit\\
\qquad\qquad\qquad\quad \mathbf{then}\ \$tick\ s\ \mathbf{else}\ \$timeout\ s\\
\qquad\qquad \mathbf{end}\\
\qquad \$stl := Stl\}),\\
end : (\lambda s.\ gen[str]\ Stream\{c := str(event);\\
\qquad \$shd := \lambda es.\ \mathbf{let}\ e = Shd\ es\ \mathbf{in}\\
\qquad\qquad \mathbf{case}\ e\ \mathbf{of}\\
\qquad\qquad\quad Coin \Rightarrow \$renew\ s\\
\qquad\qquad \mid\ Ready \Rightarrow \$warn\ s\\
\qquad\qquad \mid\ Stop \Rightarrow \$warn\ s\\
\qquad\qquad \mid\ Tick \Rightarrow \mathbf{let}\ v = \$reveal\ s\ \mathbf{in}\\
\qquad\qquad\qquad\quad \mathbf{if}\ v.time < Delay\ \mathbf{then}\ \$tick\ s\\
\qquad\qquad\qquad\quad \mathbf{else\ let}\ v = \$reveal\ s\ \mathbf{in}\\
\qquad\qquad\qquad\qquad \mathbf{if}\ v.trial\_number < Max\_trials\\
\qquad\qquad\qquad\qquad \mathbf{then}\ \$tock\ s\\
\qquad\qquad\qquad\qquad \mathbf{else}\ \$finish\ s\\
\qquad\qquad \mathbf{end}\\
\qquad \$stl := Stl\}))
\end{array}
$$

A simulator for the Reflex game is the function

$$cohom[quiet]\ reflex\ transition : \ Game \to str(event) \to str(Game).$$

□

The domain constraints needed for the example of the Reflex game can be established by structural (Hindley-Milner) type checking. Note that the simulator is not expected to terminate, in the usual sense, but rather to make finite progress in response to each external event that it receives.

Programming the Reflex game in terms of coalgebras is straightforward once the type of the solution and of the component functions has been determined. The structure of the coalgebra does not allow guesswork.

3.1 A verification logic for the Reflex game simulator

One of the most significant advantages of formulating a finite-state systems such as the Reflex game simulator as a coalgebra morphism is that the coalgebraic structure induces a complementary deductive logic in which properties of the system can be proved by coinduction. As we shall see, the coinduction rules induced by the coalgebraic structure provide a fine-grained decomposition of proof obligations that must be discharged to establish a conjectured property. We believe this structure will make verification significantly easier by removing most of the guesswork. We expect it to be amenable to the application of automatic proof discovery methods.

Corresponding to each carrier in the coalgebra signature declaration, we declare a predicate symbol whose interpretation will characterize a specific property in the major state (or sort) to which the carrier is bound. For the reflex game example, these will be unary* predicates, each relating an external event stream and a game state. The game state will be a minor state of the major state characterized by the predicate.

A coinduction rule for a coalgebra is formulated as a sequent clause. In the consequent are clauses for each sort of a multi-sorted coalgebra; in the antecedent are sets of hypotheses for each sort. The hypotheses for a given sort correspond one-for-one to the projectors defined for that sort. The structure of a coinduction rule is induced directly by the signature of a coalgebra.

Each clause in the consequent of a coinduction rule extends the interpretation of a predicate to encompass all of the states of the corresponding sort in a potentially infinite tree or sequence. There will be one such clause for each sort of a multi-sorted coalgebra, allowing characterization of a property specified at each of the major states of a finite-state model, throughout all minor states that are reachable from a given initial state.

Each individual clause of an antecedent implies the transfer of a property under a projection. For instance, referring to the Reflex game, a clause that implies the transfer of a property via the transition *$ready* is:

$$\forall u : s,\ es : str(event).\, S(u) \Rightarrow W(\$ready\, u)$$

where S and W are the predicate symbols associated with sorts s and w, respectively. Upon substituting the binding for the transition *$ready* as given in the declaration of the coalgebra *reflex*, the clause becomes

$$\forall u : s,\ es : str(event).\, S(u) \Rightarrow W(u \oplus \{state \oplus \{time := 0\}\})$$

When the coinduction rule is for a general coalgebra morphism (a *cohom*), each hypothetical implication must be qualified by a guard for the transition that can be read from the declaration of the control for the morphism. Again referring to the reflex game, the clause above, extended as a hypothetical clause for the simulator, becomes

*In this example, the initial state is fixed in each game. More generally, use of a two-place predicate would allow the simulator to be characterised as a function from an arbitarily specified initial state to the ensuing behavior.

$$\forall u : q,\ es : str(event).\,(Shd\, es = Coin) \Rightarrow Q(u) \Rightarrow S(initial\_state)$$
$$\forall u : q,\ es : str(event).\,(Shd\, es = Ready) \Rightarrow Q(u) \Rightarrow Q(u)$$
$$\forall u : q,\ es : str(event).\,(Shd\, es = Stop) \Rightarrow Q(u) \Rightarrow Q(u)$$
$$\forall u : q,\ es : str(event).\,(Shd\, es = Tick) \Rightarrow Q(u) \Rightarrow Q(u)$$

$$\forall u : s,\ es : str(event).\,(Shd\, es = Coin) \Rightarrow S(u) \Rightarrow S(initial\_state)$$
$$\forall u : s,\ es : str(event).\,(Shd\, es = Ready) \Rightarrow S(es, u) \Rightarrow W(u \oplus \{state \oplus \{time := 0\}\})$$
$$\forall u : s,\ es : str(event).\,(Shd\, es = Stop) \Rightarrow S(es, u) \Rightarrow S(u \oplus \{sigs := [ring\_bell]\})$$
$$\forall u : s,\ es : str(event).\,(Shd\, es = Tick) \Rightarrow (u.state.time < Time\_limit) \Rightarrow S(u) \Rightarrow S(u \oplus \{state \oplus \{time := s.time + 1\}\})$$
$$\forall u : s,\ es : str(event).\,(Shd\, es = Tick) \Rightarrow (u.state.time \geq Time\_limit) \Rightarrow S(u) \Rightarrow Q(tilt\_game)$$

$$\forall u : w,\ es : str(event).\,(Shd\, es = Coin) \Rightarrow W(u) \Rightarrow S(initial\_state)$$
$$\forall u : w,\ es : str(event).\,(Shd\, es = Ready) \Rightarrow W(u) \Rightarrow W(u \oplus \{sigs := [ring\_bell]\})$$
$$\forall u : w,\ es : str(event).\,(Shd\, es = Stop) \Rightarrow W(u) \Rightarrow Q(tilt\_game)$$
$$\forall u : w,\ es : str(event).\,(Shd\, es = Tick) \Rightarrow (u.state.time < C\_random) \Rightarrow W(u) \Rightarrow W(u \oplus \{state \oplus \{time := s.time + 1\}\})$$
$$\forall u : w,\ es : str(event).\,(Shd\, es = Tick) \Rightarrow (u.state.time \geq C\_random) \Rightarrow W(u) \Rightarrow W(u \oplus \{state \oplus \{time := 0\};\ sigs := [go\_on]\})$$

$$\forall u : r,\ es : str(event).\,(Shd\, es = Coin) \Rightarrow R(u) \Rightarrow S(initial\_state)$$
$$\forall u : r,\ es : str(event).\,(Shd\, es = Ready) \Rightarrow R(u) \Rightarrow R(u \oplus \{sigs := [go\_on]\})$$
$$\begin{aligned}\forall u : r,\ es : str(event).\,(Shd\, es = Stop) \Rightarrow R(u) \Rightarrow\ & S(u \oplus \{state \oplus \{time := 0; \\ & \quad total\_time := s.state.total\_time + s.state.time; \\ & \quad trial\_number := s.state.trial\_number + 1\}; \\ & \quad signs := [go\_off];\ display := s.state.time\})\end{aligned}$$
$$\forall u : r,\ es : str(event).\,(Shd\, es = Tick) \Rightarrow (u.state.time < Time\_limit) \Rightarrow R(u) \Rightarrow R(u \oplus \{state \oplus \{time := u.time + 1\}\})$$
$$\forall u : r,\ es : str(event).\,(Shd\, es = Tick) \Rightarrow (u.state.time \geq Time\_limit) \Rightarrow R(u) \Rightarrow Q(tilt\_game)$$
$$\forall u : t,\ es : str(event).\,(Shd\, es = Coin) \Rightarrow T(u) \Rightarrow S(initial\_state)$$
$$\forall u : t,\ es : str(event).\,(Shd\, es = Ready) \Rightarrow T(u) \Rightarrow T(u \oplus \{sigs := [ring\_bell]\})$$
$$\forall u : t,\ es : str(event).\,(Shd\, es = Stop) \Rightarrow T(u) \Rightarrow T(u \oplus \{sigs := [ring\_bell]\})$$
$$\forall u : t,\ es : str(event).\,(Shd\, es = Tick) \Rightarrow (u.state.time < Delay) \Rightarrow T(u) \Rightarrow T(u \oplus \{state \oplus \{time := s.time + 1\}\})$$
$$\begin{aligned}\forall u : t,\ es : str(event).\,(Shd\, es = Tick) \Rightarrow\ & (u.state.time \geq Delay) \wedge (u.trial\_number < Max\_trials) \Rightarrow \\ & T(u) \Rightarrow S(u \oplus \{state \oplus \{time := 0\} \\ & \quad display := 0\}))\end{aligned}$$
$$\begin{aligned}\forall u : t,\ es : str(event).\,(Shd\, es = Tick) \Rightarrow\ & (u.state.time \geq Delay) \wedge (u.trial\_number \geq Max\_trials) \Rightarrow \\ & T(u) \Rightarrow Q(u \oplus \{sigs := [game\_over\_on]; \\ & \quad display := s.state.total\_time / Max\_trials\}))\end{aligned}$$

Figure 2—Antecedent clauses for the Reflex coinduction rule

$$\forall u : s,\ es : str(event).\,(transition.start\,u\,(Shd\,es) = \$ready\,u) \Rightarrow \\ S(u) \Rightarrow W(u \oplus \{state \oplus \{time := 0\}\})$$

Further substituting the guard clause by its binding in the declaration of *transition*, the hypothetical implication now relates the transition to the occurrence of an external event:

$$\forall u : s,\ es : str(event).\,(Shd\,es = Ready) \Rightarrow S(u) \Rightarrow W(u \oplus \{state \oplus \{time := 0\}\})$$

This recipe gives us the following coinduction rule for the Reflex game simulator. The antecedent clauses are given in Figure 2. The consequents are:

$$\forall u_0 : Game,\ es : str[event].\,Q(u_0) \Rightarrow \Box Q(cohom[quiet]\ reflex\ transition\ u_0\ es)$$
$$\forall u_0 : Game,\ es : str[event].\,S(u_0) \Rightarrow \Box S(cohom[start]\ reflex\ transition\ u_0\ es)$$
$$\forall u_0 : Game,\ es : str[event].\,W(u_0) \Rightarrow \Box W(cohom[wait]\ reflex\ transition\ u_0\ es)$$
$$\forall u_0 : Game,\ es : str[event].\,R(u_0) \Rightarrow \Box R(cohom[react]\ reflex\ transition\ u_0\ es)$$
$$\forall u_0 : Game,\ es : str[event].\,T(u_0) \Rightarrow \Box T(cohom[end]\ reflex\ transition\ u_0\ es)$$

The temporal operator $\Box$ (*always*) in the consequent formulas expresses precisely the sense in which the predicate over game states is extended by coinduction to a predicate over a stream of game states.

The textual extent of this coinduction rule is imposing, but keep in mind that it is amenable to mechanical calculation from the three parts of the formal declaration of the Reflex game simulator: the signature, the coalgebra specification and the control. When given a conjectured proposition of a property of the potentially infinite behaviors of the simulator, the rule yields a finite set of finitary propositions that must be discharged to prove the proposition. It accomplishes a logical destructuring that is essential to constructing a formal proof, and it does so in a way that suggests mechanization.

(a) Proving safety properties of the Reflex game

The consequents of the coinduction rule for the Reflex game assert invariant properties of states of the game. These are its so-called *safety* properties.

A simple safety property is that in every state, u,

$$Q_t(u) \doteq \frac{C\_random \leq Time\_limit \qquad Delay \leq Time\_limit}{u.state.time \leq Time\_limit}$$

In this clause, the antecedent conditions relate the values of constants of the Reflex game. Without these relations, the property does not hold. To prove this property of a game started in the quiescent state, we formulate the conjectured property as a consequent:

$$\forall u_0 : Game,\ es : str[event].\,(u_0.state.time \leq Time\_limit) \Rightarrow \\ \Box(state.time \leq Time\_limit)(cohom[quiet]\ reflex\ transition\ u_0\ es)$$

for which we seek a proof by Reflex game coinduction.

In the coinduction rule stated in the preceding section, choose $Q \equiv S \equiv W \equiv R \equiv T \equiv Q_t$ and attempt to discharge each of the antecedents of the rule. Most of the antecedent clauses discharge trivially, either because they do not refer to the *time* parameter explicitly or they set it to zero. There are five antecedent clauses in which the *time* parameter is incremented, however. Each of these clauses is guarded by a condition that *time* is strictly less than one of the constants *Time_limit*, *C_random* or *Delay*. Using the antecedent condition relating the latter two constants to *Time_limit*, it can be established that the implicand in each of the clauses is satisfied and the clause can be discharged. Thus the property is proved to hold for every game state reachable from an initial state that satisfies the property, by condinduction.

A related safety property that can be established is

$$Q_{tt}(u) \doteq u.state.total\_time \leq Max\_trials * Time\_limit$$

We can also state safety properties consequent to a restriction on the external event stream. For instance we might assert

$$\begin{array}{l} \forall u_0 : Game,\ es : str(event). \\ \qquad \Box(next\ event \neq Coin)es \Rightarrow Q(u_0) \wedge (u_0.state.time = 0) \Rightarrow \\ \qquad\quad \Box(state.time = 0)(cohom[quiet]\ reflex\ transition\ u_0\ es) \end{array}$$

for a game started from the quiescent state. To prove this assertion, we must infer from the temporal logic assertion, $\Box(next\ event \neq Coin)\ es$, the proposition $\forall es : str(event).\ Shd\ es \neq Coin$. This derived proposition can then be used to restrict the domain of antecedent clauses in a proof using the Reflex game coinduction rule.

Verification logics have also been developed for proving safety properties of systems specified in *Lustre* [17, 16] and *Esterel* [5].

3.2 Liveness properties of the Reflex game

Liveness properties, which assert that a state or state sequence with the property is eventually reached in every unfolding of the game, require for their proof a specific measure of progress. A monotonically increasing count of any external event can provide a suitable measure, provided that the timing event occurs *almost everywhere* in the event stream. Occuring almost everywhere means that at every point in the stream, the next timing event will occur after at most a finite number of non-timing events. The almost everywhere restriction assures that the observation of advancing time is never obscured by an infinite stream of non-timing events.

In the Reflex game, intuition tells us that the *Tick* event is a reasonable choice for the timing event. We assume that it occurs almost everywhere in every possible stream of external events. This assumption is essential; it cannot be proved from weaker assumptions.

A liveness property we should like to prove is that every game started by a coin drop eventually terminates. We adopt for our definition of termination that either (a) the game enters the quiescent state or (b) another coin is dropped. Note that we have no direct characterization of the quiescent state (or any other major state) in terms of the program's state variables. The *time* attribute of the game state is only locally monotonic. It is monotonic with respect to transitions from any state to itself, but is reset to zero on many transitions from one state to another. Although the attribute *trial_number* is monotonic throughout all transitions that do not enter the quiescent state, we cannot use this attribute to characterize the quiescent state, because it is not incremented immediately upon leaving the quiescent state.

States can be characterized by sets of initial sequences of event streams, but this is not very convenient. It is more convenient to introduce a pseudo-variable, *game_over : bool*, which is set to *true* when the event *game_over_on* is signalled, and to *false* when *game_over_off* is signalled. The quiescent state is then characterized by a *true* value of *game_over*.

The liveness property asserting termination can be formally stated as:

$$\forall u_0 : Game,\ es : str(event).\ \Box(next\ event \neq Coin)es \Rightarrow \\ \qquad \Diamond(state.game\_over = true)(cohom[quiet]\ reflex\ transition\ u_0\ es)$$

There is an accompanying safety property asserting that once a game terminates, *game_over* remains false if no more coins are dropped. We shall address only the liveness property.

The most successful way yet developed to verify temporal properties of a finite state system uses model checking of temporal logic formulas [11, 10]. The safety and liveness properties of the Reflex game example can obviously be verified by symbolic model checking. We describe a variant of the standard technique that uses symbolic inference to check monotonicity properties of state variables over transition paths. We have not yet implemented this method.

An ordered, symbolic binary decision diagram (BDD)[6] can be used to construct a proof of a liveness property. Boolean pseudo-variables are introduced to represent the boolean-typed expressions on which local control decisions are based. The nodes of the BDD correspond to major states of the Reflex game, split in cases in which more than one boolean condition controls transitions from the state. The boolean control expressions for each state are identified by inspecting the control specification.

$$
\begin{array}{ll}
(start) & x_1 \doteq state.time < Time\_limit \\
(wait) & x_2 \doteq state.time < C\_random \\
(react) & x_3 \doteq state.time < Time\_limit \\
(end) & x_4 \doteq state.time < Delay \\
(end') & x_5 \doteq state.trial\_number < Max\_trials
\end{array}
$$

The pseudo-variables are ordered by $x_1 < x_2 < x_3 < x_4 < x_5$.

A nondeterministic BDD for the Reflex game is shown in Figure 3(a). Its nodes correspond to states of the Reflex game, but are labelled in the diagram by single letters S, W, R, E, E' to save space. The solid arcs indicate transitions possible when the value of the controlling pseudo-variable is positive; the dashed arcs represent transitions possible on negative values of the control variables.

Notice that there are multiple positive (or negative) arcs from some nodes. This BDD represents a nondeterministic FSA because transitions of the Reflex machine also depend upon external events which have not been represented in the control expressions bound to pseudo-variables. Note also that in constructing Figure 3(a), transitions that require the *Coin* event have been omitted because the *Coin* event is precluded by the antecedent clause of the liveness assertion. Nondeterminism allows us to represent with the BDD all of the transitions possible with event sequences that are restricted only by the assumptions that *Tick* events occur almost everywhere and *Coin* events are never present. The liveness property that we seek will be proved if we can show that the BDD of Figure 3(a) can be reduced to the single node, **1**.

(a) Reducing a BDD with repeated nodes

We shall describe (informally) how to reduce the BDD of Figure 3(a), which represents the asserted liveness property of the Reflex game. Notice that this BDD contains paths from ancestor nodes to leaf nodes that carry the same labels. We call these *repeated nodes.* A path from an ancestor to a repeated node occurrence represents a loop in the state transition diagram. To reduce the BDD, each of these paths must be shown to be only finitely extensible as it is elaborated by repeating transitions of the state machine.

To establish that a path to a repeated node is only finitely extensible, we examine the control expressions bound to the pseudo-variables that label the arcs of the path. In our example, these expressions are less-than inequalities. If the value of the program variable on the left of the inequality grows to reach the expressed bound after a finite number of repetitions of the path then the corresponding pseudo-variable will eventually become 0. Sufficient conditions for this to occur are that the program variable is (1) monotonic with respect to executions of the transition function corresponding to the path and (2) increasing almost everywhere in any sequence of repetitions of the path.

Consider the path from the first occurrence of a node labeled W to its repeated occurrence, controlled by pseudo-variable x_2. The program variable that appears in the corresponding inequality is *state.time*. The path controlled by x_2 represents only the transitions *\$warn* and *\$tick*, which are enabled by

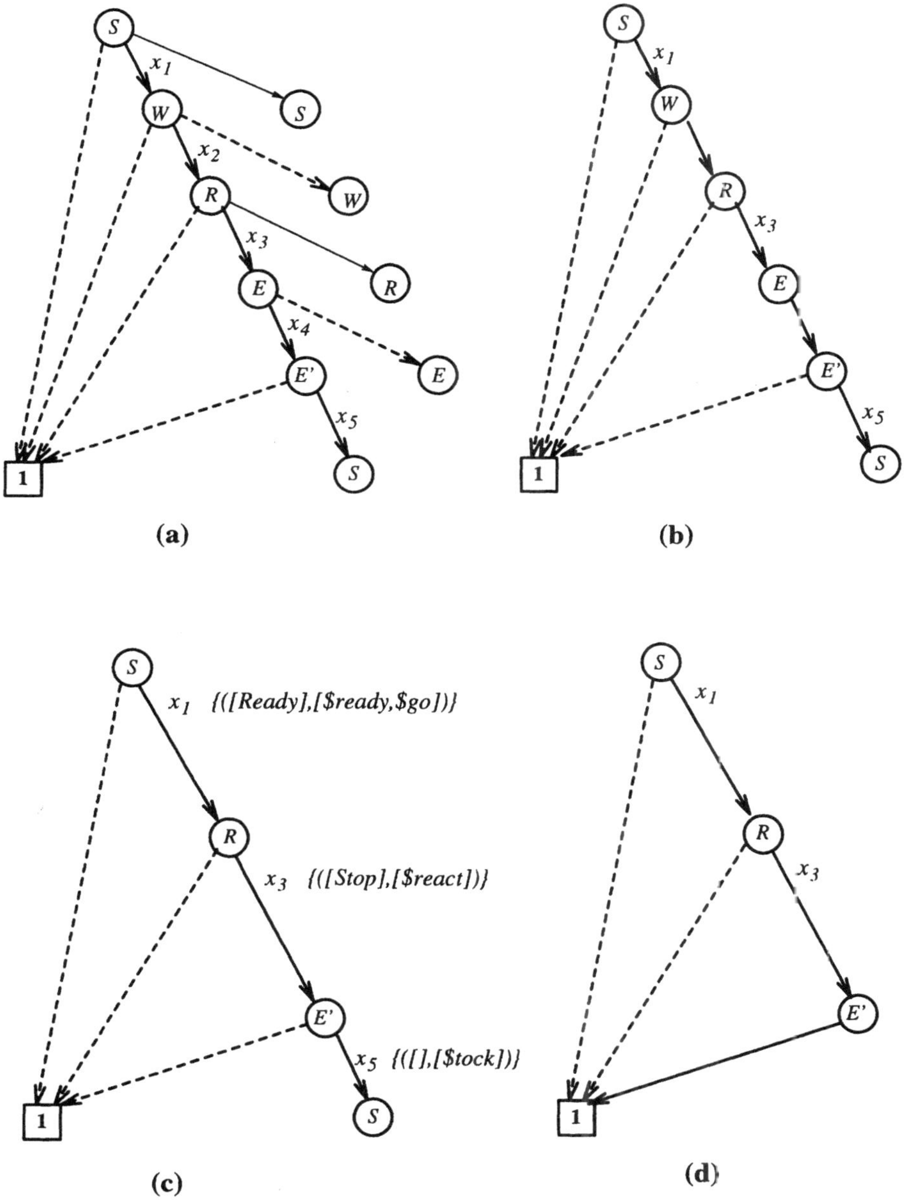

Figure 3

external events *Ready* and *Tick*, respectively. Inspection of the coalgebra specification *Reflex* reveals that a *$warn* transition does not change *state.time*, while a *$tick* transition increments its value. Thus the path satisfies condition (1), monotonicity of the program variable. Furthermore, since the *Tick* event occurs almost everywhere in an external event stream, the *$tick* transition will occur almost everywhere in a sequence of transitions from state W to itself, thus the path also satisfies condition (2). This argument proves the temporal assertion $\diamond(x_2 = 0)$.

This allows the BDD of Figure 3(a) to be reduced by removing the repeated occurrence of node W and the arc leading to it. Similar reasoning justifies removal of the repeated occurrence of nodes R, E, and the first repeated occurrence of node S leaving the BDD depicted in Figure 3(b). The paths not controlled by a pseudo-variable in this BDD are not of interest and can be reduced to single arcs.

In Figure 3(c), the arcs have been labelled with sets of the pairs of event sequences and corresponding transition actions represented by an interpretation of the arc in the *Reflex* coalgebra. The set of transition sequences from the root node to its repeated occurrence is gotten by taking the cartesian product of the sequece of set-valued labels. As the labels on individual arcs are all singletons, so is the composite label, which is {([*Ready, Stop*], [*$ready, $go, $react, $tock*])}.

We examine the expressions x_1, x_3 and x_5 in the context of the path transition sequence. The program variable *state.time* is not monotonic with respect to the transition sequence, hence we cannot conclude that repeated extensions of the path would cause the variables x_1 or x_3 to assume zero values. However, the program variable *state.trial_number* is monotonically increasing over this transition sequence, thus the arc labeled by x_5 and the repeated node S can be eliminated. The resulting BDD, depicted in Figure 3(d), is reducible to the singleton node **1** as its canonical form. This constitutes a proof of the conjectured liveness property.

4 CONCLUSIONS

We have introduced a functional programming notation that does not depend upon explicit recursion in definitions but uses instead the structure of signature coalgebras. The important contributions of this notation and the mathematical structures that underlie it are:

- It provides a framework in which control and data transformation are separately specified. A program is specified by the transitions of a finite-state system.
- All familiar iteration schemes can be modeled by varieties of coalgebras.
- Each variety of coalgebra has associated with it proof rules that virtually dictate the form of proofs of safety properties of algorithms that conform to its structure.

- Liveness properties can be verified through a hybrid deduction scheme in which temporal logical inference is used in conjunction with symbolic model checking.

REFERENCES

[1] Samson Abramsky. A domain equation for bisumulation. *Information and Computation*, 92:161–218, 1992.

[2] Edward A. Ashcroft and William W. Wadge. Lucid: A non-procedural language with iteration. *Communications of the ACM*, 20(7):519–526. 1977.

[3] G. Berry and G. Gonthier. The Esterel synchronous programming language: Design, semantics, implementation. *Science Of Computer Programming*, 19(2):87–152, 1992.

[4] Richard S. Bird. An introduction to the theory of lists. In M. Broy, editor, *Logic of Programming and Calculi of Discrete Design*, volume 36 of *NATO Series F*. Springer-Verlag, 1986.

[5] G. Boudol, V. Roy, R. de Simone, and D. Vergamini. Process calculi, from theory to practice: Verification tools. In *Automatic Verification Methods for Finite State Systems, LNCS 407*, pages 1–10. Springer-Verlag, 1990.

[6] R. E. Bryant. Symbolic boolean manipulation with ordered binary decision diagrams. *ACM Computing Surveys*, 24(3):293–318, September 1992.

[7] R M. Burstall and P. J. Landin. Programs and their proofs: an algebraic approach. In *Machine Intelligence 4*, pages 17–44. Edinburgh University Press, 1969.

[8] Rod Burstall. Inductively defined functions in functional programming languages. *Journal of Computer and System Sciences*, 34(2/3):409–421, 1987.

[9] P. Caspi and M. Pouzet. Synchronous Kahn networks. In *Proceedings of ACM SIGPLAN Internat. Conf. on Functional Programming*, pages 226–238. ACM Press, May 1996.

[10] E. M. Clarke, O. Grumberg, and D. Long. Verification tools for finite-state concurrent systems. In *A Decade of Concurrency: Reflections and Perspectives*, volume 803 of *Lecture Notes in Computer Science*, pages 124–175. Springer Verlag, 1992.

[11] E. A. Emerson and E. M. Clarke. Using branching time temporal logic to synthesize synchronizations skeletons. *Science of Computer Programming*, 2:241–266, 1982.

[12] Marcelo P. Fiore. A coinduction principle for recursive data types based on bisimulation. *Information and Computation*, 127(2):186–198, 1996.

[13] Peter Freyd. Recursive types reduced to inductive types. In *Fifth IEEE Symposium on Logic in Computer Science*, pages 498–507. IEEE Computer Society Press, 1990.

[14] Andrew Gordon. Bilimilarity as a theory of functional programming. In *Proceedings of 11th Conference on Mathematical Foundations of Programming Semantics*, volume 1 of *Electronic Notes in Theoretical Computer Science*. Elsevier, URL: www.pigeon.elsevier.nl/mcs/tcs/pc/volume1.htm, 1995.

[15] N. Halbwachs, P. Caspi, P. Raymond, and D. Pilaud. The synchronous dataflow programming language Lustre. *Proceedings of the IEEE*, 79(9):1305–1320,

1991.

[16] N. Halbwachs, J.-C. Fernandez, and A. Bouajjanni. An executable temporal logic to express safety properties and its connection with the language Lustre. In *Sixth International Symp. on Lucid and Intensional Programming, ISLIP'93*, Quebec City, Canada, April 1993. Université Laval.

[17] N. Halbwachs, F. Lagnier, and C. Ratel. Programming and verifying real-time systems by means of the synchronous data-flow programming language lustre. *IEEE Transactions on Software Engineering*, 18(9), 1992.

[18] Bart Jacobs. Mongruences and cofree coalgebras. In *Algebraic Methodology and Software Technology - AMAST'95*, volume 936 of *Lecture Notes in Computer Science*, pages 245–260. Springer Verlag, 1995.

[19] Bart Jacobs and Jan Rutten. A tutorial on (co)algebras and (co)induction. *EACTS Bulletin*, 62:222–259, 1997.

[20] Gilles Kahn. The semantics of a simple language for parallel programming. In *IFIP'74 Congress.* North Holland, 1974.

[21] Richard B. Kieburtz and Jeffrey Lewis. Algebraic Design Language—Preliminary definition. Technical report, Pacific Software Research Center, Oregon Graduate Institute of Science & Technology, January 1994.

[22] Richard B. Kieburtz and Jeffrey Lewis. Programming with algebras. In *Advanced Functional Programming*, volume 925 of *Lecture Notes in Computer Science*, pages 267–307. Springer Verlag, 1995.

[23] Erik Meijer, Maarten Fokkinga, and Ross Paterson. Functional programming with bananas, lenses, envelopes and barbed wire. In *Proc. of 5th ACM Conf. on Functional Programming Languages and Computer Architecture*, volume 523 of *Lecture Notes in Computer Science*, pages 124–144. Springer-Verlag, August 1991.

[24] Robin Milner and Mads Tofte. Co-induction in relational semantics. *Theoretical Computer Science*, 87:209–220, 1992.

[25] Lawrence C. Paulson. Mechanizing coinduction and corecursion in higher-order logic. *Journal of Logic and Computation*, 7(2):175–204, 1997.

[26] Andrew Pitts. A coinduction principle for recursively defined domains. *Theoretical Computer Science*, 124(2):195–219, 1994.

About the Author

Richard B. Kieburtz is Professor of Computer Science and Engineering at the Oregon Graduate Institute. His research interests are in the areas of functional programming; formal methods for specification and construction of software; verification and its application to hardware and software systems.

20

Imperative Objects and Mobile Processes

J. Kleist
BRICS, Department of Computer Science, Aalborg University
Fredrik Bajers Vej 7E, DK-9220 Aalborg Ø, Denmark, Phone: +45 9635 8080, fax: +45 9815 9889, Email:kleist@cs.auc.dk

D. Sangiorgi
INRIA, Sophia-Antipolis, Project Meije
BP 93, F-06902 Sophia-Antipolis Cedex, France, Phone: +33 4 9238 7639, fax: +33 4 9238 7998, Email:davide.sangiorgi@sophia.inria.fr

Abstract

An interpretation of Abadi and Cardelli's first-order *Imperative Object Calculus* into a typed π-calculus is presented. The interpretation validates the subtyping relation and the typing judgements of the Object Calculus, and is computationally adequate. The proof of computational adequacy makes use of (a π-calculus version) of *ready simulation*, and of a *factorisation* of the interpretation into a functional part and a very simple imperative part. The interpretation can be used to compare and contrast the Imperative and the Functional Object Calculi, and to prove properties about them, within a unified framework.

Keywords

Imperative objects, π-calculus, types, ready simulation, bisimulation.

1 INTRODUCTION

In their book (Abadi & Cardelli 1996), Abadi and Cardelli present and investigate a *Functional* and an *Imperative Object Calculus*, and type systems for them. These calculi can express, as primitive or derived forms, various major object-oriented idioms; they have simple but interesting typing and subtyping rules. The syntactic simplicity of the calculi, and their clear object-oriented flavour, makes them an important basis for understanding object-oriented languages. All Object Calculi are sequential.

In this paper we study the interpretation of the (first order) Imperative Object Calculus (IOC) into a *typed π-calculus*. Our main motivations are:

- There is a general lack of mathematical techniques for giving the semantics to, and proving properties about, object-oriented languages, especially the imperative ones. (For instance, it seems difficult to come up with reasonable notions of

Programming Concepts and Methods D. Gries, & W-P. de Roever (Eds.)

bisimulation for IOC. This contrasts with the Functional Object Calculus (FOC), for which one such notion has been developed (Gordon & Rees 1996).) However, most "real world" programming languages are imperative.
The π-calculus has a rich algebraic theory and a high expressive power. Its emphasis on the notions of name and of mobility makes it appealing for describing objects and their local states.

- IOC is an interesting core object-oriented language, because it is small and yet very expressive; for instance, classes and functions, as well as the Functional Object Calculus (FOC), can be encoded in it. A study of IOC can provide a solid basis for investigating more complex languages, that may include also, for instance, constructs for distribution and concurrency.
- We wish to understand what are objects from a π-calculus (and more generally, a process calculus) point of view.

The only work on behavioural equivalences for IOC that we are aware of is Gordon, Hankin & Lassen (1997). In this work, however, IOC is *untyped*. Gordon et al. study contextual equivalence for this untyped IOC, prove that it coincides with a variant of Mason and Talcott's CIU ("Closed Instances of Use") equivalence (Mason & Talcott 1991), and use the latter to validate some basic laws of the calculus.

More work exists on the semantics of the Functional Object Calculus FOC. Typed contextual equivalence and applicative bisimulation for FOC have been examined by Gordon & Rees (1996), who show that these two notions of equivalence coincide. They also show that Abadi and Cardelli's equational theory for FOC (Abadi & Cardelli 1996) is sound w.r.t. operational equivalence. Abadi & Cardelli (1996, Chapter 14) shows that the equational theory for FOC is also sound with respect their denotational semantics of FOC. Aceto, Hüttel, Ingólfsdóttir & Kleist (1997) show that the denotational semantics is sound but not fully abstract w.r.t. operational equivalence. Extending the above-mentioned techniques, based on applicative bisimulation and denotational models, to the Imperative Object Calculus IOC appears rather hard.

An interpretation of IOC into a form of imperative polymorphic λ-calculus with subtyping, recursive types and records has been found by Abadi, Cardelli & Viswanathan (1996). This interpretation has been used to validate the subtyping and typing judgements of IOC. However, it would be difficult to prove behavioural properties of IOC from this interpretation, because very little is known of the theory of the target imperative λ-calculus.

Some previous studies of encodings of imperative and Object Oriented Langauges into process calculi, namely (Milner 1989, Chapter 8), (Vaandrager 1990), (Jones 1993), (Walker 1995, Liu & Walker 1996), and (Sangiorgi 1996), are an important basis for our work. We briefly comment on the differences. Milner (1989, Chapter 8) showed how to translate a small imperative language into CCS. Vaandrager (1990), Jones (1993), Walker (1995), Liu & Walker (1996) and Philippou & Walker (1996) have gone further, by translating parallel object-oriented languages derived from the POOL family. Walker, Liu and Philippou have also used the encodings for proving the validity of certain program transformations on the source languages. The main limitation of these works is that they do not show how to handle *typed* object-oriented languages — the source languages have rather simple type systems and the translations do not act on types. Dealing with types is important when the type system of the object-oriented language contains non-trivial features like subtyping and polymorphism, otherwise many useful program equalities are lost and the semantics cannot be used to validate the typing rules of the language. By contrast, types play a central role in our interpretation. For this reason, our interpretation of objects is different from those in the above-mentioned works. In (Sangiorgi 1996) an interpretation of typed FOC into the π-calculus is given. No use is made of the π-calculus interpretation for validating behavioural properties of the source Object Calculus.

The syntax of FOC and IOC are similar, but their operational semantics are very different (for instance, the operational semantics of IOC makes extensive use of stores and stacks, not needed for FOC because it is functional). Remarkably, despite these differences in the operational semantics, the π-calculus interpretation of IOC in this paper can be derived with a simple change from that of FOC in (Sangiorgi 1996). As a consequence we can use the π-calculus interpretations to compare and contrast the Imperative and Functional Object Calculi — for instance, their discriminating power — and to prove properties about them, within a single framework.

The type language we use for the π-calculus is taken from (Pierce & Sangiorgi 1993, Sangiorgi 1996). In these type systems, as well as other type systems for the π-calculus like (Kobayashi, Pierce & Turner 1996, Vasconcelos & Tokoro 1994, Honda 1996), types are assigned to names. The types in (Pierce & Sangiorgi 1993) show the arity and the directionality of a name and, recursively, of the names carried by that name; the difference in (Sangiorgi 1996) is *variant types* in place of tupling. All values are "simple", in the sense that they are built out of names only, and cannot contain, for instance, process expressions.

The main technical contents of this paper are the following. We give a translation of both IOC terms and IOC types and type environments into the typed π-calculus. We then provide correctness proofs. Precisely, we prove that (1) the translation validates the subtyping judgements of IOC, that is, A is a subtype of B iff the translation of A is a subtype of the translation of B; (2) an IOC type judgement $E \vdash a{:}A$, asserting that object a has type A under the type assumptions E, is true iff its π-calculus translation is true, and (3) a well-typed IOC term reduces to a value iff its π-calculus interpretation does so (computational adequacy). From these results and the compositionality of the encoding, as a corollary we get the soundness of the translation w.r.t. behavioural equivalences like Morris-style contextual equivalence (Morris 1968) or barbed congruence (Milner & Sangiorgi 1992). Soundness assures us that the equalities on IOC terms provable from the interpretation are operationally valid on IOC. As for the translations of λ-calculi into π-calculus (Sangiorgi 1995), the opposite implication fails.

The IOC language we interpret into the π-calculus has a first-order type system. The interpretation can be easily extended to accommodate other features, like recursive types, variant tags, and polymorphism.

Technically, the hardest part of our work is the proof of computational adequacy. The proof is split into two parts. First we factorize our encoding into a functional part, where processes are "stateless", and a very simple imperative part, where processes have a state. This factorisation is useful because: (1) it allows us to take full advantage of various π-calculus proof techniques for functional processes; (2) it shows what — we believe — are the simplest non-functional π-calculus processes that are needed for translating the imperative features of IOC. This factorised encoding is less compact than the original one; but it allows us to establish a close correspondence with Abadi-Cardelli's operational semantics of IOC.

The second part of the proof of computational adequacy is to establish a relation between the original encoding and the factorised one. To this end, we could not use known behavioural equivalences of the π-calculus (for instance, known bisimilarities were too strong; trace equivalence too weak to yield the desired property). We solved the problem by adapting (a weak version of) the notion of *ready simulation* (Bloom, Istrail & Meyer 1995, Larsen & Skou 1991) to the π-calculus. Roughly, ready simulation was introduced in CCS-like languages as the least congruence contained in trace inclusion induced by certain classes of operators. To our knowledge, our application of ready simulation to derive properties of processes is novel.

Having established the correctness of our interpretation, we give some examples of how the theory of the π-calculus can be used to reason about IOC. By using the π-calculus for the proofs we can take advantage of the already available theory, including its algebraic laws and its co-inductive proof techniques. Here, we use the π-calculus to validate some basic equational theory for IOC. Something interesting about the coinductive π-calculus proofs is that non-trivial equalities can be proved using finitary relations (this is more rare with CIU equivalence on untyped IOC (Gordon et al. 1997) or applicative bisimulation on FOC (Gordon & Rees 1996) because the definition, or the transition system, on which they are based, contains an infinite quantification on contexts, or terms, of the language).

Among the laws we prove is (EQ SUB OBJECT). This law allows us to eliminate methods of objects that are not visible in the type assigned to the object. We are not aware of proposals of this, or similar laws, for IOC. In Abadi-Cardelli's book, the analogous of law (EQ SUB OBJECT) is at the heart of the equational theory of FOC, but no equational theory for IOC is proposed (in the book or, as far as we know, elsewhere). Strikingly, we can prove (EQ SUB OBJECT) using a bisimulation relation consisting of just two elements. Essentially the same proof can be used for (EQ SUB OBJECT) on FOC.

In this short version of the paper, for lack of space most of the proofs are omitted.

2 THE IMPERATIVE OBJECT CALCULUS

In this section we briefly present the (first-order) Imperative Object Calculus (IOC). The reader is referred to (Abadi & Cardelli 1996, Chapter 11) for details.

Syntax. An object $[l_i{=}\varsigma(x_i{:}A)b_i \;^{i\in 1..n}]$ consists of a collection of named methods

$l_i = \varsigma(x_i{:}A)b_i$ for distinct names l_i, and where x_i's are the self parameters. The letter ς (sigma) is a binder for the self variable in a method; $\varsigma(x{:}A)b$ is a method that when activated evaluates its body b with x bound to the enclosing object. A method activation $a.l$ results in the activation of the method bound to l in a; this method is evaluated with a as argument for self. A method update $a.l \Leftarrow \varsigma(x{:}A)b$ replaces the method named l in the object a with $\varsigma(x{:}A)b$ and evaluates to the modified object. Cloning creates a copy of the original object. An expression $\texttt{let}\ x{:}A = a\ \texttt{in}\ b$ first evaluates the let-part, binding the result to x, then evaluates the in-part with the variable x in its scope.

Operational semantics. The semantics for IOC is given as a relation that relates a store σ, a stack $\mathcal{S}$ (usually called environment, but we stick to the name used by Abadi and Cardelli), and a term a with a value v and an updated store σ'. The relation is written $\sigma \cdot \mathcal{S} \vdash a \rightsquigarrow v \cdot \sigma'$ and is read: "the term a will under the store σ and stack $\mathcal{S}$ reduce to the value v and store σ'.

Values v are of the form $[l_i{=}\iota_i\ ^{i\in 1..n}]$ mapping method names l_i to locations ι_i. A store σ maps locations to closures. A closure is the pair $\langle\varsigma(x)b, \mathcal{S}\rangle$ of a method body $\varsigma(x)b$ together with a local stack. A stack $\mathcal{S}$ maps variables to values. For any mapping f we let dom(f) denote the domain of f.

We shall often read stores and stacks as lists with $\emptyset$ denoting the empty store or stack, respectively. If σ is a store, then $\sigma, \iota \mapsto \langle\varsigma(x)b, \mathcal{S}\rangle$ denotes the extension of σ with the new entry $\langle\varsigma(x)b, \mathcal{S}\rangle$ on the *new* location ι.

The operational semantics is untyped; type annotations are simply removed when evaluating terms. We write $a{\Downarrow}v \cdot \sigma$ ("a converges to the value v and store σ") if we can deduce $\emptyset \cdot \emptyset \vdash a \rightsquigarrow v \cdot \sigma$ and $a{\Downarrow}$ iff $a{\Downarrow}v \cdot \sigma$ for some v and σ. If there is no v and σ such that $a{\Downarrow}v \cdot \sigma$ we write $a{\Uparrow}$ ("a diverges").

Type system. There are two forms of judgments for IOC: Type judgments and subtyping judgments. *Type judgments* are of the form $E \vdash a{:}A$ and state that the object a has type A under the assumptions in E, where E describes typing assumptions for free self variables. *Subtype judgments* $\vdash A <: B$ state that the type A is a subtype of B. Subtyping allows an object to be replaced by another with additional methods,

Type Environments $E ::= \emptyset \mid E, x : A$ *Types* $A, B ::= [l_i{:}B_i\ ^{i\in 1..n}]$

Method names l *Variables* x, y, z

Terms

a, b	$::=$	x	Variable
	$\mid$	$[l_i{=}\varsigma(x_i{:}A)b_i\ ^{i\in 1..n}]$	Object
	$\mid$	$a.l$	Method activation
	$\mid$	$a.l \Leftarrow \varsigma(x{:}A)b$	Method override
	$\mid$	$\texttt{clone}(a)$	Cloning
	$\mid$	$\texttt{let}\ x{:}A = a\ \texttt{in}\ b$	Local definition

Table 1 Syntax of IOC

Names

$p, q, r..x, y, z$

Variant Tags

$\ell, l,$ h

Types

T	::=	$\mu(X)T$	recursive type
	|	X	type variable
	|	$[\,\ell_1\_T_1..\ell_n\_T_n\,]$	variant type
	|	$\langle T_1..T_n\rangle$	tuple type
	|	T^I	channel type

I/O Tags

I	::=	r	input only
	|	w	output only
	|	b	either

Values

v	::=	x	name
	|	$\langle v_1..v_n\rangle$	tuple value
	|	ℓ_v	variant value

Processes

P	::=	$\mathbf{0}$	nil process
	|	$P\|P$	parallel
	|	$(\nu x{:}T)P$	restriction
	|	$p(x).P$	input
	|	$\overline{p}v.P$	output
	|	$!P$	replication
	|	let $x_1..x_n = v$ in P	tuple destructor
	|	case v of $[_{j\in 1..n}\ \ell_j\_(x_j) \rhd P_j]$	case
	|	wrong	error

where:

- In a recursive type $\mu(X)T$, variable X must be guarded in T, i.e., occur underneath a I/O-tag or underneath a variant tag;
- in the case statement, the tags ℓ_i ($i \in 1..n$) are pairwise distinct.

Table 2 The syntax of the typed π-calculus

but the common methods must have the same type. This invariance is necessary for the soundness of the reduction rules, i.e., avoiding requests on non-existing methods.

3 A TYPED MOBILE CALCULUS

In this section, we present the typed π-calculus on which we shall interpret IOC. The reader is referred to (Sangiorgi 1996) for details.

Syntax. The syntax of the typed π-calculus is given in Table 2. The process constructs are those of the monadic π-calculus (Milner, Parrow & Walker 1992) with matching replaced by a case construct. The latter can be thought of as a more disciplined form of matching, in which all tests on a given name are localised to a single place. The construct wrong stands for a process in which a run-time type error has occurred, i.e., for instance a communication in which the variant tag or the arity of the transmitted value was unexpected by its recipient. A soundness theorem guarantees that a well-typed process expression cannot reduce to an expression containing wrong.

Operational semantics. For the semantics of the π-calculus we adopt a labelled transition system. The advantage of a labelled semantics, compared to a reduction semantics (Milner 1991, Sangiorgi 1996), is that it easily allows us to define labelled forms of bisimulation. Process transitions are of the form $P \xrightarrow{\mu} P'$, where μ is given by the following syntax:

$$\mu ::= (\nu\tilde{n}{:}\tilde{T})\bar{p}v \mid pv \mid \tau \mid \texttt{wrong}$$

The label $(\nu\tilde{n}{:}\tilde{T})\bar{p}v$ denotes the output of the value v on the name p. The restriction $(\nu\tilde{n}{:}\tilde{T})$ where $\tilde{n}$ must be a subset of the names in v indicates that the names $\tilde{n}$ are bound names having types $\tilde{T}$. The label pv denotes the input of the value v over the name p. The action τ denotes an internal action. Finally, `wrong` denotes a run-time error. The rules for the early binding operational semantics are standard early rules of the π-calculus. The new, but expected, rules are those for `let` and `case`, in which run-time errors may be generated. For `case` we have (`let` is similar):

(CASE)

$$\frac{\ell_j \in \{\ell_1..\ell_n\}}{\texttt{case}\ \ell_j\_v\ \texttt{of}\ [\,\ell_1\_(x_1) \rhd P_1; \ldots; \ell_n\_(x_n) \rhd P_n\,] \xrightarrow{\tau} P_j\{v/x_j\}}$$

(CASE-W)

$$\frac{v \neq \ell_j\_v' \text{ or } \ell_j \notin \{\ell_1..\ell_n\}}{\texttt{case}\ v\ \texttt{of}\ [\,\ell_1\_(x_1) \rhd P_1; \ldots; \ell_n\_(x_n) \rhd P_n\,] \xrightarrow{\texttt{wrong}} \texttt{wrong}}$$

We write $P \xrightarrow{\mu}_d Q$ if $P \xrightarrow{\mu} Q$ is the only transitions that P can perform. And as usual we let $\xRightarrow{\mu}$ denote weak transitions, and $P \Longrightarrow P'$ means "$P \xRightarrow{\tau} P'$ or $P = P'$". Furthermore $\xRightarrow{\hat{\mu}} \overset{\text{def}}{=\!=} \Longrightarrow$ if $\mu = \tau$ and $\xRightarrow{\mu}$ otherwise.

Typing and subtyping. We recall that I/O annotations (Pierce & Sangiorgi 1993) are to separate the capabilities of reading and writing on a channel (we use "read" and "write" as synonymous for "input" and "output", respectively). For instance, a type $p : \langle S^{\mathrm{r}}\ T^{\mathrm{w}}\rangle^{\mathrm{b}}$ (for appropriate type expressions S and T) says that name p can be used *both* to read and to write and that any message at p carries a pair of names; moreover, the first component of the pair can be used by the recipient *only to read*, the second *only to write*.

Subtyping judgements are of the form $\Sigma \vdash S <: T$, where Σ represents the subtyping assumptions. Note that type annotation r (an input capability) gives covariance, w (an output capability) gives contravariance, and b (both capabilities) gives invariance.

A typing judgement $\Gamma \vdash P$ asserts that process P is well-typed in Γ, and $\Gamma \vdash v : T$ that value v has type T in Γ. A *type environment* Γ is a finite assignment of types to names. There is one typing rule for each process construct except `wrong`. There is one typing rule for each process construct except `wrong`. In the rules for input and output prefixes, the subject of the prefix is checked to possess the appropriate input or output capability in the type environment. For lack of space we omit the rules, see for instance (Sangiorgi 1996).

A subject reduction theorem guarantees us that if P is well-typed and $P \Longrightarrow Q$, then Q does not contain the process `wrong`.

Some derived constructs. In the translation we shall use: *Recursive definitions* $A(\tilde{x}) \stackrel{\text{def}}{=} P$, which can be defined the standard way using replication (c.f. (Milner 1991)); *polyadic inputs* $a(x_1..x_n).P$, defined as $a(y).\mathtt{let}\ \langle x_1..x_n\rangle = y\ \mathtt{in}\ P$ for $y \notin \mathrm{fn}(P)$; *variant inputs*, like $p\big[_{j\in 1..n}\ \ell_j\_\big[_{i\in 1..m}\ \ell_{i,j}\_(\tilde{x}_{i,j}) \rhd P_{i,j}\big]\big]$. The last abbreviation allows us to go down two levels within the structure of a variant value received in an input at p; in fact, this term interacts with output particles of the form $\overline{p}\ell_r\_\ell_{r,s}\_\tilde{w}$ (with $r \in 1..n$, $s \in 1..m$, and tuple $\tilde{w}$ of the same length as $\tilde{x}_{r,s}$) and, in doing so, it reduces to $P_{r,s}\{\tilde{w}/\tilde{x}_{r,s}\}$.

Barbed bisimulation and congruence. The behavioural equality we adopt for the π-calculus is *barbed congruence*. Barbed congruence is a bisimulation-based relation that has been used for a broad variety of calculi; its main advantage is that it can be uniformly defined on different calculi, for it requires of the calculus little more than a notion of reduction – the τ-step of the π-calculus.

Barbed congruence is defined as the congruence induced by *barbed bisimulation*. We write $P\Downarrow_q$ if P is *observable at* q, that is P can accept an input or an output communication with the environment along q; formally $P\Downarrow_q$ is true if $P \stackrel{\mu}{\Longrightarrow} P'$, for some P' and μ where μ is an input or output action at q.

Definition 1 (barbed bisimulation and congruence) Barbed bisimulation *is the largest symmetric relation $\dot{\approx}$ on processes such that $P \dot{\approx} Q$ implies:*

1. *whenever $P \Longrightarrow P'$ then there exists Q' such that $Q \Longrightarrow Q'$ and $P' \dot{\approx} Q'$;*
2. *for each name q, $P\Downarrow_q$ iff $Q\Downarrow_q$.*

Two processes P and Q are barbed congruent, *written $P \approx Q$, if $C[P] \dot{\approx} C[Q]$ for all contexts C.*

In an untyped calculus, no constraint is made on processes or contexts. In a typed setting, processes compared should have the same type, and should only be tested in contexts which respect such a type. We write $P \approx_\Gamma Q$ if $\Gamma \vdash P, Q$ and $C[P] \dot{\approx} C[Q]$ holds, in all contexts that respect Γ. We omit the formal definitions of the typed relations.

Barbed congruence requires a quantification over all contexts. Therefore proving process equalities can be heavy. Against this, it is important to have powerful proof techniques. One such a technique consists in using *labelled bisimilarities* whose definition does not require context quantification. For instance, in the untyped π-calculus barbed congruence can be recovered using the well-known *early labelled bisimilarity*. Its typed version, *typed early labelled bisimulation*, is studied by Boreale & Sangiorgi (n.d.). These techniques of labelled bisimilarities can be made more powerful by combining them with up-to techniques, like "up to parallel composition" and "up to injective substitutions".

4 THE INTERPRETATION

To understand the π-calculus interpretation, it is helpful to see first an intermediate interpretation into the *Higher-Order π-calculus* (HOπ) (Sangiorgi 1992), an extension of the π-calculus where arguments of communications and recursive definitions may be, besides names, also *abstractions*, i.e., parameterised processes. For the interpretation of IOC, we only need abstractions in recursive definitions. More precisely, we need certain parameters of recursive definitions to be functions from names to processes. An example of such a recursive definition is $K\langle f, p\rangle \stackrel{\mathrm{def}}{=} p(x).(f\langle p\rangle | K\langle f, x\rangle)$. Here, f is a function parameter, and p a name parameter; $f\langle p\rangle$ is the process obtained by applying function f to name p. We write functions from names to processes using a lambda notation, like in $\lambda(x, y).P$. The interpretation into HOπ is shown in Table 3. We have omitted the type annotations*.

$$
\begin{aligned}
\{\![[l_i{=}\varsigma(x_i)b_i\ ^{i\in 1..n}]]\!\}_p &\stackrel{\mathrm{def}}{=} (\nu s)(\overline{p}s \mid \mathtt{OB}\langle \lambda(x_1, r).\{\![b_1]\!\}_r, \ldots, \lambda(x_n, r).\{\![b_n]\!\}_r, s\rangle)\\
\{\![a.l_j]\!\}_p &\stackrel{\mathrm{def}}{=} (\nu q)(\{\![a]\!\}_q \mid q(x).\overline{x}l_j\mathtt{\_sel\_}p)\\
\{\![a.l_j{\Leftarrow}\varsigma(x_j)b]\!\}_p &\stackrel{\mathrm{def}}{=} (\nu q)(\{\![a]\!\}_q \mid q(x).\overline{x}l_j\mathtt{\_upd\_}\langle p, \lambda(x_j, r).\{\![b]\!\}_r\rangle)\\
\{\![x]\!\}_p &\stackrel{\mathrm{def}}{=} \overline{p}x\\
\{\![\mathtt{clone}(a)]\!\}_p &\stackrel{\mathrm{def}}{=} (\nu q)(\{\![a]\!\}_q \mid q(x).\overline{x}\mathtt{clone\_}p)\\
\{\![\mathtt{let}\ x = a\ \mathtt{in}\ b]\!\}_p^E &\stackrel{\mathrm{def}}{=} (\nu q)(\{\![a]\!\}_q \mid q(x).\{\![b]\!\}_p)
\end{aligned}
$$

where OB is defined as:

$$
\begin{aligned}
&\mathtt{OB}(f_1..f_n, s) \stackrel{\mathrm{def}}{=}\\
&\quad s\Big[_{i\in 1..n}\ l_i\mathtt{\_}[\ \mathtt{sel\_}(x) \rhd f_i\langle s, x\rangle \mid \mathtt{OB}\langle f_1..f_n, s\rangle;\\
&\qquad\qquad\qquad \mathtt{upd\_}(x, y) \rhd \bar{x}s \mid \mathtt{OB}\langle f_1..f_{i-1}, y, f_{i+1}..f_n, s\rangle\ ];\\
&\qquad\quad \mathtt{clone\_}(x) \rhd \mathtt{OB}\langle f_1..f_n, s\rangle \mid (\nu s')(\bar{x}s' \mid \mathtt{OB}\langle f_1..f_n, s'\rangle)\Big]
\end{aligned}
$$

Table 3 The intermediate translation into HOπ (sketch)

*We are omitting type annotations for ease of reading; they would be however necessary to make the definition formal. Types are taken into account in the interpretations into the π-calculus in Table 4.

The translation $\{\!\![a]\!\!\}_p$ of an IOC term a is located at a channel p. When a is an object value, with methods l_i ($i \in 1..n$), its translation is a process whose first action is to signal its valuehood by providing an access name s to its value-core, which is a process of the form $\mathtt{OB}\langle f_1..f_n, s\rangle$. This process is ready to accept along the access name s requests of selection, update and cloning for the methods l_j. The body of a method l_j is the function f_j; the set of these functions form the state of $\mathtt{OB}\langle f_1..f_n, s\rangle$.

We explain the behaviour of $\mathtt{OB}\langle f_1..f_n, s\rangle$ on the operations of selection, update and cloning. In case of a select operation $l_j\_\mathtt{sel}\_p$ (which reads "activate method l_j and use p as location for the resulting object") the body f_j of method l_j is activated, with arguments $\langle s, p\rangle$; argument s, the access name of the value-core $\mathtt{OB}\langle f_1..f_n, s\rangle$, represents the self-parameter. An update request $l_j\_\mathtt{upd}\_\langle p, f\rangle$ (which reads "replace current method body for l_j with f, and use p as the location of the resulting object") results in a side effect on $\mathtt{OB}$, whereby the j-th component of its state is updated to f. In a clone request $\mathtt{clone}\_p$ (which reads "create a copy of the current object with location p"), a new object is created that has the same value-core $\mathtt{OB}\langle f_1..f_n, s\rangle$. Note the recursive definition of $\mathtt{OB}\langle f_1..f_n, s\rangle$, which shows that $\mathtt{OB}\langle f_1..f_n, s\rangle$ may accept arbitrarily many requests at s.

Now, following the translation of HOπ into π-calculus (Sangiorgi 1992), we can turn the previous interpretation into a π-calculus one. For this, it suffices to make a recursive call with a functional argument, like $K\langle\lambda x.P\rangle$, into a first-order recursive call whose argument is a pointer to the function, like in: $(\nu b)(K\langle b\rangle \,|\, !b(x).P)$. Correspondingly, a function application becomes an output of the arguments of the function along the pointer to the function. The result of this transformation, with the addition of type annotations, is presented in Table 4.

As for the interpretations of Object Calculi into the λ-calculus (Abadi et al. 1996), so our translation of terms has an environment E as parameter in order to put the necessary type annotations in the translation of method selection. This parameter could be avoided by having, for instance, more type information on the syntax of method selection. We assume that $p, q, r, b, s \ldots$ are not IOC variables.

In the remainder of the paper, we shall call processes of the form $\mathtt{OB}^A\langle b_1..b_n, s\rangle$ an *object manager* (in the interpretation of an object, $\mathtt{OB}^A\langle b_1..b_n, s\rangle$ acts like an administrator for the object; it "owns" the object methods, in the sense that it is the only process which can reach them, via names b_i's).

Finally we need to show how to translate types. The translation of an object type must be a type that specifies repeated selection, update and clone operations.

$$\{\!\![[l_i{:}B_i\ ^{i\in 1..n}]]\!\!\} \stackrel{\text{def}}{=} \mu X.\Big[_{i\in 1..n}\ l_i\_[\ \mathtt{sel}\_\{\!\![B_i]\!\!\}^{\mathrm{w}^{\mathrm{w}}};\ \mathtt{upd}\_\langle X^{\mathrm{w}^{\mathrm{w}}}, \langle X^{\mathrm{w}}, \{\!\![B_i]\!\!\}^{\mathrm{w}^{\mathrm{w}}}\rangle^{\mathrm{w}}\rangle\ ];\ \mathtt{clone}\_X^{\mathrm{w}^{\mathrm{w}}}\Big]$$

The pattern of occurrences of w tags is determined by the protocol which implements select and update operations. What is important, however, is the level of nesting of w tags: An even number of nesting gives covariance, whereas an odd number of nesting gives contravariance. Thus, the component $\{\!\![B_i]\!\!\}$ is in covariant position on selection, and in contravariant position on update: This explains the invariance of

$$\{\![[l_i{=}\varsigma(x_i{:}A)b_i\ ^{i\in 1..n}]]\!\}^E_p \stackrel{\text{def}}{=} (\nu s{:}\{\![A]\!\}^{\mathrm{b}})(\overline{p}s \mid (\nu b_i{:}T^{\mathrm{b}}_{A,i}\ ^{i\in 1..n})(\mathrm{OB}^A\langle b_1..b_n, s\rangle \mid \prod_{i\in 1..n} !b_i(x_i, r).\{\![b_i]\!\}^{E,x_i:A}_r))$$

$$\{\![a.l_j]\!\}^E_p \stackrel{\text{def}}{=} (\nu q{:}\{\![[l_j{:}B_j]]\!\}^{\mathrm{w^b}})(\{\![a]\!\}^E_q \mid q(x).\overline{x}l_j\mathtt{\_sel\_}p)$$

$$\{\![a.l_j \Leftarrow \varsigma(x_j{:}A).b]\!\}^E_p \stackrel{\text{def}}{=} (\nu q{:}\{\![A]\!\}^{\mathrm{w^b}})(\{\![a]\!\}^E_q \mid (\nu b{:}T^{\mathrm{b}}_{A,j})q(x).(\overline{x}l_j\mathtt{\_upd\_}\langle p, b\rangle \mid !b(x_j, r).\{\![b]\!\}^{E,x_j:A}_r))$$

$$\{\![x]\!\}^E_p \stackrel{\text{def}}{=} \overline{p}x$$

$$\{\![\mathtt{clone}(a)]\!\}^E_p \stackrel{\text{def}}{=} (\nu q{:}\{\![A]\!\}^{\mathrm{w^b}})(\{\![a]\!\}^E_q \mid q(x).\overline{x}\mathtt{clone\_}p)$$

$$\{\![\mathtt{let}\ x{:}A = a\ \mathtt{in}\ b]\!\}^E_p \stackrel{\text{def}}{=} (\nu q{:}\{\![A]\!\}^{\mathrm{w^b}})(\{\![a]\!\}^E_q \mid q(x).\{\![b]\!\}^{E,x:A}_p)$$

The object manager OB^A is defined as:

$$\mathrm{OB}^A(b_1{:}T^{\mathrm{w}}_{A,1}..b_n{:}T^{\mathrm{w}}_{A,n}, s{:}\{\![A]\!\}^{\mathrm{b}}) \stackrel{\text{def}}{=}$$
$$s\Big[_{i\in 1..n}\ l_i\mathtt{\_}\big[\ \mathtt{sel\_}(x) \rhd \bar{b}_i\langle s, x\rangle \mid \mathrm{OB}^A\langle b_1..b_n, s\rangle;\ \ \mathtt{upd\_}(x, y) \rhd \bar{x}s \mid \mathrm{OB}\langle b_1..b_{i-1}, y, b_{i+1}..b_n, s\rangle\ \big];$$
$$\mathtt{clone\_}(x) \rhd \mathrm{OB}^A\langle b_1..b_n, s\rangle \mid (\nu s'{:}\{\![A]\!\}^{\mathrm{b}})(\bar{x}s' \mid \mathrm{OB}^A\langle b_1..b_n, s'\rangle)\Big]$$

and where

- $A = [l_i{:}B_i\ ^{i\in 1..n}]$ and $T_{A,j} \stackrel{\text{def}}{=} \langle \{\![A]\!\}^{\mathrm{w}}, \{\![B_j]\!\}^{\mathrm{w^w}}\rangle$
- in the encoding of selection, B_j is the unique type s.t. $E \vdash a{:}[\ldots, l_j{:}B_j, \ldots]$ holds, if one such judgement exists (the unicity of this type if a consequence of the minimum-type property of IOC), B_j can be any type otherwise;
- in the rule for update, x does not occour free in b.

Table 4 The interpretation of IOC into π-calculus

object types on the common components, in rule (OSUB OBJ) (the interpretation of IOC into the λ-calculus (Abadi et al. 1996) does the same). Type environments are then interpreted componetwise as $\{\![E, x{:}A]\!\} \stackrel{\text{def}}{=} \{\![E]\!\}, x{:}\{\![A]\!\}^{\mathrm{w}}$ and $\{\![\emptyset]\!\} \stackrel{\text{def}}{=} \emptyset$.

5 SIMPLIFYING THE IMPERATIVE PART OF THE ENCODING

In the interpretations of IOC in Section 4, the key process is the object manager OB. This process is given as a recursive definition in which certain parameters may change during time. Having a state, these processes may be regarded as "imperative". In this section we modify the encoding, so that the only imperative processes are cell-like processes, each of which just stores a name. All remaining processes will be stateless, and therefore may be regarded as "functional". We thus obtain a clean separation of the interpretation into a functional part and a very simple imperative part. Technically, this factorisation allows us take full advantage of various π-calculus proof techniques for functional names and functional processes, discussed below.

A π-calculus name is *functional* if its response to incoming messages does not change over time. Typically, a name a is functional if it only appears in subexpressions of the form $(\nu a)(!a(p).P|Q)$ where P and Q only possess the output capability on a, or of the form $(\nu a)(a(p).P|Q)$ if, in addition, a can only be used once in output. (In (Sangiorgi 1997) names obeying these constraints are called *uniformly receptive*.)

Functional names have advantages. First, they can be implemented more efficiently than arbitrary names as done, for instance, in the language PICT (Pierce & Turner 1997). Another advantage of functional names is their algebraic properties, among which copying or distributivity laws like

$$(\nu a)(!a(b).P|Q|R) = (\nu a)(!a(b).P|Q) \mid (\nu a)(!a(b).P|R),$$

whose effect is to localise computation. Another property is τ-insensitiveness: Interactions along a functional name may not affect a process behaviour. As a consequence, when comparing the behaviour of two processes there are fewer configurations to take into account. Let us call a process *functional* if all inputs made by the process during its lifetime are at functional names. Functional languages (the λ-calculus, the Functional Object Calculus FOC) may be interpreted into a sublanguage of the π-calculus in which all names are functional.

The new, factorised, encoding is defined in Table 5. To enhance readability we drop types, as they are the same as in the previous encoding. Only the clause for evaluated objects changes. Previously, the access name of the methods was part of (the state of) the object manager. By contrast, now a level of indirection is introduced, such that when updating a method, the indirection, instead of the object manager, changes; this way the object manager becomes functional.

A cell $\texttt{Cell}\langle\iota, n\rangle$ stores a pointer n to a method; and can be accessed for read and write operations at ι. The cells are the only imperative processes in the encoding. Being imperative, a cell may be *shared* by several clients, but may not be *copied* among them. By contrast, all other resources are functional and they may be copied among their clients. The copy operator `Copy` is used to create new cells in a clone operation and signal completion after this has been performed. To save space we omit the definition of `Cell` and `Copy`.

This factorised encoding is less compact, but has a simpler correctness proof, than the previous encoding of Section 4. In the next section, we use this factorised encoding for proving the correctness of the original one.

$$[\![[l_i{=}\varsigma(x_i{:}A)b_i\ ^{i\in 1..n}]]\!]_p \stackrel{\text{def}}{=} (\nu s)(\bar{p}s \mid (\nu\iota_1..\iota_n)(\mathtt{OB}_f\langle\iota_1\ldots\iota_n, s\rangle \mid \prod_{i\in 1..n}(\nu b_i)(\mathtt{Cell}\langle\iota_i, b_i\rangle \mid !b_i(x_i, r).[\![b_i]\!]_r)))$$

The other clauses are as for the original translation in Table 4.

The object manager is now defined as follows, with $\tilde{\iota}$ denoting $\iota_1..\iota_n$, and $\tilde{\iota}'$ denoting $\iota'_1..\iota'_n$:

$$\begin{array}{l}\mathtt{OB}_f(\tilde{\iota}, s) \stackrel{\text{def}}{=} \\ !s\Big[_{i\in 1..n}\ l_i\text{\_}\big[\ \mathtt{sel\_}(x) \rhd (\nu g)(\overline{\iota_i}\mathtt{read\_}g.g(m).\overline{m}\langle s, x\rangle); \\ \qquad\qquad\quad \mathtt{upd\_}(x, y) \rhd \overline{\iota_i}\mathtt{write\_}y.\overline{x}s)\ \big]; \\ \qquad\quad \mathtt{clone\_}(x) \rhd (\nu\tilde{\iota}', s')(\mathtt{OB}_f\langle\tilde{\iota}', s'\rangle \mid \mathtt{Copy}^n\langle\tilde{\iota}, \tilde{\iota}', x, s'\rangle)\ \Big]\end{array}$$

Table 5 The factorised encoding

6 CORRECTNESS OF THE INTERPRETATION

6.1 Correctness of the interpretation of types

The proofs for the correctness of the interpretation of types is a straightforward adaption of the proofs for the similar properties in (Sangiorgi 1996).

Theorem 2 (correctness for subtyping) *For all A, B, it holds that $\vdash A <: B$ iff $\emptyset \vdash \{\![A]\!\} <: \{\![B]\!\}$.*

Theorem 3 (correctness on type judgements)

1. *If $E \vdash a{:}A$ then, for all p, it holds that $\{\![E]\!\}, p{:}\{\![A]\!\}^{\mathrm{w^w}} \vdash \{\![a]\!\}^E_p$.*
2. *If $\{\![E]\!\}, p{:}\{\![A]\!\}^{\mathrm{w^w}} \vdash \{\![a]\!\}^E_p$, then $E \vdash a{:}A$.*

6.2 Operational correctness

We first prove the operational correctness of the factorised encoding of Section 5; then we relate this encoding to the original one of Section 4.

Operational correctness of the factorised encoding. The proof of the correctness of the interpretation w.r.t. Abadi and Cardelli's operational semantics has a few tricky points. First of all we need to extend the translation to deal with configurations (objects plus stores plus stacks) in the semantics. We therefore need to add translations of stores (σ), stacks ($\mathcal{S}$) and values (v). We found it quite difficult to make such an extension of the original encoding of Table 4 due to sharing of closures. We solve this problem by using instead the factorised encoding of Section 5. A location ι of a store holds a method closure (which is a method together with its stack); we translate it using a cell located at ι that holds the address of the method closure (which is the translation of the method together with a private stack).

$$[\![\sigma, \iota \mapsto \langle \varsigma(x)b, \mathcal{S}\rangle]\!] \stackrel{\text{def}}{=} [\![\sigma]\!] \mid (\nu \mathrm{dom}(\mathcal{S}), m)(\mathtt{Cell}\langle \iota, m\rangle \mid !m(x,r).[\![b]\!]_r \mid [\![\mathcal{S}]\!])$$

A stack binds values to variables, so we translate it as an object manager located on the variable name.

$$[\![\mathcal{S}, x \mapsto [l_i{=}\iota_i\ ^{i\in 1..n}]]\!] \stackrel{\text{def}}{=} [\![\mathcal{S}]\!] \mid \mathrm{OB}_f\langle \iota_1 \ldots \iota_n, x\rangle$$

We have two types of configurations in the operational semantics for Imperative Object Calculus; initial configurations of the form $\sigma \cdot \mathcal{S} \vdash a$ and final configurations of the form $v \cdot \sigma$. They are translated as follows:

$$\begin{aligned}
[\![\sigma \cdot \mathcal{S} \vdash a]\!]_p &\stackrel{\text{def}}{=} (\nu \mathrm{dom}(\sigma))([\![\sigma]\!] \mid (\nu \mathrm{dom}(\mathcal{S}))([\![\mathcal{S}]\!] \mid [\![a]\!]_p)) \\
[\![[l_i{=}\iota_i\ ^{i\in 1..n}] \cdot \sigma]\!]_p &\stackrel{\text{def}}{=} (\nu s, \mathrm{dom}(\sigma))(\bar{p}s \mid \mathrm{OB}_f\langle \iota_1 \ldots \iota_n, s\rangle \mid [\![\sigma]\!])
\end{aligned}$$

That is, in both cases we simply translate each component of the configurations and appropriately hide their access. Below, $\sim$ is the strong version of barbed congruence.

Theorem 4 *If* $\sigma \cdot \mathcal{S} \vdash a \leadsto v \cdot \sigma'$ *then* $[\![\sigma \cdot \mathcal{S} \vdash a]\!]_p \Longrightarrow_d \sim [\![v \cdot \sigma']\!]_p$.

Lemma 5 *Suppose a is well-typed. If* $a\Uparrow$ *then* $[\![\emptyset \cdot \emptyset \vdash a]\!]_p$ *has an infinite computation* $[\![\emptyset \cdot \emptyset \vdash a]\!]_p \xrightarrow{\tau}_d P_1 \ldots \xrightarrow{\tau}_d P_n \xrightarrow{\tau}_d \ldots$.

Theorem 6 *Suppose a is well-typed. If* $[\![\emptyset \cdot \emptyset \vdash a]\!]_p \Downarrow_p$, *there exists a value* v, *and a store* σ, *s.t.* $\sigma \cdot \mathcal{S} \vdash a \leadsto v \cdot \sigma$

Relating the original and the factorised encodings. We have not been able to prove that the translations of an IOC object, according to the factorised encoding and to the original encoding are equated by some known behavioural equivalence of the π-calculus — the factorised encoding yields richer behaviours. However, we have been able to extend the notion of *ready simulation* (Bloom et al. 1995, Larsen & Skou 1991) to the π-calculus and prove that the two translations of an object are in a ready simulation relation. This is a rather weak result, but, together with the correctness of the factorised encoding, it suffices to prove the operational correctness of the original encoding.

Definition 7 (Ready simulation) Ready simulation *is the largest relation* $\prec$ *s.t.* $P \prec Q$ *implies:*

1. *If* $P \xrightarrow{\mu} P'$*; then there exist a* Q' *s.t.* $Q \stackrel{\hat{\mu}}{\Longrightarrow} Q'$ *and* $P' \prec Q'$.
2. *If* $Q \xrightarrow{\mu}$*; then* $P \stackrel{\mu}{\Longrightarrow}$.

Theorem 8 $\{\!\![a]\!\!\}_p \prec [\![\emptyset \cdot \emptyset \vdash a]\!]_p$.

Theorem 9 *Suppose a is well-typed, then* $\{\!\![a]\!\!\}_p \Uparrow$ *iff* $[\![\emptyset \cdot \emptyset \vdash a]\!]_p \Uparrow$ *and* $\{\!\![a]\!\!\}_p \Downarrow$ *iff* $[\![\emptyset \cdot \emptyset \vdash a]\!]_p \Downarrow$

Proof. We first argue that $\{\!\![a]\!\!\}_p$ cannot deadlock. Assume that $\{\!\![a]\!\!\}_p$ can deadlock, that is there exists a P such that $\{\!\![a]\!\!\}_p \Longrightarrow P \not\xrightarrow{\mu}$. Now since $\{\!\![a]\!\!\} \prec [\![\emptyset \cdot \emptyset \vdash a]\!]_p$ there must exist a Q such that $[\![\emptyset \cdot \emptyset \vdash a]\!]_p \Longrightarrow Q$ with $P \prec Q$.

By Theorem 4 if a converges then $[\![\emptyset \cdot \emptyset \vdash a]\!]_p$ will also converge and by Lemma 5 if a diverges then $[\![\emptyset \cdot \emptyset \vdash a]\!]_p$ will also diverge; so $[\![\emptyset \cdot \emptyset \vdash a]\!]_p$ cannot deadlock. Then there must exist a μ s.t. $Q \xrightarrow{\mu}$. By the second clause of the definition of ready simulation we infer $P \stackrel{\mu}{\Longrightarrow}$, which is a contradiction.

Now the theorem follows from Theorem 8 and the fact that $[\![\emptyset \cdot \emptyset \vdash a]\!]_p$ either converges or diverges (it cannot do both, because of Theorem 4 and Lemma 5). □

Adequacy and soundness of the original interpretation. From Theorems 4 and 6 and Corollary 9, we infer:

Corollary 10 (computational adequacy) *If a is well-typed, then* $a \Downarrow$ *iff* $\{\!\![a]\!\!\}_p \Downarrow_p$.

Behavioural equivalences like barbed congruence or the Morris-style contextual equivalence can also be defined in IOC (in fact, on IOC the two equivalences coincide). We write $a \simeq_B b$ if a and b are closed terms of IOC of type B and are barbed congruent.

We can show soundness of the translation using compositionality of the encoding and adequacy. This tells us that the equalities that can be proven using the translation are valid equalities.

Theorem 11 (soundness) *Assume* $\emptyset \vdash a, b{:}A$. *If* $\{\!\![a]\!\!\}_p \approx_{p:\{\!\![A]\!\!\}^{ww}} \{\!\![b]\!\!\}_p$, *then* $a \simeq_A b$.

As for the encodings of λ-calculi into π-calculus, so in the case of FOC and IOC the converse of soundness does not hold ((Sangiorgi 1995, Sangiorgi 1996)).

7 COMPARISONS WITH THE INTERPRETATION OF FOC

In their book, Abadi and Cardelli consider not only the imperative, but also the functional paradigm for Object Calculi. In this section we briefly compare the (first-order) Imperative and Functional Object Calculi, and their encodings into the π-calculus. The syntax of the *Functional Object Calculus* (FOC) is the same as for the imperative except that we do not have the `let` and `clone` constructs. The operational semantics, however, is very different. In the functional case, stores and stacks are not necessary and a simple reduction semantics can be given, using the rules below, where $a = [l_i{=}\varsigma(x_i{:}A_i)b_i \ ^{i \in 1..n}]$:

$$a.l_j \leadsto b_j\{^a\!/\!_{x_j}\} \qquad (j \in 1..n)$$
$$a.l_j{\Leftarrow}\varsigma(x{:}A)b \leadsto [l_j{=}\varsigma(x{:}A)b,\ l_i{=}\varsigma(x_i{:}A_i)b_i \ ^{i \in 1..n \setminus \{j\}}] \qquad (j \in 1..n)$$

As a consequence of the differences in the operational semantics, certain basic laws of FOC, like $a.l_j \ = \ b_j\{^a\!/\!_{x_j}\}$ $(j \in 1..n)$, do not hold in IOC.

In (Sangiorgi 1996), FOC is translated onto the same typed π-calculus we use in this paper. Remarkably, despite the strong differences in the operational semantics, the interpretations of IOC and FOC into the π-calculus are structurally very close. Roughly, the only difference between the two translations is in the object manager. The FOC manager, reported below, is a functional process. This difference has consequences on the update requests: On such a request, the FOC manager always generates a new object manager, whereas the IOC manager works by having side effect on itself.

$$\mathrm{OB}^A_f(b_1{:}T^{\mathrm{w}}_{A,1}..b_n{:}T^{\mathrm{w}}_{A,n}, s{:}\{\![A]\!\}^{\mathrm{b}}) \stackrel{\mathrm{def}}{=} !s\Big[_{i \in 1..n} l_i\_\big[\mathtt{sel\_}(x) \rhd \bar{b}_i\langle s, x\rangle;$$
$$\mathtt{upd\_}(x, y) \rhd (\nu s'{:}\{\![A]\!\}^{\mathrm{b}})(\overline{x}s' \mid \mathrm{OB}^A_f\langle b_1..b_{i-1}, y, b_{i+1}..b_n, s'\rangle)\big]\Big]$$

The functional and the imperative nature of, respectively, FOC and IOC, is reflected in the functional and the imperative nature of the object managers of the π-calculus interpretations. The commonalities between the interpretations of FOC and IOC allow us to reuse certain proofs, most notably those on types (see Theorem 2 and 3), but also certain proofs about behavioural properties of objects (a good example of this is the proof of the law (EQ SUB OBJ), in Section 8).

8 REASONING ABOUT OBJECTS

In this section we give some examples of how the π-calculus interpretation can be used to validate some basic behavioural properties of IOC.

Lemma 12 *Let* $o = [l_i{=}\varsigma(x_i{:}A)b_i \ ^{i \in 1..n}]$, $A = [l_i{:}B_i \ ^{i \in 1..n}]$, *and* $o{:}A$. *Then*

1. $o.l_j \simeq_{B_j}$ `let` $x_j{:}A = o$ `in` b_j
2. *If* $x{:}A \vdash b{:}B_j$ *then* $o.l_j{\Leftarrow}\varsigma(x{:}A)b \simeq_A [l_j{=}\varsigma(x{:}A)b,\ l_i{=}\varsigma(x_i{:}A)b_i \ ^{i \in 1..n \setminus \{j\}}]$

3. $\texttt{clone}(o) \simeq_A o$
4. *If* $a\Downarrow$, $a{:}B$, $b{:}C$ $x \notin \mathrm{fv}(b)$, *then* $\texttt{let}\ x{:}B = a\ \texttt{in}\ b \simeq_C b$.
5. *If* $x \notin \mathrm{fv}(o)$, $y \notin \mathrm{fv}(a)$, $a{:}B$ *and* $(\texttt{let}\ x{:}B = a\ \texttt{in}\ \texttt{let}\ y{:}A = o\ \texttt{in}\ b) : C$, *then*

$$(\texttt{let}\ x{:}B = a\ \texttt{in}\ \texttt{let}\ y{:}A = o\ \texttt{in}\ b) \simeq_C (\texttt{let}\ y{:}A = o\ \texttt{in}\ \texttt{let}\ x{:}B = a\ \texttt{in}\ b)$$

6. *(law (*EQ SUB OBJECT*)): If* $m \geq n$, *then* $o \simeq_A [l_i{=}\varsigma(x_i{:}B)b_i\ ^{i \in 1..m}]$.

It is interesting to look at the difference between FOC and IOC on objects of the form $o.l_j$, for $o = [l_i{=}\varsigma(x_i{:}A)b_i\ ^{i \in 1..n}]$ $(j \in 1..n)$, using the π-calculus interpretations of FOC and IOC . In the case of FOC, o is interpreted as a functional process and we can therefore apply copy laws to derive $\{\![o.l_j]\!\}_p \approx \{\![b_j\{^o/_{x_j}\}]\!\}_p$. By contrast, in the case of IOC, object o is interpreted as a process with a state, and we can only infer $\{\![o.l_j]\!\}_p \approx \{\![\texttt{let}\ x_j{:}A = o\ \texttt{in}\ b_j]\!\}_p$, as by Lemma 12(1).

Laws 1.-5. can be validated using the theory of the untyped π-calculus. Law (EQ SUB OBJECT) of Lemma 12 can be validated using the typed labelled bisimulation technique (Boreale & Sangiorgi n.d.). Roughly, a typed bisimulation relation consists of triples (Γ, P, Q), and (Γ, P, Q) being in a typed bisimulation means that P and Q are undistinguishable by an observer whose use of names respect the type informations in Γ.

This is the first proof of (EQ SUB OBJECT) for IOC we are aware of. The proof can be easily adapted to the analogous law for FOC.

9 EXTENSIONS AND FURTHER WORK

Our interpretation of IOC can be extended to accommodate other type features discussed in (Abadi & Cardelli 1996), like variant tags, recursive types, polymorphic types. *Variant tags* are tags on method names which allow only selection or update operations on a method, so to have a richer subtyping relation. These tags yield the same form of subtyping on IOC types as that induced by the tags {r, w, b} on the π-calculus types. We can capture them with a simple refinement of the encoding of types. For *recursive types*, we just map type variables of a IOC type to type variables of the π-calculus types. Similarly, it is possible to handle *polymorphic types*, using polymorphic extensions of the π-calculus (Turner 1996).

The extensibility of the interpretation of imperative objects, and its resemblance to the interpretation of functional objects, suggests that the representation of objects into the π-calculus is a robust one, and that it could be used for giving the semantics to, and proving properties of, a wide range of object-oriented languages, possibly combining imperative, functional and concurrent features. We have begun examining the case of Obliq (Cardelli 1995), which has imperative objects and constructs for concurrency and distribution.

We hope the study of the Object Calculi from within the π-calculus will help to develop concurrent or distributed versions of the Object Calculi.

An interesting and challenging question is finding a direct characterisation of the equivalence induced on IOC terms by the encoding into the π-calculus (where two IOC terms are equated if their process translations are behaviourally equivalent).

Acknowledgments. Thanks to Uwe Nestmann, Martín Abadi and the anonymous referees for their comments on an earlier draft.

REFERENCES

Abadi, M. & Cardelli, L. (1996). *A Theory of Objects.* Monographs in Computer Science, Springer Verlag.

Abadi, M., Cardelli, L. & Viswanathan, R. (1996). An interpretation of Objects and Objects Types. *In* '23rd POPL', ACM Press.

Aceto, L., Hüttel, H., Ingólfsdóttir, A. & Kleist, J. (1997). Relating semantic models for the object calculus. *In* 'Express 97 Workshop', Vol. 7 of *ENTCS*, Elsevier Science B.V.

Bloom, B., Istrail, S. & Meyer, A. R. (1995). 'Bisimulation can't be traced'. *Journal of the Association for Computing Machinery* **42**(1), 232–268.

Boreale, M. & Sangiorgi, D. (n.d.). Bisimulation without matching. To appear.

Cardelli, L. (1995). 'A language with distributed scope'. *Computing Systems* **8**(1), 27–59.

Gordon, A. D., Hankin, P. D. & Lassen, S. B. (1997). Compilation and equivalence of imperative objects. *In* '17th FST&TCS Conference'.

Gordon, A. D. & Rees, G. D. (1996). Bisimilarity for a first-order calculus of objects with subtyping. *In* '23rd POPL', ACM Press.

Honda, K. (1996). Composing processes. *In* '23rd POPL', ACM Press.

Jones, C. (1993). A π-calculus semantics for an object-based design notation. *In* 'CONCUR '93', Vol. 715 of *LNCS*, Springer Verlag.

Kobayashi, N., Pierce, B. & Turner, D. (1996). Linearity and the pi-calculus. *In* '23rd POPL', ACM Press.

Larsen, K. G. & Skou, A. (1991). 'Bisimulation through probabilistic testing'. *Information and Computation* **94**(1), 1–28.

Liu, X. & Walker, D. (1996). Partial confluence of processes and systems of objects. Submitted for publication.

Mason, I. A. & Talcott, C. L. (1991). 'Equivalence in functional languages with effects'. *Journal of Functional Programming* **1**(3), 287–327.

Milner, R. (1989). *Communication and Concurrency.* Prentice Hall.

Milner, R. (1991). The polyadic π-calculus: a tutorial. Technical Report ECS–LFCS–91–180, University of Edinburgh.

Milner, R., Parrow, J. & Walker, D. (1992). 'A calculus of mobile processes, (Parts I and II)'. *Information and Computation* **100**, 1–77.

Milner, R. & Sangiorgi, D. (1992). Barbed bisimulation. *In* '19th ICALP', Vol. 623 of *LNCS*, Springer-Verlag.

Morris, J. H. (1968). Lambda-Calculus Models of Programming Languages. PhD thesis, MIT.

Philippou, A. & Walker, D. (1996). On transformations of concurrent object programs. *In* 'CONCUR'96', LNCS, Springer Verlag.

Pierce, B. C. & Sangiorgi, D. (1993). Typing and subtyping for mobile processes. *In* 'LICS'93', IEEE Computer Society Press.

Pierce, B. C. & Turner, D. N. (1997). Pict: A programming language based on the pi-calculus. Technical report CSCI 476, Indiana University.

Sangiorgi, D. (1992). Expressing Mobility in Process Algebras: First-Order and Higher-Order Paradigms. PhD thesis, University of Edinburgh.

Sangiorgi, D. (1995). Lazy functions and mobile processes. Technical Report RR-2515, INRIA-Sophia Antipolis.

Sangiorgi, D. (1996). An interpretation of typed objects into typed π-calculus. Technical report RR-3000, INRIA-Sophia Antipolis.

Sangiorgi, D. (1997). The name discipline of uniform receptiveness. *In* 'ICALP'97' Vol. 1256 of *LNCS*, Springer Verlag.

Turner, D. (1996). The polymorphic pi-calculus: Theory and Implementation. PhD thesis, University of Edinburgh.

Vaandrager, F. (1990). A process algebra semantics of POOL. *In* 'Applications of process algebra', Vol. 17 of *Tracts in Theoretical Computer Science*, Cambridge University Press.

Vasconcelos, V. & Tokoro, M. (1994). Typed concurrent objects. *In* 'ECOOP'94', Vol. 821 of *LNCS*, Springer Verlag.

Walker, D. (1995). 'Objects in the π-calculus'. *Information and Computation* **116**, 253–271.

10 BIOGRAPHY

Josva Kleist got his Masters degree in 1994 from Aalborg University, where he is currently a PhD student. His primary research interests are mobile and higher-order process calculi, models of object-oriented programming languages and type systems.

Davide Sangiorgi got his Masters degree from University of Pisa 1987 and his PhD from University of Edinburgh in 1993. He is currently a member of Scientific Staff in the Meije Project at INRIA-Sophia Antipolis, France. His research interests are concurrent systems, especially mobile and higher-order: semantics, verification techniques; high-level languages for specifying and programming concurrent activities; systolic automata and systems.

21

Relating Linear and Branching Model Checking

O. Kupferman
UC Berkeley
EECS Department, Berkeley CA 94720-1770, U.S.A.
Email: orna@eecs.berkeley.edu, URL: www.eecs.berkeley.edu/~orna

M.Y. Vardi
Rice University
Department of Computer Science, Houston, TX 77005-1892, U.S.A.
Email: vardi@cs.rice.edu, URL: www.cs.rice.edu/~vardi

Abstract

The difference in the complexity of branching and linear model checking has been viewed as an argument in favor of the branching paradigm. In particular, the computational advantage of CTL model checking over LTL model checking makes CTL a popular choice, leading to efficient model-checking tools for this logic. Can we use these tools in order to verify linear properties? In this paper we relate branching and linear model checking. With each LTL formula ψ, we associate a CTL formula ψ_A that is obtained from ψ by preceding each temporal operator by the universal path quantifier A. We first describe a number of attempts to utilize the tight syntactic relation between ψ and ψ_A in order to use CTL model-checking tools in the process of checking the formula ψ. Neither attempt, however, suggests a method that is guaranteed to perform better than usual LTL model checkers. We then claim that, in practice, LTL model checkers perform nicely on formulas with equivalences of CTL. In fact, they often proceed essentially as the ones for CTL.

1 INTRODUCTION

Temporal logics, which are modal logics geared towards the description of the temporal ordering of events, have been adopted as a powerful tool for specifying and verifying concurrent programs [Pnu77, Pnu81]. One of the most significant developments in this area is the discovery of algorithmic methods for verifying temporal-logic properties of *finite-state* programs [CE81, LP85, QS81]. This derives its significance both from the fact that many synchronization and communication protocols can be modeled as finite-state programs, as well as from the great ease of use of fully algorithmic methods. Finite-state programs can be modeled by transition systems where each state has a bounded de-

Programming Concepts and Methods D. Gries, & W-P. de Roever (Eds.)

scription, and hence can be characterized by a fixed number of boolean atomic propositions. In temporal-logic *model checking*, we verify the correctness of a finite-state program with respect to a desired behavior by checking whether a labeled transition system that models the program satisfies a temporal logic formula that specifies this behavior (for a survey, see [CGL93]).

Two possible views regarding the nature of time induce two types of temporal logics [Lam80]. In *linear* temporal logics, time is treated as if each moment in time has a unique possible future. Thus, linear temporal logic formulas are interpreted over linear sequences and we regard them as describing a behavior of a single computation of a program. In *branching* temporal logics, each moment in time may split into various possible futures. Accordingly, the structures over which branching temporal logic formulas are interpreted can be viewed as infinite computation trees, each describing the behavior of the possible computations of a nondeterministic program.

In the linear temporal logic LTL, formulas are composed from the set of atomic propositions using the usual Boolean connectives as well as the temporal operators G ("always"), F ("eventually"), X ("next"), and U ("until"). For example, the LTL formula $\psi = G(req \rightarrow F grant)$ refers to the atomic propositions *req* and *grant* and is true in a computation iff every state in the computation in which request is valid is followed by some state in the future in which grant is valid. The branching temporal logic CTL* augments LTL by the path quantifiers E ("there exists a computation") and A ("for all computations"). For example, the CTL* formula $\varphi = AG(req \rightarrow EF grant)$ is true in a computation tree iff in all its computations, every state in which request is valid branches to at least one computation in which grant is eventually valid. The branching temporal logic CTL is a fragement of CTL* in which every temporal operator is preceded by a path quantifier. For example, while φ above is a CTL formula, the CTL* formula $AG(req \rightarrow F grant)$ is not a CTL formula. Finally, the branching temporal logic $\forall$CTL is a fragement of CTL in which only universal path quantification is allowed. Formally, one introduces a positive normal form for CTL formulas so that $\forall$CTL is the syntactic fragement of CTL that does not employ the path quantifier E. For an LTL formula ψ, we denote by ψ_A the $\forall$CTL formula obtained from ψ by preceding each temporal operator by the path quantifier A. For example, ψ_A for ψ above is $AG(req \rightarrow AF grant)$.

Given a transition system M and a linear temporal logic formula ψ, the model-checking problem for M and ψ is to decide whether ψ holds in all the computations of M. When ψ is a branching temporal logic formula, the problem is to decide whether ψ holds in the computation tree of M. The complexity of model checking for both linear and branching temporal logics is well understood: suppose we are given a transition system of size n and a temporal logic formula of size m. For the branching temporal logic CTL, model-checking algorithms run in time $O(nm)$ [CES86], while, for the linear temporal logic LTL, model-checking algorithms run in time $n2^{O(m)}$ [LP85]. Since LTL model checking is PSPACE-complete [SC85], the latter bound probably cannot be improved.

The difference in the complexity of linear and branching model checking has been viewed as an argument in favor of the branching paradigm. In particular, the computational advantage of CTL model checking over LTL model checking makes CTL a popular choice, leading to efficient model-checking tools for this logic. Can we use these tools in order to verify linear properties? A straightforward relation between LTL and CTL model checking follows from the fact that LTL model checking can be reduced to the language-containment problem [VW86], which itself can be reduced to searching for fair paths, and hence to CTL model checking [VW86, CDK93]. Such an approach, however, involves the definition of a new transition system whose size is exponential in the length of the LTL formula. As such, it does not enjoy the computational advantage of CTL. The real challenge is to relate CTL and LTL model checking in a practical way, one that would enable us to use CTL model-checking tools in order to perform efficient model checking on some fragement of LTL.

A straightforward approach is as follows: given a transition system M and an LTL formula ψ to be checked with respect to M, try to translate the CTL* formula $A\psi$ to an equivalent CTL formula φ, and then check M with respect to φ. This approach has two drawbacks. First, the problem of deciding whether $A\psi$ has an equivalent CTL formula φ is still open, and so, of course, is the harder problem of constructing φ in cases it exists. Second, even when such φ exists, it may be substantially longer than ψ, making the whole effort useless. A partial success for this approach is presented in [KG96, Sch97], which identify fragments of CTL* that can be easily translated in to CTL.

In this paper we study a more modest approach: instead looking for some equivalent CTL formula to $A\psi$, we restrict ourselves to the specific candidate ψ_A. This approach is weaker, in the sense that $A\psi$ may have an equivalent CTL formula and still not be equivalent to ψ_A. For example, $\psi = (Xp) \vee (Xq)$ is not equivalent to $\psi_A = (AXp) \vee (AXq)$, yet is equivalent to the CTL formula $AX(p \vee q)$. Nevertheless, this approach does not suffer from the drawbacks mentioned above: we know how to decide whether $A\psi$ and ψ_A are equivalent, the construction of ψ_A from ψ is straightforward, and the length of ψ_A is at most double the length of ψ. In addition, $A\psi$ is always weaker than ψ_A (that is, the implication $\psi_A \rightarrow A\psi$ is valid for all ψ), which would turn out to be useful for some heuristics.

We first study the problem of deciding whether $A\psi$ and ψ_A are equivalent. As $A\psi$ and ψ_A are CTL* formulas, the known 2EXPTIME upper bound for CTL* satisfiability [ES84, EJ88] suggests an obvious 2EXPTIME upper bound for the above equivalence problem. Moreover, as $A\psi$ and ψ_A are $\forall$CTL* formulas, the problem can be solved in EXPSPACE [KV95]. We present here an EXPSPACE algorithm that is much simpler than the one in [KV95], as it avoids Safra's complicated co-determinization construction [Saf89] that is used in the definition of the maximal models described there. Our hopes to use the tight syntactic relation between $A\psi$ and ψ_A in order to improve this bound were not fulfilled. We conjecture that the problem can be solved in polynomial space, which would match our lower bound.

So, the first attempt, of checking the sensitivity of the LTL specification to branching, does not seem very appealing. We then turn to consider the second operand of the model-checking problem, namely the transition system M. We say that a transition system M is *indifferent* iff for all LTL formulas ψ, we have that M satisfies $A\psi$ iff M satisfies ψ_A. Indifference is a helpful property: in order to model check either an LTL or an ∀CTL formula in an indifferent transition system, one can use both LTL and CTL model-checking tools. We characterize transition systems that are indifferent and show that the problem of determining whether a transition system is indifferent is NLOGSPACE-complete. Hence, it is easy check a given transition system for having this property. On the other hand, our characterization shows that it is unlikely for a practical transition system to be indifferent. Thus, this second attempt does not seem very appealing as well.

In the context of model checking, however, we do not care about the equivalence of $A\psi$ and ψ_A with respect to all transition systems, neither about the indifference of M with respect to all formulas. Rather, we care only about the equivalence of $A\psi$ and ψ_A in the transition system M we wish to check. This can be checked by solving the model-checking problem $M \models A\psi \leftrightarrow \psi_A$. The model-checking problem $M \models A\psi \leftrightarrow \varphi$ for ψ in LTL and φ in ∀CTL can be solved in PSPACE [EL85]. What about the special case where $\varphi = \psi_A$? One could hope that the tight syntactic relation between $A\psi$ and ψ_A would make it easier. We show that the problem of deciding whether $A\psi$ and ψ_A are equivalent with respect to a given transition system M is PSPACE-complete, thus it is not easier than performing LTL model checking of ψ with respect to M.

There is, however, a method to avoid the equivalence check of $A\psi$ and ψ_A and still use the relation between the two formulas in order to benefit from CTL model-checking tools. The idea is very similar to an idea used in the model checker SPIN [Hol97]. In order to use its partial-order reductions, SPIN has to check its specifications for closure under stuttering. SPIN avoids the expensive check but still employs its partial-order reductions. For that, SPIN first closes the given specification under stuttering, then it model checks (with partial-order reductions) the closed specification, and it uses the relation between the closed specification and the original one in order to deduce either the satisfaction of the original specification or its not being closed under stuttering [HK96]. We follow the same lines: instead of checking $A\psi$, verification starts by checking M with respect to ψ_A. If M satisfies ψ_A, we deduce that M satisfies $A\psi$ as well. If M does not satisfy ψ_A, we use the counterexample that the model checker provides in order to determine whether it is the case that M satisfies $A\psi$ or whether it is the case that $A\psi$ and ψ_A are not equivalent. Thus, sometimes we do end up performing LTL model checking, yet the transition system to be checked then is the counterexample, which is typically much smaller than the original transition system.

So far, we considered several ways for using ψ_A in the process of ψ model checking. Unfortunately, neither ways suggests a method that is guaranteed to perform better than usual LTL model checkers. Our motivation, recall, is the computational advantage of CTL over LTL. This advantage, however, refers to worst-case complexity. In the second part of the paper we claim that, in practice, standard LTL model checkers perform nicely on most formulas ψ for which $A\psi$ and ψ_A are equivalent. In fact, model checking of ψ often proceeds essentially as model checking of ψ_A. Thus, in practice, there is no need to relate linear and branching model checking and the question whether $A\psi$ is equivalent to ψ_A is not that important. In order to prove our claim, we compare the behavior of the bottom-up CTL model-checking algorithm of [CES86] with the behavior of the automata-based LTL model-checking algorithm of [VW86]. We show that most LTL formulas ψ for which $A\psi$ is equivalent to ψ_A induce a special type of automata. Solving the nonemptiness problem of these automata involves essentially the same steps required for solving the model-checking problem for ψ_A. Intuitively, both model checkers proceed according to the semantics of the formula and are insensitive to the syntax in which it is given.

2 PRELIMINARIES

2.1 Temporal logics

The logic *CTL** is a branching temporal logic. Formulas of CTL* are defined with respect to a set AP of atomic propositions and describe the evolution of these propositions. We present here a positive normal form for CTL* formulas where negation may be applied only to atomic propositions. In this form, a path quantifier, E ("for some path") or A ("for all paths"), can prefix an assertion built from the set of atomic proposition using the usual Boolean connectives and the temporal operators X ("next time"), U ("until"), and $\tilde{U}$ ("duality of until"). There are two types of formulas in CTL*: ***state formulas***, whose satisfaction is related to a specific state, and ***path formulas***, whose satisfaction is related to a specific path. Formally, let AP be a set of atomic proposition names. A CTL* state formula is either:

- **true**, **false**, p or $\neg p$, for $p \in AP$.
- $\psi \vee \varphi$ or $\psi \wedge \varphi$ where ψ and φ are CTL* state formulas.
- $E\psi$ or $A\psi$, where ψ is a CTL* path formula.

A CTL* path formula is either:

- A CTL* state formula.
- $\psi \vee \varphi$, $\psi \wedge \varphi$, $X\psi$, $\psi U \varphi$, or $\psi \tilde{U} \varphi$, where ψ and φ are CTL* path formulas.

The logic CTL* consists of the set of state formulas generated by the above rules. The logic *CTL* is a restricted subset of CTL*. In CTL, the temporal operators X, U, and $\tilde{U}$ must be immediately preceded by a path quantifier. Formally, it is the subset of CTL* obtained by restricting the path formulas to be $X\psi$, $\psi U \varphi$, or $\psi \tilde{U} \varphi$, where ψ and φ are CTL state formulas.

The logic $\forall CTL^\star$ is a restricted subset of CTL* that allows only the universal path quantifier A. Note that since negation in CTL* can be applied only to atomic propositions, assertions of the form $\neg A\psi$, which is equivalent to $E\neg\psi$, are not possible. Thus, the logic ∀CTL* is not closed under negation. The logic ∀CTL is defined similarly, as the restricted subset of CTL that allows the universal path quantifier only. The logics ∃CTL* and ∃CTL are defined analogously, as the existential fragments of CTL* and CTL, respectively. Note that negating a ∀CTL* formula results in an ∃CTL* formula. For example, $\neg ApU(AXq)$ is equivalent to $E(\neg p)\tilde{U}(EX\neg q)$.

The logic *LTL* is a linear temporal logic. Given a set AP, an LTL formula is defined as follows:

- **true**, **false**, p, or $\neg p$, for $p \in AP$.
- $\psi \vee \varphi$, $\psi \wedge \varphi$, $X\psi$, $\psi U \varphi$, or $\psi \tilde{U} \varphi$, where ψ and φ are LTL formulas.

Thus, each LTL formula ψ corresponds to a CTL* formula $A\psi$ in which ψ is a path formula with no path quantifiers. Hence, LTL can be viewed as a fragment of CTL*. For an LTL formula ψ, we denote by ψ_A the ∀CTL formula obtained from ψ by preceding each temporal operator by the universal path quantifier A. For example, $(Xp \vee Xq)_A = AXp \vee AXq$. The formula ψ_E is defined similarly for the existential path quantifier E. We denote the size of a formula φ by $|\varphi|$ and we use the following abbreviations in writing formulas: $\rightarrow$ and $\leftrightarrow$, interpreted in the usual way, $F\psi = \mathbf{true} U \psi$ ("eventually"), and $G\psi = \neg F \neg \psi$ ("always").

We define the semantics of CTL* and its sublanguages with respect to *fair Rabin modules* (*modules*, for short). A module $M = \langle AP, W, W_0, R, L, \alpha \rangle$ consists of a set AP of atomic propositions, a set W of states, a set $W_0 \subseteq W$ of initial states, a total transition relation $R \subseteq W \times W$ (i.e., for every state $w \in W$, there exists at least w' with $R(w, w')$), a labeling function $L : W \rightarrow 2^{AP}$, and a Rabin fairness condition $\alpha \subseteq 2^W \times 2^W$, which defines a subset of W^ω. The module M is of *branching degree 1* iff for every state $w \in W$, there exists a single w' with $R(w, w')$. A *computation* of a module is an infinite sequence of states, $\pi = w_0, w_1, \ldots$ such that for every $i \geq 0$, we have that $R(w_i, w_{i+1})$. When $w_0 \in W_0$, we say that π is an *initialized computation*. For a computation π, let $Inf(\pi)$ denote the set of states that repeat infinitely often in π. That is,

$$Inf(\pi) = \{w : \text{ for infinitely many } i \geq 0, \text{ we have } w_i = w\}.$$

A computation of M is *fair* iff it satisfies the fairness condition. Thus, if the fairness condition is $\alpha = \{\langle G_1, B_1\rangle, \ldots, \langle G_k, B_k\rangle\}$, then π is fair iff there exists $1 \leq i \leq k$ for which $Inf(\pi) \cap G_i \neq \emptyset$ and $Inf(\pi) \cap B_i = \emptyset$. In other words, iff π visits G_i infinitely often and visits B_i only finitely often. Each computation $\pi = w_0, w_1, \ldots$ of M induces a *trace* $L(\pi) = L(w_0), L(w_1), \ldots$ in $(2^{AP})^\omega$. We sometimes refer to the *language*, $\mathcal{L}(M)$, of a module M, meaning the set of traces induced by M's initialized fair computations. We say that M is *nonempty* if $\mathcal{L}(M) \neq \emptyset$. For a module M and a state $w \in W$, we use M^w to denote the module obtained from M by taking the set of initial states to be the singleton $\{w\}$. For simplicity, we assume that each initial state $w_0 \in W_0$ is the first state of at least one initialized fair computation. Thus, M^{w_0} is nonempty.

Assuming an agreed module M, we use $w \models \varphi$ to indicate that a state formula φ holds at state w, and we use $\pi \models \varphi$ to indicate that a path formula φ holds at path π. The formal definition of the relation $\models$ can be found in [Eme90]. A module M satisfies a formula ψ iff ψ holds in all the initial states of M. The *model-checking problem* is to decide, given M and ψ, whether $M \models \psi$.

2.2 Simulation relation and maximal models

In [GL94], Grumberg and Long define an order relation between modules that captures what it means for a module M' to have "more behaviors" than a module M. The definition in [GL94] extend previous definitions [Mil71], which relate modules with no fairness conditions. Let $M = \langle AP, W, R, W_0, L, \alpha\rangle$ and $M' = \langle AP, W', R', W'_0, L', \alpha'\rangle$ be two modules and let w and w' be states in W and W', respectively. A relation $H \subseteq W \times W'$ is a *simulation relation* from $\langle M, w\rangle$ to $\langle M', w'\rangle$ iff the following conditions hold:

(1) $H(w, w')$.
(2) For all s and s', we have that $H(s, s')$ implies the following:

  (2.1) $L(s) \cap AP' = L(s')$.
  (2.2) For every fair computation $\pi = s_0, s_1, \ldots$ in M, with $s_0 = s$, there exists a fair computation $\pi' = s'_0, s'_1, \ldots$ in M', with $s'_0 = s'$, such that for all $i \geq 0$, we have $H(s_i, s'_i)$.

A simulation relation H is a *simulation from M to M'* iff for every $w \in W_0$, there exists $w' \in W'_0$ such that $H(w, w')$. If there exists a simulation from M to M', we say that M' *simulates* M and we write $M \leq M'$. Intuitively, it means that the module M' has more behaviors than the module M. In fact, every possible behavior of M is also a possible behavior of M'. The following theorem is proved in [GL94] for modules with a Streett fairness condition. The proof is independent of the type of the fairness condition being used and it holds also for fair Rabin modules.

Theorem 2.1 *For every M and M' such that $M \leq M'$, and for every $\forall CTL^\star$ formula φ, we have that $M' \models \varphi$ implies $M \models \varphi$.*

A module M is a *maximal model* for an $\forall$CTL* formula φ if it allows all behaviors consistent with φ. Formally, M_φ is a maximal model of φ if $M_\varphi \models \varphi$ and for every module M we have that $M \leq M_\varphi$ if $M \models \varphi$. Note that by the preceding theorem, if $M \leq M_\varphi$, then $M \models \varphi$. Thus, M_φ is a maximal model for φ if for every module M, we have that $M \leq M_\varphi$ iff $M \models \varphi$.

Let φ and ψ be two $\forall$CTL* formulas. The implication $\varphi \rightarrow \psi$ is valid iff ψ holds in all modules M in which φ holds. Since the more behaviors M has the less likely it is to satisfy ψ, it makes sense to examine the implication by checking ψ in a maximal model of φ:

Theorem 2.2 [GL94] *Let φ and ψ be $\forall CTL^\star$ formulas, and let M_φ be a maximal model of φ. Then φ implies ψ iff $M_\varphi \models \psi$.*

2.3 Büchi word automata

A *Büchi automaton over infinite words* is $\mathcal{A} = \langle \Sigma, Q, Q_0, \delta, F \rangle$, where Σ is the input alphabet, Q is a finite set of states, $Q_0 \subseteq Q$ is a set of initial states, $\delta : Q \times \Sigma \rightarrow 2^Q$ is a transition function, and $F \subseteq Q$ is an acceptance condition. Intuitively, $\delta(q, \sigma)$ is the set of states that $\mathcal{A}$ can move into when it is in state q and it reads the letter σ. Given an input infinite word $\rho = \sigma_0, \sigma_1, \sigma_2, \ldots$ in Σ^ω, a *run* of $\mathcal{A}$ on ρ is an infinite sequence $r = q_0, q_1, q_2, \ldots$ in Q^ω where $q_0 \in Q_0$ (i.e., the run starts in one of the initial states) and for every $i \geq 0$, we have $q_{i+1} \in \delta(q_i, \sigma_i)$ (i.e., the run obeys the transition function). Each run r induces a set $Inf(r)$ of states that r visits infinitely often. As Q is finite, it is guaranteed that $Inf(r) \neq \emptyset$. The run r *accepts* ρ iff $Inf(r) \cap F \neq \emptyset$. Note that $\mathcal{A}$ can have many runs on ρ. An automaton $\mathcal{A}$ accepts an input word ρ iff there exists a run r of $\mathcal{A}$ on ρ such that r accepts ρ. The *language* of $\mathcal{A}$, denoted $\mathcal{L}(\mathcal{A})$, is the set of infinite words that $\mathcal{A}$ accepts.

Theorem 2.3 [VW94] *Given an LTL formula ψ, there exists a Büchi automaton $\mathcal{A}_\psi$ of size $2^{O(|\psi|)}$, such that $\mathcal{L}(\mathcal{A}_\psi)$ is exactly the set of computations satisfying ψ.*

3 RELATING ψ AND ψ_A

In this section we describe a number of attempts to utilize the tight syntactic relation between ψ and ψ_A in order to relate linear and branching model checking. In other words, we are given a module M and an LTL formula ψ, and we try to make use of ψ_A and to benefit from CTL model-checking tools in the process of deciding whether M satisfies ψ. A natural thing to start with is to check the equivalence of $A\psi$ and ψ_A. For an LTL formula ψ, we say that ψ is *branchable* iff $A\psi$ and ψ_A are equivalent. Clearly, if ψ is branchable, then checking whether M satisfies ψ can be reduced to checking whether M satisfies ψ_A. We first claim that modules with no branches can not distinguish between $A\psi$ and ψ_A.

Lemma 3.1 *For a module M of branching degree 1 and an LTL formula ψ, we have that $M \models A\psi$ iff $M \models \psi_A$.*

Proof. Let $M = \langle AP, W, W_0, R, L, \alpha\rangle$. Since M is of branching degree 1, it contains a single initialized fair computation π. We can associate with each state $w \in W$ a suffix π^w of π that starts in w. It is easy to prove, by induction on the structure of ψ, that for every state w, we have that $\pi^w \models \psi$ iff $w \models \psi_A$. It follows that $M \models A\psi$ iff $M \models \psi_A$. □

We now claim that $A\psi$ is weaker than ψ_A:

Lemma 3.2 *For every LTL formula ψ, the implication $\psi_A \rightarrow A\psi$ is valid.*

Proof. Consider a module M that satisfies ψ_A. We show that all the initialized fair computations of M satisfy ψ. Then, by the semantics of $\forall$CTL*, we have that M satisfies $A\psi$. Let π be an initialized fair computation of M. The computation π can be viewed as a module of branching degree 1. Since π is simulated by M, it satisfies ψ_A. Hence, by Lemma 3.1 that π satisfies ψ as well. □

By Lemma 3.2, deciding whether ψ is branchable can be reduced to checking the implication $A\psi \rightarrow \psi_A$. This implication is not valid for all LTL formulas ψ. For example, the formula $AFGp$ does not imply the formula $AFAGp$. We now solve this implication problem. As $A\psi$ and ψ_A are CTL* formulas, the known 2EXPTIME upper bound for CTL* satisfiability [ES84, EJ88] suggests an obvious 2EXPTIME upper bound for the problem. Moreover, as $A\psi$ and ψ_A are $\forall$CTL* formulas, the problem can be solved in EXPSPACE [KV95]. Can we hope for a better bound? This at first seems unlikely: the implication problem $\psi \rightarrow \varphi$ is EXPSPACE-hard already for ψ in LTL and φ in $\forall$CTL [KV95]. Here, however, we handle the special case where $\varphi = \psi_A$. Hopefully, the tight syntactic relation between ψ and ψ_A would enable a more efficient check. We conjecture that the problem can be solved in polynomial space, which matches our lower bound. The algorithm we present below requires exponential space, and in the worst case shows no improvement over the known EXPSPACE upper bound. Yet, it is much simpler than the algorithm in [KV95], as it avoids Safra's complicated co-determinization construction that is used in the definition of the maximal models described there.

Theorem 3.3 *For an LTL formula ψ, checking $A\psi \rightarrow \psi_A$ is in EXPSPACE and is PSPACE-hard.*

Proof. We start with the upper bound. By Theorem 2.2, checking the implication $A\psi \rightarrow \psi_A$ can be reduced to model checking of ψ_A in the maximal model $M_{A\psi}$ of $A\psi$. To complete the reduction of implication to model checking, we have to describe the construction of maximal models for LTL formulas. A construction of maximal models for $\forall$CTL* formulas is described in [KV95]. The restriction to LTL formulas enables us to come with a much simpler construction.

Given an LTL formula ψ, let $\mathcal{A}_\psi = \langle 2^{AP}, Q, Q_0, \delta, F\rangle$ be the Büchi automaton that corresponds to ψ (see Theorem 2.3). Following the construction in [VW94], each state s of $\mathcal{A}_\psi$ is a set of subformulas of ψ. When in state s, the automaton $\mathcal{A}_\psi$ accepts exactly all the computations that satisfy all the formulas in s. In particular, for every state s, the set $\delta(s, \sigma)$ is not empty iff $s \cap AP = \sigma$. Defining the maximal model M_ψ, we apply to $\mathcal{A}_\psi$ the classical *subset construction* of [RS59], that is, we extend δ to a mapping from $2^Q \times 2^{AP}$ to 2^Q where $\delta(S, a) = \{q \in Q : q \in \delta(s, a) \text{ for some } s \in S\}$. We also extends δ to words in $(2^{AP})^*$, where $\delta(S, \varepsilon) = S$ and for $w \in (2^{AP})^*$ and $a \in 2^{AP}$, we have $\delta(S, w \cdot a) = \delta(\delta(S, w), a)$. We define $M_\psi = \langle AP, W, W_0, R, L, \alpha\rangle$ as follows.

- $W \subseteq 2^Q \times Q \times \{0, 1\}$ is such that $\langle S, s, b\rangle \in W$ iff $s \in S$. Intuitively, the 2^Q-element S follows the subset construction. Since the Q-element s is always a member of S, then whenever we move from the state $\langle S, s, b\rangle$ to a state $\langle S', s', b'\rangle$, it may be the case that the update of the Q-element is consistent with δ (i.e., s' is a successor of s in $\mathcal{A}_\psi$), and it may also be the case that the update of the Q-element is not consistent with δ (i.e., s' is a successor of some other state in S). The Boolean flag b distinguishes between the two cases.
- $W_0 = \{\langle Q_0, q_0, 0\rangle : q_0 \in Q_0\}$.
- $L(\langle S, s, b\rangle) = s \cap AP$. Thus, the label of each state is the set of atomic propositions that hold in its Q-element.
- $R(\langle S, s, b\rangle, \langle S', s', b'\rangle)$ if $\delta(S, L(\langle S, s, b\rangle)) = S'$, $s' \in S'$, and one of the following holds

  - $s' \in \delta(s, L(\langle S, s, b\rangle))$ and $b' = 0$, or

– $b' = 1$.

- $\alpha = \{\langle 2^Q \times F \times \{0,1\}, 2^Q \times Q \times \{1\}\rangle\}$. That is, a computation of M_ψ is fair iff its projection on the Q-element visits F infinitely often and its projection on the Boolean flag visits 1 only finitely often. Accordingly, a computation is fair if it has a suffix in which the Q-element describes an accepting run of $\mathcal{A}_\psi$.

We say that a computation $\langle S_0, s_0, b_0\rangle, \langle S_1, s_1, b_1\rangle, \langle S_2, s_2, b_2\rangle, \ldots$ of M_ψ is *stable* iff $b_i = 0$ for all $i \geq 0$. Note that a computation is stable only if its Q-element describes a run of $\mathcal{A}_\psi$.

We now prove that $M_\psi \models A\psi$ and that for all modules M, we have $M \models A\psi$ only if $M \leq M_\psi$. We first prove that $M_\psi \models A\psi$. Recall that each state s of $\mathcal{A}_\psi$ is a set of subformulas of ψ. When in state s, the automaton $\mathcal{A}_\psi$ accepts exactly all the computations that satisfy all the formulas in s. Therefore, for every state $\langle S, s, b\rangle$ in W and for every formula $\varphi \in s$, all the stable fair computations that leave $\langle S, s, b\rangle$ satisfy φ. Indeed, such computations describe an accepting run of $\mathcal{A}_\psi$ from the state s. Since each fair computation of M_ψ eventually becomes stable, we can associate with each initialized fair computation $\pi = \langle S_0, s_0, b_0\rangle, \langle S_1, s_1, b_1\rangle, \langle S_2, s_2, b_2\rangle, \langle S_2, s_3, b_3\rangle, \ldots$, an index k such that for all $j \geq k$, we have $b_j = 0$. Since as long as a computation of M_ψ is not stable, its 2^Q-element maintains a set of states in Q that $\mathcal{A}_\psi$ may be in, it is easy to prove, by induction on k, that π is accepted by $\mathcal{A}_\psi$.

We now prove that for all modules M, we have $M \models A\psi$ only if $M \leq M_\psi$. Consider a module $M = \langle AP, W_M, W_{M0}, R_M, L_M, \alpha_M\rangle$ and assume that $M \models A\psi$. We show a simulation H from M to M_ψ. We first need some notation. For a state $w \in W_M$, let $\Pi'(w) \subseteq W_M^*$ be the set of prefixes of initialized computations in M that lead to a state from which w is reachable in a single transition. Thus, $\Pi'(w) = \{t_0, \ldots, t_{n-1} : t_0 \in W_{M0}$, for all $0 < i < n, R_M(t_{i-1}, t_i)$, and $R_M(t_{n-1}, w)\}$. We now define, for $w \notin W_{M0}$, the set $\Pi(w) = \Pi'(w)$, and for $w \in W_{M0}$, the set $\Pi(w) = \Pi'(w) \cup \{\varepsilon\}$. Now, let $S(w) \subseteq 2^Q$ be the set of sets of states for which $S \in S(w)$ iff there exists a computation $\rho \in \Pi(w)$ such that $\mathcal{A}_\psi$ may visit any of the states in S after traversing ρ. That is, $S(w) = \{S \subseteq Q :$ there exists $\rho \in \Pi(w)$ such that $S = \delta(Q_0, L_M(\rho))\}$. We can now define the simulation relation H. For a state $w \in W_M$ and a state $\langle S, s, b\rangle \in W$, we have $H(w, \langle S, s, b\rangle)$ iff $L_M(w) = s \cap AP$ and $S \in S(w)$. We prove that H is indeed a simulation. Consider an initial state $w_0 \in W_{M0}$. Recall that for every state s of $\mathcal{A}_\psi$, the set $\delta(s, \sigma)$ is not empty iff $s \cap AP = \sigma$. Since $w_0 \models A\psi$, there exists $q_0 \in Q_0$ such that $q_0 \cap AP = L(w_0)$. Hence, as $Q_0 \in S(w_0)$, the state w_0 is related by H to some initial state of M_ψ. For the second condition, let w and $w' = \langle S, s, b\rangle$ be such that $H(w, w')$. By the definition of H, we have that $L_M(w) = s \cap AP$. Hence, the states w and w' agree on their labels. Let $\pi = w_0, w_1, \ldots$ be a fair computation in M with $w_0 = w$. Since $S \in S(w)$, the set $\Pi(w)$ contains a (possibly empty) prefix $\rho = t_0, t_1, \ldots, t_{n-1}$ such that $S = \delta(Q_0, L_M(\rho))$. The computation $\rho \cdot \pi$ is an initialized fair computation in M. Hence, since $M \models A\psi$, the computation $\rho \cdot \pi$ satisfies ψ, and therefore, $L_M(\rho \cdot \pi)$ is accepted by $\mathcal{A}_\psi$. Let $s_0, s_1, \ldots$ be an accepting run of $\mathcal{A}_\psi$ on $L_M(\rho \cdot \pi)$. By the construction of $\mathcal{A}_\psi$, for every $i \geq 0$, we have that $s_{n+i} \cap AP = L_M(w_i)$. For $i \geq 0$, let S_i be the set of states that $\mathcal{A}_\psi$ may be in after reading the prefix of length i of $L_M(\rho \cdot \pi)$; i.e. $S_i = \delta(Q_0, L_M(\rho \cdot \pi)[1 \ldots i])$. Consider the sequence $\pi' = \langle S_n, s, b\rangle, \langle S_{n+1}, s_{n+1}, b_1\rangle, \langle S_{n+2}, s_{n+2}, b_2\rangle, \langle S_{n+3}, s_{n+3}, b_3\rangle, \ldots$, where $b_1 = 1$ and for all $i \geq 2$ we have $b_i = 0$. Note that $S_n = S$, thus $\langle S_n, s, b\rangle = w'$. We show that π' is a fair computation of M_ψ. First, since for all $i \geq 0$, we have that $s_{n+i} \in S_{n+i}$, all the triples in the sequence are states of M_ψ. Also, since for all $i \geq 0$, we have $\delta(S_{n+i}, w_i) = S_{n+i+1}$, and the for all $i \geq 1$, we have $s_{n+i+1} \in \delta(s_{n+1}, w_i)$, the sequence π' is a computation of M_ψ. Finally, since the sequence $s_0, s_1, \ldots$ is accepted by $\mathcal{A}_\psi$ and visits F infinitely often and since π' has a stable suffix, π' satisfies α and is therefore fair. Now, since, by the definition of H, we have that $H(w_i, \langle S_{n+i}, s_{n+i}, b_i\rangle)$ holds for all $i \geq 1$, we are done.

Since the size of $\mathcal{A}_\psi$ is exponential in ψ, the size of M_ψ is $2^{2^{O(|\psi|)}}$. The model-checking problem for CTL with respect to fair Rabin modules with a single pair can be solved in space that is polynomial in the length of the formula and is polylogarithmic in the size of the module [KV95]. Moreover, the algorithm described in [KV95] proceeds on-the-fly, without keeping the whole module in memory at once. Therefore, the EXPSPACE upper bound follows.

For the lower bound, we do a reduction from LTL satisfiability, proved to be hard for PSPACE in [SC85]. Consider the LTL formula $\theta = (Xp) \vee (Xq) \vee X((\neg p) \wedge (\neg q))$. It is easy to see that while θ is valid, the $\forall$CTL formula $\theta_A = (AXp) \vee (AXq) \vee AX((\neg p) \wedge (\neg q))$ is not valid. Given an LTL formula φ (we assume that the set of φ's atomic propositions does not contain p and q), let $\psi = \varphi \wedge \theta$. While ψ is equivalent to φ, it is not necessarily true that ψ_A is equivalent to φ_A. We prove that $A\psi \rightarrow \psi_A$ iff φ is not satisfiable.

Assume first that φ is not satisfiable. Then, ψ is not satisfiable as well, making $A\psi \rightarrow \psi_A$ valid. Assume now that φ is satisfiable. Let π be a computation that satisfies φ. Let π_p be the computation obtained from π by labeling its second state with p. Similarly, let π_q be the computation obtained from π by labeling its second state with q. Since π_p and π_q agree on the labeling of their first states, we can arrange them in a module M with a single initial state that branches into two infinite computations. While M satisfies $A\varphi$, and hence also $A\psi$, it does not satisfy θ_A, and hence it does not satisfy ψ_A either. Thus, M does not satisfy $A\psi \rightarrow \psi_A$, and the implication is not valid. $\square$

In practice, the algorithm in Theorem 3.3 requires time that is double exponential in the length of ψ. A naive check of a module M with respect to ψ requires time that is polynomial in the size of M and only exponential in the length of ψ. So, though ψ is usually much smaller than M, checking ψ for being branchable may be more expensive than checking M with respect to ψ, making our first attempt not very appealing. The model-checking problem has two operands: the specification ψ and the module M. Our first attempt concerns the sensitivity of the specification to branching. We now turn to discuss the second operand of the model-checking problem, namely the module M. We say that a module M is *indifferent* iff for every LTL formula ψ, we have $M \models A\psi \rightarrow \psi_A$. Indifference is a helpful property: in order to model check either an LTL or an $\forall$CTL formula in a module that is indifferent, one can use both LTL and CTL model-checking tools. In the theorem below we characterize modules that are indifferent.

Theorem 3.4 *Given a module $M = \langle AP, W, W_0, R, L, \alpha \rangle$, the following are equivalent:*

(1) *M is indifferent.*
(2) *For every initial state $w_0^i \in W_0$, the language of the module $M_i = \langle AP, W, \{w_0^i\}, R, L, \alpha \rangle$ is a singleton.*

Proof. For the direction (1) $\rightarrow$ (2), assume, by way of contradiction, that there exists a state $w_0^i \in W_0$ such that $\mathcal{L}(M_i)$ is neither empty nor a singleton. Then, there exists $k \geq 0$ such that all the traces in $\mathcal{L}(M_i)$ agree on their prefixes of length k, yet there are at least two traces in $\mathcal{L}(M_i)$ that do not agree on their $k+1$'s letter. Consider the LTL formula $\psi = X^k \bigvee_{\sigma \in 2^{AP}} X\sigma$. While $M \models A\psi$, we have that $M_i \not\models \psi_A$ and thus $M \not\models \psi_A$. It follows that M is not indifferent.

For the direction (2) $\rightarrow$ (1), consider an LTL formula ψ. Let $M_{\psi_A} = \langle AP, W', W'^0, R', L', \alpha' \rangle$ be a maximal model of the formula ψ_A. Assume that $M \models A\psi$. We first prove that $\mathcal{L}(M) \subseteq \mathcal{L}(M_{\psi_A})$. Consider an initialized fair computation π of M. We can regard π as a module of branching degree 1. Since π satisfies ψ then, by Lemma 3.1, it satisfies ψ_A as well. Hence, $\pi \leq M_{\psi_A}$. Since simulation implies trace-containment [GL94], it follows that the trace induced by π is a member of $\mathcal{L}(M_{\psi_A})$. So, $\mathcal{L}(M) \subseteq \mathcal{L}(M_{\psi_A})$. Therefore, for every state $w_0^i \in W_0$, we have $\mathcal{L}(M_i) \subseteq \mathcal{L}(M_{\psi_A})$. Consider a module M_i for which $\mathcal{L}(M_i) \neq \emptyset$. Let $H_i \subseteq W \times W'$ be such that $H_i(w, w')$ iff $L(w) = L'(w')$ and $\mathcal{L}(M_i^w) \subseteq \mathcal{L}(M_{\psi_A}^{w'})$. We prove that the relation H_i is a simulation from M_i to M_{ψ_A}. We first show that w_0^i is related by H_i to some initial state of M_ψ. Recall that $\mathcal{L}(M_i) \subseteq \mathcal{L}(M_{\psi_A})$. Since $\mathcal{L}(M_i)$ is a singleton, there exists an initialized fair computation $\rho = w_0, w_1, \ldots$ in M_ψ such that $\mathcal{L}(M_i) = L'(\rho)$. Hence, $\mathcal{L}(M_i) \subseteq \mathcal{L}(M_{\psi_A}^{w_0})$, and $H_i(w_0^i, w_0)$. Let w and w' be such that $H(w, w')$. First, by the definition of H, the states w and w' agree on their labels. Let $\pi = w_0, w_1, \ldots$ be a fair computation in M_i with $w_0 = w$. Since $\mathcal{L}(M_i^w) \subseteq \mathcal{L}(M_{\psi_A}^{w'})$, there exists a fair computation $\pi' = w_0', w_1', \ldots$ in M_{ψ_A} such that $w_0' = w'$ and $L(\pi) = L'(\pi')$. We prove that for all $j \geq 0$, we have $H(w_j, w'_j)$. First, since $L(\pi) = L'(\pi')$, then clearly $L(w_j) = L'(w'_j)$. In addition, as $\mathcal{L}(M_i)$ is a singleton, it must be that $\mathcal{L}(M_i^{w_j}) \subseteq \mathcal{L}(M_{\psi_A}^{w'_j})$. It follows that $M_i \leq M_{\psi_A}$. Then, the relation $\bigcup_i H_i$ is a simulation relation from M to M_{ψ_A}. Hence, $M \leq M_{\psi_A}$, implying that $M \models \psi_A$, and we are done. □

We now use the characterization of indifferent modules in order to check a given module M for being indifferent.

Theorem 3.5 *Given a module M, the problem of checking M for indifference is NLOGSPACE-complete.*

Proof. For the upper bound, we show that checking whether M is not indifferent can be done in NLOGSPACE. The result then follows from the NLOGSPACE = co-NLOGSPACE equivalence [Imm88, Sze88]. Let $M = \langle AP, W, W_0, R, L, \alpha \rangle$. By Theorem 3.4, M is not indifferent iff there exists an initial state $w_0^i \in W_0$ such that the language $\mathcal{L}(M_i)$ is not a singleton. The algorithm searches for a witness for M not being indifferent. For that, it guesses an initial state w_0^i and two prefixes $\rho_1 \cdot w_1$ and $\rho_2 \cdot w_2$ of computations (ρ_1 and ρ_2 are sequences in W^*, and w_1 and w_2 are states in W) such that $L(\rho_1) = L(\rho_2)$, $L(w_1) \neq L(w_2)$, and both $\mathcal{L}(M^{w_1})$ and $\mathcal{L}(M^{w_2})$ are nonempty. Membership in NLOGSPACE then follows from the known NLOGSPACE complexity for the reachability problem and the nonemptiness problem for fair Rabin modules. The lower bound follows by an easy reduction from the graph reachability problem [Jon75]. □

By Theorem 3.5, it is easy to check a given module M for being indifferent. On the other hand, by the characterization in Theorem 3.4, we are unlikely to find indifferent modules in practice. Indeed, branches in M originate from nondeterminism in the program that M models. As such, different branches usually induce different traces. So, the idea of looking at the modules to be checked does not seem very appealing too.

So far, we examined two approaches for relating $A\psi$ and ψ_A. The first checks the equivalence of $A\psi$ and ψ_A with respect to all models, and the second checks the indifference of M with respect to all formulas. Neither approach seems too appealing. In the context of model checking, however, we do not care about the equivalence of $A\psi$ and ψ_A with respect to all models, neither about the indifference of M with respect to all formulas. Rather, we care only about the equivalence of $A\psi$ and ψ_A in the module M we wish to check. This equivalence can be checked by solving the model-checking problem $M \models A\psi \leftrightarrow \psi_A$. The model-checking problem $M \models A\psi \leftrightarrow \varphi$ for ψ in LTL and φ in $\forall$CTL can be solved in PSPACE [EL85]. What about the special case where $\varphi = \psi_A$? One could hope that the tight syntactic relation between ψ and ψ_A would make it easier. In the next theorem we refute this hope.

Theorem 3.6 *Given a module M and an LTL formula ψ, solving the model-checking problem $M \models A\psi \rightarrow \psi_A$ is PSPACE-complete.*

Proof. The upper bound follows from CTL* model-checking complexity [EL85]. For the lower bound, we do a reduction from polynomial space Turing machines. In order to prove that the model-checking problem for LTL is hard for PSPACE, Sistla and Clarke associate with a polynomial space Turing machine T, a module M and an LTL formula ψ, such that $M \models E\psi$ iff T accepts the empty tape [SC85]. The language of M consists of all the possible sequences of configurations of T, and the formula ψ is a conjunction, $\psi = \psi^1 \wedge \psi^2$, of two requirements: ψ^1, which requires the sequence of configurations to encode a legal computation of T on the empty tape, and ψ^2, which requires the sequence of configurations to visit an accepting configuration. Consider the CTL* formula $E\psi^1 \wedge E\psi^2$. The formula holds in M independent of whether T accepts the empty tape. Indeed, it must be that some sequence of configurations encodes a legal computation of T on the empty tape, and it must also be that some sequence of configurations visits an accepting configuration. Consider now the formula $\psi_E = \psi_E^1 \wedge \psi_E^2$. By dualizing Lemma 3.2, we know that $E\psi^1 \rightarrow \psi_E^1$, and $E\psi^2 \rightarrow \psi_E^2$. Hence, the formula ψ_E also holds in M independent of whether T accepts the empty tape. Let $\tilde{\psi}$ be the LTL formula (in our positive normal form) that is equivalent to $\neg\psi$. The $\forall$CTL formula $\tilde{\psi}_A$ holds in exactly these modules that do not satisfy ψ_E. Therefore, by the above, the formula $\tilde{\psi}_A$ does not hold in M independent of whether T accepts the empty tape. Hence, $M \models A\tilde{\psi} \rightarrow \tilde{\psi}_A$ iff $M \not\models A\tilde{\psi}$, which holds iff T accepts the empty tape. □

So, checking whether $A\psi$ and ψ_A are equivalent with respect to a given model is not easier than performing LTL model checking of ψ with respect to M. There is, however, a method to avoid this check, or the $A\psi \rightarrow \psi_A$ implication check, and still use the relation between ψ and ψ_A in order to benefit from CTL model-checking tools. The idea is very similar to an idea used in the model checker SPIN. There, SPIN avoids the check of its specifications for being closed under stuttering and is still able to use its partial-order reductions [HK96]. Given a module M and an LTL formula ψ, we suggest to proceed as follows (see Figure 1).

Instead of checking $A\psi$, verification starts by checking M with respect to ψ_A. This can be done using a CTL model checker. If $M \models \psi_A$, then, by Lemma 3.2, $M \models A\psi$ as well, in which case M is correct. If $M \not\models \psi_A$, the model checker provides a counterexample. This counterexample is a witness that M does not satisfy the formula ψ_A. As such, it is some module M' embedded in M (formally, $M' \leq M$) that satisfies the $\exists$CTL formula $\neg\psi_A$. The fact that M' satisfies $\neg\psi_A$ does not imply that M' satisfies $\neg A\psi$ as well. Verification then should continue, by checking M' with respect to $A\psi$. For this check, we do need an LTL model checker. If $M' \not\models A\psi$, then, as $M' \leq M$,

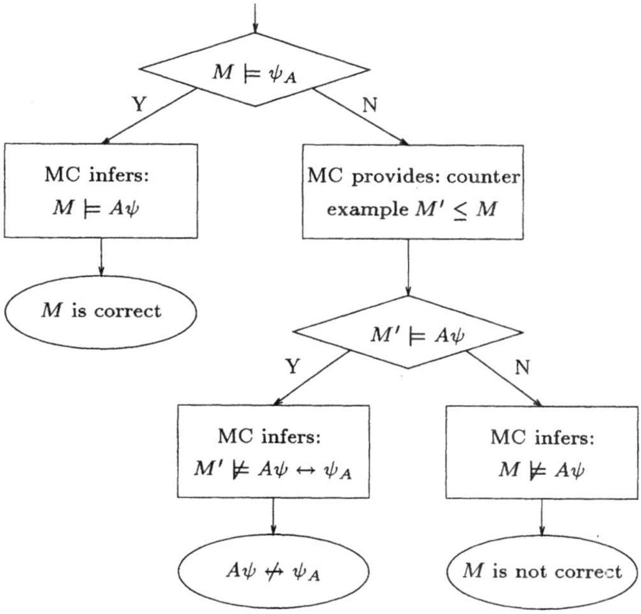

Figure 1 The algorithm.

it follows that $M \not\models A\psi$ as well, in which case M is not correct. If $M' \models A\psi$, then, as $M' \not\models \psi_A$, the module M' is a witness that ψ is not branchable. The user can then choose to repeat the last step with a different counterexample, or to repeat the verification with a revised specification with which he may be luckier*, or to give up and check $A\psi$ in M.

Note that in some cases, the check of M with respect to $A\psi$ proceeds successfully using ψ_A and avoiding LTL model checking even when ψ is not branchable (and even when $A\psi$ has no equivalence of CTL). Our algorithm is not a good one for merely checking whether ψ is branchable. First, when M is proved to be either correct or incorrect, no information on being ψ branchable is obtained. Second, as M is usually much bigger than ψ, executing our algorithm may be more expensive than a checking whether ψ is branchable directly, as described in Theorem3.3. The question we want to answer, however, is not whether ψ is branchable, but whether M is correct with respect to ψ, and we want to do so as efficiently as possible. Note also that even in the unfortunate case, where verification employs an LTL model checker, the module M' that is checked is typically much smaller than the original module

*There are heuristics that make ψ_A likely to be equivalent to $A\psi$ whenever $A\psi$ has a CTL equivalent. For example, one can try to push disjunction inward, thus transforming $Xp \vee Xq$ to $X(p \vee q)$.

M^*. Finally, even in the very unfortunate case, where verification employs an LTL model checker and ends up without a solution to the original model-checking problem, the amount of work being invested is not greater than the one required for the ordinary LTL model-checking algorithm, which can now be performed.

4 IN PRACTICE

In the previous section, we describe a number of attempts to utilize the relation between ψ and ψ_A in order to use CTL model-checking tools in the process of model checking ψ. Our motivation, recall, is the computational advantage of CTL over LTL. Indeed, while the model-checking problem $M \models \psi$ can be solved in time $O(|M| \cdot |\psi|)$ for ψ in CTL, it requires time $|M| \cdot 2^{O(|\psi|)}$ for ψ in LTL. These bounds, however, refer to worst-case complexity. In this section we claim that, in practice, LTL model checkers perform nicely on branchable LTL formulas. In fact, they often proceed essentially as the ones for CTL.

We cannot state formally that if an LTL formula ψ is branchable, then checking ψ can be done efficiently. The reason is that ψ may contain some subformulas that are not branchable and that are hard to be checked. For example, ψ may be of the form $\theta \wedge (\varphi \vee \neg\varphi)$ where θ is branchable and φ is an LTL formula whose model checking requires polynomial space. Though ψ is equivalent to θ, LTL model checkers may not detect this equivalence and may not check ψ efficiently.

What we do claim is that for a natural branchable LTL specification ψ, LTL model checkers that check ψ do essentially the same work as CTL model checkers that check ψ_A. For simplicity, we consider modules M with no fairness conditions; i.e., modules in which all the computations are fair. As the "representative" CTL model checker we take the bottom-up labeling procedure of [CES86]. There, in order to check whether M satisfies φ, we label the states of M by subformulas of φ, starting from the innermost formulas and proceeding such that, when labeling a formula, all its subformulas are already labeled. Labeling subformulas that are atomic propositions, Boolean combinations of other subformulas, or of the form $AX\theta$ or $EX\theta$ is straightforward. Labeling subformulas of the form $A\theta_1 U\theta_2$, $E\theta_1 U\theta_2$, $A\theta_1 \tilde{U}\theta_2$, or $E\theta_1 \tilde{U}\theta_2$ involves a backward reachability test. As the "representative" LTL model checker, we take the automata-based algorithm of [VW86]. There, in order to check whether M satisfies ψ, we construct a Büchi word automaton $\mathcal{A}_{\neg\psi}$ for $\neg\psi$ and check whether the intersection of the language of M with that of $\mathcal{A}_{\neg\psi}$ is nonempty. In practice, the latter check proceeds by checking whether there

*Since it is known that M' does not satisfy ψ_A, one could hope that checking $A\psi$ in M' would be easier than checking $A\psi$ in an arbitrary module. Theorem 3.6, however, refutes this hope.

exists an initial state in the intersection that satisfies CTL formula $EG\mathbf{true}$. For the construction of $\mathcal{A}_{\neg\psi}$, we follow the definition in [GPVW95], which improves [VW86] by being demand-driven; that is, the state space of $\mathcal{A}_{\neg\psi}$ is restricted to states that are reachable from the initial state.

We say that a Büchi automaton $\mathcal{A}$ is a *weak automaton* iff there exists a partition of Q into disjoint sets, $Q_1, \ldots, Q_n$, such that for each set Q_i, either $Q_i \subseteq F$, in which case Q_i is an *accepting set*, or $Q_i \cap F = \emptyset$, in which case Q_i is an *rejecting set*. In addition, there exists a partial order on the collection of the Q_i's such that for every $q \in Q_i$ and $q' \in Q_j$ for which q' occurs in $\delta(q, \sigma)$ for some $\sigma \in \Sigma$, we have $Q_j \leq Q_i$. Thus, transitions from a state in Q_i lead to states in either the same set Q_i or a lower one. It follows that every run of a weak automaton ultimately gets trapped within some set Q_i. The run is accepting iff Q_i is accepting. We say that a weak automaton $\mathcal{A}$ with state space Q is a 1-weak automaton iff all the sets in the partition of Q are singletons.

In the examples below we demonstrate that for natural LTL specifications ψ, the automaton $\mathcal{A}_{\neg\psi}$ is a 1-weak automaton.

Example 4.1 Consider the LTL formula $\psi = G(p \rightarrow Xq)$. The formula $\varphi = F(p \wedge X\neg q)$ complements ψ. The automaton that corresponds to φ by Theorem 2.3 is the 1-weak automaton

$$\mathcal{A}_\varphi = \langle 2^{\{p,q\}}, \{\varphi, \neg q, \mathbf{true}, \mathbf{false}\}, \{\varphi\}, \delta, \{\mathbf{true}\}\rangle,$$

where δ is as follows.

- $\delta(\varphi, \{p,q\}) = \delta(\varphi, \{p\}) = \{\varphi, \neg q\}$.
- $\delta(\varphi, \{q\}) = \delta(\varphi, \emptyset) = \{\varphi\}$.
- $\delta(\neg q, \{p,q\}) = \delta(\neg q, \{q\}) = \{\mathbf{false}\}$.
- $\delta(\neg q, \{p\}) = \delta(\neg q, \emptyset) = \{\mathbf{true}\}$.
- For all $\sigma \in 2^{AP}$, we have $\delta(\mathbf{true}, \sigma) = \{\mathbf{true}\}$.
- For all $\sigma \in 2^{AP}$, we have $\delta(\mathbf{false}, \sigma) = \{\mathbf{false}\}$.

Example 4.2 Consider the LTL formula $\psi = G(p \rightarrow Gq)$. The formula $\varphi = F(p \wedge F\neg q)$ complements ψ. The automaton that corresponds to φ by Theorem 2.3 is the 1-weak automaton

$$\mathcal{A}_\varphi = \langle 2^{\{p,q\}}, \{\varphi, F\neg q, \mathbf{true}\}, \{\varphi\}, \delta, \{\mathbf{true}\}\rangle,$$

where δ is as follows.

- $\delta(\varphi, \{p,q\}) = \{\varphi, F\neg q\}$.
- $\delta(\varphi, \{p\}) = \{\mathbf{true}\}$.
- $\delta(\varphi, \{q\}) = \delta(\varphi, \emptyset) = \{\varphi\}$.
- $\delta(F\neg q, \{p,q\}) = \delta(F\neg q, \{q\}) = \{F\neg q\}$.
- $\delta(F\neg q, \{p\}) = \delta(F\neg q, \emptyset) = \{\mathbf{true}\}$.

- For all $\sigma \in 2^{AP}$, we have $\delta(\mathbf{true}, \sigma) = \{\mathbf{true}\}$.

Example 4.3 Consider the LTL formula $\psi = G(p \rightarrow rUq)$. The formula $\varphi = F(p \wedge ((\neg r)\tilde{U}(\neg q))$ complements ψ. The automaton that corresponds to φ by Theorem 2.3 is the 1-weak automaton

$$\mathcal{A}_\varphi = \langle 2^{\{p,r,q\}}, \{\varphi, (\neg r)\tilde{U}(\neg q), \mathbf{true}, \mathbf{false}\}, \{\varphi\}, \delta, \{(\neg r)\tilde{U}(\neg q), \mathbf{true}\}\rangle,$$

where δ is as follows.

- For $\sigma \in 2^{AP}$ with $p \notin \sigma$ or $q \in \sigma$, we have $\delta(\varphi, \sigma) = \{\varphi\}$.
- For $\sigma \in 2^{AP}$ with $p \in \sigma$ and $q \notin \sigma$, we have $\delta(\varphi, \sigma) = \{\varphi, (\neg r)\tilde{U}(\neg q)\}$.
- For $\sigma \in 2^{AP}$ with $r \in \sigma$ and $q \notin \sigma$, we have $\delta((\neg r)\tilde{U}(\neg q), \sigma) = \{(\neg r)\tilde{U}(\neg q)\}$.
- For $\sigma \in 2^{AP}$ with $r \notin \sigma$ and $q \notin \sigma$, we have $\delta((\neg r)\tilde{U}(\neg q), \sigma) = \{\mathbf{true}\}$.
- For $\sigma \in 2^{AP}$ with $q \in \sigma$, we have $\delta((\neg r)\tilde{U}(\neg q), \sigma) = \{\mathbf{false}\}$.
- For all $\sigma \in 2^{AP}$, we have $\delta(\mathbf{true}, \sigma) = \{\mathbf{true}\}$.
- For all $\sigma \in 2^{AP}$, we have $\delta(\mathbf{false}, \sigma) = \{\mathbf{false}\}$.

Note that in all the three examples, each state of $\mathcal{A}_\varphi$ is associated with a single subformula θ of φ. As such, the size of $\mathcal{A}_\varphi$ is linear in the length of φ. Each state θ constitutes a singleton set $\{\theta\}$ in the partition of the state space. Also, the partial order on the sets in the partition is such that $\{\theta_1\} \leq \{\theta_2\}$ iff θ_1 is a subformula of θ_2 (we regard **true** and **false** as subformulas of all formulas).

Consider a module M and a branchable LTL formula ψ. We claim that when $\mathcal{A}_{\neg\psi}$ is a 1-weak automaton as above, then checking the nonemptiness of the product automaton $M \times \mathcal{A}_{\neg\psi}$ proceeds essentially as the bottom-up CTL model-checking algorithm when performed on M and ψ_A. Checking a weak automaton $\mathcal{A}$ for nonemptiness proceeds in phases as follows (see [BVW94]). Let $Q_1 \leq \ldots \leq Q_n$ be the partial order on the sets of $\mathcal{A}$. The algorithm proceeds up the partial order. In phase i, each state q in Q_i is labeled with either 'T' (in the case that the automaton $\mathcal{A}$ with initial state q is nonempty) or 'F' (in the case that $\mathcal{A}$ with initial state q is empty). The label of q depends on labels of states in sets lower than Q_i as well as on the classification of Q_i as either an accepting or a rejecting set. The nonemptiness of $\mathcal{A}$ is then determined according to the labels of its initial states.

Let $M = \langle AP, W, W_0, R, L\rangle$ and let $\mathcal{A}_{\neg\psi} = \langle 2^{AP}, Q, Q_0, \delta, F\rangle$ be a 1-weak automaton. The product automaton $\mathcal{A} = M \times \mathcal{A}_{\neg\psi}$ has state space $W \times Q$ and is a weak automaton. Indeed, if $\{q_1\} \leq \ldots \leq \{q_n\}$ is the partial order on the (singleton) sets of $\mathcal{A}_\varphi$, then $W \times \{q_1\}, \ldots, W \times \{q_n\}$ is a partition of $W \times Q$ into sets, and $W \times \{q_1\} \leq \ldots \leq W \times \{q_n\}$ is a partial order on the sets. When, as in the examples above, each of the states q_i is a subformula θ of φ, then each set Q_i of $\mathcal{A}$ is a copy of M annotated by θ. Recall that when we check $\mathcal{A}$ for nonemptiness, each phase of the algorithm handles a set and labels its states with either 'T' or 'F'. Labeling a state $\langle w, \theta\rangle$ with 'T' means that the state w does not satisfy $A\neg\theta$. Dually, labeling a state $\langle w, \theta\rangle$ with 'F' means that the state w satisfies $A\neg\theta$. When we model check M with respect to ψ_A we follow essentially the same steps: labeling starts from the innermost subformulas and proceeds, as the partial order in $\mathcal{A}_\varphi$, to outer subformulas. The way in which the nonemptiness algorithm decides the label of a state $\langle w, \theta\rangle$ in $\mathcal{A}$ coincides with the way in which the CTL model checker decides whether to label the state w of M with $(\neg\theta)_A$. In both algorithms, the decision for a formula θ that is either a propositional assertion, a Boolean combination of other formulas, or involve the X temporal operator is immediate, and the decision for the more complicated U and $\tilde{U}$ formulas involves a reachability test. It follows that the running time of the two algorithms coincides as well.

We claim that most of the LTL formulas ψ that are used in practice are such that $\mathcal{A}_{\neg\psi}$ is a 1-weak automaton. We conjecture that if an LTL formula ψ is such that all the subformulas φ of ψ are branchable, then $\mathcal{A}_{\neg\psi}$ is a 1-weak automaton. The restriction to branchable subformulas takes care of formulas like $\theta \wedge (\varphi \vee \neg\varphi)$ discussed above, and still leaves us with the bulk of LTL formulas used in practice.

5 CONCLUSIONS

The discussion of the relative merits of linear versus branching temporal logics is almost as early as these paradigms [Lam80]. We mainly refer here to the linear temporal logic LTL and the branching temporal logic CTL. One of the beliefs dominating this discussion has been "while specifying is easier in LTL, model checking is easier for CTL". The attractive complexity of CTL model checking have compensated for its lack of expressive power and branching-time model-checking tools that can handle systems with more than 10^{120} states [McM93, CGL93] are incorporated into industrial development of new designs [BBG$^+$94].

If we examine the history of these issues more closely, we find that things are not that simple. On one hand, the inability of LTL to quantify computations existentially is considered by many a serious drawback [EH86]. In addition, the introduction of fair-CTL [CES86] and of many other extensions to CTL [Lon93, BBG$^+$94, KG96], have made CTL a basis for specification languages that maintain the efficiency of CTL model checking and yet overcome many of its expressiveness limitations. On the other hand, the computational superiority of CTL is also not that clear. For example, comparing the complexities of CTL and LTL model checking for concurrent programs, both are in PSPACE [VW86, BVW94]. As shown in [Var95, KV95], the advantage that CTL enjoys over LTL disappears also when the complexity of modular verification is considered. The distinction between closed an open systems questions the computational superiority of the branching-time paradigm further. As shown in [KV96, KV97], while for LTL specifications, the model-checking paradigm is applicable also for the verification of open systems, this is not true for CTL specifications. The ability of CTL to quantify computations existentially requires a more careful check, in which all possible environments are taken into considerations. The corresponding problem, module checking, is EXPTIME-complete for CTL. Moreover, in the presence of incomplete information, when the system has variables that the environment can not read, the time complexity is exponential in the size of the system.

In this paper, we went back to the original model-checking problem and examined the computational advantage of CTL over LTL there. We first tried to relate LTL and CTL model checking, aiming to utilize CTL model-checking tools in the process of LTL model checking. Neither of our attempts suggested a method that is guaranteed to perform better than usual LTL model checkers. Then, we showed that, in practice, LTL model checkers perform nicely on the bulk of LTL formulas. In fact, they often proceed essentially as the ones for CTL. It follows that linear and branching model checkers do not need to be related: practically, the complexity of checking most LTL formulas is the same as the one required for checking their equivalent CTL formulas. Intuitively, both model checkers proceed according to the semantics of the formula and are insensitive to the syntax in which it is given. Experimental results of LTL and CTL model checking of common specifications support our observation and show no advantage to the branching paradigm [Cla97]. The computational disadvantage of LTL originates from formulas that do not have equivalent CTL formulas and from less common specifications that we rarely meet in practice.

ACKNOWLEDGMENT O. Kupferman is supported in part by ONR YIP award N00014-95-1-0520, by NSF CAREER award CCR-9501708, by NSF grant CCR-9504469, by AFOSR contract F49620-93-1-0056, by ARO MURI grant DAAH-04-96-1-0341, by ARPA grant NAG2-892, and by SRC contract 95-DC-324.036. M.Y. Vardi is supported in part by NSF grants CCR-9628400 and CCR-9700061, and by a grant from the Intel Corporation.

REFERENCES

[BBG+94] I. Beer, S. Ben-David, D. Geist, R. Gewirtzman, and M. Yoeli. Methodology and system for practical formal verification of reactive hardware. In *Proc. 6th CAV*, LNCS 818, pp. 182–193, 1994.

[BVW94] O. Bernholtz, M.Y. Vardi, and P. Wolper. An automata-theoretic approach to branching-time model checking. In *Proc. 6th CAV*, LNCS 818, pp. 142-155, 1994.

[CDK93] E. M. Clarke, I. A. Draghicescu, and R. P. Kurshan. A unified approach for showing language containment and equivalence between various types of ω-automata. *IPL* **46**, pp 301–308, 1993.

[CE81] E.M. Clarke and E.A. Emerson. Design and synthesis of synchronization skeletons using branching time temporal logic. In *Proc. Work-*

shop on Logic of Programs, LNCS 131, pp. 52–71, 1981.

[CES86] E.M. Clarke, E.A. Emerson, and A.P. Sistla. Automatic verification of finite-state concurrent systems using temporal logic specifications. *Transactions on Programming Languages and Systems*, 8(2):244–263, 1986.

[CGL93] E.M. Clarke, O. Grumberg, and D. Long. Verification tools for finite-state concurrent systems. In Proc. *REX School*, LNCS 803, pp. 124–175, 1993.

[Cla97] E. Clarke. Private communication, 1997.

[EH86] E.A. Emerson and J.Y. Halpern. Sometimes and not never revisited: On branching versus linear time. *Journal of the ACM*, 33(1):151–178, 1986.

[EJ88] E.A. Emerson and C. Jutla. The complexity of tree automata and logics of programs. In *Proc. 29th FOCS*, pp. 368–377, 1988.

[EL85] E.A. Emerson and C.-L. Lei. Modalities for model checking: Branching time logic strikes back. In *Proc. 20th POPL*, pp. 84–96, 1985.

[Eme90] E.A. Emerson. Temporal and modal logic. *Handbook of theoretical computer science*, pp. 997–1072, 1990.

[ES84] E.A. Emerson and A. P. Sistla. Deciding branching time logic. In *Proc. 16th STOC*, 1984.

[GL94] O. Grumberg and D.E. Long. Model checking and modular verification. *ACM Trans. on Programming Languages and Systems*, 16(3):843–871, 1994.

[GPVW95] R. Gerth, D. Peled, M.Y. Vardi, and P. Wolper. A simple on-the-fly automatic verification for linear temporal logic. In *Protocol Specification, Testing, and Verification*, pp. 3–18. Chapman & Hall, 1995.

[HK96] G. Holzmann and O. Kupferman. Not checking for closure under stuttering. In *Proc. 2nd SPIN*, pp 163–169, 1996.

[Hol97] G.J. Holzmann. The model checker SPIN. *IEEE Trans. on Software Engineering*, 23(5):279–295, 1997.

[Imm88] N. Immerman. Nondeterministic space is closed under complement. *SIAM Journal on Computing*, 17:935–938, 1988.

[Jon75] N.D. Jones. Space-bounded reducibility among combinatorial problems. *Journal of Computer and System Sciences*, 11:68–75, 1975.

[KG96] O. Kupferman and O. Grumberg. Buy one, get one free!!! *Journal of Logic and Computation*, 6(4):523–539, 1996.

[KV95] O. Kupferman and M.Y. Vardi. On the complexity of branching modular model checking. In *Proc. 6th CONCUR*, LNCS 962. pp. 408–422,1995.

[KV96] O. Kupferman and M.Y. Vardi. Module checking. In *Proc. 8th CAV*, LNCS 1102, pp. 75–86, 1996.

[KV97] O. Kupferman and M.Y. Vardi. Module checking revisited. In *Proc. 9th CAV*, LNCS 1254, pp. 36–47, 1997.

[Lam80] L. Lamport. Sometimes is sometimes "not never" - on the temporal logic of programs. In *Proc. 7th POPL*, pp. 174–185, 1980.

[Lon93] D.E. Long. *Model checking, abstraction and compositional verification*. PhD thesis, Carnegie-Mellon University, Pittsburgh, 1993.

[LP85] O. Lichtenstein and A. Pnueli. Checking that finite state concurrent programs satisfy their linear specification. In *Proc. 12th POPL*, pp. 97–107, 1985.

[McM93] K.L. McMillan. *Symbolic model checking*. Kluwer Academic Publishers, 1993.

[Mil71] R. Milner. An algebraic definition of simulation between programs. In *Proc. 2nd IJCAI*, pp. 481–489, 1971.

[Pnu77] A. Pnueli. The temporal logic of programs. In *Proc. 18th FOCS*, pp. 46–57, 1977.

[Pnu81] A. Pnueli. The temporal semantics of concurrent programs. *Theoretical Computer Science*, 13:45–60, 1981.

[QS81] J.P. Queille and J. Sifakis. Specification and verification of concurrent systems in Cesar. In *Proc. 5th International Symp. on Programming*, LNCS 137, pp. 337–351, 1981.

[RS59] M.O. Rabin and D. Scott. Finite automata and their decision problems. *IBM Journal of Research and Development*, 3:115–125, 1959.

[Saf89] S. Safra. *Complexity of automata on infinite objects*. PhD thesis, Weizmann Institute of Science, Rehovot, Israel, 1989.

[SC85] A.P. Sistla and E.M. Clarke. The complexity of propositional linear temporal logic. *Journal ACM*, 32:733–749, 1985.

[Sch97] K. Schneider. CTL and equivalent sublanguages of CTL*. In *Proc. IFIP Conference on Computer Hardware Description Languages and Applications*, pp. 40–59, 1997.

[Sze88] R. Szelepcsinyi. The method of forced enumeration for nondeterministic automata. *Acta Informatica*, 26:279–284, 1988.

[Var95] M.Y. Vardi. On the complexity of modular model checking. In *Proc. 10th LICS*, pp. 101-111, 1995.

[VW86] M.Y. Vardi and P. Wolper. An automata-theoretic approach to automatic program verification. In *Proc. 1st LICS*, pp. 322–331, 1986.

[VW94] M.Y. Vardi and P. Wolper. Reasoning about infinite computations. *Information and Computation*, 115(1):1–37, November 1994.

BIOGRAPHIES

Orna Kupferman is a postdoctoral scholar at the department of electrical engineering and computer science in UC Berkeley. She received her Ph.D. from the Technion in 1995.

Moshe Y. Vardi is a Noah Harding Professor and Chair of Computer Science at Rice University. Prior to joining Rice in 1993, he was at the IBM Almaden Research Center, where he managed the Mathematics and Related Computer Science Department. His research interests include database theory, finite-model theory, multi-agent systems, and design specification and verification. Vardi received his Ph.D. from the Hebrew University of Jerusalem in 1981. He is the author and co-author of about 100 technical papers, as well as a book titled "Reasoning about Knowledge". Vardi is the recipient of 3 IBM Outstanding Innovation Awards. He is an editor of several international journals.

22

Verifying Duration Properties of Timed Transition Systems

Z. Liu
Department of Mathematics and Computer Science, University of Leicester, University Road, Leicester LE1 7RH, U.K.; E-mail: *Z.Liu@mcs.le.ac.uk.*
A. P. Ravn
Department of Information Technology, Technical University of Denmark, Building 344, Lyngby, Denmark; E-mail: *apr@it.dtu.dk.*
X. Li
Faculty of Science and Technology, University of Macau, P.O. Box 3001, Macau; E-mail: *fstxsl@umac.mo.*

Abstract
This paper proposes a method for formal real-time systems development: Requirements and high level design decisions are time interval properties and are therefore specified in the Duration Calculus (DC), while implementations are described by timed transition systems (TTS). A link from implementation properties to the requirement and design properties is given by interpreting a DC formula in a model of the executions of a TTS and then providing rules for lifting properties proved by structural induction for a TTS to DC formulas. The method is illustrated by the Gas Burner case study.

Keywords
Real-time systems; Duration Calculus; Timed Transition Systems, Specification, Verification.

1 INTRODUCTION

Duration calculus (DC) was introduced to specify and reason about properties of embedded real-time systems (Zhou, Hoare & Ravn 1991, Ravn, Rischel & Hansen 1993), it has also been successfully used to reason about circuits and digital designs and hybrid systems (Ravn & Rischel 1991, Zhou, Ravn & Hansen 1993). Introductions to the applications are found in (Zhou 1993) while the logic and its foundation is given a thorough presentation in (Hansen & Zhou 1997).

A system is in DC modelled within a conventional dynamical systems framework with states that are functions of time, the non-negative reals. A Boolean state is observed through its duration in a bounded interval, i.e. the integral of an indicator function. A property for a single interval is specified by an arithmetic relation among durations and real numbers. Properties for sequences of intervals are expressed by

Programming Concepts and Methods D. Gries, & W-P. de Roever (Eds.)

the associative binary "chop" operator of the Interval Temporal Logic (Moszkowski 1985).

In a specification of requirements, the dynamical systems model is beneficial, because it focuses on relevant observable states. Furthermore, the interval logic has simple interpretations in timing diagrams for the states. The requirements will thus focus on sequencing of durational relations between observable states rather than on state transitions. A typical real-time property is *bounded critical duration*: in every interval of at most length δ the duration of a state P should not be more than γ time units. In DC this is expressed by the formula:

$$\ell \leq \delta \Rightarrow \int P \leq \gamma$$

However, when dealing with an implementation represented as a state machine such formulas do not lend themselves directly to structural induction proof methodologies. Also, at a design level, stronger assumptions may be made about timing. For example, a finite number of state changes may be assumed to occur simultaneously at a point of time, though the order in which they occur is still significant. Therefore, properties at a real-time point becomes significant when one introduces time into widely accepted transition systems models for reactive systems in general, e.g. (Keller 1976). While transition systems and the linear temporal logic (LTL), e.g. (Manna & Pnueli 1981), have been used successfully for specification and verification of reactive systems, they are not expressive enough for systems with real-time constraints, typically *bounded invariance* and *bounded responsiveness*.

Real-time is introduced into transition systems either by associating lower and upper bounds on enabled transitions (e.g. (Lamport 1977)) or by introducing explicit clocks, e.g. (Abadi & Lamport 1992). The first approach has led to extensions of LTL with bounded operators (Koymans, Vytopil & de Roever 1983), and the second has used LTL with explicit clocks, e.g. (Abadi & Lamport 1992). The relationship between the two approaches is investigated in (Henzinger, Manna & Pnueli 1994).

An advantage of TTS frameworks is that they are quite close to implementations using digital hardware and thus directly reflect semantics of programming languages. Another advantage is that safety properties and time bounded properties can be easily checked by structural induction over the transitions. However, this framework is inherently operational and less abstract than a dynamical systems based framework. For instance, properties that relate states across several transitions have to be expressed using auxiliary state variables (Lamport 1993). Thus it seems well justified to link the two formalisms such that one may use DC for high level specification and reasoning and TTS for implementation and refinement.

In a previous work (Sørensen, Hansen & Løvengreen 1994), a link is demonstrated through definition of a combination of the logics of TLT and Duration Calculus. That work investigated some of the techniques presented here. However, the current work differs by focusing on the proof system and proof techniques, which turns out to be the difficult and important part when combining theories.

After this introduction, Section 2 gives an overview of DC and its application to high level specification. Section 3 introduces TTS and a model of their executions called trajectories, which allows us to define the satisfaction of a DC formula by a

TTS in Section 4. In Section 5, we provide the rules for proving duration properties of a TTS. In Section 6, the Gas Burner example illustrates the approach and allow comparisons between this mixed approach and DC-only (Ravn et al. 1993) or TTS-only (Lamport 1993) methods.

2 REQUIREMENT AND DESIGN SPECIFICATION IN DC

A dynamic system is traditionally modelled by its state functions which are *evaluations* (or interpretations)of the system *state variables* Π over the time domain, each of them has a signature $\mathcal{V}(x) : Time \longmapsto V$, where V is the value domain of $x \in \Pi$.

The $Time$ domain must be totally ordered, and any interval $[t_1, t_2]$ between two time points is measurable by a non-negative real number called the *length* of the interval. The usual interpretation is the set of non-negative real numbers $\mathbf{R}^{\geq 0}$, but we extend it to $\mathbf{R}^{\geq 0} \times \mathbf{N}$ later in this paper.

A state function $\mathcal{V}(x)$ must be sectionally continuous and locally bounded. Sectional continuity means that in a bounded interval there is a finite number of discontinuities. For discrete state variables, which are the only variables that we use in this paper, a state function is a step function.

A *state assertion* P is a first order predicate over the state variables Π and interpreted a Boolean valued function $\mathcal{V}(P) : Time \longmapsto \{0, 1\}$; $\mathcal{V}(P)(t) = 1$ if the evaluations of the variables in P at t make P hold, and $\mathcal{V}(P)(t) = 0$ otherwise. The sectional continuity implies that $\mathcal{V}(P)$ is a step function.

The elementary observation of a state assertion P is its *duration*, written $\int P$. It denotes for a given time interval $[t_1, t_2]$, the integral $\int_{t_1}^{t_2} \mathcal{V}(P)(t)dt$. In particular, the largest duration corresponding to the length of the real-time interval is $\int 1$, which we abbreviate as ℓ. The duration is a real number and a measure. It satisfies all the properties of a measure.

Elementary formulas are arithmetic relations in durations and real valued rigid variables and constants. An example is that P holds throughout an interval: $\int P = \ell$.

The propositional connectives and quantification over rigid variables are used to generate composite formulas. An example is that P holds on a proper (non-point) interval:

$$\lceil P \rceil \stackrel{\text{def}}{=} (\int P = \ell) \wedge (\ell > 0)$$

Analogously, we introduce the abbreviation for a 'point':

$$\lceil\,\rceil \stackrel{\text{def}}{=} \ell = 0$$

Properties of subintervals are specified by the binary 'chop'-operator, denoted by '; '. A formula D_1 ; D_2 holds on an interval $[t_1, t_2]$ just when there exists an intermediate t such that the formula D_1 holds on $[t_1, t]$ and the formula D_2 holds on $[t, t_2]$.

The chop operator and durations are linked by the key property of summation over subintervals: for any real numbers $\gamma, \delta \geq 0$

$$(\int P = \gamma + \delta) \Leftrightarrow ((\int P = \gamma) \; ; \; (\int P = \delta))$$

For more details about the semantics, axioms and rules of DC, we refer the reader to (Hansen & Zhou 1997).

2.1 Specification of the Gas Burner

We use the Gas Burner example in (Ravn et al. 1993) to show the simplicity in writing requirement and design specifications in DC. This case study formulate the safety requirement of a gas burner in terms of a variable *Leak* denoting an undesirable but unavoidable state where unlit gas escapes from the nozzle. Safety requires that '*gas must never leak for more than 4 seconds in any period of at most 30 seconds*':

$$Req \stackrel{\text{def}}{=} \ell \leq 30 \Rightarrow \textstyle\int Leak \leq 4$$

To meet the requirement *Req*, we make two design decisions:

$$\begin{aligned} Des_1 &\stackrel{\text{def}}{=} \lceil Leak \rceil \Rightarrow \ell \leq 4 \\ Des_2 &\stackrel{\text{def}}{=} \lceil Leak \rceil \;;\; \lceil \neg Leak \rceil \;;\; \lceil Leak \rceil \Rightarrow \ell \geq 26 \end{aligned}$$

Des_1 is a bounded response property: it says that any occurrence of *Leak* must be stopped within 4 seconds. The other formula Des_2 is a bounded invariance: it says that once a *Leak* is stopped, this persists for at least 26 seconds.

The correctness of the design, i.e. implication of the validity of *Req* by that of $Des \stackrel{\text{def}}{=} Des_1 \wedge Des_2$, is shown in (Zhou et al. 1991) and for a more complex design in (Ravn et al. 1993).

The formula *Des* may be interpreted as a real-time automaton or a real-time program, which is refined further in a detailed design. However, this is in general a 'big' formula and a direct proof of refinement in DC may be tedious, because many of the steps deals with encoding of the behaviour of the automaton. We propose to deal with these steps by adopting the inductive proof techniques of the TTS framework.

3 TRANSITION SYSTEMS

This section starts with an overview of transition systems, as given in (Manna & Pnueli 1992). As in (Henzinger et al. 1994) a transition system is then extended to a timed version by imposing timing constraints on its transitions. We deviate slightly from these sources when we define the behaviour of a TTS in a trajectory model which is convenient to use as a semantic model for DC in Section 4.

3.1 Transition systems

A *transition system* $S = \langle \Pi, \Sigma, \Theta, \mathcal{T} \rangle$ consists of four components:

1. Π is a finite set of *state variables*.

2. Σ is a set of *states*. A state s in Σ assigns to every variable $u \in \Pi$ a value $s[u]$.
3. The *initial condition* Θ is a state assertion that defines a subset of Σ called the *initial states*.
4. A finite set $\mathcal{T}$ of *transitions*. Every transition τ in $\mathcal{T}$ is a binary relation on Σ; it defines for every state s, a (possibly empty) set of τ-successors $\tau(s)$. We use $en(\tau)$ to denote the enabling condition of a transition τ, and transition τ is *enabled* on a state s just when $\tau(s) \neq \emptyset$. When a τ holds between states s and s' this is often written $s \xrightarrow{\tau} s'$.

A *computation* (execution, run) of a transition system S is an infinite state sequence $\sigma = \sigma_0, \sigma_1, \cdots$ which satisfies the following two conditions:

Initiation: σ_0 satisfies Θ.
Consecution: For all $i \geq 0$, either $\sigma_i = \sigma_{i+1}$ (a *stuttering step*) or there is a transition τ in $\mathcal{T}$ such that $\sigma_i \xrightarrow{\tau} \sigma_{i+1}$ (a *diligent step*). In the later case, we say that a τ step is *taken* at position i of σ.

Thus, a computation either contains infinitely many diligent steps, or it *terminates* with an infinite stuttering-only suffix. The set $[\![S]\!]$ of all computations of S is *stuttering closed*: if an infinite state sequence σ is a computation of the program, then so is any state sequence obtained from σ by adding or deleting a finite number of stuttering steps. Stuttering closure is the key to relate system specifications (or models) (Abadi & Lamport 1991) at different level of abstractions by *refinement mappings*.

As in Manna and Pnueli's Linear Temporal Logic (LTL) (Manna & Pnueli 1992) or Lamport's Temporal Logic of Actions (TLA) (Lamport 1994), we represent transition τ of a system S as first order Boolean-valued over the state variables Π and their 'primed versions' Π', which is interpreted over pairs of states:

$$\langle s, s' \rangle \models \tau(\Pi, \Pi') \text{ iff } \tau(s[\Pi]/\Pi, s'[\Pi]/\Pi') \text{ holds}$$

3.2 Timed transition systems

We incorporate time in the transition systems models by assuming that all transitions happen "instantaneously", while timing constraints require transitions to be performed neither *too early* nor *too late*. Each transition τ is given a *lower time bound* l_τ, and an *upper time bound* u_τ. The lower time bound is a value from $\mathbf{R}^{\geq 0}$, which we take to be the set of non-negative real numbers, and the upper time bound is either a value from $\mathbf{R}^{\geq 0}$ or the special symbol ∞, which denotes the absence of an upper bound. Any real number in $\mathbf{R}^{\geq 0}$ is assumed to be less than ∞, and the lower bound is assumed not to exceed the upper bound for any transition.

A *timed transition system* $TS = \langle \Pi, \Sigma, \Theta, \mathcal{T}, l, u \rangle$ consists of an underlying transition system $S = \langle \Pi, \Sigma, \Theta, \mathcal{T} \rangle$ and two functions l and u defining the transition time interval for each transition.

3.3 Trajectories

Instead of defining a computations as a *timed state sequence* (Henzinger et al. 1994), we introduce the notion of a trajectory in order to interpret DC formulas over behaviours of a TTS. A *trajectory* over a set Π of state variables is a state function: $\rho : Time \longmapsto \Sigma$, where Σ is the set of states.

The time domain is $Time \stackrel{\text{def}}{=} \mathbf{R}^{\geq 0} \times \mathbf{N}$ in this framework. We refer to a pair $\langle t, n\rangle \in Time$ as a *position*, and $\rho(t, n)$ as the state at position $\langle t, n\rangle$ in ρ. Positions in $Time$ are ordered by the lexicographic ordering: $\langle t_1, n_1\rangle \prec \langle t_2, n_2\rangle$ iff $t_1 < t_2$ or $(t_1 = t_2) \wedge (n_1 < n_2)$. We write $\langle t_1, n_1\rangle \preceq \langle t_2, n_2\rangle$ if $\langle t_1, n_1\rangle \prec \langle t_2, n_2\rangle$ or $\langle t_1, n_1\rangle = \langle t_2, n_2\rangle$. For two positions p_1 and p_2 such that $p_1 \preceq p_2$, the *super-dense time interval* $[p_1, p_2]$ between p_1 and p_2 is the set of positions $\{p : p_1 \preceq p \preceq p_2\}$. We also define the *length* $d_1(\langle t_1, n_1\rangle, \langle t_2, n_2\rangle)$ of an interval $[\langle t_1, n_1\rangle, \langle t_2, n_2\rangle]$ as $t_2 - t_1$.

In order to make a trajectory ρ isomorphic to a timed state sequence in (Henzinger et al. 1994), we impose onto it the *sectional continuity* (or *finite variability*) condition: For any interval $[\langle a, m\rangle, \langle b, n\rangle]$, there exits a finite number of positions $\langle t_1, n_1\rangle, \cdots, \langle t_k, n_k\rangle$ such that

1. $a = t_1 < t_2 <, \cdots, < t_k = b$, and
2. ρ is constant on each interval $[\langle t_i, n_i\rangle, \langle t_{i+1}, 0\rangle]$.

Define the projection $\rho(t)$, $t \in \mathbf{R}^{\geq 0}$, as $\rho(t, 0)$. Then the above two conditions ensure that: (a) a state change can only occur between two consecutive positions $\langle t, n\rangle$ and $\langle t, n+1\rangle$, for some $t \in \mathbf{R}^{\geq 0}$ and some $n \in \mathbf{N}$; (b) the state sequence at a time point $t \in \mathbf{R}^{\geq 0}$ terminates with a constant state, denoted as $\rho(t, \infty)$; and (c) the first state $\rho(t)$ at a time point t equals the constant state of the preceding evolution: $\rho(t) = \rho(t^-)$; and the final state is the value of the succeeding evolution: $\rho(t, \infty) = \rho(t^+)$.

If $\rho(t, n) \xrightarrow{\tau} \rho(t, n+1)$, we say transition τ is *taken* at position $\langle t, n\rangle$ in ρ, and τ is taken at time point t in ρ if there exists a n such that τ is taken at $\langle t, n\rangle$ in ρ.

A trajectory $\rho : Time \longmapsto \Sigma$ is a *trajectory* of a timed transition system, $TS = \langle \Pi, \Sigma, \theta, \mathcal{T}, l, u\rangle$, if it satisfies the following conditions.

Initiation: $\rho(0, 0)$ satisfies Θ.

Consecution: For any position $\langle t, n\rangle$, either $\rho(t, n) = \rho(t, n+1)$ (a stuttering step) or there is a $\tau \in \mathcal{T}$ such that $\rho(t, n) \xrightarrow{\tau} \rho(t, n+1)$ (a diligent step).

Lower bound: if τ is taken at position p, there must exist a $p_1 \preceq p$ such that $d_1(p, p_1) \geq l_\tau$, and for any p_2 such that $p_1 \preceq p_2 \prec p$, τ is not taken.

Upper bound: if τ is enabled at position p, there exists $p_1 \succeq p$ such that $d_1(p_1, p) \leq u_\tau$ and τ is taken or is disabled at p_1.

A trajectory ρ of TS that satisfies the first two conditions is a trajectory of its underlying transition system. It is easy to see that the set $[\![TS]\!]^{traj}$ of all trajectories of a system TS is isomorphic to the set of timed state sequences of TS defined in (Henzinger et al. 1994).

Intuitively, the design decisions of Des for the Gas Burner system are implemented by a two-state and two-transition TS, denoted as GB_1, which is formally described below in terms of its initial condition and transitions with their time bounds:

$$\begin{array}{lcll} GB_1 & = & \langle & \Theta_1 : true \\ & & & \tau_1 : Leak \wedge \neg Leak', \quad l_{\tau_1} = 0, \quad u_{\tau_1} = 4 \\ & & & \tau_2 : \neg Leak \wedge Leak', \quad l_{\tau_2} = 26, \quad u_{\tau_2} = \infty \\ & & \rangle & \end{array}$$

The problem is, within a DC framework, to formally prove that GB_1 satisfies Des and then how to refine it.

4 SATISFACTION OF A DC FORMULA BY A TTS

To deal with a TTS in DC, we need to extend DC to cope with instantaneous transitions, and thus sequences of point properties. This section defines DC in terms of trajectories of transition systems and define the satisfaction relation of a duration formula by a TTS. This semantic definition preserves all the validity of the original DC axioms and rules.

4.1 Syntax

We keep the concept of a state assertion P, its duration $\int P$, rigid variables v, and define as usual an atomic duration formula F as any arithmetic relation over real valued constants, durations and rigid variables.

To describe state changes in a point interval, a transition τ, as well as an integer arithmetic relation over the *step counter* $\hbar$ and rigid variables, are also atomic formulas.

In addition to the binary "chop" modality, denoted by '; ', for specifying properties of subintervals, We introduce the unary modality $\triangleright$ which allows us to either prefixing or extending an interval.

A DC formula D is generated from the atomic formals by the Boolean connectives, the binary chop modality, the unary modality $\triangleright$, and quantification over rigid variables.

4.2 Semantics

A formula of this extended logic is to be interpreted over a trajectory ρ and a super-dense interval $[p_1, p_2]$ between two positions $p_1 = \langle t_1, n_1 \rangle$ and $p_2 = \langle t_2, n_2 \rangle$. We define two measures of such an interval by the two-valued function

$$d(p_1, p_2) \stackrel{\text{def}}{=} \begin{cases} (t_2 - t_1, n_2) & \text{if } t_1 < t_2 \\ (0, n_2 - n_1) & \text{if } t_1 = t_2 \wedge n_1 \leq n_2 \end{cases}$$

We shall use $d_1(p_1, p_2)$ and $d_2(p_1, p_2)$ to denote the first (the length of the interval) and second (the steps of the interval) values of $d(p_1, p_2)$ respectively.

For a trajectory ρ over a state space Σ, an observation over an interval $[p_1, p_2]$ consists of the states $\{\rho(t, n) \ : \ p_1 \preceq \langle t, n\rangle \preceq p_2\}$. In particular, at any *time point* t, every observation over an interval $[\langle t, n_1\rangle, \langle t, n_2\rangle]$ (which is a *point interval*) is a finite non-empty state sequence $\rho(t, n_1), \cdots, \rho(t, n_2)$. The observation of ρ over $[\langle t, n\rangle, \langle t, n\rangle]$ is the single state $\rho(t, n)$, i.e. a state sequence of 'length 0' is a single state.

Durations of states

The duration $\int P$ for a state assertion P over a super-dense interval $[\langle t_1, n_1\rangle, \langle t_2, n_2\rangle]$ is still used to define the accumulated time when P holds within the super-dense interval:

$$\int_{t_1}^{t_2} P(\rho(t, 0))dt$$

Thus, a duration ignores all the discontinuous positions, and its existence is guaranteed by the finite variability of the trajectory*. Under these definitions, all the conventional DC axioms in (Zhou et al. 1991) remain valid.

State properties and transitions

A state property P which is a first order predicate assertion (no quantification is allowed over state variables) holds for a trajectory ρ over an observation if it holds at the first position of the observation:

$$\rho, [\langle t_1, n_1\rangle, \langle t_2, n_2\rangle] \models P \quad \text{iff} \quad \rho(t_1, n_1) \models P$$

A transition τ is treated as an interval formula as for the case of a state predicate:

$$\rho, [\langle t_1, n_1\rangle, \langle t_2, n_2\rangle] \models \tau \quad \text{iff} \quad \langle \rho(t_1, n_1), \rho(t_1, n_1 + 1)\rangle \models \tau$$

Obviously, a state predicate is a special transition which does not refer to primed variables, and all axioms in the first order predicate logic remain valid for reasoning about state properties and transitions.

The composite formula $\lceil\,\rceil \wedge (\hbar = 0) \wedge \tau$ specifies the point observations containing a single state in which τ is enabled; and the formula $\lceil\,\rceil \wedge (\hbar > 0) \wedge \tau$ defines the point observations consisting of a sequence of more than one state such that the first two of them is a τ-step.

The Hoare Triple $\{P\}\tau\{Q\}$ for any state assertions P and Q and any state transition τ will be used in structural induction reasoning, and it is defined here as the

---

*The logic remains the same if $\int P$ is defined as $\int_{t_1}^{t_2} \forall n \in \mathbf{N} \bullet P(\rho(t, n))dt$ or as $\int_{t_1}^{t_2} \exists n \in \mathbf{N} \bullet P(\rho(t, n))dt$.

state transition

$$\{P\}\tau\{Q\} \stackrel{\text{def}}{=} P \wedge \tau \Rightarrow Q'$$

where Q' is obtained from Q by replacing each state variable x of Q by its primed version x'.

The length of a state sequence in an interval is given by the step counter $\hbar$:

$$\rho, [p_1, p_2] \models \hbar = n \quad \text{iff} \quad d_2(p_1, p_2) = n$$

The bounded version of the temporal formula $\bigcirc D$ (i.e. the 'next' operator) can be defined in terms of $\lceil\,\rceil$, $\hbar$ and the chop operator as $(\lceil\,\rceil \wedge \hbar = 1)\ ;\ D$.

Modalities

The 'chop' operator now chops a super-dense interval. A formula $D_1\ ;\ D_2$ holds on such an interval $[p_1, p_2]$ just when there exists an intermediate position p such that the formula D_1 holds on $[p_1, p]$ and the formula D_2 holds on $[p, p_2]$:

$$\begin{array}{l}\rho, [p_1, p_2] \models D_1\ ;\ D_2 \text{ iff} \\ \quad \exists p \bullet (p_1 \preceq p \preceq p_2) \wedge (\rho, [p_1, p] \models D_1) \wedge (\rho, [p, p_2] \models D_2)\end{array}$$

A formula $\rhd D$ holds on an interval $[b, e]$ there is an interval $[b, f]$ which is either a prefix or an extension of $[b, e]$ such that D holds on $[b, f]$:

$$\rho, [b, e] \models \rhd D \quad \text{iff} \quad \exists f \succeq b \bullet (\rho, [b, f] \models D)$$

This operator distributes over disjunction and is monotone. It comes as a combination $\Diamond_l \Diamond_r$ of the two neighbourhood modalities $\Diamond_l$ and $\Diamond_r$ from (Zhou & Hansen 1996*a*). In this paper, we are only concerned about future properties which can be treated sufficiently by the combined operator. Axioms and properties for the chop operator and the $\rhd$ operator (treated as $\Diamond_l \Diamond_r$) given in (Zhou et al. 1991) and (Zhou & Hansen 1996*a*) remain valid under the new interpretation.

With operator $\rhd$, the *conventional linear temporal formulas* $\Diamond D$ and $\Box D$ can be defined as follows $\rhd(\mathit{true}\ ;\ D)$ and $\neg\Diamond\neg D$, respectively.

A trajectory ρ *satisfies* a formula D if for any $\langle r, n\rangle \in \mathit{Time}$ $\rho, [\langle 0, 0\rangle, \langle r, n\rangle] \models D$. *Valid* formulas are satisfied by any trajectory. A formula D is *valid for* (or *satisfied by*) a TTS, TS, denoted by $TS \models D$, iff any trajectory $\rho \in [\![TS]\!]^{traj}$ satisfies D.

4.3 Proof System

We have just said that in the extended logic, the validity of the axioms and rules in the original DC in (Moszkowski 1985, Zhou et al. 1991, Zhou & Hansen 1996*a*) for durations and the two modalities is preserved as well as the validity of the axioms and rules in first predicate logic is for state properties and transitions at a time point. For example, it is easy to see that as in original DC and ITL, 'chop' is associative, distributes over disjunction, and has *false* as zero. Furthermore, for any durational formula D, $\lceil\,\rceil$ is the unit of 'chop': $\lceil\,\rceil\ ;\ D \Leftrightarrow D\ ;\ \lceil\,\rceil \Leftrightarrow D$. However, we need axioms to link point properties with interval properties. The following axioms about temporal variable $\hbar$ play this role:

A1 :	$\exists n : \mathbf{N} \bullet (\hbar = n)$	
A2 :	$(D \Leftrightarrow \lceil\rceil \wedge (\hbar = 0) \ ; \ D) \wedge (D \Leftrightarrow D \ ; \ \lceil\rceil \wedge (\hbar = 0))$	unit of chop
A3 :	$\lceil\rceil \wedge (\hbar = n > 0) \Leftrightarrow (\lceil\rceil \wedge \hbar = 1 \ ; \ \lceil\rceil \wedge (\hbar = n-1))$.	
	$\lceil\rceil \wedge (\hbar = n > 0) \Leftrightarrow (\lceil\rceil \wedge \hbar = n-1 \ ; \ \lceil\rceil \wedge (\hbar = 1))$	chop a point
A4 :	$(\ell = r) \Rightarrow \exists n \bullet (\lceil\rceil \wedge (\hbar = n) \ ; \ (\ell = r))$	super-dense
A5 :	$\neg(\lceil\rceil \wedge \hbar = 0) \Rightarrow ((\{P\}\tau\{Q\}) \ \Leftrightarrow \ (P \wedge \tau \Rightarrow \bigcirc Q))$	link positions

For a state predicate P we use $P^{\bullet}$ to denote that P holds *anywhere* in a interval:

$$P^{\bullet} \stackrel{\text{def}}{=} \neg(true \ ; \ \neg P \ ; \ true)$$

5 LIFTING PROPERTIES OF TTS TO DURATION PROPERTIES

The 'yardstick' properties of a timed transition system include *bounded invariance properties*, and *bounded progress properties*. These properties and the structural induction proof rules for them are given in (Henzinger et al. 1994) in timed linear temporal logic (TLTL). This section shows how these properties are incorporated into the extended DC framework.

A state property P is an *invariant* of a transition system S if P holds at any position in any interval for all trajectories of S. Thus, an unbounded invariance property is of the form $\Box\, P$, where P is a state predicate. P is an invariant of a transition system S iff P is implied by Θ, and P is preserved by all transitions in $\mathcal{T}$. Let $\{P\}\mathcal{T}\{Q\}$ hold iff $\mathcal{T}\{P\}\tau\{Q\}$ holds for each $\tau \in \mathcal{T}$. An induction rule for proving an invariant of S is given in (Manna & Pnueli 1981) as:

$$\textbf{UB-INV} \qquad \frac{\Theta \Rightarrow P, \ \ \{P\}\mathcal{T}\{P\}}{\Box\, P}$$

which is still sound in the interval logical setting, i.e. any transition system satisfying the premises also satisfies the conclusion.

There are other induction rules for proving untimed properties which we leave out of this paper, because our goal is the time bounded properties. We are mainly concerned with *bounded properties*.

As in (Henzinger et al. 1994), we are interested in proving bounded-invariance and bounded-response properties, and thus restrict ourselves to the following bounded temporal formulas:

Primitive formulas: State formulas and state transitions are (*linear*) *temporal formulas*.

Boolean connectives: Every Boolean combination of temporal formulas is a temporal formula.

Bounded-eventually formulas: If ϕ is temporal formula and $u \in \mathbf{R}^{\geq 0}$, then so is $\Diamond_{\leq u}\phi$; it is true over a trajectory ρ with an initial position $\langle t_0, n_0\rangle$ iff there is a position $p = \langle t, n\rangle$ such that $t \leq t_0 + u$ and ϕ holds for the suffix of ρ starting with

p. We thus define

$$\Diamond_{\leq u}\phi \stackrel{\text{def}}{=} (\ell < u) \vee (\ell \leq u \;;\; \phi) \quad \text{or equivalently}$$
$$\Diamond_{\leq u}\phi \stackrel{\text{def}}{=} \rhd(\ell \leq u \;;\; \phi)$$

Bounded-unless formulas: If P is a state properties, ϕ is a temporal formula, and $l \in \mathbf{R}^{\geq 0}$, then $P\,\mathcal{U}_{\geq l}\phi$ is a temporal formula; it is true over a trajectory ρ iff P holds at the initial position $\langle t_0, n_0\rangle$ of ρ and either P holds for all positions in ρ, or there there is some position p such that $t \geq t_0 + l$, and ϕ holds for the suffix starting with p, and P holds at every position $q \prec p$. This formula can thus be defined as

$$P\,\mathcal{U}_{\geq l}\phi \stackrel{\text{def}}{=} (P^{\bullet} \vee (P^{\bullet} \wedge (\ell \geq l) \;;\; \bigcirc\phi))$$

We use the convention that the letters P, Q, R, as well as φ, denote state formulas; τ and its indexed versions denote state transitions; ϕ, ψ and χ stand for temporal formulas; and D, F and their indexed versions, denote general formulas in the extended logic. We also denote $P\,\mathcal{U}_{\geq l}\mathit{true}$ by $\Box_{<l}P$ when $l > 0$, and define $\Box_{<0}P$ to be true.

5.1 Induction rules for bounded properties

We start with *bounded invariance properties*. A bounded invariance property asserts that when some state occurs a condition holds continuously for a certain amount of time. Such a property is specified by a temporal formula of the form $P \Rightarrow \Box_{<l}Q$. Therefore, to prove a bounded invariance property, we often have to prove a *bounded unless* property. There are five main rules for bounded unless in (Henzinger et al. 1994) given in Table 1, which are still sound in our setting.

$\mathcal{U}$-**MON**	$\dfrac{P \Rightarrow P_1, \quad \phi \Rightarrow \phi_1, \quad l_1 \leq l}{(P\,\mathcal{U}_{\geq l}\phi) \Rightarrow (P_1\,\mathcal{U}_{\geq l_1}\phi_1)}$
$\mathcal{U}$-**TRAN**	$\dfrac{\varphi \Rightarrow P\,\mathcal{U}_{\geq l_1}\chi, \quad \chi \Rightarrow Q\,\mathcal{U}_{\geq l_2}\psi}{\varphi \Rightarrow (P \vee Q)\,\mathcal{U}_{\geq l_1+l_2}\psi}$
$\mathcal{U}$-**SS**	$\dfrac{P \Rightarrow \neg en(\tau), \quad P \Rightarrow \varphi, \quad \varphi \Rightarrow Q, \quad \{\varphi\}\mathcal{T}-\tau\{\varphi\}, \quad \{\varphi \wedge en(\tau)\}\tau\{R\}}{P \Rightarrow Q\,\mathcal{U}_{\geq l_\tau}R}$
$\mathcal{U}$-**CSS**	$\dfrac{P \Rightarrow \neg en(\tau), \quad \{Q\}\mathcal{T}-\tau\{\neg R\}}{P\,\mathcal{U}_{\geq l}Q\,\mathcal{U}\,(R \wedge \phi) \Rightarrow P\,\mathcal{U}_{\geq l}Q\,\mathcal{U}_{\geq l_\tau}(R \wedge \phi)}$
$\mathcal{U}$-**COLL**	$(P\,\mathcal{U}_{\geq l_1}Q\,\mathcal{U}_{\geq l_2}\phi) \Rightarrow ((P \vee Q)\,\mathcal{U}_{\geq l_1+l_2}\phi)$

Table 1 Rules for bounded unless

A *bounded progress property* asserts that once P occurs, Q must occur within a certain amount of time, and thus is specified in the form $P \Rightarrow \Diamond_{\leq u}P$. Again, the rules for bounded progress properties in (Henzinger et al. 1994) can be brought into our framework, which are given in Table 2.

$\Diamond$-MON	$\dfrac{\phi \Rightarrow \phi_1, \quad u_1 \geq u}{\Diamond_{\leq u}\phi \Rightarrow \Diamond_{\leq u_1}\phi_1}$
$\Diamond$-TRAN	$\dfrac{\phi \Rightarrow \Diamond_{\leq u_1}\chi, \quad \chi \Rightarrow \Diamond_{\leq u_2}\psi}{\phi \Rightarrow \Diamond_{\leq u_1+u_2}\psi}$
$\Diamond$-SS	$\dfrac{P \Rightarrow (\varphi \vee Q), \ \varphi \Rightarrow en(\tau), \ \{\varphi\}\mathcal{T} - \tau\{\varphi \vee Q\}, \ \{\varphi\}\tau\{Q\}}{P \Rightarrow \Diamond_{\leq u_\tau} Q}$
$\Diamond$-CSS	$\dfrac{P \Rightarrow en(\tau), \ \{P\}\mathcal{T}\{\neg P\}}{P\,\mathcal{U}\,\phi \Rightarrow \Diamond_{\leq u_\tau}\phi}$
$\Diamond$-COLL	$(P_1 \Rightarrow \Diamond_{\leq l_1}\phi) \wedge (P_2 \Rightarrow \Diamond_{\leq l_2}\phi) \Rightarrow ((P_1 \vee P_2) \Rightarrow \Diamond_{\leq max\{l_1,l_2\}}\phi)$

Table 2 Rules for bounded progress

5.2 Linking rules

Now we are ready to provide the rules which link temporal properties to the DC-*invariance* properties, DC-*bounded response* properties, and the DC-*minimal separation* properties. The rules are presented in the form such that the premises of a rule are temporal formulas (including first order predicates) and the conclusion is an formula in DC. This indicates that an establishment of a DC property can be achieved from some TLTL properties which can be proven by the structural induction rules.

The DC-invariance property $\lceil\,\rceil \vee \lceil P \rceil$ can also be derived from the temporal invariance property $\Box\, P$:

LINK-1 $\qquad \dfrac{\Box\, P}{\lceil\,\rceil \vee \lceil P \rceil}$

A DC-bounded response property is of the form $\neg(\lceil P \rceil \ ; \ (\lceil \neg Q \rceil \wedge \ell > u))$, asserting that P must be followed within u time units by an occurrence of Q, and can be proved by the following linking rule:

LINK-2 $\qquad \dfrac{\begin{array}{l} P \Rightarrow \Diamond_{\leq u} Q \\ \neg Q \Rightarrow \neg Q\,\mathcal{U}\,Q\,\mathcal{U}_{\geq l}\neg Q, \qquad \text{for some } l > 0 \end{array}}{\neg(\lceil P \rceil \ ; \ (\lceil \neg Q \rceil \wedge \ell > u))}$

A *minimal separation* property is described as a DC-formula of the form

$$\neg((\lceil P \rceil \ ; \ \lceil Q \rceil) \wedge (\ell < l) \ ; \ D \ ; \ true)$$

which asserts that D cannot hold until Q has been stable for at least l time units since the change from a P-state to a Q-state took place. Using bounded unless properties, we can prove a minimal separation property by the following link:

LINK-3 $\qquad \dfrac{\begin{array}{l} Q \Rightarrow \neg P, \qquad \phi \Rightarrow \neg Q \\ \psi \Rightarrow P\,\mathcal{U}_{\geq l_1}\,Q\,\mathcal{U}\,\phi \\ P\,\mathcal{U}_{\geq l_1}\,Q\,\mathcal{U}\,\phi \Rightarrow P\,\mathcal{U}_{\geq l_1}\,Q\,\mathcal{U}_{\geq l_2}\phi \end{array}}{(\psi \ ; \ true) \Rightarrow \neg((\lceil P \rceil \ ; \ \lceil Q \rceil) \wedge (\ell < l_1 + l_2) \ ; \ \phi \ ; \ true)}$

This rule is inductive in the sense that ϕ and ψ are temporal formulas which may be linked further to DC-formulas. The first two premises $Q \Rightarrow \neg P$ and $R \Rightarrow \neg Q$

ensure the pattern $(\lceil P \rceil \; ; \; \lceil Q \rceil \; ; \; \phi)$ does not collapse, the premise in the second line says that a ψ-state sequence pattern can only proceed with P lasting for at least l_1 time units followed by a Q-state and then a ϕ pattern, the premise in the third line then ensures that Q lasts for at least l_2 time units.

The last two premises in the rule may be combined into one. However, the one in the second line have to be established which then can be used to establish the last one by rule $\mathcal{U}$ -CSS. The special case when $l_1 = 0$ and ψ is P is often used. In this case the rule becomes

$$\textbf{LINK-3}' \qquad \frac{\begin{array}{l} Q \Rightarrow \neg P \qquad R \Rightarrow \neg Q \\ P \Rightarrow P\,\mathcal{U}\,Q\,\mathcal{U}\,R \\ P\,\mathcal{U}\,Q\,\mathcal{U}\,R \Rightarrow P\,\mathcal{U}\,Q\,\mathcal{U}_{\geq l}R \end{array}}{(\lceil P \rceil \; ; \; \lceil Q \rceil \; ; \; \lceil R \rceil) \Rightarrow (\ell \geq l)}$$

6 IMPLEMENTATION AND REFINEMENT OF THE GAS BURNER

This section shows how the linked methods are used in the development of the Gas Burner. We first show that the timed transition system GB_1 given in Section 3.2 satisfies the specification Des in Section 2.1. Then we show how GB_1 is *refined* into an implementation that may have only ignition failure. Finally, we present an implementation of Des which tolerates both ignition and flame failures.

Theorem 1 *The timed transition system GB_1 given in Section 3.2, satisfies Des_1 and Des_2.*

This theorem follows from the following lemma:

Lemma 1 *The time transition system GB_1 satisfies the following TLTL properties:*

$$\begin{array}{ll} (T_1): & Leak \Rightarrow \Diamond_{\leq 4} \neg Leak \\ (T_2): & Leak \Rightarrow Leak\,\mathcal{U}\,\neg Leak\,\mathcal{U}\,Leak \\ (T_3): & Leak \Rightarrow Leak\,\mathcal{U}\,\neg Leak\,\mathcal{U}_{\geq 26} Leak \end{array}$$

Proof: (T_1) is proven by applying $\Diamond$**-SS** to $\tau_1 \stackrel{\text{def}}{=} Leak \wedge \neg Leak'$ and $u_{\tau_1} = 4$, with the following premises:

$$\begin{array}{ll} Leak \Rightarrow en(\tau_1) & \text{as } en(\tau_1) = Leak \\ \{Leak\}\tau_2\{Leak\} & \text{as } Leak \wedge \neg Leak \wedge Leak' \Rightarrow Leak' \\ \{Leak\}\tau_1\{\neg Leak\} & \text{as } Leak \wedge Leak \wedge \neg Leak' \Rightarrow \neg Leak' \end{array}$$

(T_2) is obviously valid in the untimed LTL proof system. From (T_2), we then have (T_3) by applying $\mathcal{U}$ **-CSS** for τ_2 with $l_{\tau_2} = 26$. ♡

Proof of Theorem 1: Des_1 is deduced by **LINK-2** with (T_1) and (T_3) as the premises. Des_2 follows from **LINK-3'** by letting P, Q, and R in the rule be $Leak$, $\neg Leak$ and

Leak, respectively, to establish the first two premises of the rule; while (T_2) and (T_3) are the last two premises.

An implementation without flame failure

After the initial implementation, GB_1 can be refined in the traditional TTS framework. For example, the transition system GB_2 in Figure 1 is a refinement of GB_1.

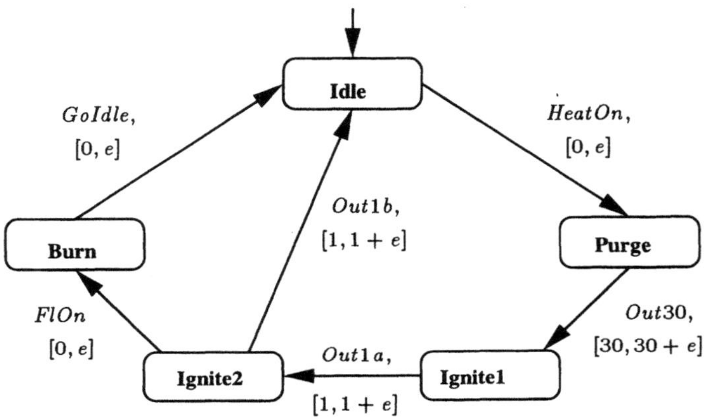

Figure 1 A refinement of GB_1

GB_2 has the following *phases*:

Idle: Await heat request, no gas and ignition. It enters **Purge** within e time units on heat request. The constant parameter e in this example is the system wide upper bound for *reacting**.

Purge: Pauses for 30 seconds and then enters **Ignite1** within e time units.

Ignite1: Turns on ignition and gas supply and enters after one second the **Ignite2** phase within e.

Ignite2: Monitors the flame and enters **Burn** if it is sensed within 1 second, otherwise returns to **Idle** while turning the gas off within e.

Burn: Ignition is switched off but gas is still on. The **Burn** phase is stable until heat request goes off. Gas is then turned off and **Idle** is entered within e.

We use a simple error recovery: return to **Idle** from **Ignite2**. We assume no flame failure in the **Burn** phase. Therefore, in this implementation, *Leak* can only occur in the **Ignite1** and **Ignite2** phases.

*In (Ravn et al. 1993, Lamport 1993), a lower bound is also given. It is not needed for proving the correctness of this design.

With the convention that the value of a variables x is changed by a transition τ only if τ names x', the formal definition of this refined transition systems is as follows.

$$
\begin{array}{lll}
GB_2 = \langle & \Pi & \stackrel{\text{def}}{=} \{gas, ignition, sensor, phase\} \\
& \Theta & \stackrel{\text{def}}{=} (gas, ignition, sensor, phase) = (\text{off}, \text{off}, \text{off}, \mathbf{Idle}) \\
& HeatOn & \stackrel{\text{def}}{=} HeatReq \wedge (phase = \mathbf{Idle}) \wedge (phase' = \mathbf{Purge}) \\
& Out30 & \stackrel{\text{def}}{=} (phase = \mathbf{Purge}) \wedge \\
& & \quad (phase', gas', ignition') = (\mathbf{Ignite1}, \text{on}, \text{on}) \\
& Out1a & \stackrel{\text{def}}{=} (phase = \mathbf{Ignite1}) \wedge (phase' = \mathbf{Ignite2}) \wedge \\
& & \quad (sensor' = \text{on}) \\
& Out1b & \stackrel{\text{def}}{=} (phase = \mathbf{Ignite2}) \wedge (phase' = \mathbf{Idle}) \wedge \\
& & \quad (ignition' = \text{off}) \wedge (gas' = \text{off}) \\
& FlOn & \stackrel{\text{def}}{=} (phase = Ignite2) \wedge Flame \wedge (phase' = \mathbf{Burn}) \wedge \\
& & \quad (ignition' = \text{off}) \\
& GoIdle & \stackrel{\text{def}}{=} (phase = \mathbf{Burn}) \wedge \neg HeatReq \wedge (phase' = \mathbf{Idle}) \wedge \\
& & \quad (gas' = \text{off}) \wedge (sensor' = \text{off}) \\
& \rangle &
\end{array}
$$

The time bounds are given by Figure 1.

Let $Leak_1$ hold iff $phase = \mathbf{Ignite1}$ holds and $Leak_2$ hold iff $phase = \mathbf{Ignite2}$ holds. In the following, we present the properties of these two *leak* states of GB_2 which *correspond* to the properties of *Leak* and have same proof routines as those for GB_1.

Lemma 2 *The timed transition system GB_2 satisfies the following TLTL properties provided $e \leq 1$:*

	Property of GB_2	*Property of GB_1*
(T_{11}) :	$Leak_1 \Rightarrow \Diamond_{\leq 1+e} \neg Leak_1$	T_1 of *Leak*
(T_{12}) :	$Leak_1 \Rightarrow Leak_1\ \mathcal{U}\ \neg Leak_1\ \mathcal{U}\ Leak_1$	T_2 of *Leak*
(T_{13}) :	$Leak_1 \Rightarrow Leak_1\ \mathcal{U}\ \neg Leak_1\ \mathcal{U}_{\geq 31} Leak_1$	T_3 of *Leak*
(T_{21}) :	$Leak_2 \Rightarrow \Diamond_{\leq 1+e} \neg Leak_2$	T_1 of *Leak*
(T_{22}) :	$Leak_2 \Rightarrow Leak_2\ \mathcal{U}\ \neg Leak_2\ \mathcal{U}\ Leak_2$	T_2 of *Leak*
(T_{23}) :	$Leak_2 \Rightarrow Leak_2\ \mathcal{U}\ \neg Leak_2\ \mathcal{U}_{\geq 31} Leak_2$	T_3 of *Leak*

By the induction rules, Lemma 2 leads to the following corollary:

Corollary 1 (GB_2 **refines** GB_1:) *Let $Leak \stackrel{\text{def}}{=} Leak_1 \vee Leak_2$ and $e \leq 1$. GB_2 satisfies the properties (T_1), (T_2) and (T_3) in Lemma 1.*

Thus, we have the following theorem corresponding to Theorem 1 for GB_1.

Theorem 2 *Let Leak* $\stackrel{\text{def}}{=}$ $Leak_1 \vee Leak_2$ *and* $e \leq 1$. GB_2 *satisfies* Des_1 *and* Des_2, *as well as Req, of the Gas Burner system.*

Lemma 3 *The timed transition system* GB_2 *has the following properties if* $e \leq 1$*:*

	Property of GB_2	*Property of* GB_1
$(Des_{11}):$	$\lceil Leak_1 \rceil \Rightarrow \ell \leq 1 + e$	Des_1 of $Leak$
$(Des_{12}):$	$\lceil Leak_1 \rceil ; \lceil \neg Leak_1 \rceil ; \lceil Leak_1 \rceil \Rightarrow \ell \geq 31$	Des_2 of $Leak$
$(Des_{21}):$	$\lceil Leak_2 \rceil \Rightarrow \ell \leq 1 + e$	Des_1 of $Leak$
$(Des_{22}):$	$\lceil Leak_2 \rceil ; \lceil \neg Leak_2 \rceil ; \lceil Leak_2 \rceil \Rightarrow \ell \geq 31$	Des_2 of $Leak$

Using Lemma 2, the proofs of Des_{11} and Des_{21} are the same as the proof of Des_1 of GB_1, while the proofs of Des_{12} and Des_{22} are the same as that of Des_2 for GB_1, in Theorem 1.

Using the linking rules as in the proof of Theorem 1, Lemma 3 has the corollary below:

Corollary 2 *The timed transition system* GB_2 *has the following properties if* $e \leq 1$*:*

	Property of GB_2	*Property of* GB_1
(Req_{11})	$\ell \leq 30 \Rightarrow \int Leak_1 \leq 1 + e$	*Req* of *Leak* in GB_1
(Req_{21})	$\ell \leq 30 \Rightarrow \int Leak_2 \leq 1 + e$	*Req* of *Leak* in GB_1

It is interesting to notice that *Req* of the Gas Burner (which is already deduced from Corollary 1 in Theorem 2) can be also deduced from Corollary 2 and the valid formula

$$\int (Leak_1 \vee Leak_2) = \int Leak_1 + \int Leak_2 = 2 + 2e \leq 4$$

An implementation with flame failure

When flame may disappear in the phase **Burn**, we can add another simple error recovery procedure which enters **Idle** from **Burn** by switching off the gas. Formally, we only have to redefine the action *GoIdle* in GB_2 as

$$\begin{aligned} GoIdle \stackrel{\text{def}}{=} & (phase = \textbf{Burn}) \wedge (\neg Flame \vee \neg HeatReq) \wedge (phase' = \textbf{Idle}) \\ & \wedge (gas' = \text{off}) \wedge (sensor' = \text{off}) \end{aligned}$$

Let $Leak_3$ denote $(phase = \textbf{Burn}) \wedge \neg Flame$. The corresponding timed transition system GB_3 satisfies Corollary 2 and the following property

$$(Req_{31}): \quad \ell \leq 30 \Rightarrow \int Leak_3 \leq e$$

which is of the same form as *Req* for the abstract state *Leak* in GB_1 and can be proved by the same proof routine by which *Req* is proved for GB_1.

Let *Leak* be the disjunction $Leak_1 \vee Leak_2 \vee Leak_3$. By the valid formulas

$$\begin{aligned} \int Leak &= \int (Leak_1 \vee Leak_2 \vee Leak_3) \\ &= \int Leak_1 + \int Leak_2 + \int Leak_3 = 2 + 3e \end{aligned}$$

this gives the following correctness theorem for GB_3:

Theorem 3 **(Correctness of** GB_3) *Assume that* $e \leq 2/3$, *the transition system* GB_3 *satisfies the requirement* Req *of the Gas Burner system.*

However, we should mention that GB_3 is not a refinement of GB_1 or GB_2. It does not implement Des as it does not meet Des_2. In other words, we do not have a corollary for GB_3 corresponding to Corollary 1 or a theorem for GB_3 corresponding to Theorem 2.

7 CONCLUSION

We have proposed an approach to combine the DC approach and the TLTL approach to specification and verification of embedded real-time systems. The combination provides both the advantage of DC for directly modelling conventional dynamical systems with state that are functions of time, and the advantage of TTS for modelling computations in reactive systems. A central point is that the link between the approaches are formulated as syntactical rules

Within this framework, DC is used for specifying the system requirements and an initial design which intuitively corresponds to a simple TTS. Then we can refine (e.g. from GB_1 to GB_2) or adjust (e.g. from GB_2 to GB_3) the initial design within the TTS framework until we obtain an implementation which is a program.

The approach is illustrated by solving the Gas Burner example. The advantage of the combined approach becomes obvious if we compare with the solution in the single DC framework in (Ravn et al. 1993), and the solution in the single TLTL framework in (Lamport 1993): specifications of the system at different levels are simpler and better structured; the proofs of the correctness of the systems at different levels are easier as they directly reflect the structural induction of each step in the refinement/implementation, and *concrete* states (e.g. $Leak_1$, $Leak_2$ and $Leak_3$ in GB_2 and GB_3) at a lower level are reasoned about in the same way as the corresponding *abstract* state (e.g. $Leak$ in GB_1) at a higher level.

The combined logic allows us to describe multiple instantaneous transitions at a time point. For the same purpose, papers (Zhou & Hansen 1996*b*) and (Xu 1997) introduce a *dense-chop operator* which can define the meaning of the sequential composition of state transitions. However, in both papers the intermediate states of a sequentially composite statement are hidden, and thus the semantics of $x := 1;\ x := x+2$ is the same as that of $x := 3$. This is a nice property if the approaches are used to deal with concurrent systems with no shared variables. However, in shared memory based models such as TTSs, the semantics of $(x := x + 1;\ x := x + 2) \mid\mid (x := 0)$ should be quite different from that of $x := 3 \mid\mid x := 0$; therefore we define DC over trajectories of a TTS.

Further work includes development of a full combined logic and extension of it to deal with hybrid transition systems (Manna & Pnueli 1993).

Acknowledgements We wish to thank Xu Qiwen for the comments and discussions about the finite variability of a trajectory, and the anonymous referees for their comments.

REFERENCES

Abadi, M. & Lamport, L. (1991). The existence of refinement mapping. *Theoretical Computer Science* **83**(2), 253–284.

Abadi, M. & Lamport, L. (1992). An old-fashioned recipe for real-time. *In* J. de Bakker, C. Huizing, W. de Rover & G. Rozenberg, eds, Real-Time: Theory in Practice, Lecture Notes in Computer Science 600, Springer-Verlag, pp. 1–27.

Hansen, M. & Zhou, C. (1997). Duration calculus: logical foundations. *Formal Aspects of Computing* **9**(3), 283–330.

Henzinger, T., Manna, Z. & Pnueli, A. (1994). Temporal proof methodologies for timed transition systems. *Information and Computation* **112**(2), 273–337.

Keller, R. (1976). Formal verification of parallel programs. *Communication of the ACM* **19**(7), 371–384.

Koymans, R., Vytopil, J. & de Roever, W.-P. (1983). Real-time programming and asynchronous message passing. *In* Proc. 2nd Annual Symposium on Principles of Distributed Computing, ACM press, pp. 187–197.

Lamport, L. (1977). Proving the correctness of multiprocess programs. *IEEE Transactions on Software Engineering* **3**(2), 125–143.

Lamport, L. (1993). Hybrid systems in TLA^+. *In* R. Grossman, A. Nerode, A. Ravn & H. Rischel, eds, Hybrid Systems, Lecture Notes in Computer Science 736, Springer-Verlag, pp. 77–102.

Lamport, L. (1994). The temporal logic of actions. *ACM Transactions on Programming Languages and Systems* **16**(3), 872–923.

Manna, Z. & Pnueli, A. (1981). The temporal framework for concurrent programs. *In* R. Boyer & J. Moore, eds, The Correctness Problem in Computer Science, Academic Press, pp. 215–274.

Manna, Z. & Pnueli, A. (1992). *The Temporal Logic of Reactive and Concurrent Systems: Specification*, Springer-Verlag.

Manna, Z. & Pnueli, A. (1993). Verifying hybrid systems, *In* R. Grossman, A. Nerode, A. Ravn & H. Rischel, eds, Hybrid Systems, Lecture Notes in Computer Science 736, Springer-Verlag, pp. 4–35.

Moszkowski, B. (1985). A temporal logic for multilevel reasoning about hardware. *IEEE Computer* **18**(2), 10–19.

Ravn, A. & Rischel, H. (1991). Requirements capture for embedded real-time systems. *In* Proc. IMACS-MCTS'91 Symposium on Modelling and Control of Technical Systems, Vol 2, pp. 1147–152.

Ravn, A., Rischel, H. & Hansen, K. (1993). Specifying and verifying requirements of real-time systems. *IEEE Transactions on Software Engineering* **19**(1), 41–55.

Sørensen, M., Hansen, O. & Løvengreen, H. (1994). Combining temporal specification techniques. *In* Temporal Logic ICTL 94, Lecture Notes in Artificial Intelligence 827, Springer-Verlag, pp. 1–16.

Xu, Q. (1997). A semantics and verification of extended phase transition systems in duration calculus, *In* O. Maler, ed., International Workshop on Hybrid and Real-Time Systems, Lecture Notes in Computer Science 1201, Springer-Verlag, pp. 301–315.

Zhou, C. (1993). Duration calculi: an overview, *In* D. Bjørner, M. Broy & I. Pottosin, eds, Proc. Formal Methods in Programming and Their Application, Lecture Notes in Computer Science 735, Springer-Verlag, pp. 256–266.

Zhou, C. & Hansen, M. (1996*a*). An adequate first order interval logic. Technical Report 91, UNU/IIST, P.O. Box 3058, Macau.

Zhou, C. & Hansen, M. (1996*b*). Chopping a point. *In* J. He, J. Cooke & P. Wallis, eds, Proc. BCS FACS 7th Refinement Workshop: Theory and Practice of System Design.

Zhou, C., Hoare, C. & Ravn, A. (1991). A calculus of durations. *Information Processing Letters* **40**(5), 269–276.

Zhou, C., Ravn, A. & Hansen, M. (1993). An extended duration calculus for hybrid real-time systems. *In* R. Grossman, A. Nerode, A. Ravn & H. Rischel, eds, Hybrid Systems, Lecture Notes in Computer Science 736, Springer-Verlag, pp. 36–59.

BIOGRAPHIES

Zhiming Liu is a lecturer in Computer Science at the University of Leicester. He obtained his MSc in Computer Science from the Software Institute of the Chinese Academy of Sciences (Beijing, 1987) and Ph.D in Computer Science from the University of Warwick (UK, 1991). His research interest is in Theories of Distributed Real-Time Systems. He has worked and had long visits to the University of Warwick and the Technical University of Denmark.

Anders P. Ravn is a Reader at the Technical University of Denmark (DTU). He works on methods for engineering of embedded real-time systems based on coherent mathematical theories and techniques. He holds a MSc in Computer Science from the University of Copenhagen (1973) and is dr. techn from DTU (1995). He has worked in industry and had long visits to IBM T.J. Watson Research Center, Oxford University, and Kiel University.

Xiaoshan Li is an assistant professor of Software Engineering at University of Macau. He received his PhD degree at Institute of Software, the Chinese Academy of Sciences (Beijing, 1993). He worked in the University of Newcastle upon Tyne from October 1995 to March 1998. His research interests include formal methods in software engineering, hardware verification, specification of concurrent, real-time and hybrid systems.

23

Towards Squiggly Refinement Algebra

D. A. Naumann
Stevens Institute of Technology
Hoboken, NJ 07030 USA. E-mail: naumann@cs.stevens-tech.edu

Abstract

The algebra of functions and relations has been used so successfully in program construction that textbooks have appeared. Despite the importance of predicate transformers in imperative programming, the algebra of transformers has been less explored. To show its promise, we prove results on exponents and recursion on inductive data types, sufficient for carrying out a polytypic derivation that has been given as a substantial example for functions and relations. We also give a data refinement from exponents of specifications to the concrete exponents needed for program semantics.

Keywords

Specification and verification, abstraction and refinement, polytypism, categorical foundations, predicate transformers, data refinement

1 INTRODUCTION

The program-level algebra of functions and relations has proved quite useful in the derivation of functional programs, and has been explored to the extent that there are now textbooks on the subject (Bird & de Moor 1996). In a particularly interesting exercise, de Moor (1996) uses the algebra of functions and relations to derive a solution to the repmin problem. The repmin problem is to replace each node of a tree of numbers with the minimum value in the tree, and to do so in a single pass over the tree. The derivation is *polytypic*, meaning that it is parameterized not just by the data type (numbers could be replaced by any suitably ordered type) but by the type-constructor 'tree-of': any inductive type-constructor will do. More striking is de Moor's observation that the derivation is also paradigm-parameterized in that the resulting program can be interpreted in two different categories, giving quite different programs: a higher-order functional program and a first-order logic program. Just as striking is the absence of an imperative interpretation. Our contribution is to justify such an interpretation, and more broadly to argue that the algebra of predicate transformers may be of practical use. In so arguing, we use a higher-order data

Programming Concepts and Methods D. Gries, & W-P. de Roever (Eds.)

refinement, i.e. refinement of a constructor rather than a primitive type, which is of independent interest.

The reader is supposed to be familiar with constructive functional programming in the categorical style – known as Squiggol – pioneered by Meertens, Backhouse et al. (Bird & de Moor 1996) and with the refinement calculus of Back, Morgan et al. (Morgan 1994). Refinement calculus and Squiggol are both algebraic in the sense that programs are developed from specifications by (in)equational calculations, in a setting where specifications are viewed as abstract programs. Derivations in refinement calculus involve heavy use of state predicates and program expressions involving state variables. By contrast, derivations in Squiggol are entirely at the level of programs, which facilitates concision and generality. But refinement calculus deals with imperative programming, for which predicate-transformer semantics is an accurate model.

There is an important connection between predicate transformers and the algebra of functions and relations. Every relation can be factored as a composite $(f^o \ ; g)$ of a function g with the *reciprocal* (relative converse) f^o of a function f. This allows the category **Rel** of relations to be constructed from the category **Fun** of functions in such a way that type-structure can be lifted from functions to relations (Bird & de Moor 1996). Refinement calculus is based on the category of what we shall call *powerset transformers*, i.e. monotonic functions $f : \wp A \rightarrow \wp B$ between powersets. Every powerset transformer can be factored as a composite $([R] \ ; \langle S \rangle)$ of the direct-image $\langle S \rangle$ and inverse-image $[R]$ of relations R, S. This allows the type-structure of **Rel** to be lifted to powerset transformers (Gardiner, Martin & de Moor 1994).

Lifting from **Fun** to **Rel** can yield weaker laws; e.g. Cartesian products are not categorical products in **Rel**. Lifting from **Rel** to powerset transformers leads to even weaker laws, as it should in an accurate model of imperative programs. Consider, e.g. the program $A \xrightarrow{f \vartriangle g} B \times C \xrightarrow{\pi} B$ which forms a pair by executing programs f and g and then projects out just the first component of the pair. It is not necessarily equal to f, because g could diverge. The refinement $(f \vartriangle g) \ ; \pi \sqsubseteq f$ does hold, but only if g obeys the law of the 'excluded miracle'. Deterministic programs satisfy the other fundamental law of categorical products, $h \ ; \pi_0 \vartriangle h \ ; \pi_1 = h$, which says that for pair-producing h the components of an output pair can be constructed separately and combined to yield the same pair. But this weakens to an inequality if h is nondeterministic, because two independent executions of h may have different outcomes. Fortunately, a small number of conditional inequalities, generalizing the familiar universal properties, sufficies to axiomatize the weak product for powerset transformers (see Proposition 5).

Coproducts do lift to categorical coproducts of powerset transformers, and de Moor (1992) shows that initial algebras (inductive data types) also lift without weakening. Martin (1995) shows that some of the 'fusion' laws of Squiggol lift in weakened form to powerset transformers. Morgan (1994) uses (monomorphic) inductive data types and Martin (1995) spells out the interpretation of map-like operations and fusion laws in the notation of refinement-calculus, but derivations at the program level are not given. This author was surprised to succeed at a nontrivial derivation in a category that is only slightly different from powerset transformers.

The repmin derivation uses initial algebras and exponents. The categorical notion of *exponent* internalizes the homset $\mathbf{Fun}(B, C)$ as an object $B \to C$ axiomatized in terms of Currying, i.e. the bijection between $\mathbf{Fun}(A \times B, C)$ and $\mathbf{Fun}(A, B \to C)$. Exponents are usually internalized homsets, but not always. De Moor's logic-programming interpretation of repmin is based on the bijection between $\mathbf{Rel}(A \times B, C)$ and $\mathbf{Rel}(A, B \times C)$ which has the formal properties of an exponent but corresponds to shuffling inputs and outputs in first-order logic programs. Function-spaces lift from $\mathbf{Fun}$ to $\mathbf{Rel}$ (and to powerset transformers), yielding a different (weak) exponent that is not the homset of $\mathbf{Rel}$ (nor of transformers). But we want an imperative interpretation of repmin as a higher-order program. If programs denote transformers, then a data type of programs should be a set of transformers, i.e. a homset of the category of transformers. Homsets of powerset transformers do carry an exponent structure but in quite weak form; by contrast with lifted products there is no simple axiomatization (Naumann 1995*b*). The evaluation rule for exponents, used in the repmin derivation, fails to hold in general. That derivation also uses a recursion theorem which is proved using exponents, and for powerset transformers we do not get a unique solution to the recursion equation (Naumann 1994*b*). Worse yet, data refinement is not preserved by the weak exponent. So much for powerset transformers.

A better-behaved category of predicate transformers (just *transformers* henceforth) can be obtained by changing the base category from $\mathbf{Fun}$ to the ordered category $\mathbf{MFun}$ of monotonic functions between preordered sets. As is explained in §2, order-absorbing relations factor into pairs of monotonic functions, and transformers on ordered data types factor into pairs of such relations. Such transformers act on predicates φ that are monotonic in the sense that x' satisfies φ whenever $x' \succeq x$ for x satisfying φ. This is certainly true of predicates used in specification, if $x' \succeq x$ means that x approximates x'. Because predicates on the exponent are restricted to be compatible with the refinement order – i.e. internalization of the homset takes its ordering into account – the properties of the weak exponent are improved. There is a complete axiomatization (Naumann 1996) (usually we shall omit the qualifier 'weak'), and data refinement is sound (Naumann 1995*a*). Transformers give an accurate semantics for a conventional higher order imperative language with specifications as abstract programs and higher types modeled by the weak exponent (Naumann 1994*a*).

This paper's first contribution is to show that inductive data types lift to transformers, and to prove the recursion theorem needed for the repmin derivation. Aside from problem-specific facts, the only other ingredient needed for repmin is a 'banana split' law that expresses a pair of recursions in terms of a single one (loop fusion). The general result weakens somewhat for transformers, but one gets a conditional law that is adequate for repmin. A companion paper (Naumann 1998) uses the present results to prove some general lemmas that are then used along with problem-specific results to derive the repmin program: de Moor's polytypic derivation can indeed be interpreted in an imperative setting.

This paper's other contribution deals with the connection between the model and concrete programs. Because the category of transformers is rich enough to interpret infeasible constructs including pre–post specifications as abstract programs, the homset is not appropriate as a concrete type. So we give a data refinement from that abstract exponent to an exponent of healthy transformers, those having a well-understood connection with operational semantics of conventional languages. This step can always be taken, which means the issue can be ignored in practice: Programs can be derived by calculation using the exponent in the category of specifications, and the final program can be interpreted concretely.

The paper is organized as follows: §2 reviews basic definitions for transformers and order-absorbing relations called ideals; §3 shows that initial algebras for ideals are final coalgebras; §4 reviews the weak product and weak exponent for transformers; §5 lifts initial algebras and proves the recursion theorem; §6 briefly sketches the repmin program; §7 discusses data refinement and defines the concrete exponent; §8 gives the data refinement between exponents; §9 discusses the results.

2 BACKGROUND ON PROSETS, PROCATS, AND IDEAL RELATIONS

This section defines the three categories **MFun**, **IRel**, and **Spec** along with quite a number related notions. Complete definitions and proofs appear in Naumann (1996); many of the ideas are based on Gardiner et al. (1994).

First, some basics. Application of function f to argument x is written fx, and associates to the left. Composition of relation $R : A \rightarrow B$ with $S : B \rightarrow C$ is denoted by $(R\,;S)$ even in the special case that R and S are functions. Composition binds less tightly than application but more tightly than other binary operators like $\Delta, \otimes, \rightsquigarrow$ introduced later. The pairing comma binds very weakly, e.g. $(x, y \otimes z)$ means $(x, (y \otimes z))$.

Data types (state spaces) are taken to be *prosets*, i.e. sets A equipped with a preorder relation $\preceq_A$. The intended interpretation of $x \preceq y$ is that x approximates y or y refines x. No further properties of $\preceq$ are required; the induced order for transformers suffices for semantics of recursion, and data types in specifications need not be restricted to CPOs. In particular, sets ordered discretely (i.e. by equality) are allowed; it is only for exponents that nontrivial order is needed. Predicates on data type A are taken to be *updeals*, i.e. subsets φ of A that are upward closed: $x \in \varphi \wedge x \preceq y \;\Rightarrow\; y \in \varphi$. (This is called monotonicity in §1.) The proset of updeals in A, ordered by $\subseteq$, is denoted by $\mathcal{U}A$. It is a complete lattice. Note that $\mathcal{U}A$ is the powerset $\wp A$ if and only if A is ordered discretely.

The repmin problem involves nonempty trees, for example defined by

$$Ltree\; B = Leaf\; B \mid Bin(Ltree\; B, Ltree\; B)$$

With B instantiated to be the naturals, the appropriate approximation ordering on trees is equality. The repmin program involves minimum values with respect to numerical magnitude, not approximation – and the same is true if, for example, B is a type of extensible records, for which the record-extension order induces a nontrivial approximation order on trees. The repmin problem is parameteric not just in B but in the constructor $Ltree$; polytypism is addressed in §3.

A *procat* is a category $\mathcal{C}$ with each homset $\mathcal{C}(A, B)$ preordered and composition monotonic. The procat **MFun** has prosets as objects and monotonic functions as arrows, ordered pointwise. The procat **Rel** has binary relations as arrows, ordered by $\subseteq$. An arrow $m : A \to B$ in a procat is a *map* just if there is an arrow $c : B \to A$, called its *comap*, such that $\mathsf{id}_A \preceq (m \,;\, c)$ and $(c \,;\, m) \preceq \mathsf{id}_B$. The maps of **Rel** are the total functions, and comaps are reciprocals of functions. We write R^o for the *reciprocal* or relative converse of any relation R.

A *transformer* is a monotonic function $\mathcal{U}A \to \mathcal{U}B$ for prosets A, B. To facilitate comparison between the algebra of relations and the algebra of transformers, we define a procat **Spec** with arrows the other way around. For prosets A, B, define $\mathbf{Spec}(A, B)$ to be the set of transformers $\mathcal{U}B \to \mathcal{U}A$, ordered pointwise (written $\sqsubseteq$). In short, $\mathbf{Spec}(A, B) = \mathbf{MFun}(\mathcal{U}B, \mathcal{U}A)$. We write the symbol $⨾$ for composition in **Spec**, so $(f ⨾ g)$ in **Spec** is the composite $(g \,;\, f)$ of functions. A powerset transformer is just a transformer on discretely ordered data types.

As mentioned in §1, every powerset transformer can be written in the form $\langle R\rangle ⨾ [S]$ where $\langle R\rangle$ is the direct-image function for some relation R and $[S]$ is the inverse-image function for some S. This factorization extends to transformers on non-discrete prosets, but the relations involved must be compatible with order in the following sense. If A, B are prosets, a relation $R : A \to B$ is an *ideal* if $(\preceq \,;\, R \,;\, \preceq) = R$. At the level of points this means $a' \preceq a \wedge aRb \wedge b \preceq b' \Rightarrow a'Rb'$. Ideals are just a mathematical tool for intermediate purposes: If one tries to interpret the ideal property for relations as a model of nondeterministic state transformers then there is clear justification for $(R \,;\, \preceq) = R$ and no justification for $(\preceq \,;\, R) = R$. Later we explain how the ideal property makes sense for pre–post specifications.

Define the category **IRel** of ideal relations to have prosets for objects and ideals for arrows, with homsets ordered by $\subseteq$. Composition is the same as in **Rel**, but the identity arrow on A is the relation $\preceq_A$ (and we refrain from writing id for that).

Whereas **Fun** is a subcategory of **Rel**, **MFun** is not a subcategory of **IRel** because a monotonic function $f : A \to B$ is not an ideal in general. But $(f \,;\, \preceq)$ is an ideal, and the maps of **IRel** are exactly the ideals of this form. For any f in **MFun**, the comap of $(f \,;\, \preceq)$ is the ideal $(\preceq \,;\, f^o)$. Every ideal factors as $(\preceq \,;\, f^o \,;\, g \,;\, \preceq)$ for some f, g in **MFun**. Monotonic functors on **IRel** preserve maps.

For ideals $S : A \to C$ and $R : B \to C$ we write S/R for the so-called *quotient* such that $Q \subseteq S/R \equiv Q \,;\, R \subseteq S$ for all Q. At the level of points, quotients in **IRel** are the same as in **Rel**. We use only one property of quotients, namely $Q \,;\, R/S = (Q \,;\, R)/S$ for all maps Q (we let / bind more tightly than ;).

The direct-image function of R in $\mathbf{IRel}(A, B)$ is a transformer $\langle R\rangle : \mathcal{U}A \to \mathcal{U}B$, i.e. an element of $\mathbf{Spec}(B, A)$. The inverse-image $[R]$ is in $\mathbf{Spec}(A, B)$. Direct-images (resp. inverse-images) are universally disjunctive (resp. conjunctive). The maps of **Spec** are the transformers of the form $[R]$, and comaps have the form $\langle R\rangle$. Readers familiar with junctivity properties of maps (left adjoints) may find this confusing. It may help to keep in mind that **Spec** is the arrow-dual of a category of functions and that, roughly speaking, maps $[R]$ correspond to weakest-precondition transformers for programs just like maps of **Rel** correspond to functional programs.

Several other potentially-confusing complications are the consequence of objects being ordered. For proset A, we write $\widetilde{A}$ for the order-dual proset: $x \preceq_A y \equiv y \preceq_{\widetilde{A}} x$. For R in $\mathbf{IRel}(A, B)$, the reciprocal R^o does not have the ideal property in general; rather, it is an ideal with respect to the order-dual prosets. We define the *op-reciprocal* $R^\ominus$ to be R^o construed as an element of $\mathbf{IRel}(\widetilde{B}, \widetilde{A})$. (Let $^\ominus$ bind more tightly than function application). Op-reciprocation is involutive and order-contravariant. It is also arrow-contravariant: $(R\,;S)^\ominus = S^\ominus\,; R^\ominus$ and $(\preceq_B)^\ominus = \preceq_{\widetilde{B}}$.

For R in $\mathbf{Rel}(A, B)$ there is function $\Lambda R : A \to \wp B$ sending a to the image of a through R. The direct image function $\langle R\rangle : \wp A \to \wp B$ can be defined by $\langle R\rangle = \Lambda(\ni;R)$ where $\ni$ is the reciprocal of the membership relation $(\in) : A \to \wp A$. The structure $\wp$, Λ, and $\ni$ in **Rel** is characterized by the *power adjunction* law

$$f = \Lambda R \equiv f\,; \ni = R \quad \text{for all relations } R \text{ and functions } f \tag{1}$$

(of appropriate type) (Bird & de Moor 1996). This implies naturality properties

$$\Lambda R\,; \langle S\rangle = \Lambda(R\,; S) \quad \text{and} \quad \Lambda(f\,; R) = f\,; \Lambda R \quad . \tag{2}$$

Updeal lattices can be described by the power adjunction on **IRel**, which facilitates calculational proofs about transformers, but there are complications due to order.

We want to axiomatize the membership relation $\ni : \mathcal{U}A \to A$ restricted to updeals, but $\ni$ does not have the ideal property with respect to the order $\subseteq$ on $\mathcal{U}A$. It is an ideal of type $\widetilde{\mathcal{U}A} \to A$ (recall that $\widetilde{\mathcal{U}A}$ is the set of updeals ordered by $\supseteq$). If R is in $\mathbf{IRel}(A, B)$ and $a \in A$ then ΛRa is an updeal, and $a \preceq a'$ implies $\Lambda Ra \supseteq \Lambda Ra'$ (these are precisely the properties $R\,; \preceq\, = R$ and $\preceq\,; R = R$). So we can take ΛR to be in $\mathbf{MFun}(A, \widetilde{\mathcal{U}B})$, and (1) holds for ideals R and monotonic functions f.

Just as the power adjunction is used to define $\langle R\rangle = \Lambda(\ni\,; R)$, it is also used to define $[R] = \Lambda(\ni/R)$. Strictly speaking these formulations are type-incorrect; e.g. $\Lambda(\ni/R)$ has type $\widetilde{\mathcal{U}B} \to \widetilde{\mathcal{U}A}$ for R of type $A \to B$, whereas we shall take $[R]$ to be $\mathcal{U}B \to \mathcal{U}A$, so that $\langle R\rangle$ is in $\mathbf{Spec}(B, A)$ and $[R]$ is in $\mathbf{Spec}(A, B)$. Precise formulations require that $\sim$ be extended to a functor on **MFun**, giving for f in $\mathbf{MFun}(A, B)$ the same mapping considered as a function $\widetilde{f}$ in $\mathbf{MFun}(\widetilde{A}, \widetilde{B})$, but we omit that. We also write $[f]$ for $[f\,;\preceq]$ and $\langle f^o\rangle$ for $\langle\preceq\,; f^o\rangle$. In the case $f = \mathsf{id}$ we are more careful, e.g. writing $[\preceq] = \mathsf{id}$ and $[R\,;S] = [R] \circ [S]$ to express functoriality of $[-]$.

Lemma 1 *(a) For any ideal R, $\langle R\rangle$ is a comap in* **Spec** *and $[R]$ is a map. (b) If f is in* **MFun** *then $[f]$ is a bimap in* **Spec** *and $[f] = \langle f^o\rangle$.*

Every transformer in $\mathbf{Spec}(A, B)$ factors as $\langle R \rangle \,⨾\, [S]$ for some proset C and ideals R in $\mathbf{IRel}(C, A)$ and S in $\mathbf{IRel}(C, B)$. In terms of specifications, R is a precondition and S a postcondition; C is an index set or specification variable linking initial and final states. The ideal properties $R \,;\, \preceq \; = \; R$ and $S \,;\, \preceq \; = \; S$ say that the predicates are updeals (monotonic) in their right argument. The ideal properties $\preceq \,;\, R = R$ and $\preceq \,;\, S = S$ are hard to justify, except that for specifications one may always choose C to be ordered by equality, making the properties vacuous.

3 INDUCTIVE DATA TYPES FOR IDEAL RELATIONS

The Cartesian product, disjoint sum, and function-space constructs lift from $\mathbf{MFun}$ to $\mathbf{IRel}$ in much the same way as they do from $\mathbf{Fun}$ to $\mathbf{Rel}$ (Bird & de Moor 1996, Naumann 1996). This section shows that inductive data types also lift.

A functor $F : \mathcal{C}^2 \to \mathcal{C}$ *has fixpoints* if for each object B there is an object $\mathsf{fix}B$ and arrow $\mathsf{in}B : F(B, \mathsf{fix}B) \to \mathsf{fix}B$ that is *initial* for B in the following sense. For each A and $R : F(B, A) \to A$ there is $(\![R]\!) : \mathsf{fix}B \to A$ such that for all S

$$S = (\![R]\!) \;\equiv\; \mathsf{in}B \,;\, S = F(\preceq, S) \,;\, R \qquad \begin{array}{ccc} F(B, \mathsf{fix}B) & \xrightarrow{\mathsf{in}B} & \mathsf{fix}B \\ {\scriptstyle F(\preceq, S)}\big\downarrow & & \big\downarrow{\scriptstyle S} \\ F(B, A) & \xrightarrow[R]{} & A \end{array} \tag{3}$$

We call $(\![R]\!)$ a *catamorphism*. Dependence on F is suppressed in the notation. Note that $\mathsf{fix}B$ is not the fixpoint of B but rather of the functor $F(B, -)$.

As an example, for each B the type $Ltree\ B$ is the least fixpoint of the functor $F(B, -)$ with F defined by $F(B, A) = B + (A \times A)$. From a function $min : F(\mathbb{N}, \mathbb{N}) \to \mathbb{N}$ giving the numerical minimum of one or two naturals we get function $(\![min]\!) : Ltree\, \mathbb{N} \to \mathbb{N}$ which gives the numerical minimum of a tree.

If F is a monotonic functor and its restriction to $\mathbf{Fun}$ (i.e. the maps of $\mathbf{Rel}$) has an initial algebra then that algebra is initial in $\mathbf{Rel}$. This can be proved using power adjunction without reciprocation (Bird & de Moor 1996). The same proof shows that fixpoints lift from $\mathbf{MFun}$ to $\mathbf{IRel}$, which we state as follows.

Proposition 2 *If F is a monotonic functor* $\mathbf{IRel}^2 \to \mathbf{IRel}$, *and it has fixpoints in the subcategory of maps, then it has fixpoints in* $\mathbf{IRel}$.

It is well known that initial algebras for relations are final coalgebras. The corresponding result for ideals is slightly more complicated. We say a functor F on $\mathbf{IRel}$ *commutes with op-reciprocation* if $F\widetilde{B} = (FB)^{\sim}$ and $FR^{\ominus} = (FR)^{\ominus}$. The result below is that if F commutes with op-reciprocation then an initial algebra $\mathsf{in}\widetilde{B}$ for $\widetilde{B}$

gives a *final coalgebra* $(\mathsf{in}\widetilde{B})^{\ominus}$ for B. That is, for each A and $R : A \to F(B, A)$ there is a so-called *anamorphism* $[\![R]\!] : A \to (\mathsf{fix}\widetilde{B})^{\sim}$ with

$$S = [\![R]\!] \;\equiv\; S\,;(\mathsf{in}\widetilde{B})^{\ominus} = R\,; F(\preceq, S) \qquad \text{for all } S. \tag{4}$$

Note that the final coalgebra for B is the op-reciprocal of the initial algebra $\mathsf{in}\widetilde{B} : F(\widetilde{B}, \mathsf{fix}\widetilde{B}) \to \mathsf{fix}\widetilde{B}$ for $\widetilde{B}$. The type of $(\mathsf{in}\widetilde{B})^{\ominus}$ is $(\mathsf{fix}\widetilde{B})^{\sim} \to (F(\widetilde{B}, \mathsf{fix}\widetilde{B}))^{\sim}$, but if F commutes with op-reciprocation then we get the type shown in this diagram:

$$\begin{array}{ccc}
A & \xrightarrow{\quad R \quad} & F(B, A) \\
{\scriptstyle [\![R]\!]}\big\downarrow & & \big\downarrow{\scriptstyle F(\preceq, [\![R]\!])} \\
(\mathsf{fix}\widetilde{B})^{\sim} & \xrightarrow[(\mathsf{in}\widetilde{B})^{\ominus}]{} & F(B, (\mathsf{fix}\widetilde{B})^{\sim})
\end{array}$$

The types can be further simplified by using initiality to show $(\mathsf{fix}\widetilde{B})^{\sim} = \mathsf{fix}B$.

Proposition 3 *The following functors on* $\mathbf{IRel}$ *commute with op-reciprocation:* $+$, $\times$, id, *the projections* $\mathbf{IRel}^2 \to \mathbf{IRel}$, *and those constant-valued functors whose value is an equivalence relation.*

Proof. For the functor constantly B, we have $x \preceq_{F\widetilde{A}} y \equiv x \preceq_B y$ and $x \preceq_{(FA)^{\ominus}} y \equiv y \preceq_B x$, hence $\preceq_B$ needs to be symmetric. The other cases are easy. □

Theorem 4 *Suppose* $F : \mathbf{IRel}^2 \to \mathbf{IRel}$ *has fixpoints and commutes with op-reciprocation. Then for each* B *the functor* $F(B, -)$ *has a final coalgebra.*

Proof. Given any A, B and $R : A \to F(B, A)$, define $[\![R]\!] = (\![R^{\ominus}]\!)^{\ominus}$. If F commutes with op-reciprocation we have $R^{\ominus} : F(\widetilde{B}, \widetilde{A}) \to \widetilde{A}$, whence $(\![R^{\ominus}]\!)\ \ \mathsf{fix}\widetilde{B} \to \widetilde{A}$ and $[\![R]\!] : A \to \mathsf{fix}B$ as explained above. For any S,

$$\begin{array}{cll}
 & S = [\![R]\!] & \\
\equiv & S = (\![R^{\ominus}]\!)^{\ominus} & \text{definition of } [\![-]\!] \\
\equiv & S^{\ominus} = (\![R^{\ominus}]\!) & {}^{\ominus}\text{ involution} \\
\equiv & \mathsf{in}\widetilde{B}\,; S^{\ominus} = F(\preceq, S^{\ominus})\,; R^{\ominus} & \text{catamorphism (3) } B, S, R := \widetilde{B}, S^{\ominus}, R^{\ominus} \\
\equiv & S\,;(\mathsf{in}\widetilde{B})^{\ominus} = R\,;(F(\preceq, S^{\ominus}))^{\ominus} & {}^{\ominus}\text{ arrow-contravariant involution} \\
\equiv & S\,;(\mathsf{in}\widetilde{B})^{\ominus} = R\,; F(\preceq, S) & F \text{ commutes with } {}^{\ominus}, {}^{\ominus}\text{ involution}
\end{array}$$

which proves (4). □

4 WEAK PRODUCTS AND WEAK EXPONENTS IN Spec

Results in this section are proved in Gardiner et al. (1994) or Naumann (1996).

An *upfunctor* F on $\mathbf{Spec}$ is a monotonic graph morphism that preserves identities and satisfies the inequation $F(g \,⨾\, h) \sqsubseteq Fg \,⨾\, Fh$. Let $F : \mathbf{IRel} \to \mathbf{IRel}$ be a monotonic functor. There is a minimum upfunctor $\widehat{F}$ on $\mathbf{Spec}$ that agrees with F on ideals, given by $\widehat{F}A = FA$ and $\widehat{F}g = [FR]\,;\langle FS\rangle$ where R, S factor g as $g = [R]\,;\langle S\rangle$. (Similarly for bifunctors.) Agreeing with ideals means $\widehat{F}[R] = [FR]$. Moreover, $\widehat{F}$ satisfies

$$\widehat{F}(m \,⨾\, g \,⨾\, c) = \widehat{F}m \,⨾\, \widehat{F}g \,⨾\, \widehat{F}c \quad \text{if } m \text{ is a map and } c \text{ a comap.} \tag{5}$$

The lifted coproduct $\widehat{+}$ is monotonic and is a categorical coproduct, but the lifted product, which we write as $\otimes$, weakens as discussed in §1.

Define $A \otimes B$ to be the product $A \times B$ of prosets. The left projection is $[\pi_0] \in \mathbf{Spec}(A \otimes B, A)$ where π_0 is the projection function. For $f \in \mathbf{Spec}(D, A)$ and $g \in \mathbf{Spec}(D, B)$, the 'pairing' $(f \vartriangle g) \in \mathbf{Spec}(D, A \otimes B)$ generalizes the pairing of functions, but we do not need the explicit definition. As usual, we define $f \otimes g = [\pi_0] \,⨾\, f \vartriangle [\pi_1] \,⨾\, g$.

We say $f \in \mathbf{Spec}(A, B)$ is *strict* if $f\emptyset = \emptyset$ and *costrict* if $fB = A$. Comaps are strict.

Proposition 5 *For all transformers* d, e, f, g, h *of suitable types we have*

$$\begin{array}{rcll}
(f \vartriangle g) \,⨾\, [\pi_0] & \sqsubseteq & f & \textit{if } g \textit{ is strict} \qquad (6)\\
(f \vartriangle g) \,⨾\, [\pi_0] & \sqsupseteq & f & \textit{if } g \textit{ is costrict}\\
h \,⨾\, [\pi_0] \vartriangle h \,⨾\, [\pi_1] & \sqsupseteq & h & \textit{if } h \textit{ is a comap (and } \sqsubseteq \textit{ if } h \textit{ is a map)}\\
h \,⨾\, f \vartriangle h \,⨾\, g & \sqsupseteq & h \,⨾\, (f \vartriangle g) & \textit{if } h \textit{ is a comap} \qquad (7)\\
h \,⨾\, f \vartriangle h \,⨾\, g & \sqsubseteq & h \,⨾\, (f \vartriangle g) & \textit{if } h \textit{ is a map}\\
d \,⨾\, f \vartriangle e \,⨾\, g & \sqsubseteq & (d \vartriangle e) \,⨾\, (f \otimes g) & \qquad (8)\\
d \,⨾\, f \vartriangle e \,⨾\, g & = & (d \vartriangle e) \,⨾\, (f \otimes g) & \textit{if } f, g \textit{ are maps or all are comaps}
\end{array}$$

Moreover, $\vartriangle, \otimes$ *preserve maps and comaps. Such a structure is is unique up to natural isomorphism.*

Define the proset $B \rightsquigarrow C$ to be $\mathbf{Spec}(B, C)$ ordered by $\sqsubseteq$. This is not (in any direct sense) a lifting from $\mathbf{IRel}$. 'Application' is an arrow $\mathsf{ap}_{B,C}$ in $\mathbf{Spec}((B \rightsquigarrow C) \otimes B\,,\, C)$; operationally, it executes a stored program from a given initial state. We do not need the definition of ap, just its properties, and the same for 'Currying'. For f in $\mathbf{Spec}(A \otimes B, C)$, $\mathsf{cur} f$ is in $\mathbf{Spec}(A, B \rightsquigarrow C)$. For h in $\mathbf{Spec}(C, A)$, define $B \rightsquigarrow h = \mathsf{cur}(\mathsf{ap} \,⨾\, h)$, so that $B \rightsquigarrow h$ is in $\mathbf{Spec}((B \rightsquigarrow C), (B \rightsquigarrow A))$.

Proposition 6 *For any* f, $\mathsf{cur} f$ *is a bimap. Also,* $(B \rightsquigarrow) : \mathbf{Spec} \to \mathbf{Spec}$ *is a* *monotonic functor and for all f, g of suitable types we have*

$$
\begin{array}{rcll}
(\mathsf{cur} f \otimes \mathsf{id}) \mathbin{;} \mathsf{ap} & = & f & \quad (9)\\
\mathsf{cur}((f \otimes \mathsf{id}) \mathbin{;} \mathsf{ap}) & \sqsubseteq & f \quad \textit{if } f \textit{ is a map} & \quad (10)\\
\mathsf{cur}((f \otimes \mathsf{id}) \mathbin{;} \mathsf{ap}) & = & f \quad \textit{if } f \textit{ is a bimap} & \quad (11)\\
\mathsf{cur}(g \mathbin{;} f) & = & g \mathbin{;} (B \rightsquigarrow f) & \\
\mathsf{cur}((f \otimes \mathsf{id}) \mathbin{;} g) & \sqsubseteq & f \mathbin{;} \mathsf{cur}\, g \quad \textit{if } f \textit{ is a map} & \\
\mathsf{cur}((f \otimes \mathsf{id}) \mathbin{;} g) & = & f \mathbin{;} \mathsf{cur}\, g \quad \textit{if } f \textit{ is a bimap} & \quad (12)
\end{array}
$$

Such a structure is unique up to natural isomorphism.

Note that not even (10) holds for all transformers, but the evaluation rule (9) does: Currying a program and then executing it is the same as just executing it, even for nondeterministic and possibly-divergent programs.

5 INDUCTIVE DATA TYPES IN Spec

After the lifting of products and coproducts was well understood, the problem of lifting inductive data types to transformers remained open for some time. The solution found for powerset transformers by de Moor (1992) works here as well: Initial algebras in **Spec** are obtained from initial algebras in **MFun** by applying the inverse image operator $[-]$ and using the final coalgebra property in **IRel**. There are minor differences in the proof due to the absence of reciprocation and the presence of order. In this section we assume that $F : \mathbf{IRel}^2 \to \mathbf{IRel}$ is a monotonic functor that has fixpoints and commutes with op-reciprocation.

Theorem 7 *The upfunctor $\widehat{F} : \mathbf{Spec}^2 \to \mathbf{Spec}$ has fixpoints.*

Proof. The initial algebra for B is the inverse image $[\mathsf{in}\widetilde{B}]$ of the initial algebra for $\widetilde{B}$ in **IRel**. Being an initial algebra, $\mathsf{in}\widetilde{B}$ is an isomorphism, hence a map in **IRel**. Thus by Lemma 1(b) we have $[\mathsf{in}\widetilde{B}] = \langle(\mathsf{in}\widetilde{B})^{o}\rangle$, which exhibits the initial algebra for B in **Spec** as the direct image of the final coalgebra for B in **IRel** (by Theorem 4). Let g be in $\mathbf{Spec}(F(B, A), A)$. We will derive the definition of catamorphism $(\!|g|\!)$ in terms of an anamorphism in **IRel**. We need to show for any h in $\mathbf{Spec}(\mathsf{fix}B, A)$

$$
h = (\!|g|\!) \;\equiv\; [\mathsf{in}\widetilde{B}] \mathbin{;} h = \widehat{F}(\mathsf{id}, h) \mathbin{;} g
\qquad
\begin{array}{ccc}
F(B, \mathsf{fix}B) & \xrightarrow{[\mathsf{in}\widetilde{B}]} & \mathsf{fix}B \\
{\scriptstyle \widehat{F}(\mathsf{id},h)}\downarrow & & \downarrow{\scriptstyle h} \\
F(B, A) & \xrightarrow[g]{} & A
\end{array}
\qquad (13)
$$

We calculate in **IRel**, so (13) takes the form

$$h = (\![g]\!) \equiv h \, ; [\mathsf{in}\widetilde{B}] = g \, ; \widehat{F}(\mathsf{id}, h) \qquad \begin{array}{ccc} \mathcal{U}(F(B, \mathsf{fix}B)) & \xleftarrow{[\mathsf{in}\widetilde{B}]} & \mathcal{U}(\mathsf{fix}B) \\ {\scriptstyle \widehat{F}(\mathsf{id},h)} \uparrow & & \uparrow {\scriptstyle h} \\ \mathcal{U}(F(B, A)) & \xleftarrow[g]{} & \mathcal{U}A \end{array} \tag{14}$$

Any h factors as $h = [\ni] \, ; \langle h \, ; \ni \rangle$, and id factors as $[\preceq] \, ; \langle \preceq \rangle$. Thus we have

$$\begin{array}{cll} & g \, ; \widehat{F}(\mathsf{id}, h) & \\ = & g \, ; [F(\preceq, \ni)] \, ; \langle F(\preceq, (h \, ; \ni)) \rangle & \text{factorization, definition of } \widehat{F} \\ = & g \, ; \Lambda(\ni / F(\preceq, \ni)) \, ; \langle F(\preceq, (h \, ; \ni)) \rangle & \text{definition of } [-] \\ = & \Lambda(g \, ; \ni / F(\preceq, \ni) \, ; F(\preceq, (h \, ; \ni))) & g \text{ function, power calculus (2)} \\ = & \Lambda((g \, ; \ni) / F(\preceq, \ni) \, ; F(\preceq, (h \, ; \ni))) & g \text{ function, quotient property} \end{array}$$

We also have

$$\begin{array}{cll} & h \, ; [\mathsf{in}\widetilde{B}] & \\ = & h \, ; \langle (\mathsf{in}\widetilde{B})^{o} \rangle & \mathsf{in}\widetilde{B} \text{ map in } \mathbf{IRel}, \text{ Lemma 1(b)} \\ = & h \, ; \Lambda(\ni \, ; (\mathsf{in}\widetilde{B})^{\ominus}) & \text{definitions of } \langle - \rangle \text{ and } {}^{\ominus} \\ = & \Lambda(h \, ; \ni \, ; (\mathsf{in}\widetilde{B})^{\ominus}) & h \text{ function, power calculus (2)} \end{array}$$

Now (14) is shown by

$$\begin{array}{cll} & h \, ; [\mathsf{in}\widetilde{B}] = g \, ; \widehat{F}(\mathsf{id}, h) & \\ \equiv & \Lambda(h \, ; \ni \, ; (\mathsf{in}\widetilde{B})^{\ominus}) = \Lambda((g \, ; \ni) / F(\preceq, \ni) \, ; F(\preceq, (h \, ; \ni))) & \text{above} \\ \equiv & h \, ; \ni \, ; (\mathsf{in}\widetilde{B})^{\ominus} = (g \, ; \ni) / F(\preceq, \ni) \, ; F(\preceq, (h \, ; \ni)) & \text{power calc. (1)} \\ \equiv & h \, ; \ni = [\![(g \, ; \ni) / F(\preceq, \ni)]\!] & \text{anamorphism (4)} \\ \equiv & h = \Lambda[\![(g \, ; \ni) / F(\preceq, \ni)]\!] & \text{power calc. (1)} \end{array}$$

and we have found the definition $(\![g]\!) = \Lambda[\![(g \, ; \ni) / F(\preceq, \ni)]\!]$. □

Lemma 8 *If g is a bimap then so is* $(\![g]\!)$.

The proof, by tedious manipulations using Lemma 1(b), is omitted.

On the face of it, catamorphisms embody only a very simple form of structural recursion. In combination with exponents, however, catamorphisms give recursion with an extra parameter. A rather general formulation is needed for repmin.

Theorem 9 *Suppose* $F : \mathbf{IRel}^2 \to \mathbf{IRel}$ *is a monotonic functor with fixpoints and* $G : \mathbf{Spec}^2 \to \mathbf{Spec}$ *is an upfunctor such that*

$$G(\mathsf{id}, \mathsf{id}, (f \,;\, h)) = G(\mathsf{id}, \mathsf{id}, f) \,;\, G(\mathsf{id}, \mathsf{id}, h) \quad \textit{for all } h \textit{ and all bimaps } f. \tag{15}$$

Suppose further that there is a family ψ *of arrows* $\psi_{A,B,C} : (\widehat{F}(A, B) \otimes C) \to G(A, C, B \otimes C)$ *with the following naturality property:*

$$\psi \,;\, G(\mathsf{id}, \mathsf{id}, f \otimes \mathsf{id}) = (\widehat{F}(\mathsf{id}, f) \otimes \mathsf{id}) \,;\, \psi \quad \textit{for all bimaps } f.$$

Then for any A, B, C, *and* h *in* $\mathbf{Spec}(G(B, A), C)$ *there is a unique* x *solving the equation* $([\mathsf{in}\widetilde{B}] \otimes \mathsf{id}) \,;\, x = \psi \,;\, G(\mathsf{id}, \mathsf{id}, x) \,;\, h$.

The types in the following picture indicate how the result gives a parameterized form of the catamorphism recursion, and why ψ is needed to rearrange arguments.

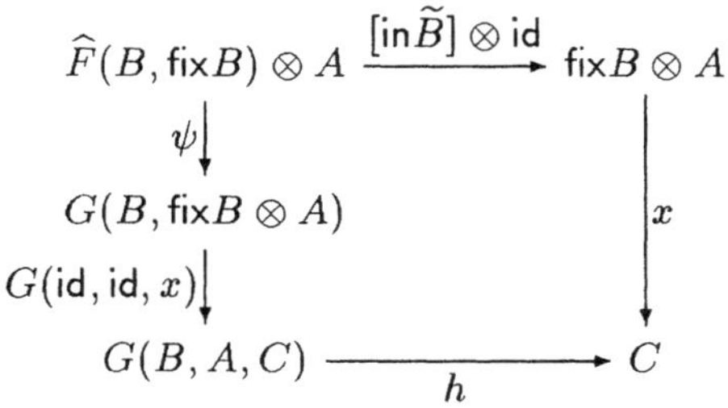

The hypotheses for F, G and ψ are satisfied for functors lifted from $\mathbf{MFun}$ and $\mathbf{IRel}$ (recall (5)). For the repmin derivation the theorem is used twice, once with $G(B, A, C) = \widehat{F}(A, C)$ and once with $G(B, A, C) = \widehat{F}(B \otimes A, C)$. In both cases ψ is defined in terms of a so-called *distributor* $dist\ \widehat{F} : \widehat{F}B \times A \to \widehat{F}(B \times A)$, which determines a distributor $dist\ \mathsf{fix} : \mathsf{fix}B \times A \to \mathsf{fix}(B \times A)$ that pairs an element $a \in A$ with each node of a tree of Bs.

Proof. We calculate in $\mathbf{Spec}$:

	$([\mathsf{in}\widetilde{B}] \otimes \mathsf{id}) \,;\, x = \psi \,;\, G(\mathsf{id}, \mathsf{id}, x) \,;\, h$	
$\equiv$	$\mathsf{cur}(([\mathsf{in}\widetilde{B}] \otimes \mathsf{id}) \,;\, x) = \mathsf{cur}(\psi \,;\, G(\mathsf{id}, \mathsf{id}, x) \,;\, h)$	cur injective, by (9)
$\equiv$	$[\mathsf{in}\widetilde{B}] \,;\, \mathsf{cur}\ x = \mathsf{cur}(\psi \,;\, G(\mathsf{id}, \mathsf{id}, x) \,;\, h)$	$[\mathsf{in}\widetilde{B}]$ bimap, (12)
$\equiv$	$[\mathsf{in}\widetilde{B}] \,;\, \mathsf{cur}\ x = \widehat{F}(\mathsf{id}, \mathsf{cur}\ x) \,;\, k$	assumption for k below
$\equiv$	$\mathsf{cur}\ x = (\!\lbrack k \rbrack\!)$	catamorphism (13)
$\Rightarrow$	$x = ((\!\lbrack k \rbrack\!) \otimes \mathsf{id}) \,;\, \mathsf{ap}$	exponent (9)

In the third step, we assume there is some $k : \widehat{F}(B, A \rightsquigarrow C) \to A \rightsquigarrow C$ such that $\mathsf{cur}(\psi \fatsemi G(\mathsf{id}, \mathsf{id}, x) \fatsemi h) = \widehat{F}(\mathsf{id}, \mathsf{cur}\ x) \fatsemi k$. So it remains to discharge the assumption about k and show the reverse implication. We derive k as follows, using that $\widehat{F}$ and $\otimes$ preserve bimaps (from the theory of lifting).

$$
\begin{array}{lll}
 & \mathsf{cur}(\psi \fatsemi G(\mathsf{id}, \mathsf{id}, x) \fatsemi h) & \\
= & \mathsf{cur}(\psi \fatsemi G(\mathsf{id}, \mathsf{id}, (\mathsf{cur}\ x \otimes \mathsf{id}) \fatsemi \mathsf{ap}) \fatsemi h) & \text{exponent (9)} \\
= & \mathsf{cur}(\psi \fatsemi G(\mathsf{id}, \mathsf{id}, \mathsf{cur}\ x \otimes \mathsf{id}) \fatsemi G(\mathsf{id}, \mathsf{id}, \mathsf{ap})) \fatsemi h) & \text{hypoth. (15), } \mathsf{cur}\ x \text{ bimap} \\
= & \mathsf{cur}((\widehat{F}(\mathsf{id}, \mathsf{cur}\ x) \otimes \mathsf{id}) \fatsemi \psi \fatsemi G(\mathsf{id}, \mathsf{id}, \mathsf{ap}) \fatsemi h) & \mathsf{cur}\ x \text{ bimap, } \psi \text{ natural} \\
= & \widehat{F}(\mathsf{id}, \mathsf{cur}\ x) \fatsemi \mathsf{cur}(\psi \fatsemi G(\mathsf{id}, \mathsf{id}, \mathsf{ap}) \fatsemi h) & \text{exp. (12), } \mathsf{cur}\ x \text{ bimap}
\end{array}
$$

We have derived $k = \mathsf{cur}(\psi \fatsemi G(\mathsf{id}, \mathsf{id}, \mathsf{ap}) \fatsemi h)$. Because k is $\mathsf{cur}(\ldots)$, it is a bimap, hence so is $(\![k]\!)$ (Lemma 8), which we use to show the reverse of the implication step in the first calculation.

$$
\begin{array}{lll}
 & x = ((\![\mathsf{cur}(\psi \fatsemi G(\mathsf{id}, \mathsf{id}, \mathsf{ap}) \fatsemi h)]\!) \otimes \mathsf{id}) \fatsemi \mathsf{ap} & \\
\Rightarrow & \mathsf{cur}\ x = \mathsf{cur}(((\![k]\!) \otimes \mathsf{id}) \fatsemi \mathsf{ap}) & \text{Leibniz, definition of } k \\
\Rightarrow & \mathsf{cur}\ x = (\![k]\!) & \text{exponent (11), } (\![k]\!) \text{ bimap}
\end{array}
$$

□

For powerset transformers, the closed form derived above is only a least solution for x (Naumann 1994*b*). The difference is that k need not be a bimap in the powerset setting, so the proof does not go through as above.

6 APPLICATION TO THE REPMIN PROBLEM

The companion paper (Naumann 1998) develops problem-specific results and gives the repmin derivation in detail. Here we just sketch and assess the result.

Let us begin with an informal description in terms of functions. From the distributor $dist\,\mathsf{fix} : \mathsf{fix}B \times A \to \mathsf{fix}(B \times A)$ one obtains rep defined as the composite $(dist\,\mathsf{fix}\ ;\ \mathsf{fix}\,\pi_1) : \mathsf{fix}B \times A \to \mathsf{fix}A$ which replaces every node of a tree with a given value $a \in A$. The composite $(\mathsf{id} \vartriangle (\![min]\!))\ ;\ rep$ replaces every node of a tree with the minimum (according to min) of the tree. This definition for repmin involves two traversals because $dist\,\mathsf{fix}$ is defined from $dist\ F$ by catamorphism. But the recursion theorem can be used to derive a single-traversal program, which applies a Curried program. In terms of functional combinators, with F instantiated to the base for type $Ltree$, the result can be expressed in ML as follows.

```
datatype 'b tree = Leaf of 'b | Bin of ('b tree) * ('b tree);
fun repm (Leaf x)    = (x, Leaf)
 |  repm (Bin(u,v)) = let val (x,f) = repm u
                          val (y,g) = repm v
                         in ( min(x,y), fn w => Bin (f w, g w) )
                        end;
fun repmin t = let val (m,r) = repm t in r(m) end;
```

Function `repmin` works by constructing a pair consisting of the minimum `m` of the tree and a closure `r` which is then applied to `m`. Although the input is traversed just once, the closure is built from tree constructors in the same shape as the input.

The ML code is not polytypic, but polytypism has been implemented in functional languages (Jansson & Jeuring 1997). Polytypism aside, what is the imperative interpretation? Alas, the derived program is not directly expressible in conventional languages. It is the composite of transformers

$$Ltree\,\mathbb{N} \xrightarrow{(\!|h \vartriangle [min]|\!)} (\mathbb{N} \rightsquigarrow Ltree\,\mathbb{N}) \otimes \mathbb{N} \xrightarrow{\mathsf{ap}} Ltree\,\mathbb{N}$$

(where $h \vartriangle [min]$ corresponds to the body of `repm` above); but transformers model commands, and commands in conventional languages have the same final as initial state space.* Moreover, it is usually procedures rather than commands that can be stored or passed as parameters. Roughly speaking, however, the imperative interpretation is the same as the ML code above. The point is not that we derive an imperative program different from the functional one, but that it can be done in a setting where imperative constructs can be used in conjunction with $\rightsquigarrow$ and $(\!|-|\!)$.

As an aside, conventional imperative languages like C, C++, and Modula-3 do not allow closures to reference local variables like `f` and `g` above that are not in outermost scope, to simplify the runtime stack. In Naumann (1994*a*) this restriction helps avoid the much-studied problems of Algol, and constants (single-assignment variables) are used to express programs like that above. Variables in ML are single-assignment, but there are reference types for mutable cells.

It would be more striking to derive an essentially imperative repmin. For example, the following ML program constructs, in a single pass, a tree of references all to the same cell `m`. Program `repminr` initializes that cell, which is then updated to maintain the invariant that it is the minimum of the leaves that have been visited.

*In his talk at POPL 1998, John Reynolds remarked that it may be time to consider allowing commands that change the shape of their state space; at the 1996 MFPS workshop the author presented such a language, with stored commands modeled by the exponent of transformers.

```
datatype 'b tr = Leafr of 'b ref | Binr of ('b tr) * ('b tr);
val m = ref 0; (* arbitrary value *)
fun repmr (Leaf x) = ( m := min(x,!m); Leafr m  )
 |  repmr (Bin(u,v)) = let val t = repmr u
                           val s = repmr v
                          in Binr (t,s)
                         end;
fun repminr t = ( m := maxint; repmr t );
```

It is also possible to deal with trees of references without aliasing. The traversal can build a list of references to the nodes; that list is then traversed to set each leaf's cell to the minimum. The list could be stored as a singly linked list and accessed as a stack, resulting in better performance than the original program with two traversals. But such programs do not come from an interpretation of the exponent as a procedure type. Perhaps it is possible to treat heap storage and references as some form of exponent. Alternatively, one could use a data refinement transform the tree-structured closures into a concrete tree – but the functional program might be an adequate starting point for that.

Rather than explore either alternative, we turn to the more general question of whether the homset of transformers is a sensible model for stored procedures in program derivation.

7 DATA REFINEMENT AND THE CONCRETE EXPONENT

Let us assume there is some sub-procat **Prog** of **Spec** such that arrows in **Prog** correspond to concrete programs. For example, **Prog** could be the strict, positively conjunctive, continuous transformers. We assume **Prog** is closed under $\otimes$. So if f', g' are in **Prog** and $f \sqsubseteq f', g \sqsubseteq g'$, then $f' \Delta g'$ is a concrete refinement of $f \Delta g$. But for $f \in \mathbf{Spec}(A \otimes B, C)$ and f' in **Prog**, the refinement $f \sqsubseteq f'$ does not imply that $\mathsf{cur} f'$ is a concrete refinement of $\mathsf{cur} f$, because cur introduces the rather abstract type $B \rightsquigarrow C$. In this section we consider the exponent $B \rightsquigarrow' C = \mathbf{Prog}(B, C)$. We define the associated constructs ap' and cur' and we show how data refinement can be used to justify the following rule:

Suppose f is in $\mathbf{Prog}(A, B)$ for exponent-free A, B, and f' is f with all occurrences of $\mathsf{ap}, \mathsf{cur}, \rightsquigarrow$ replaced by their concrete counterparts $\mathsf{ap}', \mathsf{cur}', \rightsquigarrow'$. Then $f \sqsubseteq f'$. (16)

Section 8 gives the specific data refinement justifying the rule. The rule licenses us to ignore the distinction between $\rightsquigarrow$ and $\rightsquigarrow'$ in practice.

First, we need the definitions of ap and cur. For all $\psi \in \mathcal{U}C$, $b \in B$, and $g \in B \rightsquigarrow C$, define $(b, g) \in \mathsf{ap}\psi \equiv b \in g\psi$. For all $a \in A$ and $\varphi \in \mathcal{U}(B \rightsquigarrow C)$, define $a \in \mathsf{cur} f \varphi \equiv \mathsf{cu} f a \in \varphi$, where $\mathsf{cu} f a \in \mathbf{Spec}(B, C)$ is defined by $b \in \mathsf{cu} f a \psi \equiv (a, b) \in f\psi$. The definition of ap' in $\mathbf{Prog}((B \rightsquigarrow' C) \otimes B, C)$ is the same as for ap

but with $\rightsquigarrow$ replaced by $\rightsquigarrow'$. For any f in **Prog**, the definition of $\mathsf{cur}' f$ is the same as for $\mathsf{cur}\, f$ but with φ ranging over $\mathcal{U}(B \rightsquigarrow' C)$. For ap' and cur' to have reasonable properties, $\mathsf{cu} f a$ should be in **Prog** for every a, if $f \in$ **Prog**. This is true if **Prog** is defined by healthiness. Note that $\mathsf{cur}' f$ is not defined for f not in **Prog**; cur' can be extended to **Spec** but with poor properties.

For f in $\mathbf{Spec}(A, B)$ to be *data-refined* by f' in $\mathbf{Spec}(A', B')$ *via simulation s* means that $s_A \in \mathbf{Spec}(A', A)$ and $s_B \in \mathbf{Spec}(B', B)$ are comaps such that

$$s_A \fatsemi f \sqsubseteq f' \fatsemi s_B \qquad \begin{array}{ccc} A' & \xrightarrow{\;f'\;} & B' \\ {\scriptstyle s_A}\downarrow & \sqsubseteq & \downarrow{\scriptstyle s_B} \\ A & \xrightarrow[\;f\;]{} & B \end{array} \tag{17}$$

Any comap $A' \to A$ is $\langle R \rangle$ for some $R \in \mathbf{IRel}(A, A')$, and the ideal property makes sense if aRa' means that a is simulated by a' and $\preceq$ means refinement or approximation. The conjunction of (17) and the comap requirement has been called *total simulation*; note that it does not require the underlying relations to be total or functional.

Data refinement is normally used as follows: for primitive types A, B and operations f, one explicitly defines s_A and s_B and proves (17). For constructed f, there should be a general result to the effect that constructed arrows are data refined via suitably constructed simulations; such constructs are said to *preserve data refinement*. For example, suppose (17) holds and also $g : A \to C$ is data-refined to $g' : A' \to C'$ by s_A, s_C. Then $f \vartriangle g$ should be data-refined by $f' \vartriangle g'$ via s_A and $s_{B \otimes C}$ where $s_{B \otimes C} = s_B \otimes s_C$.

The product and exponent in **Spec** preserve data refinement (Naumann 1995*a*); in particular, $s_{B \rightsquigarrow C}$ is defined as $s_B^* \rightsquigarrow s_C$ where s_B^* is the map determined by comap s_B. The usual imperative constructs preserve data refinement (Gardiner & Morgan 1991). The catamorphism construct preserves data refinement, because it can be expressed using general recursion which preserves data refinement. The local variable construct has been shown to preserve data refinement, but the proofs in the literature are at the level of predicates. We give a proof here because it demonstrates program-level calculation in **Spec** and because it provides a simple proof of soundness as explained below.

In the context of some 'global' state space(s), the local variable construct augments the state space with a new variable initialized in terms of the global state space, and then it executes the command and drops the new variable. Thus it takes an arrow $f : A \otimes B \to A \otimes C$ in **Spec** and an initialization $i : B \to A$ and yields the arrow $\mathsf{var}(i, f) : B \to C$ defined as $(i \vartriangle \mathsf{id}_B) \fatsemi f \fatsemi [\pi]$.

Theorem 10 *Local variables preserve data refinement. That is, if we have both* $s_{A \otimes B} \fatsemi f \sqsubseteq f' \fatsemi s_{A \otimes C}$ *and* $s_B \fatsemi i \sqsubseteq i' \fatsemi s_A$ *then* $\mathsf{var}(i, f)$ *is data-refined by* $\mathsf{var}(i', f')$ *via* s_B *and* s_C.

Proof. The result follows by pasting together the inequalities for the three components of $\mathsf{var}(i, f)$, depicted as follows.*

$$\begin{array}{ccccccc}
B' & \xrightarrow{i' \,\Delta\, \mathsf{id}'_B} & A' \otimes B' & \xrightarrow{f'} & A' \otimes C' & \xrightarrow{\pi} & C' \\
{\scriptstyle s_B}\downarrow & \sqsubseteq & \downarrow{\scriptstyle s_{A \otimes B}} & \sqsubseteq & \downarrow{\scriptstyle s_{A \otimes C}} & \sqsubseteq & \downarrow{\scriptstyle s_C} \\
B & \xrightarrow[i \,\Delta\, \mathsf{id}_B]{} & A \otimes B & \xrightarrow[f]{} & A \otimes C & \xrightarrow[\pi]{} & C
\end{array}$$

The middle inequality is by hypothesis, the right one follows from law (6), and

$$\begin{array}{lll}
 & s_B \,\text{;}\, (i \,\Delta\, \mathsf{id}) & \\
\sqsubseteq & s_B \,\text{;}\, i \,\Delta\, s_B & s \text{ comap, law (7)} \\
\sqsubseteq & i' \,\text{;}\, s_A \,\Delta\, s_B & \text{hypothesis (simulation for } i) \\
\sqsubseteq & (i' \,\Delta\, \mathsf{id}) \,\text{;}\, s_{A,B} & \text{law (8), } s_{A \otimes B} = s_A \otimes s_B
\end{array}$$

which proves the left inequality. □

Data refinement is used to prove ordinary refinement of programs in which the refined data is encapsulated as local variables, which is usually described as follows.

Corollary 11 (Soundness) *If* $i' : B \to A'$ *is data-refined by* $i : B \to A$ *via* s_A *and* $f' : A' \otimes B \to A' \otimes C$ *by* $f : A \otimes B \to A \otimes C$ *via* s_A *then* $\mathsf{var}(i, f) \sqsubseteq \mathsf{var}(i', f')$.

Proof. Take $R_A = \mathsf{id}_A$ and $R_C = \mathsf{id}_C$ in the theorem. □

A very similar notion of soundness justifies rule (16). If $s_A = \mathsf{id}$ and $s_B = \mathsf{id}$ then (17) is just $f \sqsubseteq f'$. So one can prove $f \sqsubseteq f'$ by data-refining constituents of f to corresponding constituents of f', and then conclude $f \sqsubseteq f'$ provided that the 'observable' types A, B are simulated by identities and the constructs preserve data refinement. We refrain from formalizing the result or its proof.

8 FROM Spec-EXPONENT TO Prog-EXPONENT

Typically, a simulation is the identity on observable types because it is built inductively from simulations on primitive types, with identity simulations for observable types and constructors that preserve identities. But here we need to refine a constructor itself (namely $\leadsto$). We shall give non-identity simulations for $\leadsto$-types, but take all simulations on primitives to be identity. Thus if $f : A \to B$ is simulated by

*Here we assume that $s_{A,B} = s_A \otimes s_C$ and $s_{A,C} = s_A \otimes s_C$ for some s_A, s_B, s_C. The assumption is reasonable: if $s_{A,C}$ involves A, C in combination then A will not be localized separately.

$f' : A' \rightarrow B'$ and A', B' are exponent-free then $A = A'$, $B = B'$, and $f \sqsubseteq f'$. That is why rule (16) needs the proviso that type are $\leadsto$-free.

Define $\mathsf{inc} : (B \leadsto' C) \rightarrow (B \leadsto C)$ to be the inclusion function. The simulation will be its inverse image $[\mathsf{inc}]$ in $\mathbf{Spec}((B \leadsto' C), (B \leadsto C))$, which is a bimap by Lemma 8(b). For any $g \in B \leadsto' C$ and $\varphi \in \mathcal{U}(B \leadsto C)$ we have $g \in [\mathsf{inc}]\varphi \equiv g \in \varphi$. Put differently, $[\mathsf{inc}]\varphi = \varphi \cap (B \leadsto' C)$. Informally, if φ is a predicate on programs then $[\mathsf{inc}]\varphi$ is the predicate 'satisfies φ and is in $\mathbf{Prog}$'.

Formal proof of rule (16) is by induction on the structure of f, and simulations are defined by induction on the structure of types (needed because $\leadsto$-types can be nested). The interesting case is the simulation $s_{A \leadsto B}$ which needs to have type $(A' \leadsto' B') \rightarrow (A \leadsto B)$ using $s_A : A' \rightarrow A$ and $s_B : B' \rightarrow B$. One defines $s_{A \leadsto B}$ as

$$A' \leadsto' B' \xrightarrow{[\mathsf{inc}]} A' \leadsto B' \xrightarrow{s_A^* \leadsto s_B} A \leadsto B$$

But the second half, i.e. $s_A^* \leadsto s_B$, is treated in Naumann (1995*a*) to show that $\leadsto$ preserves data refinement. To focus on what is new, we treat only the special case $s_A = \mathsf{id}_A$ and $s_B = \mathsf{id}_B$ so that $s_{A \leadsto B}$ is just $[\mathsf{inc}]$ (because $\leadsto$ preserves identities).

Theorem 12 ap' *data-refines* ap *via* $[\mathsf{inc}]$. *And for any f in* $\mathbf{Prog}(A \otimes B, C)$, $\mathsf{cur} f$ *is data-refined by* $\mathsf{cur}' f$ *via* $[\mathsf{inc}]$.

The proof is a straightforward calculation at the level of predicates. The pictures are as follows (the righthand diagram is actually an equality).

$$\begin{array}{ccc} A \otimes (A \leadsto' B) & \xrightarrow{\mathsf{ap}'} & B \\ \mathsf{id} \otimes [\mathsf{inc}] \downarrow & \sqsubseteq & \downarrow \mathsf{id} \\ A \otimes (A \leadsto B) & \xrightarrow[\mathsf{ap}]{} & B \end{array} \qquad \begin{array}{ccc} A & \xrightarrow{\mathsf{cur}' f} & B \leadsto' C \\ \mathsf{id} \downarrow & \sqsubseteq & \downarrow [\mathsf{inc}] \\ A & \xrightarrow[\mathsf{cur} f]{} & B \leadsto C \end{array}$$

9 DISCUSSION

Although some algebraic laws of imperative programming are weaker than those of functional and relational programming – e.g. for product and exponent – Theorem 9 for recursion on inductive data types is no weaker than for functions, despite applying to all transformers. Because the exponent includes specifications as well as concrete programs, it is not a concrete data type, and the exponent of concrete programs does not have adequate algebraic properties. Thanks to Theorem 12, it is always sound to derive a program using laws of the abstract exponent and to interpret the result in terms of the concrete one.

An application to the repmin problem was briefly sketched. It is encouraging that the laws are adequate for a nontrivial example. But the gap between implemented imperative languages and the notations used in methodological studies remains larger than for functional languages, perhaps because command typing has been neglected (not to mention polytypism).

The repmin example does not make a strong case for the algebra of transformers, because with our interpretation of the exponent the derived program is essentially the same as its functional counterpart. Much more striking would be derivation of a first-order program using pointers. Perhaps a relational theory of pointers like that of Möller (1997) can be lifted. Is there a connection between pointers and exponents beyond the writing of arrows?

REFERENCES

Bird, R. & de Moor, O. (1996) *Algebra of Programming*. Prentice-Hall.

de Moor, O. (1992) Inductive data types for predicate transformers. *Information Processing Letters* **43**(3), 113–118.

de Moor, O. (1996) An exercise in polytypic programming: repmin. Typescript, www.comlab.ox.ac.uk/oucl/publications/books/algebra/papers/repmin.ps.gz.

Gardiner, P. H., Martin, C. E. & de Moor, O. (1994) An algebraic construction of predicate transformers. *Science of Computer Programming* **22**, 21–44.

Gardiner, P. & Morgan, C. (1991) Data refinement of predicate transformers. *Theoretical Computer Science* **87**, 143–162.

Jansson, P. & Jeuring, J. (1997) PolyP — a polytypic programming language extension. *In* Proceedings, POPL, ACM Press, pp. 470–82.

Martin, C. (1995) Towards a calculus of predicate transformers. *In* Proceedings, MFCS, Vol. 969 of *Springer LNCS*, pp. 489–49.

Möller, B. (1997) Calculating with pointer structures. *In* IFIP TC2/WG2.1 Working Conference on Algorithmic Languages and Calculi.

Morgan, C. (1994) *Programming from Specifications, second edition*. Prentice Hall.

Naumann, D. A. (1994*a*) Predicate transformer semantics of an Oberon-like language. *In* E.-R. Olderog, ed., *Programming Concepts, Methods and Calculi*, IFIP Transactions A-56, Elsevier.

Naumann, D. A. (1994*b*) A recursion theorem for predicate transformers on inductive data types. *Information Processing Letters* **50**, 329–336.

Naumann, D. A. (1995*a*) Data refinement, call by value, and higher order programs. *Formal Aspects of Computing* **7**, 652–662.

Naumann, D. A. (1995*b*) Predicate transformers and higher order programs. *Theoretical Computer Science* **150**, 111–159.

Naumann, D. A. (1996) A categorical model for higher order imperative programming. *Mathematical Structures in Computer Science*. To appear.

Naumann, D. A. (1998) Beyond fun: Order and membership in polytypic imperative programming. *In* Mathematics of Program Construction.

10 BIOGRAPHY

Too little of software practice rests on a scientific foundation, as the author learned through experience as a professional programmer. His goal is to bridge the gap between methodological studies and the languages and tools used in practice. After completing his doctoral study at the University of Texas at Austin he joined the faculty of nearby Southwestern University, where formal methods were being integrated throughout the undergraduate curriculum. He is writing an undergraduate textbook on data structures and data refinement based on this experience. He is now Assistant Professor of Computer Science at Stevens Institute of Technology.

24

Towards a Theory of Sequential Hybrid Programs

P.K. Pandya, H.-P. Wang and Q.-W. Xu
International Institute for Software Technology
United Nations University
P.O. Box 3058, Macau
E-mail: qxu@iist.unu.edu

Abstract

A theory of Sequential Hybrid Programs (SHP) is studied. SHP is a programming notation for representing hybrid systems. It contains a phase statement and the normal sequential programming constructs such as assignments, conditionals and iterations. Time dependent dynamical activities of the system are specified by phase statements. Intermixing of these two features leads to programs with a rich diversity of behaviours including super dense computations, infinite executions, finitely divergent executions and instantaneously divergent executions. Duration calculus is extended with super dense states, fixed point operators and infinite intervals to give a logic μSDCI. A compositional semantics of SHP programs is defined using the logic μSDCI. Several high level proof rules are derived for establishing specific kinds of properties of SHP programs such as total correctness and invariance. These high level proof rules provide a modular and syntax directed method for establishing the properties of SHP programs with the program structure guiding the proof of correctness.

Keywords

Duration Calculus, hybrid system, recursion, compositional semantics, modular verification

1 INTRODUCTION

Increased application of computer technology has led to novel computing systems which call for investigation of new modelling and verification techniques. Among these are the hybrid systems which consist of interacting discrete and continuous components. Typical examples of hybrid systems are embedded computer systems in which digital programs are used to control the physical devices. The physical states evolve over time in accordance with some dynamical laws, whereas discrete actions, such as computation steps or switches

Programming Concepts and Methods D. Gries, & W-P. de Roever (Eds.)

between phases of dynamical activities, are usually considered instantaneous. Such an abstraction provides an essential simplification in reasoning about hybrid systems (Manna & Pnueli 1993).

This paper presents a theory for reasoning about hybrid systems using the framework of Duration Calculus (DC). A programming notation for hybrid systems, called Sequential Hybrid Programs (SHP), is proposed. It contains the usual constructs of sequential programming such as assignments, conditionals and iterations. These are called control actions. In addition, there are phase statements which model the time dependent dynamics. The control actions are assumed to take no time. Phase statements evolve according to some specified dynamical laws, and they may take time. Control actions govern the initiation and termination of phase statements. We use the Extended Duration Calculus (EDC) formulae (Zhou, Ravn & Hansen 1993) to specify phase statements. Thus, phase statements may be used to specify the dynamics of a single continuous phase or the behaviours of a complex sub-program. Control actions contain the usual features of sequential programs, and these can be used to realise complex controllers incorporating numerical algorithms.

SHP programs can exhibit a rich variety of behaviours including super dense computations and infinite executions. Super dense computations arise when a number of instantaneous actions occur at the same time. Iteration can give rise to infinite executions. For example, depending on whether the body P takes time, the iteration statement while b do P od can

(1) terminate in finite time after finitely many iterations,
(2) iterate a finite number of times and the last iteration does not terminate,
(3) iterate infinitely and the total execution time is not bounded,
(4) iterate infinitely and each iteration does not take time, or
(5) iterate infinitely and although infinitely many iterations takes nonzero time, the total execution time is bounded.

The fourth case, called instantaneous divergence, happens when the control program enters an infinite loop, or the system is switched repeatedly among several phases without spending any time in any of them. The last behaviour is the so called zeno behaviour, or finite divergence. For a more concrete impression of SHP programs, we refer to the toy example in Section 4.

In this paper, we give an adequate semantics which captures all the five behaviours listed above. It should be noted that although in general divergent behaviours are not desirable, to prove that they indeed do not occur, they must be modelled in the first place. For giving the semantics, we propose a version of DC with several additional features. The logic μSDCI has super dense states, infinite intervals and recursion. By super dense states, we mean the system is defined as a function from time to a pair of states where the first state represents the conditions at the beginning of control actions, and the second state represents the conditions at the end of all the control actions occurring at that time point. The intermediate states are not recorded, because in a sequential setting, the internal details during the execution of control actions are unimportant. (There is some similarity with relational semantics for sequential programs here). Fixed point operators are used to model recursive behaviours and infinite intervals capture infinite executions.

In principle, the proof rules of μSDCI can be used to derive properties of an SHP program as logical consequences of its semantics. However, this is usually not an effective method of reasoning, as the semantics can be complex. Instead, we propose a more high level modular approach. The low level logical semantics is used to derive several high level proof rules for establishing properties of interest. These include partial and total correctness, invariance and some temporal properties. Familiar logics such as Hoare Logic can be embedded within the proof method, and the normal patterns of syntax directed reasoning can be carried out using these. This is especially useful for reasoning about complex control actions, for they are modelled as sequential programs.

The rest of the paper is organised as follows. Section 2 defines the logic μSDCI after briefly reviewing the classical DC. The SHP programs and their semantics are given in Section 3. The high level proof rules for modular verification are derived in Section 4 and applied to a toy example. The paper ends with a summary and discussion.

2 LOGICS

Duration Calculi are a family of real time logics, based on the Interval Temporal Logic (ITL) (Moszkowski 1985). Formulae are constructed from the following sets of symbols: A set of global variables $GVar=\{x, y, \ldots\}$ and the meaning of a global variable is independent of time; A set of state variables $SVar=\{S, U, \ldots\}$; A set of global function symbols $FSymb=\{f^n, g^m, \ldots\}$, equipped with arities $n, m \geq 0$, and the meaning of a global function symbol f^n, $n > 0$, is an n-ary function $\underline{f}^n \in R^n \to R$; A set of global relation symbols $RSymb=\{G^n, H^m\}$, equipped with arities $n, m \geq 0$, and the meaning of a global relation symbol G^n, $n > 0$, is an n-ary relation $\underline{G}^n \subseteq R^n$; A set of temporal propositional letters $PLetter=\{X, Y, \ldots\}$.

The meaning of global variables is given by a value assignment,

$$\mathcal{V} \in GVar \to \text{Values}$$

associating a value with each global variable. In different variants of Duration Calculi, the interpretation of state variables and propositional letters are different.

The Classical DC

In the classical DC (Zhou, Hoare & Ravn 1991), intervals, interpretations of state variables and propositional letters are defined as follows

$$\begin{array}{l}\mathrm{Intv} \stackrel{\mathrm{def}}{=} \{[c,d] \in \mathrm{Time} \times \mathrm{Time} \mid c \leq d\}, \\ \mathcal{I} \in SVar \to \mathrm{Time} \to \{0{,}1\}, \qquad \mathcal{J} \in PLetters \to \mathrm{Intv} \to \{0{,}1\}.\end{array}$$

where Time denotes the set of non-negative reals. A model is a tuple of four elements $(\mathcal{I}, \mathcal{J}, \mathcal{V}, [c,d])$. The terms and formulae are defined as follows. A Boolean state expression B is constructed from (Boolean) state variables with Boolean connectives and its duration in a model

$$(\int B)(\mathcal{I}, \mathcal{J}, \mathcal{V}, [c,d]) \stackrel{\mathrm{def}}{=} \int_c^d (B)(\mathcal{I}, \mathcal{V})(t)dt$$

where $(B)(\mathcal{I}, \mathcal{V})(t)$ denotes the value of B at time t under state interpretation $\mathcal{I}$ and valuation $\mathcal{V}$. Primitive formulae of DC are constructed from terms using comparison operators in arithmetics, such as $<$, $=$ etc, and can be combined by Boolean connectives and modality operators. The length ℓ of an interval in a model is defined as $\ell \stackrel{\mathrm{def}}{=} \int 1$ and it is easy to prove that $(\ell)(\mathcal{I}, \mathcal{J}, \mathcal{V}, [c,d]) = d - c$. Boolean state expression B holds almost everywhere (i.e., except possibly a finite number of points) over an interval, denoted as $\lceil B \rceil$, is defined as, $\lceil B \rceil \stackrel{\mathrm{def}}{=} \int B = \ell \wedge \ell > 0$. A point interval is characterised by $\ell = 0$, shortened as $\lceil\rceil$. The modality 'chop' of ITL is defined as follows: for any formulae α and β,

$$\begin{array}{l}(\mathcal{I}, \mathcal{J}, \mathcal{V}, [c,d]) \models \alpha; \beta \text{ iff there exists } m \text{ such that } c \leq m \leq d \text{ and} \\ \qquad\qquad (\mathcal{I}, \mathcal{J}, \mathcal{V}, [c,m]) \models \alpha \text{ and } (\mathcal{I}, \mathcal{J}, \mathcal{V}, [m,d]) \models \beta.\end{array}$$

A property of DC, which becomes particularly important when extending the calculus with fixed point operators, is the following substitution lemma:

Substitution Lemma 1 For DC formulae $\alpha(X)$ and ϕ, where X is a propositional letter, $(\mathcal{I}, \mathcal{J}, \mathcal{V}, [c,d]) \models \alpha(\phi/X)$ iff $(\mathcal{I}, \mathcal{J}', \mathcal{V}, [c,d]) \models \alpha(X)$, where for any interval $[g,h]$, $\mathcal{J}'(X)([g,h]) = 1$ iff $(\mathcal{I}, \mathcal{J}, \mathcal{V}, [g,h]) \models \phi$, and $\mathcal{J}'(Y)([g,h]) = \mathcal{J}(Y)([g,h])$ for any $Y \neq X$. Note that substitution $\alpha(\phi/X)$ is not simple replacement of X by ϕ, because ϕ may contain free variables which become bound in α. In such cases, the bound variables in α must be appropriately renamed. The precise definition of substitution can be found in standard text books, such as (Apt & Olderog 1997).

The SDC

Hybrid systems contain physical variables which typically are of the type real. To describe and reason about hybrid systems, DC has been extended to

EDC (Zhou, Ravn & Hansen 1993), where state variables can be functions over arbitrary domains. To model state transitions, several of which may occur at one time point, DC is extended to SDC, where an interpretation of state variables is

$$\mathcal{I} \in SVar \rightarrow \text{Time} \rightarrow (\text{Values} \times \text{Values}).$$

Let $S_{\mathcal{I}}$ denote the set of all state interpretations. Let $\mathcal{I}_{\_1}$ and $\mathcal{I}_{\_2}$ respectively be $\mathcal{I}$ projected to the first and the second values. At any point t where $\mathcal{I}_{\_1}$ or $\mathcal{I}_{\_2}$ is continuous, we require that $\mathcal{I}_{\_1}(S)(t) = \mathcal{I}_{\_2}(S)(t)$. In the following diagram, the upper and lower curves represent respectively $\mathcal{I}_{\_2}(S)(t)$ and $\mathcal{I}_{\_1}(S)(t)$ as functions of time (but for visual convenience, we draw them slightly apart at continuous points).

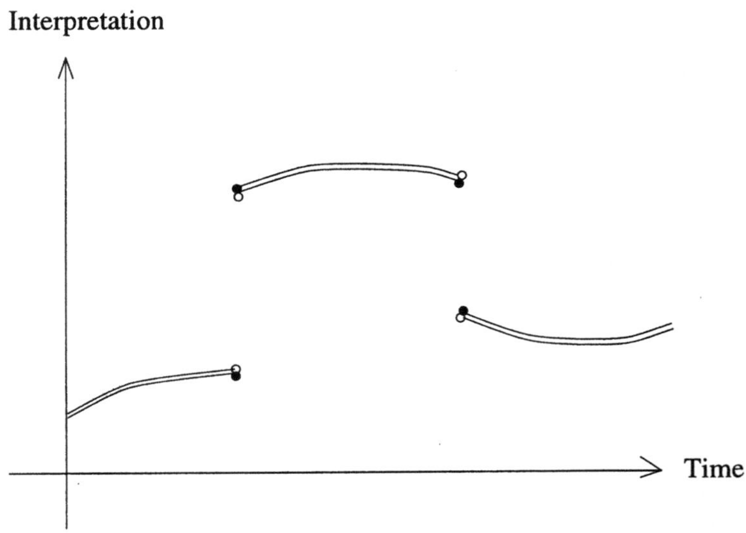

Fig. 1: Timing diagram of a state interpretation

Boolean state expressions, also called state predicates, can be constructed from state variables and global variables with usual comparison operators over the value domain and Boolean connectives. An example of a Boolean state expression could be $(\mathsf{speed} > \mathsf{high}) \wedge \mathsf{brake\_on}$, where speed and brake_on are state variables and high is a global variable. Two unary modalities are introduced to describe the pre- and post-conditions of discrete actions. For any model $(\mathcal{I}, \mathcal{J}, \mathcal{V}, [c, d])$ and a Boolean state expression B, let

$$(\mathcal{I}, \mathcal{J}, \mathcal{V}, [c, d]) \models \nwarrow B \quad \text{iff} \quad c = d \text{ and } (B)(\mathcal{I}_{\_1}, \mathcal{V})(c) = 1,$$
$$(\mathcal{I}, \mathcal{J}, \mathcal{V}, [c, d]) \models \nearrow B \quad \text{iff} \quad c = d \text{ and } (B)(\mathcal{I}_{\_2}, \mathcal{V})(c) = 1$$

where $(B)(\mathcal{I}_{\text{-}i}, \mathcal{V})(c)$ denotes the value of B at time c under the interpretation $\mathcal{I}_{\text{-}i}$ and valuation $\mathcal{V}$. A state transition can be specified by a pair of pre- and post-conditions, e.g., $\nwarrow (x = 0) \wedge \nearrow (x > 8)$. The chop modality is defined as follows: for any SDC formulae α and β

$$\begin{aligned}(\mathcal{I}, \mathcal{J}, \mathcal{V}, [c, d]) \models \alpha; \beta \text{ iff there exist } & m, \mathcal{I}', \mathcal{I}'' \text{ such that } c \leq m \leq d \text{ and} \\ & (\mathcal{I}', [c, m]) \otimes^{\mathcal{I}} (\mathcal{I}'', [m, d]) \text{ and} \\ & (\mathcal{I}', \mathcal{J}, \mathcal{V}, [c, m]) \models \alpha \text{ and } (\mathcal{I}'', \mathcal{J}, \mathcal{V}, [m, d]) \models \beta\end{aligned}$$

where $(\mathcal{I}', [c, m]) \otimes^{\mathcal{I}} (\mathcal{I}'', [m, d])$ iff for any state variable S

$$\begin{aligned}&\mathcal{I}'(S)(t) = \mathcal{I}(S)(t) \text{ if } c \leq t < m, \ \mathcal{I}'_{\text{-}1}(S)(m) = \mathcal{I}_{\text{-}1}(S)(m), \\ &\mathcal{I}''(S)(t) = \mathcal{I}(S)(t) \text{ if } m < t \leq d, \ \mathcal{I}''_{\text{-}2}(S)(m) = \mathcal{I}_{\text{-}2}(S)(m), \\ &\text{and } \mathcal{I}'_{\text{-}2}(S)(m) = \mathcal{I}''_{\text{-}1}(S)(m).\end{aligned}$$

This chop modality satisfies the following properties

$$\begin{aligned}&(\nwarrow B_1 \wedge \nearrow B_2); (\nwarrow B_3 \wedge \nearrow B_4) \Leftrightarrow \nwarrow B_1 \wedge \nearrow B_4 && \text{if } B_2 \wedge B_3 \text{ is satisfiable,} \\ &(\nwarrow B_1 \wedge \nearrow B_2); (\nwarrow B_3 \wedge \nearrow B_4) \Leftrightarrow \mathsf{false} && \text{if } B_2 \wedge B_3 \text{ is not satisfiable.}\end{aligned}$$

In Duration Calculi, state functions are usually assumed to satisfy the finite variability condition, which says that they are continuous almost everywhere, i.e., everywhere except for a finite number of points in any finite interval. Under this assumption, $\int_c^d (B)(\mathcal{I}_{\text{-}1}, \mathcal{V})(t)dt = \int_c^d (B)(\mathcal{I}_{\text{-}2}, \mathcal{V})(t)dt$, for a Boolean expression B, and we can define the duration of B as

$$(\int B)(\mathcal{I}, \mathcal{J}, \mathcal{V}, [c, d]) \stackrel{\text{def}}{=} \int_c^d (B)(\mathcal{I}_{\text{-}1}, \mathcal{V})(t)dt\,.$$

For any term z which only involves global variables and piece-wise continuous state function variables, $\lim_{t \to c^-} (z)(\mathcal{I}_{\text{-}1}, \mathcal{V})(t) = \lim_{t \to c^-} (z)(\mathcal{I}_{\text{-}2}, \mathcal{V})(t)$ and $\lim_{t \to c^+} (z)(\mathcal{I}_{\text{-}1}, \mathcal{V})(t) = \lim_{t \to c^+} (z)\ (\mathcal{I}_{\text{-}2}, \mathcal{V})(t)$. We define the limit values of such a term at the beginning and the end of a non-empty interval as

$$\begin{aligned}(\mathbf{b}.z)(\mathcal{I}, \mathcal{J}, \mathcal{V}, [c, d]) &\stackrel{\text{def}}{=} \lim_{t \to c^+} (z)(\mathcal{I}_{\text{-}1}, \mathcal{V})(t), \\ (\mathbf{e}.z)(\mathcal{I}, \mathcal{J}, \mathcal{V}, [c, d]) &\stackrel{\text{def}}{=} \lim_{t \to d^-} (z)(\mathcal{I}_{\text{-}1}, \mathcal{V})(t).\end{aligned}$$

The definition of $\lceil B \rceil$ remains the same, i.e., $\lceil B \rceil \stackrel{\text{def}}{=} \int B = \ell \wedge \ell > 0$.

In EDC, the following MT rule allows mathematical theories to be imported into the calculus:

Let $R(\lceil H(z) \rceil, \mathbf{b}.z, \mathbf{e}.z, l)$ be a EDC formula without chop.
If in mathematics $(\forall c \leq d) R(\forall c \leq t \leq d. H(z(t)), z(c^+), z(d^-), d - c)$ then
$\lceil\rceil \vee R(\lceil H(z) \rceil, \mathbf{b}.z, \mathbf{e}.z, \ell)$

where $z(c^+)$ and $z(d^-)$ denote limits of z from the right of c and left of d respectively.

Substitution Lemma 1, as stated in the last section, is not valid for SDC. Below is a counterexample: let S be a state variable and $\mathcal{I}\_2(S)(t) = 0$ for any t, we have $(\mathcal{I}, \mathcal{J}, \mathcal{V}, [c,d]) \models \nearrow S; \mathsf{true}$, but $(\mathcal{I}, \mathcal{J}', \mathcal{V}, [c,d]) \not\models X; \mathsf{true}$, because for any interval $[g,h]$, $\mathcal{J}'(X)([g,h]) = 0$ as $(\mathcal{I}, \mathcal{J}, \mathcal{V}, [g,h]) \not\models \nearrow S$. The complication in SDC is that in the definition of chop, not only the interval but also the state interpretation $\mathcal{I}$ may be changed. Therefore, the interpretation of propositional letters should be defined as

$$\mathcal{J} \in \mathit{PLetters} \to (S_{\mathcal{I}} \times \mathrm{Intv}) \to \{0,1\}.$$

Under the new definition, we have

Substitution Lemma 2 For SDC formulae $\alpha(X)$ and ϕ, $(\mathcal{I}, \mathcal{J}, \mathcal{V}, [c,d]) \models \alpha(\phi)$ iff $(\mathcal{I}, \mathcal{J}', \mathcal{V}, [c,d]) \models \alpha(X)$, where for any interpretation of state variables $\mathcal{I}'$ and interval $[g,h]$, $\mathcal{J}'(X)(\mathcal{I}', [g,h]) = 1$ iff $(\mathcal{I}', \mathcal{J}, \mathcal{V}, [g,h]) \models \phi$ and $\mathcal{J}'(Y)(\mathcal{I}', [g,h]) = \mathcal{J}(Y)\ (\mathcal{I}', [g,h])$ for any $Y \neq X$.

μSDCI

The standard way to describe the semantics of a recursive program is to define it as a fixed point (Scott & Strachey 1971) of an appropriate functional. Fixed points operators have also been introduced in propositional and modal logics, see e.g., (Kozen & Parikh 1981, Stirling 1995), and in Duration Calculus (Pandya & Ramakrishna 1995). In this section, we propose an extension of SDC, called μSDCI, which includes fixed points operators and infinite intervals. The syntax of μSDCI contains two additional constructs $(\mu X)\alpha$ and $(\nu X)\alpha$, where the occurrence of X in α is positive (i.e., X is preceded by even number of negation symbols).

To give the semantics of fixed point operators by Knaster-Tarski theorem, we consider the complete lattice $(2^{(S_{\mathcal{I}} \times \mathrm{Intv})}, \subseteq)$, where

$$\mathrm{Time}^+ \stackrel{\mathrm{def}}{=} \mathrm{Time} \cup \{\infty\},$$
$$\mathrm{Intv} \stackrel{\mathrm{def}}{=} \{[c,d] \in \mathrm{Time} \times \mathrm{Time}^+ \mid c \leq d\}.$$

For notational convenience, we regard an interpretation of propositional letters $\mathcal{J}$ as a function in $\mathit{PLetters} \to 2^{(S_{\mathcal{I}} \times \mathrm{Intv})}$. For a given interpretation of propositional letters $\mathcal{J}$, a valuation of global variables $\mathcal{V}$, we define a function $\mathcal{E}_{\mathcal{V}}^{\mathcal{J}}$ from the set of μSDCI formulae to $2^{(S_{\mathcal{I}} \times \mathrm{Intv})}$ by induction:

$$\mathcal{E}_{\mathcal{V}}^{\mathcal{J}}(G^n(z_1, \ldots, z_n)) \stackrel{\mathrm{def}}{=}$$
$$\{(\mathcal{I}, [c,d]) \mid ((z_1)(\mathcal{I}, \mathcal{J}, \mathcal{V}, [c,d]), \ldots, (z_n)(\mathcal{I}, \mathcal{J}, \mathcal{V}, [c,d])) \in \underline{G^n}\}$$

where $(z_i)(\mathcal{I}, \mathcal{J}, \mathcal{V}, [c,d])$ denotes the value of term z_i in the model,

$\mathcal{E}^{\mathcal{J}}_{\mathcal{V}}(X) \stackrel{\text{def}}{=} \mathcal{J}(X),$
$\mathcal{E}^{\mathcal{J}}_{\mathcal{V}}(\nwarrow B) \stackrel{\text{def}}{=} \{(\mathcal{I},[c,d]) \mid c = d \neq \infty \text{ and } (B)(\mathcal{I}_{-1},\mathcal{V})(c) = 1\},$
$\mathcal{E}^{\mathcal{J}}_{\mathcal{V}}(\nearrow B) \stackrel{\text{def}}{=} \{(\mathcal{I},[c,d]) \mid c = d \neq \infty \text{ and } (B)(\mathcal{I}_{-2},\mathcal{V})(c) = 1\},$
$\mathcal{E}^{\mathcal{J}}_{\mathcal{V}}(\neg\alpha) \stackrel{\text{def}}{=} 2^{(S_{\mathcal{I}}\times \text{Intv})} - \mathcal{E}^{\mathcal{J}}_{\mathcal{V}}(\alpha),$
$\mathcal{E}^{\mathcal{J}}_{\mathcal{V}}(\alpha_1 \vee \alpha_2) \stackrel{\text{def}}{=} \mathcal{E}^{\mathcal{J}}_{\mathcal{V}}(\alpha_1) \cup \mathcal{E}^{\mathcal{J}}_{\mathcal{V}}(\alpha_2),$
$\mathcal{E}^{\mathcal{J}}_{\mathcal{V}}(\alpha_1;\alpha_2) \stackrel{\text{def}}{=} \quad (\mathcal{E}^{\mathcal{J}}_{\mathcal{V}}(\alpha_1) \cap \{(\mathcal{I},[c,d]) \mid c \in \text{Time},\ d = \infty\})$
$\qquad\qquad \cup(\mathcal{E}^{\mathcal{J}}_{\mathcal{V}}(\alpha_1) \otimes \mathcal{E}^{\mathcal{J}}_{\mathcal{V}}(\alpha_2))$
where $(\mathcal{I},[c,d]) \in \mathcal{E}^{\mathcal{J}}_{\mathcal{V}}(\alpha_1) \otimes \mathcal{E}^{\mathcal{J}}_{\mathcal{V}}(\alpha_2)$ if and only if there are $m \in$ Time, state interpretations $\mathcal{I}'$ and $\mathcal{I}''$ such that $c \leq m < d$ and $(\mathcal{I}',[c,m]) \otimes^{\mathcal{I}} (\mathcal{I}'',[m,d])$, $(\mathcal{I}',[c,m]) \in \mathcal{E}^{\mathcal{J}}_{\mathcal{V}}(\alpha_1)$, and $(\mathcal{I}'',[m,d]) \in \mathcal{E}^{\mathcal{J}}_{\mathcal{V}}(\alpha_2)$,
$\mathcal{E}^{\mathcal{J}}_{\mathcal{V}}((\exists x)\alpha) = \bigcup_{a\in D} \mathcal{E}^{\mathcal{J}}_{\mathcal{V}(x\mapsto a)}(\alpha)$ where D is value domain of variable x,
$\mathcal{E}^{\mathcal{J}}_{\mathcal{V}}((\mu X)\alpha) = \bigcap\{\chi \mid \mathcal{E}^{\mathcal{J}(X\mapsto\chi)}_{\mathcal{V}}(\alpha) \subseteq \chi\},$
$\mathcal{E}^{\mathcal{J}}_{\mathcal{V}}((\nu X)\alpha) = \bigcup\{\chi \mid \mathcal{E}^{\mathcal{J}(X\mapsto\chi)}_{\mathcal{V}}(\alpha) \supseteq \chi\}.$

The set theoretical semantics is related to satisfaction and validity in obvious ways, namely, for any α,

$$(\mathcal{I},\mathcal{J},\mathcal{V},[c,d]) \models \alpha \text{ iff } (\mathcal{I},[c,d]) \in \mathcal{E}^{\mathcal{J}}_{\mathcal{V}}(\alpha),$$
$$\models \alpha \text{ iff } \mathcal{E}^{\mathcal{J}}_{\mathcal{V}}(\alpha) = 2^{(S_{\mathcal{I}}\times \text{Intv})} \text{ for any } \mathcal{J} \text{ and } \mathcal{V}.$$

In this setting, the substitution lemma is expressed as

$$\mathcal{E}^{\mathcal{J}}_{\mathcal{V}}(\alpha(\phi)) = \mathcal{E}^{\mathcal{J}(X\mapsto\mathcal{E}^{\mathcal{J}}_{\mathcal{V}}(\phi))}_{\mathcal{V}}(\alpha(X)).$$

Finite and infinite intervals are characterised by

$$\mathsf{inf} \stackrel{\text{def}}{=} (\forall x)(\ell \geq x), \qquad \mathsf{fin} \stackrel{\text{def}}{=} \neg\mathsf{inf}.$$

It is easy to prove the following theorems

$$\models ((\alpha \wedge \mathsf{inf});\beta) \Leftrightarrow (\alpha \wedge \mathsf{inf}), \qquad \models \mathsf{inf} \Leftrightarrow (\mathsf{true};\mathsf{false}),$$
$$\models \mathsf{inf};\alpha \Rightarrow \mathsf{inf}, \qquad \models \alpha;\mathsf{inf} \Rightarrow \mathsf{inf}.$$

For any interpretation of propositional letters $\mathcal{J}$, global valuation $\mathcal{V}$, μSDCI formula α and propositional letter X, let $(F^{\mathcal{J}}_{\mathcal{V}})^{\alpha}_{X}$ be the function in $2^{(S_{\mathcal{I}}\times \text{Intv})} \longrightarrow 2^{(S_{\mathcal{I}}\times \text{Intv})}$ such that:

$$(F^{\mathcal{J}}_{\mathcal{V}})^{\alpha}_{X}: \quad \chi \longmapsto \mathcal{E}^{\mathcal{J}(X\mapsto\chi)}_{\mathcal{V}}(\alpha) \quad \text{for any } \chi \in 2^{(S_{\mathcal{I}}\times \text{Intv})}.$$

It is easy to prove that if X is positive in α then $(F^{\mathcal{J}}_{\mathcal{V}})^{\alpha}_{X}$ is monotonic with respect to the set inclusion order. Therefore by Knaster-Tarski fixed point theorem, we have

Theorem 1 *For any interpretation of propositional letters $\mathcal{J}$, valuation $\mathcal{V}$, μSDCI formula α and propositional letter X, $\mathcal{E}_{\mathcal{V}}^{\mathcal{J}}((\mu X)\alpha)$ and $\mathcal{E}_{\mathcal{V}}^{\mathcal{J}}((\nu X)\alpha)$* are respectively the least and greatest fixed points of $(F_{\mathcal{V}}^{\mathcal{J}})_X^{\alpha}$ in $(2^{(S_{\mathcal{I}} \times Intv)}, \subseteq)$.*

It follows from this theorem and Substitution Lemma 2 that

Theorem 2 *For any μSDCI formula $(\mu X)\alpha$, $\models \alpha((\mu X)\alpha) \Leftrightarrow (\mu X)\alpha$, and $\models \alpha((\nu X)\alpha) \Leftrightarrow (\nu X)\alpha$.*

Theorem 3 *Let α be a μSDCI formula and X a propositional letter such that the occurrence of X in α is positive.*
(1) If $\models \alpha(\phi/X) \Rightarrow \phi$ then $\models (\mu X)\alpha \Rightarrow \phi$;
(2) If $\models \phi \Rightarrow \alpha(\phi/X)$ then $\models \phi \Rightarrow (\nu X)\alpha$.

Theorem 4 *Let X be a propositional variable, α_1 and α_2 be two formulae in which X is positive. If $\models \alpha_1 \Rightarrow \alpha_2$, then $\models ((\mu X)\alpha_1) \Rightarrow ((\mu X)\alpha_2)$ and $\models ((\nu X)\alpha_1) \Rightarrow ((\nu X)\alpha_2)$.*

Theorem 5 *Let α, ϕ and ψ be μSDCI formulae, and X a propositional letter positive in α. If $\models \phi \Rightarrow \psi$, then $\models \alpha(\phi/X) \Rightarrow \alpha(\psi/X)$.*

The last four theorems provide some simple syntactic rules for reasoning about μSDCI formulae. For example, they can be used to prove that the following formulae are valid.

Example 1

$$
\begin{array}{ll}
(\mu X)(\mathsf{true}; X) \Leftrightarrow \mathsf{inf}, & (\nu X)(\mathsf{true}; X) \Leftrightarrow \mathsf{true}, \\
(\mu X)(\mathsf{inf}; X) \Leftrightarrow \mathsf{inf}, & (\nu X)(\mathsf{inf}; X) \Leftrightarrow \mathsf{inf}, \\
(\mu X)(\mathsf{fin}; X) \Leftrightarrow \mathsf{false}, & (\nu X)(\mathsf{fin}; X) \Leftrightarrow \mathsf{true}, \\
(\mu X)(X; \alpha) \Leftrightarrow \mathsf{false}, & (\nu X)(\alpha; (X \wedge \mathsf{inf})) \Rightarrow \mathsf{inf}.
\end{array}
$$

3 SEQUENTIAL HYBRID PROGRAMS

We propose a language for describing hybrid systems based on the earlier work in (Xu 1997). The language supports constructive design by allowing specification statements to be mixed with program constructs, in the tradition of the well established theories of program development such as refinement

*Recall that for $(\mu X)\alpha$ and $(\nu X)\alpha$ to be well formed, X must be positive in α

calculus (Back 1980, Morgan 1990). In addition to usual program constructs, the language includes a specification statement for describing (instantaneous) state transitions and a specification statement using an EDC formula for describing a possibly hybrid component with time dependent dynamics.

The abstract syntax and informal interpretation of the basic commands are as follows, where for simplicity, we assume $\bar{x}$ contains all the system variables.

$$P ::= \langle R(\bar{x}, \bar{x}') \rangle \mid \ll C \gg \mid P_1;P_2 \mid P_1 \,[]\, P_2 \mid \textsf{while } B \textsf{ do } P \textsf{ od}.$$

$\langle R(\bar{x}, \bar{x}') \rangle$ is the nondeterministic assignment; its execution is instantaneous and the state transition satisfies the binary predicate R; Sequential composition is represented by $P_1;P_2$ and its meaning is that if P_1 terminates then P_2 is executed immediately afterwards; $[]$ is the nondeterministic choice; Statement $\ll C \gg$ describes a component by an EDC formula C. Continuous evolution can be specified by an invariant expressing the dynamical laws. The effect of the statement is like skip if no time is elapsed during its execution; Iteration statement is executed repeatedly until the boolean guard becomes false. Other commands can be defined from the basic ones, e.g.,

$$\begin{aligned}
&\bar{x} := exp(\bar{x}) \stackrel{\text{def}}{=} \langle \bar{x}' = exp(\bar{x}) \rangle,\\
&\textsf{skip} \stackrel{\text{def}}{=} x := x,\\
&\textsf{if } B_1(\bar{x}) \to P_1 \,[]\, \cdots \,[]\, B_n(\bar{x}) \to P_n \textsf{ fi}\\
&\stackrel{\text{def}}{=} (\langle B_1(\bar{x}) \wedge \bar{x}' = \bar{x} \rangle; P_1) \,[]\, \cdots \,[]\, (\langle B_n(\bar{x}) \wedge \bar{x}' = \bar{x} \rangle; P_n),\\
&\textsf{delay } t \stackrel{\text{def}}{=} \ll l = t \gg .
\end{aligned}$$

We shall abbreviate $\langle B(\bar{x}) \wedge \bar{x}' = \bar{x} \rangle$ as $\langle B(\bar{x}) \rangle$. The semantics is defined as follows

$$\begin{aligned}
[\![\langle R(\bar{x}, \bar{x}') \rangle]\!] &\stackrel{\text{def}}{=} (\exists \bar{u}\bar{v})(R(\bar{u}, \bar{v}) \wedge \nwarrow (\bar{x} = \bar{u}) \wedge \nearrow (\bar{x} = \bar{v})),\\
[\![\ll C \gg]\!] &\stackrel{\text{def}}{=} (\exists \bar{u}\bar{v})(\nwarrow (\bar{x} = \bar{u})\\
&\qquad ; (\mathbf{b}.\bar{x} = \bar{u} \wedge C \wedge (\ell > 0) \wedge \mathbf{e}.\bar{x} = \bar{v})\\
&\qquad ; \nearrow (\bar{x} = \bar{v}))\\
&\quad \vee (\exists \bar{v})(\nwarrow (\bar{x} = \bar{v}) \wedge \nearrow (\bar{x} = \bar{v}) \wedge C \wedge (\ell = 0)),\\
[\![P_1;P_2]\!] &\stackrel{\text{def}}{=} [\![P_1]\!]; [\![P_2]\!],\\
[\![P_1 \,[]\, P_2]\!] &\stackrel{\text{def}}{=} [\![P_1]\!] \vee [\![P_2]\!],\\
[\![\textsf{while } B \textsf{ do } P \textsf{ od}]\!] &\stackrel{\text{def}}{=} (\mu X)(([\![\langle B \rangle]\!]; [\![P]\!]; X) \vee [\![\langle \neg B \rangle]\!])\\
&\quad \vee (\nu X)((([\![\langle B \rangle]\!]; [\![P]\!]) \wedge \textsf{fin}); (X \wedge \textsf{inf})).
\end{aligned}$$

The semantics of the iteration statement needs some elaboration. The least fixed point (μX) $(([\![\langle B \rangle]\!]; [\![P]\!]; X) \vee [\![\langle \neg B \rangle]\!])$ characterises the executions with finitely many iterations of the loop, where the Boolean guard becomes false eventually or the last iteration takes infinite time. We take the view that if the body does not take time, then finitely many iterations of the loop also do not take time. The least fixed point formula evaluated to false if the number of iterations is infinite. The greatest fixed point $(\nu X)(((\llbracket \langle B\rangle \rrbracket;\llbracket P\rrbracket)\wedge \mathsf{fin});(X\wedge \mathsf{inf}))$, on the other hand, describes executions with infinitely many iterations. Normally, infinitely many iterations altogether take infinite time. In our model, we also record divergent behaviours which arise either because infinitely many iterations of instantaneous actions or because infinitely many iterations with total execution time bounded (e.g., if the nth iteration takes time $\frac{1}{2^n}$, then within 2 units there will be infinitely many iterations). We follow a CSP-like approach (Hoare 1985) to divergence and consider the behaviour after infinitely many iterations as nonterminating but totally arbitrary, and model it by the formula inf.

The above modelling of divergence can be justified as follows: We regard infinitely many iterations of instantaneous actions undesirable, because if this happens the plant will not receive any control signals. The other case of zeno behaviour also seems undesirable, and therefore we consider the behaviour after the limit time point of a zeno computation arbitrary. This view is technically convenient, and certainly safe. We have not yet come across serious applications with zeno computations either to test or to challenge it. It appears that to model zeno behaviour more accurately, the notion of limit of a convergent sequence of reals has to be incorporated into the logic (Hansen, Pandya & Zhou 1995).

Example 2 We show $\llbracket x := x+1; x := x+2\rrbracket \Leftrightarrow \llbracket x := x+3\rrbracket$.

This is because

$$\begin{array}{l}
\llbracket x := x+1; x := x+2\rrbracket \\
\Leftrightarrow \llbracket x := x+1\rrbracket;\llbracket x := x+2\rrbracket \\
\Leftrightarrow ((\exists v)(\nwarrow(x=v)\wedge\nearrow(x=v+1)));((\exists v)(\nwarrow(x=v)\wedge\nearrow(x=v+2))) \\
\Leftrightarrow (\exists v_1,v_2)((\nwarrow(x=v_1)\wedge\nearrow(x=v_1+1));(\nwarrow(x=v_2)\wedge\nearrow(x=v_2+2))) \\
\Leftrightarrow (\exists v_1,v_2)((v_1+1=v_2)\wedge\nwarrow(x=v_1)\wedge\nearrow(x=v_2+2)) \\
\Leftrightarrow (\exists v)(\nwarrow(x=v)\wedge\nearrow(x=v+3)) \\
\Leftrightarrow \llbracket x := x+3\rrbracket.
\end{array}$$

Example 3 We show $\llbracket \mathsf{while\ true\ do\ skip\ od}\rrbracket \Leftrightarrow \mathsf{inf}$.

We have

$$\begin{array}{ll}
(\mu X)((\llbracket\langle \mathsf{true}\rangle\rrbracket;\llbracket \mathsf{skip}\rrbracket;X)\vee\llbracket\langle\neg\mathsf{true}\rangle\rrbracket) & \{\llbracket\langle\mathsf{true}\rangle\rrbracket\Leftrightarrow\llbracket\mathsf{skip}\rrbracket,\llbracket\mathsf{skip}\rrbracket\Rightarrow\mathsf{fin}\} \\
\Rightarrow (\mu X)(\mathsf{fin};X) & \{\text{Example 1 in previous section}\} \\
\Leftrightarrow \mathsf{false} &
\end{array}$$

and $(\nu X)(((\llbracket\langle\mathsf{true}\rangle\rrbracket;\llbracket\mathsf{skip}\rrbracket)\wedge\mathsf{fin});(X\wedge\mathsf{inf}))\Leftrightarrow(\nu X)(\llbracket\mathsf{skip}\rrbracket;(X\wedge\mathsf{inf}))$. Because $\mathsf{inf}\Rightarrow\llbracket\mathsf{skip}\rrbracket;(\mathsf{inf}\wedge\mathsf{inf})$, it follows from Theorem 3 that $\mathsf{inf}\Rightarrow(\nu X)(\llbracket\mathsf{skip}\rrbracket;(X\wedge\mathsf{inf}))$. Example 1 in the previous section shows that $(\nu X)(\llbracket\mathsf{skip}\rrbracket;(X\wedge\mathsf{inf}))\Rightarrow\mathsf{inf}$. Therefore, $\llbracket\mathsf{while\ true\ do\ skip\ od}\rrbracket\Leftrightarrow\mathsf{inf}$. □

Unfolding Law The iteration statement can be unfolded as usual, formally,

$\models \alpha([\![W]\!]) \Leftrightarrow [\![W]\!]$, where $\alpha(X) = ([\![\langle B\rangle]\!]; [\![P]\!]; X) \vee [\![\langle\neg B\rangle]\!], \beta(X) = (([\![\langle B\rangle]\!]; [\![P]\!]) \wedge \mathsf{fin}); (X \wedge \mathsf{inf})$ and $[\![W]\!] = ((\mu X)\alpha(X)) \vee ((\nu X)\beta(X))$.

4 MODULAR VERIFICATION

To effectively reason about SHP programs, we use the familiar notations from Hoare logic. Let p and q be state predicates, and α a formula. Define

$$\{p\}\ P\ \{q\} \stackrel{\text{def}}{=} \nearrow p; [\![P]\!] \Rightarrow \mathsf{fin}; \nearrow q, \qquad \{p\}\ P\ \alpha \stackrel{\text{def}}{=} \nearrow p; [\![P]\!] \Rightarrow \alpha$$

4.1 Total Correctness

A discrete component is an SHP statement which does not use the phase statement $\ll C \gg$. Consequently, if the execution is not divergent, it takes no time. For discrete components, the Hoare triple $\{p\}\ \ D\ \ \{q\}$ of total correctness is equivalent to

$$\nearrow p; [\![D]\!] \Rightarrow \nearrow q.$$

Rules of Hoare Logic for sequential discrete programs can be considered as abbreviations of μSDCI theorems.

$$\{p\}\ < R(\bar{x}, \bar{x}') >\ \{(\exists \bar{v})p(\bar{v}) \wedge R(\bar{v}, \bar{x})\}$$
$$\nearrow p; (\exists \bar{u}\bar{v})(R(\bar{u}, \bar{v}) \wedge \nwarrow (\bar{x} = \bar{u}) \wedge \nearrow (\bar{x} = \bar{v})) \Rightarrow \nearrow ((\exists \bar{v})p(\bar{v}) \wedge R(\bar{v}, \bar{x}))$$

$$\frac{\{p\}\ D_1\ \{r\} \qquad \{r\}\ D_2\ \{q\}}{\{p\}\ D_1; D_2\ \{q\}}$$
$$\frac{\nearrow p; [\![D_1]\!] \Rightarrow \nearrow r \qquad \nearrow r; [\![D_2]\!] \Rightarrow \nearrow q}{\nearrow p; [\![D_1; D_2]\!] \Rightarrow \nearrow q}$$

$$\frac{\{p\}\ D_1\ \{q\} \qquad \{p\}\ D_2\ \{q\}}{\{p\}\ D_1 [\,]\ D_2\ \{q\}}$$
$$\frac{\nearrow p; [\![D_1]\!] \Rightarrow \nearrow q \qquad \nearrow p; [\![D_2]\!] \Rightarrow \nearrow q}{\nearrow p; [\![D_1 [\,]\ D_2]\!] \Rightarrow \nearrow q}$$

$$\frac{\begin{array}{c} r(i) \wedge i > 0 \Rightarrow B \qquad r(0) \Rightarrow \neg B \\ \{r(i) \wedge i > 0\}\ D\ \{(\exists j < i) r(j)\} \end{array}}{\{\exists i. r(i)\}\ \mathsf{while}\ B\ \mathsf{do}\ D\ \mathsf{od}\ \{r(0)\}}$$
$$\frac{\begin{array}{c} r(i) \wedge i > 0 \Rightarrow B \qquad r(0) \Rightarrow \neg B \\ \nearrow (r(i) \wedge i > 0); [\![D]\!] \Rightarrow \nearrow ((\exists j < i) r(j)) \end{array}}{\nearrow (\exists i. r(i)); [\![\mathsf{while}\ B\ \mathsf{do}\ D\ \mathsf{od}]\!] \Rightarrow \nearrow r(0)}$$

$$\frac{p \Rightarrow p_1 \quad \{p_1\}\ D\ \{q_1\} \quad q_1 \Rightarrow q}{\{p\}\ D\ \{q\}}$$

$$\frac{p \Rightarrow p_1 \quad \nearrow p_1; [\![D]\!] \Rightarrow \nearrow q_1 \quad q_1 \Rightarrow q}{\nearrow p; [\![D]\!] \Rightarrow \nearrow q}$$

We only prove the soundness of iteration rule. Let $W \stackrel{\text{def}}{=} \textsf{while}\ B\ \textsf{do}\ D\ \textsf{od}$.

$$\begin{array}{ll} \nearrow r(0); [\![W]\!] & \{\text{unfolding law}\} \\ \Rightarrow \nearrow r(0); (([\![\langle B \rangle]\!]; [\![D]\!]; [\![W]\!]) \vee [\![\langle \neg B \rangle]\!]) & \{r(0) \Rightarrow \neg B\} \\ \Leftrightarrow \nearrow r(0). & \end{array}$$

For any $i > 0$

$$\begin{array}{ll} \nearrow r(i); [\![W]\!] & \{\text{unfolding law}\} \\ \Rightarrow \nearrow r(i); (([\![\langle B \rangle]\!]; [\![D]\!]; [\![W]\!]) \vee [\![\langle \neg B \rangle]\!]) & \{r(i) \Rightarrow B\} \\ \Leftrightarrow \nearrow r(i); ([\![\langle B \rangle]\!]; [\![D]\!]; [\![W]\!]) & \\ \Rightarrow (\exists j < i) \nearrow r(j); [\![W]\!]. & \end{array}$$

It follows from induction that $\nearrow (\exists i.r(i)); [\![W]\!] \Rightarrow \nearrow r(0); [\![W]\!]$ and subsequently $\nearrow (\exists i.r(i)); [\![W]\!] \Rightarrow \nearrow r(0)$. □

4.2 Temporal Properties

We propose a number of rules which can be used to verify properties that are not restricted to pre-conditions and post-conditions. In the following, P, P_1 and P_2 may contain continuous components.

$$\{\textsf{true}\} \quad < R(\bar{x}, \bar{x}') > \quad \lceil\rceil$$

$$\frac{\{p\}\ P_1\ \alpha \qquad \{p\}\ P_2\ \alpha}{\{p\}\ P_1 [] P_2\ \alpha}$$

$$\frac{\{p\}\ P_1\ \{r\} \qquad \{p\}\ P_1\ \alpha_1 \qquad \{r\}\ P_2\ \alpha_2}{\{p\}\ P_1; P_2\ (\alpha_1; \alpha_2)}$$

$$\frac{\{p\}\ P_1\ (\alpha \wedge \textsf{inf})}{\{p\}\ P_1; P_2\ (\alpha \wedge \textsf{inf})}$$

One particularly interesting property is invariance, expressed as $\lceil S \rceil \vee \lceil\rceil$. The following rule says that an iteration statement satisfies an invariant if the body always takes at least some non-zero constant time c (this ensures that there is no divergence or zeno) and satisfies the invariant.

$$\frac{\{B \wedge r\}\ P\ ((\lceil S \rceil \wedge l > c > 0); \nearrow r)}{\{r\}\ \text{while } B \text{ do } P \text{ od}\ (\lceil S \rceil \vee \lceil\rceil)}$$

The correctness of the invariant rule follows from the unfolding law.

$$\begin{array}{ll}\nearrow r; [\![W]\!] & \{\text{unfolding law}\}\\ \Rightarrow \nearrow r; (([\![\langle B \rangle]\!]; [\![P]\!]; [\![W]\!]) \vee [\![\langle \neg B \rangle]\!]) & \\ \Rightarrow (\lceil S \rceil \wedge l > c > 0); \nearrow r; [\![W]\!] \ \vee\ \lceil S \rceil \ \vee\ \lceil\rceil. & \end{array}$$

By induction

$$\begin{array}{l}\nearrow r; [\![W]\!]\\ \Rightarrow (\forall n)((\lceil S \rceil \wedge l > n \times c \wedge c > 0); \nearrow r; [\![W]\!]) \ \vee\ \lceil S \rceil \ \vee\ \lceil\rceil\\ \Rightarrow \lceil S \rceil \ \vee\ \lceil\rceil.\end{array}$$

4.3 A Simple Example

We consider the following toy example, named CRUISE for convenience in exposition. In the system, the current speed of the car V is continuous and is controlled by a computer by periodically calculating the acceleration a which must be applied for the next time unit. The sampling of the current speed, is denoted by the statement $v := V$. If $v < 80$, the car can accelerate and the rate of acceleration is computed by a control algorithm A. Similarly, if $v \geq 70$, the car may decelerate at a rate determined by a control algorithm D. When accelerating, the behaviour of the car is defined by the phase statement $\ll \exists x.x = \mathbf{b}.a \wedge \lceil |\dot{V} - x| \leq 3 \wedge \dot{V} \geq 1 \rceil \wedge \ell = 1 \gg$. Due to hardware limitations, the actual acceleration $\dot{V}$ may not be exactly the same as specified. Condition $|\dot{V} - x| \leq 3 \wedge \dot{V} \geq 1$ states that $\dot{V}$ is within an error of 3 from the value of x and that it is at least 1. The design task is to construct components A and D such that the speed never exceeds 100.

The requirement can be expressed by the following correctness formula

$$\{\text{true}\}\quad \text{CRUISE}\quad (\lceil V < 100 \rceil) \vee \lceil\rceil)$$

Due to compositionality of our method, we can verify the correctness of the system based on the specifications of A and D. We record the verification by what is commonly called proof outline in program verification. In the outline, the formulae, marked by shaded boxes, represent conditions and conclusions of various verification rules used. For example, the formula in line (2) is obtained by applying the assignment axiom to the statement in line (1). The formula in turn serves as the pre-condition for the statement in line (3). Formula in line (6) is carried over from line (4), and is used as the pre-condition of the iteration body; line (19) denotes the property that the body has, and by the iteration rule, the iteration statement satisfies the property in line (21).

$$V := 0; \tag{1}$$
$$\{V = 0\} \tag{2}$$
$$\mathsf{alarm} := \mathsf{off}; \tag{3}$$
$$\{V < 100\} \tag{4}$$
$$\mathsf{while\ true\ do} \tag{5}$$
$$\quad \{V < 100\} \tag{6}$$
$$\quad v := V; \tag{7}$$
$$\quad \{V < 100 \wedge v = V\} \tag{8}$$
$$\quad \mathsf{if}\ \ v < 80 \rightarrow\ \{V < 80\}\ A;\ \{V < 80 \wedge a < 15\} \tag{9}$$
$$\qquad \ll \exists x.x = \mathbf{b}.a \wedge \lceil |\dot{V} - x| \leq 3 \wedge \dot{V} \geq 1 \rceil \wedge \ell = 1 \gg \tag{10}$$
$$\qquad (\lceil V < 100 \rceil \wedge l > 0.5); \nearrow (V < 100) \tag{11}$$
$$\quad [\,]\ v \geq 70 \rightarrow\ \{V < 100\}\ D;\ \{V < 100\} \tag{12}$$
$$\qquad \ll \exists x.x = \mathbf{b}.a \wedge \lceil |\dot{V} - x| \leq 3 \wedge \dot{V} \leq -1 \rceil \wedge \ell = 1 \gg \tag{13}$$
$$\qquad (\lceil V < 100 \rceil \wedge l > 0.5); \nearrow (V < 100) \tag{14}$$
$$\quad [\,]\ v > 100 \rightarrow\ \{\mathsf{false}\} \tag{15}$$
$$\qquad \mathsf{alarm} := \mathsf{on} \tag{16}$$
$$\qquad (\lceil V < 100 \rceil \wedge l > 0.5); \nearrow (V < 100) \tag{17}$$
$$\quad \mathsf{fi} \tag{18}$$
$$\quad (\lceil V < 100 \rceil \wedge l > 0.5); \nearrow (V < 100) \tag{19}$$
$$\mathsf{od} \tag{20}$$
$$(\lceil V < 100 \rceil \vee \lceil\,\rceil) \tag{21}$$

The proof outline indicates that to guarantee the simple invariant requirement, it is sufficient that algorithm A does not assign a value bigger than 15 to a, or formally

$$\{V < 80\}\ A\ \{V < 80 \wedge a \leq 15\}$$

It is preferable to accelerate fast when the speed is low and accelerate slowly when the speed is high. Therefore, we calculate the value of a based on function $0.1 * e^{100/(v+20)}$. To this end, we let

$$\{\mathsf{true}\}\ A\ \{0.1 * e^{100/(v+20)} - 1 \leq a \leq 0.1 * e^{100/(v+20)}\}$$

Correctness of the system is maintained, because

$$0.1 * e^{100/(v+20)} \leq 15 \qquad \text{for any } v \geq 0$$

Finally, the control algorithm A is developed. It can be verified using Hoare Logic which has been embedded.

$c := 100/(v+20);$
$k := 1;$
$a := 0.1;$
$r := 0.6 * 5;$
$\{a = 0.1 * \sum_{n=0}^{k-1} \frac{1}{n!}(\frac{100}{v+20})^n \wedge r = 0.6 * 5^k/k!\}$
while $k \leq 5 \vee r \geq 1$ do
  $a := a + 0.1 * c;$
  $k := k + 1;$
  $c := (100 * c)/((v+20) * k);$
  $r := (5 * r)/k$
od
$\{a = 0.1 * \sum_{n=0}^{k-1} \frac{1}{n!}(\frac{100}{v+20})^n \wedge r = 0.6 * 5^k/k! \wedge k > 6 \wedge r < 1\}$
$\{0.1 * e^{100/(v+20)} - r \leq a \leq 0.1 * e^{100/(v+20)}\}$
$\{0.1 * e^{100/(v+20)} - 1 \leq a \leq 15\}$

5 DISCUSSION

This paper presents a theory for reasoning about Sequential Hybrid Programs. These include the usual sequential programming constructs as well as phase statements which are Extended Duration Calculus specifications of time dependent dynamics. A compositional semantics of SHP is given using an extension of the Duration Calculus. Some high level rules are defined for modular verification of properties like total correctness and invariance.

An initial formulation of these ideas was given in (Xu 1997). Since then, the base logic used for formalising the semantics has significantly evolved. The original formulation used infinite conjunctions and disjunctions, causing the logic to be more complex than necessary, and the treatment of infinite behaviours was somewhat cumbersome.

Based on several previous papers, the present logic μSDCI incorporates super dense states, greatest and least fixed point operators, and infinite intervals. Duration Calculus with super dense states has been studied in (Zhou &Hansen 1996), and in (Xu 1997). The fixed point operators have been introduced in Duration Calculus in (Pandya & Ramakrishna 1995), and used to model the terminating and divergent behaviours of programs. Our approach to infinite intervals follows the work (Moszkowski 1995) in Interval Temporal Logic.

In the literature, hybrid systems are often represented as Automata or as Phase Transition Systems (Manna & Pnueli 1993, Henzinger, Manna & Pnueli 1994). In our approach, we work with a notation for hybrid systems which is closer to how hybrid systems are programmed. In particular, complex digital control algorithms can be directly incorporated in our framework as subprograms. Similar description languages have been proposed in (He 1994, Fix & Schneider 1994, Zhou, Wang & Ravn 1995), but they all assume that every action takes non-zero time. In contrast, we allow instantaneous actions, which together with recursion have led to complex behaviours such as termination, infinite executions, finite and instantaneous divergence. We formalise the semantics using a mixture of the greatest and the least fixed points. This appears to be novel as compared to the usual approach of using a single fixed point.

Using the logical semantics, we have derived several high level proof rules for establishing specific kinds of properties of hybrid systems. These rules provide a modular and syntax directed method for verification of SHP programs, extending to hybrid systems the design and verification paradigm, proposed originally by Dijkstra, Gries and Hoare for sequential programs. Well established methods such as Hoare Logic can be embedded within our proof method. These are especially useful and also complete for reasoning about complex discrete components incorporating algorithms for digital control. In contrast to most of the existing work which assumes that divergent behaviours do not exist, usually by ruling out instantaneous actions altogether or by an axiom which states that time is never bounded, we can prove that divergent behaviours indeed do not occur. Properties studied so far include total correctness and invariance. Further investigation is needed for other properties.

Our theory is developed for sequential systems. One way to reason about concurrent systems is to first transform them into sequential ones. The techniques in this paper can then be applied. However, this approach may lead to state explosion and therefore modular verification methods for concurrent hybrid systems should be studied. Adding concurrency, nevertheless, is non-trivial, as intermediate states arising during the control actions of one process can be significant for the other processes. This requires the logic to be able to describe the sequences of states occurring at a single time point, leading to the notion of the so-called weakly monotonic time, which was first studied in real-time temporal logic (Koymans 1992). A Duration Calculus of Weakly Monotonic Time has been proposed in (Pandya & Dang 1996) where compositional semantics of concurrent systems have also been formalised, and in (Liu, Ravn & Li 1998). In future, we plan to extend our theory to Concurrent Hybrid Programs using a logic similar to μSDCI with weakly monotonic time.

Acknowledgements We thank a number of researchers for comments and discussions, especially R. Barua, M.R. Hansen, Dang Van Hung, B. von Karger, A. Ravn, W.-P. de Roever, Zhou Chaochen and anonymous referees.

REFERENCES

Apt, K. & Olderog, E.-R. (1997), *Verification of Sequential and Concurrent Programs (2nd edition)*, Springer–Verlag.

Back, R. (1980), *Correctness Preserving Program Refinements: Proof Theory and Applications*, Vol. 131 of *Mathematical Center Tracts*, Mathematical Centre, Amsterdam.

Fix, L. & Schneider, F. (1994), Hybrid verification by exploiting environment, *in* H. Langmack, W.-P. de Roever & J. Vytopil, eds, 'Formal Techniques in Real-Time and Fault-Tolerant Systems', LNCS 863, Springer-Verlag, pp. 1–18.

Hansen, M., Pandya, P. & Zhou Chaochen. (1995), 'Finite divergence', *Theoretical Computer Science* **138**, 113–139.

He Jifeng. (1994), From csp to hybrid systems, *in* A. Roscoe, ed., 'A Classical Mind, Eassy in Honour of C.A.R. Hoare', Prentice-Hall International, pp. 171–189.

Henzinger, T., Manna, Z. & Pnueli, A. (1994), 'Temporal proof methodologies for timed transition systems', *Information and Computation* **112**(2), 273–337.

Hoare, C. A. R. (1985), *Communicating Sequential Processes*, Prentice–Hall.

Koymans, R. (1992), *Specifying Message Passing and Time-Critical Systems with Temporal Logic*, LNCS 651, Springer–Verlag.

Kozen, D. & Parikh, R. (1981), 'Results on the propositional μ-calculus', *Theoretical Computer Science* **14**, 113–118.

Liu, Z., Ravn, A. & Li, X.-S. (1998), Verifying duration properties of timed transition systems, this volume.

Manna, Z. & Pnueli, A. (1993), Verifying hybrid systems, *in* 'Hybrid Systems, R.L. Grossman, A. Nerode, A.P. Ravn, H. Rischel (Eds.)', LNCS 736, Springer-Verlag, pp. 36–59.

Morgan, C. (1990), *Programming from Specifications*, Prentice-Hall.

Moszkowski, B. (1985), 'A temporal logic for multilevel reasoning about hardware', *IEEE Computer* **18**(2), 10–19.

Moszkowski, B. (1995), Compositional reasoning about projected and infinite time, *in* 'Proc. the First IEEE International Conference on Engineering of Complex Computer Systems (ICECCS'95)', IEEE Computer Society Press, pp. 238–245.

Pandya, P. & Dang, V.H. (1996), Duration calculus with weakly monotonic time, Technical Report Detfors 6, UNU/IIST, P.O. Box 3058 Macau.

Pandya, P. & Ramakrishna, Y. (1995), A recursive duration calculus, Technical report, CS-95/3, Computer Science Group, TIFR, Bombay.

Scott, D. & Strachey, C. (1971), Toward a mathematical semantics for computer languages, *in* J. Fox, ed., 'Proc. Symp. Computer and Automata', Polytechnic Institute of Brooklyn Press, pp. 19–46.

Stirling, C. (1995), Modal and temporal logics, *in* S. Abramsky, D. M. Gabbay & T. Maibaum, eds, 'Handbook of Logic in Computer Science Volume 2 Background: Computational Structures', Clarendon Press - Oxford, pp. 476–563.

Xu, Q.-W. (1997), Semantics and verification of extended phase transition systems in duration calculus, *in* O. Maler, ed., 'International Workshop on Hybrid and Real-Time Systems', LNCS 1201, Springer–Verlag, pp. 301–315.

Zhou Chaochen, & Hansen, M. R. (1996), Chopping a point, *in* J.-F. He, J. Cooke & P. Wallis, eds, 'Proc. BCS FACS 7th Refinement Workshop:Theory and Practice of System Design', Electronic Workshops in Computing, Springer–Verlag, Bath, U.K.

Zhou Chaochen, Hoare, C. & Ravn, A. (1991), 'A calculus of durations', *Information Processing Letters* **40**(5), 269–276.

Zhou Chaochen, Wang Ji, & Ravn, A. (1995), A formal description of hybrid systems, *in* R. Alur, T. Henzinger & E. Sontag, eds, 'Hybrid Systems III: Verification and Control', LNCS 1066, Springer–Verlag, pp. 511–530.

Zhou Chaochen, Ravn, A. & Hansen, M. (1993), An extended duration calculus for hybrid systems, *in* 'Hybrid Systems, R.L. Grossman, A. Nerode, A.P. Ravn, H. Rischel (Eds.)', LNCS 736, Springer-Verlag, pp. 36–59.

6 BIOGRAPHY

Pandya, Paritosh K. is a Reader in the Computer Science Department of the Tata Institute of Fundamental Research, Mumbai, India. He obtained a Ph.D. in Computer Science from Bombay University in 1988. He has worked as a research officer at Oxford University Computing Laboratory, U.K., and as visiting researcher at UNU/IIST, Macau. His research interests are logics of programs, analysis of real-time systems, concurrency theory and formal methods in programming.

Wang, Hanpin is a faculty member in the Department of Computer Science and Technology, Beijing University, P.R. China. He obtained a Ph.D. in Mathematical Logic from Beijing Normal University, P.R. China in 1993. He was a fellow of UNU/IIST from February 1997 to August 1997. His research interests are mathematical logic especially model theory, computational complexity and logics of programs.

Xu, Qiwen is a Research Fellow of UNU/IIST. He obtained a D.Phil. in Computing from Oxford University Computing Laboratory, U.K., in 1992. He has worked as a research associate at Christian Albrechts Universität zu Kiel, Germany and Åbo Akademi, Finland. His research interests are program verification and refinement, theory of real-time and concurrent systems.

Test Selection for Object-Oriented Software Based on Formal Specifications

C. Péraire, S. Barbey and D. Buchs

Swiss Federal Institute of Technology, Software Engineering Laboratory, 1015 Lausanne, Switzerland, phone: +41 (21) 693.52.43, fax: +41 (21) 693.50.79, email: {Cecile.Peraire, Stephane.Barbey, Didier.Buchs} @ epfl.ch, url: hhtp:// lglwww.epfl.ch

Abstract

We propose a method of test selection based on formal specifications, for specification-based testing of object-oriented software. This method is based on rigorous theoretical foundations. To limit the size of test sets, we present several hypotheses specific to object-oriented systems, used to reduce an exhaustive test set into a pertinent test set. Regularity hypotheses are used to constrain the shape of test cases while uniformities, with or without subdomain decomposition, are used to limit the values of the variables appearing in the test cases. Care is taken to provide a method for which operational techniques can be implemented.

Keywords

Specification-based testing, test set selection, object-orientation, formal methods, operational methods.

Programming Concepts and Methods D. Gries, & W-P. de Roever (Eds.)

1 INTRODUCTION

Testing is obviously one of the answers to address the issue of quality in software, even developed using object-oriented (O-O) methods. However, given the complexity of today's software, a good test selection cannot be performed without a rigorous foundation for the theoretical, methodological and operational aspects.

For specification-based testing of O-O software, test selection is made difficult because the behavior of the objects does not only depend on the input domain, but also on the history of the objects, because of their persistent state. Thus, operations must not be tested individually, but in interaction. This combinatorial explosion implies to carefully determine that only necessary test cases are provided.

In this paper, we propose a testing method to take this issue into account. It is based on the theory of testing presented in [Barbey et al., 1996]. This theoretical framework, is an adaptation to O-O software of the Bernot, Gaudel and Marre theory of testing [Bernot et al., 1991]. Its essence is to reduce an exhaustive test set into a finite and pertinent test set by applying reduction hypotheses. The aim of this paper is mainly to show how to determine test shapes that are appropriate for the system under test, and to describe some of the applicable hypotheses for O-O software, while taking care that the test selection can be (semi-) automated.

In section 2, we present other research that addresses the same topic. (A comparison with our approach is made in the conclusion.) The third section is devoted to the presentation of already published results about our approach [Barbey et al., 1996] as well as a short informal introduction to our specification language, *CO-OPN/2*. The fourth section presents the test selection process, which is based on choosing hypotheses of two kinds — regularity and uniformity— and deriving constraints from those choices. Examples of hypotheses, together with their strategy, are described in section 5. In section 6, we present a refined uniformity hypothesis which increases the quality of the test sets by performing subdomain decomposition.

2 STATE OF THE ART

Many methods have already been proposed for the test selection of O-O software. A good survey of the state of the art can be found in [Binder, 1996]. For the purpose of this article, we will however limit ourselves to the two methods that are closer to ours.

The ASTOOT method [Doong and Frankl, 1994] proposes a testing strategy and a tool based on traces for specifications written in an algebraic O-O language, LOBAS. A test case consists of pairs of sequences of calls to the operations of one class, and a flag indicating the relationship between the sequences (equivalent or not). The test set generation is performed by selecting interesting sequences of operations and generating equivalent sequences by term rewriting of the axioms of the specification. Thus, the test sequences are directly derived from the specification. The test set generation is partly automated, but the equivalence relationship (oracle) must be provided by the tester.

Another method has been proposed by Kirani [Kirani, 1994]. This approach is based on the specification of MtSS, Method Sequence Specification, which describes valid sequences of invocations of operations of a single class under the form of a regular expression. Those regular expressions can be developed from many kinds of specifications such as state transition diagrams or object diagrams. Given these expressions, test cases can be selected by generating all possible sequences of invocations. The test set is reduced by using standards methods, such as random, partition and data flow testing. However, this method only includes a strategy for generating sequences, and does not cover the choice of parameter values. Moreover, Kirani does not tackle the development of an oracle for his method.

3 THEORETICAL GROUNDS

Specification-based testing is an approach to find errors in a program by verifying its functionalities, without analyzing the details of its code, but by using the specification of the system only. It can be summarized as the equation:

$$(P \not\models_O T \Rightarrow P \not\models SP)$$

i.e. that the test set T applied on a program P will reveal that P does not implement correctly the specification SP. The goal in selecting T is to uncover the cases where the program does not satisfy the test cases, and thus reveal errors wrt the specification.

Test selection is based on the properties of the specification language, which must be theoretically well founded. Usually, specification languages have a notion of formula representing the properties that all desired implementations satisfy. Test cases can be expressed using the same language, however this is not necessary. The most interesting solution is to have a specification language well adapted to the expression of properties, and another language to describe test cases that can be easily applied to an oracle, as long as there is a full agreement between these two languages. In the remaining of this section, we will present a specification language, *CO-OPN/2*, and a language for expressing test cases, *HML*.

3.1 Specifying Object Systems with *CO-OPN/2*

This section presents a concurrent O-O specification language, called *CO-OPN/2* (Concurrent O-O Petri Nets) that will be used to demonstrate the testing principles. *CO-OPN/2* is a formalism developed for the specification and design of large O-O concurrent systems [Biberstein et al., 1997]. Such system consists of a possibly large number of entities, which communicate by triggering parameterized events (sending messages). The events to which an object can react are also called its methods. The behavior of the system is expressed with algebraic Petri nets.

A *CO-OPN/2* specification consists of a collection of two different kinds of modeling entities: algebraic abstract data types (*ADTs*) and classes. Algebraic sorts are defined together with related functions, in *ADT* modules. Algebraic sorts are used to specify values such as the primitive sorts (integer, boolean, enumeration types, etc.) or purely functional sorts (stacks, etc.). Class' type sorts are defined together with their methods in a distinct class module. Such a module corresponds to the notion of encapsulated entity that holds an internal state and provides the outside with various services.

Cooperation between objects is performed by means of a synchronization mechanism, i.e. each event may request synchronization with the methods of one or of a group of partners using a synchronization expression. Three synchronization operators are defined: "//" for simultaneity, ".." for sequence, and "+ " for alternative. The syntax of the behavioral axiom that includes synchronization is

[Condition =>] Event [**with** SynchroExpression]: Precondition -> Postcondition

Condition is a condition on algebraic values, expressed with a conjunction of equalities between algebraic terms. Event is an internal transition name or a method with term parameters. SynchroExpression is the (optional) expression described above, in which the keyword **with** plays the role of an abstraction operator. Precondition and Postcondition correspond respectively to what is consumed and to what is produced in the different places within the net (*in* arcs and *out* arcs in the net).

To illustrate *CO-OPN/2*, we introduce an example that will be used through this paper: a phonecard system. This example models the behavior of a telephone machine that can be used with a phonecard. We model this system using several *ADTs* (Pin, Money, Bool and Nat) and classes (PhoneCard and Telephone).

```
Class PhoneCard;
Interface
   Use Pin, Money;
   Type phonecard;
   Creation create _ : pin;
   Methods
      get-pin _ : pin;
      withdraw _ ,
      get-balance _ : money;
Body
   Places
      balance : money;
      id : pin;
   Initial
      balance 20;
   Axioms
      create p : -> id p;
      get-pin p : id p -> id p;
      get-balance b : balance b -> balance b;
      (b >= m) = true => withdraw m :
            balance b -> balance b - m;
   Where b, m:money; p:pin;
End PhoneCard;
```

```
Class Telephone;
Interface
   Use Pin, Money, PhoneCard, Booleans;
   Type telephone; Object cabin : telephone;
   Creation create;
   Methods
      insert _ : phonecard;
      enter _ : pin;
      buy _ : money;
Body
   Places
      idle : money;
      wait-for-pin: phonecard money;
      wait-for-buy: phonecard money;
      ready-to-eject: phonecard money;
   Initial idle 0;
   Transition eject;
   Axioms
      insert c: idle s -> wait-for-pin c s;
      (pp = p) = true => enter p With c.get-pin pp :
            wait-for-pin c s -> wait-for-buy c s;
      (pp = p) = false => enter p With c.get-pin pp :
            wait-for-pin c s -> ready-to-eject c s;
      (m >= b) = true => buy m With c.get-balance b :
            wait-for-buy c s -> ready-to-eject c s;
      (m >= b) = false => buy m
         With c.get-balance b .. c.withdraw m:
            wait-for-buy c s -> ready-to-eject c s+m;
      eject: ready-to-eject c s -> idle s;
   Where s, m, b: money; c: phonecard; p, pp : pin;
End Telephone;
```

Figure 1. Textual specification of the classes Phonecard and Telephone

The figure 1 shows the textual description of the class Phonecard. The state of a phonecard is described by the place balance, which stores the money available on the card, and id, which stores the pin-code. The balance is initialized (keyword **Initial**) to a constant value 20 for each new card. Four methods are exported by this class: to create the phonecard (create), to get the pin-code (get-pin), to access the balance (get-balance), and to reduce it (withdraw). In the field **Axioms**, the behavior of the

methods is given by the behavioral axioms described above. The class Telephone specifies the behavior of the automaton which accepts a card, waits for and checks a pin-code, and, as long as the pin-code is correct, reduces the balance of the card of a given amount corresponding to the price of a phone call.
The semantics of a *CO-OPN/2* specification is based on labeled transition systems. These rules are expressed as *structured operational semantics* and they build a deduction system over the axioms. The semantics expressed by the rules is that the behavior of a set of objects is calculated by starting from the lowest object in the hierarchy and repeatedly adding a new object to the system. We may thus build the graph of all the possible behaviors of a specification, and build proof trees, which allow both selecting cases of satisfaction and non satisfaction for *CO-OPN/2* formulae containing variables, and validating test cases, for ground *CO-OPN/2* formulae.

3.2 The Theory of Testing

The theory of testing is elaborated on specifications *SPEC*, programs *PROG* and test cases *TEST*, and on adequate compatible satisfaction relationships between programs and specifications, $\models$, and between programs and test cases, $\models_O$ This is defined by the following equation:

$$(P \models_O T_{SP} \Leftrightarrow P \models SP).$$

The equivalence relationship $\Leftrightarrow$ is satisfied when the test set T_{SP} is pertinent, i.e. valid (any incorrect program is discarded) and unbiased (it rejects no correct program). However, a pertinent test set T_{SP} can only be used to test a program P if T_{SP} has a "reasonable" finite size. Limiting the size of a test sets is performed by sampling. In our theory, sampling is performed by applying hypotheses on P, i.e. by making assumptions that the program reacts in the same way for some inputs.

Expressing Test Cases with HML Formulae

For *CO-OPN/2*, the test cases can be expressed with the *HML* Logic introduced by Hennessy-Milner in [Hennessy and Milner, 1985][1]. *HML* formulae built using the operators *Next* (<_>), *And* ($\wedge$), *Not* ($\neg$), *T* (always true constant), and the events *EVENT* (*SP*) of the specification $SP \in SPEC$, are noted HML_{SP}. An advantage of this approach is to have an observational description of the valid implementation through the test cases. A test case is a formula which is valid or not in the specification, and which must be experimented in the program, i.e. a correct implementation behaves similarly on the test cases.

An elementary test case for a program under test $P \in PROG$ and a specification $SP \in SPEC$ can be defined as a couple <*Formula*, *Result*> where:

- *Formula* $\in HML_{SP}$: (ground) temporal logic formula.
- *Result* $\in \{true, false\}$: boolean value showing whether the expected result of the evaluation of *Formula* (from a given initial state) is *true* or *false*.

[1] It exists a full agreement between the bisimulation equivalence and the HML^∞ equivalence (HML^∞ is *HML* with the infinite conjunction (see [Hennessy and Stirling, 1985])). The bisimulation equivalence identifies correct implementations with respect to the specifications. Bisimulation is stronger than other equivalence relationships, such as some of those proposed in [de Nicola and Hennessy, 1984], in that it assumes that non specified behaviors are not acceptable for the implementation.

A test case <*Formula, Result*> is successful if *Result* reflects the validity of *Formula* in the labeled transition system modeling the expected behavior of *P*, for instance:

T1: <<c.create 1234> (<c.withdraw 20> <c.get-balance 0>*T* and <c.get-pin 1234>*T*), true>

In all other cases, a test case <*Formula, Result*> is a fail. It is important to note that the test case definition will allow the test procedure to verify that a non-acceptable scenario cannot be produced by the program (for instance, to make a call even though the identification code of the phonecard is wrong), i.e.

T2: <<c.create 1234> <cabin.insert c> <cabin.enter 5629> <cabin.buy 5>*T*, false>

For test cases expressed using HML_{SP}, we can define the exhaustive test set $\text{EXHAUST}_{SP,\,H_0} \subseteq \text{TEST}$, which includes all possible behaviors derivable from the specification, as:

$\text{EXHAUST}_{SP,\,H_0} = \{ \langle Formula, Result \rangle \in HML_{SP} \times \{true, false\} \mid (SP \models_{HML_{SP}} Formula \text{ and } Result = true) \text{ or } (SP \not\models_{HML_{SP}} Formula \text{ and } Result = false)\}$.

Practicable Test Context and Hypotheses

Assuming that hypotheses *H* have been made on *P*, the following formula has to be verified for any selected test sets $T_{SP,\,H}$:

$$(P \text{ satisfies } H) \Rightarrow (P \models_O T_{SP,\,H} \Leftrightarrow P \models SP).$$

Thus, the test selection problem is reduced to applying hypotheses to a program until a test set of reasonable size is selected. For that purpose, we build a test context, called practicable because it is pertinent and can be effectively applied to the oracle. Given a specification *SP*, a practicable test context $(H, T)_O$ is defined by a set of hypotheses *H* on a program under test *P*, a test set *T* of "reasonable" finite size and an oracle *O* defined for each element of *T*. The selection of a practicable test set *T* is made by successive refinements of an initial test context $(H_0, T_0)_O$ which has a pertinent test set T_0 (possibly of not "reasonable" size), until obtaining a practicable test context $(H, T)_O$: $(H_0, T_0)_O \le \dots (H_i, T_i)_O \le (H_j, T_j)_O \dots \le (H, T)_O$.

At each step, the preorder refinement context $(H_i, T_i)_O \le (H_j, T_j)_O$ is such that:

- The hypotheses H_j are stronger than the hypotheses H_i
- The test set $T^j_{SP,\,H_j}$ is included in the test set $T^i_{SP,\,H_i}$
- If *P* satisfies H_j then $(H_j, T_j)_O$ detects no more errors than $(H_i, T_i)_O$
- If *P* satisfies H_j then $(H_j, T_j)_O$ detects as many errors than $(H_i, T_i)_O$

Therefore, if T^i is pertinent then T^j is pertinent. Since the exhaustive test set is pertinent, we can use it for the initial context T^0.

Test Selection

From a practical point of view, the reduction process is implemented as a selection process: to each reduction hypothesis on the program corresponds a constraint on the test set. Indeed, the exhaustive test set can be defined as a couple $\langle f, r \rangle$ where *f* is a HML_{SP} formula with variables universally quantified. The aim of the test selection becomes the reduction of the level of abstraction of *f* by constraining the instantiation of its variables. This will be presented in details in section 5.

For that purpose we define *Var (f)*, the set of variables in the formula *f*, and we introduce the language HML_{SP} with variables, $HML_{SP,\,X}$, build using the standard *HML* operators, the events with variables $\text{EVENT}\ (SP, X_S)$ of the specification $SP \in$

SPEC, and variables. The variables of $HML_{SP,\ X}$ belong to $X = X_{HML} \cup X_{event} \cup X_S$ where:

- X_{HML}: variables of type $HML_{SP,\ X}$ formula,
- X_{event}: variables of type event,
- $X_S = X_{adt} \cup X_c$: variables of type ADT and class (reference to objects).

For instance, in the telephone example, the $HML_{SP,\ X}$ formula f = <cabin.insert (o)> <cabin.enter (p)> <e> g has the variables g $\in X_{HML}$, e $\in X_{event}$, c, o $\in X_c$, and p $\in X_{adt}$. We note $HML_{SP,\ X_S}$ the $HML_{SP,X}$ language in which X is restricted to X_S.

To replace those variables by values, we use interpretations (the set of all the interpretations is called *INTER*). To replace those variables by terms, we use substitutions (the set of all the substitutions is called *SUBS*). The evaluation of a term in the domain D is performed using the function $[\![\ ]\!]_D$: term-D -> D. We also define the concatenation $f \mid g$ of a $HML_{SP,\ X_S}$ formula f and *a* $HML_{SP,\ X}$ formula g as the $HML_{SP,X}$ formula obtained by replacing all T in f by g.

The Oracle

Once a test set has been selected, its elements are executed on the program under test. The choice of the *HML* logic to express test cases allows executing easily those test cases. A logic with more complex modalities could have led to nonexecutable test cases. Then the results collected from this execution are analyzed. It is the role of the oracle to perform the analysis, i.e. to decide the success or the failure of the test set. The oracle O is a partial decision predicate of a formula in a program P. Since oracles are not always able to compare all the necessary elements to determine the success or the failure of a test we introduce oracle hypotheses H_O as part of the possible hypotheses and collect all power limiting constraints imposed by the realization of the oracle. More information about the construction of oracles for our approach is given in [Barbey et al., 1996] and [Barbey, 1997].

4 THE TEST SELECTION PROCESS

The previous description of the test selection process was mainly concerned with the theoretical justification of the approach correctness. In the next sections we will emphasize the practical problems that appear when practical test sets have to be produced. The test selection process is performed in the following steps:

- Focus on a particular unit (class) of interest to test in details, the class under test. This unit must be an independent unit (which does not use any other unit), or a unit which uses other units **already tested** or replaced by **stubs**.The introduction of stubs should be avoided by introducing a test order that allows the integration of already tested components. This minimizes the testing effort and focus the test process on successive enrichments of the specification. The class under test will be tested through one of its instances. Possibly more instances of the class can appear if needed in methods parameters.
- Deduce the test environment from the focus: The test environment is the set of all the units used (directly and indirectly) by the focus.
- Define a system of constraints on the exhaustive test set with the help of reduction hypotheses as follows:

  - For the focus: use 'weak' reduction hypotheses (like regularity, see section 5.2) to preserve as much as possible the quality of the test set.
  - For the other units: use 'strong' reduction hypotheses (like uniformity, see section 5.3) to minimize as much as possible the size of the test set. Uniformity hypotheses can be used on subdomains, which implies the computation of the variables' subdomains of validity (following a given criteria of test coverage) by unfolding techniques (see section 6).
- Solve the system of constraints previously defined, based on the inference rules of *CO-OPN/2*. This results in a test set of 'reasonable' size.

Of course, to select a complete test set for a given class, it may be necessary to define several systems of constraints that exercise different aspects of the specification. Throughout the test process, the test cases can be validated by computation of the value of the variable *Result*.

Because of the definition of a test as a couple $<HML_{SP}\ formula, Result>$, and because of its construction's mechanism, a test set could contain redundant test cases. A redundant test is a test which can be suppressed from the test set without altering its pertinence (validity and unbiais). For instance, the test cases $<f, true>$ and $<\neg f, false>$ are redundant, as well as the test cases $<f \wedge g, true>$ and $<g \wedge f, true>$. To eliminate such structural redundancies, a test set can be transformed into a test set free of redundant test cases, called a *minimal test set.* This transformation can occur at any time during the process when it is possible to perform it.

5 HYPOTHESES AND STRATEGIES FOR TEST SELECTION

It is often reasonable to start the test set selection process by applying regularity hypotheses on the program, i.e. by constraining the $HML_{SP,\ X}$ formulae. Then uniformity hypotheses can be applied, i.e. the instantiation of the remaining variables of the $HML_{SP,\ X}$ formulae can be constrained. This section presents these different reduction hypotheses and constraints, and the associated strategies used in practice. Note that, as mentioned in [Arnould, 1997], the strategies need to be carefully built to implement the corresponding hypotheses. The danger is to obtain test sets which do not keep the pertinence of the initial exhaustive test set.

5.1 Language of Constraints

The constraints are expressed in a language called $\textit{CONSTRAINT}_{SP,\ X}$, which includes the set of all the constraints applicable on $HML_{SP,\ X}$. The syntax and the semantics of $\textit{CONSTRAINT}_{SP,\ X}$, are defined by means of elementary constraints applicable either on the events or on the shape of the $HML_{SP,\ X}$ formulae. The elementary constraints are built using numeric functions like *nb-events or nb-occurrences*, boolean functions like *only* or *shape* and *HML* functions like | *(concatenation)*. The satisfaction relationship $\models_C^I \subseteq \textit{CONSTRAINT}_{SP}$ is partially defined as follows:

$$\models_C^I (C_1 \wedge C_2) \Leftrightarrow (\models_C^I C_1 \wedge \models_C^I C_2)$$
$$\models_C^I (\textit{nb-events}\ (f) = k) \Leftrightarrow ([\![\textit{nb-events}\ (f)]\!]_{I\!N} = [\![k]\!]_{I\!N})$$
$$\models_C^I (\textit{nb-events}\ (f) = x) \Leftrightarrow ([\![\textit{nb-events}\ (f)]\!]_{I\!N} = \mathbf{I}\ (x))$$

where $f \in HML_{SP,\ X_S}$, $k \in I\!N$, x is a variable of type $I\!N$ and $\mathbf{I} \in \textit{INTER}$

Other constraints will be presented in the following text. The complete definition of $\mathit{CONSTRAINT}_{SP,\,X}$ can be found in [Barbey, 1997].

5.2 Regularity Hypotheses

The regularity hypotheses stipulate that if a test $<f, r>$ in which the formula f contains a variable v, is successful for all instances of v satisfying a constraint C, then it is successful for all possible instances of v. For instance, in the case of the telephone system and a constraint *"the number of insertions of a phonecard is equal to 20"*, if all test cases $<f, r>$, in which the constraint is satisfied, are successful, then the system behaves correctly for all possible numbers of insertions.

Definition: Regularity hypothesis
Given a specification $SP \in \mathit{SPEC}$, a test $<f, r> \in \mathit{HML}_{SP,\,X} \times \{\mathit{true}, \mathit{false}\}$, a variable $v \in \mathit{Var}\,(f)$, a constraint $C \in \mathit{CONSTRAINT}_{SP,\,X}$. A regularity hypothesis of constraint C on a variable v for a test $<f, r>$ and a program P, is such that:

$$\forall\, r \in \{\mathit{true}, \mathit{false}\},\ ((\forall\, (v_0 / v) \in \mathit{SUBS},\ (\forall\, \mathbf{I}_0 \in \mathit{INTER},\ (\models_C^{I_0}\ (v_0 / v)\ (C) \Rightarrow P \models_o <\mathbf{I}_0((v_0 / v)\ (f)),\ r>))) \Rightarrow (\forall\, (v_1 / v) \in \mathit{SUBS},\ (\forall \mathbf{I}_1 \in \mathit{INTER},(P \models_o <\mathbf{I}_1((v_1 / v)\ (f)),\ r>)))).$$

This definition means that if for all substitutions $(v_0\ /\ v)$ the satisfaction of the constraint C implies that P satisfies the formula f in which v is replaced by v_0, then for all substitutions $(v_1\ /\ v)$ P will satisfy the formula f in which v is replaced by v_1. The role of the two interpretations $\mathbf{I}_0$ and $\mathbf{I}_1$ is just to replace the remaining variables by values, to deal with ground constraints and formulae during the evaluations. For instance, if the constraint C and the substitution $(v_0\ /\ v)$ force the *HML* formula f to have the structure: $f = <e>\ g$ where e is an event and g a variable of type *HML*, g must be replaced by all its possible interpretations $\mathbf{I}_0$ to obtain ground formulae which could be evaluated. For instance:

$\mathbf{I}_{0,\,\alpha}(g) = <e>\ \mathrm{T} \Rightarrow f = <e>\ <e>\ \mathrm{T}$,

$\mathbf{I}_{0,\,\beta}(g) = \mathrm{not}\ <e>\ \mathrm{T} \Rightarrow f = <e>\ \mathrm{not}\ <e>\ \mathrm{T}$,...

To each regularity hypothesis on the program is associated a predicate and a strategy. According to the former definition, the predicate is a constraint $C \in \mathit{CONSTRAINT}_{SP,\,X}$ and the strategy aims at finding the test cases which satisfy this constraint.

Regularity on Events

This section gives some examples of hypotheses having constraints on the events of the HML_{SP,X_S} formulae.

a. Number of Events

Hypothesis: If a test $<f, r>$ is successful for all instances of f having a number of events equal to a bound k, then it is successful for all possible instances of f. The number of events is computed recursively with the function *nb-events* as follows:

Definition: Semantics of *nb-events*: $\mathit{HML}_{SP,\,X_S} \rightarrow I\!N$

- *nb-events* $(T) = 0$
- *nb-events* $(\neg f) =$ *nb-events* (f)
- *nb-events* $(f \wedge g) =$ *nb-events* (f) + *nb-events* (g)

- *nb-events* (<e> *f*) = *nb-events* (*f*) + 1

where $e \in$ EVENT (SP, X_S).

Thus the constraint $C \in$ CONSTRAINT$_{SP,\, X}$ is the predicate: *nb-events* (*f*) = *k*.

Strategy: The strategy used to solve the former constraint *C* generates all the $HML_{SP,\, X_S}$ formulae with a number of events equal to *k*, without redundancy. With this strategy, only skeletons are generated and nothing is imposed by the specification. Later, free variables will be instantiated to events based on methods of the environment. For instance, the constraint *nb-events* (*f*) = 2 produces the four following test cases (where the variable V_0, and V_1 are of type event):

T0: <(not <V_0> T) and (not <V_1> T), *result*>

T1: <(not <V_0> T) and (<V_1> T), *result*>

T2: <(<V_0> T) and (<V_1> T), *result*>

T3: <<V_0> <V_1> T, *result*>

b. Occurrences of a Given Method

Another way to reduce the size of the test sets is to constrain the number of occurrences of a given method in each test.

Hypothesis: If a test <*f*, *r*> is successful for all instances of *f* having a number of occurrences of a given method *m* equal to a bound *k*, then it is successful for all possible instances of *f*.

The number of occurrences of a given method *m* is recursively computed with the function *nb-occurrences*: $HML_{SP,\, X_S} \times$ METHOD $\rightarrow \mathbb{N}$, which is defined like the function *nb-events*. The constraint $C \in$ CONSTRAINT$_{SP,\, X}$ is the predicate *nb-occurrences* (*f*, *m*) = *k*.

Strategy: The strategy used to solve the former constraint *C* generates all the $HML_{SP,\, X_S}$ formulae with a number of events based on the method *m* equal to *k*. For instance, for a phonecard c we can do the assumption:

nb-occurrences (*f*, get-balance) = 1 -- 1 occurrence of get-balance

which leads to this kind of test cases:

T: <<c.create V_0> <c.get-balance V_1> <c.withdraw V_2> T, *result*>

where the variables V_0, V_1, V_2 are of type ADT.

c. Event Classification

The events used in the test cases can be based on the kinds of the methods of the environment. The kinds of actions that are performed by the events are classified into *creators* (creators allow to create the state of the objects), *modifiers* (modifiers allow to modify the state of the objects) and *observers* (observers allow to observe the state of the objects but not to modify it). For instance, in the class Phonecard, the events based on create are creators, the events based on withdraw are modifiers and the events based on get-pin and get-balance are observers.

Hypothesis: If a test <*f*, *r*> is successful for all instances of *f* which are a combination of creators followed by a combination of modifiers and terminated by a combination of observers, then it is successful for all possible instances of *f*.

Thus the constraint $C \in$ CONSTRAINT$_{SP,\, X}$ is the following:

$(f = (f_c \mid (f_m \mid f_o))) \wedge only_{creator}(f_c) \wedge only_{modifier}(f_m) \wedge only_{observer}(f_o)$,

where the function $only_i$: $HML_{SP,\, X_S} \rightarrow \{true, false\}$ (i = {*creator*, *modifier*, *observer*}) is recursively defined in a fashion similar to the function *nb-events*.

Strategy: The strategy used to solve the former constraint C generates all the $HML_{SP,\ X_S}$ formulae which are a combination of creators (used to create the objects of the system) followed by a combination of modifiers (used to describe state evolution) and terminated by a combination of observers. For instance using this strategy on a phonecard c with the creator create, the modifier withdraw and the observers get-pin and get-balance, allows to generate this kind of test:

<<c.create V_0> <c.withdraw V_1> <c.get-balance V_2> T, *result*>

where the variables V_0, V_1, V_2 are of type ADT.

d. State Classification

We can divide the methods of a class in sets according to the places that are connected to them. If there is no interaction between those sets in the specification and in the implementation, testing those interactions will not help much in discovering errors. This division can be based on the pre- and post conditions of the axioms, which define how events read and modify the contents of places.

For example, the methods of PhoneCard can be divided in two sets, according to whether they are based on balance or on id: the method get-pin is involved in the security of the card and is connected to the place id, while the methods get-balance and withdraw are involved in the accounting of the card, and are connected to the place balance (see figure 2).

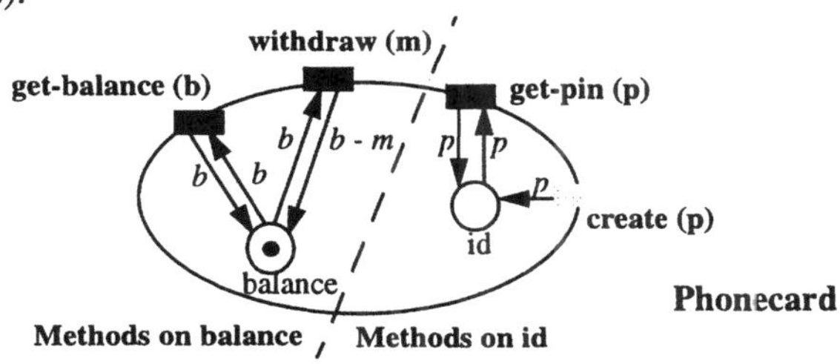

Figure 2. Classification of methods wrt to their state of interest

Hypothesis: Given M (P_i) the set of methods applied to the set of places P_i such that $\forall$ i, j, i $\neq$ j, $P_i \cap P_j = \emptyset$, a formula f_i containing only methods included in M (P_i) will not uncover more errors in the methods of M (P_i) than a formula f_j made of f_i interleaved with methods of M (P_j), i $\neq$ j. Thus, if a test set for M (P_i) and another test set for M (P_j) are successful, all test cases for M ($P_i \cup P_j$) are successful too.

In the above example, we can make the hypothesis that the behavior of M ({balance}), i.e. withdraw and get-balance, is independent from that of M ({id}), i.e. get-pin, and that these methods need not be tested in interaction (i.e. we need not generate test cases for M ({balance, id})). Thus, the constraint $C \in CONSTRAINT_{SP,\ X}$ is the predicate: *only* $(f,\ Methods\ (P_i)) = true$ where the function *only*: $HML_{SP,\ X_S} \times \mathcal{P}\ (METHOD) \rightarrow \{true, false\}$ is recursively defined akin to the function *nb-events*.

Strategy: The strategy used to apply the former constraint C generates only $HML_{SP,\ X}$ formulae that are bound to a particular place or set of places. For instance, applying the constraint on the place balance, i.e. $(f = (f_c \mid f_b)) \wedge only_{creator}(f_c) \wedge only\ (f_b,\ \{withdraw,\ get\text{-}balance\}) = true$, will provide test cases like

<<c.create V_0> <c.withdraw V_1> <c.get-balance V_2> <c.withdraw V_3> T, result>

This hypothesis is strong, because it assumes that the program follows the specification, in that the lack of interaction in the specification is conveyed in the program.

However, in some cases, it can be shown by a static analysis of the program or simply by a code review, assuming that there is a simple morphism between the places in the specification and the class components in the program. The algorithm to find the sets of methods must take into account connected objects.

Regularity on the Shape of HML Formulae

This section presents a constraint applicable on the shape of the $HML_{SP,\,X}$ formulae, i.e. a constraint allowing to force the shape of the test cases.

Hypothesis: If a test case <*f*, *r*> is successful for all instances of *f* having a given shape *s*, then it is successful for all possible instances of *f*. The formulae *f* of shape *s* are detected using the function *shape:* $HML_{SP,\,X} \times HML_{SP,\,X} \rightarrow \{true, false\}$ recursively defined like the function *nb-events*. The constraint $C \in CONSTRAINT_{SP,\,X}$ is the predicate: *shape (f, s) = true*

Strategy: The strategy used to solve the constraint *C* = (*shape (f, s) = true*) generates all the $HML_{SP,\,X}$ formulae *f* of shape *s*. For instance, for a phonecard c with the pin-code 1234 and the initial balance 20, we can express the following constraint:

shape (f, <c.create 1234> ($f_0 \wedge \neg$ <c.get-balance 25> f_1))=*true*

which leads to test cases of the shape:

<<c.create 1234> (f_0 and not <c.get-balance 25> f_1), result>

in which the two variables f_0 and f_1 are $HML_{SP,\,X}$ formulae.

This section shows that the combinatorial explosion can be reduced by constraining the shape of the $HML_{SP,\,X}$ formulae. Obviously, we can imagine a lot of other constraints of this type, for instance "$HML_{SP,\,X}$ *formulae with a given number of 'and' operators*" or "$HML_{SP,\,X}$ *formulae with a given number of 'not' operators*", ...

Choosing Regularity Hypotheses

During the test selection process, the tester selects regularity hypotheses with respect to his own knowledge of the type of faults that can occur in the program. For instance, this knowledge can be derived from a graphical representation of the specification, which allows an intuitive comprehension and an easy understanding of the behavior of each unit of the system. This is very helpful for hypotheses like *nb-events, nb-occurences, shape*. For instance, for the Telephone, a phone call always begins by the insertion of a phonecard (method insert) followed by the entrance of the pin-code (method enter). Thus for the test of the class Telephone, the tester can choose to have test cases satisfying the constraint:

shape (f, <c.create 1234> <cabin.insert c> <cabin.enter p> *g) = true*

and test cases satisfying the constraint

shape (f, <c.create 3961> <cabin.buy m> *g) = true.*

This second test set will only contain test cases that verify that the implementation does not allow events to happen if the user omits to insert his phonecard.

Other hypotheses less dependent of the tester's knowledge of the specification, like "*event classification*" and "*state classification*", can be applied systematically.

5.3 Uniformity Hypotheses

The application of constraints on the exhaustive test set generates test cases with variables. These variables can be replaced using various strategies, like *exhaustive-*

ness or *uniformity*. Exhaustiveness implies that each variable is replaced by all its possible instances. It can be useful, but it can lead to a test set infinite or having an 'unreasonable' size. To overcome this problem, uniformity hypotheses can be used.

The uniformity hypotheses stipulate that if a test case $<f, r>$ in which the formula f contains a variable v, is successful for a given value of v, then it is successful for all possible values of v. Thus uniformity hypotheses are performed to limit the test cases selected for the variables in a formula f by selecting a unique instance of each variable v in $Var(f)$.

Definition: Uniformity hypothesis

Given a specification $SP \in \mathit{SPEC}$, a test case $<f, r> \in HML_{SP,X} \times \{true, false\}$, a variable $v \in Var(f)$. An uniformity hypothesis on a variable v for a test case $<f, r>$ and a program P, is such that:

$\forall\, r \in \{true, false\},\ \forall\, (v_0 / v) \in \mathit{SUBS},$

$((P \models_o <(v_0 / v)(f), r>) \Rightarrow (\forall\, (v_1 / v) \in \mathit{SUBS},\ P \models_o <(v_1 / v)(f), r>)).$

This definition means that for all result r of $\{true, false\}$ and for all substitution (v_0 / v) we have: if P satisfies the formula f in which v is replaced by v_0, then for all substitution (v_1 / v) P will satisfied the formula f in which v is replaced by v_1.

Four kinds of variables can occur in a formula f: $HML_{SP,X}$ formulae, events, objects (class instances), and algebraic values (ADT instances). The strategy for uniformity of the four kinds of variables is the following:

- uniformity on $HML_{SP,X}$ formulae: Any $HML_{SP,X}$ formula can be randomly selected, with respect to the constraints applied on the enclosing test formula.
- uniformity on events: Any event can be randomly selected, with respect to the constraint that it is applied to an object in the focus environment.
- uniformity on algebraic values: Any algebraic value can be generated by applying a random combination of the functions defined in the corresponding ADT.
- uniformity on objects: An object in any state can be generated. Generating randomly a sequence of events including first a creation method, and then a (possibly empty) sequence of modifiers produce such object. The observers s are not relevant This sequence must be injected in the formula in construction at a place before the event containing the variable to which the uniformity is applied.

Uniformity hypotheses are very strong, because the coverage of the signature of methods is weak for the domain of the units under test. Therefore, they are usually not applied to the component under test, but to the components imported into the specification, which we suppose being already tested. Uniformities can only be applied with a satisfying coverage when the semantics of the operation include no calculation based on the variable on which the hypothesis is applied — e.g. the observer methods — or if the operation only considers the reference to the object, and not its state — e.g. the stored item in most container classes—. In some cases, a static analysis of the program can show the validity of a uniformity hypothesis by examining the use of the object on which the uniformity hypotheses are applied.

6 UNIFORMITY AND SUBDOMAIN DECOMPOSITION

The coverage of the tested unit can be very low when applying a uniformity hypothesis if, by selecting an unique instance, cases of the specification are not covered.

For example, the method enter of the class Telephone specifies a different behavior depending on the condition (pp = p): if the condition is true, the telephone will be ready to accept a call, if not, it will eject the card. For a good coverage of the method enter, test cases must be performed to verify the behavior by introducing a valid code ((pp = p) = true) and an invalid code ((pp = p) = false). A uniformity on the parameter p of the method enter will only select one value of pp, and will miss one of the two specified behaviors. Thus, applying a uniformity hypothesis on pp will result in not covering all specified behaviors, leading to a test set of low quality.

The strategy to obtain a good coverage of a formula *f* whenever constraints exist on the domain of any free variable *v* of *f*, is to apply uniformity hypotheses with subdomain decomposition. The subdomains for the different variables are considered as constraints, and are handled in conjunction to form sets of constraints on formulae on which uniformity hypotheses are then applied to select ground formulae. For a formula *f* with free variables $Var_{X_S}(f)$, it consists in finding the possible behaviors encompassed in *f*, and, for each found behavior, to select a test case in which the variables in $Var_{X_S}(f)$ are assigned values that will cause this behavior. In *CO-OPN/2*, variables with a domain belong to X_S, i.e. to algebraic values (of ADTs) and objects (of classes), excluding variables in X_{Event} and X_{HML}. It is difficult to analyze the possible behaviors and consequently to perform subdomain decomposition on a formula if the event and *HML* variables have not been fixed.

Finding the behaviors of a formula *f* is performed by enumerating the *valid* and *invalid* sequences in the transition system of the specification under test and to find the constraints on the elements of $Var_{X_S}(f)$ that will result in the execution of these sequences. Thus, uniformity subdomains are *sets of constraints on the variables of a formula f*. The union of all the uniformity subdomains should include all the possible sequences of transition derivable from the axioms of the events in the formula.

Subdomain decomposition on a formula *f* is a three steps process:

Step 1: **Derivation of constraints from the specification:** Find out the possible behaviors of the formula *f*, i.e. the constraints on the variables in *f* found in the behavioral axioms.

Step 2: **Computation of subdomains from the constraints:** Unfold the constraints to find uniformity subdomains on algebraic axioms.

Step 3: **Test set selection from the subdomains:** For each uniformity subdomain, solve the constraints and select values for the variables.

6.1 Derivation of constraints from the specification

The constraints can be divided in two groups: β-constraints and σ-constraints.

- β-constraints — behavioral constraints — drive the possible executions. They can influence the ability to trigger an event, and are algebraic or synchronization conditions. β-constraints are found by performing a case analysis of the behavioral axioms. Generally, we will discern two choices for each construct: the case of a success (i.e. valid behavior), and the case of failure (invalid behavior).
- σ-constraints — substitution constraints — are constraints that must hold between variables, given the β-constraints. σ-constraints make up the "glue" between the different events in a formula. The constraints are equalities between the variables in the derivation trees.

The β-constraints are found in the constructs of the behavioral axioms:

- Algebraic condition and method parameters on an axiom limit its domain of validity. Since our approach also deals with failures, two β-constraints are drawn up, in concordance with the results of the condition. We include a β-constraint for which the condition yields true and another one for which it yields false.
- β-constraints can be drawn up from synchronization expressions by enumerating the possible synchronization cases.
- Pre- and postconditions give information on what the state of an object will be after triggering the event, assuming that the initial state (i.e. before triggering) satisfies the precondition. Thus, they are helpful in selecting β-constraints based on the preconditions, and will also provide σ-constraints based on an analysis of the relationships between the initial state and the preconditions.

The semantics of an event can be described with several behavioral axioms (Axiom_i). When enumerating the possible sequences in the transition system, this leads to as many possible choices for a given method as axioms for this method, unless the axioms cover each other, in which case the system is not deterministic, and it may not be possible to ensure the coverage of all axioms.

Therefore, this first step can be divided in two sub-steps:

Step 1.1: decide upon β-constraints for each event in the formula. To each β-constraint corresponds a possible (valid or invalid) execution. Since we are not only interested in selecting test cases in the domains of validity of the formula, but also in its possible failures, we will not only consider the cases where the constraints are satisfied, but also the cases when the constraints are not satisfied.

Step 1.2: calculate the σ-constraints corresponding to β-constraints. These constraints can be calculated from the derivation tree deducted from the inference rules, given the β-constraints.

6.2 Computation of subdomains from the constraints

The second step in the strategy is to unfold the constraints to extract subdomains. The constraints must be solved in conjunction using logical properties such as transitivity to take into account the entire formula and the properties of the axioms. Two cases can occur:

- The constraint is an algebraic condition. In this case, unfolding is performed as described in [Bernot et al., 1991].
- The constraint involves objects. In this case, a formula must possibly be generated to select an object that satisfies the constraint.

Since β-constraints express behaviors that must hold, these constraints are only unfolded in their domain of validity, and must remain in the constraints. σ-constraints however express basic substitutions, that occur at a single step when calculating the derivation trees, and thus may disappear from the constraints. To find out invalid behaviors, σ-constraints will also be unfolded outside their domains of validity, which means, since they are equalities, that we will consider uniformity subdomains with the corresponding inequality.

Of course, when unfolding constraints, several uniformity domains can appear given the number of variables appearing in the constraint.

6.3 Test set selection from the subdomains

The third step in the strategy is to solve constraints and to select values. For each subdomain, values that satisfy the conditions in the uniformity subdomain must be assigned to the variables. Uniformity subdomains for which the constraints cannot be solved will be dropped. For each free variable, a single instance uniformity hypothesis is applied per uniformity subdomain.

6.4 Example

Given the following formula, which includes an *HML And* operator, and satisfies the constraint ($f=((f_c \mid f_m) \mid f_o) \wedge only_{creator}(f_c) \wedge only_{modifier}(f_m) \wedge only_{observer}(f_o)) = true$):
f = <c.create V_0> <c.withdraw V_1>(<c.get-pin V_2> and <c.get-balance V_3>)T

Step 1.1. The only constraint is on the method withdraw, from which we extract two β-constraints, β_1 and β_2, corresponding to the case of the balance bigger than the withdrawn money, and the opposite case. We decompose f in two sequences of events. This decomposition is equivalent to the original formula, and makes calculations simpler because of the determinism of the sequence R1 (<c.create V_0> <c.withdraw V_1>). We show on figure 3 the inference trees for β_1.

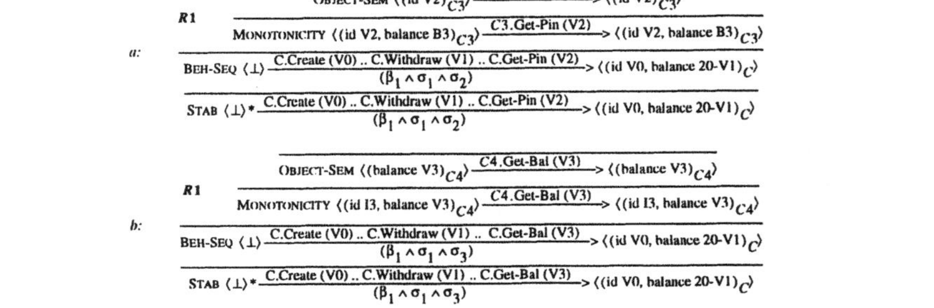

Figure 3. Inference trees for β_1

- *a:* <c.create V_0> <c.withdraw V_1> <c.get-pin V_2> T
- *b:* <c.create V_0> <c.withdraw V_1> <c.get-balance V_3> T.

Step 1.2. From the derivation trees for β_1 and β_2 (which is not shown), we can extract the set of subdomains S.

$$S = \left\{ \begin{array}{l} \langle \beta_1 = (B1 \geq V1), \sigma = \sigma_1 \wedge \sigma_2 \wedge \sigma_3 \rangle, \\ \langle \beta_2 = \neg(B1 \geq V1), \sigma = \begin{pmatrix} c = c1 \\ V0 = I1 \\ 20 = B1 \end{pmatrix} \rangle \end{array} \right\} \quad \sigma_1 = \begin{pmatrix} c = c1 \\ V0 = I1 \\ 20 = B1 \end{pmatrix}, \sigma_2 = \begin{pmatrix} c2 = c3 \\ V2 = I2 \\ B2 = V3 \end{pmatrix}, \sigma_3 = \begin{pmatrix} c = c2 \\ V0 = V2 \\ V3 = 20 - V1 \end{pmatrix}$$

We drop the constraints on the reference ($c = c1 = c2 = c3$) because they are always true. From the first tuple of *S*, we extract that for ($20 \geq V_1$) = true, ($V_0 = V_2$) = true and ($V_3 = 20\text{-}V_1$) = true, and from the second tuple, that for ($20 \geq V_1$) = false, Result will always be false, whatever the values of V_0 and V_2 are.

Step 2. For the first member of *S*, we unfold the second and the third conditions into true and false equalities. This leads to four uniformity subdomains:

1: <{V_0, V_1, V_2, V_3}, {($20 \geq V_1$) = true, ($V_0 = V_2$) = true, ($20 - V_1 = V_3$) = true}, *f*, true>

2: <{V_0, V_1, V_2, V_3}, {($20 \geq V_1$) = true, ($V_0 = V_2$) = true, ($20 - V_1 = V_3$) = false}, *f*, false>

3: <{V_0, V_1, V_2, V_3}, {($20 \geq V_1$) = true, ($V_0 = V_2$) = false, ($20 - V_1 = V_3$) = true}, *f*, false>

4: <{V_0, V_1, V_2, V_3}, {($20 \geq V_1$) = true, ($V_0 = V_2$) = false, ($20 - V_1 = V_3$) = false}, *f*, false>

No unfolding is performed on the second member. This leads to one additional uniformity subdomain:

5: <{V_0, V_1, V_2, V_3}, {($20 \geq V_1$) = false}, *f*, false>

Step 3. After selecting values by applying uniformity hypotheses on each subdomain, we get the following test cases:

1: <<c.create 1234> <c.withdraw 12> (<c.get-pin 1234> T and <c.get-balance 8> T), true>

2: <<c.create 4123> <c.withdraw 6> (<c.get-pin 4123> T and <c.get-balance 5> T), false>

3: <<c.create 111> <c.withdraw 17> (<c.get-pin 1234> T and <c.get-balance 3> T), false>

4: <<c.create 45> <c.withdraw 17> (<c.get-pin 5371> T and <c.get-balance 6> T), false>

5: <<c.create 53> <c.withdraw 50> (<c.get-pin 53873> T and <c.get-balance 6> T), false>

7 CONCLUSION

In [Barbey et al., 1996], we have presented a generalization and an adaptation of the Bernot, Gaudel, and Marre theory of testing to object oriented software. In this paper, we presented the methodological grounds for applying this theory in practice. We have described a practical process for test selection, based on the construction of constraints. First, we have presented several regularity hypotheses, including the strategies to put them into practice. Those constraints are used to select test formulae based on its global shape, or on its events. Elementary constraints can be combined to form complex constraints. We have also shown how the variables not fixed by these constraints can be instantiated using uniformity hypotheses, and how to enhance the quality of the selection with subdomain decomposition. Although our method solves the most common problems in testing O-O software, it does not deal with polymorphism and inheritance. These issues are examined in [Barbey, 1997].

Our approach has similarity with the approaches presented in section 2. Like Kirani, we have a model for possible sequences of messages. However, unlike Kirani, we use the axioms of the specifications to partition the parameter values, like ASTOOT. Unlike ASTOOT, we do not limit ourselves to term rewriting, but generate longer combinations of invocations corresponding to repetitions and interleaving of events. We take better advantage of the specification,e.g. by using axioms for classifying methods (state of interest, category). Also, our approach is different in that it does not specify what to test, but what not to test (i.e. which test cases to remove from the exhaustive test set) based on the hypotheses. Thus, the quality of the test set only depends on the quality of the hypotheses. However, in the present state of the art, how to measure the quality of hypotheses is still an open issue.

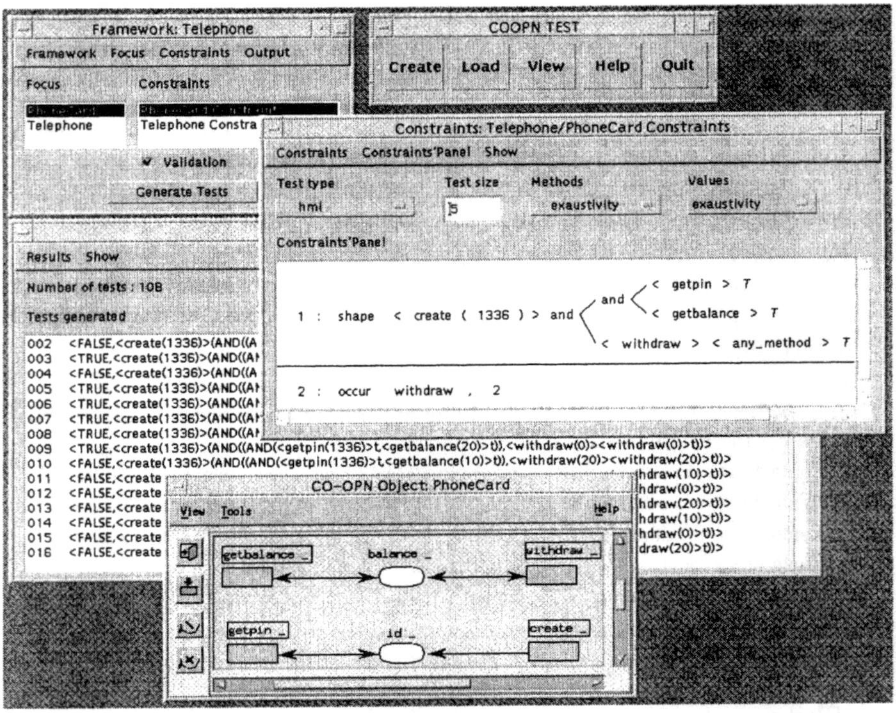

Figure 4. Snapshot of the test selection for the class PhoneCard with *CO-OPNTest*

Our theory and method also exhibit the advantage of being formal enough to semi-automate the test selection. A Prolog tool, called *CO-OPNTest*, is being implemented, by coding the *HML* semantics rules and the *CO-OPN/2* class semantics into equational logic: resolution techniques allow us to compute test sets from a *CO-OPN/2* system and the constraints presented in this paper. A front-end, written in Java, allows a user-friendly definition of the constraints. The figure 4 displays the snapshot of the test of a phone card. The 108 test cases generated are constrained by the constraints *shape* and *occur* (*nb-occurrences* in the text), and by a size (*nb-events*) of 5. They have been generated in a few seconds. Moreover, the tool allows a graphical representation of the Petri nets of the objects in the system. This representation is useful because it allows an intuitive comprehension of the specification and thus guides the tester during the test selection process.

Although *CO-OPNTest* is still under development, it already allowed us to generate test sets for several case studies in a simple, rapid and efficient way. Moreover, it shows how to apply our theory and demonstrates the pertinence of our approach.

8 ACKNOWLEDGMENTS

We wish to thank Bruno Marre, Pascale Thévenod, Hélène Waeselynck, and the anonymous referees for their numerous and valuable comments on previous versions of this paper.

This work has been supported partially by the Esprit Long Term Research Project 20072 "Design for Validation" (DeVa) with the financial support of the OFES, and by the FNRS project 20-43648.95 "Research in O-O Software Development".

9 REFERENCES

Arnould, A. (1997). *Test à partir de spécifications de structures bornées: une théorie du test, une méthode de sélection, un outil d'assistance à la sélection.* PhD thesis, Université de Paris-Sud, U.F.R. scientifique d'Orsay.

Barbey, S. (1997). *Test Selection for Specification-Based Testing of Object-Oriented Software Based on Formal Specifications.* PhD thesis, Swiss Federal Institute of Technology in Lausanne (EPFL). Ph.D. Thesis 1753.

Barbey, S., Buchs, D., and Péraire, C. (1996). A theory of specification-based testing for object-oriented software. In *Proceedings of EDCC2 (European Dependable Computing Conference)*, LNCS (Lecture Notes in Computer Science) 1150, pages 303–320, Taormina, Italy. Springer verlag.

Bernot, G., Gaudel, M.-C., and Marre, B. (1991). Software testing based on formal specifications: a theory and a tool. *IEE Software Engineering Journal*, 6(6):387–405.

Biberstein, O., Buchs, D., and Guelfi, N. (1997). COOPN/2: A concurrent object-oriented formalism. In Bowman, H. and Derrick, J., editors, *Proc. of FMOODS '97*, pages 57–72, Canterbury, UK. Chapman and Hall, London.

Binder, R. V. (1996). Testing object-oriented software: a survey. *Journal of Testing, Verification and Reliability*, 6:125–252.

de Nicola, R. and Hennessy, M. (1984). Testing equivalences for processes. *Theoretical Computer Science*, 34:83–133. North-Holland (Elsevier).

Doong, R.-K. and Frankl, P. G. (1994). The ASTOOT approach to testing object-oriented programs. *ACM Transactions on Software Engineering and Methodology*, 3(2):101–130.

Hennessy, M. and Milner, R. (1985). Algebraic laws for nondeterminism and concurrency. *Journal of the ACM*, 32(1):137–161.

Hennessy, M. and Stirling, C. (1985). The power of the future perfect in program logics. *Information and Control*, 67(1-3):23–52.

Kirani, S. (1994). *Specification and Verification of Object-Oriented Programs.* PhD thesis, University of Minnesota.

10 BIOGRAPHY

Cécile Péraire is a research assistant at the Software Engineering Laboratory of EPFL. She graduated from EPFL in 1993. She is a doctoral candidate.

Stéphane Barbey is a research assistant at the Software Engineering Laboratory of EPFL. He graduated from EPFL in 1992 and holds a Ph.D. since 1997.

Didier Buchs is a senior researcher at the Software Engineering Laboratory of EPFL since 1993. He obtained a Ph.D. degree in Computer Science from the University of Geneva in 1989.

26
Logical Foundations for Typed Object-Oriented Languages

Arnd Poetzsch-Heffter and Peter Müller
Fernuniversität Hagen, D-58084 Hagen, Germany
email: [poetzsch,peter.mueller]@fernuni-hagen.de

Abstract
This paper presents logical foundations for the most important object-oriented language features, including abstract types, dynamic binding, subtyping, and inheritance. These foundations are introduced along with an object-oriented kernel language. We show how object environments of such languages can be formalized in an algebraic way. Based on this foundation, we develop a Hoare-style logic for formal verification of object-oriented programs.

Keywords
Programming logic; verification; object-oriented programming language; programming language semantics

1 INTRODUCTION

Typed object-oriented programming languages like C++, Java, Eiffel, Oberon, Modula-3, BETA, and Ada95 form an important practical class of languages. This paper presents the logical foundations needed to formally verify object-oriented programs from that class. This introduction sketches the motivation for this work, the approach taken, and related work.

Motivation The language class mentioned above is increasingly important, in particular, because OO-techniques support reuse and adaptation via inheritance. Reuse and adaptation of software components have been shown to be very useful for application frameworks and component-based architectures. There are three reasons why formal verification techniques are especially interesting for OO-programs: 1. Verification techniques are needed for software certification in the quickly developing software component industry, which is based on OO-technology. 2. The potential for reuse in OO-programming carries over to reusing proofs. 3. *Formal* verification is important because of the complexity of the underlying languages. Without tool support, large program proofs are tedious to handle and can hardly be kept error-free. Formality is a prerequisite for the construction of computer-based tools.

Programming Concepts and Methods D. Gries, & W-P. de Roever (Eds.)

Approach Three aspects make verification of OO-programs more complex than verification of programs with just recursive procedures and arbitrary pointer data structures: Subtyping, abstract types, and dynamic binding. Subtyping allows variables to hold objects of different types. Abstract types have different or incomplete implementations. Thus, techniques are needed to formulate type properties without referring to implementations. Dynamic binding destroys the static connection between the calls and body of a procedure.

Our solutions to these problems build on well-known techniques. Object environments are specified as an abstract data type with operations to create objects and to read and write instance variables/attributes. Based on object environments, abstraction of object structures can be expressed. Using such abstractions, the behavior of abstract types can be formulated. Our programming logic refines a Hoare-logic for procedural languages. To express the relation between environments in pre- and poststates the current object environment can be referenced through a special variable.

Object-oriented languages use dynamically bound method invocations where procedural languages use statically bound calls. Consider e.g. the invocation `x.m()` where variable x is of type T with subtypes T1 and T2 and where m belongs to the interface of T (and consequently to the interfaces of T1 and T2). If x holds an object of type T1 at method invocation time, the implementation associated with T1:m is executed; if it holds a T2-object, T2:m is executed. The basic idea for the verification of method invocations is to consider them as statically bound calls to virtual methods; e.g., the above method invocation is considered as a call to the virtual method T:m, the properties of which are used to verify the call. The distinction between the virtual behavior of a method and the behavior of the associated implementation allows the transfer of verification techniques for procedures to OO-programs.

Related Work In [Lei97], a wlp-calculus for an OO-language is presented that is semantically similar to the language considered here. But the underlying methodology is different. Method specifications are part of the programs. The calculus is used to check that programs satisfy their specifications Changing the specifications modifies the program and makes a new check of the entire program necessary. In our approach, programs and specifications are separated. The programming logic is used to verify theorems about programs. In section 5, we show that the approach in [Lei97] can be considered as restricting our approach to a certain program development strategy. Thereby, it becomes simpler and more appropriate for automatic checking, but gives up flexibility that seems important to us for general program verification.

A different logic for OO-programs that is related to type-systems is presented and proved sound in [AL97]. It is developed for an OO-language in the style of the lambda calculus whereas our language aims to be close to practical OO-languages. In particular, our language supports inheritance.

The programming logic presented in the following is essentially an extension of the partial correctness logic described in [Apt81]. The extension to object-orientation profited from other papers about verification of imperative languages with complex data structures, especially [Suz80].

In practice, formal verification requires elaborate formal specification techniques. Our goal is to verify implementations w.r.t. program specifications according to the two-tiered specification approach developed in the Larch project (cf. [GH93]). In [MPH97], we outline the connection between Larch-style program specifications and our logical foundations. To automate proof steps, weakest precondition transformations are very important (cf. [Gri81]). We apply such techniques for the classical rules. An extension to the new rules is considered future work.

Overview Section 2 introduces the simple kernel object-oriented language SKOOL. Section 3 contains a formalization of object environments. The axiomatic semantics of SKOOL is presented in section 4. Section 5 demonstrates how the logic can be used to verify OO-programs. In section 6, SKOOL is extended by inheritance and the logic is adapted to this new feature.

2 AN OBJECT-ORIENTED KERNEL LANGUAGE

The common features of typed OO-programming languages are (a) type/class declarations that combine records and type-local procedures, so-called *methods*, (b) subtyping, and (c) code inheritance. In this paper, we develop a logic for a kernel of object-oriented languages called KOOL supporting these features. KOOL is presented in two steps. This section presents the sublanguage SKOOL featuring type declarations and subtyping. Section 6 adds inheritance.

Types and Methods A *type* describes a collection of objects together with their operations. In the context of OO-programming, it is helpful to distinguish between *concrete* and *abstract* types: A concrete type is associated with a complete implementation; an abstract type expresses common behavior of its subtypes. In SKOOL, an abstract type declaration has the form:

```
abstract type TA subtype of <AbsTypeList> is <MethSigList> end
```

A method signature consists of the method name, a parameter list, and a result type. If the result of a method is irrelevant, the result type may be omitted. The signature list is called the *interface* of type TA, denoted by IF(TA). The declaration of a concrete type has the form:

```
type TC subtype of <AbsTypeList> is <MethList> <AttrList> end
```

A method is a type-local procedure with an *implicit parameter* having the enclosing type; the implicit parameter is denoted by `this`. A method definition consists of a method signature, a list of local variable declarations, and a body:

$$\texttt{m(}\ p_1\texttt{:}T_{p_1}\texttt{,}\dots\texttt{,}\ p_q\texttt{:}T_{p_q}\ \texttt{):}T_m\ \ \texttt{is}\ \ v_1\texttt{:}T_{v_1}\texttt{;}\dots\texttt{;}v_r\texttt{:}T_{v_r}\texttt{;}\ \ \texttt{<Body>}\ \ \texttt{end}$$

The list of local variables implicitly contains a variable `result` of type T_m. The value of result is returned as result of `m`.The body of a method is either *predefined* or a (usually compound) statement.

Attribute declarations have the form `attr a:TR` where `a` is the attribute name and `TR` is a type name, the *range type* of `a`. A declaration `attr a:TR` is considered as an abbreviation for the following two method declarations:

```
get_a(): TR  is  predefined        set_a( p:TR ) is  predefined
```

In addition to this, a concrete type may contain the predefined method `equ` comparing objects of that type with other objects, and `new` creating objects of that type. Method `new` is a typical case of a static or class method, i.e., a method that does not need an implicit parameter. We avoid a special treatment of such methods here to keep the number of logical rules in later sections small. Such methods can be called using the null-object that is predefined for each concrete type (see below).

The *interface of a concrete type* consists of the signatures of the declared methods and of the attribute access methods. All method names in interfaces must be distinct.

A *SKOOL program* is a finite set of type declarations containing an abstract type OBJECT with equality `equ(p:OBJECT):BOOL` and the concrete types INT and BOOL with appropriate operations. The `subtype`-clause defines a binary relation on the types of a program. The reflexive and transitive closure of this relation is called the *subtype relation* (denoted by $\preceq$). In SKOOL, three conditions have to be satisfied: 1. The subtype relation has to be a partial ordering. 2. Concrete types have to be minimal in the subtype relation. 3. Every type has to be a subtype of OBJECT (for INT and BOOL this property is only claimed to avoid separate treatment of these types).

A method signature with (explicit) parameter types $S_1, \ldots, S_z$ and result type SR is called a *subsignature* of a signature with (explicit) parameter types $T_1, \ldots, T_z$ and result type TR, if they have the same method name and $T_j \preceq S_j$ and SR $\preceq$ TR. An interface IF(S) is called *subinterface* of interface IF(T) if for each signature in IF(T) there is a subsignature in IF(S). In SKOOL programs, IF(S) has to be a subinterface of IF(T) if S $\preceq$ T.

Expressions and Statements SKOOL supports only atomic expressions. An expression is either an INT or BOOL constant, a variable or parameter of the enclosing method, or a null-object: For each user-declared concrete type TC there is exactly one null-object denoted by null(TC). Null-objects have no attributes; they are needed for initialization of attributes and to handle recursive types. Typed null-objects can also be used to simulate static methods by using the null-object of the corresponding type as implicit argument in the invocation. For brevity, compound expressions are not considered here. They can be broken up into atomic expressions by introducing auxiliary variables for subexpressions. SKOOL provides if- and while-statements and sequential statement composition with the usual syntax. Assignments with casting and method invocations are written as follows:

`v := (T) EXP`   `v :=` EXP_0 . T:m($\text{EXP}_1, \ldots, \text{EXP}_q$)

The type T in an assignment must be a subtype of both the left-hand side's and the expression's type. If T equals the expression type, it can be omitted. Casts are provided by KOOL because they occur in most OO-languages. An invocation statement is type-correct, if the type of EXP_0 equals type T and the interface of T contains a method m such that the types of the EXP_i are subtypes of the parameter types, and the result type of T:m is a subtype of the type of the left-hand side. We use the redundant type prefix "T:" for methods to simplify the verification. If it is clear from the context, it may be omitted. To come closer to notational conventions, we write `v:= EXP.a` instead of `v:= EXP.T:get_a()`, and `v.a:= EXP` instead of `v.T:set_a(EXP)`.

3 FORMALIZING OBJECT ENVIRONMENTS

An object environment describes the states of all objects in a program at a certain point of execution. In particular, it describes how objects are linked via references and which objects are alive. A formalization of object environments is important as the semantic foundation of program specifications and is central for the verification of OO-programs. This section summarizes the formal background used and formalizes objects, object states, and object environments.

Formal Background The general techniques underlying our work can be formulated in different formal frameworks. In this paper, we use many-sorted first-order specifications (cf. e.g. [Wir90]) and recursive data type specifications (see below). A *(many-sorted) signature* Σ is a tuple $\langle S, F \rangle$ where S is a set of *sort symbols* and F is a set of *function symbols*. We assume that all many-sorted signatures contain a sort *Bool* with constants TRUE and FALSE as well as an appropriate integer data type with sort *Int*.

The set of Σ-*formulas* contains (1) every term of sort *Bool*, (2) $\neg G, (G \wedge H), (G \vee H), (G \Rightarrow H)$, and $(G \Leftrightarrow H)$, and (3) $(\forall X : G)$ and $(\exists X : G)$, where G and H are Σ-formulas, and X is a logical variable. Substitution of all free occurrences of a variable or constant X by a term t in formula $\mathbf{P}$ is denoted by $\mathbf{P}[t/X]$, where the sort of t has to be equal to the sort of X.

For the specification of recursive data types, we use the following notation:

data type
$DSrt = constr_1(USrt_1^1, \ldots, USrt_1^{m_1}) \mid \ldots \mid constr_n(USrt_n^1, \ldots, USrt_n^{m_n})$
end data type

Such a definition introduces the sort *DSrt* with constructor functions $constr_j$. We assume rules to reason about recursive data types; these rules allow in particular to prove the in-/equality of two terms and support term induction.

Notation We use the following notational conventions: Σ-formulas are denoted by bold capital letters **P**, **Q**, etc. Functions, constants, and program variables are written in lower case. Logical variables are written in upper case.

Objects The set of objects in a given program depends on the declared types, attributes, and their relation. The simplest approach is to assume that a program is fixed and to define the objects for this program. The disadvantage of this approach becomes apparent when new types are added. By such program extensions, the set of objects is enlarged. Thus, formulas quantifying over all objects that are valid in the original program may become invalid in the extended program. To avoid this, we consider a program to be part of all its extensions. I.e., we assume infinite sorts *TypId* and *ATypId* of type identifiers for concrete and abstract types resp., and an infinite sort *AttId* of attribute identifiers where attributes with the same name, but different object types, are considered to be different. A program determines the relation between its types and attributes, but leaves the relation between types and attributes not occurring in the program un(der)specified. Extending a program then means refining the type-attribute relation. To distinguish different objects of the same type, we assume an infinite sort *ObjId* of object identifiers:

```
data type                         data type
  Type  =  BOOL                     Object  =  bool( Bool )
        |  INT                              |  int( Int )
        |  ct( TypId )                      |  null( TypId )
        |  at( ATypId )                     |  mkobj( TypId, ObjId )
end data type                     end data type
```

As can be seen from the definition of data type *Object*, an object of a declared type T is either the null-object of T or a typed object identifier. Notice that all objects are of concrete types. Furthermore, we assume an appropriate axiomatization of the subtype relation $\preceq$ on sort *Type*.

Object States Object states are modeled via *object locations*: For each attribute of its type, an object has a location. Locations can be considered as anonymous variables, i.e., variables that can only be referenced through the object they belong to. Locations are often called instance variables.

```
data type
  Location  =  mkloc( AttId, ObjId )
end data type
```

The relations between objects, types, and attributes, and their basic properties are expressed by the following functions: *typ* yields the type of an object; *isnull* asserts that an object is a null-object; *otyp* and *rtyp* yield the object and range type of an attribute; *ltyp* yields the type of a location; *obj* yields the object a location belongs to; given an object and an attribute, *loc* yields the corresponding location; *static* asserts that an object is not subject to object creation.

$$
\begin{array}{lcl}
typ : Object \to Type & & \\
\quad typ(bool(B)) & = & BOOL \\
\quad typ(int(I)) & = & INT \\
\quad typ(null(T)) & = & ct(T) \\
\quad typ(mkobj(T, OI)) & = & ct(T)
\end{array}
$$

$$
\begin{array}{lcl}
ltyp : Location \to Type & & \\
\quad ltyp(mkloc(A, OI)) & = & rtyp(A)
\end{array}
$$

$$
\begin{array}{l}
obj : Location \to Object \\
\quad obj(mkloc(A, OI)) = mkobj(otyp(A), OI)
\end{array}
$$

$$
\begin{array}{l}
loc : Object \times AttId \to Location \\
\quad loc(mkobj(otyp(A), OI), A) = mkloc(A, OI)
\end{array}
$$

$$
\begin{array}{l}
static : Object \to Bool \\
\quad static(X) \quad \Leftrightarrow \quad typ(X) = BOOL \vee typ(X) = INT \vee isnull(X)
\end{array}
$$

$$
\begin{array}{l}
isnull : Object \to Bool \\
\quad \neg isnull(bool(B)) \\
\quad \neg isnull(int(I)) \\
\quad \neg isnull(mkobj(T, OI)) \\
\quad isnull(null(T))
\end{array}
$$

$$
\begin{array}{l}
otyp : AttId \to TypId \\
rtyp : AttId \to Type
\end{array}
$$

$$
\begin{array}{lcl}
init : Type \to Object & & \\
\quad init(BOOL) & = & false \\
\quad init(INT) & = & int(0) \\
\quad init(ct(T)) & = & null(T) \\
\quad typ(init(at(T))) \preceq at(T) & & \\
\quad static(init(at(T))) & &
\end{array}
$$

All functions except *otyp* and *rtyp*, are program-independent. The object and range types of attributes do not change if a program is extended. We assume that *otyp* and *rtyp* are specified by enumeration for all attributes of a given program.

Object Environments Object environments are modeled by an abstract data type with main sort *ObjEnv* and the following operations: $E\langle L := X\rangle$ denotes updating the object environment E at location L with object X. $E(L)$ denotes reading location L in environment E; $E(L)$ is called the *object held by* L *in* E. $new(E,T)$ returns a new object of type T in environment E. $E\langle T\rangle$ denotes the environment after allocating a new object of type T in E. $alive(X, E)$ yields true if and only if object X has been allocated in E:

$$
\begin{array}{ll}
\_\langle\_ := \_\rangle & : ObjEnv \times Location \times Object \to ObjEnv \\
\_\langle\_\rangle & : ObjEnv \times TypId \to ObjEnv \\
\_(\_) & : ObjEnv \times Location \to Object \\
alive & : Object \times ObjEnv \to Bool \\
new & : ObjEnv \times TypId \to Object
\end{array}
$$

In the following, we present and explain the axiomatization of these functions. Location update and object allocation construct new environments from given ones; location read and liveness test allow the observation of environments. We first consider the properties of environments observable by location reads, then the liveness properties, and finally the properties of the *new*-operation.

Axiom env1 states that updating one location does not affect the objects held by other locations. Axiom env2 states that reading a location updated by an object X yields X, if the object of the location and X are both alive. We restrict this property to living objects in order to guarantee that locations never hold non-living objects and that locations of non-living objects are initialized as described by axiom env3. Axiom env4 states that updates by non-living objects do not modify the environment. The assumptions and requirements about the liveness of objects in axioms env2, env3, env4 simplify the definition of equivalence properties on environments. Axiom env5 states that allocation does not affect the objects held by locations:

$$\begin{array}{ll} \text{env1}: & L1 \neq L2 \;\Rightarrow\; E\langle L1 := X\rangle(L2) = E(L2) \\ \text{env2}: & alive(obj(L),E) \wedge alive(X,E) \;\Rightarrow\; E\langle L := X\rangle(L) = X \\ \text{env3}: & \neg alive(obj(L),E) \;\Rightarrow\; E(L) = init(ltyp(L)) \\ \text{env4}: & \neg alive(X,E) \;\Rightarrow\; E\langle L := X\rangle = E \\ \text{env5}: & E\langle T\rangle(L) = E(L) \end{array}$$

Axiom env6 states that location updates do not influence liveness of objects. Axiom env7 specifies that an object is alive after allocation if and only if it was alive before allocation or it is the newly allocated object. Axiom env8 ensures that objects held by locations are alive. Together with env2, env3, and env4, this simplifies proofs. Finally, static objects, i.e., objects that are not subject to creation, are considered to be alive:

$$\begin{array}{ll} \text{env6}: & alive(X, E\langle L := Y\rangle) \;\Leftrightarrow\; alive(X,E) \\ \text{env7}: & alive(X, E\langle T\rangle) \;\Leftrightarrow\; alive(X,E) \vee X = new(E,T) \\ \text{env8}: & alive(E(L),E) \\ \text{env9}: & static(X) \;\Rightarrow\; alive(X,E) \end{array}$$

The following two axioms specify properties of the new-operation. A newly created object is not alive in the environment in which it was created (env10) and it has the correct type (env11).

$$\begin{array}{ll} \text{env10}: & \neg alive(new(E,T),E) \\ \text{env11}: & typ(new(E,T)) = ct(T) \end{array}$$

A model for these axioms can be found in [PH97].

4 A LOGIC FOR OBJECT-ORIENTED PROGRAMS

This section presents a programming logic for SKOOL. In particular, we show how method invocation and subtyping can be handled.

Program Specific Signatures To specify program properties, we have to refer to variables, attributes, and types in formulas. This is enabled by introducing constant symbols for these entities. More precisely, let Π be a SKOOL program and let Σ denote a signature that includes the signature of the object environment as introduced above, a constant symbol T of sort *TypId* or *ATypId* for each concrete or abstract type T declared in Π, and a constant symbol T:att of sort *AttId* for each attribute att declared in type T. To refer to the current object environment in formulas, the constant symbol \$ of sort

ObjEnv is used, and Γ denotes $\Sigma \cup \{\$\}$. The current object environment \$ can be considered as a global variable.

Furthermore, we treat program variables and parameters syntactically as constant symbols of sort *Object* to simplify quantification and substitution rules*. The following signatures are used to define context conditions for pre- and postconditions (see below). Let m be a method: 1. The extension of Γ by constant symbols for the parameters of m (in particular, *this*) is denoted by $\Gamma_{pre(m)}$. 2. The extension of Γ by constant symbols for each parameter and local variable of m is denoted by $\Gamma_{body(m)}$. 3. The extension of Γ by the constant symbol result is denoted by Γ_{post}.

Triples and Sequents A *program component* is a method signature occurrence or a statement occurrence within a given program. I.e., we assume that the program context in which each program component occurs is given implicitly. In particular, we can refer to the method enclosing a statement. A *Hoare triple* or simply *triple* has the form { **P** } COMP { **Q** } where COMP is a program component and **P** and **Q** are first-order formulas, called *pre-* and *postconditions*, respectively. If the component in a triple **A** is a method, we call **A** a *method annotation*; otherwise **A** is called a *statement annotation.* Pre- and postconditions of statement annotations are formulas over $\Gamma_{body(m)}$ where m is the enclosing method; pre- and postconditions in annotations of method m are $\Gamma_{pre(m)}$-formulas and Γ_{post}-formulas, respectively.

A triple { **P** } COMP { **Q** } specifies the following *refined* partial correctness property: If **P** holds in a state before executing COMP, then execution of COMP either

1. terminates and **Q** holds in the state after execution or
2. aborts because of errors or actions that are beyond the semantics of the programming language (e.g., memory allocation problems, stack overflow, external interrupts from the execution environment), or
3. runs forever.

In particular, execution of COMP does not abort because of dereferencing of null-objects or illegal casts. Thus, this refined partial correctness logic can be used to prove that a program does not produce such runtime errors.

A *sequent* has the form $\mathcal{A} \vdash \mathbf{A}$ where $\mathcal{A}$ is a set of method annotations and **A** is a triple. Triples in $\mathcal{A}$ are called *assumptions* of the sequent and **A** is called the *consequent* of the sequent. A sequent expresses the fact that we can prove a triple based on some assumptions about methods. Sequents are necessary to handle recursive procedures and subtyping (see below).

Axiomatic Semantics The axiomatic semantics of SKOOL consists of axioms for the predefined methods, a cast axiom that adapts the classical as-

*This treatment imitates the distinction between global (i.e. logical) variables and local variables in temporal logic (cf. [GU91], p. 233ff.)

signment axiom, and rules explaining statement and method behavior. We concentrate here on the most interesting axioms and rules.

Predefined Methods In SKOOL, there are predefined methods for equality test, object creation, and attribute access. The specifications of these methods illustrate the use of the object environment in triples. In the axioms for the attribute access methods, we use this.T:a as abbreviation for $loc(\text{this}, \text{T:a})$ and $prec(\text{this}, \text{T})$ as abbreviation for $\neg isnull(\text{this}) \wedge typ(\text{this}) = \text{T}$:

$\vdash \{\ \mathbf{P}[bool(\text{this} = \text{p})/\text{result}]\ \}$ T:equ(p:OBJECT):BOOL $\{\ \mathbf{P}\ \}$

$\vdash \{\ \mathbf{P}[new(\$, \text{T})/\text{result}\ ,\ \$\langle \text{T}\rangle/\$]\ \}$ T:new():T $\{\ \mathbf{P}\ \}$

$\vdash \{\ prec(\text{this}, \text{T}) \wedge \mathbf{P}[\$(\text{this.T:a})/\text{result}]\ \}$ T:get_a():TR $\{\ \mathbf{P}\ \}$

$\vdash \{\ prec(\text{this}, \text{T}) \wedge \mathbf{P}[\$\langle \text{this.T:a} := \text{p}\rangle/\$]\ \}$ T:set_a(p:TR) $\{\ \mathbf{P}\ \}$

Statements Assignments in SKOOL may be combined with casts to narrow the static type of the right-hand side. The semantics of a cast is only defined if the (dynamic) type of the object denoted by the right-hand side expression is a subtype of the given type T:

cast-axiom:

$\vdash \{\ typ(\text{EXP}) \preceq T \wedge \mathbf{P}[\text{EXP}/\text{v}]\ \}$ v := (T) EXP $\{\ \mathbf{P}\ \}$

The rules for the loop, conditional, and sequential statement are standard and not presented here. Because of the syntactical conditions discussed above, the rule for the invocation statement becomes very intuitive. Formal parameters are substituted by the actual parameter expressions and the result variable is substituted by the left-hand side variable:

invocation-rule:

$$\frac{\mathcal{A} \vdash \{\ \mathbf{P}\ \}\ \ \text{T:m}(\text{p}_1 : \text{T}_1, \ldots, \text{p}_q : \text{T}_q)\text{:TR}\ \ \{\ \mathbf{Q}\ \}}{\mathcal{A} \vdash \{\ \mathbf{P}[\text{E}_0/\text{this}, \text{E}_1/\text{p}_1, \ldots, \text{E}_q/\text{p}_q]\ \}\ \ \text{v} := \text{E}_0\ .\ \text{T:m}(\text{E}_1, \ldots, \text{E}_q)\ \ \{\ \mathbf{Q}[\text{v}/\text{result}]\ \}}$$

The fact that program variables different from v are not modified by an invocation is expressed by the following rule. Local variables and parameters w of the enclosing method different from v may be substituted for logical variables:

var-rule:

$$\frac{\mathcal{A} \vdash \{\ \mathbf{P}\ \}\ \ \text{v} := \text{E}_0\ .\ \text{T:m}(\text{E}_1, \ldots, \text{E}_q)\ \ \{\ \mathbf{Q}\ \}}{\mathcal{A} \vdash \{\ \mathbf{P}[\text{w}/Z]\ \}\ \ \text{v} := \text{E}_0\ .\ \text{T:m}(\text{E}_1, \ldots, \text{E}_q)\ \ \{\ \mathbf{Q}[\text{w}/Z]\ \}}$$

Methods There are two rules explaining the derivation of method annotations in SKOOL. The first rule deals with methods of concrete types, i.e., with methods having a body. The second rule deals with methods of abstract types, i.e., with *virtual methods.*

Essentially, an annotation of an implemented method m holds if it holds for its body. This basic rule is strengthened in two aspects: 1. In order to handle recursion, the method annotation may be assumed for the proof of the body. Informally, this is sound, because, in any terminating execution, the last incarnation does not contain a recursive invocation of the method. 2. The requirement that local variables are initialized to static objects of the correct type is established:

implementation-rule:

$$\frac{\mathcal{A},\ \{\mathbf{P}\}\ \text{T:m(..)}\ \{\mathbf{Q}\}\ \vdash\ \{\mathbf{P} \wedge \bigwedge_i (v_i = \mathit{init}(\text{TV}_i))\}\ \text{BODY(T:m)}\ \{\mathbf{Q}\}}{\mathcal{A} \vdash \{\mathbf{P}\}\ \ \text{T:m(..)}\ \ \{\mathbf{Q}\}}$$

where v_i are the local variables of method T:m and TV_i denotes the static type of v_i.

In OO-languages with subtyping and dynamic binding, annotations for virtual methods must be derived. The basic idea is simple: To prove something for a virtual method T:m, we have to prove it for all the corresponding methods T*i*:m in the subtypes. In order to get the type assumptions right, we consider a pseudo-implementation of T:m and derive the subtype-rule using the programming logic without a subtype-rule. The pseudo-code performs a case distinction according to the type of the this-object. Depending on the type, the this-object is cast to one of T's subtypes and the corresponding method associated with the subtype is called. A simple example, in which T has only two subtypes T1 and T2, is illustrative:

```
meth  T:m( p: TP ): TR is
   v1: T1 ;   v2: T2 ;
   if  typ(this) ≼ T1       then  v1      := (T1) this ;
                                  result := v1.T1:m(p)
   else if  typ(this) ≼ T2 then  v2      := (T2) this ;
                                  result := v2.T2:m(p)
                            else  abort              end end
end
```

Applying the programming logic to prove $\{\ \mathbf{R}\ \}$ T:m(p:TP):TR $\{\ \mathbf{Q}\ \}$ leads to the following proof obligations:

$\{\ \tau \preceq \text{T1} \wedge \mathbf{R}\ \}$	T1:m(p:TP1):TR1	$\{\ \mathbf{Q}\ \}$
$\{\ \tau \preceq \text{T2} \wedge \mathbf{R}\ \}$	T2:m(p:TP2):TR2	$\{\ \mathbf{Q}\ \}$
$\{\ \tau \not\preceq \text{T1} \wedge \tau \not\preceq \text{T2} \wedge \mathbf{R}\ \}$	abort	$\{\ \mathbf{Q}\ \}$

where τ abbreviates *typ*(this). The last triple can only be proved for arbitrary **R** if its precondition is falsified. If the program is complete, we can use the knowledge that T1 and T2 are the only subtypes of T, i.e. $\tau \preceq \text{T} \Rightarrow \tau \preceq \text{T1} \vee \tau \preceq \text{T2}$. Substituting $\tau \preceq \text{T} \wedge \mathbf{P}$ for **R** and applying the implication, the precondition of the abort statement becomes false so that this triple can be proved (see false-axiom in appendix). Because of $\tau \preceq \text{T}i \Rightarrow \tau \preceq \text{T}$, this development can be summarized by the following rule:

$$\frac{\begin{array}{lll}\{\ \tau \preceq \text{T1} \wedge \mathbf{P}\ \} & \text{T1:m(p:TP1):TR1} & \{\ \mathbf{Q}\ \} \\ \{\ \tau \preceq \text{T2} \wedge \mathbf{P}\ \} & \text{T2:m(p:TP2):TR2} & \{\ \mathbf{Q}\ \}\end{array}}{\begin{array}{lll}\{\ \tau \preceq \text{T} \wedge \mathbf{P}\ \} & \text{T:m(p:TP):TR} & \{\ \mathbf{Q}\ \}\end{array}}$$

This rule can be generalized to abstract types with an arbitrary, but known number of subtypes. But what happens, if the program is not complete? Extending a program Π means adding new subtypes to some of Π's abstract types AT. In general, this invalidates the proofs of AT's methods, since these proofs were based on the assumption that all subtypes of AT were present. To handle program extensions, we collect proof obligations that have to be met by all future subtypes. To cover these obligations in the logic, we weaken the above rule by adding an assumption to the conclusion. As an aside, the use of assumptions allows us to avoid an arbitrary number of antecedents in the subtype-rule. In summary, we get the following compact form for the subtype-rule:

subtype-rule:

$$\frac{\mathrm{T}' \preceq \mathrm{T} \qquad \mathcal{A} \vdash \{\, \tau \preceq \mathrm{T}' \wedge \mathbf{P} \,\}\ \mathrm{T}'{:}\mathrm{m}\ \{\, \mathbf{Q} \,\}}{\{\, \tau \preceq \mathrm{T} \wedge \tau \not\preceq \mathrm{T}' \wedge \mathbf{P} \,\}\ \mathrm{T}{:}\mathrm{m}\ \{\, \mathbf{Q} \,\}, \mathcal{A} \ \vdash \{\, \tau \preceq \mathrm{T} \wedge \mathbf{P} \,\}\ \mathrm{T}{:}\mathrm{m}\ \{\, \mathbf{Q} \,\}}$$

The elimination of the assumptions and the application of the rules for program verification is treated in section 5.

Programming Logic The programming logic for SKOOL is the union of axioms and rules described above and of the language-independent rules given in the appendix. The language-independent rules are essentially an adaptation of the proof systems G and G_0 presented in [Apt81].

5 VERIFICATION OF OBJECT-ORIENTED PROGRAMS

In this section we discuss the verification of "open" programs, the subtype-rule, and top-down development of types.

Open vs. Closed Programs In section 4, the notion of program execution was used to explain the meaning of a triple. To be more precise, we have to define what the executions of a SKOOL program are. We consider two cases: 1. A program may be declared to be *closed* (e.g., by adding some suitable keyword to the program). A closed program is considered complete and can be executed by calling some method of the program that takes only integer and boolean arguments as explicit parameters (recall from section 4 that methods can be invoked in a static fashion by using a null-object as implicit parameter). This defines all executions of a closed program. In a closed program, the subtype relation is complete; this is axiomatized as follows: For all abstract types T we add the following axiom to our programming logic:

$$S \prec \mathrm{T} \Leftrightarrow S \preceq \mathrm{T}_1 \vee \ldots \vee S \preceq \mathrm{T}_k$$

where $\mathrm{T}_1, \ldots, \mathrm{T}_k$ are the direct subtypes of T.

2. A program that is not closed is called *open*. It can be extended by adding new types. Open programs are very common in OO-programming. In particular, all libraries are open programs. The executions of an open program Π are all executions of all closed extensions of Π. Intuitively, open OO-programs are more difficult to verify because extensions can influence abstract types.

Bottom-up Verification According to the semantics of OO-languages, the properties of a virtual method in type T depend on the properties of the corresponding methods in T's subtypes. This kind of bottom-up verification, reflected by the subtype-rule, is illustrated in this paragraph: Let us assume a closed program declaring an abstract container type CO with an insert method and two subtypes: LI, a list implementation, and AR, an array-based implementation. LI and AR possess abstraction functions aL and aA that map their objects in a given object environment to elements of an abstract data type $Multiset$ with an insertion operation ins. Assume we have proved

$$\{\ \tau \preceq ct(\mathrm{LI}) \wedge aL(\mathrm{this}, \$) = M \wedge \mathrm{o} = O\ \}\ \ \mathrm{LI{:}insert(o)}\ \ \{\ aL(\mathrm{result}, \$) = ins(M, O)\ \}$$

i.e., if multiset M is the abstraction of *this* in the state before execution of `LI:insert` and O denotes the actual parameter object, the abstraction of the result is $ins(M, O)$. In order to prove a similar triple for `CO:insert`, we have to define an abstraction function for CO that works for objects of LI and AR (we write $\mathrm{LI_c}$ for ct(LI), $\mathrm{AR_c}$ for ct(AR), and $\mathrm{CO_a}$ for at(CO)):

$$\begin{array}{l} aC : Object \times ObjEnv \rightarrow Multiset \\ \quad typ(X) \preceq \mathrm{LI_c} \quad \Rightarrow \quad aC(X, E) = aL(X, E) \\ \quad typ(X) \preceq \mathrm{AR_c} \quad \Rightarrow \quad aC(X, E) = aA(X, E) \end{array}$$

Using this definition and the fact that the result of `LI:insert` is correctly typed (the latter assumption can be made w.l.g., because we can prove within the logic that SKOOL is a type-safe language; cf. [PH97] for proving type annotations), we can derive

$$\vdash \{\ \tau \preceq \mathrm{LI_c} \wedge aC(\mathrm{this}, \$) = M \wedge \mathrm{o} = O\ \}\ \ \mathrm{LI{:}insert(o)}\ \ \{aC(\mathrm{result}, \$) = ins(M, O)\}$$

The subtype rule with $\mathrm{LI_c} \preceq \mathrm{CO_a}$ yields:

$$\{\ \tau \preceq \mathrm{CO_a} \wedge \tau \not\preceq \mathrm{LI_c} \wedge \mathbf{P}\ \}\ \mathrm{CO{:}insert(o)}\ \{\ \mathbf{Q}\ \} \vdash \{\ \tau \preceq \mathrm{CO_a} \wedge \mathbf{P}\ \}\ \mathrm{CO{:}insert}\ \{\ \mathbf{Q}\ \}$$

where $\mathbf{P}$ abbreviates $aC(\mathrm{this}, \$) = M \wedge \mathrm{o} = O$ and $\mathbf{Q}$ abbreviates $aC(\mathrm{this}, \$) = ins(M, O)$. If we start from a specification of AR:insert similar to that given above for LI:insert and add $\tau \not\preceq \mathrm{LI_c}$ to the preconditions, we can use the same steps to derive:

$$\begin{array}{l} \{\ \tau \preceq \mathrm{CO_a} \wedge \tau \not\preceq \mathrm{AR_c} \wedge \tau \not\preceq \mathrm{LI_c} \wedge \mathbf{P}\ \}\ \mathrm{CO{:}insert(o)}\ \{\ \mathbf{Q}\ \} \\ \qquad \vdash \{\ \tau \preceq \mathrm{CO_a} \wedge \tau \not\preceq \mathrm{LI_c} \wedge \mathbf{P}\ \}\ \mathrm{CO{:}insert(o)}\ \{\ \mathbf{Q}\ \} \end{array}$$

The consequent of the derived sequent equals the assumption of the sequent derived first. Thus, we conclude:

$$\begin{array}{l} \{\ \tau \preceq \mathrm{CO_a} \wedge \tau \not\preceq \mathrm{AR_c} \wedge \tau \not\preceq \mathrm{LI_c} \wedge \mathbf{P}\ \}\ \mathrm{CO{:}insert(o)}\ \{\ \mathbf{Q}\ \} \\ \qquad \vdash \{\ \tau \preceq \mathrm{CO_a} \wedge \mathbf{P}\ \}\ \mathrm{CO{:}insert(o)}\ \{\ \mathbf{Q}\ \} \end{array}$$

As we assumed that the program is closed, the precondition of the assumption is false, so that the assumption can be eliminated (see false-axiom and assumpt-elim-rule in appendix). Thus, we have derived a property of the virtual method `CO:insert`.

Top-down Verification Usually, OO-programs are developed by refining existing types in open programs, i.e. by adding new subtypes to the program. Verification then means proving that a new subtype satisfies the specification of its supertypes. I.e., programs are developed together with their verified properties in a top-down manner. This methodology can be realized in our logic by the following ***strategy***: 1. Provide a specification for each method of the program. We assume that a method specification SPEC(T:m) is a triple of the form $\{\tau \preceq \mathrm{T} \wedge \mathbf{P}_{\mathrm{T:m}}\}$ T:m $\{\mathbf{Q}_{\mathrm{T:m}}\}$. 2. If a new type S is added to the program, prove that the methods of S satisfy the specifications of supertype methods, i.e. for all direct supertypes T of S and all methods T:m show SPEC(S:m) $\vdash \{\tau \preceq \mathrm{S} \wedge \mathbf{P}_{\mathrm{T:m}}\}$ S:m $\{\mathbf{Q}_{\mathrm{T:m}}\}$. 3. If S is a concrete type prove in addition that method implementations satisfy their specifications. In these proofs, the method specifications of the original program can be used.

Lemma: All methods of a closed program Π that was developed according to the strategy sketched above satisfy their specifications.

Proof: To prove the lemma, we show that all methods of Π satisfy their specification under certain assumptions that can be discarded for closed programs. Let DST(T, Π) denote the direct subtypes of type T in program Π and VM(Π) the virtual methods of Π. By $\mathcal{A}_\Pi$ we denote the following set of triples:

$$\bigcup_{\mathrm{T:m} \in \mathrm{VM}(\Pi)} \{\tau \preceq \mathrm{T} \wedge \bigwedge_{\mathrm{T'} \in \mathrm{DST}(\mathrm{T},\Pi)} \tau \not\preceq \mathrm{T'} \wedge \mathbf{P}_{\mathrm{T:m}}\}\ \mathrm{T:m}\ \{\mathbf{Q}_{\mathrm{T:m}}\}$$

$\mathcal{A}_\Pi$ formalizes the assumption that new subtypes satisfy the supertype specification. We show that $\mathcal{A}_\Pi \vdash$ SPEC(T:m) can be derived for all T:m in a program Π that is developed together with its specification according to the above strategy, i.e. this sequent is a development invariant. The lemma is proved by induction on the number of extension steps*.

Induction Base: In the minimal program containing the types OBJECT, BOOL, and INT, the specifications of the predefined methods are given by axioms.

Induction Step: Let Π' be an extension of Π by type S. We have to prove $\mathcal{A}_{\Pi'} \vdash$ SPEC(U:m) for all U:m in Π'. We distinguish three cases: 1. U:m is a method of Π. 2. U = S and S is a concrete type. 3. U = S and S is abstract. The last case is trivial because DST(S, Π') is empty, so that SPEC(S:m) $\in \mathcal{A}_{\Pi'}$.

---

*To focus on the application of the subtype-rule, we assume here that programs are extended type by type, i.e., we do not consider extensions by mutually recursive types.

For the first two cases we can assume $\mathcal{A}_{\Pi} \vdash$ SPEC(U:m) (induction hypothesis in case 1, part 3 of strategy in case 2). Thus, it suffices to show $\mathcal{A}_{\Pi'} \vdash \mathcal{A}_{\Pi}$. To do that, we prove for each virtual method T:m $\in$ VM(Π) that the corresponding assumption can be derived from $\mathcal{A}_{\Pi'}$: If S $\notin$ DST(T, Π'), then DST(T, Π') = DST(T, Π) and the triple about T:m is the same in $\mathcal{A}_{\Pi}$ and $\mathcal{A}_{\Pi'}$. The interesting case is S $\in$ DST(T, Π'). Starting with the subtype requirement guaranteed by the strategy (part 2), applying precondition strengthening, the subtype rule, and enlarging the assumption set, we derive (EXT(this) denotes $\bigwedge_{T' \in DST(T,\Pi)} \tau \not\preceq T'$):

$$\frac{\frac{\frac{\text{SPEC(S:m)} \quad \vdash \quad \{\, \tau \preceq S \wedge \mathbf{P}_{T:m} \,\}\ \text{S:m}\ \{\, \mathbf{Q}_{T:m} \,\}}{\text{SPEC(S:m)} \quad \vdash \quad \{\, \tau \preceq S \wedge \text{EXT(this)} \wedge \mathbf{P}_{T:m} \,\}\ \text{S:m}\ \{\, \mathbf{Q}_{T:m} \,\}}}{\begin{array}{l}\text{SPEC(S:m)}\ ,\ \{\, \tau \preceq T \wedge \tau \not\preceq S \wedge \text{EXT(this)} \wedge \mathbf{P}_{T:m} \,\}\ \text{T:m}\ \{\, \mathbf{Q}_{T:m} \,\} \\ \qquad\qquad \vdash \quad \{\, \tau \preceq T \wedge \text{EXT(this)} \wedge \mathbf{P}_{T:m} \,\}\ \text{T:m}\ \{\, \mathbf{Q}_{T:m} \,\}\end{array}}}{\text{SPEC(S:m)}\ ,\ \mathcal{A}_{\Pi'} \quad \vdash \quad \{\, \tau \preceq T \wedge \text{EXT(this)} \wedge \mathbf{P}_{T:m} \,\}\ \text{T:m}\ \{\, \mathbf{Q}_{T:m} \,\}}$$

If S:m is a virtual method, we are finished because SPEC(S:m) $\in \mathcal{A}_{\Pi'}$. If S:m has an implementation, we can eliminate SPEC(S:m) from the assumptions using the implementation-rule together with the fact that part 3 of the strategy guarantees the existence of a proof of $\mathcal{A}_{\Pi} \vdash$ SPEC(S:m). For brevity, we omit the technical details here. **end of proof**

This lemma shows that our logic can be used as the foundation for program development methods and that the assumptions occurring in the subtype rule can be kept implicit.

6 TREATING INHERITANCE

This section defines the kernel language KOOL by adding inheritance to SKOOL and presents the logical rules for verifying KOOL programs.

Inheritance Inheritance means using implementation parts from a type T to implement a type S. We impose the restriction that S has to be a subtype of T. (In most OO-languages S has to be a direct subtype.) To keep the definition of KOOL simple, we support only single inheritance, i.e., a type may only inherit from one type, as it is e.g. in Java.

A *KOOL program* is a finite set of type declarations of the following form (brackets indicate that the surrounded syntactic construct is optional):

```
[abstract] type T subtype  of    <AbsTypeList>
                  inherits from  <AbsType>
                  is             <MethDeclList> <AttrList> end
```

The `inherits`-clause defines a binary relation on types, denoted by $\sqsubset_{inh}$, i.e., S $\sqsubset_{inh}$ T means that the implementation of S directly inherits from T. The reflexive and transitive closure of this relation is denoted by $\sqsubseteq$. A method declaration in KOOL is either a method signature or method definition, i.e., abstract types may have implementations as well. These are defined as in SKOOL except that KOOL supports an additional invocation statement (see below). The *interface* IF(S) of a type S consists of (1) the signatures of methods declared in S (including attribute access methods) and (2) all signatures in the interface of T, S $\sqsubset_{inh}$ T, that are not overridden in S where *overridden* means that S contains a signature with the same method name. A method name may appear only once in an interface.

We say that a method S:m in IF(S) is *associated with implementations* if it is declared in S and has a (possibly predefined) body or if it is not declared in S and S $\sqsubset_{inh}$ T and T:m is associated with an implementation. In the first case, we say that S:m is *defined in* S. In concrete types, all methods must be associated with an implementation.

It is important to understand the relation between method signatures, implementations, and invocations in OO-programs. The implementation associated with a method T:m is not necessarily the implementation being executed on invocations of T:m. We illustrate this by a small example:

```
abstract type  T  subtype of OBJECT    is
  m(): OBJECT          is  result := false   end
  mm( x: T ): OBJECT   is  result := x.T:m()  end

type S  subtype of T   inherits from T  is
  m(): S               is  result := null(S)  end
end
```

Method T:m is overridden in S. An invocation `T:mm( null(S) )` would lead to the execution of the implementation associated with S:m. In particular, to verify properties of invocations like `result:= x.T:m()` one has to use the properties of the virtual method T:m that are derived from the subtypes and cannot rely on the implementation associated with T:m. To be able to distinguish between a virtual method and its associated implementation, we write T@m to refer to the implementation associated with m in T.

Most OO-languages make it possible to invoke overridden methods from overriding methods, mostly via static binding (e.g., in C++ overridden methods can be invoked using the scope resolution operator, in Java it can be done using the keyword `super`). In KOOL, implementations associated with overridden methods can be called with the following syntax*:

```
v :=  this . T@m( .. )
```

*This syntax can be considered as a verbose form of the Java syntax `super.m(..)`, because `super` refers to the superclass of the static type of `this`.

Such a *call-statement* is context-correct, if the parameter types are covariant, if the result type of T:m is a subtype of v, if the enclosing type of the call inherits from T, and if T:m is associated with an implementation.

Logic for KOOL The specification of the object environment is as in SKOOL. The sort *AttId* needs clarification: A concrete type TC contains all attributes being declared in TC or in a type from which TC inherits. As overriding of attributes is possible, there may exist several different attributes with the same name in TC. To avoid such ambiguities, attribute identifiers in KOOL are not only prefixed by the concrete type (as in SKOOL), but as well by the type the attribute is declared in. I.e., we write TC:T@a for an attribute a that is declared in type T and belongs to objects of type TC.

KOOL distinguishes between virtual methods and method implementations. Thus, we introduce implementation annotations as a third form of triples. Implementation annotations have the form $\{\mathbf{P}\}$ T@m(..) $\{\mathbf{Q}\}$ where **P** and **Q** are $\Gamma_{pre(m)}$-formulas and Γ_{post}-formulas, respectively. They may be used as assumptions in sequents. The programming logic of KOOL is described by modifying and extending the logic presented in section 4.

In SKOOL, the predefined implementations could be associated only with concrete types, but KOOL provides more flexibility. The predefined implementation of equ can be used for any type and can possibly be overridden in subtypes. Thus, we have to replace T:equ by T@equ in the axiom for equ, where T are the types in which equ is defined. In the axiom for new, we replace T:new by T@new, but T may only range over concrete types. The predefined implementations of the access methods for an attribute a declared in type T can operate on all objects of concrete types TC with TC $\sqsubseteq$ T . Abbreviating *loc*(this, TC:T@a) by this.TC:T@a, we get:

$$\vdash \{\ prec(\text{this}, \text{TC}) \wedge \text{TC} \sqsubseteq \text{T} \wedge \mathbf{P}[\$(\text{this.TC:T@a})/\text{result}]\ \}\ \text{T@get\_a():TR}\ \ \{\mathbf{P}\}$$

$$\vdash \{\ prec(\text{this}, \text{TC}) \wedge \text{TC} \sqsubseteq \text{T} \wedge \mathbf{P}[\$\langle\text{this.TC:T@a} := \text{p}\rangle/\$]\ \}\ \text{T@set\_a(p:TR)}\ \{\mathbf{P}\}$$

These axioms enable overriding and dynamic binding of attribute access methods. In Java and C++, attributes are statically bound. We didn't use this semantics for KOOL since it leads to more rules. On the other hand, such rules become simpler, at least if inheritance and subtyping are strongly connected as e.g. in Java and C++.

The two rules given in section 4 for the invocation-statement hold the same way for the call-statement with method implementations instead of virtual methods. We show here the call-rule:

call-rule:

$$\frac{\mathcal{A} \vdash \{\mathbf{P}\}\ \ \text{T@m}(\text{p}_1, \ldots, \text{p}_z)\ \{\mathbf{Q}\}}{\mathcal{A} \vdash \{\ \mathbf{P}[\text{E}_1/\text{p}_1, \ldots, \text{E}_z/\text{p}_z]\ \}\ \text{v} := \text{this .T@m}(\text{E}_1, \ldots, \text{E}_z)\ \{\ \mathbf{Q}[\text{v/result}]\ \}}$$

We also use a similar adaptation of the var-rule. An implementation S@m is either defined in S or inherited from a type T. In the first case, properties of

S@m can be proved by the adapted implementation-rule, which is obtained from the rule for SKOOL by substituting T@m for T:m. In the second case, the properties of S@m are derived from those of T@m by the inheritance-rule, given below. Finally, we have to relate properties of implementations to properties of virtual methods. This can be done in concrete types where the behavior of virtual methods is defined by the associated implementation:

inheritance-rule:

$$\frac{\mathcal{A} \vdash \{\mathbf{P}\} \quad \text{T@m} \quad \{\mathbf{Q}\}}{\mathcal{A} \vdash \{\mathbf{P}\} \quad \text{S@m} \quad \{\mathbf{Q}\}}$$

if S@m is inherited from T.

concrete-type-rule:

$$\frac{\mathcal{A} \vdash \{\mathbf{P}\} \quad \text{T@m} \quad \{\mathbf{Q}\}}{\mathcal{A} \vdash \{\mathbf{P}\} \quad \text{T:m} \quad \{\mathbf{Q}\}}$$

if T is a concrete type.

7 CONCLUSIONS

This paper has presented logical foundations for the essential OO-language features: abstract types, multiple-subtyping, single-inheritance, and dynamic binding. We have shown how object environments can be formalized as first-order values. Based on this foundation, we presented a Hoare-style programming logic that allows one to prove properties of OO-programs. In particular, we discussed how subtyping, inheritance, and abstract types can be handled.

Our logic can be used for verifying OO-programs. This requires specifications of program properties, which are usually given as pre- and postconditions of methods, and as class invariants. [PH97] shows how such specifications can be transformed into triples of the logic and thus be verified.

We validated the logic by simulating dynamic binding via dispatching in pseudo-code. A formal validation against a complete operational semantics of the programming language would be desirable, in particular, if logics using these techniques are to be applied to realistic size languages like Java.

Acknowledgments

We are glad to thank the referees for their helpful comments.

REFERENCES

[AL97] M. Abadi and K. R. M. Leino. A logic of object-oriented programs. In M. Bidoit and M. Dauchet, editors, *TAPSOFT '97: Theory and Practice of Software Development, 7th International Joint Conference CAAP/FASE, Lille, France*, volume 1214 of *Lecture Notes in Computer Science*, pages 682–696. Springer-Verlag, 1997.

[Apt81] K. R. Apt. Ten years of Hoare logic: A survey — part I. *ACM Trans. on Prog. Languages and Systems*, 3:431–483, 1981.

[GH93] J. V. Guttag and J. J. Horning. *Larch: Languages and Tools for Formal Specification.* Springer-Verlag, 1993.

[Gri81] David Gries. *The Science of Programming.* Springer-Verlag, 1981.

[GU91] T. Gergely and L. Úry. *First-Order Programming Theories.* Springer-Verlag, 1991.

[Lei97] K. R. M. Leino. Ecstatic: An object-oriented programming language with an axiomatic semantics. In B. Pierce, editor, *Proceedings of the Fourth International Workshop on Foundations of Object-Oriented Languages*, 1997. Available from: www.cs.indiana.edu/hyplan/pierce/fool/.

[MPH97] P. Müller and A. Poetzsch-Heffter. Formal specification techniques for object-oriented programs. In M. Jarke, K. Pasedach, and K. Pohl, editors, *Informatik 97: Informatik als Innovationsmotor*, Informatik Aktuell. Springer-Verlag, 1997. Available from www.informatik.fernuni-hagen.de/pi5/publications.html.

[PH97] A. Poetzsch-Heffter. Specification and verification of object-oriented programs. Habilitation thesis, Technical University of Munich, January 1997.

[Suz80] N. Suzuki, editor. *Automatic Verification of Programs with Complex Data Structures.* Garland Publishing, 1980.

[Wir90] M. Wirsing. Algebraic specification. In J. van Leeuwen, editor, *Handbook of Theoretical Computer Science*, volume B, pages 675–788. North-Holland, Amsterdam, 1990.

APPENDIX 1 SUMMARY OF PROGRAMMING LOGIC

In addition to the axioms and rules described in the sections above, the programming logic consists of the usual rules for if, while, sequential statements, strengthening/weakening of pre-/postconditions, and the following language-independent axioms and rules:

assumpt-axiom:

$$\mathbf{A} \vdash \mathbf{A}$$

false-axiom:

$$\vdash \{\ \mathrm{FALSE}\ \}\ \mathrm{COMP}\ \{\ \mathrm{FALSE}\ \}$$

assumpt-intro-rule:

$$\frac{\mathcal{A} \vdash \mathbf{A}}{\mathbf{A_0}\,,\ \mathcal{A} \vdash \mathbf{A}}$$

assumpt-elim-rule:

$$\frac{\mathcal{A} \vdash \mathbf{A_0} \qquad \mathbf{A_0}\,,\ \mathcal{A} \vdash \mathbf{A}}{\mathcal{A} \vdash \mathbf{A}}$$

conjunct-rule:

$$\frac{\mathcal{A} \vdash \{\ \mathbf{P_1}\ \}\ \mathrm{COMP}\ \{\ \mathbf{Q_1}\ \} \qquad \mathcal{A} \vdash \{\ \mathbf{P_2}\ \}\ \mathrm{COMP}\ \{\ \mathbf{Q_2}\ \}}{\mathcal{A} \vdash \{\ \mathbf{P_1} \wedge \mathbf{P_2}\ \}\ \mathrm{COMP}\ \{\ \mathbf{Q_1} \wedge \mathbf{Q_2}\ \}}$$

disjunct-rule:

$$\frac{\mathcal{A} \vdash \{\ \mathbf{P_1}\ \}\ \mathrm{COMP}\ \{\ \mathbf{Q_1}\ \} \qquad \mathcal{A} \vdash \{\ \mathbf{P_2}\ \}\ \mathrm{COMP}\ \{\ \mathbf{Q_2}\ \}}{\mathcal{A} \vdash \{\ \mathbf{P_1} \vee \mathbf{P_2}\ \}\ \mathrm{COMP}\ \{\ \mathbf{Q_1} \vee \mathbf{Q_2}\ \}}$$

inv-rule:

$$\frac{\mathcal{A} \vdash \{\, \mathbf{P} \,\}\ \text{COMP}\ \{\, \mathbf{Q} \,\}}{\mathcal{A} \vdash \{\, \mathbf{P} \wedge \mathbf{R} \,\}\ \text{COMP}\ \{\, \mathbf{Q} \wedge \mathbf{R} \,\}}$$

where **R** is a Σ-formula, i.e. does not contain program variables.

all-rule:

$$\frac{\mathcal{A} \vdash \{\, \mathbf{P}[Y/Z] \,\}\ \text{COMP}\ \{\, \mathbf{Q} \,\}}{\mathcal{A} \vdash \{\, \mathbf{P}[Y/Z] \,\}\ \text{COMP}\ \{\, \forall Z : \mathbf{Q} \,\}}$$

where Z, Y are arbitrary, but distinct logical variables.

subst-rule:

$$\frac{\mathcal{A} \vdash \{\, \mathbf{P} \,\}\ \text{COMP}\ \{\, \mathbf{Q} \,\}}{\mathcal{A} \vdash \{\, \mathbf{P}[t/Z] \,\}\ \text{COMP}\ \{\, \mathbf{Q}[t/Z] \,\}}$$

where Z is an arbitrary logical variable and t a Σ-term.

ex-rule:

$$\frac{\mathcal{A} \vdash \{\, \mathbf{P} \,\}\ \text{COMP}\ \{\, \mathbf{Q}[Y/Z] \,\}}{\mathcal{A} \vdash \{\, \exists Z : \mathbf{P} \,\}\ \text{COMP}\ \{\, \mathbf{Q}[Y/Z] \,\}}$$

where Z, Y are arbitrary, but distinct logical variables.

BIOGRAPHIES

Arnd Poetzsch-Heffter is Professor at the University of Hagen. He received a Doctor in Computer Science from the Technical University of Munich in 1991 with a thesis about specification techniques for static semantics of programming languages. During a post-doc year at the CS department of Cornell University he developed an approach to integrate program specification and verification techniques for object-oriented programs. This is the topic of his Habilitation thesis. His main research interests include programming techniques and methods, language design, and system support. Currently, his work focuses on the construction of provably correct programs from correct components.

Peter Müller is a member of the Lopex project at the University of Hagen, Germany. He works in the field of specification and verification of object-oriented programs. In particular, he studies the verification of component-based programs. Before that, he worked at the Technical University of Munich, where he received a diploma in computer science. Topic of his thesis was the formal semantics of Sather and the development of an operational assertion language.

27

Verifying a Self-Stabilizing Mutual Exclusion Algorithm

S. Qadeer
University of California at Berkeley
Department of EECS, Berkeley CA 94720 U.S.A.
Phone: (510) 642-1490 Email: shaz@eecs.berkeley.edu

N. Shankar
SRI International
Computer Science Laboratory, Menlo Park CA 94025 U.S.A.
Phone: (650) 859-5272 Email: shankar@csl.sri.com

Abstract

We present a detailed description of a machine-assisted verification of an algorithm for self-stabilizing mutual exclusion that is due to Dijkstra [Dij74]. This verification was constructed using PVS. We compare the mechanical verification to the informal proof sketch on which it is based. This comparison yields several observations regarding the challenges of formalizing and mechanically verifying distributed algorithms in general.

Keywords

Self-stabilization, mutual exclusion, theorem proving, PVS.

1 INTRODUCTION

A self-stabilizing algorithm is one that ensures that the system behavior eventually stabilizes to a safe subset of states regardless of the initial state. In Dijkstra's original paper [Dij74] introducing distributed self-stabilization, he gave three self-stabilizing mutual exclusion algorithms and left their proofs as exercises for the reader. Subsequently, Dijkstra [Dij86] proffered a proof of self-stabilization of one of his algorithms while conceding that the proofs were in fact nontrivial. In this paper, we take on the challenge of mechanically verifying the self-stability of one of Dijkstra's other algorithms. This algorithm poses an interesting challenging for formalization and mechanical verification for several reasons. The self-stabilization argument involves a nontrivial amount of mathematics. Self-stability is a convergence property whereas typical attempts at the mechanical verifications of distributed algorithms mainly involve safety properties or simple progress reasoning. The use of model checking in the verification of distributed algorithms, even non-finite-state ones, is a recent trend, but there is no obvious way to apply model checking in this context. It is hard to draw substantive conclusions from the verification of

Programming Concepts and Methods D. Gries, & W-P. de Roever (Eds.)

one self-stabilization algorithm but we wish to use this example to touch on some of the important themes in formal verification such as:

1. What is the difference in effort between constructing a convincing informal argument and mechanically verifying it?
2. What are some of the specific obstacles to effective formalization?
3. How much of the formal verification involves only conventional mathematics as opposed to temporal reasoning?
4. Can the temporal reasoning be carried out within the framework of a conventional predicate calculus or is there a need for temporal or modal logics?

The heart of this paper is a careful elucidation of the formalization and mechanically verified proof of self-stability for Dijkstra's algorithm. The informal proof of this algorithm is itself quite interesting. A survey of the literature revealed only one attempt at a proof by Varghese [Var92][1] who presents an informal sketch of an argument that is similar to the one used in this paper. As with any distributed algorithm, the verification requires careful attention to details that are easily overlooked in an informal sketch. Our verification was conducted using PVS but our explanation of the verified proof will be presented in a conventional style thus requiring no prior knowledge of PVS [ORS92].[2]

We only consider the first of Dijkstra's three algorithms for self-stabilizing mutual exclusion. In this algorithm, there are N processes for $N > 1$ numbered 0 to $N - 1$ arranged in a unidirectional ring where each process can observe its own state and that of its predecessor. Each process i maintains a counter $v(i)$ of values from 0 to $M - 1$, where $N \leq M$. Process 0 is a distinguished process that is enabled when $v(0) = v(N-1)$, and when enabled, it can make a transition by incrementing its counter modulo M. A nonzero process i is enabled when $v(i) \neq v(i-1)$, and when enabled, it can update its counter value so that $v(i) = v(i-1)$. The transitions of the individual processes are interleaved. Despite the absence of a central controller, the system can be shown to converge or *self-stabilize* from an arbitrary initial state to a stable behavior where exactly one process is enabled at any state. The one enabled process in a state in such a stable behavior is allowed exclusive access to its critical section.

2 AN INFORMAL PROOF SKETCH

The reader is invited to set aside this paper and contemplate a proof of self-stability for the above algorithm by showing that any computation leading out of an arbitrary initial state eventually stabilizes to a computation where exactly one process is enabled in a state. In our initial verification attempts,

---

[1]See the URL `dworkin.wustl.edu/~varghese/PAPERS/dijk.ps.Z`.

[2]The URL `www.csl.sri.com/pvs/examples/self-stability/` contains the PVS specification and proofs.

we had some difficulty merely constructing a reliable, informal proof sketch. Even with a proof sketch that withstood informal scrutiny, we had a lot of difficulty formalizing the needed concepts in a form that was elegant enough to support feasible mechanical verification. We finally restarted our verification with a proof sketch consisting of the following sequence of claims:

1. *There is always at least one enabled process.* Otherwise, for each $i, i < N-1$, $v(i) = v(i+1)$ yet $v(0) \neq v(N-1)$.
2. *The number of enabled processes never increases.* Each transition due to process i affects the enabledness of at most i and $i+1 \, mod \, N$, and definitely disables i.
3. *The enabledness of each process is eventually toggled.* This is a crucial observation. For each i, let $p(i)$ be the sum over the enabled processes j of the unidirectional distance from j to i, i.e., $i - j$ for $j \leq i$, and $N - j + i$ for $j > i$. Then, whenever an enabled process $j, j \neq i$, makes a transition, $p(i)$ decreases. If i is initially enabled but never taken, then $p(i)$ eventually becomes 0. By Claim 1, i is the only remaining enabled process, which must therefore be taken leaving i disabled. If i is initially disabled, then when $p(i)$ is 0, it must be enabled by Claim 1.
4. *Process 0 is eventually incremented.* This follows trivially from Claim 3.
5. *Process 0 eventually takes on any value below M.* Follows by induction from Claim 4.
6. *There is some value x below M so that for any $i, i \neq 0$, we have $v(i) \neq x$.* This is a consequence of the pigeonhole principle which is the key property used to guarantee self-stability.
7. *Eventually $v(0) = x$ and for all $i, i \neq 0$, we have $v(i) \neq x$.* Let x be chosen as in Claim 6. By Claim 5, eventually $v(0) = x$. Up to (and including) the earliest point where $v(0) = x$, we have $v(i) \neq x$ for any $i, i \neq 0$
8. *Once $v(0) \neq v(i)$ for all $i, i \neq 0$, then process 0 is not enabled again until for all processes $i, v(i) = v(0)$.* This is because given Claim 7, there eventually is a prefix of n processes, for any $n < N$, so that $v(i) = v(0)$ holds for $i \leq n$.
9. *The system eventually reaches a stable state with exactly one enabled process.* By Claim 8, there is eventually a state where only process 0 is enabled, and by Claims 1 and 2, the system will remain stable in a state where there is exactly one enabled process.

Though this informal proof sketch is fairly convincing, the formalization and mechanical verification of Dijkstra's self-stabilizing mutual exclusion protocol using PVS are not straightforward. The formalization and verification are described in Sections 3 and 4.

3 THE FORMALIZATION OF THE PROBLEM

Both the algorithm and self-stability property are formalized as predicates on sequences of states. The global *state* in this case consists of an array with indices in the subrange 0 to $N - 1$ and with elements in the subrange 0 to

$M-1$. A sequence of such states is a function from the type of natural numbers (i.e., non-negative integers) to the *state* type.

A process i is *enabled* in state v when the curried predicate $E(v)(i)$ holds. For process 0, the predicate $E(v)(0)$ holds when $v(N-1) = v(0)$. For a nonzero process i, $E(v)(i)$ holds when $v(i) \neq v(i-1)$. The curried form $E(v)(i)$ is chosen so that we can also employ the predicate $E(v)$ as (the characteristic predicate of) a set of processes.

A sequence of states σ is a function from natural numbers to the *state* type. A sequence of states σ is a *run*, i.e., $run(\sigma)$ holds, when each pair of adjacent states is in U. Two states v and v' are in the next-state relation U (for *update*), i.e., $U(v, v')$, if there exists a process i that is enabled in state v and $UP(i)(v, v')$ holds. The relation $UP(i)(v, v')$ (for *update process*) holds if (1) $i = 0$ and $v'(0) = v(N-1) + 1 \, mod \, M$ and $v'(j) = v(j)$ for $j \neq 0$, or (2) $i \neq 0$ and $v'(i) = v(i-1)$ and $v'(j) = v(j)$ for $j \neq i$.

The variables u, v, v' range over states. The variables x, y, z range over counter values. All increment operations applied to $v(i)$, x, y, z are assumed to be modulo M. The variables i, j, and k range over process numbers in the subrange 0 to $N-1$. All increment and decrement operations applied to i, j, k are assumed to be modulo N. The various definitions that are used in the proof are summarized in Figure 1.

Term	Definition
$E(v)(i)$	$\begin{cases} v(N-1) = v(0), & \text{if } i = 0 \\ v(i) \neq v(i-1) & \text{otherwise} \end{cases}$
$UP(i)(v, v')$	$\begin{cases} v' = v\{0 \leftarrow v(0) + 1\}, & \text{if } i = 0 \\ v' = v\{i \leftarrow v(i-1)\} & \text{otherwise} \end{cases}$
$U(v, v')$	$\exists i \colon UP(i)(v, v')$
$run(\sigma)$	$\forall n \colon U(\sigma(n), \sigma(n+1))$
$d(i)(j)$	$\begin{cases} i - j, & \text{if } j \leq i \\ N + i - j, & \text{otherwise} \end{cases}$
$D(v)(i)$	$\sum_{j=0}^{N-1} d(i)(j) \colon j \in E(v)$
$\sigma[n]$	$\lambda \, m \colon \sigma(m+n)$
$S(v)$	$\{x \mid x < M \wedge \exists i \colon i \neq 0 \wedge v(i) = x\}$
$prefix(v)(j)$	$(\forall i \colon i \leq j \equiv v(i) = v(0))$

Figure 1 Summary of Definitions

4 THE MECHANICAL VERIFICATION

We informally describe the steps in the mechanical verification using PVS. It is worth noting that PVS was used interactively to discover the detailed justifications based on the informal sketch above. The elaboration of the informal sketch is not at all intellectually trivial. First, the formalization, namely the choice of representations and the form of definitions and theorems, has to be carried out with a tremendous amount of care since otherwise the formal justifications can easily become unmanageably large. Second, it can be quite difficult to come up with formal justifications even for informal steps that seem intuitively obvious. It is this latter aspect of the informal to formal transition that we wish to highlight in presenting the details of the mechanical verification below.

Initial proof attempts such as the ones described below tend to be verbose as they represent the form in which the proofs were discovered. It is customary to devote some effort to polishing PVS proofs so as to enhance their conciseness while exploiting the available automation. We indicate the number of interactions needed to construct the mechanically checked proof of individual formulas in order to convey a rough idea of the effort needed. This number does not have any precise significance since some interactions consist of commands with many inputs that invoke complex proof strategies, while others consist of simple atomic inference steps. Note that the verification relies on pre-existing PVS libraries for the *mod* operation and for finite cardinalities.[3]

Lemma 4.1 corresponds to Claim 1.

Lemma 4.1 *There is always at least one enabled process. Formally,* $\forall v : \exists i : E(v)(i)$.

Proof. Suppose that $\forall j : v(j) = v(0)$, then in particular, $v(N-1) = v(0)$, but this would imply that process 0 is enabled. Otherwise, when $\forall j : v(j) = v(0)$ does not hold, there is a least j, $j \neq 0$ such that $v(j) \neq v(0)$ and since $v(j) \neq v(j-1)$, process j is enabled. The second part of this proof is actually formally proved by induction on j.

The mechanization of this entire proof consists of ten interactions. The first two steps are universal quantifier elimination and case splitting. The first case involves five interactions for existential quantifier instantiation and simplification. The second case involves three interactions for induction/simplification and quantifier instantiation followed by simplification. □

Lemma 4.2 is a step in the proof of Lemma 4.3 which corresponds to Claim 2.

---

[3]The URL `www.csl.sri.com/pvs.html` contains links relevant to PVS including pointers to the groups using PVS, several example verifications, and an extensive bibliography of papers by PVS users.

Lemma 4.2 *An update to an enabled process i removes i and could otherwise at most insert or remove i + 1 from the set of enabled processes. Formally,*

$$UP(i)(v, v') \supset E(v') = \begin{cases} E(v) - \{i\} \bigcup \{i+1\}, & \textit{if } E(v')(i+1) \\ E(v) - \{i, i+1\}, & \textit{otherwise} \end{cases}$$

Proof. There are two parts to this proof. First, we establish that $i \notin E(v')$. This is trivial when $i \neq 0$ since $v'(i) = v'(i-1)$. When $i = 0$, a previously proved lemma yields $v(0)+1 \neq v(0) \bmod M$ which is used to show that $v'(0) \neq v'(N-1)$. The second part of the proof essentially demonstrates that only the enabledness of i and $i+1$ are affected when i is updated. The extensionality rule for set equality is applied to the conclusion which then follows from the lemmas $x < N \supset x \bmod N = x$ and $N \bmod N = 0$ by definition expansion and simple set-theoretic reasoning.

The mechanization has three preliminary interactions for quantifier elimination, definition expansion (for *UP*) and propositional simplification. The next step introduces the case analysis for splitting the proof into two parts. The first part is propositionally simplified into two cases. The first case is proved by introducing a lemma instance followed by simplification and definition expansion. The second case is proved directly by expansion/simplification. The second part of the proof has three interactions for using extensionality, introducing a lemma instance, and brute-force expansion/simplification. The last brute-force step is not entirely pleasant since a lot of essential detail has been buried in the automation. A more careful argument would be to show that when $UP(i)(v, v')$, then for $j \notin \{i, i+1\}$, $j \in E(v')$ iff $j \in E(v)$. □

Lemma 4.3 *A transition never increases the cardinality of the set of enabled processes. Formally,* $U(v, v') \supset |E(v')| \leq |E(v)|$.

Proof. This lemma is of course a simple consequence of Lemma 4.2. There is, however, one minor complication. The cardinality operation applies only to finite sets and the sets $E(v)$ and $E(v')$ have to be shown to be finite. The typechecker generates proof obligation to this effect. This proof obligation is discharged by exhibiting an injection from these sets to some bounded initial segment of the natural numbers. Since the elements of $E(v)$ are already chosen from the subrange of numbers below N, we can choose N as the bound and the identity function on these sets as the required injection. The proof of the lemma follows from Lemma 4.2 using the above proof obligations (which have to be proved separately) as lemmas. This proof also invokes simple cardinality lemmas regarding the operations of adding and removing elements from a finite set: $|E(v) - \{i\}| = |E(v) - 1|$ when $i \in E(v)$, and hence, $|(E(v) - \{i\}) \bigcup \{i+1\}| \leq |E(v)|$.

The mechanization uses three interactions to bring in Lemma 4.2 and the finiteness proof obligations. A single `GRIND` step, the catch-all brute-force strategy[4] completes most of the proof while leaving one trivial subgoal. This is however quite misleading because the arguments to GRIND are quite specific about which lemmas and definitions are to be used, and which ones excluded. The main observation is that though such reasoning about cardinalities is entirely trivial in informal terms, there are a number of bookkeeping details that are needed in the formal proof to ensure that all the sets involved are indeed finite. □

We now formally define the measure that is used in Claim 3 to demonstrate that each process is always eventually enabled and eventually disabled. The formalization deviates slightly from the informal script. We can avoid the case analysis in Claim 3 but use the very same measure to show the equivalent fact that each process is always eventually updated. The measure is defined in terms of a summation operation $\sum_{i=0}^{n} f(i){:}\, i \in P$ which takes a function f, a set P, and an upper bound n and adds up the $f(i)$ for $0 \leq i \leq n$ such that $i \in P$ holds. It is easy to prove the following lemmas by induction on n followed by a handful of simplification steps.

Lemma 4.4

$$\sum_{i=0}^{n} f(i){:}\, i \in (P - \{j\}) = \begin{cases} \sum_{i=0}^{n} f(i){:}\, i \in P - f(j), & \textit{if } j \leq n \wedge j \in P \\ \sum_{i=0}^{n} f(i){:}\, i \in P, & \textit{otherwise} \end{cases}$$

Lemma 4.5

$$\sum_{i=0}^{n} f(i){:}\, i \in (P \bigcup \{j\}) = \begin{cases} \sum_{i=0}^{n} f(i){:}\, i \in P, & \textit{if } j > n \vee j \in P \\ \sum_{i=0}^{n} f(i){:}\, i \in P + f(j), & \textit{otherwise} \end{cases}$$

Let $d(i)(j)$ be the unidirectional distance from i to j defined as $i - j$ when $j \leq i$ and $N + i - j$, otherwise.

Then for any process i, the measure for i in state v is given by $D(v)(i)$ which is defined as $\sum_{j=0}^{N-1} d(i)(j){:}\, j \in E(v)$. In words, this measure is the sum of the unidirectional distance of the enabled processes from i in state v. This simple definition of the measure function was constructed after several failed attempts at mechanization. In our earlier attempts, we tried to define the measure by summation over the processes k steps away from j and this made all the inductions very complicated.

Lemma 4.6 *The measure $D(v)(j)$ for j decreases with any update to an enabled non-j process. Formally,*

$$i \neq j \wedge UP(i)(v, v') \supset D(v')(j) < D(v)(j).$$

[4]The GRIND strategy performs quantifier elimination and instantiation, propositional simplification, rewriting using lemmas as rewrite rules, definition expansion, explicit case analysis according to the case structure in the goal, and does many of these steps repeatedly until no further simplification is possible.

Proof. First, note that $i \in E(v)$. By Lemma 4.2, the goal simplifies to considering $E(v')$ to either be $E(v) - \{i\} \bigcup \{i+1\}$ or $E(v) - \{i\}$. In the first case, we have a further case analysis according to whether $j = i + 1$. If $j = i + 1$, then since $i \in E(v)$, we have by Lemmas 4.2 and 4.4 that $D(v')(j)$ is $D(v)(j) - d(j)(i) + 0$. Since $i \neq j$, we have $d(j)(i) > 0$ and $D(v')(j) < D(v)(j)$. If $j \neq i + 1$, then by Lemmas 4.2, 4.4, and 4.5, $D(v')(j)$ is at most $D(v)(j) - d(j)(i) + d(j)(i+1)$. We can prove that when $i \neq j$, $d(j)(i) > d(j)(i+1)$ and hence $D(v')(j) < D(v)(j)$. In the second case when $E(v')$ is $E(v) - \{i\}$ and since $i \in E(v)$ and $D(v')(j) = D(v)(j) - d(j)(i)$, we again have by $d(j)(i) > 0$ that $D(v')(j) < D(v)(j)$.

The mechanical verification carries out a similar case analysis. Of the four cases, three are trivially discharged by the GRIND strategy and the remaining case has three further steps using a lemma about the *mod* operation. □

Lemma 4.7 *No non-j process is enabled when the measure for j is* 0 *in state v. Formally,* $D(v)(j) = 0 \supset (\forall i\colon i \neq j \supset i \notin E(v))$.

Proof. This is proved by first expanding the definition of D in terms of summation and generalizing the theorem to bound the summation by some n that is below N (rather than $N - 1$) so that the theorem can now be proved by induction. The induction proof is then straightforward since if $i \neq j$, then $d(j)(i) > 0$ so if the summation $\sum_{k=0}^{n+1} d(j)(k)\colon k \in E(v)$ equals 0, then if $i = n + 1$ it must be because $n + 1 \notin E(v)$. If $i \leq n$, then since $\sum_{k=0}^{n} d(j)(k)\colon k \in E(v)$ equals 0, the induction hypothesis can be used to demonstrate that $i = j$ or $i \notin E(v)$.

The mechanical proof requires ten interactions that follow the above outline. The default brute-force induction strategy fails primarily because the definition of summation defeats a heuristic that bounds the depth to which recursive definitions are expanded, and also the instantiation heuristic is unable to find the correct instantiation for the quantified variables. □

Up to this point, we have merely proved basic mathematical facts or theorems about a single transition step in a conventional mathematical style. We have not introduced any temporal properties such as invariants or eventualities. We now show the first temporal property (Claim 3) that a process i is eventually updated in any run of the system. A run of the system is a sequence σ such that $\forall n\colon U(\sigma(i), \sigma(i+1))$ holds. Note that any suffix of a run is also a run. The statement of the theorem is that if σ is a run, then $\exists n\colon UP(i)(\sigma(n), \sigma(n+1))$. We did this proof in two different ways. In the first attempt, we proved it directly by measure induction on the measure function. In the second case, we established an eventuality rule that was used to prove the goal. Somewhat unexpectedly, the latter proof attempt turned out to be less straightforward than the first one. The main reason is that the overhead of using the eventuality rule outweighed the savings. We explain the verification using the eventuality rule below.

Let the suffix of σ which is the sequence $\sigma(n), \sigma(n+1), \ldots$ be denoted by $\sigma[n]$. The eventuality rule establishes $\exists n: R(\sigma[n])$ for a given trace predicate R by requiring a measure function f on a trace with a well-founded ordering on the range type (such as the usual $<$ relation on natural numbers) such that for any run θ, either $R(\theta)$ or $f(\theta[1]) < f(\theta)$.

Theorem 4.8 *If there is a function f from sequences to natural numbers such that*

$$\forall \theta: run(\theta) \supset R(\theta) \vee f(\theta[1]) < f(\theta)$$

then

$$\forall \sigma: run(\sigma) \supset \exists n: R(\sigma[n]).$$

Proof. The conclusion is proved by measure induction on $f(\sigma)$. By the premise, $R(\sigma)$ or $f(\sigma[1]) < f(\sigma)$. When $R(\sigma)$ holds, we already have the conclusion $R(\sigma[0])$ since $\sigma[0] = \sigma$. When $f(\sigma[1]) < f(\sigma)$ holds, we can apply the induction hypothesis on $\sigma[1]$ to get $R(\sigma[1][n])$ which is the same as $R(\sigma[n+1])$ and hence the conclusion.

The eventuality rule is easily proved in about thirteen steps mainly for invoking measure induction and providing quantifier instantiations, expanding definitions, and applying extensionality to demonstrate equality between sequences. □

Lemma 4.9 *Each process i is eventually updated in any run. Formally,* $run(\sigma) \supset \exists n: UP(i)(\sigma(n), \sigma(n+1))$.

Proof. With the eventuality rule, we can avoid measure induction in the proof that in any run σ, process i is eventually updated, i.e., $\exists n: UP(i)(\sigma(n), \sigma(n+1))$. This removes one major intellectual obstacle from the proof. We still need to identify the measure in terms of σ. In this case, the measure is $D(\sigma(0))(i)$. Four interactions are needed to introduce and properly instantiate the eventuality rule. Four more interactions are needed to show that the conclusion of the eventuality rule $run(\sigma) \supset \exists n: R(\sigma[n])$ can be instantiated to yield the conclusion $run(\sigma) \supset \exists n: UP(i)(\sigma(n), \sigma(n+1))$. The corresponding premise of the eventuality rule

$$UP(i)(\sigma(0), \sigma(1)) \vee D(\sigma(1))(i) < D(\sigma(0))(i)$$

can be proved by first expanding run to get $\exists j: UP(j)(\sigma(0), \sigma(1))$. If $i = j$ then we have $UP(i)(\sigma(0), \sigma(1))$. Otherwise, we have to invoke Lemma 4.6 to get $D(\sigma(1))(i) < D(\sigma(0))(i)$. The mechanical proof of this use of the eventuality rule takes about twelve interactions. Overall, the proof of this lemma takes twenty interactions, whereas the direct proof of this theorem by measure induction and without using the eventuality rule took 21 interactions. □

Lemma 4.10 corresponds to Claim 4.

Lemma 4.10 *Process 0 is eventually incremented in any run. Formally,*

$$run(\sigma) \supset \exists n: \sigma(n)(0) = \sigma(0)(0) + 1.$$

Proof. This claim is a consequence of Lemma 4.9 but not obviously so. We know from Lemma 4.9 that process 0 will eventually be updated but only the first such update will lead to the desired increment. We also need to ensure that none of the intervening transitions affects the state of process 0. If σ is a run, let m be given by Lemma 4.9 so that $UP(0)(\sigma(m), \sigma(m+1))$ holds. We instead prove that

$$\forall m, \sigma: run(\sigma) \wedge UP(0)(\sigma(m), \sigma(m+1)) \supset \exists n: \sigma(n)(0) = \sigma(0)(0) + 1$$

by induction on m. If m is 0 then we can let n be 1 since by the definition UP, $\sigma(1)(0) = \sigma(0)(0) + 1$. In the induction step when $m > 0$, we know by the definition of *run* that $UP(i)(\sigma(0), \sigma(1))$ holds for some i. If i is 0, then once again, we can let n be 1 since by the definition of UP, $\sigma(1)(0) = \sigma(0)(0) + 1$. If $i \neq 0$ then $\sigma(1)(0) = \sigma(0)(0)$. Since in $c[1]$, the occurence of $UP(0)(\sigma(m), \sigma(m+1))$ is reachable in $m - 1$ steps, we can instantiate the induction hypothesis by $\sigma[1]$. Since we know that $run(\sigma[1])$ and $UP(0)(\sigma[1](m-1), \sigma[1](m))$ hold, we can conclude by the induction hypothesis that there is an n' such that $\sigma[1](n')(0) = \sigma[1](0)(0) + 1$ and since $\sigma(1)(0) = \sigma(0)(0)$ we have $\sigma(n'+1)(0) = \sigma(0)(0) + 1$ yielding $n' + 1$ as the desired witness for n.

The mechanical proof essentially follows each step of the above outline. The proof could not be carried out more automatically since some of the quantifier instantiations were not found by the simple syntactic matching techniques used by PVS to instantiate quantifiers. This is the first example of a theorem that is fairly obvious but whose proof requires a fair amount of formal machinery for extracting the induction scheme that underlies the intuitive reasoning and for carefully instantiating quantifiers. □

Lemma 4.10 can be used to prove Lemma 4.11 which corresponds to Claim 5.

Lemma 4.11 *Process* 0 *can eventually take on any counter value. The formal statement is*

$$\forall x: run(\sigma) \supset \exists n: \sigma(n)(0) = x.$$

Proof. The proof is by measure induction on the number of increments needed to reach x from $\sigma(0)(0)$. If none are needed, then we can clearly choose n to be 0. Otherwise, by Lemma 4.10 we have an n' such that $\sigma(n')(0) = \sigma(0)(0) + 1$. We can now apply the induction hypothesis to $\sigma[n']$ since we one fewer increment is needed to reach x. By the induction hypothesis, we have an n'' such that $\sigma[n'](n'')(0) = x$. The witness n for the main conclusion then can be chosen to be $n' + n''$.

The primary points where the mechanical proof has to be carried out delicately are in some of the definition expansions, the quantifier instantiations, and in some steps involving properties of *mod*. Although the proof involves 27 interactions, many of these involve simple but important details such as type correctness proof obligations. The outline of the proof matches the above description and the details are quite straightforward. □

The pigeonhole principle (Claim 6) is a classic example of a theorem that is substantially more obvious than its proof. The principle can be stated in many forms but the one that is useful to us is shown below. Informally, the principle states that if each of $n + 1$ pigeons is assigned one of n pigeonholes, then some hole must contain at least 2 pigeons.

Lemma 4.12 (Pigeonhole principle) *There is no injection from the segment of numbers below $n + 1$ to the segment of numbers below n.*

Proof. The proof is by contradiction using a straightforward induction on n. If $n = 0$ then the range type of the required injection is empty so there is no function to such a range type. Otherwise, if $n \neq 0$ and there is an injection f from the segment below $n + 1$ to the segment below n, then we can construct an injection from the segment below n to the segment below $n - 1$ as follows. Define a function g over the domain type of the segment below n so that $g(k)$ is $f(k)$ for $f(k) < f(n)$ and $f(k) - 1$ otherwise. The range type of g is the segment below $n - 1$. The function g can be shown to also be an injection by the the case analysis used in its definition. This contradicts the induction hypothesis that there is no injection from the segment below n to the segment below $n - 1$.

The primary creative input in the mechanical proof is the definition of g. Otherwise, the proof is a straightforward induction followed by an easy case analysis. This proof required 16 interactions.[5] □

The following is yet another example of a seemingly obvious theorem that does not have a simple formal argument. Let $S(v)$ denote the set $\{x|x < M \wedge \exists i{:}\, i \neq 0 \wedge v(i) = x\}$.

Lemma 4.13 *The nonzero processes do not contain all the possible counter values. The formal statement of the theorem is $\exists x{:}\, x < M \wedge x \notin S(v)$.*

[5]The PVS proof should be compared with a similar proof carried out by Boyer and Moore [BM84] using the Boyer-Moore theorem prover. In the latter proof, the injection is represented as a list with some complicated conditions that constrain it to behave as an injection.

Proof. The intuitive reason is that there are at most $N-1$ nonzero processes and hence at most $N-1$ distinct counter values. If there are M possible counter values where $N \leq M$, then there must be some x below M such that $x \notin S(v)$.

A detailed description of the mechanized proof is as follows. First, there exists an injection f from $S(v)$ to the segment below $N-1$. Such a function f can be defined as the inverse of the mapping from i to $v(i+1)$ since $S(v)$ is the image set of such a mapping. Note that the inverse function f^{-1} is defined on the image of f so that $f^{-1}(j) = i$ for some i such that $f(i) = j$. An inverse of any mapping is injective on the image of the mapping.

If the conclusion of the theorem is false, then $S(v)$ coincides with the segment below M and the identity function I is an injection from the segment below M to $S(v)$. Since the composition of injections is an injection, we have an injection $f \circ I$ from the segment below M to the segment below $N-1$ and hence the segment below $M-1$. This contradicts the pigeonhole principle (Lemma 4.12).

The mechanical proof carries out the above construction but a large number of type correctness proof obligations are generated due to the sophisticated use of predicate subtyping. The proof has 51 interactions out of which all but 15 interactions deal with simple type correctness proof obligations. □

At this point we have established that there is a counter value that does not occur in the nonzero processes and we also know that through successive increments, process 0 can take on any counter value. The next step is to show (Claim 7) that process 0 can acquire a counter value that does not occur in any of the nonzero processes, and furthermore once this value is acquired, it is propagated along a growing prefix of processes until all processes have the same counter value (Claim 8). At this point, process 0 is the only enabled process and the system has entered a stable state.

Let *prefix*$(v)(j)$ be defined as $(\forall i{:}\, i \leq j \equiv v(i) = v(0))$. The first step is to show that process 0 can acquire a counter value that is different from the counter value of any other process. We know by Lemma 4.13 that there is a value x below M that does not occur as the counter value of any nonzero process. We know by Lemma 4.11 that process 0 does eventually take on value x in the nth state of the computation, for some n, but the lemma does not imply that no other process has value x at this point. We need to prove the statement that 0 acquires a counter value that is distinct from those of other processes by induction on the number of steps n given by Lemma 4.11.

Lemma 4.14 *In any run σ, eventually process 0 acquires a counter value that is distinct from those of the nonzero processes. Formally,*

$$\forall n, \sigma{:}\, run(\sigma) \wedge \sigma(n)(0) = x \wedge x \notin S(\sigma(0)) \supset (\exists n'{:}\, (\forall i{:}\, i = 0 \equiv \sigma(n')(i) = x)).$$

Proof. Note that the formal statement has an extra antecedent asserting that

$\sigma(n)(0) = x$ which we know can be discharged by Lemma 4.11, but is required here since the proof is by induction on n. In the base case when $n = 0$, the proof follows easily by letting n' be 0 since $\sigma(0)(0) = x$ but $x \notin S(\sigma(0))$. In the induction step, when $n > 0$ we instantiate σ in the induction hypothesis with $\sigma[1]$. This yields an induction hypothesis

$$\begin{aligned} & run(\sigma[1]) \wedge \sigma[1](n-1)(0) = x \wedge x \notin S(\sigma[1](0)) \\ \supset \quad & (\exists n''\colon (\forall i\colon i = 0 \equiv \sigma[1](n'')(i) = x)). \end{aligned}$$

If $x \in S(\sigma[1](0))$, then it must be the case $\sigma(0)(0) = x$ and the transition from $\sigma(0)$ to $\sigma(1)$ is on process 1. In this case, we let n' be 0 since $\sigma(0)(0) = x$ but $x \notin S(\sigma(0))$. Otherwise, when $x \notin S(\sigma[1])$, we obtain an n'' from the induction hypothesis so that $(\forall i\colon i = 0 \equiv \sigma[1](n'')(i) = x)$. We let n' be $n''+1$ to prove the required conclusion.

The corresponding PVS proof is constructed with 25 interactions. □

The next claim is needed in the induction step for showing that if we have a homogeneous prefix from 0 to j where $j < N - 1$, then it can be extended to a homogeneous prefix from 0 to $j + 1$. Note that the claim in the previous sentence is incorrect unless the definition of *prefix* ensures that the prefix value does not occur outside the prefix.

Lemma 4.15 *If process $j + 1$ is eventually updated in a run where there initially is a homogeneous prefix from 0 to j, a homogeneous prefix from 0 to $j + 1$ is eventually obtained. Formally,*

$$\begin{aligned} & \forall n, \sigma\colon run(\sigma) \wedge UP(j+1)(\sigma(n), \sigma(n+1)) \wedge prefix(\sigma(0))(j) \\ \supset \quad & (\exists n'\colon prefix(\sigma(n'))(j+1)). \end{aligned}$$

Proof. This claim is proved by induction on n. When $n = 0$, $UP(j + 1)(\sigma(0), \sigma(1))$ holds. If we take n' to be 1, then the conclusion follows by noting that $\sigma(1)(j + 1) = \sigma(0)(j) = \sigma(0)(0)$ and for $i > j + 1$, $\sigma(1)(i) = \sigma(0)(i) \neq \sigma(0)(0)$. The quantifier instantiation in the proof of the base case is quite tricky and the mechanical proof requires six interactions.

In the induction step when $n > 0$, we have to show that the conclusion follows from the induction hypothesis

$$\begin{aligned} & \forall \sigma'\colon run(\sigma') \wedge UP(j+1)(\sigma'(n-1), \sigma'(n)) \wedge prefix(\sigma'(0))(j) \\ \supset \quad & (\exists n''\colon prefix(\sigma'(n'')(j+1))). \end{aligned}$$

We have by $run(\sigma)$ that there is some k such that $UP(k)(\sigma(0), \sigma(1))$ holds. This k cannot be in the subrange from 0 to j since these processes are not enabled in $\sigma(0)$. If $k = j + 1$, then we can repeat the reasoning carried out in the base case. If $k > j + 1$, then we instantiate the induction hypothesis with $\sigma[1]$ for σ'. Clearly $run(\sigma[1])$ and $UP(j + 1)(\sigma[1](n - 1), \sigma[1](n))$ follow from the corresponding formulas in the induction conclusion. The antecedent of the induction hypothesis, $prefix(\sigma[1](0))(j)$, also follows from the corresponding formula since $\forall i: i < j \supset \sigma(1)(i) = \sigma(0)$. The induction hypothesis therefore yields an n'' such that $prefix(\sigma[1](n''))(j + 1)$ holds. We can therefore prove the induction conclusion by instantiating n' with $n'' + 1$.

This entire proof is fairly sizable and requires 33 interactions. □

Lemma 4.16 *In any run, it is always possible to reach a state where the processes from 0 to j have the same counter value and this counter value does not occur in the processes numbered from i+1 to N−1. The formal statement is*

$$\forall j, \sigma: run(\sigma) \supset \exists n: prefix(\sigma(n))(j).$$

Proof. The proof is by induction on j. In the base case, when $j = 0$, we know by Lemma 4.13 that there is at least one x such that $x \notin S(\sigma(0))$. We know by Lemma 4.11 that there is an n'' where $\sigma(n'')(0) = x$. We can use Lemma 4.14 with n'' for n to get an n' such that $prefix(\sigma(n'))(0)$ holds.

Next we turn to the induction step when $j > 0$. The formula to be proved here is

$$run(\sigma) \land prefix(j - 1)(\sigma(n)) \supset (\exists m: prefix(\sigma(m))(j)).$$

By instantiating σ in Lemma 4.9 with $\sigma[n]$ we get an n'' at which process j is updated and $UP(j)(\sigma[n](n''), \sigma[n](n'' + 1))$ holds. We can therefore apply Lemma 4.15 with $\sigma[n]$ for σ, n'' for n, and $j - 1$ for j, to obtain an n' where $prefix(\sigma[n](n'))(j)$ holds. Thus, $n + n'$ serves a witness for m in our desired conclusion. □

At this point, we have all the ingredients needed to prove the self-stabilization property (Claim 9). Again, one might think that this is an obvious consequence of the claims presented thus far but the details are by no means straightforward.

Theorem 4.17 *In any run, there is a point beyond which the cardinality of the set of enabled processes is exactly one. The theorem is formally stated as*

$$\forall \sigma: run(\sigma) \supset (\exists m: \forall n: |E(\sigma[m](n))| = 1).$$

Proof. The first step in the proof is to invoke Theorem 4.16 with $N-1$ for j to obtain a state $\sigma(m)$ where the counter values of all the processes are identical. This leaves us with the task of proving that if $prefix(\sigma[m](0))(N - 1)$ then $\forall n: |E(\sigma[m](n))| = 1$. This is proved by induction on n. In the base case, we first show that $E(\sigma[m](0)) = \{0\}$. This follows by applying extensionality and using the homogeneous prefix property twice: once on i to show that for any

i, if $i \in E(\sigma[m](0))$ then $i = 0$, and again on 0 to show that $0 \in E(\sigma[m](0))$. The second step is a trivial one of showing that the cardinality of the set $\{0\}$ is 1, but it requires the use of some lemmas concerning finite cardinalities. The mechanical verification of the base case takes ten interactions.

In the induction step, we need to show that the cardinality of enabled process remains 1 under a transition from $\sigma[m](n)$ to $\sigma[m](n+1)$. We know by Lemma 4.3 that $|E(\sigma[m](n+1))| \leq |E(\sigma[m](n))|$ which means $|E(\sigma[m](n+1))|$ is either 0 or 1. It cannot be 0, since this contradicts Lemma 4.1 which asserts that there is always at least one enabled process. Hence the conclusion. The induction step takes up about eleven interactions, and about eight more interactions are needed to discharge the type-correctness proof obligations that come up, particularly those that require the demonstration that certain intermediate set constructions are finite, i.e., possess a bijection to a finite segment of the natural numbers. □

5 DISCUSSION

Related work. The study of self-stabilizing algorithms was initiated by Dijkstra in 1974 [Dij74]. He presented three algorithms for distributed N-process mutual exclusion arranged in a ring. These algorithms ensured that the system converged to stable behavior with at most one privileged or active process in any state. The study of self-stabilizing algorithms was dormant for a while following Dijkstra's work but there has been a recent flurry of activity in the subject. Schneider [Sch93] presents a survey of the issues in the design of self-stabilizing algorithms. Arora and Gouda [AG93] describe a uniform formal framework for verifying fault-tolerance and self-stability. Varghese [Var92] presents various systematic techniques for designing fault-tolerant algorithms including one based on the algorithm studied in this paper. He also provides an informal proof sketch for the correctness of this algorithm that is loosely similar to the one described here.

Prasetya [Pra97] verifies a self-stabilizing minimum-cost routing algorithm in a variant of the UNITY logic [CM88] that is formalized in the HOL proof checking system [GM93]. He presents an elegant development of the theory needed to verify this algorithm but reports a prohibitively high level of verification effort. His verification needed 8900 lines of specification and proof for the basic theories, 9300 lines for formalizing various aspects of the UNITY logic, and 5500 lines for the verification itself. Even though his verification takes some implementation details such as the communication mechanisms into account, the algorithm he verifies is roughly comparable in complexity to the one verified here. Since Prasetya's verification differs from ours in style and content, a sensible comparison of the two proof efforts is not viable. However, in the following discussion, we would like to dispel the impression that the mechanical verification of distributed algorithms, particularly self-stabilizing ones, necessarily requires an unreasonable amount of time and effort.

The challenge of formalization. Having struggled with the formalization of this self-stabilization problem, we certainly do not feel that formalization is a trivial matter. It took us quite a bit of effort to resolve even simple questions such as how to state the pigeonhole principle in its most relevant and usable form, how to formulate the measure function, and when to use measure induction rather than ordinary induction. The proof effort is extremely sensitive to the exact form of the formalization. It took us several false starts and not-so-near misses before we finally arrived at the formalization presented here. The construction of informal proof outline given by the claims in Section 2 was guided by insights gained from the failed attempts but was written without the aid of mechanization.

The final formalization does not dilute the intuitive clarity of the informal presentation. We have given a detailed informal outline of the formal steps in the mechanical verification. Nothing in this outline runs counter to informal intuitions, and indeed the formal proof is a faithful elaboration of these informal intuitions. Several serious gaps in the informal proof sketch were addressed in the formalization without loss of intuitive clarity. It is, of course, quite easy to construct informal or formal definitions and proofs that are completely obscure. However, it is not the case that the clarity of an informal presentation must be lost in formalization.

The formal script is not unreasonably long. The entire specification is fewer than 200 lines including generous amounts of white space and blank lines. The proof script consisting of all of the interactive commands for all of the proofs, including those of the type-correctness proof obligations that were generated and proved automatically, is fewer than 600 lines when pretty-printed with lots of white space and blank lines. This level of conciseness and faithfulness to the informal outline would be impossible without the use of the automation that is available in PVS in terms of typechecking, proof obligation generation, rewriting, decision procedures, and proof strategies. Even this proof script could be made more robust and concise through modest improvements to the automation that is available in PVS.

The mechanization was first fully completed with about four to six days of effort, and another two days were spent streamlining some of the proofs. Automated tools provide quite a bit of help in getting the details right by highlighting both syntactic and semantic errors. In the case of PVS, we use it to actively explore and discover proofs and not merely check existing proofs. This activity is quite enjoyable. The parts that are routine and mechanical are usually handled by means of the automation. The construction of a crisp and taut formal argument requires a number of mental leaps that are essentially similar to the creative effort needed to construct a convincing informal proof. In making these leaps, the mechanization helps construct explanations why some of these leaps are problematic and how they can be refined.

The main conclusion, one that has been observed earlier by de Bruijn [dB80] and others, is that the machine-checked proofs are of manageable size and linearly track the informal argument, and with modern automation, the expansion factor can actually be made quite small.

The challenge of mechanical verification. There is a widespread belief that mechanized deductive verification is too hard. Even those who advocate formal techniques are skeptical about the value of mechanical verification. The primary objection is that the achievable level of automation is inadequate for productive proof construction. In the case of the self-stabilization proof, even with the extensive automated support in PVS, we were repeatedly confronted with subgoals that were obvious but where the automation in PVS was unable to expand just the right definitions or supply the right instantiations for quantified variables. Through experiments such as these, we are constantly learning about the problems and drawbacks of the current automated support. There is no reason why the automation cannot be improved to a point where most obvious subgoals are indeed proved automatically.

The existing state of automated support is not an indication of what is in fact possible. To quote Dana Scott, *"formalization is an experimental science"* and the same holds for mechanization. Current automated tools are already being used quite effectively by a large body of users. The progress so far in understanding the tradeoffs between automation and interaction has been quite encouraging.

Is self-stability hard to verify? Prasetya [Pra97] claims the verification of self-stability to be especially hard. We can only speak of this particular experience. The main challenge for us was in coming up with a clean and crisp informal proof sketch. The mechanization based on this proof sketch was certainly not a mere formality, but there is no reason to believe that there is anything especially hard about deductively verifying self-stability. Self-stability is a global progress property of a system and requires reasoning about global progress measures which makes it different from the usual local progress properties that are proved for individual processes, but the techniques used are not that dissimilar.

How much of the proof was conventional mathematical reasoning? We would estimate that more than half the verification involved conventional mathematical reasoning about sets, cardinalities, modulo arithmetic, injective maps, pigeonhole principle, and well-founded measure functions. There were only four truly temporal proofs and even some of these involved a fair amount of combinatorial reasoning.

Would a special-purpose temporal formalism have helped? Although we initially felt that this proof would not have derived a significant benefit from a special-purpose temporal formalism [MP92, CM88] because large parts of the proof involved conventional mathematical reasoning, we did find some situations where a temporal framework would have been handy. After we completed our first pass at the verification, we observed that all the temporal properties following Lemma 4.9 employed instances of a single temporal rule, a generalization of the WHILE rule, which allows $\Diamond(p \wedge q)$ to be derived from $\Diamond q$ and $p \wedge \Box(p \wedge \neg q \supset \bigcirc p)$. We have not tried out the proof with this proof rule, but believe that the ability to identify and employ such powerful and generic proof rules provides sufficient methodological justification for embedding a temporal framework within the general-purpose one used here. Temporal logic can be quite easily embedded in the higher-order logic of PVS.

Could model checking be used? Model checking is often the easiest way to automatically verify a distributed algorithm. PVS has support for model checking but we were unable to reduce the problem here to one that could be model checked. While there are some finite-state techniques for verifying parametric systems of the form shown here [CGL94, WL89], they do not appear to be useful for this example. We were also unable to reduce the other two protocols presented by Dijkstra [Dij74] to model checkable form even though these are systems composed only of finite-state processes.

We pose this as an open problem: *Find a way to combine deduction and model checking to verify this and other self-stabilization properties/algorithms, or show that such a reduction is impossible?*

6 CONCLUSION

We have presented a proof of one of Dijkstra's self-stabilizing mutual exclusion algorithms that has been verified using PVS. We started with an informal proof sketch and constructed a formalization and mechanical verification that preserves the structure and enhances the clarity of the original proof sketch. This serves as a useful existence proof that the challenges of formalization and mechanization are not unreasonably daunting. Dijkstra's algorithm is particularly interesting since its justification employs a nontrivial amount of combinatorial mathematics. This kind of mathematics has typically been thought to be easier to present informally than formally. We have shown that this is not the case and that the formalization can closely follow the informal development. We have also shown exactly where the formal development loses succinctness when compared with the informal one. Such an analysis is useful in developing automated decision procedures and strategies that can more effectively close the informal/formal gap.

Acknowledgment. This work was supported by the Air Force Office of Scientific Research under contract F49620-95-C0044 and by the National Science Foundation under contract CCR-9509931. The views and conclusions contained herein are those of the authors and should not be interpreted as necessarily representing the official policies or endorsements, either expressed or implied, of the Air Force Office of Scientific Research, the National Science Foundation, or the U.S. Government. We are grateful to John Rushby for his encouragement, advice, and careful reading of drafts of this paper, to Sam Owre for help with PVS and LaTeX, and to Nikolaj Bjørner and the anonymous reviewers for their insightful comments and suggestions.

REFERENCES

[AG93] Anish Arora and Mohamed Gouda. Closure and convergence: A foundation of fault-tolerant computing. *IEEE Transactions on Software Engineering*, 19(11):1015–1027, November 1993.

[BM84] R. S. Boyer and J. S. Moore. Proof checking the RSA public key encryption algorithm. *American Mathematical Monthly*, 91(3):181–189, 1984.

[CGL94] E.M. Clark, O. Grumberg, and D.E. Long. Model checking and abstraction. *ACM Transactions on Programming Languages and Systems*, 16(5):1512–1542, September 1994.

[CM88] K. Mani Chandy and Jayadev Misra. *Parallel Program Design: A Foundation.* Addison-Wesley, Reading, MA, 1988.

[dB80] N. G. de Bruijn. A survey of the project AUTOMATH. In J. P. Seldin and J. R. Hindley, editors, *Essays on Combinatory Logic, Lambda Calculus and Formalism*, pages 589–606. Academic Press, New York, NY, 1980.

[Dij74] Edsger W. Dijkstra. Self-stabilizing systems in spite of distributed control. *Communications of the ACM*, 17(11):643–644, November 1974.

[Dij86] E. W. Dijkstra. A belated proof of self-stabilization. *Distributed Computing*, 1:5–6, 1986.

[GM93] M. J. C. Gordon and T. F. Melham, editors. *Introduction to HOL: A Theorem Proving Environment for Higher-Order Logic.* Cambridge University Press, Cambridge, UK, 1993.

[MP92] Zohar Manna and Amir Pnueli. *The Temporal Logic of Reactive and Concurrent Systems, Volume 1: Specification.* Springer-Verlag, New York, NY, 1992.

[ORS92] S. Owre, J. M. Rushby, and N. Shankar. PVS: A prototype verification system. In Deepak Kapur, editor, *11th International Conference on Automated Deduction (CADE)*, volume 607 of *Lecture Notes in Artificial Intelligence*, pages 748–752, Saratoga, NY, June 1992. Springer-Verlag.

[Pra97] I. S. W. B. Prasetya. Mechanically verified self-stabilizing hierarchical algorithms. In Ed Brinksma, editor, *Tools and Algorithms for the Construction and Analysis of Systems (TACAS '97)*, volume 1217 of *Lecture Notes in Computer Science*, pages 399–415, Enschede, The Netherlands, April 1997. Springer-Verlag.

[Sch93] Marco Schneider. Self stabilization. *ACM Computing Surveys*, 25(1):45–67, March 1993.

[Var92] George Varghese. *Self-Stabilization by Local Checking and Correction.* PhD thesis, MIT, 1992.

[WL89] P. Wolper and V. Lovinfosse. Verifying properties of large sets of processes with network invariants. In *Proceedings of the International Workshop on Automatic Verification Methods for Finite State Systems*, number 407 in Lecture Notes in Computer Science, pages 68–80, Grenoble, France, 1989. Springer Verlag.

Shaz Qadeer is a graduate student in Electrical Engineering and Computer Sciences at the University of California at Berkeley. His research interests are formal methods applied to verification and synthesis of concurrent hardware and software systems. He graduated with a B.Tech. in Electrical Engineering and received the President's Gold Medal from the Indian Institute of Technology, Kanpur in 1994.

He received an M.S. in Electrical Engineering and Computer Sciences from the University of California at Berkeley in 1997.

Natarajan Shankar is a computer scientist at the SRI International computer science laboratory in Menlo Park. His main research interests are in formal methods and automated deduction. He graduated with a B.Tech. in Electrical Engineering from IIT Madras in 1980, and a Ph.D. in Computer Science from the University of Texas at Austin in 1986.

28

A Combination of Interval Logic and Linear Temporal Logic

*Z. Qiu**
Department of Informatics, School of Mathematics, Peking University, Beijing 100871, China. E-Mail: zyqiu@pku.edu.cn

*C. Zhou***
International Institute for Software Technology, The United Nations University, P.O.Box 3058, Macau. E-Mail: zcc@iist.unu.edu

Abstract

The *super-dense computation* model provides an abstraction of real-time behaviour of computing systems. We present a combination of a linear temporal logic and an interval logic that uses super-dense computation and demonstrate how it can be used to specify real-time semantics and real-time properties of an OCCAM-like programming language.

Keywords

Temporal Logic, Interval Logic, Duration Calculus, Real-time semantics and specifications, Super-dense computation, OCCAM

1 INTRODUCTION

A *super-dense behaviour* consists of a series of continuously evolving phases in which a sequence of discrete actions can take place at the juncture of any two successive phases. The discrete actions are assumed to be instantaneous (they take no time), but ordered. Time, as a sequence of real numbers, is dense, and the assumption that ordered action sequences can happen at time points introduces additional structure into the already dense time domain. Thus the name *super-dense.*

The super-dense computation model is an important abstract model for real-time systems [7]. Many articles deal with this model [5, 7, 8, 16], and some industrially applicable programming languages (e.g. Esterel [1]) adopt similar models.

---

*The work was done when this author visited UNU/IIST.

**On leave of absence from Software Institute, Beijing.

Programming Concepts and Methods D. Gries, & W-P. de Roever (Eds.)

Control systems can be used to explain the concept of a super-dense model. The main part of a process in a control system can be expressed as:

while TRUE **do**
$wait(SAMPLING\_TIME)$;
$x := get\_sample(sensor)$;
$y := calculate\_output(x)$;
$send\_output(actuator, y)$

Execution of the process consists of continuous evolution (waiting between samplings) and discrete actions (computer calculations). The interaction frequency of the process with its environment is measured in seconds, while the discrete actions are performed in a computer with speed counted in nanoseconds. Thus, there is a 10^6–10^9 gap between sampling and calculation speeds. Control engineers therefore prefer to assume that the calculations take no time, and the super-dense model applies to this class of systems.

The super-dense model is reasonable and can make analyses of system behaviour more tractable under two conditions: (1) No infinite sequence of discrete actions takes place at a time point; and (2) the time consumed by each discrete action sequence is negligible in comparison to the continuous phases.

The literature contains several proposals to describe super-dense model mathematically. Some researchers use a timed sequence of actions to describe the behaviour of a real-time system (e.g. [7]). Here, a timed action is represented as a pair $\langle a, t \rangle$, where a is the action and t the time consumed by a. Thus, timeless discrete actions are special cases of pairs with $t = 0$. Article [12] adopts a similar view and suggests combining TLA [4] with the duration calculus [14] in describing the super-dense model.

Article [16] formalizes the intuition of two different levels of time measurement as a modal logic. By a modality named ***super-dense chop***, a point in the *coarse* time space can be chopped into a sequence of points in the *fine* time space. The ***intervals*** in the fine time space are invisible at the coarse level, which achieves the hiding of internal states. However, because of the hiding, different action sequences become indistinguishable, causing inconvenience for describing the behaviour of concurrent systems with shared variables.

We take a view similar to that of [2]. We view a process under the super-dense model as a trajectory in a two-dimensional time space and establish a logic to describe and reason about it. We assume there are countably infinite time axes, which are indexed by natural numbers. A process starts at some time on a time axis. When the process executes time-consuming actions, time progresses horizontally and the process stays on the same axis. When the process executes a timeless action, it jumps to another axis and changes to a new state. These jumps are instantaneous, and they can happen sequentially when necessary. Thus, real-time behaviour is divided into two classes as far as time is concerned: staying on an axis (when time evolves) and jumping instantaneously to another axis. A trajectory of a super-dense behaviour is shown in the following figure:

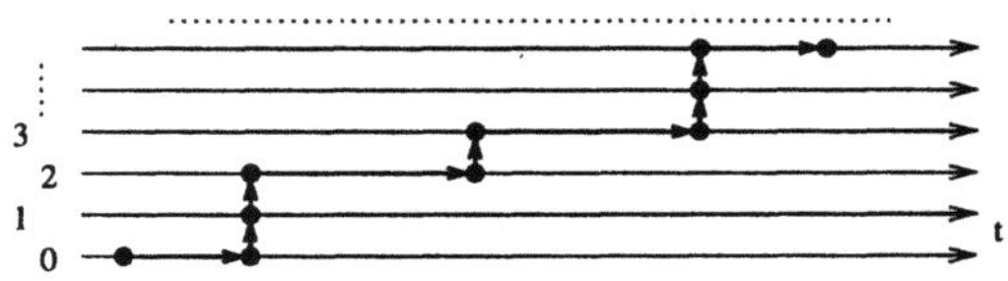

For this two-dimensional time space, we need a logic for a single axis, where continuous time is assumed, and we need modalities to travel among axes. We use an interval logic for behaviours on a single axis and a linear temporal logic for traveling between axes. In the following sections, we define the combined logic and then use it to define the semantics of a real-time OCCAM-like programming language. We close with a discussion of future work.

2 TWO-DIMENSIONAL TEMPORAL LOGIC

We present the syntax and semantics of the logic, give an inference system, and prove a number of theorems.

2.1 Syntax

(a) Symbols

Symbols of the logic include those presented below. Note that there are two kinds of variables: a global variable has a fixed value on all time axes over all time intervals, while a temporal variable represents a function of intervals on each time axis.

- Global (or rigid) variables: $Gvar$. $u, u_1, \ldots \in Gvar$.
- Temporal variables: $Tvar$. $x, y, x_1, \ldots \in Tvar$.
- Interval length: ℓ, which is a specific temporal variable.
- Function symbols: $f, g, f_1, \ldots$, including $0, 1, +, -, \ldots$.
- Relation symbols: $F, G, F_1, \ldots$, including $tt, ff, =, <, \ldots$.

(b) Terms

In the presentation of the form of terms below, $\theta, \theta_1, \theta_2, \ldots$ represent arbitrary terms, f is an n-ary function symbol, and $\bigcirc$ is the next moment operator from linear temporal logic [6]:

$$\theta \ ::= \ u \mid x \mid \ell \mid f(\theta_1, \ldots, \theta_n) \mid \bigcirc \theta$$

(c) Formulas

We use $\mathcal{D}$ to denote the set of formulas of the logic and $\varphi, \psi, \varphi_1, \varphi_2, \ldots \in \mathcal{D}$ to represent arbitrary formulas. In the following formation rules for formulas, F is an n-ary predicate symbol, $\bigcirc$ is the *next* modality and $\mathcal{U}$ the *until* modality (from linear temporal logic [6]), and $\Diamond_l$ and $\Diamond_r$ are two interval modalities (from neighbourhood logic [15]).

$$\varphi ::= F(\theta_1, \ldots \theta_n) \mid \neg\varphi \mid \varphi_1 \vee \varphi_2 \mid \exists u.\varphi \mid \bigcirc \varphi \mid \varphi_1 \,\mathcal{U}\, \varphi_2 \mid \Diamond_l\varphi \mid \Diamond_r\varphi$$

2.2 Semantics

Our semantics assumes countably infinite time axes. Interval modalities $\Diamond_l$ and $\Diamond_r$ define accessibility of left or right neighbourhoods of the reference interval on a single axis, while temporal modalities ($\bigcirc$ and $\mathcal{U}$) define accessibility between axes. A model of the logic contains three components: a valuation, an interpretation and a reference interval. Throughout, $\mathbb{R}$ denotes the set of real numbers and $\mathbb{N}$ the set of natural numbers.

- A *valuation* $\mathcal{V}$ assigns values to all global variables:

  $$\mathcal{V} \in Gvar \to \mathbb{R}$$

- An *interval* $[b, e]$, where $(b, e \in \mathbb{R}) \wedge b \leq e$, is the set $\{x \mid b \leq x \leq e\}$. We use $Intv$ to denote the set of all intervals.
- An *interpretation* $\mathcal{I}$ gives meaning to every temporal variable on each time axis as a function from intervals to real numbers:

  $$\mathcal{I} \in \mathbb{N} \to (Tvar \to (Intv \to \mathbb{R}))$$

  Here, $\mathbb{N}$ serves as the indices of axes. An interpretation $\mathcal{I}$ can be written as an infinite sequence

  $$\mathcal{I} = \sigma_0, \sigma_1, \sigma_2, \ldots$$

  where each $\sigma_i = \mathcal{I}(i), i = 0, 1, \ldots$, assigns every temporal variable an interval function on axis i. We use $\mathcal{I}_k$ to denote the subsequence of $\mathcal{I}$ starting at σ_k: $\mathcal{I}_k \mathrel{\widehat{=}} \sigma_k, \sigma_{k+1}, \sigma_{k+2}, \ldots$. Obviously, $\mathcal{I}_k(i) = \mathcal{I}(k+i)$.

A model $\mathcal{M}$ of the logic is a triple

$$\mathcal{M} = (\mathcal{I}, \mathcal{V}, [b, e])$$

where $\mathcal{V}, \mathcal{I}$ are an arbitrary valuation and interpretation, and $[b, e]$ is an interval. In the following definitions, let: $\mathcal{M}_0 = \mathcal{M}$ and $\mathcal{M}_k = (\mathcal{I}_k, \mathcal{V}, [b, e])$. Also, $\underline{f}$ and $\underline{F}$ denote function and predicate in real arithmetic and represent the *standard* meaning of f and F. The meaning of terms and formulas are defined as follows:

(a) For model $\mathcal{M}$, the meaning $\mathcal{M}(\theta)$ of a term θ is a real number defined by: $\mathcal{M}(\theta) \mathrel{\widehat{=}} \mathcal{M}_0(\theta) \in \mathbb{R}$, and $\mathcal{M}_i(\theta)$ is defined as:
  1) $\mathcal{M}_i(u) \mathrel{\widehat{=}} \mathcal{V}(u)$.
  2) $\mathcal{M}_i(\ell) \mathrel{\widehat{=}} e - b$.
  3) $\mathcal{M}_i(x) \mathrel{\widehat{=}} \mathcal{I}(i)(x)([b, e])$.
  4) $\mathcal{M}_i(f(\theta_1, \ldots, \theta_n)) \mathrel{\widehat{=}} \underline{f}(\mathcal{M}_i(\theta_1), \ldots, \mathcal{M}_i(\theta_n))$.
  5) $\mathcal{M}_i(\bigcirc\theta) \mathrel{\widehat{=}} \mathcal{M}_{i+1}(\theta)$.

(b) Given $\mathcal{M}$, the meaning $\mathcal{M}(\varphi)$ of formula φ is one of the truth values tt and ff. We define $\mathcal{M}(\varphi) \mathrel{\widehat{=}} \mathcal{M}_0(\varphi) \in \{\mathrm{tt}, \mathrm{ff}\}$, where $\mathcal{M}_i(\varphi)$ is defined as:
  1) $\mathcal{M}_i(F(\theta_1, \ldots, \theta_n)) \mathrel{\widehat{=}} \underline{F}(\mathcal{M}_i(\theta_1), \ldots, \mathcal{M}_i(\theta_n))$.
  2) $\mathcal{M}_i(\neg\varphi) \mathrel{\widehat{=}} \mathrm{tt}$ iff $\mathcal{M}_i(\varphi) = \mathrm{ff}$.
  3) $\mathcal{M}_i(\varphi_1 \vee \varphi_2) \mathrel{\widehat{=}} \mathrm{tt}$ iff $\mathcal{M}_i(\varphi_1) = \mathrm{tt}$ or $\mathcal{M}_i(\varphi_2) = \mathrm{tt}$.
  4) $\mathcal{M}_i(\exists u.\varphi) \mathrel{\widehat{=}} \mathrm{tt}$ iff there exists $\mathcal{V}'$, $\mathcal{V}'$ u-equivalent to $\mathcal{V}$, such that $\mathcal{M}_i[\mathcal{V}'/\mathcal{V}](\varphi) = \mathrm{tt}$. By u-equivalent we mean that $\mathcal{V}'$ differs from $\mathcal{V}$ by at most the value assigned to u. $\mathcal{M}_i[\mathcal{V}'/\mathcal{V}]$ denotes the model formed from $\mathcal{M}_i$ by replacing the component $\mathcal{V}$ by $\mathcal{V}'$.
  5) $\mathcal{M}_i(\bigcirc\varphi) \mathrel{\widehat{=}} \mathrm{tt}$ iff $\mathcal{M}_{i+1}(\varphi) = \mathrm{tt}$.
  6) $\mathcal{M}_i(\varphi_1 \,\mathcal{U}\, \varphi_2) \mathrel{\widehat{=}} \mathrm{tt}$ iff there exists j, $i \leq j$, such that $\mathcal{M}_j(\varphi_2) = \mathrm{tt}$ and for every k, $i \leq k < j$, $\mathcal{M}_k(\varphi_1) = \mathrm{tt}$.
  7) $\mathcal{M}_i(\diamond_l\varphi) \mathrel{\widehat{=}} \mathrm{tt}$ iff there exists a $\delta \geq 0$ such that $\mathcal{M}_i[(b-\delta)/b, b/e](\varphi) = \mathrm{tt}$. Here we use substitution to form a new model from the original one with a revised reference interval.
  8) $\mathcal{M}_i(\diamond_r\varphi) \mathrel{\widehat{=}} \mathrm{tt}$ iff there exists a $\delta \geq 0$ such that $\mathcal{M}_i[e/b, (e+\delta)/e](\varphi) = \mathrm{tt}$.

From the definitions in (a) and (b), we see that the meanings of $\bigcirc$ and $\mathcal{U}$ correspond to their meanings in linear temporal logic: $\bigcirc$ accesses the same reference interval but on the next axis, and $\mathcal{U}$ accesses a sequence of intervals above the reference interval. Operator $\diamond_l$ (and $\diamond_r$) accesses a left (right) neighbourhood of the beginning (end) point of the reference interval. Thus, the combination $\diamond_l\diamond_l$ (and $\diamond_r\diamond_r$) can be used to access an interval to the left (right) of the reference interval, while $\diamond_l\diamond_r$ (and $\diamond_r\diamond_l$) can be used to access a right (and left) neighbourhood of the beginning (end) point of the reference interval.

We say that $\mathcal{M}$ is a *model* of formula φ, written $\mathcal{M} \models \varphi$, iff $\mathcal{M}(\varphi) = \mathrm{tt}$. Similarly, $\mathcal{M} \not\models \varphi$ is written for $\mathcal{M}(\varphi) = \mathrm{ff}$. A formula φ is called *satisfiable* iff $\mathcal{M} \models \varphi$ for some model $\mathcal{M}$, and φ is called *valid* iff $\mathcal{M} \models \varphi$ for all models $\mathcal{M}$.

Other modalities of linear temporal logic and interval logic can be defined. The $\diamond$ and $\Box$ modalities of linear temporal logic are defined as usual:

$$\diamond\varphi \mathrel{\widehat{=}} \mathrm{tt}\,\mathcal{U}\,\varphi \qquad \Box\varphi \mathrel{\widehat{=}} \neg\diamond\neg\varphi$$

The chop modality $\frown$ of interval logic is defined as:

$$\varphi_1 \frown \varphi_2 \mathrel{\widehat{=}} \exists u_1, u_2.((\ell = u_1 + u_2) \wedge \Diamond_l \Diamond_r (\ell = u_1 \wedge \varphi_1 \wedge \Diamond_r (\ell = u_2 \wedge \varphi_2)))$$

$\varphi_1 \frown \varphi_2$ holds for a reference interval with length ℓ iff this interval can be chopped into two adjacent parts, where φ_1 holds over the left part and φ_2 holds over the right part.

We also have the duals of $\Diamond_l$ and $\Diamond_r$. These modalities are used to express properties that are true over all the left and over all the right neighbourhoods:

$$\Box_l \varphi \mathrel{\widehat{=}} \neg \Diamond_l \neg \varphi \qquad \Box_r \varphi \mathrel{\widehat{=}} \neg \Diamond_r \neg \varphi$$

2.3 Inference System

We now present the axioms and inference rules of the logic. First of all, the axioms of the linear temporal logic and the neighbourhood logic are still valid. For a complete set of axioms to formalize the class of our model, the following additional axioms are necessary.

1. $\bigcirc$ retains the length of the reference interval.
   (LT1) $(\ell = u) \Leftrightarrow \bigcirc(\ell = u)$
   From this axiom and the inference system of linear temporal logic, we can prove theorems like: $(\ell = u) \Leftrightarrow \Diamond(\ell = u)$, $(\ell = u) \Leftrightarrow \Box(\ell = u)$.
2. Commutativity of the *next* modality and the neighbourhood modalities.
   (NN1) $\Diamond_l \bigcirc \varphi \Leftrightarrow \bigcirc \Diamond_l \varphi$
   (NN2) $\Diamond_r \bigcirc \varphi \Leftrightarrow \bigcirc \Diamond_r \varphi$
   To access a neighbourhood on next axis, we can either reach a neighbourhood on the current axis and then go up to the next axis or do it the other way round.
3. Distributivity of neighbourhood modalities over the *until* modality:
   (UN1) $\Diamond_l(\varphi_1 \,\mathcal{U}\, \varphi_2) \Rightarrow (\Diamond_l \varphi_1) \,\mathcal{U}\, (\Diamond_l \varphi_2)$
   (UN2) $\Diamond_r(\varphi_1 \,\mathcal{U}\, \varphi_2) \Rightarrow (\Diamond_r \varphi_1) \,\mathcal{U}\, (\Diamond_r \varphi_2)$
   The other direction of the implications are valid under certain conditions on interval length:
   (UN3) $(\Diamond_l(\ell = u \wedge \varphi_1)) \,\mathcal{U}\, (\Diamond_l(\ell = u \wedge \varphi_2)) \Rightarrow \Diamond_l(\ell = u \wedge (\varphi_1 \,\mathcal{U}\, \varphi_2))$
   (UN4) $(\Diamond_r(\ell = u \wedge \varphi_1)) \,\mathcal{U}\, (\Diamond_r(\ell = u \wedge \varphi_2)) \Rightarrow \Diamond_r(\ell = u \wedge (\varphi_1 \,\mathcal{U}\, \varphi_2))$
4. The complementary axioms of (UN1) and (UN2):
   (UN5) $(\Box_l \varphi_1) \,\mathcal{U}\, (\Box_l \varphi_2) \Rightarrow \Box_l(\varphi_1 \,\mathcal{U}\, \varphi_2)$
   (UN6) $(\Box_r \varphi_1) \,\mathcal{U}\, (\Box_r \varphi_2) \Rightarrow \Box_r(\varphi_1 \,\mathcal{U}\, \varphi_2)$
   The converse implications are not true.

Soundness of these axioms is easy to check semantically. However, we do not know whether they form a complete set.

2.4 Theorems

With the axioms described above, we can prove the theorems listed below.

- Commutativity of $\bigcirc$ and neighbourhood with length:

$$\Diamond_l(\ell = u \wedge \bigcirc\varphi) \Leftrightarrow \bigcirc\Diamond_l(\ell = u \wedge \varphi)$$
$$\Diamond_r(\ell = u \wedge \bigcirc\varphi) \Leftrightarrow \bigcirc\Diamond_r(\ell = u \wedge \varphi)$$

The proofs are simple. We give one only for $\Diamond_l$.

$$\begin{aligned}\Diamond_l(\ell = u \wedge \bigcirc\varphi) &\Leftrightarrow \Diamond_l(\bigcirc(\ell = u) \wedge \bigcirc\varphi)\\ &\Leftrightarrow \Diamond_l \bigcirc (\ell = u \wedge \varphi) \qquad \Leftrightarrow \bigcirc\Diamond_l(\ell = u \wedge \varphi)\end{aligned}$$

- $\bigcirc$ is distributive over chop.

$$\bigcirc(\varphi_1 {}^\frown \varphi_2) \Leftrightarrow \bigcirc\varphi_1 {}^\frown \bigcirc \varphi_2$$

Here is a proof:

$$\begin{aligned}&\bigcirc(\varphi_1 {}^\frown \varphi_2)\\ \Leftrightarrow\ &\bigcirc\exists u_1, u_2.((\ell = u_1 + u_2) \wedge \Diamond_l\Diamond_r(\ell = u_1 \wedge \varphi_1) \wedge \Diamond_r\Diamond_l(\ell = u_2 \wedge \varphi_2))\\ \Leftrightarrow\ &\exists u_1, u_2. \bigcirc ((\ell = u_1 + u_2) \wedge \Diamond_l\Diamond_r(\ell = u_1 \wedge \varphi_1) \wedge \Diamond_r\Diamond_l(\ell = u_2 \wedge \varphi_2))\\ \Leftrightarrow\ &\exists u_1, u_2.(\bigcirc(\ell = u_1 + u_2) \wedge \bigcirc\Diamond_l\Diamond_r(\ell = u_1 \wedge \varphi_1) \wedge \bigcirc\Diamond_r\Diamond_l(\ell = u_2 \wedge \varphi_2))\\ \Leftrightarrow\ &\exists u_1, u_2.((\ell = u_1 + u_2) \wedge \Diamond_l\Diamond_r(\ell = u_1 \wedge \bigcirc\varphi_1) \wedge \Diamond_r\Diamond_l(\ell = u_2 \wedge \bigcirc\varphi_2))\\ \Leftrightarrow\ &\bigcirc\varphi_1 {}^\frown \bigcirc \varphi_2\end{aligned}$$

- Commutativity of *eventual* modality $\Diamond$ and neighbourhood modalities:

$$\Diamond_l\Diamond\varphi \Leftrightarrow \Diamond\Diamond_l\varphi \qquad\qquad \Diamond_r\Diamond\varphi \Leftrightarrow \Diamond\Diamond_r\varphi$$

An axiom of the neighbourhood logic is:

$$\Diamond_l\varphi \;\Rightarrow\; \exists u \geq 0.\Diamond_l(\ell = u \wedge \varphi)$$

Thus:

$$\begin{aligned}\Diamond\Diamond_l\varphi &\Rightarrow \Diamond(\exists u \geq 0.\Diamond_l(\ell = u \wedge \varphi))\\ &\Rightarrow \exists u \geq 0.\Diamond\Diamond_l(\ell = u \wedge \varphi)\\ &\Leftrightarrow \exists u \geq 0.(\mathrm{tt}\ \mathcal{U}\ \Diamond_l(\ell = u \wedge \varphi))\\ &\Leftrightarrow \exists u \geq 0.((\Diamond_l(\ell = u \wedge \mathrm{tt}))\ \mathcal{U}\ (\Diamond_l(\ell = u \wedge \varphi)))\\ &\Rightarrow \exists u \geq 0.\Diamond_l(\ell = u \wedge (\mathrm{tt}\ \mathcal{U}\ \varphi))\\ &\Leftrightarrow \exists u \geq 0.\Diamond_l(\ell = u \wedge \Diamond\varphi)\\ &\Leftrightarrow \Diamond_l\Diamond\varphi\end{aligned}$$

The other direction is simpler:

$$\Diamond_l \Diamond \varphi \Leftrightarrow \Diamond_l (\mathrm{tt}\, \mathcal{U}\, \varphi) \Rightarrow (\Diamond_l \mathrm{tt})\, \mathcal{U}\, (\Diamond_l \varphi) \Leftrightarrow \mathrm{tt}\, \mathcal{U}\, (\Diamond_l \varphi) \Leftrightarrow \Diamond \Diamond_l \varphi$$

- Commutativity of *always* modality $\Box$ with $\Box_l$ and $\Box_r$:

$$\Box \Box_l \varphi \Leftrightarrow \Box_l \Box \varphi \qquad \Box \Box_r \varphi \Leftrightarrow \Box_r \Box \varphi$$

The proofs are straightforward. For example:

$$\begin{aligned} \Box \Box_l \varphi &\Leftrightarrow \neg \Diamond \neg \neg \Diamond_l \neg \varphi \Leftrightarrow \neg \Diamond \Diamond_l \neg \varphi \\ &\Leftrightarrow \neg \Diamond_l \Diamond \neg \varphi \quad \Leftrightarrow \neg \Diamond_l \neg \neg \Diamond \neg \varphi \Leftrightarrow \Box_l \Box \varphi \end{aligned}$$

- Commutativity among $\Diamond$, $\Box_l$, $\Box_r$, and their dualities:

$$\begin{array}{ll} \Diamond \Box_l \varphi \Rightarrow \Box_l \Diamond \varphi & \Diamond \Box_r \varphi \Rightarrow \Box_r \Diamond \varphi \\ \Diamond_l \Box \varphi \Rightarrow \Box \Diamond_l \varphi & \Diamond_r \Box \varphi \Rightarrow \Box \Diamond_r \varphi \end{array}$$

We give proofs of two of them. The first:

$$\Diamond \Box_l \varphi \Leftrightarrow \mathrm{tt}\, \mathcal{U}\, (\Box_l \varphi) \Leftrightarrow (\Box_l \mathrm{tt})\, \mathcal{U}\, (\Box_l \varphi) \Rightarrow \Box_l (\mathrm{tt}\, \mathcal{U}\, \varphi) \Leftrightarrow \Box_l \Diamond \varphi$$

Because $\Diamond \Box_l \neg \varphi \Rightarrow \Box_l \Diamond \neg \varphi$, then $\neg \Box_l \Diamond \neg \varphi \Rightarrow \neg \Diamond \Box_l \neg \varphi$. The third:

$$\Diamond_l \Box \varphi \Leftrightarrow \Diamond_l \neg \Diamond \neg \varphi \Leftrightarrow \neg \Box_l \Diamond \neg \varphi \Rightarrow \neg \Diamond \Box_l \neg \varphi \Leftrightarrow \Box \Diamond_l \varphi$$

3 REAL-TIME LANGUAGE

In this section, we use the logic to give semantics of a real-time programming language, thus illustrating the power of the logic and a style of real-time semantics. The chosen language is an OCCAM-like language with variables, assignments, the usual control structures, message-passing synchronous communication, choice, etc. No sharing of variables is present in the language. Similar studies can be found in, for example [3, 10, 16].

3.1 Syntax

The language uses the following symbols:

- Time: $t \in (0, \infty) = \mathbb{R}^+$. $\mathbb{R}^+$ is the set of positive real numbers.
- Variables: A finite set of *program variables*, $x, y, x_1, x_2, \ldots$.
- Communication channels: A finite set of *channels*, $c, d, c_1, \ldots$.
- Arithmetic expressions: $e, e_1, e_2, \ldots$.

- Boolean expressions: $B, B_1, B_2, \ldots$.
- Sequential processes: $S, S_1, S_2, \ldots$.
- Parallel processes: $P, P_1, P_2, \ldots$.

The syntax of the language is:

$$\begin{array}{rcl} S & ::= & (x := e) \mid S_1; S_2 \mid \textbf{if } B \textbf{ then } S \mid \textbf{while } B \textbf{ do } S \mid \textbf{wait } t \mid \\ & & c?x \mid c!e \mid (c?x \to S_1 [\!] d?y \to S_2) \mid (c?x \to S_1 [\!] \textbf{wait } t \to S_2) \\ P & ::= & S \mid (P_1 || P_2) \end{array}$$

where:

$x := e$ is an assignment.
$S_1; S_2$ is the sequential composition of processes S_1 and S_2.
if B **then** S behaves like S if B evaluates to *true*; otherwise, it does nothing.
while B **do** S is the ordinary iteration.
wait t delays a process for t time units.
$c?x$ stands for receiving a message from channel c. If the communication is confirmed (i.e. it is synchronized with a send request on c), the message passed via c is assigned to variable x; otherwise, it waits forever. We adopt the *prompt* model of communication: a communication takes place as soon as the two partners are ready.
$c!e$ stands for sending a message through channel c. The process waits (possibly forever) for confirmation and then sends the value of e.
$(c?x \to S_1 [\!] d?y \to S_2)$ is a choice. Only the communication that is confirmed first (via channel c or channel d) takes place. When two communications are confirmed at the same time, the choice is arbitrary.
$(c?x \to S_1 [\!] \textbf{wait } t \to S_2)$ is the timeout structure. If communication via channel c is confirmed in less than t time units, the first branch is chosen. Otherwise, the second branch is chosen.
$(P_1 || P_2)$ is the parallel composition of sequential processes P_1 and P_2. The two processes have no shared variables, so the only means of interaction is communication via channels. Communication channels are directed. A channel connects two processes, one at each end.

3.2 Semantic Model

(a) Variables and Channels

The semantics of the language defines *denotations* for sequential and parallel processes by formulas of the logic over specific temporal variables. First, we determine the denotations for program variables and channels.

program variable: We assume real numbers as the only data type for variables, but the value of a variable may change over time. Temporal variables of the logic are used to denote variables. For each variable x, a temporal variable x is introduced in the semantic definition, where the same name is used for simplicity. Given an interpretation $\mathcal{I}$ and a point interval $[b, b]$, $\mathcal{I}(i)(x)([b, b]) = r$ means that the value of x at time b on axis i is r.

communication channel: For each channel c, three temporal variables c, $c?$ and $c!$ are introduced, where the name c is also overloaded. All communication values are of type $\mathbb{R}$. Variable c in a point interval records the value passed over channel c at that communication time. For the 0/1 valued temporal variable $c?$, $\mathcal{I}(i)(c?)[b, b] = 1$ indicates a request at time b on axis i to receive a message from channel c, while value 0 means no request is present. Similarly, $c!$ has value 1 to denote a sending request via c and 0 otherwise.

Temporal variables $c?$ and $c!$ are called *communication ports*. The set of all ports of process P is denoted by $ports(P)$. We say that a port is *enabled* at a time when it has value 1 at that time and *disabled* otherwise. We use $vars(P)$ to designate the set of all variables of P. In a parallel process $(P_1 \mid P_2)$, P_1 and P_2 have no common ports and no shared variables. Thus, $port(P_1) \cap port(P_2) = \emptyset$ and $vars(P_1) \cap vars(P_2) = \emptyset$.

(b) Abbreviations

In order to simplify the semantic definitions, we introduce a set of abbreviations. Operator $\doteq$ denotes equality over point intervals and $\stackrel{=}{=}$ denotes equality on all points of an interval.

$$x \doteq \theta \;\widehat{=}\; (x = \theta) \wedge (\ell = 0)$$
$$x \stackrel{=}{=} \theta \;\widehat{=}\; \neg(\mathrm{tt}^\frown \neg(x \doteq \theta)^\frown \mathrm{tt})$$

The following abbreviations are used to describe value-preservation of variables and ports.

$$\dot{kp}_P\,(X) \;\widehat{=}\; \bigwedge_{q \in ((vars(P) \cup ports(P)) - X)} q \doteq \bigcirc q$$
$$\bar{kp}_P \;\widehat{=}\; \bigwedge_{q \in (vars(P) \cup ports(P))} \exists u.(q \stackrel{=}{=} u)$$

$\dot{kp}_P\,(X)$ carries values of variables and ports of process P that are not in set X from a time point of the current axis to the same point of the next axis. When P is clear from the context, we omit the subscript P and simply use $\dot{kp}\,(X)$. Furthermore, $\dot{kp}\,(\{x_1, c_2\})$ is abbreviated as $\dot{kp}\,(x_1, c_2)$. The special case $\dot{kp}\,()$ is written as $\dot{kp}$, which carries values of all variables and ports of a process into the next axis. Secondly, $\bar{kp}_P$ is used to pass values of all variables and ports at the beginning of an interval to every point of the interval. Similar abbreviations, such as $\bar{kp}$, are also used.

Abbreviation $\bar{np}\,(X)$ (shown below) indicates that no port in X is enabled in a left-closed, right-open interval, while $\bar{np}\,(c?, d?)$ means that ports $c?$ and $d?$ are disabled at all points of a half closed interval. Note that $\bar{np}$ is true for all point intervals. The abbreviation $\dot{dis}$ says that all ports in X are disabled at a point.

$$\bar{np}\,(X) \;\widehat{=}\; (\ell = 0) \vee \neg(\mathrm{tt}^\frown(\bigvee_{p \in X} (p \doteq 1))^\frown(\ell > 0))$$

$$\dot{dis}\,(X) \;\widehat{=}\; \bigwedge_{p \in X} (p \doteq 0)$$

(c) Two Non-logical Axioms

The semantic model of a process will be defined as the trajectory of the process. On the trajectory, the values of all relevant temporal variables are determined. In order to propagate the values on the trajectory to other areas of the two-dimensional space, we stipulate two non-logical axioms:

$$(\ell > 0) \Rightarrow ((x \doteq u) \Rightarrow \bigcirc((x \doteq u)^\frown(\ell > 0)))$$
$$(\ell > 0) \Rightarrow (\bigcirc(x \doteq u) \Rightarrow ((\ell > 0)^\frown(x \doteq u)))$$

The first axiom says that, for any closed non-point interval, the values will be carried upward to all corresponding left-closed, right-open intervals. The second axiom carries value downward to left-open, right-closed intervals below. Note that values at isolated points are not propagated by these axioms.

(d) Semantic Definitions

We use a *continuation* approach to describe the semantics of the language. Let S be a sequential process. We will define:

$$[\![S]\!] \in \mathcal{D} \to \mathcal{D}$$

where $\mathcal{D}$ is the set of logical formulas. Let $C \in \mathcal{D}$ be a formula defining the semantic model of a continuation of S. $[\![S]\!]C$ defines the meaning of S with continuation C. It is assumed that a program begins its execution at an arbitrary time point on time axis 0. All sequential processes start simultaneously. Semantic definitions of various processes are listed below, where the abbreviations of $\dot{kp}$ and $\bar{kp}$ are widely used in the contexts.

- $x := e$ The statement, a timeless discrete action, assigns the value of e to x on the next axis, and leaves all other variables and ports unchanged.

$$[\![x := e]\!]C \;\widehat{=}\; \dot{kp}\,(x) \wedge \bigcirc x \doteq e \wedge \bigcirc C$$

• $S_1; S_2$ With continuation, sequential composition is defined by:

$$[\![S_1; S_2]\!]C \mathrel{\widehat{=}} [\![S_1]\!]([\![S_2]\!]C)$$

• **if** B **then** S In the semantics of this process, $[\![\dot{B}]\!]$ denotes the value of B at the current time on the current axis:

$$[\![\textbf{if } B \textbf{ then } S]\!]C \mathrel{\widehat{=}} ([\![\dot{B}]\!] \wedge [\![S]\!]C) \vee (\neg [\![\dot{B}]\!] \wedge C)$$

• **wait** t This statement delays its continuation C for t time units, keeping all relevant variables and ports unchanged within this period.

$$[\![\textbf{wait } t]\!]C \mathrel{\widehat{=}} \Diamond_r((\bar{kp} \wedge \ell = t)^\frown(\ell = 0 \wedge C))$$

• $c?x$ Execution moves to next axis, where it retains the values of all variables and ports but enables $c?$. Thereafter, it looks up and rightward for $c! \doteq 1$ to reach a synchronization. When a synchronization is reached, value passing is triggered: x gets a new value from c and $c?, c!$ are disabled. Here, we assume that waiting for synchronization may take time, but value passing is a timeless action. When synchronization fails, the process goes into an infinite wait. These two cases are described by a disjunction.

$$\begin{aligned}[\![c?x]\!]C \mathrel{\widehat{=}}\; & \dot{kp}\,(c?) \wedge \bigcirc(c? \doteq 1 \wedge \\ & (\quad \Diamond_r((\dot{kp} \frown \bar{kp})\,\mathcal{U}\,(\bar{kp} \wedge (\bar{np}\,(c!)^\frown(c! \doteq 1 \wedge Com_1)))) \\ & \vee\; \Box_r(\bar{kp} \wedge c! \doteq 0)\ )\ )\end{aligned}$$

where

$$Com_1 \mathrel{\widehat{=}} \dot{kp}\,(c?, x) \wedge \bigcirc(x \doteq c \wedge \dot{dis}\,(c?, c!) \wedge C)$$

Note that when $(c! \doteq 1)$ occurs on a time axis below and/or at a time before $(c? \doteq 1)$, by the symmetric semantic definition for $c!e$, the communication partner will look for $(c? \doteq 1)$ for the synchronization.

• $c!e$ The semantics of $c!e$ is symmetric to that for $c?x$.

$$\begin{aligned}[\![c!e]\!]C \mathrel{\widehat{=}}\; & \dot{kp}\,(c!) \wedge \bigcirc(c! \doteq 1 \wedge \\ & (\quad \Diamond_r((\dot{kp} \frown \bar{kp})\,\mathcal{U}\,(\bar{kp} \wedge (\bar{np}\,(c?)^\frown(c? \doteq 1 \wedge Com_2)))) \\ & \vee\; \Box_r(\bar{kp} \wedge c? \doteq 0)\ )\ )\end{aligned}$$

where

$$Com_2 \mathrel{\widehat{=}} \dot{kp}\,(c!, c) \wedge \bigcirc(c \doteq e \wedge \dot{dis}\,(c?, c!) \wedge C)$$

• $c?x \rightarrow S_1 \,\|\, d?x \rightarrow S_2$ The semantics of this process mimics the one for $c?x$. Initially, both ports $c?$ and $d?$ are enabled. Then the process looks for $(c! \doteq 1) \vee (d! \doteq 1)$. When found, a value is passed via the synchronized channel; when both are synchronized at same time, the choice is arbitrary.

$$[\![c?x \rightarrow S_1 \,\|\, d?x \rightarrow S_2]\!]C \mathrel{\hat{=}} \dot{kp}\,(c?, d?) \wedge \bigcirc(c? \doteq 1 \wedge d? \doteq 1 \wedge \left(\begin{array}{l} \quad \Diamond_r(\,(\dot{kp} \frown \bar{kp})\,\mathcal{U} \\ \qquad (\bar{kp} \wedge (\bar{np}\,(c!, d!) \frown ((c! \doteq 1 \wedge Com_3) \vee (d! \doteq 1 \wedge Com_4))))) \\ \vee\ \Box_r(\bar{kp} \wedge c! \doteq 0 \wedge d! \doteq 0) \end{array}\right))$$

where

$$\begin{aligned} Com_3 &\mathrel{\hat{=}} \dot{kp}\,(c?, d?, x) \wedge \bigcirc(x \doteq c \wedge \dot{dis}\,(c?, d?, c!, d!) \wedge [\![S_1]\!]C) \\ Com_4 &\mathrel{\hat{=}} \dot{kp}\,(c?, d?, x) \wedge \bigcirc(x \doteq d \wedge \dot{dis}\,(c?, d?, c!, d!) \wedge [\![S_2]\!]C) \end{aligned}$$

• $c?x \rightarrow S_1 \,\|\, \textbf{wait}\, t \rightarrow S_2$ If a synchronization with $c!$ can be reached within t time units, the first branch is chosen; otherwise, the second one is chosen.

$$[\![c?x \rightarrow S_1 \,\|\, \textbf{wait}\, t \rightarrow S_2]\!]C \mathrel{\hat{=}} \dot{kp}\,(c?) \wedge \bigcirc(c? \doteq 1 \wedge \left(\begin{array}{l} \quad \Diamond_r(\ell < t \wedge ((\dot{kp} \frown \bar{kp})\,\mathcal{U}\,(\bar{kp} \wedge (\bar{np}\,(c!) \frown (c! \doteq 1 \wedge Com_5))))) \\ \vee\ (\neg\Diamond\Diamond_r(\ell < t \wedge (\mathrm{tt} \frown (c! \doteq 1))) \wedge \\ \quad \dot{kp}\,(c?) \wedge \bigcirc\Diamond_r(\ell = t \wedge (((c? \doteq 0) \frown \bar{kp}) \frown (\ell = 0 \wedge [\![S_2]\!]C)))) \end{array}\right))$$

where

$$Com_5 \mathrel{\hat{=}} \dot{kp}\,(c?, x) \wedge \bigcirc(x \doteq c \wedge \dot{dis}\,(c?, c!) \wedge [\![S_1]\!]C)$$

• **while** B **do** S To define the semantics of iteration, we extend the logic with infinite disjunction and conjunction*. Let A_i $(i \in \mathbb{N})$ be formulas. $\bigvee_{i\in\mathbb{N}} A_i$ is an infinite disjunction of A_i, which defines models satisfying at least one A_i. Similarly, $\bigwedge_{i\in\mathbb{N}} A_i$ defines models that satisfy every A_i.

For **while** B **do** S we introduce the following formulas

$$\begin{aligned} W^0_{B,S}(C) &\mathrel{\hat{=}} \neg\,[\![\dot{B}]\!] \wedge C \\ W^{n+1}_{B,S}(C) &\mathrel{\hat{=}} [\![\dot{B}]\!] \wedge [\![S]\!] W^n_{B,S}(C) \\ W^\omega_{B,S}(C) &\mathrel{\hat{=}} \bigvee_{n\in\mathbb{N}} W^n_{B,S}(C) \end{aligned} \quad \text{and} \quad \begin{aligned} F^0_{B,S} &\mathrel{\hat{=}} \mathrm{tt} \\ F^{n+1}_{B,S} &\mathrel{\hat{=}} [\![\dot{B}]\!] \wedge [\![S]\!] F^n_{B,S} \\ F^\omega_{B,S} &\mathrel{\hat{=}} \bigwedge_{n\in\mathbb{N}} F^n_{B,S} \end{aligned}$$

*We don't discuss the fixed point operator of the logic, cf. [13].

where $W^{\omega}_{B,S}(C)$ defines the finite iteration of the process and $F^{\omega}_{B,S}$ defines the infinite iterations. Then, the semantics of the **while** statement is defined as:

$$[\![\textbf{while}\, B\, \textbf{do}\, S]\!]C \mathrel{\hat{=}} W^{\omega}_{B,S}(C) \vee F^{\omega}_{B,S}$$

We can now define the semantics of parallel processes. Suppose P is a parallel composition of n sequential processes, $P = (S_1 \,||\, \ldots \,||\, S_n)$, $(n \geq 1)$. The semantics of P is defined as:

$$[\![P]\!] \mathrel{\hat{=}} \bigwedge_{i \in 1..n} [\![S_i]\!](\Box_r\, \bar{kp}_{S_i})$$

We use $\Box_r\, \bar{kp}_{S_i}$ as the continuation of process S_i. This means that, once S_i terminates, the values of all its variables and ports will stay the same forever.

3.3 Examples

We give two simple examples to illustrate the semantics defined above.

Example 1
$x := 1;$ **wait** $3;$ $x := x + 3$

We assume that x is the only program variable and that there are no communication ports. The semantics of this process can be derived as:

$$\begin{aligned}
&[\![x := 1;\ \textbf{wait}\ 3;\ x := x + 3]\!](\Box_r\, \bar{kp}) \\
=\ &\bigcirc x \doteq 1 \wedge \bigcirc([\![\textbf{wait}\ 3;\ x := x + 3]\!](\Box_r\, \bar{kp})\,) \\
=\ &\bigcirc(x \doteq 1 \wedge \Diamond_r((x \doteq 1 \wedge \ell = 3)^\frown(\ell = 0 \wedge [\![x := x + 3]\!](\Box_r\, \bar{kp})))) \\
=\ &\bigcirc(x \doteq 1 \wedge \Diamond_r((x \doteq 1 \wedge \ell = 3)^\frown(\ell = 0 \wedge (\bigcirc x \doteq 4 \wedge \bigcirc(\Box_r\, \bar{kp}))))) \\
=\ &\bigcirc(x \doteq 1 \wedge \Diamond_r((x \doteq 1 \wedge \ell = 3)^\frown(\ell = 0 \wedge \bigcirc(x \doteq 4 \wedge \Box_r(x \doteq 4)))))
\end{aligned}$$

The picture below shows the execution trajectory of this process, where it is supposed that the process starts at time point b on axis 0.

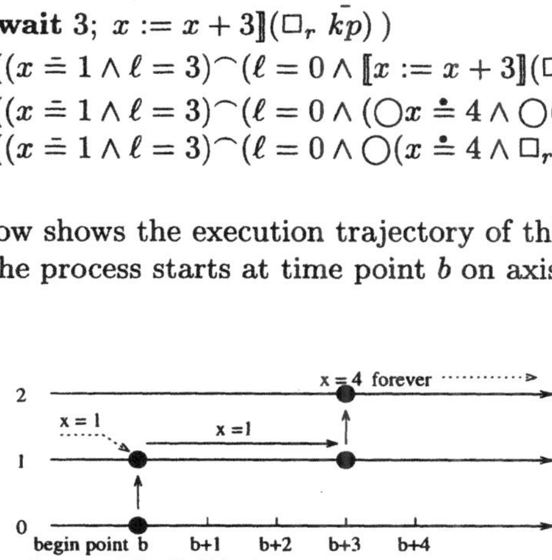

By the two non-logical axioms, the value of x is determined from time b onward on all axes. In interval $(b, b+3)$, x has value 1 on all axes. In interval $(b+3, \infty)$ of any axis, x has value 4. At points b and $b+3$, the situation is different. For example, at time b of axis 0, x has an undefined initial value, but it has value 1 on all axes from axis 1 upward.

Example 2

$x := 1;\ x := x + 1;\ c?x \parallel$ **wait** $3;$ **wait** $2;\ y := 1;\ c!(y + 3)$

Here x and $c?$ are the only program variable and communication port of the left sequential process, while y and $c!$ the only ones for the right. We give here only a picture instead of a semantic formula to explain the defined semantics of the parallel process. We assume that all ports are initially disabled.

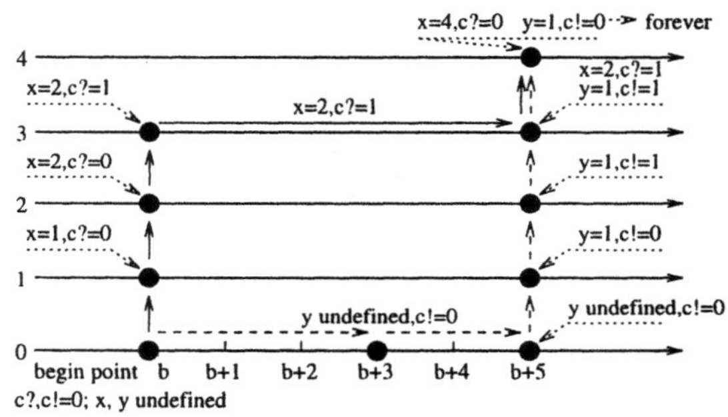

The execution trajectories of the two sequential processes are presented by solid arrows and dashed arrows respectively. We can see that the right sequential process has one stuttering step to reach synchronization with its partner.

3.4 Process Properties

We now demonstrate how to formulate various program properties in the logic.

Precondition: A precondition gives initial values to all variables and disables all ports. When $\{x_i\}$ and $\{p_j\}$ are the sets of variables and ports of the process, and $\{r_i\}$ a set of real numbers, a precondition is in the form:

$$pre \mathrel{\hat{=}} \bigwedge_{\text{all variables } x_i} (x_i \doteq r_i) \wedge \bigwedge_{\text{all ports } p_j} (p_j \doteq 0)$$

Convergence: A process is *divergent* if it performs infinite timeless discrete actions in a finite time period. For example, if x is greater than 0 initially,

while $x > 0$ **do** $x := x + 1$ will perform infinite discrete action $x := x + 1$ at a time point. Hence, a divergent process has a vertical boundary. A process is *convergent* if it is not divergent. Therefore, a convergent process can progress horizontally forever and can determine a value of any of its variables in the right half of the plane. Let P be a process and x be a variable of P. P is convergent under pre-condition *pre* if

$$pre \land [\![P]\!] \Rightarrow \Box_r \Diamond_r \Diamond_r \exists u.(x \doteq u \land \ell > 0)$$

Subsequently, we are interested only in properties of convergent processes.

Termination: Let $P = (S_1 \| \ldots \| S_n)$, $(n \geq 1)$. We introduce an additional boolean valued temporal variable tm_i into the continuation of each S_i.

$$cnt_i \mathrel{\widehat{=}} \bar{kp}_{S_i} \land (tm_i \doteq 1)$$

Then the semantics of P is changed to

$$[\![P]\!] \mathrel{\widehat{=}} \bigwedge_{i \in 1..n} [\![S_i]\!](\Box_r cnt_i)$$

Termination of P can therefore be formulated as

$$tm(P) \mathrel{\widehat{=}} \Diamond_r \Box_r \bigwedge_i (tm_i \doteq 1)$$

A postcondition of P can be specified as a relation among variables of P that eventually becomes true and stays true forever. Using $\overline{post}$ for "*post* is true everywhere in an interval where the beginning point is not taken into account", the proof obligation for total correctness of P with respect to precondition *pre* and postcondition *post* is:

$$pre \land [\![P]\!] \Rightarrow (tm(P) \land \Diamond_r \Box_r \overline{post})$$

Deadlock-Freedom: A deadlock is an endless waiting for a synchronization between, say, $c?$ and $c!$, where one of $c?$ and $c!$ always has value 1 and the other 0. Therefore, the property of deadlock-freedom of process P with private channels $c_1, c_2, \ldots, c_n$ can be formulated as:

$$\bigwedge_{j \in 1..n} \Box_r \Diamond_r \Diamond_r ((\ell > 0) \land (c_j? \doteq c_j!))$$

This formula specifies that, for every channel c_j, after any time interval, a non-point interval can be found where $c_j?$ and $c_j!$ have the same value. In fact, they are both disabled in that interval.

Real-Time Properties: We give two formulations as examples.

(1) Relation φ is never continuously true for longer than t time units:

$$\Box_r \Box_r (\overline{\varphi} \Rightarrow (\ell < t))$$

(2) Any two appearances of φ have a separation of at least t time units:

$$\Box_r \Box_r ((\overline{\varphi} ^\frown \overline{\neg\varphi} ^\frown \overline{\varphi}) \Rightarrow (\ell \geq t))$$

4 DISCUSSION

Our work aims to establish a two-dimensional modal logic that can be used as a logical foundation for specifying and reasoning about real-time systems, where super-dense computation is assumed. In this paper, we investigate a combination of linear temporal logic and interval logic. Combinations of other logics may also be interesting (see e.g. [9]).

Based on this combination, one can develop logics for system trajectories. The one shown in the paper is the execution trajectory of real-time processes. The mathematical models suggested in [5, 8, 11] provide abstractions of system trajectories, and, we believe, can be formalized as an extension of this combined logic. A general trajectory logic can be used as a logical framework for various models of real-time systems and can become an interesting research topic. How to develop a complete calculus for the combined logic is another research topic. It would be interesting to define the semantics of a synchronous language, such as Esterel, in terms of this logic.

ACKNOWLEDGEMENT

We gratefully acknowledge the instructive comments from the five referees, the carefully reading and correction of the paper by David Gries, and helpful suggestions from our colleagues in UNU/IIST.

REFERENCES

[1] G. Berry and G. Gonthier. The Esterel synchronous programming language: design, semantics, implementation. In *Science of Computer Programming 19* (2), 87–152, Elsevier, 1992.

[2] T. Bolognesi and F. Lucidi. LOTOS-like process algebras with urgent or timed interactions. In *Formal Description Techniques, IV*, 249-264, North-Holland, 1992.

[3] R. Koymans. *Specifying message passing and time-critical systems with temporal logic.* LNCS 651, Springer-Verlag, 1992.

[4] Leslie Lamport. The temporal logic of actions. Technical Report 79, DEC System Research Centre, 1991.

[5] Z. Liu, A. P. Ravn and X. Li. Duration properties of timed transition systems. Technical Report 1997/12, Leicester University, 1997.

[6] Z. Manna and A. Pnueli. *The temporal logic of reactive and concurrent systems: specification.* Springer-Verlag, 1991.

[7] Z. Manna and A. Pnueli. Models of reactivity. *Acta Informatica 30* (7), 609–678, Springer-Verlag, 1993.

[8] Paritosh K. Pandya and Dang Van Hung. Duration calculus of weakly monotonic time. Technical Report No.122, UNU/IIST, 1997.

[9] Rana Barua and Zhou Chaochen. Neighbourhood logic: NL and NL^2. Technical Report No.120, UNU/IIST, 1997.

[10] G. M. Reed and A timed model for communicating sequential processes. In *ICALP 86: Automata, Language, and Programming*, LNCS 226, 314-323, Springer-Verlag, 1986.

[11] Mahalik Swarup and Xu Qiwen. Compositional verification in duration calculus. Technical Notes, UNU/IIST, 1997.

[12] Morten U. Sørensen, Odd E. Hansen and Hans H. Løvengreen. Combining temporal specification techniques. In Dov M. Gabbay and Hans J. Ohlbach (Eds.) Proceedings of *Temporal Logic, First International Conference, ICTL'94*, 1-16, Springer-Verlag, 1994.

[13] Wang Hanpin and Xu Qiwen. Infinite duration calculus with fix-point operators. Technical Notes, UNU/IIST, 1997.

[14] Zhou Chaochen, C.A.R Hoare and A.P.Ravn. A calculus of durations. In *Information Processing Letters 40* (5), 269-276, Elsevier, 1991.

[15] Zhou Chaochen and Michael R. Hansen. An adequate first order interval logic. Technical Report No.91, UNU/IIST, 1996.

[16] Zhou Chaochen and Michael R. Hansen. Chopping a point. In J. F. He *et al* (Eds.), *BCS-FACS 7th Refinement Workshop*, Electronic Workshops in Computing, Springer-Verlag, 1996.

BIOGRAPHIES

Zongyan Qiu is an associate professor of Computer Science in the Department of Informatics in Peking University. His main interests are Programming Languages and Formal Methods.

Chaochen Zhou is the director of UNU/IIST. He is on leave of absence from the Software Institute, the Chinese Academy of Science, where he is a professor. His main interest is Formal Technique of Programming, including Formal Semantics, Specification, Verification and Design Calculi for Real-time Systems.

29

A model of real-time distributed systems

A. Wabenhorst
Software Verification Research Centre
University of Queensland QLD 4072, Australia
akw@it.uq.edu.au

Abstract

A model of real-time distributed systems using action systems is presented, with semantics given in terms of the predicate transformer semantics of non-timed action systems. An example is given to illustrate the model and to demonstrate its stepwise development from specification. A strength of the approach presented is the wide range of real-time systems which can be specified in the model.

Keywords

Real time, action systems, weakest preconditions, refinement, formal methods

1 INTRODUCTION

The problem of specifying real-time distributed systems has occupied computer scientists in recent times. This is partly because real-time systems, particularly in the area of defence, are more often safety-critical than systems without the concept of time. Real-time systems often need to react to an environment which may not always be controllable. In such cases, validation by testing may be particularly unreliable, and there is greater scope for the use of formal methods.

Real-time systems reacting to an environment present the challenge of modelling the environment and its interaction with the system, and showing that the system meets its requirements when reacting to the environment. A particular difficulty is modelling time for different processes acting in parallel, and the issue arises as to whether there is the concept of global time.

For our model, we choose the notation of action systems (Back 1989) for their developmental clarity and general expressive power, particularly of parallelism, and because their predicate transformer semantics are concise and calculational.

We begin in Section 2 by recalling the definitions of predicate transformers (Dijkstra *et al.* 1990) and action systems (Back 1989), together with the

Programming Concepts and Methods D. Gries, & W-P. de Roever (Eds.)

resulting definition of refinement. We define action sequences and give a characterisation of the semantics of iteration using them. In Section 3, we motivate and explain our model of real-time action systems and state some of its properties. The model is illustrated by a message passing example in Section 4. Finally in Section 5, we discuss our results and relate them to those of others.

2 BACKGROUND

2.1 Predicate transformers

Let $\Sigma_{\mathcal{A}}$ denote the state space of a program $\mathcal{A}$ expressed in the language of guarded commands (Dijkstra *et al.* 1990). A *predicate* is a function $f : \Sigma_{\mathcal{A}} \rightarrow \mathbb{B}$, the set of all of which will be denoted by $Pred\mathcal{A}$.

A statement S is a predicate transformer $S : Pred\mathcal{A} \rightarrow Pred\mathcal{A}$ known as the *weakest precondition* (Dijkstra *et al.* 1990) satisfying, for all $P, Q : Pred\mathcal{A}$, the axioms

- monotonicity: if $P \Rightarrow Q$, then $S(P) \Rightarrow S(Q)$;
- conjunctivity: if $I \neq \emptyset$ is an index set, then

$$(\forall \alpha \in I\ S(P_\alpha)) \Rightarrow S(\forall \alpha \in I\ P_\alpha).$$

Informally, we can regard the weakest precondition $S(P)$ for $P : Pred\mathcal{A}$ to be the weakest predicate on the variable states from which execution of the statement S guarantees termination in a state satisfying P. In particular, $S(true)$ is the weakest predicate which guarantees that S terminates. Notice that we allow statements which do not satisfy strictness $S(false) \Leftrightarrow false$.

Statements and their associated weakest precondition transformers include those in Figure 1 (Boom 1982, Dijkstra *et al.* 1990) and the specification statements of Morgan (1994).

An *action system* (Back 1989) has the form

$$\begin{array}{lll} \textbf{var} & & x_1, \ldots, x_m \\ \textbf{init} & & x_1, \ldots, x_m :\in X_1, \ldots, X_m \\ \textbf{do} & []_{i=1}^{n} & A_i \ \textbf{od}, \end{array}$$

where $x_1, \ldots, x_m$ are typed variables and $A_1, \ldots, A_n$ are actions. Sometimes we will omit the variable declaration when it can be deduced from the body of the action system. When a variable is initialised arbitrarily within its type, we will omit an explicit initialisation.

Definition 1 (Refinement) *A statement* S is refined by *a statement* S' *(notation* $S \leq S'$*) if for all* $P : Pred\mathcal{A}$, $S(P) \Rightarrow S'(P)$. □

- skip: $\mathbf{skip}(P) \ \widehat{=} \ P$.
- assertion: $(!b)(P) \ \widehat{=} \ b \wedge P$.
- abort: $\mathbf{abort} \ \widehat{=} \ !false$.
- assignment: $(\vec{x} :\in \vec{X})(P) \ \widehat{=} \ \forall \vec{y} \in \vec{X} \ P[\vec{y}/\vec{x}]$, where $\vec{x}$ is a list of variables and $P[\vec{y}/\vec{x}]$ is the predicate P with each member of $\vec{y}$ replacing the corresponding member of $\vec{x}$.
- sequential composition: $(S_1; S_2)(P) \ \widehat{=} \ S_1(S_2(P))$.
- choice: $(S_1 \ [] \ S_2)(P) \ \widehat{=} \ S_1(P) \wedge S_2(P)$.
- actions: $(g \rightarrow S)(P) \ \widehat{=} \ \neg g \vee S(P)$. Here, g is called the *guard* of the action.
- alternation: $(\mathbf{if} \ []_{i=1}^{n} \ g_i \rightarrow S_i \ \mathbf{fi})(P) \ \widehat{=} \ \bigvee_{i=1}^{n} g_i \wedge ([]_{i=1}^{n} \ g_i \rightarrow S_i)(P)$.
- iteration: $(\mathbf{do} \ []_{i=1}^{n} \ g_i \rightarrow S_i \ \mathbf{od})(P) \ \widehat{=} \ \exists \kappa : Ord \ H_\kappa(P)$, where Ord is the class of ordinal numbers and

$$\begin{aligned} H_0(P) \ &\widehat{=} \ P \wedge \neg \bigvee_{i=1}^{n} g_i, \\ H_{\kappa+1}(P) \ &\widehat{=} \ H_0(P) \vee (\mathbf{if} \ []_{i=1}^{n} \ g_i \rightarrow S_i \ \mathbf{fi}) \ (H_\kappa(P)) \text{ and} \\ H_\delta(P) \ &\widehat{=} \ \exists \kappa < \delta \ H_\kappa(P), \text{ where } \delta \text{ is a limit ordinal.} \end{aligned}$$

Figure 1 Some statements and their weakest preconditions.

2.2 Action sequences

For an action system $\mathcal{A}$, $seq\mathcal{A}$ denotes the set of all finite sequential compositions of actions in $\mathcal{A}$, while the elements of the set $seq_\omega\mathcal{A}$ are written as sequential compositions of infinitely many actions, but do not have predicate transformer semantics. These two sets are the *action sequences* of $\mathcal{A}$. For an action sequence s of length at least m, $s|_m$ is the prefix of s with length m. The predicate transformer **skip** is considered to be an action sequence of length 0. For an action A, A^m is the sequential composition of A with itself m times.

The following characterisation (Morris 1987, Butler *et al.* 1995, Wabenhorst 1996) of the weakest precondition of an action system can be thought of as a decomposition. The first conjunct is a safety condition on the finite action sequences, also known as the weakest errorfree precondition (Hesselink 1995), which states that if $\mathcal{A}$ terminates at all, then it terminates in state P. The second conjunct is a liveness condition on the infinite action sequences which states that $\mathcal{A}$ terminates eventually.

Theorem 1 *Let* $\mathcal{A} \ \widehat{=} \ \mathbf{do} \ []_{i=1}^{n} \ g_i \rightarrow S_i \ \mathbf{od}$ *be an action system. Then for all* $P : Pred\mathcal{A}$,

$$\mathcal{A}(P) \Leftrightarrow \forall s : seq\mathcal{A} \ s(P \vee \bigvee_{i=1}^{n} g_i) \ \wedge \ \mathcal{A}(\neg \bigvee_{i=1}^{n} g_i)$$

and $\mathcal{A}(\neg \bigvee_{i=1}^{n} g_i) \Leftrightarrow \exists\kappa\ \mathcal{H}^*_\kappa$, where

$$\begin{array}{rcl} \mathcal{H}^*_0 & \widehat{=} & \neg \bigvee_{i=1}^{n} g_i \\ \mathcal{H}^*_{\kappa+1} & \widehat{=} & \forall s : seq_\omega \mathcal{A}\ \exists m < \omega\ s|_m(\mathcal{H}^*_\kappa) \\ \mathcal{H}^*_\delta & \widehat{=} & \exists \kappa < \delta\ \mathcal{H}^*_\kappa . \end{array}$$

Proof:
See Wabenhorst (1996). □

2.3 The Movers Theorem

Sufficient conditions under which an iteration within an action system can be flattened are given in the Movers Theorem (Back 1989, Wabenhorst 1997), which will be used extensively in the example of Section 4.

Theorem 2 (Movers Theorem) *Let*

$$\begin{array}{llll} \mathcal{A} \ \widehat{=} & init; & & \\ & \mathbf{do} & g & \rightarrow S \\ & & []_{j=1}^{m}\ h_j & \rightarrow T_j \\ & \mathbf{od} & & \end{array} , \qquad \begin{array}{llll} \mathcal{B} \ \widehat{=} & init; & & \\ & \mathbf{do} & g & \rightarrow S_0 \\ & & []_{i=1}^{n}\ g_i & \rightarrow S_i \\ & & []_{j=1}^{m}\ h_j & \rightarrow T_j \\ & \mathbf{od} & & \end{array}$$

and $\mathcal{C} \ \widehat{=}\ \mathbf{do}\ []_{i=1}^{n}\ g_i \rightarrow S_i\ \mathbf{od}$ *such that* $!(\neg \bigvee_{i=1}^{n} g_i); g \rightarrow S \leq g \rightarrow S_0; \mathcal{C}$.

Then $\mathcal{A} \leq \mathcal{B}$*, if the following conditions hold:*

1.(a) *For all* j *such that* $1 \leq j \leq m$, $\bigvee_{i=1}^{n} g_i \Rightarrow (h_j \rightarrow T_j)(\bigvee_{i=1}^{n} g_i)$.
(b) *For all* j *such that* $1 \leq j \leq m$, $\neg \bigvee_{i=1}^{n} g_i \Rightarrow (h_j \rightarrow T_j)(\neg \bigvee_{i=1}^{n} g_i)$.
(c) $init(\neg \bigvee_{i=1}^{n} g_i) \Leftrightarrow true$.
2. $\bigvee_{i=1}^{n} g_i \Rightarrow \neg g$.
3. *The set* $\{h_j \rightarrow T_j \mid 1 \leq j \leq m\}$ *can be expressed as the disjoint union of sets* $\mathcal{L}$ *(called the* left movers*) and* $\mathcal{R}$ *(called the* right movers*), such that:*

(a) *For all* $L \in \mathcal{L}$, $L; g \rightarrow S_0 \leq g \rightarrow S_0; L$.
(b) *For all* $L \in \mathcal{L}$ *and* i *such that* $1 \leq i \leq n$, $L; g_i \rightarrow S_i \leq g_i \rightarrow S_i; L$.
(c) *For all* $L \in \mathcal{L}$ *and* $R \in \mathcal{R}$, $L; R \leq R; L$.
(d) *For all* $R \in \mathcal{R}$ *and* i *such that* $1 \leq i \leq n$, $g_i \rightarrow S_i; R \leq R; g_i \rightarrow S_i$.
(e) $\bigvee_{i=1}^{n} g_i \Rightarrow (\mathbf{do}\ []_{R \in \mathcal{R}}\ R\ \mathbf{od})(true)$.

(f) *All left movers and all* $g_i \to S_i$, $1 \leq i \leq n$, *are boundedly nondeterministic.*

□

Other refinement theorems include Monotonicity (Back 1989, Wabenhorst 1996), which permits the refinement of actions one-by-one with the result that the action system as a whole is refined also.

3 A MODEL OF TIME

3.1 Assumptions

Consider the action system

$$\begin{array}{lll} \mathcal{A} \mathrel{\widehat{=}} & \mathbf{var} & \ldots \\ & \mathbf{init} & \ldots \\ & \mathbf{do} & \mathbin{[\!]}_{i=1}^{M} \mathbin{[\!]}_{j=1}^{N_i} \; g_{i,j} \;\; \to \;\; S_{i,j} \\ & \mathbf{od} & \end{array}$$

which we wish to transform into a timed action system. The subscript i in the action $g_{i,j} \to S_{i,j}$ denotes the process which executes the action, while j labels the action within process i. As in other models of time, actions in different processes may be executed concurrently if they do not interfere, otherwise one or more actions must wait. Actions within the same process are executed in sequence.

We make the assumption of maximal parallelism: if a process is idle and able to execute one of its actions, then it does so immediately. In any case, we can add actions which explicitly delay the execution of other actions if we desire.

We propose the syntax for the timed action system corresponding to $\mathcal{A}$ in Figure 2. Here, we use dashes ——— to delineate processes and introduce a time variable t_i of type *Time*, which can be $\mathbb{R}$ or $\mathbb{Z}$, for each process i. The variable t_i contains the time at which the action last executed by process i has ceased executing; therefore this is the time at which the next action may be executed by process i. The assignment $t_i := \ldots$ updates t_i to take into account the time that the corresponding action takes, possibly depending on the states of other variables. The assignment might involve a nondeterministic choice, and could take into account the time taken to make a scheduling decision. The sets $mutex_{i,j}$ contain the names of actions which interfere with action (i, j); these are the responsibility of the developer. We use the notation **do-rt** ... **od-rt** to signal that the semantics do not correspond to those of a

var ...
init ...
do-rt $[]_{j=1}^{N_1}$ $g_{1,j}$ **without** $mutex_{1,j} \rightarrow S_{1,j};\ t_1 := \ldots$ $(1, j)$

$[]_{j=1}^{N_2}$ $g_{2,j}$ **without** $mutex_{2,j} \rightarrow S_{2,j};\ t_2 := \ldots$ $(2, j)$

...

$[]_{j=1}^{N_M}$ $g_{M,j}$ **without** $mutex_{M,j} \rightarrow S_{M,j};\ t_M := \ldots$ (M, j)
od-rt

Figure 2 Syntax for the general real-time action system.

standard action system. Otherwise, the syntax is the same as for the standard action system $\mathcal{A}$.

Our task now is to define the semantics of the real-time action system in Figure 2. To this end, we will obtain a standard action system incorporating as design decisions the assumptions made in this section. We will then define the semantics of the real-time action system to be the semantics of this standard action system.

3.2 Time variables

To the action system $\mathcal{A}$ in Section 3.1, we add the time variables t_i of Figure 2. Thus, the time variables are initialised to 0:

$$\textbf{init}\ \ldots;[]_{i=1}^{M}\ t_i := 0,$$

where the ellipses correspond to the initialisation of the original action system $\mathcal{A}$. Also, the time variables are updated during execution to take into account the time taken by an executing action: thus, $g_{i,j} \rightarrow S_{i,j}$ is modified to become $g_{i,j} \rightarrow S_{i,j}; t_i := \ldots$

We consider the current global time of an action system to be

$$T \mathrel{\widehat{=}} \min_{k=1}^{M} t_k.$$

This can be regarded as an invariant which connects the real world with the action system. Here, T is an abbreviation designed to simplify the exposition, rather than a variable which would result in extra assignment statements in the action system.

At the current global time T, there is some process which is ready to execute an action. This is because there must be at least one i for which $t_i = T$. Indeed, there may be more than one, such as upon initialisation when all time variables t_i are 0. In accordance with the semantics of action systems, a nondeterministic choice is made between the enabled actions in such processes, and the chosen action executes subsequently. The time variable of the process will be updated, which may or may not increase the current global time.

Usually the time variables will be different from each other, reflecting the fact that some processes are in advance of the current global time. However, we stipulate that the next action chosen for execution may only occur in a process which is at the current global time; this limits the extent to which one process may be in advance of other processes. Thus, we strengthen the guard of each action (i, j) as follows:

$$g_{i,j} \wedge t_i = T \;\rightarrow\; S_{i,j}; t_i := \ldots$$

3.3 Blocking actions

The concurrent execution of actions in different processes is achieved by the usual interleaving semantics of action systems. However, when interference would occur, concurrent execution must be prevented.

Recall from Section 3.2 that the new choice of an action (say b in process i) to execute in the action system may only be made at the current global time T. Suppose that previously, action a (in process m different from i) was chosen for execution, so that the update of t_m has resulted in m being ahead of the current global time. The choice of b would correspond, in the real world, to a and b executing concurrently. However in the case of interference between a and b, this should be prevented in accordance with our assumptions in Section 3.1. As a was chosen for execution previously, it must be b which is prevented from executing.

We introduce new variables which help us to deduce when interference between actions would occur. Thus, we define $mutex_b$ for each action b to be the set of names of all other actions which prevent execution of b because of interference. Normally, two actions are considered to interfere if one accesses a variable which the other writes. Also, we define $exec_i$ for each process i to be the last action chosen for execution in process i.

We assume that the potential for interference between actions does not change at run time. It could be argued that an action a with body

$$\textbf{if}\ g \rightarrow x := 1\ [\!]\ \neg g \rightarrow y := 2\ \textbf{fi}$$

interferes with an action b which accesses y, only if $\neg g$ holds. However, it may not be possible for b to evaluate g at run time because g might depend on variables which are either local to a's process or are being changed by a (such as x and y), and hence are not accessible to b. Thus, $mutex_b$ is set upon initialisation of the action system by analysing the syntax of the original action system $\mathcal{A}$, and not changed during execution.

$$\textbf{init} \ \ldots; \ \|_{i=1}^{M} t_i := 0; \ \|_{i=1}^{M} \|_{j=1}^{N_i} mutex_{i,j} := \ldots$$

Using the new variables just introduced, we deduce that an action $b = (i, j)$ would be prevented from execution by interference with action $a = (m, n)$ at the current global time T if

$$t_i < t_m \wedge exec_m \in mutex_{i,j},$$

and we strengthen the guard of action (i, j) from Section 3.2 to take this into account. As a result the guard, which we abbreviate to $h_{i,j}$, becomes

$$h_{i,j} \ \widehat{=} \ g_{i,j} \ \wedge \ t_i = T \ \wedge \ \bigwedge_{m=1}^{M} \ (t_i < t_m \Rightarrow exec_m \notin mutex_{i,j}).$$

We also update $exec_i$ in the body of (i, j), so (i, j) becomes

$$h_{i,j} \ \rightarrow \ S_{i,j}; \ t_i, exec_i := \ldots, (i, j).$$

The $exec_m$ variables may have arbitrary values initially, so they need not be initialised explicitly. This is because the value of $exec_m$ is not needed in the guard of (i, j) until $t_i < t_m$. In this case, the body of the action in process m currently executing will have updated $exec_m$.

3.4 The wait action

When a choice of an action to be executed is required at the current global time, each possible action might be blocked. This could occur either because its original guard $g_{i,j}$ is false, or because of potential interference with actions executing in other processes (see Section 3.3). If all processes are at the current global time, then there is no potential interference and termination has occurred. However, if some processes are ahead of the current global time, then increasing the current global time (that is, *waiting*) might result in at least one action becoming unblocked. The earliest when this might occur is the earliest completion time of an action after the current global time, that is

$$NT \ \widehat{=} \ \min_{\{m | t_m > T\}} t_m.$$

$$
\begin{array}{lll}
\textbf{var} & & \ldots;\ \|_{i=1}^{M}\ t_i : Time;\ \|_{i=1}^{M}\ exec_i : ActionName; \\
& & \|_{i=1}^{M}\|_{j=1}^{N_i}\ mutex_{i,j} : \mathbb{P}\,(ActionName) \\
\textbf{init} & & \ldots;\ \|_{i=1}^{M}\ t_i := 0;\ \|_{i=1}^{M}\|_{j=1}^{N_i}\ mutex_{i,j} := \ldots \\
\textbf{do} & \|_{i=1}^{M}\|_{j=1}^{N_i} & h_{i,j} \ \rightarrow\ S_{i,j};\ t_i, exec_i := \ldots, (i,j) \quad (i,j) \\
& \| & (\bigvee_{i=1}^{M} t_i \neq T)\ \wedge\ \bigwedge_{i=1}^{M}\bigwedge_{j=1}^{N_i} \neg h_{i,j} \\
& & \qquad \rightarrow\ \|_{i=1}^{M}\ (t_i = T \rightarrow t_i := NT) \quad (W) \\
\textbf{od} & &
\end{array}
$$

where

$$
\begin{array}{rcl}
T & \widehat{=} & \min_{k=1}^{M} t_k \\
NT & \widehat{=} & \min_{\{m \mid t_m > T\}} t_m \\
h_{i,j} & \widehat{=} & g_{i,j}\ \wedge\ t_i = T\ \wedge\ \bigwedge_{m=1}^{M} (t_i < t_m \Rightarrow exec_m \notin mutex_{i,j})
\end{array}
$$

Figure 3 Semantics for the general real-time action system.

With these considerations, we construct the wait action as follows:

$$
\left(\bigvee_{i=1}^{M} t_i \neq T\right)\ \wedge\ \bigwedge_{i=1}^{M}\bigwedge_{j=1}^{N_i} \neg h_{i,j}\ \rightarrow\ \|_{i=1}^{M}\ (t_i = T \rightarrow t_i := NT)
$$

The condition for blocking is the conjunction of the negations of the guards of all actions, that is $\bigwedge_{i=1}^{M}\bigwedge_{j=1}^{N_i} \neg h_{i,j}$, where $h_{i,j}$ is as defined in Section 3.3. We exclude waiting when termination has occurred, that is, when there is no process executing past the current global time. For this reason, $(\bigvee_{i=1}^{M} t_i \neq T)$ is added to the guard. All time variables t_i at the current global time (that is, $t_i = T$) are updated to NT in the body of the wait action.

Note that the body of the wait action does not change $exec_i$. This is because $exec_i$ is never used for t_i at the current global time. (See also the justification in Section 3.3 for $exec_i$ not being initialised explicitly.)

3.5 Real-time action systems

The action system constructed in the previous sections is shown in Figure 3, and incorporates the desired properties of the real-time action system of Figure 2 described informally in Section 3.1. Therefore, we define the semantics of the real-time action system in Figure 2 to be the semantics of the action system in Figure 3.

We now state some properties of real-time action systems. The following lemma, which can be proven using predicate calculus, shows that the termination condition of the real-time action system is closely related to that of the corresponding standard action system.

Lemma 1 *The disjunction of the guards of the action system in Figure 3 is*

$$\left(\bigvee_{i=1}^{M} t_i \neq T\right) \vee \bigvee_{i=1}^{M} \bigvee_{j=1}^{N_i} g_{i,j}$$

□

One would expect the real-time action system to implement the standard action system $\mathcal{A}$ in Section 3.1. This is indeed the case:

Theorem 3 *The real-time action system in Figure 3 refines the standard action system $\mathcal{A}$.*

Proof:
See the Appendix. □

The real-time action system with only one process behaves exactly like the corresponding standard action system: the guards $h_{1,j}$ are $g_{1,j}$, and the guard of the wait action is false.

3.6 The environment

Normally, we would expect an action a to interfere with an action b in a different process exactly when the second interferes with the first, that is

$$a \in mutex_b \Leftrightarrow b \in mutex_a.$$

However, there may be circumstances in which the relaxation of this symmetry property is convenient. Consider a situation where action b models part of the environment and action a is in a different process which reacts to the environment. It could be argued that execution of b should not be delayed through a accessing the environment, but that if b is executing then a should be delayed. In this case we would have $a \in mutex_b$ but not $b \in mutex_a$.

$$
\begin{array}{lll}
\textbf{var} & & in, msg : seqData;\ inchar, last : Data \cup \{\bot\};\ r : \mathbb{B} \\
\textbf{init} & & inchar, last, msg, r := \bot, \bot, \emptyset, false \\
\textbf{do-rt} & & in \neq \emptyset \wedge inchar = \bot \wedge \neg r \ \rightarrow \\
& & \qquad in, inchar, r := tl(in), hd(in), true \quad (1,1) \\
& [] & inchar \neq \bot \wedge r \ \rightarrow \ r, t_1 := false, t_1 + chdef \quad (1,2) \\
& [] & inchar \neq \bot \wedge \neg r \ \rightarrow \ inchar, t_1 := \bot, t_1 + chsep \quad (1,3) \\
& \rule{1cm}{0.4pt} & \\
& [] & inchar \neq \bot \wedge inchar \neq last \ \textbf{without}\ \{(1,3)\} \ \rightarrow \\
& & \qquad msg, last, t_2 := msg \frown inchar, inchar, t_2 + chread \quad (2,1) \\
\textbf{od-rt} & &
\end{array}
$$

Figure 4 Final message passing implementation.

The model as it stands results in the continued execution of $a = (m, n)$ after $b = (i, j)$ has been chosen for execution. However, it may be more appropriate to abort in these circumstances, so we could modify (i, j) to become

$$h_{i,j} \quad \rightarrow \quad ! \left(\bigwedge_{m=1}^{M} (t_i < t_m \Rightarrow (i,j) \notin mutex_{exec_m}) \right) ; \ S_{i,j};\ t_i, exec_i := \ldots, (i,j)$$

where an assertion $!P$, defined in Figure 1, skips if P holds and aborts otherwise. Modifying (i, j) in this way would mean that Theorem 3 would no longer hold in general, but would depend on satisfactory time updates $t_k := \ldots$

4 EXAMPLE: MESSAGE PASSING

We now illustrate the concepts in previous sections by an example, where we achieve a final implementation from a high level specification by stepwise refinement using the Movers Theorem and other results.

In this example, based on that in Hayes *et al.* (1997), a message is constructed from character-by-character input. A character appears in *inchar* for a duration *chdef* > 0, during which time the character must be added to the message *msg*. The time required for this is *chread* > 0, which we stipulate to be no larger than *chdef*. After duration *chdef*, *inchar* is undefined for duration *chsep* > 0 before the next character appears. The characters appearing in *inchar* are taken from a fixed finite channel *in*, so that termination will be guaranteed. The process constructing the message *msg* has no access to *in*, but must rely on *inchar*.

The final implementation is shown in Figure 4, where the first process implements the environment and the second constructs the message. The boolean r holds if *inchar* is readable, and acts as a synchronisation variable which helps to ensure that the actions in the first process are always executed in the order $(1,1)$, then $(1,2)$, then $(1,3)$. The action $(1,1)$ updates *inchar* from *in* instantaneously, as t_1 does not change; this technique is also used by Fidge *et al.* (1997). Here, the functions *hd* and *tl* give the head and tail of a channel respectively and $\perp$ is a special character which is different from the characters in *Data*. The action $(1,2)$ waits for duration *chdef*, during which time *inchar* may be accessed by the other process. The action $(1,3)$ represents *inchar* being undefined for time *chsep*. In action $(2,1)$, *last* is used to detect when a new character has arrived in *inchar*: *last* stores the character last received through *inchar*, which we compare with the current value of *inchar*. Here, we assume that consecutive values in *in* are different, if necessary by appending a label to each datum. Using *last*, we avoid assumptions about timing behaviour to detect when a new *inchar* has arrived.

We set $mutex_{2,1} = \{(1,3)\}$ to prevent the second process from beginning to access *inchar* while *inchar* is no longer defined. It makes no difference whether $mutex_{2,1}$ contains $(1,1)$ or not, because $(1,1)$ has duration 0. For the environment process, *mutex* is empty because the environment is not affected by the second process.

4.1 Specification and first steps

As a high level specification,

$$in, msg := \emptyset, in$$

constructs the final message *msg* directly from *in*. This can be refined to

$$\begin{array}{lllll} & msg := \emptyset; & & & \\ \textbf{do} & in \neq \emptyset & \rightarrow & in, msg := tl(in), msg \frown hd(in) \\ \textbf{od} & & & \end{array}$$

using one of the techniques of Morgan (1994), for example Exercise 5.6.

The definition of refinement permits the introduction of new variables, so we add the variable *inchar* by initialising it to $\perp$ and adding the conjunct $inchar = \perp$ to the guard of the single action. This is then refined to

$$\begin{array}{llll} & inchar, msg := \perp, \emptyset; & & \\ \textbf{do} & in \neq \emptyset \wedge inchar = \perp & \rightarrow & in, inchar := tl(in), hd(in) \\ \quad [] & inchar \neq \perp & \rightarrow & inchar, msg := \perp, msg \frown hd(in) \\ \textbf{od} & & & \end{array}$$

as a straightforward application of the Movers Theorem.

Now the variable *last* is introduced: it is initialised to $\perp$ and $last := inchar$ is added to the body of the second action. Since $inchar \neq \perp \Rightarrow inchar \neq last$ is an invariant, $inchar \neq last$ may be added as a conjunct to the guard of the second action. Theorem 3 for one process is applied to obtain Figure 5.

$$
\begin{array}{l}
inchar, last, msg := \bot, \bot, \emptyset; \\
\mathbf{do\text{-}rt} \quad in \neq \emptyset \wedge inchar = \bot \rightarrow \\
\qquad\qquad in, inchar, t_1 := tl(in), hd(in), t_1 + chdef \\
\quad [] \ inchar \neq \bot \wedge inchar \neq last \rightarrow \\
\qquad\qquad msg, last, inchar, t_1 := msg \frown inchar, inchar, \bot, t_1 + chsep \\
\mathbf{od\text{-}rt}
\end{array}
$$

$$
\begin{array}{l}
inchar, last, msg, t_1 := \bot, \bot, \emptyset, 0; \\
\mathbf{do} \quad in \neq \emptyset \wedge inchar = \bot \rightarrow \\
\qquad\qquad in, inchar, t_1, exec_1 := tl(in), hd(in), t_1 + chdef, (1,2) \\
\quad [] \ inchar \neq \bot \wedge inchar \neq last \rightarrow \\
\qquad\qquad msg, last, inchar, t_1 := msg \frown inchar, inchar, \bot, t_1 + chsep; \\
\qquad\qquad exec_1 := (1,3) \\
\mathbf{od}
\end{array}
$$

Figure 5 One process.

4.2 Two processes

The next refinement step, which splits the single process into two, is the most delicate. First, we add the time variable t_2 by appending $t_2 := t_1$ at the end of the body of the second action. We can add conjuncts $t_1 \leq t_2$ and $t_2 \leq t_1 \wedge (t_2 < t_1 \Rightarrow exec_1 \neq (1,3))$ to the guards of the first and second actions respectively because

$$inchar = \bot \Rightarrow t_1 = t_2 \quad \text{and} \quad inchar \neq \bot \Rightarrow (t_1 = t_2 + chdef \wedge exec_1 \neq (1,3))$$

are invariants of the resulting action system. Now we use the Movers Theorem with only right movers and

$$
\begin{array}{ll}
t_2 \leq t_1 \wedge (t_2 < t_1 \Rightarrow exec_1 \neq (1,3)) \wedge inchar \neq \bot \wedge inchar \neq last \rightarrow & \\
\qquad msg, last, inchar, t_1 := msg \frown inchar, inchar, \bot, t_1 + chsep; & \\
\qquad t_2, exec_1 := t_1, (1,3) & \\
\leq & \\
t_2 \leq t_1 \wedge (t_2 < t_1 \Rightarrow exec_1 \neq (1,3)) \wedge inchar \neq \bot \wedge inchar \neq last \rightarrow & \\
\qquad msg, last, t_2 := msg \frown inchar, inchar, t_2 + chread; & (2,1) \\
\mathbf{do} \quad t_1 \leq t_2 \wedge inchar \neq \bot \rightarrow & \\
\qquad inchar, t_1, exec_1 := \bot, t_1 + chsep, (1,3) & (1,3) \\
\quad [] \ t_2 < t_1 \wedge (inchar = \bot \vee inchar = last \vee exec_1 = (1,3)) \rightarrow & \\
\qquad t_2 := t_1 & (W) \\
\mathbf{od} &
\end{array}
$$

$$
\begin{array}{ll}
\multicolumn{2}{l}{inchar, last, msg := \bot, \bot, \emptyset;} \\
\textbf{do-rt} & in \neq \emptyset \wedge inchar = \bot \;\rightarrow \\
& \qquad in, inchar, t_1 := tl(in), hd(in), t_1 + chdef \\
& [\!]\quad inchar \neq \bot \;\rightarrow\; inchar, t_1 := \bot, t_1 + chsep \qquad (1,3) \\
& \overline{} \\
& [\!]\; inchar \neq \bot \wedge inchar \neq last \;\textbf{without}\; \{(1,3)\} \;\rightarrow \\
& \qquad msg, last, t_2 := msg \frown inchar, inchar, t_2 + chread \qquad (2,1) \\
\textbf{od-rt} &
\end{array}
$$

$$
\begin{array}{ll}
\multicolumn{2}{l}{inchar, last, msg, t_1, t_2 := \bot, \bot, \emptyset, 0, 0;} \\
\textbf{do} & t_1 \leq t_2 \wedge in \neq \emptyset \wedge inchar = \bot \;\rightarrow \\
& \qquad in, inchar, t_1, exec_1 := tl(in), hd(in), t_1 + chdef, (1,2) \\
[\!] & \quad t_1 \leq t_2 \wedge inchar \neq \bot \;\rightarrow \\
& \qquad inchar, t_1, exec_1 := \bot, t_1 + chsep, (1,3) \qquad (1,3) \\
[\!] & t_2 \leq t_1 \wedge (t_2 < t_1 \Rightarrow exec_1 \neq (1,3)) \\
& \wedge inchar \neq \bot \wedge inchar \neq last \;\rightarrow \\
& \qquad msg, last, t_2 := msg \frown inchar, inchar, t_2 + chread \qquad (2,1) \\
[\!] & t_2 < t_1 \wedge (inchar = \bot \vee inchar = last \vee exec_1 = (1,3)) \;\rightarrow \\
& \qquad t_2 := t_1 \qquad (W) \\
\textbf{od} &
\end{array}
$$

Figure 6 Two processes.

to obtain the action system in Figure 6. In the application of the Movers Theorem, we use the fact that $chread \leq chdef$ and four invariants,

- $(t_2 < t_1 \wedge inchar \neq \bot \wedge inchar \neq last) \Rightarrow t_1 = t_2 + chdef$ (used in the verification of the refinement above);
- $(t_1 \leq t_2 \wedge inchar \neq \bot) \Rightarrow inchar = last$ (used in the verification of condition 2.);
- $t_2 \leq t_1$ (used in the verification of conditions 1.(b) and 3.(d));
- $exec_1 = (1,3) \Rightarrow inchar = \bot$ (used to help prove the other invariants).

Some invariants are stronger than required, but we have found the stronger versions easier to prove.

Note that $mutex_{2,1}$ does not include the first action even though the first action changes *inchar* and $(2,1)$ reads it. Intuitively, the first action can be thought of as instantaneously updating *inchar* and then waiting for duration *chdef*, during which time $(2,1)$ may access *inchar*. The action W corresponds to the wait action because of the invariant $t_2 \leq t_1$.

4.3 Final implementation

In the final step, we separate the instantaneous update of *inchar* from waiting for duration *chdef*. For this, we introduce a boolean synchronisation variable r and initialise it to $false$. This allows us to add $\neg r$ to the guards of the first and second actions. Now we use the Movers Theorem with

$$\begin{array}{l}
t_1 \leq t_2 \wedge in \neq \emptyset \wedge inchar = \perp \wedge \neg r \rightarrow \\
\quad in, inchar, t_1, exec_1 := tl(in), hd(in), t_1 + chdef, (1,2) \\
\leq \\
t_1 \leq t_2 \wedge in \neq \emptyset \wedge inchar = \perp \wedge \neg r \rightarrow \\
\quad\quad in, inchar, r, exec_1 := tl(in), hd(in), true, (1,1); \quad (1,1) \\
\mathbf{do} \quad t_1 \leq t_2 \wedge inchar \neq \perp \wedge r \rightarrow \\
\quad\quad\quad r, t_1, exec_1 := false, t_1 + chdef, (1,2) \quad (1,2) \\
\mathbf{od}
\end{array}$$

to obtain an action system which corresponds to the final implementation in Figure 4. As before, there are no left movers, only right movers. The invariant $t_2 < t_1 \Rightarrow \neg r$ is used in the verification of conditions 1.(b) and 3.(d).

The wait action can be left as it is in Figure 6. A wait action corresponding to that in Figure 4 would require the addition of the disjunct

$$t_1 < t_2 \wedge inchar = \perp \wedge (in = \emptyset \vee r)$$

to the guard and changing the body to $t_1, t_2 := \max(t_1, t_2), \max(t_1, t_2)$. However, this change in the wait action is redundant because of the invariant

$$t_1 < t_2 \Rightarrow (inchar \neq \perp \wedge r \wedge t_2 = t_1 + chread).$$

This invariant also ensures that the assertion

$$!(t_1 < t_2 \Rightarrow (1,3) \notin mutex_{2,1})$$

for action $(1,3)$ according to Section 3.6 always skips, taking into account the guard of $(1,3)$, and therefore may be added to the body of $(1,3)$ as a valid refinement. (If we had $(1,1) \in mutex_{2,1}$, then the appropriate assertion for $(1,1)$ could also be added, for the same reason.)

We do not use Theorem 3 directly in obtaining the final implementation in Figure 4 because the abstract action system for Theorem 3 is not refined by Figure 4 and therefore cannot occur in the development. In the abstract action system for Theorem 3, $(1,1)$ and $(1,2)$ may execute alternately without $(2,1)$ ever occurring, with the result that the final output message *msg* remains empty.

5 DISCUSSION

Related work with similar aims is due to Abadi *et al.* (1994), de Boer *et al.* (1996), Fidge *et al.* (1997) and Broy (1997).

The approach of Abadi *et al.* (1994) uses the Temporal Logical of Actions (TLA) to reason about the real-time properties of systems. Unlike our approach, TLA has a global time variable *now*, which is advanced by a tick action. Fairness constraints are used to execute this tick action and the other actions in parallel, whereas our approach does not require reasoning about fairness. The nonZeno condition, which states that *now* is not bounded, is verified in order to help prove liveness properties.

As for our approach, Fidge *et al.* (1997) model concurrent real-time systems with action systems, but use traces for the semantics rather than weakest preconditions. The global variable *now* is incremented periodically, resulting in the uniform advance of time across all processes. The variables up_x and ac_x are similar to our t_i and $mutex_{i,j}$. A compositional Hoare-style proof system for a large class of distributed real-time systems is presented by de Boer *et al.* (1996). The proof system is shown to be sound and relatively complete.

Broy (1997) characterises the behaviour of processes by the histories of output variables relative to input variables. These histories are known as streams, and may be discrete sequences or continuous. The behaviours of processes are combined using parallel composition with feedback, and refinement is defined in terms of simulations between abstract and concrete systems.

The model in this paper is able to handle a wide variety of real-time systems while keeping the introduction of special variables to a minimum, and no assumptions are made about the types of statements. Actions associated with real-time systems such as deadlines and delays can be modelled by assertions and time updates $g \rightarrow t_i := \ldots$ respectively.

We believe we have obtained a model of real-time systems which is faithful to the intuition we have about such systems in the real world. While the semantics of the model are complicated, we believe that this reflects the complicated interactions in real-time systems, rather than a deficiency in the model.

In action systems with time, there are as yet few results which provide support for stepwise development. The complexity of the calculations in Section 4 show the desirability of being able to reason on the level of real-time action systems (Figure 2) rather than their underlying standard action systems (Figure 3), and more work is required in this area.

Acknowledgements

I wish to thank Colin Fidge and the anonymous referees for their helpful comments. This work was funded by the Information Technology Division of the Defence Science and Technology Organisation.

REFERENCES

Abadi M. and Lamport L. (1994) An Old-Fashioned Recipe for Real Time. *ACM Transactions on Programming Languages and Systems*, **16**, 1543–71.

Back R.J.R. (1989) A Method of Refining Atomicity in Parallel Algorithms, in Odijk E., Rem M. and Syre J.-C. (Eds.) *Proc. Parallel Architectures and Languages Europe (PARLE'89)*. Lecture Notes in Computer Science **366**, Springer-Verlag, New York.

de Boer F.S., Tej H., de Roever W.-P. and van Hulst M. (1996) Compositionality in Real-Time Shared Variable Concurrency, in Jonsson B. and Parrow J. (Eds.) *Proc. Formal Techniques in Real-Time and Fault-Tolerant Systems (FTRTFT'96)*. Lecture Notes in Computer Science **1135**, Springer-Verlag, New York.

Boom H.J. (1982) A Weaker Precondition for Loops. *ACM Transactions on Programming Languages and Systems*, **4**, 668–77.

Broy M. (1997) Refinement of Time, in Bertran M. and Rus T. (Eds.) *Proc. Transformation-Based Reactive System Development (ARTS'97)*, Lecture Notes in Computer Science **1231**, Springer-Verlag, New York.

Butler M.J. and Morgan C.C. (1995) Action Systems, Unbounded Nondeterminism, and Infinite Traces. *Formal Aspects of Computing*, **7**, 37–53.

Dijkstra E.W. and Scholten C.S. (1990) *Predicate Calculus and Program Semantics*. Springer-Verlag, New York.

Fidge C.J. and Wellings A.J. (1997) An Action-Based Formal Model for Concurrent Real-Time Systems. *Formal Aspects of Computing*, **9**, 175–207.

Hayes I.J. and Utting M. (1997) A Sequential Real-Time Refinement Calculus. *Technical Report 97-33, Software Verification Research Centre, University of Queensland*, http://svrc.it.uq.edu.au/Publications/Technical_reports_1997.html

Hesselink W.H. (1995) Safety and Progress of Recursive Procedures. *Formal Aspects of Computing*, **7**, 389–411.

Morgan C.C. (1994) *Programming from Specifications*, 2nd Edition. Prentice-Hall, New York.

Morris J.M. (1987) Stepwise Refinement and the Programming Calculus. *Science of Computer Programming*, **9**, 287–306.

Wabenhorst A.K. (1996) Developing Fairness in Terminating and Reactive Programs. *Technical Report TR-1-96, Programming Research Group, Oxford University*, http://www.comlab.ox.ac.uk/oucl/publications/tr/TR-1-96.html

Wabenhorst A.K. (1997) A Stepwise Development of the Alternating Bit Protocol. *Technical Report TR-12-97, Programming Research Group, Oxford University*, http://www.comlab.ox.ac.uk/oucl/publications/tr/TR-12-97.html

APPENDIX

Proof of Theorem 3:
We need to ensure that the strengthened guards in the real-time action system do not result in premature termination, and that the wait action does not prevent termination.

Let $\mathcal{B}$ be the real-time action system in Figure 3. We wish to show that $\mathcal{A} \leq \mathcal{B}$, for which we will use the characterisation of weakest preconditions in Theorem 1.

First, we prove a preliminary result. Let $\varphi : seq\mathcal{B} \to seq\mathcal{A}$ map action sequences in $\mathcal{B}$ to the corresponding action sequences in $\mathcal{A}$, discarding any wait actions. We extend φ to infinite action sequences by continuity. We show that for $s : seq\mathcal{B}$, $\varphi(s) \leq s$ by induction on the construction of s. The result clearly holds for $s =$ **skip**. For an action A and $P : Pred\mathcal{A}$,

$$\varphi(s;A)(P)$$

$\Leftrightarrow$ property of φ

$$(\varphi(s);\varphi(A))(P)$$

$\Rightarrow$ induction hypothesis

$$(s;\varphi(A))(P)$$

$\Rightarrow$ see below

$$(s;A)(P)$$

For the last step, there are two cases to consider: if $A = W$, then $\varphi(W)(P) \Leftrightarrow P \Rightarrow W(P)$, whereas if $A = (i,j)$, then $\varphi(i,j)(P) \Rightarrow (i,j)(P)$ because strengthening the guard of an action constitutes a refinement.

To show that $\mathcal{A}(P) \Rightarrow \mathcal{B}(P)$ for $P : Pred\mathcal{A}$, we show that each conjunct for $\mathcal{A}(P)$ in Theorem 1 implies the corresponding conjunct for $\mathcal{B}(P)$. For the first conjunct,

$$\forall s : seq\mathcal{A}\ s(P \vee \bigvee_{i=1}^{M} \bigvee_{j=1}^{N_i} g_{i,j})$$

$\Rightarrow$ for $s : seq\mathcal{B}$, $\varphi(s) : seq\mathcal{A}$

$$\forall s : seq\mathcal{B}\ \varphi(s)(P \vee \bigvee_{i=1}^{M} \bigvee_{j=1}^{N_i} g_{i,j})$$

$\Rightarrow$ above, since $P \vee \bigvee_{i=1}^{M} \bigvee_{j=1}^{N_i} g_{i,j} : Pred\mathcal{A}$

$$\forall s : seq\mathcal{B}\ s(P \vee \bigvee_{i=1}^{M} \bigvee_{j=1}^{N_i} g_{i,j})$$

$\Rightarrow$ monotonicity

$$\forall s : seq\mathcal{B}\ s(P \ \vee\ (\bigvee_{i=1}^{M} t_i \neq T) \ \vee\ \bigvee_{i=1}^{M} \bigvee_{j=1}^{N_i} g_{i,j})$$

which is the desired result by Lemma 1.

For the second conjunct in Theorem 1, we show that for all $\kappa : Ord$, there exists $\kappa' : Ord$ such that $\mathcal{H}^*_{\kappa,\mathcal{A}} \Rightarrow \mathcal{H}^*_{\kappa',\mathcal{B}}$. First suppose that $\mathcal{H}^*_{0,\mathcal{A}}$, and let $s : seq_\omega \mathcal{B}$. If s contains (i,j), say $s = W^n; (i,j); s'$ with $n \geq 0$, then

$$\mathcal{H}^*_{0,\mathcal{A}}$$

$$\Leftrightarrow \qquad \text{definition of } \mathcal{H}^*_{0,\mathcal{A}}$$

$$\neg \bigvee_{i=1}^{M} \bigvee_{j=1}^{N_i} g_{i,j}$$

$$\Rightarrow \qquad W \text{ does not change variables in } \neg \bigvee_{i=1}^{M} \bigvee_{j=1}^{N_i} g_{i,j}$$

$$W^n(\neg \bigvee_{i=1}^{M} \bigvee_{j=1}^{N_i} g_{i,j})$$

$$\Rightarrow \qquad \text{guard of } (i,j) \text{ is } \mathit{false} \text{ if } \neg \bigvee_{i=1}^{M} \bigvee_{j=1}^{N_i} g_{i,j}$$

$$(W^n; (i,j))((\bigwedge_{i=1}^{M} t_i = T) \wedge \neg \bigvee_{i=1}^{M} \bigvee_{j=1}^{N_i} g_{i,j})$$

$$\Rightarrow \qquad \text{definition of } \mathcal{H}^*_{0,\mathcal{B}} \text{ and Lemma 1}$$

$$\exists m < \omega \ s|_m(\mathcal{H}^*_{0,\mathcal{B}})$$

On the other hand, if s consists only of wait actions, then execution of at most M of these gives the same result.

For the step case, take $s : seq_\omega \mathcal{B}$. If $\varphi(s) : seq\mathcal{A}$, then s has a tail of wait actions, and a sequential composition of at most M of these results in termination, as in the base case. Otherwise, $\varphi(s) : seq_\omega \mathcal{A}$ and

$$\mathcal{H}^*_{\kappa+1,\mathcal{A}}$$

$$\Leftrightarrow \qquad \text{definition of } \mathcal{H}^*_{\kappa+1,\mathcal{A}}$$

$$\forall s' : seq_\omega \mathcal{A} \ \exists m < \omega \ s'|_m(\mathcal{H}^*_{\kappa,\mathcal{A}})$$

$$\Rightarrow \qquad \varphi(s) : seq_\omega \mathcal{A}$$

$$\exists m < \omega \ \varphi(s)|_m(\mathcal{H}^*_{\kappa,\mathcal{A}})$$

$$\Leftrightarrow$$

$$\exists m < \omega \ \varphi(s|_m)(\mathcal{H}^*_{\kappa,\mathcal{A}})$$

$$\Rightarrow \qquad \text{from result earlier in proof}$$

$$\exists m < \omega \ s|_m(\mathcal{H}^*_{\kappa,\mathcal{A}})$$

$$\Rightarrow \qquad \text{induction hypothesis and monotonicity}$$

$$\exists m < \omega \ s|_m(\mathcal{H}^*_{\kappa',\mathcal{B}})$$

As κ' is independent of s, we have shown $\mathcal{H}^*_{\kappa'+1,\mathcal{B}}$.

The limit case is straightforward. □

BIOGRAPHY

Axel Wabenhorst received his doctorate from the University of Oxford in 1997 with a thesis on the formal development of concurrent systems with fairness constraints. His background is in pure mathematics, having completed a science degree at Monash University and Part III Mathematics at the University of Cambridge. Currently, he is a Research Fellow in the Software Verification Research Centre at the University of Queensland, with research interests in the formal development of concurrent systems.

INDEX OF CONTRIBUTORS

KEYWORD INDEX

MIX
Papier aus verantwortungsvollen Quellen
Paper from responsible sources
FSC® C105338

If you have any concerns about our products,
you can contact us on
ProductSafety@springernature.com

In case Publisher is established outside the EU,
the EU authorized representative is:
Springer Nature Customer Service Center GmbH
Europaplatz 3, 69115 Heidelberg, Germany

Printed by Libri Plureos GmbH
in Hamburg, Germany